The Reading Process

The Reading Process
the teacher and the learner
third edition

Miles V. Zintz
University of New Mexico

ꝟꜿꜿ

Wm. C. Brown Company Publishers
Dubuque, Iowa

wcb
Wm. C. Brown
Chairman of the Board

Book Team

Wm. J. Fitzgerald
Editor

William J. Evans
Designer

Elizabeth Munger
Production Editor

Mary Heller
Visual Research Editor

Larry W. Brown
President WCB Group

Wm. C. Brown Company Publishers, College Division

Lawrence E. Cremer
President

Raymond C. Deveaux
Vice President / Product
Development

David Wm. Smith
Assistant Vice President / National
Sales Manager

Matt Coghlan
National Marketing Manager

David A. Corona
Director of Production Development
and Design

William A. Moss
Production Editorial Manager

Marilyn A. Phelps
Manager of Design

Cover photo   John Running/Flagstaff, Arizona

Copyright © 1970, 1975, 1980 by Wm. C. Brown Company Publishers

Library of Congress Catalog Card Number: 79–54038

ISBN 0–697–06184–1

Printed in the United States of America

To Mary Hatley Zintz

Contents

Preface   ix

Part One • The Overview   1

1   What Is Reading?   2
2   Psychological Foundations for Reading Instruction   18
3   Linguistic Foundations for Reading Instruction   46

Part Two • A Good Beginning   67

4   Assessment of Prereading Skills   68
5   Teaching Beginning Reading   93

Part Three • Classroom Management to Facilitate Reading   123

6   Organizing the Classroom Reading Program   124
7   Interaction in the Classroom   151
8   Parent-Teacher Cooperation   172

Part Four • The Skills of Reading   187

9   Word-Recognition Skills   188
10   Comprehension Skills   230
11   Study Skills   264
12   Developing Critical Reading Abilities   288
13   Oral Reading   304
14   Developing Permanent Reading Habits   318
15   Teaching Reading in the Content Fields   341

Part Five • Provision for All the Children   365

16   Teaching Reading to the Bilingual Child   367
17   Teaching Reading to Children Who Speak Nonstandard
     English   398
18   Exceptional Children and Reading Instruction   415

Part Six • Evaluation in the Reading Program   447

19   The Informal Reading Inventory   448
20   Corrective Reading   465
21   Evaluation in the Reading Program   489
22   Teaching Reading in Proper Perspective   509

Bibliography   520

Appendix   524

Photo Credits   527

Name Index   529

Subject Index   537

Preface

The primary purpose of this text is to help the classroom teacher to be a *diagnostic teacher of reading* every day, from the very first day of school.

Part One, The Overview, begins with a discussion of the place of reading in the elementary school. Chapters 2 and 3 are, respectively, about the psychological and the linguistic foundations for reading instruction. The two chapters in Part Two, A Good Beginning, offer the teacher techniques for assessing prereading skills and teaching beginning reading. Readiness for beginning reading is approached as a diagnostic problem in the first grade. Evaluation of children's abilities and disabilities enables those who are ready for formal reading to proceed efficiently in a well planned program. Evaluation prevents failure for those who need to build strengths and overcome weaknesses. Emphasis is given to language development. Part Three, Classroom Management to Facilitate Reading, discusses organization of the classroom for reading, group interaction in classroom learning, and parent-teacher cooperation.

How to plan for each child then becomes the focus of attention in Part Four. These chapters, 9 through 15, cover techniques the teacher of reading needs in the areas of word recognition, comprehension, study skills (reading in subject-matter areas), critical reading, oral reading, and the building of permanent reading habits. Oral reading is especially useful as both a tool and a goal. Not only does it serve many purposes in everyday life, it can help the classroom teacher do continuous evaluation of a child's developmental reading skills.

Throughout the text the importance of the affective component of learning has been emphasized. Permanent interest in reading and in critical and constructive evaluation of material read is as much a product of *affect* as of *cognition*. Teachers sometimes fail to understand and use this fact in teaching reading in the elementary school.

Good diagnostic teaching of reading in any classroom requires an eclectic approach. Some children need programmed lessons that teach and reinforce skills. Others work best with sequenced basal reader lessons that allow long periods of practice on plateaus of learning. But utilizing the experiences of the child in the language-experience approach is the best way to *introduce* the process of reading to the child.

Mainstreaming exceptional children in regular classes is right and necessary. The gifted, the retarded, the bilingual, the gifted bilingual, the child with specific learning disability—all have a place in the classroom reading program that is organized and conducted according to diagnostic principles.

The text concludes with a reaffirmation of the importance of reading in the total elementary school curriculum. Additional guides are offered to show how *each teacher* can increase the functional reading ability *each child* brings to the classroom. This is what diagnostic teaching is all about.

Diagnostic teaching is a methodology which requires that the teacher ascertain the level of functional skills and abilities of *each child* in the classroom. It will never be possible for all the children in a group to learn the same thing at the same time with the same amount of practice. To teach diagnostically, teachers must utilize important psychological concepts:

1. The varying innate abilities of children in all skills, abilities, and appreciations.
2. The role of practice in learning.
3. The importance of motivation for efficient learning.
4. Development of understanding.
5. Transfer of learning where common elements exist.
6. The problem of forgetting.

Finally, diagnostic teaching provides for the deviant child's learning needs, whether the child is linguistically different, culturally different, gifted, retarded, emotionally disturbed, or neurologically impaired.

The references at the end of each chapter offer extensive reading in any phase of the program which a teacher may find especially meaningful or necessary in day-to-day work.

Perhaps a word of explanation should be added about how the different faces and sizes of type are used in this book. Passages that are quoted from other authors are set in the Helvetica type face. When other authors are cited but their work is paraphrased rather than quoted, the paraphrases are set in a reduced size of the Times Roman type face.

Miles V. Zintz

The Reading Process

1

The Overview

Chapter 1 defines reading as a continuous developmental process. Chapter 2 then discusses the psychological foundations on which learning is based. Chapter 3 contains information about the phenomenon of language and language acquisition—that is, how children learn to talk. Teachers should have some understanding of what linguistics—the scientific study of language—teaches about the nature of language before they begin helping children develop reading skills.

1

What Is Reading?

Jack is in the first grade. He is a happy little boy who happened to be born into a comfortable, middle-class family early in May. He had one brother and no sisters. When Jack was born, his father was past thirty and already a junior executive. Often, he brought his briefcase home and worked at a desk in the extra bedroom. Jack's mother had graduated from a two-year college course with an A.A. degree and then worked for a few years as a secretary in a large telephone company office before she married. Jack's father was a very curious, interested, "always learning" kind of man who read a great deal. His mother read too, usually about subjects which would give her practical hints. When Jack was an infant his mother spent all her time with him while his father was at work. They laughed and played, and she *talked to him* a great deal. By the time he was able to walk around a bit, his mother was pregnant a second time. During her pregnancy she continued to spend a great deal of time *talking to Jack.* When he was eleven months old he was saying *mama, daddy, go, come,* and a few other words in clearly intelligible language. Jack's mother explained to him that she would be going to the hospital when his little brother was born. When that time arrived his grandmother came and lived in the house and assumed full responsibility during the mother's absence.

The grandmother bought books of the *Baby's First Book* variety and shared them with Jack. By the time Jack was eighteen months old, his mother was holding him on her lap reading *Mother Goose* to him for relatively long periods of time in the afternoon while his brother slept or in the evening while they waited for daddy to come home. By the time Jack was three, he was "demanding" a story hour at bedtime and using language confidently in complicated sentence structures. His growth in language skills was constant, and as he developed a *broad vocabulary* he could deal with concepts and problem-solving. He learned to *listen,* to *observe,* and to like books.

Even though the state in which he lived did not provide kindergarten classes for five-year-olds, Jack enjoyed many of the experiences of kindergartners with his mother and brother sixteen months younger. He learned how to *sequence ideas,* how to *explain* simply and carefully, teaching his little brother many things big boys had already mastered.

Jack entered first grade with *highly developed verbal* skills. He could *listen well with understanding* and *understand* many of the *simple jokes* his mother and father told largely for his benefit. He went most *willingly* to *school* because he felt he was getting very grown up by the time he was *six years and four months old.* When he asked his mother about words, she had always answered his questions. He usually recognized his own, his father's, and his mother's names on letters that came in the mail. He could distinguish many of his books by the pictures on the covers, but he was probably also noticing distinguishing features in the titles, too. By the time he entered school, Jack and his brother had a library of nearly 200 books, mostly of the variety picked up in the supermarket.

Needless to add, Jack entered first grade *confident and secure.* He was anxious to learn to read. With a teacher who was gentle, understanding, and efficient in the teaching of reading, he would probably read by almost any method. Fortunately, the teacher did know that all children grow at different rates, have varying needs for emotional response and security, and have different levels of mastery of language as a communication process. The teacher encouraged all the children to talk, to discuss, to explain, and to have fun at school. By the end of one month, the teacher had divided the class into groups—those who were ready for formal reading, those who needed readiness activities and a gradual introduction to formal reading, and those who would not show a great deal of interest in the printed word for several months.

The teacher continued to study the children carefully. She discussed them with her supervisor and, as problems in their learning arose, referred them to the school nurse, the school psychologist, or the school social worker. But her goal was to keep everybody learning something.

When Jack dictated an especially good experience story, she encouraged him to take it home and read it to his father and mother. When he finished each of the preprimers, she encouraged him to carry them home and read aloud to whichever *parent* would *really listen.*

Phonics, spelling, and writing developed naturally and smoothly for Jack. His manuscript writing was very legible almost from the beginning. Jack will finish first grade able to read fluently and smoothly from books more difficult than first grade readers. He may have read stories in a first-semester, second grade book or many trade books of interest to him. Also he will have written (dictated) at least one book of stories which will have been bound together with a table of contents and with his name visibly displayed on the cover distinguishing him as the author.

How fortunate Jack was to have six excellent *years of readiness* for the academic job of going to school!

Now contrast Jack's successes with the problems confronting Ernesto.

Ernesto is in the fifth grade. His grandparents speak only Spanish, and his parents learned Spanish first at home but attended only English language schools. They were never taught the structure of English as a second language and never learned to speak it confidently. As a result, Ernesto and all his brothers and sisters have difficulty with English syntax and vocabulary. While they use the superficial everyday expressions "Good morning, Miss Smith" or "How're things?" with ease, they lack both ability and confidence to compose essays in class or give good oral reports. Similarly, Ernesto neither studied Spanish nor learned to read or write it.

Consequently, in fifth grade Ernesto has confidence and understanding with the sound patterns of commonly used Spanish vernacular and he gets along with the minimum amount of English language. He is illiterate in Spanish and considerably substandard for fifth grade in reading and writing English. He is well on his way to leaving school neither monolingual nor bilingual. As Knowlton said, "He may graduate from high school illiterate in two languages!"[1]

Jack and Ernesto represent only two of the innumerable children any classroom teacher in the elementary school must be prepared to meet and guide through a school year. While all children are like each other in more ways than they are different, it is the understanding and acceptance of the degrees of difference that enable each child to grow.

Of course, the school could have provided a quite different curriculum for Ernesto. More and more schools today would be able to offer a child like Ernesto some options in first grade:

1. A language specialist in the school system could determine whether *English* or *Spanish* was his primary language. If it was Spanish, he could be encouraged to develop it through oral language usage to the

level of reading readiness and then learn to read in Spanish first. At the same time he could be learning English systematically and efficiently as a second language. However, if his primary language was English, he could be encouraged to develop it further through oral language usage to the level of prereading competence and then learn to read in English first. At the same time he could be learning Spanish systematically and efficiently as a second language. In either event, he could be proud of being a bilingual/bicultural person in our pluralistic society.

2. If a school does not provide regular instruction in a child's primary language, an extended period of time would be allotted for him to master English for the formal reading necessary for success in the school grades. Even though certified teachers of the child's primary language may not be available, the school would be responsible for providing opportunity for the child to use and extend his knowledge and understanding of it orally as another language.

3. Because the school is concerned that a child's self-concept be strengthened and not destroyed, it provides a variety of programs in which children of minority groups are encouraged to appreciate their language and culture. Children learn that their extended families are integral parts of the community. The school bolsters their self-concept and thus makes them feel important as persons. Chapter 16 is devoted to this problem.

What Is Reading?   Is reading pronouncing words correctly? Is reading getting ideas from printed pages? Here are some definitions:

> Reading is decoding written words so that they can be produced orally.
>
> Reading is understanding the language of the author of a printed passage.
>
> Reading is the ability to anticipate meaning in lines of print so that the reader is not concerned with the mechanical details but with grasping ideas from groups of words that convey meaning.

Reading encompasses all of these things. The differences in current reading programs in use today lie mainly in the relative importance assigned to each of these three definitions.

Programs strongly oriented to a phonics approach for identifying words have proved unsuccessful in motivating children strongly enough to want to continue to learn to read. Recent attempts to construct preprimers that utilize no more than 12, 15, or 20 different words have only provided further evidence that this is not a way to motivate children to learn to read as the third definition above intended they should. Savage's example of teaching spelling patterns in rigidly controlled sentences using the ridiculous "Flick the tick off the chick with a thick stick, Nick," exemplifies the possible extremes in such sentence composition.[2]

Without alert, innovative teachers, the newer reading programs in use may allow too much time for teaching beginners the names of letters, severely controlled vocabularies, and other artificial ways of encouraging the work of decoding.

Children need not start with simple sentences prepared for them by a "strange" author. They can write sentences of their own. The rationale of this "language experience" approach is that children need to learn how the process of reading works by seeing that what they can express in their own vernacular can be recorded for them and that it means what they said when they first thought of it. Allen, author of language-experience materials, said, "Children who write, read! They have to read!" He continues:

To children who have experienced authorship many times, reading is not lessons, worksheets, practice exercises, or a time each day in a time schedule (perhaps to dread). It is the continuous discovery of stepping-stones to a lifetime of enjoyment of books. It results in the conceptualizations:

What I can think about, I can say.

What I can say, I can write.

What I can write, I can read.

I can read what I can write and what other people have written for me to read.[3]

There is basic psychological value in having first or second graders use their own vocabulary and sentence structure in preparing a great deal of their reading material during the beginning of the reading program. If the reading program ended here, they would not be mature readers. Reading must take children into new areas of life and experience which are provided for their enjoyment through the writing of other people. Of course, children need all the clues they can be given in order to help them anticipate meaning in all they read.

Beyond this, children require a great deal of easy reading practice, just as in learning analogous skills, such as how to play the piano, or how to use another language fluently. As they refine their decoding skills through a great deal of interesting reading practice, more of the words they encounter in print become sight words. What happens is that by using the analytical skills they have learned and the context of what they are reading, they can immediately identify the necessary word to complete the meaning in a sentence or paragraph.

Gray identified four steps in the reading act: perception, comprehension, reaction, and integration.[4] Perception is the ability to pronounce the word as a meaningful unit. Comprehension is the ability to make individual words evoke useful ideas as they are read in context. Reaction requires judgmental action—a feeling about what the author has said. Integration, the final step, is the ability to assimilate the idea or concept into one's background of experience so that it is useful as a part of the total experience of the individual. Of course these four steps are completely interdependent for meaningful use of reading as a tool in the solution of problems. (See figure 1.1.)

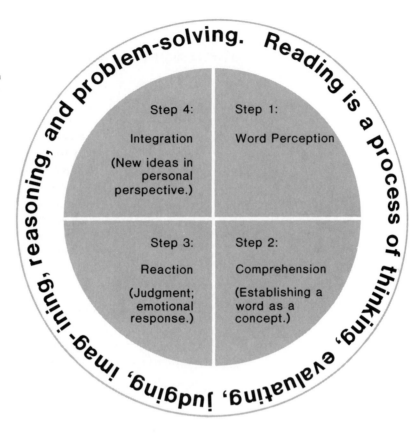

Figure 1.1 Gray's definition of reading as a four-step process.

This diagram is adapted from one written in Spanish in an unpublished language bulletin prepared for elementary teachers by Señora Coñsuelo de Escorcia, Tegucigalpa, Honduras, Ministry of Education.

Reading is a process of thinking, evaluating, judging, imagining, reasoning, and problem-solving.

Step 4:

Integration

(New ideas in personal perspective.)

Step 1:

Word Perception

Step 3:

Reaction

(Judgment; emotional response.)

Step 2:

Comprehension

(Establishing a word as a concept.)

The Language-Experience Approach

Reading is a process of thinking, evaluating, judging, imagining, reasoning, and problem-solving. It is necessary, however, to distinguish between the tasks of learning how to read as young children do it and of daily reading as mature readers do it. Teachers must provide children with learning opportunities which allow them to sense from the very beginning that reading produces meaning and that reading and writing are only extensions of the listening and speaking which the children have been doing for some years.

Reading materials for children just learning to read must be structured to allow them to anticipate and acquire meaning from context from the very first lessons. This has been explained by Burke as a process by which children utilize the grammar of their language to express ideas personal and important to them. They are not being bogged down with the sound-symbol relationships of letters until there is need for them, and then only after they have understood how the process of reading works.[5] (See figure 1.2.) This emphasis is based on the point of view that children bring to school a fully developed language and possess all the skills of thinking, reasoning, problem-solving and imagining in oral language. Instead of supposing that they do not know any words to read with, teachers must recognize that they know thousands of words, but not in their written form. By using a child's own experiences, conversation,

Figure 1.2 Meaning
must always be the
center of the reading
task. Every lesson
should be figuratively
like a wedge that
reaches to the center
as in the diagram.

From Carolyn L. Burke,
"The Language Process:
Systems or Systematic," in
*Language and Learning To
Read,* ed. Richard E.
Hodges and E. Hugh
Rudorf (Boston: Houghton
Mifflin, 1972), p. 26.

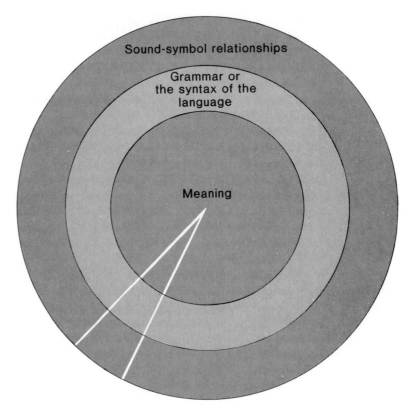

and ability to explain events, teachers can write this language for the child
to read. Seeing the written form of their own language and hearing it read
back, children understand that the written words are an extension of their
spoken language. This language-experience approach to beginning reading is
the logical way to extend the child's listening and speaking skills to include
reading and writing. As the avenue to formal reading for all children, the
language-experience approach will be discussed more fully in a later chapter.

When children read at an appropriate level of difficulty, three kinds of
feedback help them decide how accurately they are anticipating meaning.
First, the printed word must correspond to an idea or concept they already
know. They will reject any nonsense word and accept one that makes sense.
Second, they will know whether or not a pronunciation of a printed word fits
the syntax of a sentence spoken correctly in their own vernacular. If a noun
is needed but an oral reader supplies an adjective or a verb, it will be rejected
immediately because it does not fit the syntax. Third, children will be continually testing the appropriateness of meaning of a sentence the way they have
read it and reject any words that do not make sense in the context of the
passage. So, the reader's (or listener's) knowledge of words, grammar, and

semantic correctness provides not only feedback for what is being read but enables one to anticipate, to some degree, what is going to be read next.[6]

The language-experience approach helps the child make the transition from oral to written language. Recall Gray's four steps of the reading process: *perception* of words, *comprehension* of meanings, *reaction* to ideas conveyed, and *integration* into one's total experience. A child's own story or sentence dictated to a teacher is a part of the child's experience, so the teacher need not be concerned about the child's comprehension and ability to react. The child's task is only to decode the message that already belongs to him. A child whose language is already rich in concepts, vocabulary, and imagination has the potential for "writing" many stories before reading stories written by others. If the language-experience approach is used, the first 75 to 100 written words children learn may be from their own repertoire of language rather than arbitary choices of the authors of a series of readers. With this personal sight vocabulary, a child can read comfortably after developing an understanding of what the reading process is and how it works.

Naturally, young children soon exhaust their own realm of experience, and extension of their learning depends upon reading what others have written about other places and other experiences. Then it is time for children to begin acquisition of all the word recognition skills that will make them independent readers and all the evaluation skills necessary for making valid judgments about the worth of what is read.

Literacy in Today's World

Most people who become teachers in the United States have probably been fortunate enough throughout their lives to live in an environment where reading is encouraged, respected, and expected. They have developed sufficiently mature reading habits to succeed in general education courses in college. In this environment it is easy to overlook the fact that many people in this country grow up and live out their lives without learning to read.

An individual can scarcely survive in present-day society without reading skill. To participate fully, a person needs to have achieved a high level of literacy. Appreciation of the extent and seriousness of illiteracy is evidenced by special reading programs in the schools, general reading clinics, and numerous programs funded by federal grants since 1965, such as Right to Read and the National Reading Program.

Holloway has recorded the extent of failure or deficiency of reading skill in the United States:[7] "In 1971, there were some eighteen million adults who were considered functionally illiterate and seven million elementary and secondary school children who had reading deficiencies sufficient to cause a problem in the schools."

An assessment of seventeen-year-olds in 1974 continued to emphasize the fact that many young people graduate from high school each year unable to assimilate the reading materials they encounter in life outside the school, such as road signs, advertisements, blank forms, maps, etc.[8]

Carl Rowan wrote:[9]

Adult illiteracy takes a devastating toll. Unemployment, poverty, alienation are all part of its legacy. One study found that half of the unemployed 16-to-21-year-olds in major cities were functionally illiterate. A large percentage of welfare recipients—over half in some surveys—read at grade-school levels. Chief Justice Warren E. Burger has noted that "the percentage of inmates in all institutions who cannot read or write is staggering."

Chall has written:[10]

We consider that any adult is at a disadvantage when he cannot read a serious newspaper like the *New York Times,* a news magazine such as *Time* or *Newsweek,* the Federal income tax forms and instructions, and the bold and fine print on a house or apartment lease. The approximate readability level of these documents is estimated to be about twelfth grade reading level . . . it will take all our ingenuity as scientists, as teachers, as clinicians, and as administrators to bring this level of literacy about, for we are not now achieving it, even when the average educational attainment is twelfth grade.

Studies surveying populations in adult basic education programs show evidence that the person over twenty-five who attended school for seven years is apt to perform on an achievement test at about the fourth grade level. If school attendance was for four years, the person is likely to perform nearer to the second grade level.

It is obvious that current efforts of federal agencies are long overdue if the adult population is to acquire minimum literacy skills.

One of the objectives of reading instruction is to lay the groundwork for lifelong reading habits in boys and girls when they are going through school. To build such habits, to instill constructive attitudes, and to ensure that students' efforts are successful during their school attendance are a *sacred trust of classroom teachers.*

Reading Defined

Horn defined reading in this way:

. . . reading includes those processes that are involved in approaching, perfecting, and maintaining meaning through the use of the printed page. Since there are many such processes, and since each one varies in degree, the term must be elastic enough to apply to all the varieties and gradations of reading involved in the use of books.[11]

Horn, further, analyzed communication through reading as follows:

The author does not really convey ideas to the reader; he merely stimulates him to construct them out of his own experience. If the concept is already in the reader's mind, the task is relatively easy, but if, as is usually the case in school, it is new to the reader, its construction more nearly approaches problem-solving than simple association.[12]

Then he concluded:

. . . it is clear that very little improvement may be expected from formal drill in reading unless at the same time provision is made for the enrichment of experience, the development of language abilities, and the improvement of thinking.[13]

While communication skills and concept development go hand in hand, they should not be confused. Communication skills develop in children in a fixed order: (1) listening with understanding; (2) speaking; (3) reading; and (4) writing. Concept development, on the other hand, can and should be reinforced at each of those steps. Reflection, appraisal, and problem-solving need to be practiced in open-ended oral discussions, teacher-led but not teacher-dominated, as well as in reading and writing lessons.

Gates described the nature of the reading process in this way:

Reading is not a simple mechanical skill; nor is it a narrow scholastic tool. Properly cultivated, it is essentially a thoughtful process. However, to say that reading is a "thought-getting" process is to give it too restricted a description. It should be developed as a complex organization of patterns of higher mental processes. It can and should embrace all types of thinking, evaluating, judging, imagining, reasoning, and problem-solving. Indeed, it is believed that reading is one of the best media for cultivating many techniques of thinking and imagining. The reading program should, therefore, make careful provision for contributing as fully as possible to the cultivation of a whole array of techniques involved in understanding, thinking, reflecting, imagining, judging, evaluating, analyzing, and reasoning.[14]

Gates pointed out that reading is more than a mental activity; that emotional responses are also required:

. . . the child does more than understand and contemplate; his emotions are stirred; his attitudes and purposes are modified; indeed, his innermost being is involved. . . . The reading program should, therefore, make provision for exerting an influence upon the development of the most wholesome dynamic and emotional adjustments.[15]

In this text, reading is defined as the process by which the graphic symbols are translated into meaningful sound symbols in the reader's experience. *Meaning* is the key: learning to read necessitates mastery of all the linguistic clues that facilitate anticipation of meaning in a line of print.

Ability to anticipate meaning in context is stressed in order to emphasize what reading is *not*. Reading is *not* being concerned with the mechanical details; it is, rather, being concerned with perception of chunks of language that convey meaning. The main difference between the "learning how to read" process of beginners and the reading of mature readers is that beginners must give some attention to the mediating process of pronouncing words for so long as they are internalizing the nature of the process. Successful transition to mature reading depends upon the richness of a person's language, the ability to function with and extend one's language, and the ability to solve problems with language. A section in chapter 8, Teaching Beginning Reading, is devoted to extending oral language competence because this is a primary requisite to the language acquisition necessary for facile reading.

Differences among Children

Such expressions as "all children are different" and "no two are alike" have become *trite* through verbalization but not through day-by-day teacher performance in the classroom. Children vary greatly in physical, mental, emotional, and social characteristics. Teachers are admonished at every turn to recognize that children grow at different rates in all these characteristics. Greater attention to putting these known principles into practice is indicated.

Of course, children who have a vision or hearing impairment, a neurological handicap, poor general health, insufficient sleep or rest, a substandard living environment, a speech impediment, emotional upsets, inadequate language readiness for reading, or long absences from school are apt to have difficulty beyond that experienced by other children in learning to read. But the differences in normal children under normal circumstances are what teachers need to understand and plan for in their everyday work.

Since no two children can learn the same thing in the same amount of time with the same amount of practice, there can be no arbitrary standards for what constitutes first grade or fifth grade in the elementary school.

As children progress through the grades in public schools, the range of individual differences on various traits will become greater and greater, not less and less. It follows that twelve-year-olds will vary more within their age group than will six-year-olds. What happens to the range of IQs within a group will demonstrate this point. The IQ—intelligence quotient—is the arithmetic relationship between a child's chronological age and measured mental age, and it is assumed to remain relatively stable for any individual. Therefore, if the range of IQs in a given class of six-year-olds is 75 to 125, the mental ages will vary from four and a half years ($4.5/6 = $ IQ 75) to seven and a half years ($7.5/6 = $ IQ 125). The same group when twelve-year-olds will have mental ages varying from nine years ($9/12 = $ IQ 75) to fifteen years ($15/12 = $ IQ 125). And when fifteen-year-olds, they will have mental ages varying from eleven years and three months ($11.25/15 = $ IQ 75) to eighteen years and nine months ($18.75/15 = $ IQ 125).

Even though the limitations of tests which yield IQ scores are generally recognized, almost every school uses the scores as an index of general learning ability. Such a measure always demonstrates a wide range of ability in children.

The real problems in trying to teach six-, seven-, and eight-year-olds arise from the children's specific strengths and weaknesses when they are confronted with the complicated four-faceted process of learning how to read the printed word: (1) mastering a basic sight vocabulary, (2) learning phonic and structural analysis skills, (3) developing comprehension skills, and (4) getting lots of easy practice. Obviously, most teachers sufficiently understand their job, because the great majority of children do learn to read with encouraging degrees of success.

Perhaps *too much* emphasis has been placed on the techniques of teaching reading and *not enough* upon the peculiar nature of the child who does not learn what he is taught. Different methods as currently used probably do not account for the extreme range of differences in children's learning. But the idiosyncrasies of children vary extremely. Teachers, then, need to be constantly evaluating the individual *child* as well as the specific techniques used to help that child learn to read.

The Skills of Reading

It has been estimated that nearly 90 percent of a child's school day is spent on reading and writing activities. This amount of time is certainly not necessary and probably not desirable, but it is the way most classrooms are operating. This fact emphasizes that reading is not taught or practiced only during a scheduled reading class. It is taught all day long in some form. Actually, often reading is not taught at all but, more accurately, is assigned and tested. The fact that 10 to 15 percent of boys and girls have problems with reading in school may be due in greater measure to inadequate teaching than to failure to learn. No teacher can deny this charge until both sides of the issue are competently examined.

One classroom was observed where the sixth grade had been divided into three subgroups for reading: high second grade level, easy fourth level, and easy fifth level. Yet, all the sixth graders were assigned the same spelling word list of sixth grade words for regular spelling, and each member of the class was issued a sixth grade geography book adjudged to be too difficult for more than half a class in which the achievement normally fits the sixth grade achievement level. Can even the top subgroup, reading at easy fifth grade level, read with any degree of understanding a sixth grade geography book which is likely to be written at a more difficult reader level than a sixth grade reader?

It has been said that the teachers in the primary grades teach children how to read, while in later grades teachers assign reading for the children to learn the content of the course of study. This idea is not true, and teachers must be very careful to discredit it. Of course, in the first year and perhaps most of the second, children have to develop a great deal of decoding ability so they can pronounce or recognize words for the reading process. They must learn how to phrase, punctuate, and make proper uses of inflection. However, students should be improving these very same skills all the way through secondary school in a comprehensive reading program.

On the other hand, children during their very first reading lessons are going to find the primary emphasis given to "getting the idea" or "finding the meaning in the story" even while the decoding process is being learned (and no reading can happen unless the child can pronounce the words). Teaching that reading is a process of deriving meaning through interpretation of printed symbols must be given primary emphasis. Just as reading for meaning is important during the initial reading program, it remains the primary reason for reading throughout one's life. Consequently, one learns to read and reads to learn as two concurrent processes all the way through school.

Reading skills at different levels are often broken down in the following way:

A. Developmental: The how-to-read skills
   1. Word recognition skills
   2. Comprehension skills
   3. Study skills
B. Functional reading
   1. Location activities
   2. Specific skills for study/comprehension
   3. Selection and organization
   4. Summarizing
   5. Providing for remembering
C. Recreational reading
   1. Reading as a "free time" activity
   2. Locating books of interest in the library
   3. Developing tastes for a variety of reading material
   4. Giving pleasure to others through oral reading
   5. Fixing permanent habits of reading every day

Objectives of the Reading Program

The objective of teaching reading is to make each person as literate, in the broadest sense, as possible. Four levels of mastery are necessary: (1) mastering the skills necessary to decode the written word so that it is immediately pronounceable and meaningful; (2) mastering the skills necessary to comprehend so that the reader demands meaning from the passage being read; (3) developing the abilities necessary to think about and evaluate the validity or usefulness of what one reads; and (4) developing a lifelong habit of relying on reading to gather information, to substantiate one's thinking, to solve new problems, or to entertain oneself. All teachers undoubtedly have some general purposes similar to these four as global purposes of teaching.

A good school reading program would be based on the following principles:

1. Reading is communicating. So are listening, speaking, and writing. All these skills should develop in an integrated, interdependent manner in the school.

2. All school personnel teach reading; overtly or covertly, they demonstrate its value.

3. Reading development takes place within the framework of total child development.

4. Each child grows at his or her own rate and needs to follow a well worked out program from kindergarten through all the school years.

5. The reading program (a) teaches how to read, (b) provides for much reading practice, and (c) encourages both functional and recreational reading in a very wide range of interests and levels of difficulty.

6. The reading program provides other avenues for communicating learning for nonreaders and provides diagnostic and prescriptive services for those who can profitably use them.

Summary

Reading is the process by which graphic symbols are translated into meaningful sound symbols in the reader's experience. Meaning is the key: learning to read necessitates mastery of all the linguistic clues that facilitate anticipating meaning in a line of print.

The reading act as practiced by mature readers may be thought of as a four-step process: perception, comprehension, reaction, and integration.

Learning to read is a complicated developmental process that large numbers of children do not master although most do to some degree of proficiency. Children need to grow into reading. They do this by extending their communication skills from well developed listening and speaking skills to reading and writing. The language-experience method of beginning reading means that children's own ideas and concepts are presented in their own words, which they learn to read first.

Suggested Activities

1. Select a story from a basal reader and write questions for it which elicit abilities to think about and use language.
2. Think about your own public school education and try to evaluate the degree to which your school exemplified the principles of a good school reading program. Which of the six were apparent and which were not?
3. Observe a teacher teaching a reading lesson and evaluate the level of questioning used in a class discussion.
4. Take a standardized reading test and compare your results with norms provided. Do you read "better" than the average college student?

For Further Reading

Burron, Arnold, and Amos L. Claybaugh. *Basic Concepts in Reading Instruction: A Programmed Approach,* 2nd ed. Columbus: Charles E. Merrill, 1977.

Dallman, Martha, et al. *The Teaching of Reading.* 5th ed. Chapter 1, "The Teaching of Reading: A Challenge." New York: Holt, Rinehart & Winston, 1978.

Fryer, Ann. "Teaching Reading in the Infant School," in *Teaching in the British Primary School,* edited by Vincent R. Rogers. New York: Macmillan, 1970.

Guszak, Frank J. *Diagnostic Reading Instruction in the Elementary School,* 2d ed. New York: Harper & Row, 1978.

Harris, Stephen G. "Reading Methodology: What's Modern; What's Traditional." *The Reading Teacher* 27 (November 1973):134–37.

Heilman, Arthur. *Principles and Practices of Teaching Reading.* 4th ed. Chapter 1, "Principles of Teaching Reading." Columbus: Charles E. Merrill, 1977.

Hodges, Richard E., and E. Hugh Rudorf, eds. *Language and Learning to Read.* Boston: Houghton Mifflin, 1972.

Smith, Frank. *Understanding Reading,* 2d ed. New York: Holt, Rinehart & Winston, 1978.

Stauffer, Russell. *Directing Reading Maturity as a Cognitive Process.* Chapter 1, "Reading, A Thinking Process." New York: Harper & Row, 1975.

Tinker, Miles A. *Preparing Your Child for Reading.* New York: McGraw-Hill, 1976.

Zintz, Miles V. *Corrective Reading.* 3rd ed. Appendix A: "Teaching Reading: An Overview." Dubuque, Iowa: Wm. C. Brown, 1977.

Notes

1. Clark S. Knowlton, "Spanish-American Schools in the 1970's," *Newsletter,* General Department of Mission Strategy and Evangelism, Board of National Missions, United Presbyterian Church in the U.S.A., 475 Riverside Drive, New York, N.Y. 10027, July 1968, p. 4.
2. John F. Savage, ed., *Linguistics for Teachers: Selected Readings* (Chicago: Science Research Associates, 1973), p. 216.
3. Roach Van Allen and Claryce Allen, *An Introduction to a Language Experience Program, Level I* (Chicago: Encyclopaedia Britannica Press, 1966), p. 21.
4. William S. Gray, *On Their Own in Reading* (Chicago: Scott, Foresman, 1948), pp. 35–37.
5. Carolyn L. Burke, "The Language Process: Systems or Systematic," in *Language and Learning To Read,* ed. Richard E. Hodges and E. Hugh Rudorf (Boston: Houghton Mifflin, 1972), p. 26.

6. Bradford Arthur, *Teaching English to Speakers of English* (New York: Harcourt Brace Jovanovich, 1973), pp. 43–45.

7. Ruth Love Holloway, *Right to Read: The First Four Years* (Washington, D.C.: U.S. Office of Education, 1974), p. 2.

8. "Functional Literacy—Basic Reading Performance," a newsletter of The National Right to Read, National Assessment of Educational Programs, Denver, Colorado, 1975.

9. Carl T. Rowan and David M. Mazie, "Johnny's Parents Can't Read Either," *The Reader's Digest* 110 (January 1977):153.

10. Jeanne S. Chall, *Reading and Development,* Keynote Address, International Reading Association, 1975 (Newark, Del.: International Reading Assn., 1976), pp. 5–6.

11. Ernest Horn, *Methods of Instruction in the Social Studies* (New York: Charles Scribner's Sons, 1937), p. 152.

12. Ibid., p. 154.

13. Ibid., p. 156.

14. Arthur I. Gates, "Character and Purposes of the Yearbook," *Reading in the Elementary School,* ed. Nelson B. Henry, 48th Yearbook of the National Society for the Study of Education (Chicago: University of Chicago Press, 1949), p. 3.

15. Ibid., p. 4.

2

Psychological Foundations for Reading Instruction

Each classroom teacher is confronted with problems of classroom management, of motivation of learning, and of articulating this year's work with the previous and following year's work. Within the class, the teacher must expect to find the normal range of abilities in intellectual, physical, emotional, and social development.

There are a number of principles of learning that the teacher needs to understand, accept, and use in interpreting the school success of individual children.

When the teacher and child meet, a major part of the teacher's armament must be a knowledge of the principles of learning. Many normal children learn readily in spite of the repeated violations of learning principles. . . . By sharpening our awareness of some of these principles, as applied to teaching children, . . . we can anticipate broader adherence to them. . . .

Some of these major principles of learning include *overlearning, ordering,* and *sizing* (programming) of new material, *rewarding* only *desired responses, frequent review,* and avoidance of interference and negative transfer.[1] [Italics added.]

Gagné discusses eight types of learning and defines them briefly as follows:[2]

1. *Signal learning.* Learning to make a general, diffuse response to a signal.
2. *Stimulus response.* A precise response to a discriminated stimulus.
3. *Chaining.* A chain of two or more stimulus-response connections.
4. *Verbal association.* Learning of verbal chains.
5. *Multiple discrimination.* Even with n different responses to x different stimuli, the learner does discriminate.
6. *Concept learning.* Acquiring ability to respond to entire classes of objects or events with proper identification.
7. *Principle learning.* Chaining of two or more concepts.
8. *Problem-solving.* Using thinking to combine principles to obtain new solutions.

According to Hilgard, learning theory might be expected to answer questions one might ask about learning in everyday life. Any theory, then, may be appraised in terms of its attention to measuring.[3]

1. *Capacity.* What are the limits of learning? How is learning measured? What is the range of individual differences?
2. *Practice.* What is the role of practice in learning? Practice causes improvement in efficiency in performance only when the conditions of learning are suited to the one who is practicing.
3. *Motivation.* How important are drives and incentives? What about rewards and punishments? Or intrinsic vs. extrinsic motives?
4. *Understanding.* What is the place of insight? Or a hierarchy of steps leading to generalizations?
5. *Transfer.* Does learning one thing help you in learning something else?
6. *Forgetting.* What happens when we remember? When we forget?

This chapter discusses such elements of learning theory as capacity, practice, motivation, understanding, transfer, and forgetting as they relate to reading. These observations lead to principles of programmed learning, of helping children learn to generalize, and of taking into account the affective, the cognitive, and the psychomotor domains in the education of children.

Elements of Learning Theory

Capacity

The normal bell-shaped curve of distribution has become a household term. It represents the range, the extent, and the distribution of a skill or trait. This concept that the distribution of any given attribute, skill, or ability falls normally around a central or average value is an important one.

For example, if we were to stop the first 100 men passing a given street corner and measure their height, we would find out something about their sameness and their difference. Since the average American man is about five feet nine inches, most of the men measured would be about this height. Some would be shorter; some would be taller. If one were to plot this information on graph paper and generalize it to a curved line (see figure 2.1), the graphed points would tend to cluster around a central value, resulting in the normal curve.

Figure 2.1 Areas under the normal curve. (The Greek letter σ is the statistical representation for standard deviation.)

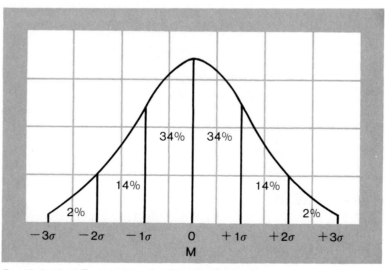

Intelligence, problem-solving abilities, length of time required to memorize nonsense syllables, or scores on a vocabulary test constitute skills and abilities that also fall in a *normal distribution* when a large unselected group is measured.

Statistically, the area under a normal curve can be divided into three equal deviations from the median or center. The standard deviation represents a given distance (in points) on the baseline which corresponds to arbitrarily predetermined *areas* for each standard deviation. One standard deviation encompasses 34 percent below or 34 percent above the median; two standard deviations encompass an additional 14 percent above or below the median; and three standard deviations include the additional 2 percent on either side. This tells a teacher that if there is a random distribution, 68 cases in 100 lie within one standard deviation above and one standard deviation below the median; 28 cases are in the second standard deviation, 14 above and 14 below the median; and 4 are in the third, 2 above and 2 below the median. (See figure 2.1.)

When the median is defined, half the class will perform above the median, and half the class will perform below the median. To try to get a class to perform in such a way that everyone is average or better is to deny the existence of this spread of abilities.

Figure 2.2 Variations of general learning abilities in relation to chronological ages.

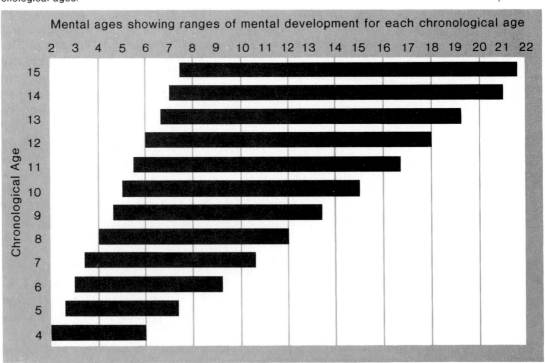

This interpretation becomes meaningful when the arithmetic average (mean) or the position of the middle child in a distribution (median) gives a value for the *typical* or *average* level of performance.

The range of differences in achievement in reading and arithmetic get wider with good teaching. For each teacher this means that the children taught should become more different in achievement, *not more alike,* during a year of instruction.

Some children grow faster academically; some children show average growth; and other children grow more slowly academically. Figure 2.2 shows the increasing spread of general learning abilities associated with chronological age range from four to fifteen years.

The Wechsler Intelligence Scale for Children is a common individually administered intelligence test in schools and children's clinics. It has been standardized so that a score of 100 is *normal* for any given chronological age. In other words, if a child of ten earns a full scale IQ score of 100, this represents normal or average intelligence and ranks him at the median, or the 50th percentile, in the distribution. Since the standard deviation for this test is 15, two standard deviations (a range from 70 IQ to 130 IQ) include 96 percent of the total sample tested as indicated in table 2.1. This corresponds to the normal curve of distribution already discussed. About 50 percent of all the people of a given age test between 90 and 110. This is called the normal intelligence range. (See table 2.1.)

The Spread of Differences

The longer a group of children the same age attend school, the *more different* they become.

Teachers may expect to find that in classes of unselected children (heterogeneous groups) the range of reading achievement measured by a standardized test will be, on the average, three years at the end of grade two, four years at the end of grade three, five years at the end of grade four, six years at the end of grade five, and seven years at the end of grade six.

Many factors in the child's total growth and development contribute to these differences in achievement. Figure 2.3 details differences in school learning attributable to constitutional factors, intellectual factors, environmental factors, educational factors, and emotional factors.

Table 2.1 Intelligence classification for WISC IQs.

From Henry E. Garrett, *Testing for Teachers,* 2d ed. (New York: American Book Co., 1965), p. 75.

IQ Ranges	Classification	Percent in Each Group
130–	very superior	2
120–129	superior	7
110–119	bright normal	16
90–109	average	50
80– 89	dull normal	16
70– 79	borderline	7
69 below	mental defective	2
		100

Figure 2.3 Factors in the range of individual differences.

From Miles V. Zintz, *Corrective Reading,* 3rd ed. (Dubuque, Ia.: Wm. C. Brown, 1977), p. 44.

Figure 2.3 content:

Constitutional
1. Chronological age (the one criterion by which pupils are most alike in classroom). 2. Physical health. Can the child see well? Hear well? Have good motor coordination? Diet? Rest? Sleep? 3. Handicapping conditions: 7 percent have speech problems; 3 percent have hearing problems; neurological handicaps.

Intellectual
The range in intelligence in any elementary class will be several years—much more crucial than chronological age. Results of intelligence tests must be used cautiously with pupils who cannot read or for whom English is a second language.

Environmental
Parental understanding of purpose of school; level of aspiration for child; high relationship between socioeconomic level of parent and achievement of child; illiteracy; foreign language background; mobility of families.

Learning
in school for any pupil is conditioned by these factors in the child's life experience.

Educational
Background of experience. More closely related to socioeconomic status than to intelligence. For some extremely meager; for others, extremely rich. Readiness for day's lesson: vocabulary, reading skills, help needed in establishing purposes for study. Foreign language background. Inadequate materials; inadequate grouping, motivation.

Emotional
Obstacles to the "normal" satisfactions in meeting psychological needs; development of the self-concept; ego-gratification; recognition; need for new and varied experiences, tension; defeatist attitude, fear of failure.

Mastery Learning

Mastery learning is a concept predicated upon the belief that students should be given an assignment with predetermined criteria of achievement and then not be permitted to move to another task until those criteria are met. For example, *mastery* could be arbitrarily defined as earning a 90 percent level of correctness on a criterion-referenced test over the material to be learned. Each learner uses *as much time as he or she needs* to master the assignment.

Bloom identifies four elements in good teaching:[4]

1. Giving the student adequate and motivational *cues.* This is the way the teacher presents and explains the assignment. Whether or not the student can use the cues depends on the breadth of the student's background and the variety of enriching materials accessible to him or her.

2. *Reinforcement* of the student's successes. A skillful teacher knows what would be a reward for a given student.

3. *Involvement* of the student in the learning process. The extent to which a student actively participates is a good index of the quality of learning taking place.

4. Giving the student immediate *feedback* with necessary correction is the ingredient that makes the first three elements work over an extended period.

With learning centers in the classroom (discussed in chapter 4), and with adequate informal diagnosis of *entering behaviors,* teachers will be able to incorporate a great deal of mastery learning for their students into the course of study. *Students who need more time can take it.* Fast learners can either move more quickly to enrichment activities or take time to be peer teachers and work with their own classmates in learning activities.

Practice

Practice provides the circumstance for conditions of learning to operate. For effective practice, essential conditions include:

1. Motivation
2. Immediate knowledge of results
3. Distributed practice
4. Elimination of error

Drill should be:

1. At the point of error
2. Spirited
3. Of short duration
4. Meaningful and purposeful

What a student practices must be meaningful to *that student.* To stay motivated, children must have some expectations of success. They cannot compete seriously if they feel they cannot win. Marks that signify merit rather than failure should be assigned to the lowest achievers in class.

Immediate knowledge of results shows a child whether or not he or she is successful; such knowledge is a strong motivational factor.

Distributed vs. Massed Practice

Ebbinghaus demonstrated that with any considerable number of repetitions of an act, a planned distribution of repetitions over a period of time is decidedly more advantageous than the massing of them at a single time. More short practice periods return greater dividends than fewer long ones.

Teachers need to be aware of the importance of *distribution of exposure* to concepts and generalizations to be taught. Summarizing at the end of the class period, reviewing each lesson on succeeding days, and helping students write summarizing statements are important in this exposure of learning. This evidence should be used by teachers to reduce the amount of procrastinating and cramming students do for tests.

For the drill included in any subject, such as spelling, handwriting, and overlearning arithmetic algorithms, the principles of distributed practice in shorter periods apply. Short, lively, motivated drills on basic sight words, consonant blend sounds, most common prefixes, or responding with synonyms or antonyms will be very profitable in the reading program.

Motivation

No learning takes place without a motive. Motives are conditions within the organism that cause it to seek satisfaction of need. The basis for the condition is obscure, generally speaking, since the real motivation a given student has for a specific learning objective may not be the same as the teacher suspects it to be. An intrinsic motive to learn something may not be as strong as the extrinsic motive the student established at home, or as strong as the many psychological needs apart from the student's intellectual growth.

Motivating students is a complex, involved process for teachers and often leaves them baffled when their plans go awry. Since there will be no one way to motivate every child, the teacher must seek ways to cause each student to set his own goals, both immediate and mediate.

The relation of education to the level of motivation in the society is more direct than most people recognize. The goals a young person sets are very heavily affected by adult expectations. The educational system provides the young person with a sense of what society expects in the way of performance. If it is lax in its demands, then the student will believe that such are the expectations of society. If the educational system expects much, the young person will probably have high expectations for himself or herself.

When the United States Office of Education completed a three-year study about methods of teaching reading in the first grade, where thousands of teachers used dozens of varying approaches, the one big generalization to be drawn was that a *good teacher,* not a special twist in methodology, was the variable that exercised most control over teaching success.

Students respect the teacher who is honest with them, the teacher who works for them, sits in on class projects as an advisor, and listens to problems and keeps them confidential.

Teachers of the highest achieving groups are positive in their approach to teaching. They encourage responses even when those responses aren't exactly what the teacher had in mind. They explore content with the students at many thinking levels.[5] Good teachers try different approaches. They allow children to demonstrate why they think they are right, and praise them for their effort. Good teachers ask open-ended questions so that there is no pat answer such as reciting "a fact." However, the kinds of questions teachers ask affect the classroom climate in ways other than providing occasions for praising a student.

The effective teacher understands that there are many bases for motivation: (1) mastery motives—desire to excel, desire to succeed, desire to overcome difficulties; (2) social approval motives—desire for approval, desire for self-esteem, desire for attention; (3) conformity motives—desire to conform, desire to avoid censure.

Motivation should:

1. Include success experiences so the student has feelings of personal worth and security.

2. Be greater in school if the school curriculum emphasizes social utility with considerable emphasis on the usefulness, here and now, of what it teaches. In addition to school being a preparation for future life, it is accepted that it is more importantly preparation for life here and now; and the result of learning to live here and now prepares one to live in an undefinable future.

3. Include methodology to reinforce self-expression and self-esteem in *all* boys and girls.

4. Maximize competition with one's own past record and minimize competition among members of a class.

Intrinsic vs. Extrinsic Motivation

When young children enter school, much of their motivation may be teacher- or adult-generated. Elementary teachers are using extrinsic motivation when one hears them say: "You'd like to do that for Miss Brown, wouldn't you?" or "Miss Brown would like you to finish that before you go out to play."

One of the goals of education in a free society is that the value of learning becomes its own reward. The extent to which the school achieves this goal will determine how successfully students are intrinsically motivated to achieve self-realization. Motivation for learning may be diagrammed as in figure 2.4, largely extrinsic in first grade and largely intrinsic in twelfth.

The hierarchy of needs described by Maslow leads to the conclusion that the well integrated personality on the top step in the hierarchy has a curiosity about life, the future, and the unknown that is satisfied through a need to know and to understand.

Figure 2.4 Growth in intrinsic motivations; acquiring the desire to learn.

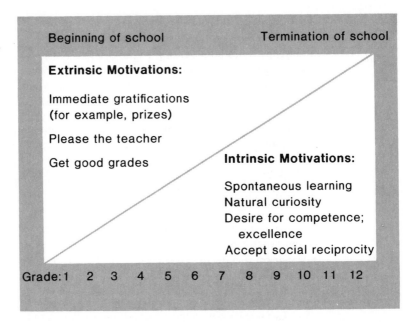

Figure 2.5 Hierarchy and prepotency of needs.

From Herbert J. Klausmeier and William Goodwin, *Learning and Human Abilities: Educational Psychology,* 4th ed. (New York: Harper & Row, 1975), p. 227. Copyright 1975 by Herbert J. Klausmeier and William Goodwin. By permission of the publisher. Drawing based on Maslow.

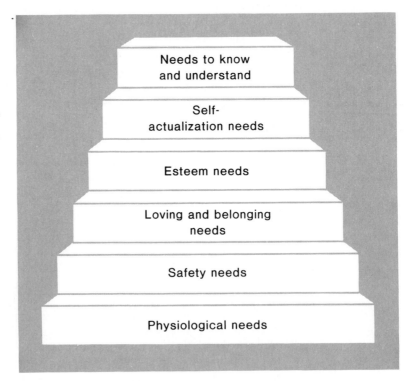

Physiological needs, safety, love and belonging, esteem, and self-actualization needs must be met to some degree before man explores his need to know and understand. When a more basic need is fairly well satisfied, the next higher order need emerges and serves as an active motivator of behavior. See figure 2.5.[6]

Maslow concluded:

These basic goals are related to each other, being arranged in a hierarchy of prepotency. This means that the most prepotent goal will monopolize consciousness and will tend of itself to organize the recruitment of the various capacities of the organism. The less prepotent needs are minimized, even forgotten or denied. But when a need is fairly well satisfied, the next prepotent (higher) need emerges, in turn, to dominate the conscious life and to serve as the center of organization of behavior, since gratified needs are not active motivators.

Thus man is a perpetually wanting animal. Ordinarily the satisfaction of these wants is not altogether mutually exclusive, but only tends to be. The average member of our society is most often partially satisfied and partially unsatisfied in all of his wants. The hierarchy principle is usually empirically observed in terms of increasing percentages of non-satisfaction as we go up the hierarchy. Reversals of the average order of the hierarchy are sometimes observed. Also it has been observed that an individual may permanently lose the higher wants in the hierarchy under special conditions. There are not only ordinary multiple motivations for usual behavior, but in addition many determinants other than motives.[7]

Rewards and Punishments

Praise works better than blame; rewards work better than punishments; and children need to experience more successes than failures.

Fear of failure can be sufficiently traumatic in children to hinder their ability to function in a given learning situation.

Jucknat has graphed the effect of experiences of success and failure on level of aspiration (figure 2.6).

Transfer of Training

Transfer of training is exhibited when the learner is able to make use of learning in circumstances that are different from the situation in which the learning initially took place. Transfer is a necessary factor in all growth in learning. Transfer is absolutely necessary in the extension of any generalized skill taught in the elementary school, such as reading, writing, and arithmetic. Thorndike explained the concept of transfer in this way: ". . . a change in one function alters any other only in so far as the two functions have as factors identical elements."[8]

The theory of identical elements explains an important condition in the probability of transfer. Judd advanced the theory of generalized training to explain the likelihood of transfer. His position was that the ability to generalize, understand, or abstract enhanced transfer.[9]

Ellis listed principles of transfer that include:[10]

1. *Overall task similarity.* Transfer of training is greatest when the training conditions are highly similar to those of the ultimate testing conditions.

Figure 2.6 Effects of failure and success on level of aspiration.

From James M. Sawrey and Charles W. Telford, *Educational Psychology* (Boston, Mass.: Allyn & Bacon, 1958), p. 356. After M. Jucknat, *Psychol. Forsh.*, 1937, pp. 22, 89.

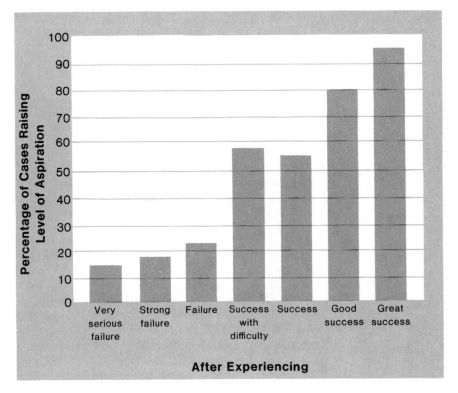

2. *Stimulus similarity.* When a task requires the learner to make the same response to new but similar stimuli, positive transfer increases with increasing stimulus similarity.
3. *Learning-to-learn.* Cumulative practice in learning a series of related tasks or problems leads to increased facility in learning how to learn.
4. *Insight.* Insight, defined behaviorally as the rapid solution of problems, appears to develop as a result of extensive practice in solving similar or related classes of problems.
5. *Amount of practice on the original task.* The greater the amount of practice on the original task, the greater the likelihood of positive transfer.
6. *Understanding and transfer.* Transfer is greater if the learner understands the general rules or principles which are appropriate in solving the problems.

Understanding

Learning progresses from the concrete to the abstract. Dale's cone of experience shows the importance of concrete, direct experiences and the difficulty of conceptualizing from only abstract verbal symbols. (See figure 2.7.)

Dale divides the cone of experience into activities of doing, observing someone else do something, and interpreting abstract visual or verbal symbols.

A. Activities of action. The child is a participant in the learning process.
1. Direct experience with a purpose. Experiences that involve the senses: touch, smell, sight, hearing, taste. For example, preparation of a meal in class or construction of a piece of furniture.

Figure 2.7 Cone of experience.

From Edgar Dale, *Audiovisual Methods in Teaching*, 3d ed. Copyright 1969 by Holt, Rinehart and Winston, Inc., p. 107. Reprinted by permission of Holt, Rinehart & Winston.

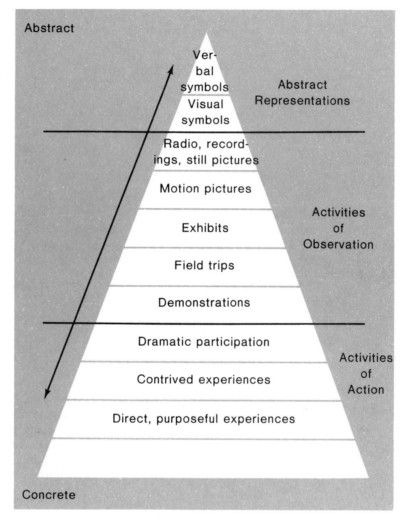

2. Contrived experiences. A method that simplifies the details. For example, a model or a small reproduction.
    3. Dramatization. Participating in a drama.
B. Activities of observation. The child only observes someone else doing the action.
    4. Demonstration. Performed by the teacher.
    5. Excursions away from the school. For example, to the dairy or to the store.
    6. Exhibitions. Collections of things in the experiences of children: stamps, coins, dolls, etc.
    7. Educational motion pictures.
    8. Vertical picture files, photos, the radio, records.
C. Abstract representations.
    9. Visual symbols. Charts, graphs, maps, diagrams, etc. Each is only a representation of an idea.

10. Verbal symbols. A word, an idea, a concept, a scientific principle, a formula. In each case, completely abstract.

Intellectual life functions primarily on a very high level of abstraction or symbolization. The point is that children need much experience at concrete levels before they can solve abstract questions and problems with good comprehension.

Process vs. Content

To enhance understanding in the school life of the child, the curriculum of the school should be based more on *process* than on *content*. When teachers are aware of how the cognitive processes of children develop and therefore understand the necessity of putting new learning to work in order for it to be remembered, they are apt to see much that is objectionable in the traditional classroom. Such teaching emphasized factual recall, parroting back explanations to the teacher, and performing on tests that require much regurgitation of factual information at the simple recall level. To point up the differences, *process* methodology is contrasted with *content* methodology below.

Process Methodology	**Content Methodology**
Learning to think clearly to solve problems.	Careful memorizing of teacher's lecture notes.
Learning to categorize the *relevant* and the *irrelevant* in a problem situation.	Depending on the teacher to decide what is important.
Learning by discovery—learning by inductive methods is more valuable than learning what the teacher says.	Relying on information learned from teachers, books, and parents.
Experimenting with, testing, and integrating subject matter information.	Studying each subject as a small isolated body of necessary information.
Evaluating—using the evidence—and accepting or rejecting the results.	Accepting the judgment of teachers and textbooks as unquestioned authority.
Emphasizing *how* to read, study, think, and learn.	Emphasizing *what* to read, study, think, and learn.
Free discussion and small group work to search for answers to the "larger" questions.	Recitation in class.

Children must learn a great deal of factual information *to use* how-to-think situations. One should not make a dichotomy of "Do we teach children *what* to think or *how* to think?" since without the *what* it will not be possible to do the *how*.

Forgetting

The most widely cited historical study of forgetting is that of Ebbinghaus, first published in 1885. He reported that 66.3 percent of what one learns is forgotten within twenty-four hours. The conditions surrounding this fact are important. He was his own subject, his materials were nonsense syllables, and his criterion was two errorless repetitions. The Ebbinghaus curve of forgetting is reproduced in figure 2.8.

Figure 2.8 Curve of retention (Ebbinghaus) for nonsense syllables after various time intervals.

From Henry E. Garrett, *Great Experiments in Psychology* (New York: Appleton-Century-Crofts, 1941), p. 273.

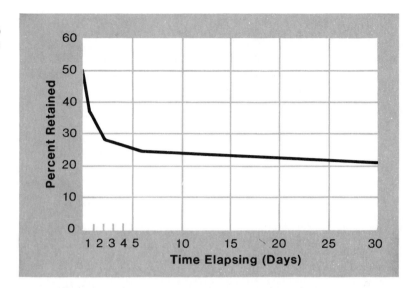

The importance of review to reduce the high rate of forgetting has been recognized for a long time. Reviewing very soon after learning and then reviewing several times at spaced intervals will help to minimize forgetting.

The practical bearing of the results obtained on education in general is that when associations have once been formed they should be recalled before an interval so long has elapsed that the original associations have lost their 'color' and cannot be recalled in the same 'shape', time, and order. In general it was found that the most economical method for keeping material once memorized from disappearing, was to review the material whenever it started to 'fade.' Here also the intervals were found to be, roughly speaking, in arithmetical proportion. For similar reasons the student is advised to review his 'lecture notes' shortly after taking them, and if possible, to review them again the evening of the same day. Then the lapse of a week or two does not make so much difference. When once he has forgotten so much that the various associations originally made have vanished, a considerable portion of the material is irretrievably lost.[11]

Spitzer's study of retention shows the importance of immediate recall and spaced review in helping sixth graders' scores on tests administered after different time intervals.[12] (See figure 2.9.)

Rules for remembering:

1. Material is easy to remember in proportion as it is meaningful.
2. Material is easier to remember if it gets well organized in the individual's mind.
3. Outlining, summarizing, or taking good notes are aids to remembering.
4. An active intention to recall is an aid to remembering.
5. A single reading is rarely enough. Reviewing and re-reading are necessary for remembering any length of time.
6. Recall must be selective. One must sift out the main points.

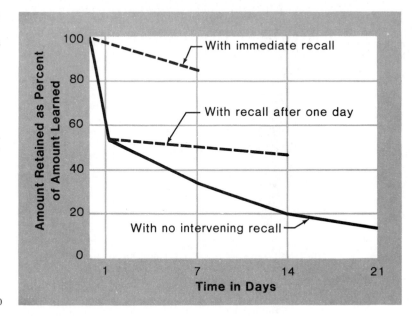

Figure 2.9 Curves of retention obtained by having equated groups read a selection and take tests at different time intervals. The solid line shows how forgetting takes place when there is no review before the test. The broken lines show the effect on retention when review follows either immediately or one day after reading.

From Sidney L. Pressey, Francis P. Robinson, and John E. Horrocks, *Psychology in Education* (New York: Harper & Row, 1959), p. 572. After H.F. Spitzer, "Studies in Retention," *Journal of Educational Psychology* 30 (1939):641–56.

7. Immediately after reading, one should reflect on what has been read and recite important points to oneself.
8. What we learn and never review is gradually forgotten. What we want to remember must be refreshed from time to time by review.[13]

Programmed Learning

Programmed learning is planned to utilize the following learning principles:

1. Easy steps.
2. Continuous response at each step of the way.
3. Immediate knowledge of results.
4. Progressing at individual rates.
5. Elimination of error.
6. Repetitive practice.

These principles are some of the most fundamental for promoting learning. Individualized lessons which are paced to the tempo and maturity of the individual student and which provide immediate feedback about correct and incorrect responses are the type of lessons conscientious teachers have been dreaming about for a long time. The greatest difficulties have arisen in the quality of programs; it has been easier to produce *programs* than to produce *high quality* programs which have adequate content that conforms to the principles.

An example of programmed reading based on these principles that has been successfully used is the following:

M.W. Sullivan and Cynthia Buchanan. *Programmed Reading.* 3d ed. New York: Webster Division, McGraw-Hill, 1973. A series of 23 student response booklets to teach reading skills from readiness through grade three level.

Traditional materials with comparable objectives are:

Science Research Associates. *Junior Reading for Understanding Laboratory.* 259 East Erie Street, Chicago, Ill. 60611: Science Research Associates, 1963.

Donald G. Anderson. *New Practice Readers.* 2d ed. New York: Webster Division, McGraw-Hill, 1978. A series of eight workbooks, A–G, with graded difficulty from 2.0 to 6.8.

William A. McCall and Lelah Mae Crabbs. *Standard Test Lessons in Reading.* New York: Teachers College Press, Columbia University, 1979. Provides six levels, from grade three through high school.

Learning to Generalize

A generalization is a statement or principle that encompasses the common characteristics of a cluster of ideas or individual statements. Teachers should help students to generalize their knowledge in a given subject. Sanders has pointed out that in a fourth grade geography book, the generalization "Life in the desert is difficult" is not stated directly but is clearly implied in such subordinate information as: (1) the home is crude and the family moves frequently; (2) medical help is not available; (3) life is close to nature and often dependent on the caprice of nature; (4) transportation is by foot or animal.[14]

Figure 2.10

Accumulative perceptual experiences grow into concepts.

From Asahel D. Woodruff, *Basic Concepts of Teaching,* con. ed. (San Francisco, Calif.: Chandler Publishing Co., 1961), p. 71.

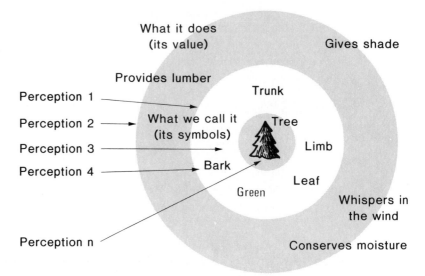

This development of generalizations from the students in the class is an inductive method of teaching. By analyzing their own experiences and forming concepts that are meaningful and useful to them, children can accumulate descriptive information to allow them to arrive at a generalized statement.

Woodruff illustrated how this process works in developing an extended understanding of the concept "tree." This process utilizes perception, conceptualization, thinking, evaluating, and selecting the contributing components to the generalization (see figure 2.10).

The most immediate perceptions about "tree" include its parts, its color, and the shade it casts. Some of the abstract ideas learned later may be that trees rustle in the wind, conserve moisture, and are either evergreen or deciduous. Accumulation of all these perceptual experiences leads to concept formation and generalizing.

In understanding many elementary concepts about weather and its components, children grow toward the ability to draw generalizations about weather and climate. This is illustrated in figure 2.11, which shows Woodruff's diagram of a major concept developed from many supporting concepts.[15]

Finally, one can construct a conceptual model based on many individual, miscellaneous experiences, grouped into simple facts or ideas contributing to broader concepts and finally leading to a generalization.

The way perceptions lead to conceptualizations, which lead to generalizations, is further discussed in chapter 10, Comprehension Skills.

The Cognitive Domain

Cognition is knowing. Knowing utilizes a hierarchy of abilities: the ability to recall facts; the ability to use factual information for solving problems; and the application of problem-solving abilities in new situations. Concrete knowl-

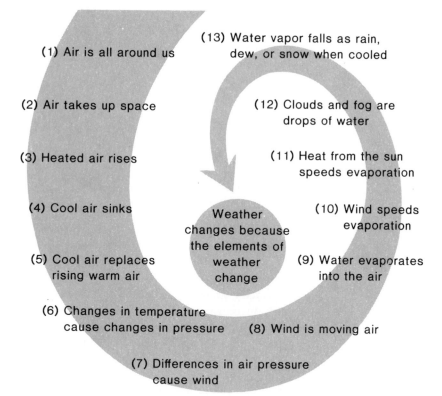

Figure 2.11 A major concept and some supporting concepts.

From Asahel D. Woodruff, *Basic Concepts of Teaching,* con. ed. (San Francisco, Calif.: Chandler Publishing Co., 1961), p. 184.

(1) Air is all around us

(2) Air takes up space

(3) Heated air rises

(4) Cool air sinks

(5) Cool air replaces rising warm air

(6) Changes in temperature cause changes in pressure

(7) Differences in air pressure cause wind

(8) Wind is moving air

(9) Water evaporates into the air

(10) Wind speeds evaporation

(11) Heat from the sun speeds evaporation

(12) Clouds and fog are drops of water

(13) Water vapor falls as rain, dew, or snow when cooled

Weather changes because the elements of weather change

edge, abstract thinking, reflection, application, and deriving generalizations are all processes in cognition.

Knowledge may be specific bits of information, terminology, methods of dealing with specific information, awareness of the arbitrary conventions of social behavior, classifying or categorizing, or stating principles and generalizations.

Intellectual skills and abilities are utilized in putting knowledge to work. Included are skills and abilities in comprehension, translation (paraphrasing, interpreting figures of speech), interpretation, application, analysis, synthesis, and evaluation.

In this frame of reference, *comprehension* is the ability to understand the idea being communicated by the speaker or writer. *Translation* is the listener's ability to paraphrase the ideas into his own thought patterns. Figures of speech have to be understood. Translation includes the ability to summarize the important points or *interpret* data reported in a study.

Application requires the ability to use a rule, a method, or a generalization in a new situation. *Critical analysis* includes ability to separate fact from opinion, to evaluate supporting evidence, to understand the relationships between ideas, and to see through persuasion, advertising, or propaganda.

Synthesis is the ability to assemble ideas into an integrated unit.

Evaluation requires the ability to establish or accept criteria for judgment and to use them objectively.

Bloom's categories of thinking include:

1. *Memory (knowledge).* The student recalls or recognizes information.
2. *Translation (comprehension).* The student changes information into a different symbolic form or language. He paraphrases.
3. *Interpretation (comprehension).* The student discovers relationships among facts, generalizations, definitions, values, and skills.
4. *Application.* The student solves a lifelike problem that requires the identification of the issue and the selection and use of appropriate generalizations and skills.
5. *Analysis.* The student solves a problem in the light of conscious knowledge of the parts and forms of thinking.
6. *Synthesis.* The student solves a problem that requires original, creative thinking.
7. *Evaluation.* The student makes a judgment of good or bad, right or wrong, according to standards he designates.[16]

The Affective Domain

In the primary grades, most children develop the attitude that reading is something to be valued. Some develop a preference for reading over some other school activity. A few—far too few—develop a real commitment to reading. In any event, reading as a value develops from the accumulation of many experiences over a long period of time. Accumulated experience produces many values which each individual must organize into a personal value hierarchy. The end result forms character as a person.

Krathwohl's outline of the development of values within the affective domain is as follows:[17]

A. Receiving
  1. Awareness
  2. Willingness to receive
  3. Selective attention
B. Responding
  1. Acquiescence in responding
  2. Willingness to respond
  3. Satisfaction in response
C. Valuing
  1. Acceptance of a value
  2. Preference for a value
  3. Commitment to a value
D. Organization
  1. Conceptualization of a value
  2. Organization of a value system
E. Characterization by a value
  1. Generalized set
  2. Characterization

Krathwohl et al.[18] have indicated ways in which the cognitive and affective domains interact, overlap, or follow parallel steps:

Cognitive
The cognitive continuum begins with the student's *recall* and *recognition* of knowledge;

Affective
The affective continuum begins with the student's merely *receiving* stimuli and giving them passive attention and then more active attention;

it extends through *comprehension* of the knowledge;

skill in *application* of the knowledge comprehended;

skill in *analysis* of situations involving this knowledge; skill in *synthesis* of this knowledge into new organizations;

skill in *evaluation* in this area of knowledge in order to judge the value of material and methods for given purposes.

the student responds to stimuli on request, willingly, and with satisfaction;

the student values the phenomenon or activity and voluntarily responds and seeks out ways to respond;

the student *conceptualizes* each value responded to;

the student organizes the values into systems and finally into a single whole, a *characterization* of the individual.

Values and Teaching

Raths et al. have defined values as those elements that show how a person has decided to use his or her life.

Values are based on three processes: choosing, prizing, and acting. One chooses freely from alternatives after thoughtful consideration of the consequences of each alternative. One prizes and cherishes one's choices, is happy with them, and is willing to affirm the choices publicly. One does something with the choice, does it repeatedly, in some pattern in his life. These criteria of valuing about one's beliefs, attitudes, activities, and feelings are based on self-directed behavior.[19]

Teachers recognize that in any group of children, individual behavior varies widely. Some children seem to know clearly what they value, while others are apathetic, flighty, uncertain, or inconsistent. Or there may be drifters, overconformers, overdissenters, or role players. Children who are unclear about their values may be said to lack a clarity of relationship to society.[20]

Teachers need to know and use a number of neutral clarifying responses to help children strengthen their choices and deepen their commitment to values.[21]

Neutral questions that help to clarify responses include:

Is this something that you prize?
Are you *glad* about that?
How did you feel when that happened?
Have you felt this way for a long time?
Did you *have* to choose that; was it a *free* choice?
Do you *do* anything about that idea?
Would you really *do* that or are you just talking?
What are some good things about that notion?
What other possibilities are there?
Is that very important to you?
Would you do the same thing over again?
Would you like to tell others about your idea?[22]

| The Affective Response to Reading | One of the surest ways to help a child develop a permanent attachment for reading is to ensure *an affective response* to the reading world. The child who lives the experience of the mongoose in its struggle to kill the cobra in Kipling's *Jungle Book;* the boy or girl who reads Laura Ingalls Wilder's *Little House on the Prairie, On the Banks of Plum Creek,* or *The Long Winter* is sure to develop strong empathy for Laura, her sisters, and her father and mother during their pioneer struggles as farmers in the Midwest. Several other examples from children's literature that emphasize affective response can be cited. |

Booker T. Washington's autobiography, *Up From Slavery,* has one recurring central theme—the struggle for education. First, his own, then his brother's, then the Indians', and finally his own people's. Interest, attitude, value, commitment, an organized value system, and a complete philosophy of life are exemplified.[23]

Elizabeth Yates, in her Newbery Medal Book *Amos Fortune, Free Man,* shows how Amos throughout his life learned to treasure freedom and education most of all. All that he earned as a free man helped others buy freedom. Freedom became the characterization of Amos as an *ultimate value.*[24]

In Doris Gates's *Blue Willow,* Janie never wanted to have to move again. She wanted to stay in one place, have a friend, and go to school. But because her father was a migrant worker, she had no friends and she did not attend school. If she could stay in one place, she could have friends to play with happily, like the children she had observed so many times as her family drove through towns between jobs. When the story ends, Janie's father gets a regular job and they will not have to move.[25]

Boys and girls find *Charlotte's Web* very sad when Charlotte explains to Wilbur, the pig, that she is going to die. Even though her babies do hatch, and Fern, the little girl, realizes she is getting too old to come to the barn to talk to the animals, it is very sad because Charlotte dies.[26]

When Travis must go out and shoot Old Yeller because he has rabies, the reader is as emotionally involved as Travis is.[27]

By the time Billy has succeeded in training his pair of coon hounds so they are the best hunting dogs around, the reader feels the same sadness Billy feels when the male of the pair is wounded and dies and the female dies of a broken heart.[28]

Cavanah creates a strong affective response to the inherent drive for learning held by young Abe when she tells how he learned *grammar:*

One morning when Abe Lincoln was having breakfast at Mentor Graham's house, he said,

"I have a notion to study English grammar."

"If you expect to go before the public, I think it would be the best thing to do."

"If I had a grammar I would commence now."

Mentor thought for a moment. "There's no one in town who owns a grammar," he said finally, "but Mr. Vaner out in the country has one. He might lend you his copy."

Abe got up from the table and walked six miles to the Vaner farm. When he returned, he carried an open book in his hands. He was studying grammar as he walked.[29]

Other books that will have value in developing the attachment for reading that is based on emotional response include Eleanor Estes' *The Hundred Dresses*, Esther Forbes's *Johnny Tremain*, Marguerite de Angeli's *Yonie Wondernose*, Joseph Krumbold's *And Now Miguel*, Jade Snow Wong's *Fifth Chinese Daughter*, William H. Armstrong's *Sounder*, Jean George's *Julie of the Wolves*, Laurence Yep's *Dragonwings*, Jane Wagner's *J.T.*, John Gunther's *Death Be Not Proud*, or Margaret Craven's *I Heard the Owl Call My Name*.[30]

Dora V. Smith, in her Kappa Delta Pi Lecture, emphasized the importance of reading in sharing experiences in these words:

Books such as these help young people the world over to share their experiences one with the other—to discover the ways in which they are very much alike and the ways in which they are different and therefore capable of making a unique contribution to the world's life. Truly the arts of communication are making possible the miracle of shared living.[31]

The Psychomotor Domain

The psychomotor domain encompasses such activities as muscular or motor skill, manipulation of materials and/or objects, or any act which requires a neuromuscular coordination. The following types of activities would be most common in elementary school physical education programs.

Dances and rhythms: fundamental movements and traditional and creative dances

Activities on equipment: jungle gym, ladder, rings, bars, swings, slides, seesaws

Games: dodge ball, circle tag, endball, ring toss

Classroom games: Simon says

Team sports: softball, soccer, touch football, volleyball

Stunts and tumbling

Calisthenics

Psychomotor objectives emphasize some muscular or motor skill, some manipulation of material and objects, or some act which requires a neuro-muscular coordination. Few such objectives are stated in education except for handwriting, physical education, and perhaps trades' skills, technical courses, and special education.

The classroom teacher could easily test some areas of psychomotor abilities in six-year-olds entering the formal reading program in order to locate areas of potential difficulty before the child fails in academic skills. The way certain skills develop as children master motor and perceptual components is illustrated in figure 2.12. These skills include the following abilities:

Distinguish the right from the left hand and copy letters, numbers, and designs correctly.

Sense (understand) the position of one's body in space.

Perceive figure-ground relationships, finding outline birds or squirrels in large pictures, recognizing what an object must be in terms of the things around it which are easily identified.

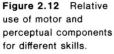

Figure 2.12 Relative use of motor and perceptual components for different skills.

From Herbert J. Klausmeier and William Goodwin, *Learning and Human Abilities: Educational Psychology,* 4th ed. (New York: Harper & Row, 1975), p. 33. Copyright 1975 by Herbert J. Klausmeier and William Goodwin. By permission of the publisher.

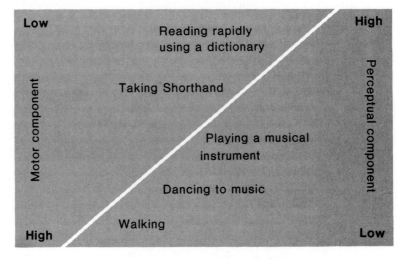

Objectives that convey most clearly what the intention is are those that tell how a student can concretely demonstrate that he has achieved the objectives. Thus, the objectives are measurable in terms of the student's behavior and are called *behavioral objectives.*

For example, after the third grade story about "Snakebite"[32] has been read, the teacher's objective might be that each member of the group be able to recall seven of the nine suggestions given in the story about what to do.

Or, after reading the story in the third reader about "Making Soap in Pioneer Days,"[33] the teacher's objective could be that each member of the group be able to recall all the ingredients needed by the pioneer woman to make her own soap.

Or, if the sixth grade story contains such words as *momentary, magical,* and *suitable,* the teacher's objective may be to teach the group that the suffix *ary* usually means "belonging to, or connected with"; the suffix *al* usually means "having to do with"; and the suffix *able* usually means "telling what kind." The objective also states the minimum acceptable level of performance. The teacher might plan to give a five-point quiz and set four right choices as the minimum acceptable performance.

A satisfactory behavioral objective meets the following criteria: (1) it indicates what the learner will do; (2) it states how the determination of achieving the objective will be measured; and (3) it establishes the minimum level of acceptable performance.

Contrast the following objectives:

Nonbehavioral	Behavioral
To find and give the meanings of idiomatic expressions.	To give the common meaning of five idiomatic expressions used in ten illustrative sentences on a ditto master.
To develop the ability to arrange ideas in a story in proper sequence.	After the story has been read, the eight ideas presented in the teacher's guide will be given to the students in the reading group in a mixed up order and they will number all eight of them in the correct order in which they appeared in the story.
To understand picturesque language.	Each member of the group will select and read aloud to the group a sentence containing picturesque language.

Should teachers learn to state their objectives behaviorally? Ojemann[34] answered the question "Yes, definitely," but cautioned that children's behavior when in the classroom is different from their behavior when satisfying their own interests:

Overt behavior in the classroom is not the same as the overt behavior when the learner is alone.

Both kinds of children's behavior should be included in teaching and testing.

Behavior in "controlled motivation" situations must not interfere with the child's feelings that what he or she is studying has personal significance.

Summary   Some general principles based on learning theory are:

1. No learning takes place without a motive. Motivation, from childhood to maturity, moves from greater to lesser *extrinsic* motivation and from lesser to greater *intrinsic* motivation.

2. Active participation in learning is better than passive reception of learning.

3. Material is more easily learned and remembered according to how well it is meaningfully understood by the learner.

4. Praise works better than blame; reward works better than punishment.

5. Generally, brighter people learn some things less bright people do not.

6. Once crucial facts have been understood, they must be overlearned to reduce loss by forgetting. Memorization is important after understanding is established.

7. Immediate knowledge of results aids learning.

8. Distributed practice is better than massed practice.

9. Nothing succeeds like success.

10. Provision for each child to grow at his or her own rate is necessary.

Educational psychologists have evolved many valuable generalizations about children and how they learn. The following principles of programming are based on some of the most important generalizations.

1. Easy steps
2. Continuous response at each step
3. Immediate knowledge of results
4. Progressing at completely individual rates
5. Elimination of error
6. Repetitive practice

Behavioral objectives can be established in the cognitive, affective, and psychomotor domains. These objectives must meet three criteria: (1) State what the learner will do. (2) State how achievement of the objectives will be measured. (3) Establish a minimum level of acceptable performance.

Suggested Activities

1. Explain clearly how each of the following relates directly to teaching reading: (a) capacity, (b) practice, (c) motivation, (d) understanding, (e) transfer, and (f) forgetting.

2. List the principles on which programmed learning is based.

3. Explain Krathwohl, Bloom, and Masia's statement of interaction, overlapping, and parallel progression of the cognitive and affective domains.

4. Demonstrate ability to write objectives for daily lessons in behavioral terms.

For Further Reading

Ausubel, David P. *Educational Psychology: A Cognitive View.* Chapter 1, "The Role and Scope of Educational Psychology," pp. 3–34. New York: Holt, Rinehart & Winston, 1968.

Bruner, J.S. *The Process of Education.* Cambridge, Mass.: Harvard University Press, 1960.

Charles, C.M. *Educational Psychology: The Instructional Endeavor,* 2d ed., pp. 3–83. St. Louis, Mo.: C.V. Mosby, 1976.

Darling, David W. "Evaluating the Affective Dimension in Reading." In Perspectives, No. 8, *The Evaluation of Children's Reading Achievement,* pp. 127–41. Newark, Del.: International Reading Assn., 1967.

Gagné, Robert M. *The Conditions of Learning.* 2d ed. New York: Holt, Rinehart & Winston, 1970.

Greer, Margaret. "Affective Growth Through Reading." In *Elementary Reading Instruction: Selected Materials,* 2d ed., edited by Althea Beery, Thomas Barrett, and William Powell, pp. 317–24. Boston, Mass.: Allyn & Bacon, 1974. Reprinted from *The Reading Teacher* 25 (January 1972):336–41.

Hilgard, Ernest R. "A Perspective on the Relationship Between Learning Theory and Educational Practices." In *Theories of Learning and Instruction,* 63rd Yearbook, National Society for the Study of Education, Part 1, pp. 402–15. Chicago: University of Chicago Press, 1964.

Powell, William. "The Nature of Individual Differences." In *Organizing for Individual Differences,* edited by Wallace Ramsey, pp. 1–17. Newark, Del.: International Reading Assn., 1968.

Smith, Frank. *Comprehension and Learning.* New York: Holt, Rinehart & Winston, 1975.

Woodruff, Asahel D. *Basic Concepts in Teaching.* San Francisco: Chandler, 1961.

Notes

1. Barbara Bateman, "Learning Disabilities—Yesterday, Today, and Tomorrow," *Exceptional Children* 31 (December 1964):176.

2. Robert M. Gagné, *The Conditions of Learning,* 2d ed. (New York: Holt, Rinehart & Winston, 1970), pp. 35–62, passim.

3. Ernest Hilgard, *Theories of Learning,* 4th ed. (New York: Appleton-Century-Crofts, 1974).

4. Benjamin Bloom, *Human Characteristics and School Learning* (McGraw-Hill, 1976), pp. 115–27.

5. See Norris M. Sanders, *Classroom Questions: What Kinds?* (New York: Harper & Row, 1966), and Frank J. Guszak, "Teachers' Questions and Levels of Reading Comprehension," in *Perspectives in Reading: The Evaluation of Children's Reading Achievement* (Newark, Del.: International Reading Assn., 1967), pp. 97–109.

6. Herbert J. Klausmeier, *Learning and Human Abilities: Educational Psychology,* 4th ed. (New York: Harper & Row, 1975), p. 227.

7. A.H. Maslow, "A Theory of Human Motivation," *Psychological Review* 50 (1943):394–95.

8. E.L. Thorndike, *Educational Psychology* (New York: Lemcke & Buechner, 1903), p. 80.

9. C.H. Judd, *Psychology of Secondary Education* (Boston: Ginn, 1927), p. 441.

10. Henry A. Ellis, *The Transfer of Learning* (New York: Macmillan, 1965), pp. 72–74.

11. D.O. Lyon, "The Relation of Length of Material to Time Taken for Learning, and the Optimum Distribution of Time," *Journal of Educational Psychology* 5 (1914):155–63, cited in J.B. Stroud, *Psychology in Education* (New York: Longman, Green, 1946), p. 521.

12. H.F. Spitzer, "Studies in Retention," *Journal of Educational Psychology* 30 (1939):641–56.

13. Albert J. Harris and E.R. Sipay, *How to Increase Reading Ability,* 6th ed. (New York: David McKay, 1975), pp. 486–87.

14. Sanders, *Classroom Questions,* p. 23.

15. Asahel D. Woodruff, *Basic Concepts of Teaching,* concise ed. (San Francisco, Calif.: Chandler Publishing Co., 1961), p. 184.

16. Benjamin S. Bloom, ed., *Taxonomy of Educational Objectives —Handbook I: Cognitive Domain* (New York: Longman, Green, 1956), pp. 201–7.

17. David R. Krathwohl, Benjamin Bloom, and Bertram Masia. *Taxonomy of Educational Objectives—Handbook II: Affective Domain* (New York: David McKay, 1964), pp. 176–85.

18. Ibid., pp. 49–50.

19. Louis E. Raths, Merrill Harmin, and Sidney B. Simon, *Values and Teaching: Working with Values in the Classroom* (Columbus, Ohio: Charles E. Merrill, 1966), p. 30.

20. Ibid., pp. 4–6.

21. Ibid., pp. 51–62.

22. Ibid., pp. 260–61.

23. Booker T. Washington, *Up From Slavery* (Boston: Houghton Mifflin, 1917).

24. Elizabeth Yates, *Amos Fortune, Free Man* (New York: E.P. Dutton, 1950).

25. Doris Gates, *Blue Willow* (New York: Viking Press, 1948).

26. E.B. White, *Charlotte's Web* (New York: Harper & Row, 1952).

27. Fred Gipson, *Old Yeller* (New York: Harper & Bros., 1956).

28. Wilson Rawls, *Where the Red Fern Grows* (Garden City, N.Y.: Doubleday, 1961).

29. Frances Cavanah, *Abe Lincoln Gets His Chance* (Chicago: Rand McNally, 1959), p. 78.

30. Eleanor Estes, *The Hundred Dresses* (New York: Harcourt, Brace & World, Inc., 1944); Esther Forbes, *Johnny Tremain* (Boston: Houghton Mifflin, 1943); Marguerite de Angeli, *Yonie Wondernose* (New York: Doubleday, 1944); Joseph Krumgold, *And Now Miguel* (New York: Thomas Y. Crowell, 1953); Jade Snow Wong, *Fifth Chinese Daughter* (New York: Scholastic Book Services, 1963); William H. Armstrong, *Sounder* (New York: Harper & Row, 1969); Jean George, *Julie of The Wolves* (New York: Harper & Row, 1972); Lawrence Yep, *Dragonwings* (New York: Harper & Row, 1975); Jane Wagner, *J.T.* (New York:

Dell, 1969); John Gunther, *Death Be Not Proud* (New York: Pyramid Books, 1949); Margaret Craven, *I Heard the Owl Call My Name* (New York: Dell, 1973).

31. Dora V. Smith, *Communication: The Miracle of Shared Living* (New York: Macmillan, 1955), p. 57.

32. Ernest Horn et al., *Progress in Reading Series,* Third Reader (Boston, Mass.: Ginn, 1940).

33. Ibid.

34. Ralph Ojemann, "Should Educational Objectives Be Stated in Behavioral Terms?" *The Elementary School Journal* 68 (February 1968):231.

3
Linguistic Foundations for Reading Instruction

Language is the system of speech sounds by which people communicate with one another in their social group. The study of the nature of language is called *linguistics*. Teachers of reading must know something of the nature and components of language. Wardhaugh wrote in 1969:

It would be true to say that most reading experts have given only token recognition to linguistics in their work, with the consequence that the vast part of what is discussed under the name of linguistics in texts, methods, and courses on reading is in reality very far from the best linguistic knowledge that is available today.[1]

Characteristics of Language

There are eight general characteristics of language that have especial implications for the classroom teacher.

1. Language is uniquely human. Only people use language as an expression of abstract thought. While bees, dolphins, and a few other animals may use sequences of signs and signals, linguists do not consider these to be language systems of communication. They do not combine sound with specific meanings.
2. Language is speech; it is oral. Writing is only a representation of the oral language. In written language, most of the important phonological features of stress, intonation, and juncture are left out. For example, "Are you going to wear that dress?" could have different kinds of stress and therefore meaning: "*Are* you going to wear that dress?" "Are you going to *wear* that dress?" "Are you going to wear *that* dress?" Each of these three sentences means something different. But just as the spoken language cannot completely express thought, so the written language cannot completely encode speech. Spoken language is the natural expression commonly used by the native speaker, with its contractions, idiomatic expressions, and slang and one-word answers. "How are you?" may be spoken as if it were one word, "Howarya?" And "It is a book" is spoken, "Itza book."

3. Language expresses a people's culture. The following examples illustrate how a people's attitudes and values are inherent in the structure of their language. For example, in English we would say, "I dropped the plate." But the equivalent in Spanish translates, "The plate fell from me." Young illustrates the need for understanding translation difficulties from Navajo to English:

> Navajo culture does not have a heritage of coercive religious, political or patriarchal family figures. In the Navajo scheme of things one does not usually impose his will on another animate being to the same extent and in the same ways as one does from the English point of view. "I *made* my wife sing" becomes, in Navajo, simply "even though my wife did not want to do so, she sang when I told her to sing." From the Navajo point of view, one can compel his children to go to school in the sense that he drives them there; or he can *place* them in school, but none of these terms reflect the imposition of one's will independently of physical force—the children do not comply with a mandate.[2]

Kaulfers has illustrated clearly how language is an integral part of people's culture. Language is the means by which thoughts and feelings are expressed; language guides our thinking about social problems and processes. Kaulfers wrote:

> How translation can defeat its own ends if words are merely transverbalized without regard for their pleasant or unpleasant associations is illustrated by the difficulties missionaries have sometimes in trying to convert remote populations to Christianity. Most Eskimos, for example, eat no bread. Few like it, because it has no taste or smell. Consequently, early missionaries found it difficult to explain the phrase, "Give us this day our daily bread." To win the natives, they had to substitute walrus, polar bear, and deer. This illustration is but one of many that could be cited to show how an expert command of a second language always requires a thorough understanding of the attitudes, likes, dislikes, customs, and standards of values of the people.[3]

4. Every language has a distinctive structure which is arbitrary and systematic. This structure determines the nature and placement of sounds that make words, and it determines the form of the words that make sentences—subjects, verbs, and objects or modifiers. The letters "blla si rde het" have no meaning. Rearrange the sounds to make English words of them, "ball the red is," and there is still no meaning. But if the words are arranged in the order "the ball is red," there is meaning. Word order is not important in all languages, but in English it is very important. However, arrangement of the sounds that make up words is important in all languages.

Children internalize the structural features of their language. These structural features include such things as the distinctive sounds of the languages and how they combine, how words are formed from sub-word units called morphemes, and the relationships of one word to another.

When they read, "The glings glongled glorgily in the goag," we can be sure that "glings" is the subject of the sentence, "glongled" is a verb, "glorgily" is an adverb, and "goag" is a noun used as the object of the preposition *in.*[4]

5. Language is unconscious, learned behavior. Native speakers are not conscious of each sound or word they say nor of the sequence of the sounds of words. They are primarily conscious of the ideas or thoughts they are trying to convey. The stringing together of sounds in certain positions is an unconscious act. The structure of a child's language is internalized and automatic by the time the child enters first grade. When children learn their first language in a free, relaxed, trial-and-error atmosphere, there is time for error, correction, and repetition without conscious effort. Whenever another language is superimposed as a second language, there is interference between the two sound patterns. Therefore, much guided repetition, self-correction, and motivated drill are indicated.

6. Language is personal. It is the reflection of the speaker's self-image. It is a person's primary means of expressing all that he or she is or aspires to be. Each person has certain expressions that are distinctively his or her own.

7. The language of a given group is neither "good" or "bad" nor "right" or "wrong"; it is communication. Dialects of English other than Standard English are referred to as *non*standard rather than *sub*standard. This topic is discussed in detail in chapter 17.

8. A language is always slowly changing its sounds, its lexicon, and its syntax. There is certainly sufficient permanence in the lexicon of any language that the elders use most of the same basic words as the young. However, the lexicon of English has increased enormously in the twentieth century to include in everyday usage such new words as *blitzkrieg, hara-kiri, television.* Some slang expressions become established and are added to the dictionary. Others disappear with the generation that created them—as, for example, calling something "the bee's knees" or "the cat's pajamas."

Teachers can easily demonstrate to boys and girls that language changes markedly through the centuries. But they must also teach that language is consistent and dependable and that change is always slow and never severe. A teacher could show passages from *Beowulf* or Chaucer or Robert Burns to show how the further away from us in time, the more different is each form of English from our own. For example, following are some lines from *Beowulf,* written about the seventh century A.D.:

Nealles him on heape handgesteallan,
ae elinga bearn, ymbe gestodon

hildecystum, ac hy on holt bugon,
ealdre burgan. (2596-99a)[5]

In modern English, they would be:

In no way did those war-comrades,
those sons of noblemen, take
their stand around him in formation as fighting-men should; no
they fell back into the forest
and took care of their own lives.

Following are some lines from the Prologue to the *Canterbury Tales* by Geoffrey Chaucer, who lived in the fourteenth century:

Whan that Aprill with his shoures soote
The droghte of March hath perced to the roote,
And bathed every veyne in swich licour
Of which vertu engendred is the flour;[6]

In modern English, they would be:

When April comes with its sweet showers
It abruptly ends the March drouth,
And bathes the spring plants in such moisture
So they burst into beautiful flowers.

Or, following are some lines from Robert Burns's poem "To a Louse," written
in 1786 after he saw a louse on a lady's bonnet in church. The poem ended
with this verse:

O wad some Power the giftie gie us
To see oursels as ithers see us!
It wad frae mony a blunder free us,
An' foolish notion:
What airs in dress an' gait wad lea'e us,
An ev'n devotion![7]

Ways to Describe Language

Linguists have given us words to use to describe language. *Phonology* is the
study of the distinctive sounds of a language, called *phonemes*. *Morphology*
is the study of the smallest meaningful units of a language, called *morphemes;*
they are mainly words and parts of words. *Syntax* is the grammar of the
language—the set of rules by which words are combined into sentences.

Table 3.1 summarizes information needed for understanding the succeeding chapters about beginning reading, phonic and structural analysis,
teaching English as a second language, teaching reading to bilinguals, and
teaching reading to speakers of nonstandard English.

Table 3.1 The structure of language.

Phonology	Morphology	Syntax	Semantics
Phonology is the study of the distinctive sounds of language.	Morphology is the study of the smallest meaningful units of language, called *morphemes,* which are mainly words or parts of words. Morphemes especially important in elementary school teaching are:	Syntax is often thought of as the grammar of a language. More precisely, it is the set of rules governing how morphemes are combined into sentences.	Semantics is the study of the meanings communicated through language.
1. There are 44 distinctive sounds, called *phonemes,* in the English language. (Sources differ: 40, 44, 45, 47.) The alphabet is an imperfect representation of those sounds.	1. Compound words. 2. Inflectional endings *er, est, ed, ing, s, es.* 3. Prefixes and suffixes. 4. The common Greek and Latin combining forms.	1. Word order, an important distinctive feature of English, is an aspect of syntax (a *pocket watch* is not the same as a *watch pocket).* 2. Basic ("kernel") sentence patterns:	1. English is a language with a rich vocabulary, or lexicon, which has many words borrowed from other languages.

2. Phonemes combine into distinctive meaningful units, called *morphemes,* which are words or parts of words.		a. Noun—transitive verb—object
		   b. Noun—linking verb—predicate noun or adjective
		   c. Noun—verb—prepositional phrase
			2. The listener or the reader must rely on context clues; meanings depend upon context.

3. Minimal pairs are two words with only one phonemic difference, which changes meaning (pick-pig, map-mat, big-pig, big-bag).		3. Transformations:
		   a. Negative statements
		   b. *Or* changes
		   c. Expansions
		   d. *There* changes
			3. The language contains many figures of speech, idiomatic expressions, and slang expressions.

4. Stress and juncture (called *suprasegmentals)* are also distinctive features of English, comparable to phonemes, which change meaning. (*You bought that. You bought that. You bought that.* A blue bird is not necessarily a bluebird.)		e. Question changes
		   f. Passive changes
		   g. Combined kernel sentences
		   h. *Until, if, because* changes
		   i. Tense changes
			4. The vocabulary contains antonyms, heteronyms, homographs, homonyms, synonyms.

5. The phoneme-grapheme relationships are often confusing in English because the same sound may have many variant spellings, and different sounds may have the same spellings.			5. Suprasegmentals, which are phonemic because they change meanings, are also semantic in communicating meaning changes.

**A Short Glossary
of Linguistic
Terms**

A brief glossary of terms that may be useful to classroom teachers is included here.

affix: A morpheme that occurs as a prefix or suffix. It is called a "bound morpheme" because it cannot stand alone.

deep structure: The "kernel" sentences underlying the grammatical transformations represented by the surface structure of a sentence.

dialect: The distinctive phonological, morphological, and syntactic patterns of a language in a given part of a country or of a given social group.

digraph: The combination of two letters (graphemes) to represent a single phoneme: vowel digraph—*read*; consonant digraph—*th*ink.

diphthong: The combination of two vowel sounds, the one gliding into the second, as *oi* in *boil.*

ethnography: Descriptive anthropology, which can include the study of language in particular cultural and social contexts. (One has to know when to talk, when to be silent, and how much to talk. One has to know how to talk to one's boss, to one's mother, to one's best friend, to one's peer, and to a total stranger.)[8]

grammar: The rules that govern the structure of a language.

grapheme: The *written symbol* used to represent a phoneme.

homographs: Words written in exactly the same way but having entirely different meanings.

homophones: Words pronounced alike but having different meanings or spellings.

intonation: Pitch of the voice to change meanings.

juncture: The "boundary" between consecutive words in a stream of speech: the juncture of *an + aim* is different from *a + name.*

lexicon: The total vocabulary of a language.

linguistics: The scientific study of language.

morpheme: The smallest meaningful units of a language—mainly words or parts of words. *Albuquerque* is one morpheme, for example; *un-dy-ing* is three morphemes.

morphology: The study of word formation of a language—the origin and functions of inflections and derivations especially.

morphophoneme: A given phoneme within a given morpheme whose pronunciation changes, bridging the gap between morphological levels and phonemic levels. Compare the vowel changes in *verbose—verbosity; divine—divinity.*[9]

morphophonemics: The study of the relationships between the sound structure and the word structure of the language. May be thought of as the bridge between morphology and phonology.

phoneme: The smallest significant unit of speech. A phoneme is technically not to be thought of as a syllable or letter. There are 44 phonemes and only 26 letters in English.

phonetics: The analysis of speech sounds with respect to their articulation and acoustic properties.

phonic analysis: Phonic analysis is the application of a knowledge of consonant and vowel sound clues to the pronunciation of a word.

phonics: The teaching of techniques about the sounds of written words so that children acquire letter-sound correlations.

phonology: The study of the patterns and distribution of speech sounds, or phonemes.

pitch: The tonal quality in speech that signals meaning variation; pitch has four discrete sound ranges in spoken English.

pragmatics: A branch of linguistic science that studies the relationship between things (facts) and verbal expressions and the people who use the verbal expression.

psycholinguistics: A study of the interdependence of linguistic and psychological behaviors of an individual or group.

semantics: The study of meaning in language.

sociolinguistics: A study of linguistics in its social context: who says what to whom, how, when, and to what purpose.

stress: The degree of prominence a syllable has, usually identified as primary, mid, and weak.

suprasegmentals: The phonological entities of pitch, stress, intonation, and juncture—equivalent to phonemes because they can signify meaning.

surface structure: The words we speak to communicate.

syntax: The rules for combining words to form grammatical sentences.

utterance: A meaningful unit of spoken language; it may or may not be a sentence.

vernacular: Pertaining to the everyday speech of one's native language and dialect.

Language Acquisition

Learning to talk the language of one's extended family appears to be a very simple task for almost everyone. One could say that speaking the language is virtually self-taught. Well before the age of six months infants begin trying to reproduce the sounds around them which represent communication, differentiating those sounds from the total range of sounds possible. From that point, children do not try to imitate their elders exactly so much as they experiment with approximations of what the elders say to see if they too can communicate meaningfully. Then, rather than merely repeating what someone else has said, they imitate sentence patterns and spontaneously produce new sentences that are their own. Psycholinguists call the process by which children test out their own abilities to express themselves "hypothesis testing."

The second step in this process is what children do with the response they elicit from others. If they ask for something or tell their mothers something and get no response, they conclude that they are not communicating the way adults around them do. However, if they get a positive response, their efforts are reinforced. Feedback is what everyone needs to encourage them to keep trying, keep learning, keep experimenting. A child may say, "Milk!" and mother asks, "Do you want more milk?" while she gets some more. The child has created communication; the mother understood and responded; and the child is rewarded for having mastered one more step in the effort to learn how to talk.

There is perhaps a third step in this process. The significant adult in the child's environment expands the child's language competence just by talking and thereby providing a model. The parent may even try consciously to expand the child's language by *correcting* it. However, the very young child is apt to pay little attention to the correction, as the following conversation reported by Cazden indicates:

Child: Nobody don't like me.
Mother: No, say "Nobody likes me."
Child: Nobody don't like me.
(Eight repetitions of this dialogue)
Mother: No, now listen carefully; say, "Nobody likes me."
Child: Oh! Nobody don't likes me![10]

Young children rely on exposure to language, from which they can make inferences about the syntax of the language and create their own set of rules regarding that language. Then, in their own speech, children hypothesize correct language usage, test their hypotheses, and eliminate incorrect patterns because they are not rewarded.

Cazden further reported:

Evidence on the role of correction in the child's learning of syntax is wholly negative. In hundreds of hours of recordings of Adam, Eve, and Sarah talking with their parents, we found corrections of misstatements of fact, but no correction of immature syntactic forms.[11]

The school needs to provide for talking so the student has a body of knowledge for hypothesis-testing. After children adjust to a talking environment, they are anxious to participate openly and naturally in fruitful ways. It seems that children initiate their own learning more than they are taught by those who try so hard to teach!

John cautions us that the learning styles of children with varying cultural backgrounds may make significant differences in their use of language when they enter school. She suggests that Indian children of the Southwest are visual in their approaches to the world and that they absorb their world through sight and touch:

Language lessons are introduced as the most valued aspect of education, but they are presented in ways that contradict aspects of Navajo children's preschool life. The shape and cold feel of the buildings in which they live and are taught deprive them of sensory impressions they are used to: the look of the sky, the feel of the wind, the smell of smoke. I was struck . . . how often the little ones clustered around each other, touching their buddies' hair and arms and holding hands even during lessons. This is one of the ways in which they keep literally in touch with the familiar.[12]

Extending Oral Language to the Child's First Reading Lessons

With only slight exaggeration, it could be said that teachers have often made learning to read very difficult for many children. They approach the task formally with prescribed lessons to make sure the children understand phonemes, sight words, and then the syntax of language before finally extracting the meaning. These teachers usually organize beginning reading programs in the following order:

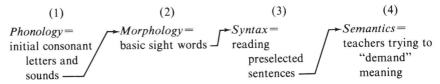

(1) *Phonology* = initial consonant letters and sounds

(2) *Morphology* = basic sight words

(3) *Syntax* = reading preselected sentences

(4) *Semantics* = teachers trying to "demand" meaning

Of course beginning reading doesn't need to happen this way. Burke has shown that *meaning* should be at the core of every reading lesson; that the syntax of the child's personal language guarantees meaning; and that grapheme-phoneme relationships become important only when the child must decode a word to get the meaning.[13] Beginning reading really should begin

with ideas or concepts that are personal and important to the child—never only with names and sounds of initial consonants. Burke's concept is diagrammed in figure 1.2.

Therefore, the linguistic schema for learning to read would look like this:

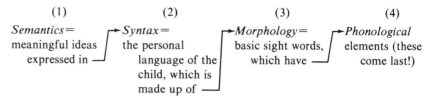

The language-experience approach to reading which is emphasized throughout this text is based on this schema.

Holt said that if parents felt as obligated to teach children to talk as first-grade teachers do to teach them to read, the results would be disastrous:

Bill Hull once said to me, "If we taught children to speak, they'd never learn." I thought at first he was joking. By now I realize that it was a very important truth. Suppose we decided that we had to "teach" children to speak. How would we go about it? First, some committee of experts would analyze speech and break it down into a number of separate "speech skills." We would probably say that, since speech is made up of sounds, a child must be taught to make all the sounds of his language before he can be taught to speak the language itself. Doubtless we would list these sounds, easiest and commonest ones first, harder and rarer ones next. Then we would begin to teach infants these sounds, working our way down the list. Perhaps, in order not to "confuse" the child—"confuse" is an evil word to many educators—we would not let the child hear much ordinary speech but would only expose him to the sounds we were trying to teach. . . .

Suppose we tried to do this; what would happen? What would happen, quite simply, is that most children, before they got very far, would become baffled, discouraged, humiliated, and fearful, and would quit trying to do what we asked them. If, outside of our classes, they lived a normal infant's life, many of them would probably ignore our "teaching" and learn to speak on their own. If not, if our control of their lives was complete (the dream of too many educators), they would take refuge in deliberate failure and silence, as so many of them do when the subject is reading.[14]

Cazden has suggested some ways in which learning to read *can* be like learning to talk:

Consider, as an example, the differences between learning to talk and learning to read. In oral language the child has to learn relationships between meanings and sounds. The raw material for the child's learning processes consists of a rich set of pairings of meanings and sound—for that is what language in the context of ongoing experience is. In reading the child must learn relationships between oral language—which he now knows—and letters of the alphabet. But a rich set of pairings of oral and written language is much less available. It is available when the child is read to while sitting on an adult's lap (not when read to as part of a group in school); it is available when the bouncing ball accompanies TV commercials; it is available whenever the child points to any writing and asks "What's that say?" and it is available whenever the child himself tries to write. Provision of a rich set of sound-word pairings can be built into deliberately planned environments—in the classroom or on TV. But the necessary pairings don't just happen for written language at school as they do for oral language at home.[15]

Minimal Pairs

Children whose first language is not English must learn to hear all the phonemes used in English that are not used in their native language. For Spanish-speakers learning English, there are several substitutions likely to be made, such as *sumb* for *thumb* or *pass* for *path,* because the phonemes of the Spanish language do not include those consonant distinctions. Vowel sounds vary from one language to the other also. The student must learn to discriminate all these differences. Discriminating minimal pairs and juncture is good practice for sharpening this ability.

Minimal pairs are two words that sound exactly the same except for one phoneme that changes the meaning. Ending consonant sounds are often troublesome. For example, *pick* is spoken as *pig, map* is spoken as *mat.* This auditory discrimination practice, important in second-language teaching, is also important to primary children learning to read.

pi*ck*-pi*g*	*t*aste-*t*est	*p*ain-*p*en	boa*t*-bo*th*
*b*ig-*p*ig	*d*ip-*d*eep	sheep-ship	*b*it-*b*eat
niece-knee*s*	ma*p*-ma*t*	for*c*e-four*s*	man-men
pri*c*e-pri*z*e	dea*th*-dea*f*	la*c*y-la*z*y	*b*ig-*b*ug
a*g*e-e*dg*e	bu*s*-bu*zz*	tu*ck*-tu*g*	po*k*e-pa*ck*

Juncture

Juncture is the name given to the "boundary" between consecutive words within a sentence (or between sentences) in speech. Written language usually expresses juncture with a space. The following examples are comparable to minimal pairs and demonstrate that juncture is phonemic because it changes meaning.

Mary was home sick.	Mary was sick at home.
Mary was homesick.	Mary wanted very much to go home.
Was that the green house?	Was it a green color?
Was that the Green house?	Do the Greens live there?
Was that the greenhouse?	Was it a place where plants are nurtured year-round?
I saw a blue bird.	The bird I saw was a blue color.
I saw a bluebird.	It was the variety called "bluebird."
Bob said he saw a horse fly.	The horse had wings.
Bob said he saw a horsefly.	It was a fly that bothers horses.

And in these:

I scream	send them aid	night rate	lighthouse keeping
ice cream	send the maid	nitrate	light housekeeping

Structure Words　　　Words that have no referent are called structure words. It is estimated that there are no more than 300 such words in the English language, but they comprise nearly half the words in an elementary context. They are termed *markers* for the type of structural element that follows them:

Noun markers: a, the, some, any, three, this, my, few, etc.
Verb markers: am, are, is, was, have, has, had, etc.
Phrase markers: up, down, in, out, above, below, etc.
Clause markers: if, until, because, that, how, when, etc.
Question markers: who, why, how, when, what, where, etc.

Structure words are also called *glue* words or *service* words because in and of themselves they do not convey meaning but are necessary connectors. They should be taught and mastered as early in the reading process as possible. They play a significant part in helping the reader to anticipate meanings of the verbs or nouns that follow in a given sentence structure.

Is It Linguistics? Is It Phonics?　　　There is no conflict between being skillful at decoding words by phonic analysis and learning whatever one can about *linguistics.*

We are proposing that linguistics encompasses knowledge about how children acquire and extend language through the hierarchy of listening, speaking, reading, and writing. We also propose that the purpose of language is to illuminate meaning. Phonics supports what the teacher does to make "decoding-encoding" of the meaning in reading and writing an efficient operation. *Phonics is never emphasized to the exclusion of meaning.* Table 3.2 should clarify some of these differences.

Sustakoski attempted to clarify for teachers of beginning reading that "letters do not have sound." This misconception is based on the notion that written language is the primary form of language, and may be further perpetuated by the misconception that it is the written form that preserves language in its "correct" form. Of course, by necessity, one must prepare much more carefully what is put down on paper. In writing, many of the signals of speech are lacking, including all the intonational features, and this causes the writer to use greater caution in the arrangement of sentences. Thus, Sustakoski wrote:

The most dangerous aspect of this confusion, as far as the teaching of reading is concerned, is that the teacher attempts to have a child "pronounce" the letters of the word as if the letters had sounds instead of allowing the written configuration to evoke the oral counterpart in the child's mind, which is the *true* nature of the process of reading.[16]

Generalizations Teachers Can Borrow from Linguists　　　Linguists have helped reading teachers understand the nature and function of language and the part reading plays in the total communication process. First, they have emphasized the distinction between *grammar* and *usage* of

Table 3.2 What teachers say compared to how linguists describe language.

Adapted from Dorothy Seymour, "The Differences Between Linguistics and Phonics," *The Reading Teacher* 23 (November 1969):99–102, 111.

In teaching phonics to children, teachers are apt to say:	The linguist would like to remind teachers that:
There are five vowels in the English language.	But this means there are five *graphemes*: *a, e, i, o,* and *u.* There are more than twice that many vowel *sounds* (phonemes).
Phonics has a set of rules to teach vowel sounds.	Each vowel grapheme represents several different phonemes. One of *several* sounds of "a" is /ey/.
Most consonants have only one *sound.*	Letters on paper do not "have" *sounds.* The "written-down" graphemes are only symbolic representations of a spoken language.
Sound out the word. Sound and connect phonemes into a chain of integrated sounds to make a new word: *s-a-nd-w-i-ch.*	Written letters are only graphic symbols of the sounds (phonemes) that the children have known and produced correctly for a long time.
We have silent letters: *k* is silent in *know; g* is silent in *sign.*	Letters make neither sound nor silence. Changes in English spellings have not kept up historically with changes in English speech (and we still need the *g* in *sign* for the related words *signal and signature*).
Look at the words. (The problem here is with meaning. If we allow children to think that words mean what is "written down," they may believe that words become language by being written.)	Language is speech. Words were oral before they were written with symbols (graphemes).
Children must learn to pronounce a controlled basic sight vocabulary.	This is illogical. Children usually begin reading only words that they have been pronouncing correctly for years.

language. Grammar is formalized language structure; usage is the preference or ethical judgment of the user of the language. People do say:

That's where it's at. It's me. No, it ain't.

Second, children do, if they are native speakers, understand the differences between the deep structure and the surface structure of language. The sentences "Time flies like an arrow" and "Fruit flies like a banana" appear very much alike on the surface but the syntax is entirely different.[17] Rutherford illustrates differences between surface structure and deep structure in many pairs of sentences that look on the surface as if they followed the same pattern:[18]

What he wants is *more* of your business. What he wants is *none* of your business.
It was a moving *train.* It was a moving *experience.*

Third, language is oral. It is speech before it is either reading or writing. Fourth, our writing system is based on an alphabet whose symbols (letters) long ago had a much closer correspondence to the sounds they represented. Spoken language changes over time at a much faster rate than does written language. This fact explains many of what we call the spelling irregularities and peculiarities of English. Nevertheless, our spelling conventions still have a fairly high degree of sound-symbol regularity.

Given these linguistic facts, some facts about reading follow:

1. Efficient reading moves directly to meaning with the least mediation possible in the process. To achieve this efficiency, the reader must learn to make intelligent guesses about what is in the line of print he is reading—anticipating meaning before he really sees the words.
2. Always teach *context*. Letters are only parts of words, words are only parts of sentences or meaningful phrases, and even sentences are only a part of the paragraph, which contains a more complete meaning.
3. We should encourage beginners to get the meaning of the sentence and not to be overconcerned about the preciseness of word-calling. Readers should be able to make mistakes without penalty.
4. Many of the phonics rules we have insisted on in the past were not nearly so important as extracting meaning from the message. Phonics is no help with "read" in the sentences "I will read the book for you" and "I read the book yesterday" since other words in the sentences determine how to pronounce "read."

Some "do's" and "don'ts," then, are:

1. Do not give emphasis to traditional "rules" of reading.
2. Do not depend on phonics rules.
3. Teach letters as parts of words; words as parts of sentences.
4. Accept sensible reproduction of print that conveys meaning.
5. Try to be sure that the context provides feedback to the reader.
6. Focus on the child, not on the method of teaching reading.

Linguists have also shown the following points to be important when teaching reading:

1. A child's dialect is that child's natural language and should be accepted completely by teachers as the place to start teaching. Probably no one *speaks* standard written English. Reading teachers need to study children's dialects in order to help them learn how to move from *their* oral language to *their* written-down language.
2. The language-experience method is undoubtedly the most natural method for learning to read because children read their own language as they "told" it. The child who dictates a story already understands it, so has optimal chances of reading it successfully. The teacher can assist

the child by using the rebus technique for some of the nouns in the story:

Daddy shot a  when he went hunting.

3. The cloze technique reveals the student's ability to sense meaning and anticipate what will happen next in the story. Cloze lessons are easy to prepare and are adaptable. They require filling in missing words in sentences. Cloze is discussed in more detail in chapter 10, "Comprehension Skills."

4. Miscue analysis is the means by which the teacher decides whether the student has adapted the reading to his or her dialect, has substituted a meaningful word that would ordinarily not have been used, or has made some other miscue that is not exactly like the printed line. In the event the reader is using the language correctly, is understanding the message, and is confidently getting the point of the story, *no error* has been made, and the miscue should be accepted without penalty. Graphic miscues, such as confusing *b* and *d* or *th* and *wh,* may cause the student to have to repeat phrases to correct the meaning in the sentence. Semantic miscues are more significant because the student will lose meaning unless the miscue is corrected. If a sentence is written "Away the bird flew and then she came back" and the child reads aloud "The bird flew away and then she came back," the meaning is clear and the miscue need not be corrected. However, if the sentence "They practiced conservation" is read as "They practiced conversation," the meaning is lost.

5. Semantics is the study of the meanings communicated through language. Helping children develop an ever larger vocabulary, both oral and written, is one way to help them increase their grasp of meaning. Teachers can also begin introducing even first graders to multiple meanings of common words, word opposites, homonyms, idiomatic expressions, similes, and other devices by which language usage conveys meaning.

Redundancy

One of the features about language that we need to analyze in helping children learn to read is its redundancy. In the sense in which the word is used here, it is *not* deprecatory and does not imply that needless or undesirable features are present. On the contrary, redundancy in linguistic structure makes anticipating meaning in the line of print easier for the reader. Osgood's theory of communication suggests that redundancies and transitional probabilities facilitate the transmission and receipt of messages:

Redundancy: For example, "man coming" means the same as the redundant statement "a man is coming this way now." It is suggested that the latter is more like ordinary English; it indicates the singular number of the subject three times (by "a," "man," and "is"), the present tense twice ("is coming" and "now"), and the direction of action twice ("coming" and "this way"). Such repetitions of meaning . . . make it possible to replace "is," "this," "way," or "now," should they be deleted.[19]

Information helpful to the reader in completing the meaning while reading may be pictorial, orthographic, syntactic, or semantic.[20] The typical efficient reader, though he may be quite unaware, makes skilled use of redundancy. There are few words that begin with *dw* or *tw;* there are fifteen common prefixes the good reader already knows; or the first three or four letters of a polysyllabic word may be the only clue necessary. Such are the details that allow the reader to hurry on with absorbing the meaning of a paragraph. "This kind of prior knowledge, which reduces the alternative number of possibilities that a letter or word can be, is termed redundancy."[21]

Hodges and Rudorf explained:

Redundancy facilitates language processing. This term, derived from information theory, means the tendency in language for information to be carried by more than one part of the signal. Language is redundant to the extent that each element carries more than a single bit of information.

In the sentence *He was watching Mary, watching* has three cues to its function as a verb: its position in the sentence, the use of *was* with it, and its *ing* ending. Sequential constraint contributes considerably to redundancy. Since *q* must always be followed by *u,* no new information is provided by the *u.* Redundancy makes it possible to sample without losing information. It also provides a possibility of verification, since multiple cues must be consistent.[22]

Summary

Linguistics is the scientific study of language. It is divided into *phonology,* the distinctive sounds of language (forty-four phonemes in English); *morphology,* the arrangement of phonemes into meaningful units, called *morphemes;* and *syntax,* the arrangement of morphemes into sentences.

The study of language as an expression of human behavior is called *psycholinguistics.* Knowledge of psycholinguistics is as important to the teacher as knowledge of *descriptive linguistics,* the study of the phenomenon of language itself. *Sociolinguistics* is the scientific study of language in the context of the cultural values, practices, attitudes, and ideals which are expressed through language, including also the social context of who says what to whom, how, when, and for what purpose. Some general principles about the nature of language and the methodology for describing language are presented briefly in this chapter. Also, an attempt has been made to derive some working principles for teachers of reading.

For Further Reading

Abrahams, Roger D., and Rudolph C. Troike, eds. *Language and Cultural Diversity in American Education.* Englewood Cliffs, N.J.: Prentice-Hall, 1972.

Arthur, Bradford. *Teaching English to Speakers of English.* New York: Harcourt Brace Jovanovich, 1973.

Carroll, John B. *Language and Thought.* Englewood Cliffs, N.J.: Prentice-Hall, 1964.

Cazden, Courtney, Vera John, and Dell Hymes. *Functions of Language in the Classroom.* New York: Teachers College Press, Columbia University, 1972.

DeStefano, Johanna S., ed. *Language, Society, and Education: A Profile of Black English.* Worthington, Ohio: Charles A. Jones, 1973.

Fries, C. C. *Linguistics and Reading.* New York: Holt, Rinehart & Winston, 1963.

Goodman, Kenneth. "The Linguistics of Reading." *Elementary School Journal* 64 (April 1964):355–61.

————. "Reading: A Psycholinguistic Guessing Game." In *Theoretical Models and Processes of Reading,* edited by Harry Singer and Robert Ruddell, pp. 259–72. Newark, Del.: International Reading Assn., 1970.

Hall, Edward T. *The Silent Language.* New York: Fawcett, 1966.

Hodges, Richard E., and E. Hugh Rudorf, eds. *Language and Learning to Read.* Boston, Mass.: Houghton Mifflin, 1972.

Horn, Thomas D., ed. *Reading for the Disadvantaged: Problems of Linguistically Different Learners.* Newark, Del.: International Reading Assn., 1970.

Laffey, James L., and Roger Shuy. *Language Differences: Do They Interfere?* Newark, Del.: International Reading Assn., 1973.

LeFevre, Carl A. *Linguistics and the Teaching of Reading.* New York: McGraw-Hill, 1964.

Loban, Walter. *Language Development, K-12.* Urbana, Ill.: National Council of Teachers of English, 1976.

Malmstrom, Jean. *Understanding Language: A Primer for the Language Arts Teacher.* New York: St. Martin's Press, 1977.

Rutherford, William E. "Deep and Surface Structure, and the Language Drill." *TESOL* (Teachers of English to Speakers of Other Languages) *Quarterly* 2 (June 1968):71–79.

Savage, John F., ed. *Linguistics for Teachers: Selected Readings.* Chicago: Science Research Associates, 1973.

Seymour, Dorothy Z. "The Difference Between Linguistics and Phonics." *The Reading Teacher* (November 1969):99–102.

Shuy, Roger, ed. *Linguistic Theory: What It Can Say About Reading.* Newark, Del.: International Reading Assn., 1977.

Smith, E. Brooks, Kenneth Goodman, and Robert Meredith. *Language and Thinking in the Elementary School,* 2d ed. New York: Holt, Rinehart & Winston, 1975.

Smith, Frank. *Comprehension and Learning.* New York: Holt, Rinehart & Winston, 1975.

————. *Understanding Reading: A Psycholinguistic Analysis of Reading and Learning to Read.* New York: Holt, Rinehart & Winston, 1971.

Smith, Frank, ed. *Psycholinguistics and Reading.* New York: Holt, Rinehart & Winston, 1973.

Venezky, R. L. "English Orthography: Its Graphical Structure and Its Relation to Sound." *Reading Research Quarterly* 2 (Winter 1967):75–106.

Notes

1. Ronald Wardhaugh, *Reading: A Linguistic Perspective* (New York: Harcourt, Brace & World, 1969), p. 30.
2. Robert Young, "Culture," in *Language and Cultural Diversity in American Education,* ed. Roger D. Abrahams and Rudolph C. Troike (Englewood Cliffs, N.J.: Prentice-Hall, 1972), p. 41.
3. Walter V. Kaulfers, "Gift of Tongues or Tower of Babel," *Educational Forum* 19 (Nov. 1954):82.
4. John F. Savage, ed., *Linguistics for Teachers: Selected Readings* (Chicago: Science Research Associates, 1973), p. 114.
5. Edward B. Irving, Jr., *A Reading of Beowulf* (New Haven, Conn.: Yale University Press, 1968), p. 7.
6. F. N. Robinson, ed., *The Works of Geoffrey Chaucer* (Boston: Houghton Mifflin, 1961), p. 17.
7. Charles Elliott, ed., *The Harvard Classics* (New York: P.F. Collier & Son, 1909), 6:199.
8. Joel Sherzer, "The Ethnography of Speaking," in *Linguistic Theory: What Can It Say about Reading?* ed. Roger Shuy (Newark, Del.: International Reading Assn., 1977), pp. 144–45.
9. Robert Hall, *Introductory Linguistics* (Philadelphia: Chilton, 1964), p. 138.
10. Courtney B. Cazden, *Child Language and Education* (New York: Holt, Rinehart & Winston, 1972), p. 92.
11. Ibid., p. 114.
12. Vera John, "Styles of Learning—Styles of Teaching: Reflections on the Education of Navajo Children," in *Functions of Language in the Classroom,* ed. Courtney Cazden, Vera P. John, and Dell Hymes (New York: Teachers College Press, Columbia University, 1972), p. 335.
13. Carolyn L. Burke, "The Language Process: Systems or Systematic," in *Language and Learning to Read,* ed. Richard E. Hodges and E. Hugh Rudorf (Boston: Houghton Mifflin, 1972), pp. 24–30.
14. John Holt, *How Children Learn* (New York: Pitman, 1967), pp. 56–57.

15. Cazden, *Child Language and Education,* pp. 140–41.

16. Henry J. Sustakoski, "Some Contributions of Linguistic Science to the Teaching of Reading," in *Oral Language and Reading,* ed. James Walden (508 South Sixth Street, Champaign, Ill. 61820: National Council of Teachers of English, 1969), p. 61.

17. Cazden, *Child Language and Education,* p. 5.

18. William E. Rutherford, "Deep and Surface Structure, and the Language Drill," *TESOL* (Teachers of English to Speakers of Other Languages) *Quarterly* 2 (June 1968): 71–79.

19. Cited in Thomas C. Potter, *A Taxonomy of Cloze Research; Part I: Readability and Reading Comprehension* (11300 La Cienega Blvd., Inglewood, California 90304: Southwest Regional Laboratory for Educational Research and Development, 1968), pp. 2–3.

20. Frank Smith, *Understanding Reading* (New York: Holt, Rinehart & Winston, 1971), p. 20.

21. Ibid., p. 7.

22. Kenneth S. Goodman, "The Reading Process: Theory and Practice," in *Language and Learning to Read,* ed. Richard E. Hodges and E. Hugh Rudorf (Boston: Houghton Mifflin, 1972), p. 153.

Part 2
A Good Beginning

A good beginning for boys and girls in the primary grades is based on adequate screening and sorting to determine which children learn best verbally, which children lack adequate motor coordination, and which children enter school emotionally immature. This is how diagnostic teaching begins.

Diagnostic teaching continues with the teacher continually examining and reexamining teaching failure in order to insure that children are taught at levels at which they can succeed. Teaching diagnostically demands that causes of reading failure be carefully analyzed to permit successful teaching.

Lee has very wisely said:

Diagnostic teaching permits the child to deal with familiar concepts and procedures as he continues his growth in the unfamiliar school setting. When the school year opens with *a* plan of procedures, *a* set of materials, *a* topic on which to focus, many children are placed at a disadvantage; the teacher loses much valuable time and a variety of opportunities for enriching the learning that children already have.

Some instructional programs are now swamping children with a multitude of experiences which their meager backgrounds ill prepare them to perceive or from which they gain little meaning.[1]

---

1. Dorris M. Lee, *Diagnostic Teaching* (1201 Sixteenth St., N.W., Washington, D.C. 20036; Department of Elementary-Kindergarten-Nursery Education, National Education Association, 1966), p. 9.

4

Assessment of Prereading Skills

Since our society is deeply entrenched in a traditional practice of starting all children in first grade at age six, chronological age has become the only criterion for deciding if children are ready for this new and exciting adventure. Chronological age will be the only characteristic that many of these children have in common even though it is the least important in assessing whether each child has the psychological, intellectual, and neurological maturity to profit from this experience.

Because the school accepts children who are chronologically six, it needs to provide for much better sorting and selecting after the children arrive so that each one can be kept learning and developing *appropriate behaviors at his or her growing edge of learning.* Children who are already reading should be encouraged to continue reading, with proper precaution that reading isn't being emphasized to the exclusion of all the other areas of growth and development. For those children who are ready to read, there is no reason to insist that they complete all the pages in a readiness workbook just because the school has a copy for each child to use. They can begin reading if they are ready to read. However, many children, perhaps a sizable minority, lack language skills, vocabulary concepts, experiences with the middle-class life pictured and assumed in most of the textbooks children will read. Moreover, for perhaps one child in ten or twelve, English has not been the first language of the home. Because of our extremely mobile population today, every elementary teacher should know something about teaching English as a second language.

There is an optimal time for learning. Skills that build upon currently developing behavior are most easily learned. A child who does not have developing behavior for learning to read is apt not to learn to read. Assessing the child's ability to perform prereading skills will help the teacher to predict the child's adjustment to the reading situation. If skills are missing at any step of the way, they should be developed before the child is confronted with the abstract process of reading.

The more mature the learner, the less adaptation is needed to attain a given level of proficiency in specific skills. This is clearly demonstrated in any large group of six-year-old children. Some few have learned how to read, some are optimally ready for learning to read, and some will not exhibit this developing behavior for some time. Children who are permitted to learn to read *when they are ready* will generally learn easily and read a great deal.

Teaching formal readiness or prereading skills before the child has appropriate neurological, psychological, or intellectual maturation is almost sure to result in failure to achieve the standards set by the school. This too early attempt may prevent the child from developing natural curiosity about reading and may be the beginning of emotional problems that will later become stumbling blocks to learning.[1]

The child who is ready to read has achieved an adequate level of intellectual development, possesses a body of relevant knowledge, and has control of the grammar of the language. Obviously, this statement is about subjective elements and has only a relative value. There is a minimal functioning level of use of concepts, verbalizing, and general understanding before the child is greatly interested in such an abstract process as deciphering the printed word.

Two important related areas which the teacher must also evaluate are the child's emotional stability and maturity and physical and neurological development. A child who has problems in vision and hearing or who lacks the visual-perceptual skills required for reading will not learn to read well.

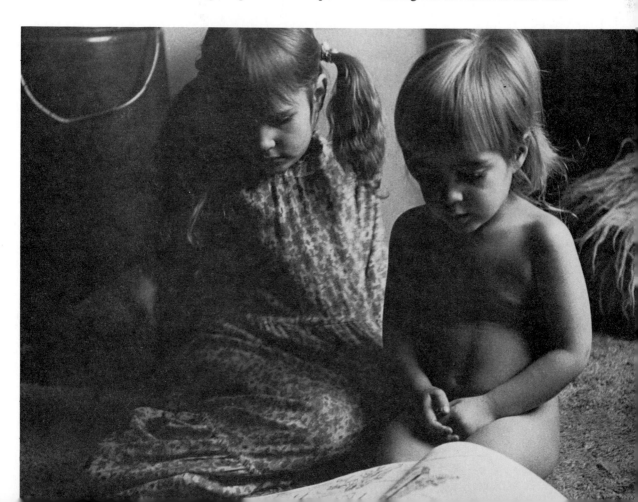

The jobs of the first grade teacher, then, are to evaluate children's skills when they come to the first grade, determine their degree of readiness for reading, and make sure that those who give evidence of lack of readiness in any area have opportunity to develop needed skills *before* they are presented formal reading tasks.

Much of what has traditionally been done in readiness programs has been ineffective because whole groups of children have been asked to work through skills which many of them already knew well and a few understood neither before nor after the teaching.

The present point of view is that teachers must evaluate—with supplemental judgments of the principal, the school nurse, school social worker, school psychologist, and reading supervisor—the learning levels of children and keep them growing toward maturity without regard to their place on a learning continuum when they enrolled in school.

The following sections discuss briefly some standardized measuring instruments that might be used in a school to provide the classroom teacher with the kinds of information that would make it possible for her to make confident judgments about the learning levels of children in her class. Language and concept development in young children is then discussed, and also the complexity of "being ready."

Evaluating Children

Psychologists have developed a number of tests that evaluate the skills and abilities known to be necessary for a child's successful performance in school.

Illinois Test of Psycholinguistic Abilities (ITPA)

The Illinois Test of Psycholinguistic Abilities[2] is designed to measure language development of young children. It was originally conceived as an instrument for assessing language in exceptional children of preschool age. Children who lack sufficient depth of cognitive language for beginning reading in first grade need some kind of assessment to discover areas of weakness so that they can be developed. This test helps determine these weaknesses. The test contains the following subtests.

1. *Auditory-Vocal Automatic Test.* This test samples the child's knowledge of standard sentence usage of inflected forms of words:
   "Here is an apple. Here are two _____ ."
   "This box is big. This box is even _____ ."
   "This man is painting. He is a _____ ."
   "Father is hanging a picture. Now the picture has been _____ ."
2. *Visual Decoding Test.* This test asks the child to locate among several pictures the stimulus picture previously presented. For example, on one page is a picture of a shoe. On the following page are many pictures, one of which is a shoe. The child must point to the shoe.
3. *Motor Encoding Test.* The child is shown a picture and must gesture to demonstrate the use of the object. For example, for the picture of a cup, the child simulates drinking; for pencil, the child simulates writing.

4. *Auditory-Vocal Association Test*. This is a test that relates verbal symbols by analogy. For example:
   "I sit on a chair. I sleep on a _____ ."
   "Cotton is soft; stones are _____ ."
   "A rabbit is swift; a turtle is _____ ."
5. *Visual-Motor Sequencing Test*. This test measures the ability to reproduce a sequence of visual stimuli from memory. For example, the examiner places in the tray, in this order, pictures of dog, potato, cat. They are then removed and the child is to arrange them as the examiner did. Geometric figures are also used to produce sequences: triangles, squares, circles, hexagons, diamonds, pentagons, and trapezoids.
6. *Vocal Encoding Test*. The child is asked to "tell all you can" about a simple object such as a block or a ball. The examiner can help the child get started by asking questions for the first object: "What is it?" "What is it made of?" "What color is it?" "What do you use it for?"
7. *The Auditory-Vocal Sequencing Test* is a test of the child's ability to reproduce a sequence of digits from memory. Digits beginning with a sequence of two are pronounced at a uniform rate of two per second.
8. *Visual-Motor Association Test*. This test measures the ability to relate a pictured stimulus to one picture in a series. For example, the stimulus picture is *sock,* to be related to either *hammer* or *shoe*.
9. *Auditory Decoding Test*. This test measures the child's understanding of oral questions.

"Do you eat?"	"Do cars cry?"
"Do you rain?"	"Do bananas telephone?"
"Do airplanes fly?"	"Do goats eat?"

The ITPA total score represents a language-age for the individual child whose chronological age is between three and nine. A profile of scores on the nine subtests makes clear in which areas the child is performing below age level, at age level, or above age level. Such information can be most useful to the classroom teacher in planning concept development, language experiences, and other kinds of diagnostic teaching for the child. It is hoped that the school language specialist will be available to administer and interpret the test for the classroom teacher.

Valett Developmental Survey of Basic Learning Abilities

The Valett Developmental Survey of Basic Learning Abilities[3] is a survey of seven major categories of readiness abilities. It is administered by the classroom teacher and can yield a profile to show areas of strength and weakness. The seven major categories are:

1. Motor Integration and Physical Development
2. Tactile Discrimination
3. Auditory Discrimination
4. Visual-Motor Coordination
5. Visual Discrimination
6. Language Development and Verbal Fluency
7. Conceptual Development

Again, a survey of abilities that can show the teacher in which areas a child is not functioning normally allows the teacher to plan a program to meet these learning needs. The object is to strengthen needed skills in children before introducing them to teaching levels where they may otherwise experience failure.

Predicting Reading Failure

De Hirsch, Jansky, and Langford selected ten tests that can be administered at the kindergarten level for determining the child's readiness for formal schooling. These ten tests can be administered in about forty-five minutes by a teacher who is familiar with them. The authors have established critical score levels below which they expect a child will have difficulty.[4] Table 4.1, which shows the critical score levels, was developed by comparing the scores of children who failed in beginning reading with the scores of children who did not fail.

De Hirsch and Jansky[5] found that six tests could identify the failing readers, the slow starters, and the high achievers with respect to school success at the end of the second grade. They were the Bender Gestalt, the drawing of a human figure, auditory discrimination, classifying or putting things in categories, presence of reversals, and word recognition. With limited study and instruction, first grade teachers could evaluate beginning first grade boys and girls on all these abilities and rank them, after some experience, with considerable confidence. Such an endeavor could be a much needed step toward prevention of failure because it could set the stage for the diagnostic teaching needed to overcome weaknesses.

Table 4.1 Critical score levels on ten kindergarten tests included in the predictive index.

Adaptation of table "Critical Score Levels on Ten Kindergarten Tests Included in the Predictive Index," p. 114, from *Predicting Reading Failure* by De Hirsch, Jansky, and Langford (New York: Harper & Row, 1966).

Test	Score Range (Best–Poorest)	Critical Score Level
1. Pencil Use	0–2	0 (level expected for age)
2. Bender Visuo-Motor Gestalt (A, 1, 2, 4, 6, 8)	0–6	(at least 5 designs copied correctly)
3. Auditory Discrimination (Wepman)	0–11	1 (X-error)
4. Number of words	594–54	226 words
5. Categories	0–3	(all series correctly categorized)
6. Reversals (Horst)	0–9	4 (at least 5 rows correctly matched)
7. Word Matching (Gates)	0–12	3 (at least 9 words correctly paired)
8. Word Recognition I (Pack)	0–2	0 (both words identified)
9. Word Recognition II (Table)	0–2	0 (both words identified)
10. Word Reproduction	6–0	3 (no. of letters reproduced correctly)

De Hirsch and Jansky, concerning early identification of school failure in children, stated:

Since development is by and large a consistent and lawful process, it seemed safe to assume that a kindergarten child's perceptuo-motor and oral language level would forecast his performance on such highly integrated tasks as reading, writing, and spelling. The tests covered several broad aspects of development: behavior and motility patterning; large and fine motor coordination; figure-ground discrimination; visuo-motor organization; auditory and visual perceptual competence; ability to comprehend and use language; and more specifically, reading-readiness.[6]

Bankson Language Screening Test

Bankson has devised a test to screen for young children who may need language development.[7] There are five parts to the test: semantic knowledge, morphological rules, syntactic rules, visual perception, and auditory perception. The test is administered on a one-to-one basis and needs about 25 minutes to administer. This language screening test resembles parts of the ITPA, already discussed, and also more traditional reading readiness tests such as the Metropolitan Reading Readiness Test, presented later in this chapter. This test might be useful in teacher-training classes to help in-service teachers devise classroom strategies for informally assessing the strengths and weaknesses of boys and girls so they can plan activities that would enrich the curriculum.

Prediction with Diagnostic Qualities

Hillerich developed a testing procedure for four- and five-year-old children which he named "Prediction with Diagnostic Qualities," or "PDQ."[8] It is based on items that would be diagnostic in that they would have direct implication for teacher instruction to overcome deficits. The test has nine parts:

1. Auditory discrimination.
2. Listening comprehension.
3. Vocabulary.
4. Ability to categorize.
5. Ability to use such "relationship" words as *in* and *on*.
6. Picture sequence.
7. Oral language development.
8. Following one-, two-, and three-step oral directions.
9. Using oral context, for example, "Daddy wrote a letter with his new _____ ."

This test was administered to entering kindergarteners, and teachers used the results to teach toward removing deficits in the children's abilities. At the end of first grade, the reading achievement was compared to a control group of first graders who did not have the PDQ test. The experimental group outperformed the control group with a statistical significance at the .01 level of confidence.[9]

Individual Tests of General Intelligence	The Revised Stanford-Binet Test of Intelligence[10] is an individually administered test of general learning ability. It yields only one total score, which is a mental age. It requires considerable manipulation at the three-and-four-year-old levels but becomes highly verbal at the older ages of childhood.

The Wechsler Intelligence Scale for Children[11] is an individually administered test of general learning ability. It obtains separate verbal and performance scores and a total score that combines the two. The verbal section measures vocabulary, comprehension, information, similarities, and arithmetic. The performance section presents pictures with missing parts to be identified; one-inch-cube blocks to be used to reconstruct designs; a series of jigsaw puzzles; pictures to be assembled in sequence to tell a story; and mazes. An observant examiner may gain many worthwhile insights into a child's behavior during the administration of the test.

The Vineland Social Maturity Scale	The Vineland Social Maturity Scale[12] is a scale for measuring social development. The information for checking the scale is obtained by a skillful interview with the parent and may be supplemented by direct observation of the child. The items evaluate self-help, locomotion, communication, self-direction, and socialization in relation to expected normal development in children. A social age is determined by the total number of items passed. A social quotient is obtained by dividing the child's social age by the chronological age. For example, children at age two may be expected to ask to go to the toilet; children at age four may be expected to wash their faces unassisted; and children at age six go to bed unassisted.

This test and the two intelligence tests mentioned above require technical preparation of whoever administers them, so are usually administered by the school counselor, psychologist, or diagnostician.

Language and Concept Development	In order that the teacher may place sufficient emphasis on developing language concepts, provide for thinking in the language, and deliberately work for expanded vocabulary, *planned sequential verbal bombardment* is called for. This is probably the only way the culturally different child can ever hope to catch up sufficiently to profit from the compulsory school classes of middle-class schools. A well planned verbal environment will keep the children on the growing edge of learning as much of their short school day as possible.

Since reading success correlates most highly with verbal behavior, it is recommended that teachers place their greatest emphasis on types of oral language lessons that will *develop and extend concepts* in children when they enter school. Exercises such as those suggested below should be helpful:

1. Using word "opposites" in meaningful ways:

big–little	winter–summer	clean–dirty
on–off	good–bad	above–below
in–out	before–after	left–right
long–short	open–close	stop–go

up–down	front–back	sick–well
over–under	first–last	push–pull
boy–girl	wide–narrow	noisy–quiet

2. Classifying things:

red, blue, and yellow	colors
two, three, four	numbers
lion, tiger, giraffe	wild animals
cat, dog, goldfish	pets
Tom, Dick, Harry	boy's names
men, woman, boy, worker, nurse	people
sofa, chair, stove, table	furniture
pants, suit, hat, socks, shirt	clothes
houses, barns, stores, restaurants, hotels, bars . .	buildings
robin, wren, blackbird, sparrow, warbler	birds

3. Counting concrete objects and recognizing numbers of things to five:

How many baby chickens?

How many cherries?

How many beads are not on the string?

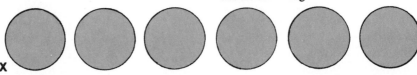

X

Which is the fifth circle from the **X?**

4. Associating words in pairs:

cow–calf	ring–finger	mail–postman
knife–fork	hen–chicken	shirt–tie
cup–saucer	cat–kitten	doll–dress
mother–baby	frog–tadpole	sheep–lamb
ball–bat	milk–milkman	horse–colt
cream–sugar	pen–pencil	dog–pup
salt–pepper	comb–hair	fire–fireman
hammer–nails	dog–bone	pan–lid

5. Using common prepositions: A large chart published by Ginn and Company (see figure 16.1) to illustrate the ten most common prepositions is useful in first grade where the children are all speakers of English. *In, out, on, between, up, down, over, across, into* and *under* are presented. Special attention needs to be given to the presentation of such prepositions when teaching English to speakers of other languages. The list of common prepositions in children's speech is not long and the teacher can provide opportunity to make sure children have control of many of them:

about	before	from	on	until
across	beneath	in	out	up
after	beside	inside	outside	upon
against	by	into	over	with
along	beyond	like	since	without

6. Finding homonyms, to control use of *both* meanings in oral language:

to–too–two	blew–blue	no–know	through–threw
knew–new	deer–dear	ate–eight	cheap–cheep
our–hour	sale–sail	son–sun	waist–waste
week–weak	he'll–heel	tale–tail	by–buy
read–red	fair–fare	rode–road	right–write

7. Using words with several meanings:

We went to the state *fair* yesterday.
The weather will be *fair* today.
Boys should play *fair*.

The leaves *fall* from the trees in October.
We start to school in the *fall*.
Please *fall* in line! (Take your place)
There is a *fire* in the furnace.
The soldiers will *fire* at the enemy.
His boss will *fire* him.

Most of the girls wear *bangs*.
Bang! went the gun.
The baby was *banging* the pots and pans together.
(If children volunteer "Tom banged the door" or "Mother says not to bang the door," very good.)

He was cutting the *bark* from the tree.
The dog will be sure to *bark*.

We sat on the river *bank*.
John put his money in a savings *bank*.
(If any children know "Bank the fire" or "Don't bank on that," be sure to praise them.)

8. Completing word association exercises:

You sit on a chair; you sleep on a _____ .
A bird flies; a fish _____ .
Soup is hot; ice cream is _____ .
Feathers are light; stones are _____ .
You have fingers on your hand; you have toes on your _____ .
You can cut with scissors; with a pencil, you can _____ .
A rabbit goes fast; a turtle goes _____ .
A mile is long; an inch is _____ .

9. Practicing word inflections:

I have one apple. There are two *apples*.
Here is a box. Now there are two *boxes*.
This one is long. This one is *longer*.
This one is big. This one is *bigger*.
This one is pretty. This one is *prettier*.
Here is a mouse. There are two *mice*.
Here is a child. There are two *children*.
Here is a goose. There are two *geese*.
I do my work every day. Yesterday I *did* it.

I go to work every day. Yesterday I *went* to work.
I throw the ball to Jack. Yesterday I *threw* it.

10. Testing readiness concepts for quantitative thinking; teachers may use the following list as a guide in informal conversations with beginners and identify which children lack the concepts:

Up and *down*	*Round*	*Kilogram*
Big and *little*	*Rectangle*	*Some*
Before and *after*	*Afternoon*	*Next*
Near and *far*	*Straight*	*One-half* of single objects
Fast and *slow*	*Above*	*Less than* and *more than*
Under and *over*	*Cupful*	*More* and *most*
Thick and *thin*	*Jarful*	*Faster* and *slower*
All and *none*	*Liter*	
Night and *day*	*Meter*	

11. Answering some comprehension questions that help teachers evaluate a child's understanding of concepts:

Why do we have books?
Why do we have stoves?
How old are you?
Where do we put the paper that is no good?
What are two things that you wear on your head?
What tells us what time it is?
Does a house have doors?
What color is the flag?
Is a baby cat a puppy? What is it?
What two things can you do with a pencil?
What things fly?
What animals have long ears?
What do we call a baby dog? cat? goat? hen? cow? sheep?
Where does the bird put her eggs?
What do you see in the sky in the daytime?
When do you need an umbrella?
Can you write with scissors? What can you do with them?
How many days do you come to school in a week?
What are all the things that you can do with a ball?
What does a car have to have to make it go?

12. Using interesting pictures to encourage conversation and discussion. Some of the major publishers of children's textbooks have sets of large pictures emphasizing elementary concepts in social studies, science, and health that can be very useful in this respect. One of the learning aids provided by the Field Enterprises Educational Corporation is a 25″ by 38″ picture with city life depicted on one side and country life on the other. Suggestions for the teacher for use of these pictures are also provided.[13]

13. Making up rhymes. After the teacher illustrates with phrases like "A *pig* can *jig*," and "A *boy* has a *toy*," the boys and girls either make up similar phrases or supply rhyming words:

A goat in a _____ .   A fox in a _____ .   A nose smells a _____ .
A hen in a _____ .   A girl has a _____ .   A horse, of _____ .

The Complexity of "Being Ready": Factors Affecting Performance in Beginning Reading

Some of the factors the teacher will observe in appraising a child's maturity for reading are (1) intelligence, (2) use of language, (3) emotional and social maturity, (4) visual discrimination, (5) auditory discrimination, (6) left-handedness, (7) attendance in kindergarten, and (8) informal reading experiences in relation to the home environment. However, the teacher's informal appraisal of these factors should not be interpreted narrowly. Rather, they should be viewed in relation to the child's total growth and development, participation in all types of activities, and communication through nonverbal signals as well as oral language.

Intelligence

While intelligence is a major factor in learning to read, teachers must be aware that the standard measures of intelligence may not be valid for a very large percentage of children who do not communicate with the standard English of the teacher and do not relate to the middle-class experiences emphasized in the school. Cultural biases are at work against the lower socioeconomic class, against those who speak nonstandard English, and against those whose first language is not English. The teacher can observe the child's general reactions in situations all day long: on the playground, in discussions, when working with mechanical devices, when solving problems not related to language expression, the type of leadership exercised among peers; and how the child's nonverbal behavior changes (facial expression, motivation, emotional response) when activities related to the prereading experience are presented. Formal intelligence tests which must be administered in selected cases have been discussed earlier in this chapter.

Use of Language

Teachers must find time to read a great deal to young children: stories, both fanciful and true, and selected poetry, rhymes, and jingles. Of course, readiness for literature depends on the child's stage of language cognition. All children in a group will not see, hear, and feel the same things when the teacher reads to them. Especially with children who have not had broad experiences, the teacher should try to compensate for the deficit. *Jam* is a poem that can be enjoyed and "tasted" until it is a meaningful experience for all the boys and girls in the class.

Jam

Jam in the morning, jam at noon,
Bread and jam by the light of the moon.
Jam
is
very
nice.
Jam on biscuits, jam on toast,
Jam is the thing I like the most.

Jam is sticky, jam is sweet,
Jam is tasty, jam's a treat—
Raspberry
Strawberry
Gooseberry,
I'm very
FOND OF JAM!—by Russell Hoban[14]

Assessment of Prereading Skills

A Good Beginning

Sources of good materials for literature in grade one include: May Hill Arbuthnot,[15] Geismer and Suter,[16] and *The Real Mother Goose.*[17]

Facility with language may be one of the most important factors in reading readiness. Language facility will vary tremendously in any unselected group of six-year-old children, of course. The gamut includes the little girl of three and one-half years, who, after playing with paper boats in nursery school one morning, asked her mother to make her a paper boat to float in the dishpan of water in the afternoon. In a few minutes she brought a crumpled piece of wet paper to her mother in the living room and said, "My boat has *disintegrated* in the water." The other end of the continuum includes both the child who has very meager language and gives one word answers or says "Me go," meaning "I want to go," and the child whose native language is not the language of the school.

Language is being developed when parents, other adults, and teachers encourage children in the use of the language; when they answer many of the child's questions; when they model for children so they can understand concepts in a conversation; and when they ask children to correctly repeat sentence patterns, to form verb phrases correctly, or to straighten out pronunciations. These are always done in an informal, encouraging way. Thus the child learns, unlearns, and relearns the language through trial and error.

One reason culturally advantaged children often seem to display more verbal fluency than other children apparently stems from the way adults talk to them, answer their questions, ask them questions, ask them to amplify answers, and so on. If, on the other hand, children are talked to in one word commands, or given instructions with minimal word usage, they respond in the same way and remain much less articulate than children who are answered, asked to amplify answers, given synonyms for many words they know, and so on.

Speaking and understanding spoken language utilizing concepts; asking questions or presenting problems; using language to formulate concepts; differentiating words that sound similar but mean different things; inferring meanings from context when one word has many meanings; and holding ideas in mind and organizing and classifying them in sequential order—all of these mental operations are evidences of language power and correlate highly with success in developing reading skills and academic learning. Needlessly carrying on an extensive readiness program for children who are already prepared is as foolish as ignoring readiness activities when they are needed. Some five-year-olds are more advanced intellectually, physically, socially, emotionally than some six-year-olds. It should be just as possible to offer a long continuum of learning experiences in a kindergarten or first grade class as in any other. In that way, some point along the continuum should match each child's optimal readiness for learning.

Environmental experiences are needed—trips and excursions; fact and fancy in stories and poems; skills and habits in visual-auditory/visual-motor discrimination; creative expression through art, music, games, and rhythms.

Telling a story, seeing it written down, hearing it read back, and listening to its contents and knowing that it is what was said before—this sequence helps the child understand what reading is.

Children can learn in many informal experiences to *extend* their vocabulary:

Not, "It's a bird"; rather, "It's a robin."
Not, "It's a tree"; rather, "It's a maple tree."
Not, "It's a dog"; rather, "It's a big collie dog."

Emotional and Social Maturity

Many activities in the first two years of school life contribute to a child's emotional and social growth. A teacher who is sensitive to such traits as timidity, aggression, fear, anxiety, and the need for success and approval can create opportunity to help each child in terms of his or her need. Children learn through planned group work experiences to work cooperatively to achieve group goals, to share with each other, and to exchange ideas through informal conversation. Comfortable emotional and socializing experiences contribute to greater maturity, stability, and confidence when a child is confronted with the formal learning-to-read process. In the informal atmosphere of a kindergarten or first grade classroom, the teacher can promote vocabulary enrichment, correct English usage, fluency in extemporaneous speaking, and the ability to give attention in listening, all of which are skills essential in the learning-to-read process.

Visual Discrimination

It is clear that good vision is an asset in becoming a good reader. Reading requires the ability to see clearly at close range for extended periods of time. Some children are sure to come to school with visual problems for which adjustments can be made. The teacher must be alert to observe whether the child appears to have vision problems and make sure that the proper referrals are made. Reading clinicians, reading clinics in large school systems, and school nurses will be able to administer such tests as the *Snellen Chart,* the *Eames Eye Test,* or the *Keystone Visual Telebinocular Survey Test.*[18] When indicated, medical referrals will then be made.

Because of the great amount of color used in pictures and in all teaching media today, the child who is color-blind has a distinct disadvantage. These children need to be identified and given special help when identification, naming, and use of color are required. Possibly auditory methods can be emphasized more with the color-blind child. About 4 percent of the children enrolled in a school are likely to be color-blind, and almost all will be boys.[19]

Olson screened 275 first grade boys at the end of the school year with the AO H-R-R Pseudo-Isochromatic Plates and identified twelve color-blind boys. She matched these with twelve boys who were not color-blind and compared their achievement on the *California Reading Test,* Lower Primary, Form W, given in May. The differences in achievement were significant at the .01 level of confidence in favor of the boys who had color vision.[20]

Schiffman[21] identified 201 color-blind boys in first grade. The teachers of fifty-one of these boys were told about the color blindness, but no other treatment was given. At the end of the year, the fifty-one whose teachers had been informed performed better than the rest of the color-blind boys, whose teachers were not informed. The difference was statistically significant at the .05 level of confidence.

Children should be screened early in their school careers for color blindness. For those identified, adjustment should be made early in the course of study to prevent failure. Parents and teachers should plan to give support to the child in meeting psychological and societal demands if adjustments are necessary.

The following are a few activities that teachers can use during the prereading period to assess visual discrimination abilities:

1. Which word is not like the others?

boy	boys	boy	boy
went	went	went	want

2. Pick out all the words in an experience story that begin with the same letter.
3. Underline a given word every time it appears in an experience story.
4. In two columns of the same words in different orders, draw lines to connect the two that are just alike.
5. Match flash cards with words in the reading chart or in sentences on the chalkboard.
6. See also the subsection "Visual Configuration" in chapter 9, "Word Recognition Skills."

Auditory Discrimination

In order to learn to read, it is necessary for children to have acquired skills in auditory discrimination. Boys and girls need to be able to identify likenesses and differences in beginning and ending sounds of words, and to hear and correctly identify consonant sounds, vowel sounds, consonant clusters, diphthongs, pitch, and intonation. The prereading program must include many nonverbal, expressive kinds of activities to compensate for grammatical or syntactical differences or confusions in verbal activities. Some oral exercises that teachers may use to strengthen auditory discrimination are:

1. List all the words you can think of that have the same beginning sound as the word *dog*.
2. Tell me the sound you hear at the beginning of *Ruth*.
3. Do *man* and *mother; dog* and *boy* begin alike?
4. Which word does not begin like the others?
   mother   money   Nancy   milk
5. Which words do not begin with the same sound as in *mother?*
   money   something   milk   never   said
6. Tell me some words that rhyme with *tall*.

7. Supply the rhyming words at the ends of lines of *Mother Goose*.
8. Name all the things you can see that start with the same sound as the beginning sound of *red*.

Minimal pairs are two words containing all the same sounds except one phoneme, which changes the meaning of the word. Several examples of minimal pairs are given in chapter 3, "Linguistic Foundations for Reading Instruction."

The importance of visual and auditory discrimination is further emphasized in chapter 9, "Word Recognition Skills."

The Left-Handed Child

Statistics have indicated for some time that about 7 percent of the children in school are left-handed. Since a relationship between changing handedness of young children and stuttering was hypothesized some decades ago, most teachers have accepted the general concept that if a child enters school using his left hand, they should accept that fact and make no attempt to change it.

If a young child doesn't demonstrate a definite handedness preference by the time he is between twenty-four and thirty months of age, mothers might well see if the practice of always handing the child objects from the right side might cause him to decide to be right-handed. If there is no strong preference, a small amount of encouragement might be all that is necessary to have a child decide to be right-handed, and he will find that society is organized for right-handed people. However, if the child enters school at age five or six with a preference for the left hand, he should certainly be encouraged to use it.

In view of the large number of children who do not learn how to write successfully with the left hand, however, it seems necessary to offer a word of advice to teachers. Rather than take a complete "hands off" attitude toward the left-handed child, they should show the child how to hold a pencil comfortably and firmly in the left hand just as they would if the child were right-handed. They can also provide affective support and encouragement. When the child is ready for cursive writing, they can demonstrate how to turn the paper at a forty-five degree angle to the right, just as the opposite arrangement is used for the right-handed child. While many children are able to work at tables where writing is comfortable with either hand, the school administrator should provide chairs with arms on the left side instead of on the right and make any other adjustments needed.

Attendance in Kindergarten

Children who attend kindergarten are exposed to many types of socializing experiences that provide for small group interaction and development of language. They hear stories and listen to records and play rhythm and singing games that develop skills in physical, emotional, social, and intellectual areas. Children who do not attend kindergarten need a longer period of time in first grade to make their adjustment to school and to participate in many of these activities. For many children who do attend kindergarten, there is a genuine need to continue their informal activities at the beginning of first grade to make the second year of school a continuation of the first but leading to more complex types of activities.

While there is some controversy about teaching reading in kindergarten, wise kindergarten teachers do not make any formal attempt for all the children to have any such lessons. All types of beginning reading experiences are available, but each child is allowed to demonstrate his or her own readiness and motivation *before* the teacher begins to place importance on "what words are." When a child points to a word and asks "What's that word?" the child should, of course, be told and commended for wanting to know. When the child draws a picture, the teacher can encourage the child to make up a sentence about it, which can be written below the picture to tell a story. But the child need not remember any of the individual words as part of a sight vocabulary. It is hoped that the child's attention span will grow to the point of wanting to hear stories read by the teacher, but a child should be permitted to leave the group when no longer interested.

Informal Reading in Relation to Home Environment

The teacher will be interested in determining the extent to which the child's parents read, because this helps determine the importance the child will place on reading. The teacher will observe whether there are books in the home and whether the parents place value on learning through reading. If a mother asks for ways she may help her child informally, she can be advised that trips to the supermarket provide opportunity for the child to identify words on signs, cans, and packages where the picture is a guide to the contents. Also, many inexpensive books are available in the supermarket that can be read to the child and that the child can then reread by studying the pictures. Teachers counseling parents might emphasize that a happy child with parents who love him, who spend time with him, and who strengthen his self-concept is likely to adjust well anywhere.

Parents need to understand that the following activities lead to readiness for formal reading:[22]

1. Many, varied opportunities for oral expression.
2. Practice in listening to other people tell about things; for example, "show and tell" time.
3. Discussing experiences or things shared by others.
4. Opportunities to hear stories and poems read by the teacher or presented on records and tapes.
5. Field trips and other excursions, preceded by preparedness directions followed by discussion and experience charts.
6. Activities such as choral speaking, dramatization, radio or television skits, and practice with a tape recorder, to promote accurate pronunciation and enunciation.
7. Arranging pictures into a story sequence. This is carried out in a variety of situations, including flannel boards and pictures mounted on individual cards.
8. Interpreting a picture by telling a story about it: what the people are doing; where they are going; do they look happy?
9. Practice in recognizing the central ideas in stories read by the teacher.

10. Extensive practice in auditory discrimination and identification of familiar sounds. This may be thinking about things in the kitchen that begin with *p* (*p*an, *p*ot, *p*itcher, *p*late). Or it may be identifying different animal or traffic sounds or sounds like wood on wood, spoons being tapped together, paper being crumpled, or shoes scraping.
11. Making children aware of reading in their daily lives by having them distinguish their own names, looking at and talking about stories, reading or seeing signs, bulletin boards, and messages.
12. Keeping records of interesting or unusual words that have been used in conversation.

Testing Readiness for Reading

Upon completing a program of activities with young children in the first grade which includes many different elements of linguistic and cognitive knowledge and skills, the teacher may wish to administer a standardized reading readiness

A Good Beginning

test. Such a test will supplement the teacher's judgment and can be used as a criterion for moving the child into more formal reading activities. It is logical to assume that a readiness test would also predict the child's success in learning to read.

Reading readiness tests currently available have rather serious limitations with respect to accurate prediction of future reading success, however. Reading success in first grade may depend less on cognitive learning than on the affective factors that surround the child's life and the extent of the child's enriched oral language competence. Attention span and experiential background may be factors too, but they are not measured on a readiness test in many cases.

Although the commonly administered readiness tests do not have high validity in predicting reading success for first graders, they may have diagnostic usefulness. Analysis of the errors made on the test may help teachers to plan subsequent exercises for the child.

Commonly used reading readiness tests are the following:

1. *Clymer-Barrett Prereading Battery* by Theodore Clymer and Thomas Barrett (Princeton, New Jersey: Personnel Press, 1969). A prereading test that measures letter recognition, shape completion, sentence-copying, discriminating ending sounds, discriminating beginning sounds, and matching words.

2. *The Metropolitan Readiness Test* by Joanne R. Nurss and Mary E. McGauvran (New York: Harcourt Brace Jovanovich, 1976). A school readiness test for end of the kindergarten year or beginning first grade. In addition to the reading readiness activities, there is a number readiness subtest, and space for a child's drawing of a man. The subtests of the reading readiness include: (1) word meaning, (2) understanding sentences, (3) using information, and (4) visual discrimination of pictures.

3. *Harrison-Stroud Reading Readiness Tests* by M. Lucille Harrison and J. B. Stroud (Boston: Houghton Mifflin, 1956). A reading readiness test that may be used in the first grade when the teacher believes the child is ready for reading. It measures visual discriminations, use of context clues, auditory discriminations, use of context and auditory clues, and identification of the letters of the alphabet.

4. *Murphy-Durrell Diagnostic Reading Readiness Tests* by Helen Murphy and D. D. Durrell (New York: Harcourt, Brace & World, 1964). A reading readiness test that measures visual discrimination, auditory discrimination, and learning rate.

Rude reminds us that attention span, cognitive learning style, and experiential background are only three important factors which are not measured by these tests.[23] For that reason, the preventive kinds of assistance to be rendered by the school psychologist become extremely important to insure the young child a successful start in school.

Figure 4.1 Back cover of the *Metropolitan Readiness Tests* showing subtests and provision for summarizing data.

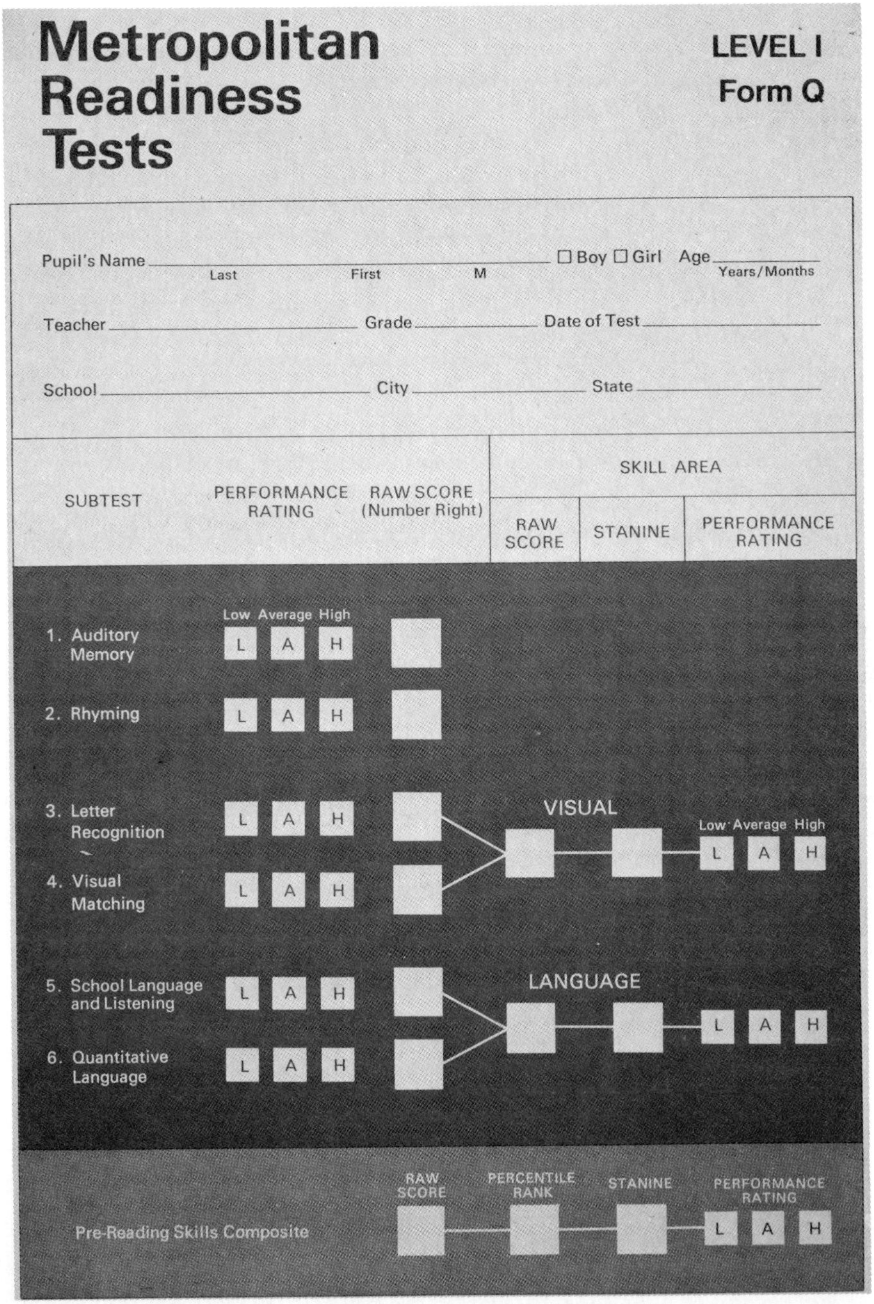

Metropolitan Readiness Tests

LEVEL I
Form Q

Pupil's Name _____ ☐ Boy ☐ Girl Age _____
Last First M Years/Months

Teacher _____ Grade _____ Date of Test _____

School _____ City _____ State _____

SUBTEST	PERFORMANCE RATING	RAW SCORE (Number Right)	SKILL AREA		
			RAW SCORE	STANINE	PERFORMANCE RATING
1. Auditory Memory	Low Average High L A H	☐			
2. Rhyming	L A H	☐			
3. Letter Recognition	L A H	☐	VISUAL		Low Average High L A H
4. Visual Matching	L A H	☐			
5. School Language and Listening	L A H	☐	LANGUAGE		L A H
6. Quantitative Language	L A H	☐			

	RAW SCORE	PERCENTILE RANK	STANINE	PERFORMANCE RATING
Pre-Reading Skills Composite	☐	☐	☐	L A H

A Good Beginning

Summary   This chapter has discussed the factors most important in the child's readiness for learning how to read. These may be summarized as: (1) *physical-neurological factors,* including the ability to see and hear well, visual and auditory discriminatory abilities, length of attention span, willingness to attend, and the presence of specific disabilities that may be neurological dysfunctioning; (2) *emotional and social factors,* such as ability to adjust to and cooperate in the group, adequate attention span, and the possible presence of behavioral disorders; and (3) *intellectual factors,* including cognitive development in relevant knowledge, comprehension, quantitative thinking, word association, story sequence, and extensiveness of vocabulary. It is in the intellectual area that the teacher hopes to develop curiosity about reading and a genuine interest in learning how to read.

It is detrimental to growth to "push" a child into reading before he or she has the prerequisite skills. The most important prerequisite is a functional language background that the child can use in reading. Children who exhibit little interest in reading the printed page need lots of opportunity to use language orally. They need to think and express their thoughts, to solve problems, to tell and guess riddles, to become curious about print, to *see purpose* in making use of reading. A delay in efforts to make children learn words and read from early readers will pay big dividends if the children are working on expanding and enriching their oral language repertoire.

Since chronological age has not been demonstrated as a defensible criterion for enrolling all children in first grade, it becomes very important that the kindergarten and first grade years be used for competent assessment of maturity for the reading process. Learning to read makes use of the child's previous learning, attention span, ability to follow instructions, and attainment in language. The first grade teacher must plan the room organization and language interaction with the class so observations about each child can be made. Does the child:

1. Talk easily and use a big vocabulary to relate experiences?
2. Have a sufficiently long attention span to become engrossed in some tasks for long periods?
3. Become engrossed in activities based entirely on language when the occasion fits?
4. Prefer active games or physical movement, and have difficulty sitting still for very long periods of time?
5. Think and spontaneously answer the teacher's questions with ease?
6. Follow directions and finish the jobs started?
7. Recognize whether sounds are alike or different?
8. Observe well and note salient features?
9. Have motor control in writing his or her name; in following the line?
10. Recognize the left-to-right progression of printed words?
11. Handle books with care?
12. Exhibit a desire to read?

Suggested Activities

1. Observe a psychologist, counselor, or reading clinician administer one of the tests recommended in this chapter for children who need special evaluation for readiness for school.
2. Study the manual for the Illinois Test of Psycholinguistic Abilities and make a list of informal types of questions first grade teachers might use to help determine a child's readiness with language for formal reading instruction.
3. Examine several teachers' manuals for first grade reading programs in basal readers and study the informal checklists of reading readiness items. Prepare a checklist that you think would be useful for a first grade teacher.
4. Administer a reading readiness test to a child of four, five, or six and try to evaluate the results in terms of his readiness for formal school.
5. As a result of No. 4 above, select specific activities from the teacher's manual designed to meet the readiness needs of the individual as revealed by the test performance.

For Further Reading

Bing, Lois. "Vision and the 'Right to Read' Effort." *Journal of Learning Disabilities* 5 (December 1972):46–50.

Book, Robert. "Predicting Reading Failure: A Screening Battery for Kindergarten Children." *Journal of Learning Disabilities* 7 (January 1974):43–47.

De Hirsch, Katrina, Jeannette Jansky, and William Langford, *Predicting Reading Failure,* chapter 9, "Recommendations," pp. 84–92. New York: Harper & Row, 1966.

Dunn, Lloyd. *Peabody Language Development Kits.* Circle Pines, Minn. 55014: American Guidance Services, Inc., 1967.

Farr, Roger, and Nicholas Anastasiow. *Tests of Reading Readiness and Achievement: A Review and Evaluation.* Newark, Del.: International Reading Assn., 1969.

Harris, Albert J., and E. R. Sipay. *Effective Teaching of Reading,* chapter 2, "Getting Ready for Reading." New York: David McKay, 1971.

Heilman, Arthur W. *Principles and Practices in Teaching Reading,* 3d ed. chapter 4, "Readiness for Reading," pp. 109–61. Columbus, Ohio: Charles E. Merrill, 1972.

Hillerich, Robert L. *Reading Fundamentals for Preschool and Primary Children.* Columbus, Ohio: Charles E. Merrill, 1977.

Pitcher-Baker, Georgia. "Does Perceptual Training Improve Reading?" *Academic Therapy* 9 (Fall 1973):41–45.

Rude, Robert T. "Readiness Tests: Implications for Early Childhood Education." *The Reading Teacher* 26 (March 1973):572–80.

Tinker, Miles A. *Preparing Your Child for Reading.* New York: McGraw-Hill, 1976.

Tonjes, Marian, and Mavis Martin. *Thinkers: A Manual of Independent Learning Activities for Kindergarten and Grade One.* Albuquerque, N.M.: Southwestern Cooperative Educational Laboratory, 1970.

Notes

1. Based on Ernest R. Hilgard, *Theories of Learning* (New York: Appleton-Century-Crofts, 1957), pp. 60–63.
2. By Samuel A. Kirk and James J. McCarthy (Champaign: University of Illinois Press, 1968).
3. Robert E. Valett, *Valett Development Survey of Basic Learning Abilities* (577 College Avenue, Palo Alto, California: Consulting Psychologist Press, 1966).
4. Katrina de Hirsch, Jeanette Jefferson Jansky, and William S. Langford, *Predicting Reading Failure* (New York: Harper & Row, 1966).
5. Katrina de Hirsch and Jeannette J. Jansky, "Early Prediction of Reading, Writing, and Spelling Ability," in *Corrective Reading in the Elementary Classroom,* ed. Marjorie Seddon Johnson and Roy A. Kress, Perspectives in Reading No. 7 (Newark, Del.: International Reading Assn., 1967), p. 50.
6. Ibid., p. 47.
7. Nicholas W. Bankson, *Bankson Language Screening Test* (Baltimore: University Park Press, 1977).
8. Robert L. Hillerich, *Prediction with Diagnostic Qualities* (Wilmette, Ill.: Eduscope, Inc., 1974).
9. ———. "A Diagnostic Approach to Early Identification of Language Skills," *The Reading Teacher* 31 (January 1978):357–64.
10. Published by Houghton Mifflin, Boston, Mass., 1960.
11. Published by the Psychological Corporation, 304 East 45th Street, New York, New York.
12. E. A. Doll, *The Measurement of Social Competence* (Philadelphia: Educational Test Bureau, 1953).
13. *Farm Life* (1963) and *City Life* (1965) (Chicago: Field Enterprises Educational Corporation).
14. Donald J. Bissett, ed., *Poems and Verses to Begin On* (124 Spear Street, San Francisco: Chandler Publishing Co., 1967), p. 31.
15. May Hill Arbuthnot, ed., *The Arbuthnot Anthology of Children's Literature* (Chicago: Scott, Foresman, 1952).
16. Barbara Geismer and Antoinette Suter, *Very Young Verses* (Boston: Houghton Mifflin, 1945).
17. *The Real Mother Goose* (Chicago: Rand McNally, 1944).
18. The Snellen Chart, American Optical Company, Southbridge, Massachusetts; The Eames Eye Test, Harcourt, Brace, & World; Keystone Visual Telebinocular Survey Test, Keystone View Division, Mast Development Co., 2210 East 12th St., Davenport, Iowa 52803.
19. A. Chapanis, "Color Blindness," *Scientific American* 184 (1951):48–53; F. E. Kratter, "Color Blindness in Relation to Normal and Defective Intelligence," *American Journal of Mental Deficiency* 62 (1957):436–41.
20. Arleen L. Olson, "An Experimental Study of the Relationship Between Color Blindness and Reading Achievement in the First Grade," Master's thesis, The Graduate School, University of New Mexico, 1963.
21. G. B. Schiffman, *The Effect of Color Blindness upon Achievement of Elementary School Males,* Experimental Research Series Report No. 106 (Towson, Maryland: Board of Education, 1963).

22. From Warren G. Cutts, *Modern Reading Instruction* (Washington, D.C.: Center for Applied Research in Education, 1964), p. 18. See also Roma Gans, "This Business of Reading," *Progressive Education* 21:70, 72, 93, 94; and Lucille M. Harrison, "Getting Them Ready to Read," *NEA Journal* 40:106–8.

23. Robert T. Rude, "Readiness Tests: Implications for Early Childhood Education," *The Reading Teacher* 26 (March 1973):579.

5
Teaching Beginning Reading

Without meaning, there is no reading. The process of reading is first and foremost a thinking process, from the very first reading lesson. Of course, the visual perception of words and the ability to call up meanings they represent make word recognition a prerequisite.

How Reading Begins

As explained in the definition of the reading process in chapter 1, the very first lessons in how to read must teach children that *ideas* are contained in the printed symbols. Children need to watch ideas being written down on paper, preserved, and then restated in exactly the way they were stated the first time. To demonstrate this process from the very first lesson, the teacher should work from the children's own experiences. Children utilizing their own grammar to express ideas personal and important to them can then see their stories recorded. All this must happen before they become concerned with the sound-symbol relationships of letters in the words authors have used to provide stories for them to read. They learn *first* how the reading process works.

It must be reemphasized that children of six or seven years bring to school a well developed language and that they possess all the skills to think and reason orally using that language. A primary responsibility of the teacher is to understand what kind of language a child has. Is it standard English, as used in school textbooks? Is it any one of many nonstandard dialects of English? Is it English spoken with interference from a second language? Or is it a language other than English? If a child's *primary* language can be categorized in any of these areas, the child should be introduced to reading through a language-experience approach using that "kind of language."

The first language-experience reading of a child whose primary language is Spanish should be in the Spanish language. The first language-experience reading of the child who speaks Black English should be in that dialect of English. Similarly, a child who speaks standard English should learn reading *first* in that dialect. (See the diagram suggested by Burke in figure 1.2.)

With every reading lesson, the child needs to relate first to meanings, next to the language used to express the meanings. Only then should the child be concerned about analysis of phonic or structural elements. When the teacher's effort is centered on meanings, the child's opportunity to see the task as a whole is enhanced. In all teaching of reading, a primary consideration must be the development of concepts—the translation of concrete experiences into abstractions. In order to be a good reader, one must be able to do abstract and critical thinking.

Harris warns us that children are apt to fail to learn the meaningful nature of reading if teachers spend undue time teaching phonic elements in isolation. If, from the child's first conscious exposure to written language, that language does not communicate, then the chances are high that the beginning reader will get a false idea of the purpose of the reading lesson. Even recently published materials often may present the alphabet or phonic skills or sight words in isolation as immediate goals of learning. It is therefore possible that children will *not* start by demanding meaning in reading, and reading groups may show evidences of boredom and low levels of motivation.[1]

The concept of developing skills sequentially has been adhered to closely in all traditional teaching materials. When children understand the reading process as an extension of their total use of language in communication, beginning with the language-experience approach, rigid sequencing loses its importance from the *child's* standpoint. If we accept two premises—(1) that the child's thinking skills are developed in oral language to a mature degree, and (2) that the language-experience approach to reading is each child's avenue to reading something that is interesting and personal—then we cannot feel bound to teach phonic and structural analysis skills in any rigid sequence. However, it is important to emphasize that the teacher must know the sequence of skills that helps a particular child move from the known to the unknown, from the simple to the complex, from the old to the new. The teacher can thus help the child develop the skill needed *when* it is needed.

Some of the characteristics of a primary reading program are:

1. It extends the communication arts from listening and speaking to reading and writing.
2. It emphasizes the principle that reading is recorded talk, that writing preserves talk.
3. It emphasizes that reading is primarily a thinking process.
4. Its primary objective is that children accumulate a vocabulary of sight words they can use.
5. It teaches appreciation so that children begin early to like to read and to anticipate enjoyment in good books.
6. It does not rely on only one method or technique for learning; a good teacher's methodology is eclectic.
7. It requires interesting, exciting, changing things in the room to read—bulletin boards, displays, labels, questions, current events.

8. It emphasizes that phoneme-grapheme relationships translate symbols into worthwhile ideas.

9. It teaches a variety of approaches to new words so the independent reader can discover new words: configuration, similarity to known words, context clues, picture clues, sounding out, analyzing the word structure.

Children who are mastering a sight vocabulary of some 50 words are already profiting from directed lessons in auditory discrimination of initial consonant sounds. From pictures, they are becoming aware of the beginning sound of "goat," "girl," "goose," and "gun" and labeling it as the *g* sound. They will learn to recognize the visual symbol as soon as they have learned to read a few *g* words in print. As soon as they associate the phoneme (sound as spoken) with the grapheme (letter as written), children can make systematic use of phonics. Most reading series will present a sequenced program in phonic analysis through the sixth grade, with the heaviest dosage in grades two and three. Structural analysis will be taught all the way through public school, but by the end of grade three, children will already have much familiarity with compound words, root words, prefixes, suffixes, and syllables.

Beginning formal reading, then, is the transition from expanding language development, through the acquisition of an acuity in auditory discrimination of English phonemes, to a knowledge of a basic sight vocabulary of from 50 to 100 words and some fluency in reading meaningfully.

Chall suggested in *Learning to Read: The Great Debate* that there have been only a few innovations in widely used reading programs through the past decade:

1. Somewhat more emphasis on learning the alphabet and its phoneme-grapheme relationship;

2. Adjusting the content of readers to make them more broadly interesting to all the children;

3. Accepting the reality of individual differences in children and providing for more individualization in teaching.[2]

Readiness

One of the most important things for a teacher of young children to bear in mind always is that six-year-olds show great variability in what they are ready to learn in school. This is true because of the great range in what they already know, in what they can already do, in the length of their attention span, and in what they value as worthwhile.

Classroom practices that are predicated on the assumption that all children of any *given age* are ready to read is false and unfair to *all* children. All teachers have probably observed such sharp differences among children as the following:

The shy, timid, self-absorbed child vs. the more aggressive, brave, gregarious child.

The child with no interest in books, print, or learning to write vs. the child who pores over pictures and illustrated books, "reading" and creating stories.

The quiet daydreamer vs. the loud, obnoxious mixer.

The socialized, demure child vs. the eternally curious child.

The undernourished child or the one with little resistance to disease vs. the "healthy" child who seems to stay well.

The child who has enjoyed few toys of his or her own vs. the child of affluence who has "too many things."

The child whose parent is busy and does not know the responsibilities of parenting vs. the one whose parent is patient, takes time, is concerned and helpful and motivating and encouraging.

These individual differences undoubtedly have more bearing on how the great majority of children will respond to future reading experiences than will the results of currently used intelligence and achievement tests.

One wonders why educators have not widely accepted the logical notion that some few children learn to read at three; more learn when they are four; some when they are five; the great majority when they are six; and some few need more time and will learn if permitted to do so when they are seven, or eight, or nine. Learning centers such as described in chapter 7 could make it possible for young children of all stages of readiness to have profitable days at school indefinitely. Those interested in reading may do so, and those who have other needs to be met first are permitted to delay formal reading until a later time.

Cutts reminds teachers of an important point about children who have had limited experiences:

Six-year-olds who cannot talk coherently can scarcely be expected to begin reading as soon as they enter school. Teachers need to approach English language instruction for underprivileged children as if they were teaching a foreign language. Children whose language is limited to grunts and crudities need extensive experiences before they are ready for any formalized reading instruction. Underprivileged children must have plenty of time to react to talk about the things they have seen and heard. Many culturally deprived children have extremely limited horizons; many have never traveled more than two blocks from home before entering school.[3]

Methods

Teachers today usually have the option of using five methods of teaching reading, with emphasis distributed as they wish: (1) a language-experience approach; (2) a basal reader approach; (3) an individualized reading approach; (4) an approach based on a modified or special writing system; and (5) an approach strongly oriented to phonics, as in some programmed materials and in some systems approaches. The strengths and weaknesses of some of these approaches are summarized in tables later in this chapter. The individualized reading approach is described more fully in chapter 6, Organizing the Classroom Reading Program.

At the same time young teachers are learning methods of teaching reading, they may be introduced to certain dogmatisms. Jastak and Jastak have some pertinent advice to teachers about two particular dogmatisms.

The literature on reading instruction contains various prescriptions as to what children should not be encouraged to do in learning to read. Sometimes such prescriptions are in the form of indirect allusions that children are slowed down when they use certain ways of learning. Among the Taboos are pointing with the finger, moving lips, oral reading, reading without comprehension, spelling aloud before reading, reading without inflection, phonic reading, breaking words up into syllables, etc. These interdictions are taught with complete confidence in their validity without evidence that they are bad habits except that they "slow children down." Furthermore, they are applied as absolute rules to persons of any age and at any point of the learning stage. We have heard of supervisors and reading specialists visiting classrooms for the sole purpose of checking whether any of the children move their lips or point with their fingers while reading. Teachers whose children move their lips are condemned as inferior and are given poor professional ratings. This strange behavior on the part of supervisors and reading experts causes more retardation in reading than any moving of the lips or pointing with the fingers has ever done. It can be demonstrated that some children who point with their fingers read faster and more accurately than when they do not. The fallacy of "being slowed down" stems from the observations that good readers do not point with their fingers but poor readers do. It is known however to students of statistics that correlation is not causation. The poor reader, finding that he loses his way or that his performance is not what it should be, hits upon the device of using his finger to help himself. Pointing with the finger becomes an important temporary aid in overcoming the coordination difficulties that exist in poor readers. Pointing with the finger is not a cause but an effect of reading disability. It is helpful in the early stages of learning to read and is spontaneously abandoned as the skill of reading gains in efficiency.[4]

The Language-Experience Approach to Reading

Writing down the language contributions of a young child is one of the most natural ways of extending the child's learning in the communication arts. The kindergarten teacher stops at a child's desk and admires a picture the child is making. When the teacher asks about the picture, the child says, "My dog has chased the cat up a tree." The teacher can say, "Billy, would you like me to write that under your picture?" Of course he would, because the teacher is preserving something personal and valuable to him. The result is presented in figure 5.1.

The kindergarten class goes to the baby animal zoo for a field trip. When they return to the classroom and talk about their trip, the teacher encourages a great deal of discussion—verbalization about whatever topics of conversation are of most interest to the children. By encouraging the children's responses, the teacher may spur each child to express one idea and illustrate it with crayon. As these pictures evolve, the teacher can write a sentence for each child's picture about what it tells. The teacher could then bind all the pictures into a big book for the reading table, which the children may peruse in their free time. Children are apt to remember their own sentences and, although they do not know individual words at this time, they will be able to "read" to the class what their own pictures "say." Children build vocabulary while gaining new ideas, discussing with others, asking questions about things they see, and listening as the teacher talks with the group. Children should be able to acquire a sight vocabulary of approximately 100 words with this approach. They then have sufficient reading power to read several books with controlled vocabularies.

The heightened effect produced by the teacher arranging to meet individually with each child, albeit for only very short periods, to write down what he would like to record, develops a sensitivity to oral and written language and encourages the child to be more observant of his environment and the language he hears, and more impressed with the recording of oral language as a means of preserving ideas.

The language-experience method of operating with small groups or individuals in the classroom has been clearly described in recent publications.[5] Nielsen's steps in developing the language-experience approach are given in chapter 6.

How to Prepare Experience Charts

Experience charts provide the teacher several avenues to language development that are practical and useful in daily activities in the classroom. They can contain: (1) short written accounts of children's experiences that can be read and reread for review; (2) announcements, directions, reminders, or lists

A Good Beginning

Figure 5.1 After a young child makes a picture that "tells" a story, the teacher should elicit an explanatory sentence and write it (in manuscript) under the picture.

My dog has chased the cat up a tree.

of duties; (3) summaries of subject matter discussed; (4) samples of children's creative writing; or (5) plans for the day or for special work periods.[6]

The following outline details the necessary steps in making experience charts.

I. Getting ready to make an experience chart
   A. The teacher needs to select an experience that has been common to all the children. Many charts can be based on usual happenings in daily school routine. A common experience of the group, such as an excursion, provides a basis for several stories. (See the story "At the Zoo" dictated by the kindergarten class in figure 5.2.)
   B. After the experience has been selected, it is necessary to develop, through group discussion, the important concepts and to state them in complete sentences.
   C. The concepts need to be analyzed and organized so that different members of the group will present the concepts in proper chronology.
   D. The teacher writes the sentences in the story as they are dictated by the children. Other children in the group may edit sentences or extend the discussion to clarify concepts.
II. The content of the chart should contain:
   A. Sentences dictated by individual children.
   B. Complete sentences.
   C. All sentences "one-line" length in early charts.
   D. Ideas clearly and accurately stated.

At The Zoo

We went to the zoo.
We went on the bus.
We saw the animals.
We saw the monkeys.
We saw the giraffe.
We saw the elephant.
We like the zoo.

The Kindergarten.

Uncle Jim's Apple Orchard

We went to visit
Uncle Jim's Apple Orchard.
Mr. Garcia drove the bus.
We rode for about an hour.
We saw Uncle Jim.
He gave us apples to eat.
He has more than
a thousand bushels.
He has twenty pickers.
He has cold rooms
in his packing shed.
He has many kinds of apples.
We like Uncle Jim's Apple Orchard.

The First Grade

Figure 5.3 Zaner-Bloser alphabet.

Used by permission of the Zaner-Bloser Company, Columbus, Ohio 43215.

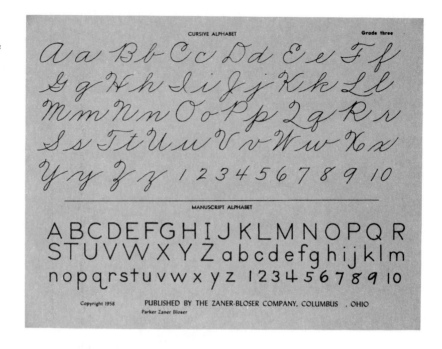

III. Making the experience chart:
   A. Use large size chart paper, 22 by 30 inches or larger. The lines should be spaced three-fourths of an inch apart. Such lined paper is available commercially for primary teachers.
   B. Center the title three spaces from top of page.
   C. Capitalize only the first letters of words in the title.
   D. Leave a two-inch margin on the left and a neat margin on the right.
   E. Begin the first line three spaces below the title.
   F. Use three spaces for each line of manuscript writing. A middle space is the base line for writing, a space above is for the tall letters and a space below for the letters with stems below. (See *Zaner-Bloser* alphabet, figure 5.3.)
   G. Leave a fourth space for separation of lines of manuscript writing.
   H. Make lines fairly uniform in length, if possible.
   I. When a sentence is too long for one line, be sure to break it between phrases without regard to length of written line. (See story *Uncle Jim's Apple Orchard,* figure 5.2.)

After children have read a number of experience stories, the teacher can identify the basic sight words that have been used several times and prepare *reading charts* using the names of the children in the room. This provides some interesting practice for overlearning the most used words in primary reading. For example, when the group has read *went, saw, to, on,* and *the,* the teacher can prepare a rebus reading chart like this:

Mary went on the bus.

John went to the zoo.

Mary saw the

John saw the

Billy went to the zoo.

Jean went to the zoo.

Billy saw the

Jean saw the

Teachers should practice appropriate editorial skills so that charts will be finished with both good form and good content. They can be displayed in the room and also reused at later times. Some of the editorial skills include organization on the page, line arrangement, spacing, the use of pictures, editing, and expanding to include additional information when indicated. An excellent handbook outlining the range of uses for, the preparation of, and the rationale for experience charts is *Using Experience Charts with Children* by Herrick and Nerbovig.[7]

Lamoreaux and Lee wrote:

In general, . . . certain principles can be drawn which distinguish good charts. First, each chart must serve the purpose it is intended to serve, and, over a period of time, charts should serve a variety of purposes. They should be simple and unified. They should be suited to the ability of the children for whom they are intended. There should be adequate word control. The mechanics should be good, the print clear and large enough, and the lines well spaced. The sentences should be correctly phrased in thought units and indented in regular paragraph form.[8]

The Basal Reader Approach

Basal reader materials generally are a series of books and auxiliary materials designed to stimulate systematic development of reading abilities. Basal reading series provide (1) carefully sequenced presentation of skills, (2) continuity of all skills through the grades, and (3) integration of materials and skills to facilitate independent learning. Series are usually organized to provide gradual progression to more difficult steps and gradual broadening of children's conceptions of social organization, vocabulary, word analysis skills, and evaluative abilities.

If a child cannot recognize a word, probably the child will have difficulty gathering meaning from a sentence containing it. For very young children beginning the reading process, it is safe to assume that if they cannot pronounce a word, they will not be able to get the full meaning of a sentence in which it appears. Therefore, reading programs generally try to teach children to recognize a small stock of sight words so they can extract meaning from the very first books of a reading series. Some first preprimers will have no more than twenty different words. The significant point is that a child will, with this limited stock of words, read meaningful sentences and little stories for which the teacher will ask guide questions and build story plots. And from the beginning, the teacher will request children to "read with their eyes and not with their lips" so that they will form the habit of recognizing all the words in a sentence and then practice saying them as they might speak instead of reading word-by-word slowly and with observable difficulty.

Stone has identified the 100 words used most in early reading in first-grade basal reading programs. (They are listed in chapter 9.) These words must be learned as sight words. They do provide a core of service words to be used in a great deal of easy reading practice.

Dolch made a list of *service* words most needed by children in all textbook reading in the elementary school. The list of 220 words contains no nouns and constitutes about *two-thirds* of all the words read by children in first and second grade books and *half* of all the words read by boys and girls in fourth, fifth, and sixth grade books. Since they appear over and over in all elementary reading, knowing them as sight words is crucial for all readers. The first 300 words of the Fry "instant words" list include the service words that appear most often in children's reading. This list, found in chapter 9, contains almost all of the Dolch words.

Basal readers have been heavily criticized as shallow, repetitive, and uninteresting. For children not from middle-class American culture, basal readers have failed to present life realistically. They have not motivated children who are culturally different. And they have portrayed too much of the comfortable easy life of children not from the lower socioeconomic classes.

Salisbury has pointed out[9] that stories which focus on American middle-class children and their interests in the United States may not have applicability in many areas of our country, in binational schools outside the United States, and in other outlying areas. This condition makes it even more difficult to write interestingly with a drastically limited vocabulary.

Nevertheless, for the *beginning* teacher who must meet the demands of all the children in the classroom each day, basal readers provide gradual introduction of skills, necessary repetition, ready-made seatwork, and tests. In other words, basal texts make it possible for inexperienced teachers to offer a well worked out reading program to a class.

Usually there are readiness materials—often in the form of a workbook for the child, three preprimers introducing the first sight vocabulary, a primer or two, and a first reader for the first grade reading program. Beyond first grade, there are usually two books for each grade, for example, *second grade, semester one* and *second grade, semester two*. For all of these books, publishers provide workbooks of exercises and teachers' editions of the readers or separate manuals. More recently, in an attempt to eliminate grade level distinctions, publishers have renumbered the books in basal reader series. The first six books might constitute the grade one program; then numbers seven through ten would be for the grade two program; eleven and twelve, the grade three program; and thirteen, fourteen, and fifteen, for grades four, five, and six, respectively.

Under the impetus of the Elementary Secondary Education Act (ESEA), Title I, which made federal money available for purchase of materials, publishers have provided text films, film strips, recordings, word and phrase cards, and many supplementary reading materials.

Many major publishers now provide reading series for use all through elementary school:

Allyn and Bacon: *Pathfinder,* K–6, 1978. Robert B. Ruddell, senior author.

American Book Company: *American Book Reading Program,* 1–6, 1977. Marjorie S. Johnson and Roy A. Kress, senior authors.

Economy Company: *Keys to Reading,* 1–8, 1975. Theodore L. Harris, senior author.

Encyclopaedia Britannica Educational Corporation: *Teacher's Resource Guide, Language Experiences in Reading,* Levels I, II, III, 1974. Roach Van Allen, senior author.

Field Educational Publications: *Field Literature Program,* 1–8, 1971. Helen Huus, Robert J. Whitehead, and Henry A. Bamman, authors.

Ginn and Company: *Ginn 720,* K–6, 1976. Theodore Clymer, senior author.

Holt, Rinehart & Winston: *Holt Basic Reading Program,* K–8, 1977. Eldonna Evertts, senior author.

Houghton Mifflin: *Reading for Meaning,* K–6, 1977. William Durr, senior author.

Lippincott: *Basic Reading,* K–8, Levels A–H, 1975; I–K, 1978; L–M, 1971. Charles Walcutt and Glenn McCracken, senior authors.

Macmillan: *Series R, The New Macmillan Reading Program,* K–6, 1975–1977. Carl Smith, senior author.

Open Court Publishing Co.: *Open Court Correlated Language Arts Program.* Foundation Program, Ann Hughes, 1976; Basic Readers, Marianne Carus, 1976–1977.

Rand McNally: *Young America Basic Reading Program,* K–8, 1978. Leo C. Fay, senior author.

Scott, Foresman: *Basics in Reading,* K–8, 1978. Ira Aaron, senior author.

Science Research Associates: *SRA Reading Program,* K–6, 1971. Donald Rasmussen and Lynn Goldberg, authors.

Many publishers of these reading series also provide many supplementary aids for teachers: placement tests for each level of achievement; mastery tests for each level of achievement; sets of overhead transparencies for skill development; reading time books; tape cassettes; spirit duplicating masters; and teacher materials for additional learning aids.

Estimates of school systems using reading series as basal readers run as high as 90 percent with many schools recommending a second and third series as co-basal and tri-basal. Basal readers also provide much material for supplementary reading.

After young teachers have taught basal reading programs and learned the skills sequences, they need to organize their own resources and venture more broadly into language-experience approaches and/or individualized reading programs. Needless to say, the confidence of teachers in their ability to carry out a competent program is the first requisite. Until they feel confident that they understand the many word recognition and comprehension skills that children need for reading in today's world, they must adhere to an organized program that will insure success for the children they teach. Their goal must be to see children as individuals, and their approach to teaching must be diagnostic with respect to the learning needs of each one.

Modified Writing Systems

The Initial Teaching Alphabet

The Initial Teaching Alphabet has 44 symbols instead of the conventional 26. Each of the 44 symbols represents only one sound. The i/t/a is basically phonemic rather than phonetic. Capital letters in i/t/a are only larger duplicates of the small letter. Thus, instead of small letters in manuscript and capital letters in manuscript, then small letters in cursive and large letters in cursive, the beginning reader has to learn only 44 symbols that always stay the *same*.

While the vowel sound in the word *pie* is called a long *i*, that same sound can be spelled many different ways in other words in traditional orthography. Not in i/t/a. This sound is spelled the same in *buy, sigh, aisle, island, kite,* etc.

Most children are ready to make the transition from i/t/a to traditional orthography by the end of the first grade. The traditional basal readers rewritten into i/t/a would serve no purpose since i/t/a vocabulary is not as severely controlled. The traditional reading program is apt to introduce the child to only 350 words the first year but i/t/a may introduce that many words in a few weeks. Once children learn the sounds and realize they remain constant, they can read much more widely much more quickly.[10] The alphabet in i/t/a and a few sentences written with the i/t/a alphabet are shown in figures 5.4 and 5.5.

Words in Color

Words-in-color is a phonemic system of writing that uses a distinct color for each phoneme. The system proved very successful in languages that have fewer phonemes than does English. Having developed the system for languages in Africa, Caleb Gattegno used it for English. This required forty-seven shades of color to fit the forty-seven phonemes which he identified in the English language. In this system, a vowel sound is always the same color regardless of how it is spelled. Long *a*, for example, may be in conventional orthography:

ey in they	*ay* in day	*ei* in vein	*aigh* in straight
ea in great	*ai* in wait	*eigh* in sleigh	*a—e* in gate

The words-in-color method will present all these spellings for long *a* in the same color.

Figure 5.4 Pitman's Initial Teaching Alphabet, with its 44 symbols and words illustrating the sounds these symbols represent.

Reproduced by permission of Initial Teaching Alphabet Publications, Inc., New York, N.Y.

A Good Beginning

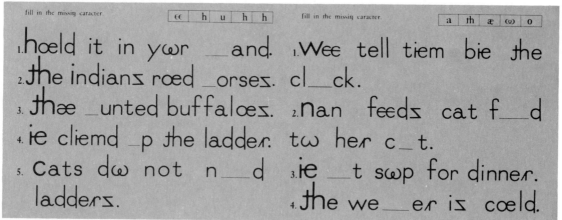

Figure 5.5 Two pages from a primary workbook written in i/t/a.

From *Workbook to Accompany Houses,* pp. 53–54 (New York: Initial Teaching Alphabet Publications, 1965.)

On the other hand, the sound of *a* in *ago, ran, rain, arm,* and *call* would be represented by a different color in each word. Similarly, *s* in *sell* and *say* is the "s" sound; *s* in *his* and *turns* is the "z" sound; *s* in *sugar* and *sure* is the "sh" sound; and *s* in *pleasure* and *treasure* is the "zh" sound. "S" appears, then, in four different colors, according to its sound in a word.

In the words-in-color system, eight charts present the forty-seven different phonemes in English in forty-seven different colors or color combinations. It is doubtful that such a complicated system of matching colors to sounds will prove very useful for the teaching of reading as a thinking process as expounded throughout this text. After making all the phoneme-grapheme associations, one will only be able to pronounce words. Perceiving how words are pronounced is only the first step of the reading process.

Use of the Rebus in Beginning Reading

The Peabody Rebus Reading Program, American Guidance Services, Inc., Circle Pines, Minnesota 55014, is a method of using pictographs so a child can read a sentence without all the English words being presented in their printed form. The technique is described also in chapter 18, devoted to children with special problems in reading. With the rebus technique, pupils first learn to read pictures of objects that stand for words (rebuses). They can thus direct their first learning efforts to how the reading process works. After learning to read the rebuses and understanding the way the reading process works, the pupils proceed through a controlled transition process in which spelled words are substituted for the pictures.

Either rebus or structured phonics materials may be especially appropriate for emotionally disturbed or neurologically impaired children who need to work in tightly structured situations, sheltered from the confusion of many other children working near them. (See figures 5.6 and 5.7.)

Figure 5.6 The vocabulary used in Books One and Two, The Peabody Rebus Reading Program.

From Richard W. Woodcock, *Teacher's Guide: Introducing Reading, Books One and Two*, the Peabody Rebus Reading Program (Circle Pines, Minn.: American Guidance Service, Inc., 1967), back cover.

a	a		can		have		run
	airplane		car		here		see
	and		cat		house		sit
	are		chair	I	I		table
	at		coat		in		the
	ball		come		is		they
	banana		dog		it	3	three
	big		down		little		to
	bird		eat		look		tree
	black	5	five		me	2	two
	blue		floor		my		under
	boat	4	four		no		up
	book		girl		on		walk
	box		go	1	one		what
	boy		green		play		with
	brown		ground		red		yellow
	cake		hat		ride		yes

Approaches That Are Strongly Phonics-Oriented

Many phonics systems have been published through the years to provide children with methods of decoding printed words for reading. Fifty years ago the Beacon Charts[11] were widely used to teach children many isolated sounds and then to provide practice in integrating these sounds into family endings and sight words.

Usually the pages in the primers contained sentences unrelated to each other. They were prepared for the specific purposes of giving the child a number of repetitions in pronouncing the phonic element being taught.

Figure 5.7 Four frames from a programmed reader using the rebus vocabulary of the Peabody Rebus Reading Program.

From Richard W. Woodcock, *Introducing Reading—Book Two,* Peabody Rebus Reading Program (Circle Pines, Minn.: American Guidance Service, 1967), frames 381–84.

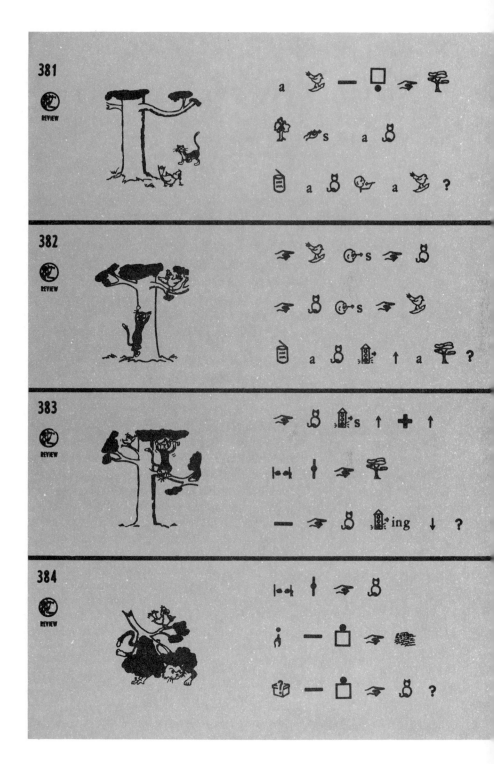

Figure 5.8 Phonics, as traditionally presented, will be helpful only at the word-perception level in demanding meaning in the reading process.

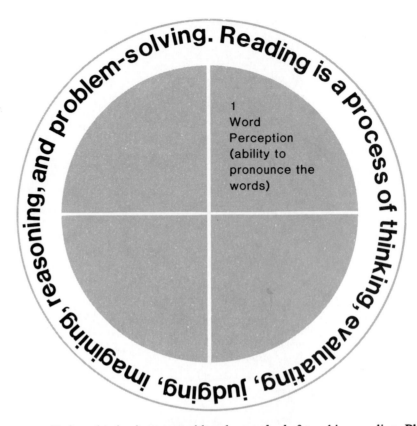

Today phonics is not considered a *method* of teaching reading. Phonics is a very necessary skill in word analysis and word identification. As emphasized throughout this text, this is not *reading*. With respect to Gray's four-step definition—"Reading is perception, comprehension, reaction, and integration"—phonics can possibly be of help only with the first step. Of course it is necessary to perceive words before reading can take place, but perceiving what words are is not reading. This is illustrated in figure 5.8, which repeats the circle presented in figure 1.1, but with only one quadrant identified to show that word perception helps the child only with the first quarter of the circle.

Any child who has low word-recognition abilities after being taught developmental reading might profit from some instruction specifically in phonic skills. Such workbooks as those provided by Rand McNally, *Phonics We Use,* and by McCormick Mathers, *Building Reading Skills,* are useful.

Some phonic systems intended for classroom use are:

Programmed Reading, McGraw-Hill.
The Phonovisual Method, Phonovisual Products, Inc., 4708 Wisconsin Avenue, N.W., Washington, D.C. (See the Phonovisual Consonant and Vowel Charts, figures 5.9 and 5.10.)
The SRA Basic Reading Series, Workbooks Level A, B, C, D, E, Science Research Associates, Chicago, Illinois.

Figure 5.9 The Phonovisual Consonant Chart sometimes used as part of a supplementary phonics program.

Copyright 1972, Phonovisual Products, Inc., P.O. Box 2292, Rockville, Md.

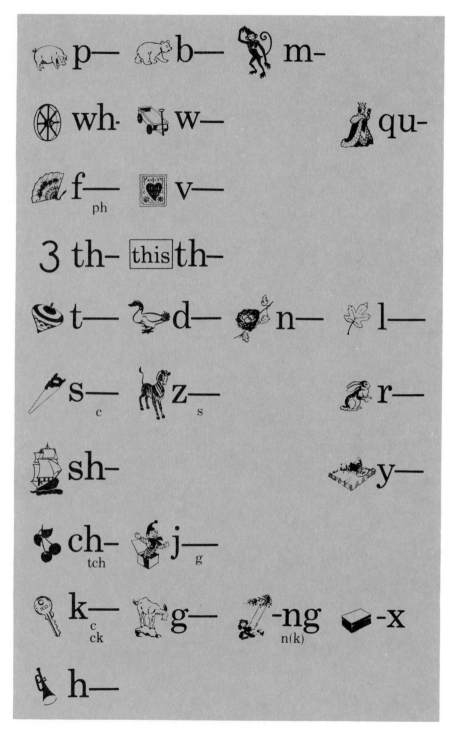

Figure 5.10 The Phonovisual Vowel Chart is sometimes used as a supplementary phonics program in the primary grades.

Copyright 1972, Phonovisual Products, Inc., P.O. Box 2292, Rockville, Md.

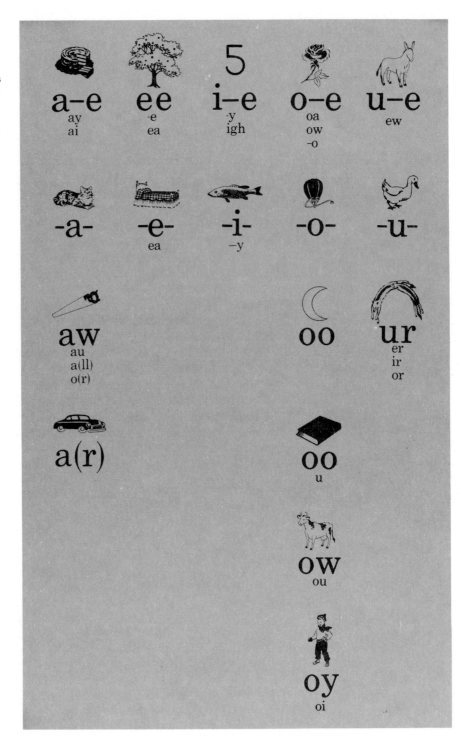

These systems are not intended to take the place of a regular reading program which expands sight vocabulary, develops meaning vocabulary, and provides a great deal of easy reading practice. These materials should be used as parallel teaching materials.

Evaluation of First Grade Reading Programs

By observing in elementary schools, one can see that the differences among classrooms are greater than the differences among the methods being used to teach reading. The most important factors are the teachers themselves and their individual abilities to relate to the children being taught.

Nevertheless, some evaluation of different methods for teaching reading is in order. The strengths and weaknesses of various methodologies are summarized below in tables 5.1, 5.2, 5.3, and 5.4.[12]

Sex Differences in First Grade

Until recently, children were expected to behave in accordance with stereotyped sex roles. The Mother Goose Rhyme was only a mild exaggeration:

What are little girls made of?
Sugar and spice and all that's nice
That's what little girls are made of.
What are little boys made of?
Snaps and snails and puppy dog tails
That's what little boys are made of.

These sex roles were often evident in the ways parents, especially fathers, expected their sons to be little men when the boys really felt like crying! Boys were supposed to learn to defend themselves, never to act like sissies, and to display some masculine aggression. Little girls were expected to wear dresses, sit quietly like little ladies, and be agreeable. A mother whose little girl turned out to be a tomboy sometimes expressed disappointment.

Whatever may be the causes, girls are likely to speak in sentences, use longer sentences and more of them, and achieve clear enunciation of all the phonemes of the language at an earlier age than are boys.

These differences mean that girls may enter first grade with two distinct advantages over boys: (1) greater ability to sit still and do seatwork, and (2) greater facility with language. Add to this the probability of a child having a woman teacher, who may emphasize traditional female values, and it is apparent that girls *do* have an advantage. Perhaps these facts explain why girls are apt to have a more favorable attitude toward school all the way through. Boys are more apt to rebel, become belligerent, or fail to see reasons why school should be largely unrelated to life.

Table 5.1 Summary of strengths and weaknesses of the language-experience approach to teaching reading.

Adapted from James F. Kerfoot, ed., *First Grade Reading Programs,* Perspectives in Reading, No. 5.

Strengths	Weaknesses
1. Shows children that reading is just talk written down.	1. Vocabulary may be too uncontrolled.
2. Encourages communication—free and easy talk.	2. May not provide continuity in teaching phonics skills.
3. Makes reading a personal and meaningful experience.	3. May not learn thinking, problem-solving skills in comprehension.
4. It is flexible.	4. Important gains in child progress may not be measured on standardized test at end of school.
5. Encourages greater creative experience in writing original stories.	5. Classroom may seem disorganized during reading class.
6. Children provide their own source of materials.	6. Charts used must seem to the children to have specific purposes.
7. Gives opportunity for the teacher to emphasize the left-to-right direction in beginning sentence reading.	7. Requires extra preparation by the teacher: chart-making, planning first-hand experiences.
8. Children learn to share their own ideas—but, more importantly, they learn to listen to the ideas of others.	
9. Children learn use of punctuation marks.	
10. Pitch, intonation, and stress can be more meaningful using child's natural spoken language in his sentences.	

Table 5.2 Summary of strengths and weaknesses of the basal reader approach to teaching reading.

Adapted from James F. Kerfoot, ed., *First Grade Reading Programs,* Perspectives in Reading, No. 5.

Strengths	Weaknesses
1. Eclectic in nature with practices integrated from all systems.	1. Too much vocabulary control—dull, repetitious.
2. *Sequential* order in presentation of skills.	2. Limited content in preprimers: shallow, unrealistic, lack of literary style.
3. *Continuity* of all skills through the grades.	3. Lack of visibility in the way skills are developed.
4. *Integration*—coordination of materials and skills.	4. Stories often not related to children's interests.
5. Gradual introduction of vocabulary and word analysis skills.	5. Sentence patterns appear haphazardly without repetition or mastery.
6. Organization is horizontal (coordination of materials) and vertical (social organization, vocabulary, word analysis skills, comprehension).	6. Race and ethnic groups are stereotyped and stylized.
	7. Tell only easy and comfortable life.
	8. Attitudes: society not realistic.
	9. Not enough done to stimulate curiosity.
	10. Need to make important things *interesting.*

A Good Beginning

Table 5.3 Summary of strengths and weaknesses of the individualized reading approach to teaching reading.

Adapted from James F. Kerfoot, ed., *First Grade Reading Programs,* Perspectives in Reading, No. 5.

Strengths	Weaknesses
1. Self-selected books are more likely to satisfy reading interests.	1. Inadequate library materials in the schools.
2. Greater opportunity for interaction among students in bringing together ideas gained from independent reading.	2. Danger of insufficient skill development.
	3. Puts heavy clerical burden on the teacher.
3. Children progress at their own rate.	4. Difficult to find time for enough individual conferences.
4. Individual teacher-pupil conferences develop rapport.	5. Young children need much guidance in material selection.
5. Diminishes competition and comparison; avoids stigma of being in lowest group.	6. Hard to judge difficulty of books.
6. Each child experiences greater self-worth; takes more initiative.	7. Is only one of possible ways to accommodate for differences in children.
7. Flexible—no ceiling on the learning.	8. Teacher needs to have read many books in children's literature.
8. Some children can be introduced to a much greater variety of reading materials.	9. Teacher needs to be able to teach skills as needed.
9. Small groups are formed as needed for specific purposes.	10. Inefficient to teach a skill to an individual that half a dozen need at that time.
10. Through time, teachers should develop greater skill and flexibility in teaching.	11. May encourage carelessness in reading and lack of thoroughness.
11. Some children can be guided in more oral and written expression and in critical thinking.	12. Difficult to administer written seatwork.
	13. Control (discipline) of room may be more difficult for teacher.
12. Combines well with other methods.	14. Teacher must do a good job of interpreting program to the parents.

Table 5.4 Summary of strengths and weaknesses of a strong phonics approach to teaching beginning reading.

Adapted from James F. Kerfoot, ed., *First Grade Reading Programs,* Perspectives in Reading, No. 5.

Strengths	Weaknesses
1. Aids in auditory perception.	1. Inhibits other skills if overemphasized in the beginning.
2. Aids in visual-auditory discrimination.	
3. Aid to word recognition.	2. Over-reliance narrows flexibility in reading.
4. Aid to unlocking new, strange words.	
5. Systematic system of learning letter sounds.	3. Memorizing phonics rules *does not* assure ability to use them.
6. Builds confidence in word recognition.	4. Meaning is really much more important than sounding.
7. Useful in spelling and composition.	5. Too many sounds are spelled alike.
	6. Too many rules—and most of them have exceptions.
	7. No good for children with hearing defects.
	8. Intensive drill can kill interest in reading.

Teaching Beginning Reading

There is some evidence that women have greater difficulty giving birth to male babies. It has been theorized that the male baby may be larger and the head therefore subject to greater danger of injury during the birth process, with resulting minimal brain dysfunction, neurological impairment, or brain lesions. Statistically, about 53 births in 100 are male, which may be nature's way of compensating for the "weaker" sex in order to insure equal numbers of males and females in the population.

While, on the average, girls have more school success than boys (whatever the causes), individual differences within each sex are just as great as between the sexes. In other words, boys fall along the whole continuum of readiness for reading in school, as do girls. Therefore, it is clear that *some* boys at age six are much more ready for formal school than *some* girls of the same chronological age. The suggestion, occasionally voiced, that girls might enter school a year younger than boys cannot be generalized to *all* six-year-olds.

The average girl of six is more advanced than the average boy of that age in general development, including skeletal structure, and she maintains this superiority throughout the usual span of ages of the primary grades. In both height and weight, as well as in other aspects of size, the average boy surpasses the average girl.[13]

Tests measuring success in school generally show girls superior in performance all the way through high school in English and courses heavily dependent on language concepts. In high school, boys overtake girls in science and mathematics courses.

Deutsch found important sex differences among black children in severely culturally deprived areas.[14] Black girls could aspire to jobs as clerks, clerk typists, and secretaries with some likelihood of achieving them. Black boys were apt to see that black men were usually thwarted in job opportunities if whites were available to fill them. Also, black children more often saw the mother as the family authority figure. The man, more often less able to contribute to the family's needs, and with no economic value to the family, had little ego strength and was a negative psychological force rather than a positive one. We recognize today that both sex differences and ethnic or racial differences are the result of social forces. Such attribution was beyond the scope of Deutsch's work, however.

Stanchfield reported a study designed to determine whether boys might experience greater success in reading if taught in classes of boys only.

Using 550 children in the first grades of the Los Angeles City Schools, reading was taught in sex-segregated groups. Care was taken to provide a wide range of socio-economic levels. Two reading periods were offered, one in the morning and one in the afternoon. The outcome of this study was that, after statistical analyses of reading achievement and reading growth, boys taught in the absence of girls did not show more significant gains in achievement or in growth than boys taught in mixed groupings. Again, the girls as a group achieved more significantly than boys and showed greater reading growth.[15]

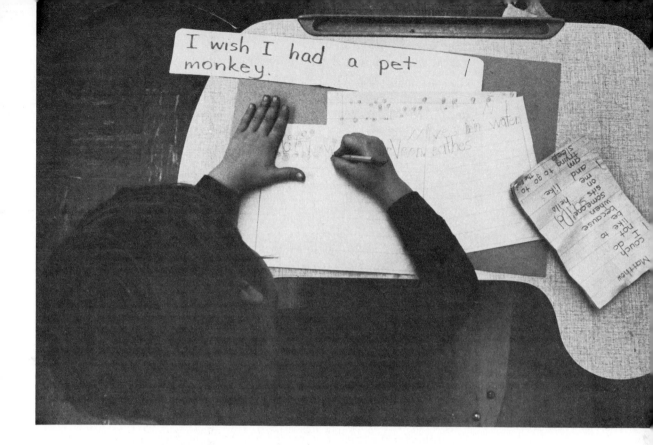

Following are comments of teachers who taught "boys only" groups in Stanchfield's study.

"Boys are so overwhelmingly active, so frighteningly energetic, so terribly vigorous, so utterly strenuous." "It's so hard for a six-year-old boy to keep himself occupied with reading a book." "Boys tend to wiggle, twist, push, turn, shove, and, in general, bother each other instead of reading."

"Girls are so quiet and controlled—they can sit quietly and read a book." "Girls are easier to teach—so ladylike and easy to handle."

Generally, boys were less anxious to please the teacher, less motivated to develop good work habits, lacked desire to assume responsibility and were less self-motivated in learning to read. Gates . . . suggested that boys in the culture have had less goal-direction for the act of reading than the girls, while they have more motivation for physical involvement and activity.[16]

Betts made these observations about sex differences and beginning reading:

First, there is some evidence to the effect that girls are promoted on lower standards of achievement than boys are. Second, girls use reading activities for recreation more often than boys do. Third, there is a need for more reading materials to challenge the interests of boys.[17]

Yet, at the same time, Betts cautioned:

Sex differences in readiness for reading may be over-emphasized. After all, there is considerable overlap between sexes. Girls as well as boys may be characterized by speech defects and delayed language development.[18]

Statistics have been reported for some time showing that boys referred to reading clinics or for special reading instruction outnumber girls by large ratios. Koppitz reported, for example, that the ratio of boys to girls in special classes for learning-disabled was six to one.[19]

Another study questioned whether all the *girls* who would profit from remediation get reported in the literature. Naiden examined the results of the Metropolitan Reading Tests for all fourth, sixth, and eighth graders in the Seattle public schools. She found that there were only three boys to every two girls among the disabled readers. Then she found that boys outnumbered girls four to one in remedial classes. These findings suggest that boys without skills get referred more often than do girls without skills. Naiden suggested:[20]

1. Boys in general tend to display more overt undesirable behaviors. Teachers do not readily refer underachieving children if they are not discipline problems.
2. Teacher expectation for boys and girls may differ. Do teachers feel that boys need to learn to read more than girls in order to be successful in later years?

Summary

Beginning reading instruction should include all the methodological skills it is possible for the teacher to incorporate. Teaching reading should begin with the language-experience approach to written language. This places the emphasis on *meaning* as the core of the reading process. Children's personal language is used for whatever message they wish to convey. They need to learn phoneme-grapheme relationships only after trying to interpret their own messages in written form. Language-experience gives children the opportunity to select the vocabulary they wish to read *first* instead of having to read a controlled vocabulary selected by others.

To go beyond reading their own experiences, children need to develop a sight vocabulary of the most commonly used words; to learn a set of skills for phonic and structural analysis of strange words (any words decoded become a child's own sight words); to develop skills of selection, comprehension, and evaluation; and to practice reading in many rewarding situations.

The problems of teaching developmental reading stem much more from the complexity of children and their learning processes than from the deficiencies of any particular teaching method.

This chapter emphasizes introduction of reading by the use of language-experience stories, then discusses basal reader approaches, modified writing systems, and phonic approaches to developing reading skill.

Sex differences in children's behavior, language skills, and ability to absorb different kinds of learning may have been exaggerated in the past. Sex-role expectations imposed by the culture can have profound influence on both the children and the adults who teach or observe them.

Suggested Activities	1. Compare and contrast the teaching of beginning reading with teaching reading at successively higher levels.
	2. Enumerate the major strengths and weaknesses of the three main methods of teaching beginning reading.
	3. Compare teaching for readiness to read with teaching beginning reading.

For Further Reading

Allen, R. V., and Clarice Allen. *Language Experiences in Reading: Teacher's Resource Book.* Levels I through VI. Chicago: Encyclopaedia Britannica, 1965–67.

Aukerman, Robert C. *Approaches to Beginning Reading.* New York: John Wiley & Sons, 1971.

———. ed. *Some Persistent Questions on Beginning Reading.* Newark, Del.: International Reading Assn., 1972.

Chall, Jeanne. *Learning to Read: The Great Debate.* New York: McGraw-Hill, 1967.

Durkin, Dolores. *Teaching Them to Read.* Chapter 9, "Teaching Beginning Reading," pp. 195–232. Boston: Allyn & Bacon, 1970.

First Grade Reading Studies. U.S. Office of Education. *The Reading Teacher* 19 (May 1966) and 20 (October 1966).

Graebner, Dianne Bennett. "A Decade of Sexism in Readers." *The Reading Teacher* 26 (October 1972):52–58.

Hall, Mary Anne. *The Language-Experience Approach to Teaching Reading: A Research Perspective,* 2d ed. Newark, Del.: International Reading Assn., 1978.

Heilman, Arthur W. *Principles and Practices in Teaching Reading.* 4th ed. Chapter 5, "Beginning Reading," and Chapter 6, "Beginning Reading—The Instructional Program." Columbus, Ohio: Charles E. Merrill, 1977.

Kerfoot, James F., ed. *First Grade Reading Programs.* Perspectives in Reading, No. 5. Newark, Del.: International Reading Assn., 1965.

Klineberg, Otto. "Life is Fun in a Smiling, Fair-Skinned World." *Saturday Review* 46(1963):75–77.

Koppitz, Elizabeth M. "Special Class Pupils with Learning Disabilities: a Five-year Follow-up Study." *Academic Therapy* 8(1972–1973):133–39.

Lee, Dorris M. *Diagnostic Teaching.* 1201 Sixteenth St., N.W., Washington, D.C. 20036: National Education Association, Department of Elementary-Kindergarten-Nursery Education, 1966.

Lee, Dorris M., and Roach Van Allen. *Learning to Read Through Experience.* New York: Appleton-Century-Crofts, 1963.

McCracken, Robert A., and Marlene J. McCracken. *Reading Is Only the Tiger's Tail.* San Rafael, Calif.: Leswing Press, 1972.

McKee, Paul. *Reading: A Program of Instruction for the Elementary School.* Part II, "The First Major Phase of Instruction," pp. 45–220. Boston, Mass.: Houghton Mifflin, 1966.

Naiden, Norma. "Ratio of Boys to Girls Among Disabled Readers." *The Reading Teacher* 29 (February 1976): 439–42.

Rogers, Vincent R. *Teaching in the British Primary School.* New York: Macmillan, 1970.

Smith, Nila Banton. *American Reading Instruction.* Newark, Del.: International Reading Assn., 1965.

Stauffer, Russell. *The Language-Experience Approach to the Teaching of Reading.* New York: Harper & Row, 1970.

Tinker, M. A., and Constance McCullough. *Teaching Elementary Reading.* 3d ed. Chapter 21, "Recommended Practices in First Grade," pp. 439–72. New York: Appleton-Century-Crofts, 1968.

Veatch, Jeannette, Florence Sawicki, Geraldine Elliott, Eleanor Barnette, and Janis Blakey. *Key Words to Reading: The Language Experience Approach Begins.* Columbus, Ohio: Charles E. Merrill, 1973.

Notes

1. Stephen G. Harris, "Reading Methodology: What's Radical, What's Traditional," *The Reading Teacher* 27 (November 1973):135.

2. Jeanne S. Chall, *Learning to Read: The Great Debate* (New York: McGraw-Hill, 1967), pp. 305–14.

3. Warren G. Cutts, "Reading Unreadiness in the Underprivileged," *NEA Journal* 52 (April 1963):24–25.

4. Careth Ellingson, *The Shadow Children* (Five North Wabash Avenue, Chicago, Illinois 60602: Topaz Books, 1967), pp. 92–93, quoted from J. F. Jastak and S. R. Jastak, *Wide Range Achievement Test—Manual of Instructions* (Wilmington, Del.: Guidance Associates).

5. See Russell Stauffer, *The Language Experience Approach to the Teaching of Reading* (New York: Harper & Row, 1970); Robert A. McCracken and Marlene J. McCracken, *Reading Is Only the Tiger's Tail* (San Rafael, Calif.: Leswing Press, 1972); Jeannette Veatch et al., *Key Words to Reading: The Language Experience Approach Begins* (Columbus, Ohio: Charles E. Merrill, 1973); Mary Anne Hall, *The Language-Experience Approach to Teaching Reading: A Research Perspective,* 2d ed. (Newark, Del.: International Reading Assn., 1978).

6. Virgil E. Herrick and Marcella Nerbovig, *Using Experience Charts with Children* (Columbus, Ohio: Charles E. Merrill, 1964), pp. iii–iv.

7. Ibid.

8. Lillian A. Lamoreaux and Dorris M. Lee, *Learning to Read Through Experience* (New York: Appleton-Century-Crofts, 1943), p. 180.

9. Lee H. Salisbury, "Teaching English to Alaska Natives," *Journal of American Indian Education* 6 (January 1967):4–5.

10. Albert J. Mazurkiewicz, *New Perspectives in Reading Instruction,* "The Initial Teaching Alphabet (Augmented Roman) for Teaching Reading," pp. 539–44 (New York: Pitman Publishing Corp., 1964).

11. James H. Fassett, *The Beacon Primer* (Boston: Ginn and Company, 1912).

12. Kerfoot, James F., ed. *First Grade Reading Programs,* Perspectives in Reading, No. 5 (Newark, Del.: International Reading Assn., 1965).

13. Martha Dallman, *Teaching the Language Arts in the Elementary School* (Dubuque, Iowa: Wm. C. Brown, 1971).

14. Martin Deutsch, *Minority Group and Class Status as Related to Social and Personality Factors in Scholastic Achievement*, Society for Applied Anthropology, Monograph No. 2 (Ithaca, New York: Cornell University, 1960), pp. 8–13.

15. Jo M. Stanchfield, "Do Girls Learn to Read Better Than Boys in the Primary Grades?" in *New Directions in Reading,* ed. Ralph Staiger and David Sohn (New York: Bantam Books, 1967), p. 60; see also, Jo M. Stanchfield, "Boys' Achievement in Reading," in *Reading and Inquiry,* ed. J. Allen Figurel, International Reading Association Conference Proceedings 10 (1965):290–93.

16. Stanchfield, "Do Girls Learn to Read Better Than Boys in the Primary Grades?" pp. 60–61; see also, Arthur I. Gates, "Sex Differences in Reading Ability," *Elementary School Journal* 61 (May 1961):431–34.

17. Emmett Albert Betts, *Foundations of Reading Instruction* (New York: American Book Company, 1950), p. 137.

18. Ibid.

19. Elizabeth M. Koppitz, "Special Class Pupils with Learning Disabilities: a Five-year Follow-up Study," *Academic Therapy* 8 (1972–1973):133–39.

20. Naiden, Norma, "Ratio of Boys to Girls among Disabled Readers," *The Reading Teacher* 29 (February 1976): 439–42.

3
Classroom Management to Facilitate Reading

6

Organizing the Classroom Reading Program

The primary goal for the teacher is to organize the classroom to permit each child to learn. The teacher needs both methodology and materials to help each child progress in the acquisition of sequenced, developmental reading skills.

The teacher needs to complete an informal reading inventory for each child in order to assign the child to an appropriate working group. Finding an oral instructional reading level, a silent reading level with adequate comprehension, and an estimated capacity for understanding for each child is a comprehensive task for the teacher. By the end of the first month of school, the teacher will have determined at least the oral instructional reading level for each student and completed as much additional informal testing as time permits.

The teacher must often use less than exact group methods for finding out approximate reading abilities of boys and girls. During the first week of school the teacher can ask groups of children to read a selected story orally. The teacher should give a synopsis of the story and then ask the members of the group to read around the circle, taking turns and passing the book along to each succeeding person to read. Children who read well can read a long passage. Children who have difficulty can read a short one. If the level is obviously frustrating for a child, only one sentence need be read. Any child who does not wish to read or can't *should not be required to do so* but should be given priority for a personal conference. The child can try the informal reading inventory then, by which method the teacher can establish temporarily the level of difficulty appropriate for that child, and for most members of the class. The few children who cannot read can be given worksheet types of assignments until further testing is completed.

Cumulative records, standardized test results, and conversations with children's previous teachers and principals are also sources of evidence, both cognitive and affective, for grouping children at the beginning of the year. These supplement, but do not substitute for, the teacher's listening to children read individually or in small groups.

The teacher can expect to find in the classroom a wide range of differences in reading performance. Since differences in mental, physical, emotional, and social development are completely normal in children, the teacher *must accept* as normal the great variability in school achievement. With good teaching the *differences get greater, not less,* as the year progresses.

Principles for Planning a Reading Program

The teacher will surely allow for flexibility in planning the reading program in order to incorporate a variety of activities to best develop the range of abilities within a class. The teacher will probably rely on basal readers but will also utilize an individualized reading program, a language-experience approach, and a writing way to reading while at the same time providing activities to keep each child profitably working. The following principles should be kept in mind:

1. The basal reader program is not sufficient to provide for all the children in a given classroom.
2. The same amount of time need not be spent with each child. Equal time is not to be equated with providing equal opportunity.
3. The notion that for any given grade there is a *basic book* that all the children must finish is absurd and must be discarded.
4. Having children read in a group and then answer memory questions about the story is a superficial activity that must be changed so reading can be followed by higher levels of questioning which evaluate the story read.
5. A whole set of study skills must be developed for the process to constitute developmental reading.

Some suggestions for adapting basal readers made by Dallmann and colleagues[1] are appropriate here:

. . . reliance should not be placed on a single basal reader for the whole class; indeed, it should not be placed on an entire single series. In any given class basal readers designed for many levels of reading ability and containing many different kinds of material should be provided. It is fortunate that, increasingly, newer reading textbook series have, as their basic plan of organization, levels of reading which cut across grade designations. If a series is organized by grade levels, with arrangements for variations in needs of boys and girls, the reader should not be labeled according to grade level of difficulty, although the publisher's estimate of difficulty level may be indicated by some code device. All basal readers should be amply supplemented with general reading materials on many subjects and representing many levels of reading difficulty. . . . Basal readers should not be used for mere oral drill, in smaller or larger groups, in which everyone marks time while one pupil struggles through a passage. Pupils who are able to complete the material in the basal reader rapidly and without instructional assistance should be permitted to go on to more difficult materials.

Teachers often share their experiences about procedures in teaching reading. One may emphasize learning how to handle reading groups. This procedure gets things compartmentalized well, and once the organization is taken care of, the operation runs smoothly. These teachers usually manage three groups. Others talk about having four or five groups, and occasionally a teacher refers to a classroom as a "regular three-ring circus." Many listeners to such a conversation might wonder what a teacher does to adequately *manage* a room with many things going on.

More and more teachers are talking about individualized reading in their rooms. Different problems are sure to arise if the teacher organizes the room for individual teacher-pupil conferences.

Then there are those teachers who are committed to the language-experience approach to reading. How do they operate?

Knowing that children are all different from each other, and that the longer the children attend school the greater the range of difference becomes in all types of skills, abilities, interests, and ambitions, teachers cannot rely on teaching any *one* thing to all members of a given class. Consequently, any teacher who *accepts the facts* about the way children grow, develop, learn, and satisfy their curiosities must be searching for ways to manage the classroom so that each child does have opportunity to stretch outward on the growing edge of learning.

Figure 6.1 illustrates why it is impossible for the classroom teacher today to think of a group of boys and girls as "doing fourth grade work" or "doing second grade work." The boxes labeled "Conventional Grade Competence" represent the narrow limit of what may be thought of as appropriate to that grade, while the shaded horizontal bars show the *range* of achievement in general knowledge to be *expected* in any single grade. The appalling dilemma of the sixth grade teacher who tries to teach only the content of "the sixth grade textbooks" is obvious because the group probably has an achievement range extending over almost eight years of knowledge, skills, and abilities.

Some tangible supports to which to anchor lesson plans, however, will help the novice teacher learn and develop security. It may well be that dividing a class into three reading groups using the previous teacher's recommendations and the informal reading inventory is the most practical way to get a good year underway. Teacher's manuals contain storehouses of worthwhile information that many beginning teachers do not know. There can be nothing wrong in first acquiring that information.

There is no three-group plan which could provide for all the individual differences that exist in a class. Nevertheless, each teacher must decide what the limits are in organizing the classroom for productive learning. The beginning teacher will probably plan the reading program around the use of a basal reading series as a starting point. However, the teacher sensitive to needs will soon begin to borrow from other reading approaches, and the plan will become more flexible.

Figure 6.1 Range of achievement in general knowledge among elementary school children at indicated grade levels.

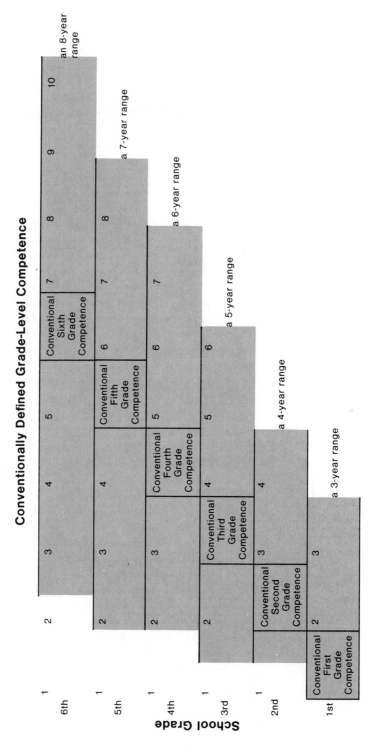

Conventionally Defined Grade-Level Competence

School Grade

The teacher's first job is to develop techniques that work well. Having gained some confidence and security in teaching developmental reading-skills, the teacher can then explore ways to direct the enthusiasm, interests, and aptitudes of all the boys and girls in his or her charge. Some of these ways are sure to involve individualized work, language-experience assignments, and small groups organized for specific teaching purposes during the year.

The most efficient interaction between teacher and groups of children takes place when the teacher meets children in groups of no more than five or six. This is the maximum number with which there can be personal exchange, eye contact, and opportunity for full exchange of ideas. Therefore, teachers must continually search out management techniques that work with large groups. Peer teaching is one. Having teachers' aides direct small group work is another. The teacher can set up varieties of learning centers in the room, being sure to change the content or the objectives of the centers often. Cross-age grouping can be used. And programmed materials that provide for needed practice in skill development for all levels of difficulty and all types of skill exercises are useful.

Beyond these challenges lie more complicated tasks: (1) planning a program in corrective reading for the child who has missed many needed skills; (2) planning an adjusted reading program for the educable mentally retarded child who is not provided for in the special education program; (3) providing an environment in which the emotionally disturbed child can spend at least a part of the day in the regular classroom; and (4) providing for the child of normal intelligence who has some physical handicap such as minimal brain dysfunction, limited vision, or defective hearing.

The teacher is also responsible for all the special activities that are related to the reading lessons themselves. These may include (1) preparing a TV program in which parts of stories are dramatized; (2) promoting reading of interesting books through oral book reports or panel discussions of books read; (3) compiling reports by committees about authors of favorite children's books and about books awarded the Newbery Medal or the Caldecott Medal; and (4) tape recording each child's voice reading a passage at the child's instructional level of reading.[2]

The primary consideration is that teachers decide what they can do and how they can best function within their limitations. Teachers have individual differences, just as do the children they teach. They vary considerably in the amount of noise they can tolerate in the classroom and in the amount of freedom they can allow to the committees or small groups talking among themselves across the room. Such statements as "Nothing *shakes* him" and "She's *so* conscientious" suggest different levels of tolerance.

In the sections of this chapter which follow, a few specific ideas are outlined for different types of lessons: (1) the directed reading lesson in the graded reader; (2) the individualized reading period; (3) the language-experience approach; and (4) the monitored programmed reading-study period.

There are inherent limitations of schedules, such as shown in figure 6.2, but improvement of instruction by meeting the needs of a classroom of boys and girls depends on *the skills the teacher can develop to fulfill the responsibilities* of the job. A new teacher may be able to plan carefully how to teach reading lessons for assigned reading groups in the classroom but may have considerable difficulty with the rest of the class because their time has not been sufficiently planned. As every teacher can testify, "idle hands do often get into mischief." Knowing how to plan specifically for each child's work period without direct supervision by the teacher may be more crucial than careful study of the teacher's manual for teaching one subgroup. This chapter discusses later on how the teacher can manage this problem.

The Basal Reader Program: The Directed Reading Lesson

A directed reading lesson requires more time than many new teachers realize. Such a lesson may be introduced and the guided silent reading completed during one period. It can be recalled and finished in a second session. Some stories need more time than others, and some lessons may be guided during one period with the teacher and then finished independently. The teacher's manual will include for each lesson one or two specific skills to be stressed—phonic analysis, structural analysis, comprehension, or interpretation. Manuals also afford many opportunities for teachers to evaluate children's development in the affective as well as the cognitive areas.

One set of teacher's guides contains the following outline for teaching the directed reading lesson:

I. Teaching the selection
    1. New words
    2. Decoding skills
    3. Specific objectives
    4. Special materials
    5. Preparation for reading
    6. Reading the story
    7. Discussion of purposes
    8. Purposeful rereading
    9. Related language activities
    10. Supplementary materials
II. Developing reading skills
III. Adjusting to individual needs[3]

Most reading lesson plans follow similar outlines. The teacher will attempt to motivate an interest in reading the story; teach the new vocabulary and review difficult words; guide the silent reading of the story and discuss the content; interpret the story through questioning or rereading parts; and provide related activities as a follow-through for the lesson.

Figure 6.2 Planning work for the reading period. What independent seatwork will each child do?

	Group 1	**Group 2**	**Group 3**
5 minutes	The teacher answers questions and reminds individuals and groups about work to be done in independent work periods. The students ask questions and get ready to complete independent seatwork.		
Period I 15 minutes	Directed teaching of a reading lesson—probably for the least able readers first, because they will be least able to plan independently. The teacher may plan to develop only some of the steps in a directed reading lesson.	Interest centers, exercises to practice skills; free reading; committee work; preparing reports; games to teach skills.	
3 minutes	Teacher gives attention to progress of individual and group work; answers questions.		
Period II 15 minutes	Interest centers, etc.	Directed teaching of a reading lesson. Less attention should be given to formal teaching in how to read the lesson than to free discussion of ideas in the story and making value judgments about it.	Interest centers, etc.
3 minutes	Teacher gives attention to progress of individual and group work; answers questions.		
Period III 15 minutes	Interest centers, etc.		If this group is the highest achieving group, greater attention can be given to vocabulary development, evaluating, and making critical judgments.

Classroom Management to Facilitate Reading

Motivating an Interest	Thumbing through the pages may show that the story is accompanied by colored illustrations which reveal incidents in the story that can be discussed. The teacher may have related pictures from the materials center, or may talk about new or unusual words in the story, or perhaps raise questions to guide children's thinking. The incident around which the story is built needs to be related to the experience of the class so the children can decide whether it is fact or fiction, real or imaginary. Finally, the teacher must establish a purpose for reading. The child starts reading to "find out something."
Making Sure of Vocabulary	New words should be presented in context and discussed so that they are meaningful to the boys and girls. The words can then be reviewed with flash card drills or games that give practice in matching, comparing, or using them in sentences. Children should be led to discover new words for themselves if they have sufficient word analysis skills to do so. If they use their skills to unlock new words, there will be fewer and fewer strange words to present as they gain in reading independence.
Guiding the Silent Reading	In the first books, very young children need to be guided sentence by sentence or section by section to make sure they are learning that the words on the page are telling them something, just as a conversation using these words would. Guide questions should be specific enough to cause children to look carefully for specific information. As children gain in reading power, they can read longer and longer parts of stories without detailed teacher guidance. In the intermediate grades, students reading at grade level should be able to read the entire story after adequate preparation and after the purpose is established.
Interpreting the Story	It is important for the teacher to ask questions to make sure the reader understood the story, but that is only a minor part in evaluation. Understanding the sequence of events and what the author said is prerequisite to using the story information for evaluation of ideas requiring judgment, reasoning, and analysis of values.

Most teachers' questions have tended to fall in the memory and translation (paraphrase) levels, according to Bloom's taxonomy (see chapter 2).

While memory and translation questions are necessary to establish common understandings and sequence of story events, it is at the higher, integrative, levels of thinking that interpretation, reflection, application, and evaluation can be developed. As teachers require application, analysis, and evaluation of ideas read, they more closely approach the affective life of the child and require him to reflect on his acceptance of, preference for, and commitment to *values*. There is opportunity for the teacher to use the story as a basis for interpreting other happenings in the light of the children's values. The teacher could analyze at the children's level why the author ended the story as he or she did. Or the teacher could help the children see analogies between the story and actual happenings in their lives or community. Original thinking can be evoked with such questions as "What would you have done if you had been in Bob's shoes?" or "What would have been a more realistic ending for this story?"

Providing Related Activities

Related cognitive activities include comprehension exercises, further work on vocabulary, or practice of phonic or structural analysis skills. Related affective activities require children to connect story incidents to their own experiences and feelings. Children learn that ideas are not *all* right or *all* wrong, *all* good or *all* bad, or *all* true or *all* false; that they have shades of meaning that relate to personal attitudes and position in time and space.

The lesson may be extended through the search for additional information in general references, free reading at the book table, or shared oral reading.

Individualized Reading

The recognition that reading is an active, thinking process—a complex developmental process—an individual, personal experience—has led to changing concepts of teaching reading in the schools. One response that has evolved from this change is commonly called *individualized reading*. Individualized reading programs show an effort, at least, to let children proceed at their own rates of learning and select the material they want to read. Individualized reading is a broad approach, not entirely new to many competent teachers, and not limiting or restricting insofar as other reading activities are concerned.

Recreational reading is not individualized reading. Recreational reading is easy reading practice to develop greater fluency, to learn that reading is fun, and that there are lots and lots of interesting books.

Individualized reading promotes the principles of self-motivation, self-selection, self-pacing, and self-evaluation. Teachers achieve their objectives in such a program if the children are learning independence in purposeful reading and building lasting reading interests.

In order to initiate a system of self-motivation, self-selection and self-pacing of reading for each member of the class, it is necessary that the following criteria be met.

1. The classroom provides a variety of all types of reading to meet the needs, interests, and abilities of all the members of the group. Administering and evaluating informal reading inventories for each individual is the best way to obtain this information.
2. Types of reading materials include (a) trade books (library books) of adventure, animals, family life, humor, mystery, history, travel, science, folktales, myths and legends, biography, and poetry; (b) basal and supplementary readers; (c) standard reference books; and (d) newspapers and magazines.
3. The teacher either takes sufficient time with the total group to work out purposes, methods of operating, and ways of reporting or arranges for part of the group to continue with traditional ways of working while one subgroup at a time is introduced to the process of self-selection and independent study.

Figure 6.3 A reading program based primarily on the use of basal readers and teachers' guides.

Basal Readers

A basal reader approach with reading groups provides the new teacher with direction, well planned lessons, and source materials.

This well planned framework will give teachers security, as they learn through experience what constitutes an adequate program, they will gain self-confidence.

Through the year, as varying levels of ability and different kinds of reading problems become apparent, the teacher will move toward more individualizing of children's work.

Language-Experience Reading

Utilizing learning experiences in reading helps the beginner understand that reading is talk written down, and that written down, it is preserved and can be read back.

Older boys and girls can utilize and extend writing skills by well illustrated booklets about the units of work they are doing in school.

Corrective Reading

Corrective reading is the remedial work done by the regular class teacher to help children develop sequentially their reading skills— filling in what has been missed and relearning what has been forgotten.

Individualized Reading

Self-motivation, self-selection, and self-pacing are the key words in helping children develop individual reading habits. Each child reads what he or she enjoys, wants to learn about, and finds useful.

Lots of trade books and some kind of reading record are important.

Special Reading Activities

Dramatizing parts of stories.

Collecting information about books; making book week displays; studying favorite authors.

Using reading games and puzzles.

Using standard references.

4. A system of assigning or checking out books needs to be devised so that it is monitored entirely by selected members of the group. This process must continue while the teacher works with other aspects of the program.

5. The reading program should be planned with a week as the basic unit of time. For example, perhaps each child is assured of at least one individual conference each week with Monday, Tuesday, and Wednesday being the individual conference days. If there are thirty children in one room, an average of ten conferences must be held each day. If the conferences average from three to ten minutes each, it may be possible for the teacher to hold ten conferences in one reading hour. Some teachers would prefer to have only six conferences on each of the five days and utilize some time each day for a group discussion or special reports given to the whole class.

Figure 6.4 A sample weekly schedule for individual reading conferences.

Group	Monday	Tuesday	Wednesday	Thursday	Friday
I	Conferences 45 min.	Silent reading	Skills exercises	Silent reading and reporting	Weekly Reader 30 min. and reporting 30 min.
II	Silent reading	Conferences 45 min.	Silent reading and reporting	Skills exercises	Weekly Reader 30 min. and reporting 30 min.
III	Skills exercises	Silent reading and reporting	Conferences 45 min.	Silent reading	Weekly Reader 30 min. and reporting 30 min.
IV	Silent reading and reporting	Skills exercises	Silent reading	Conferences 45 min.	Weekly Reader 30 min. and reporting 30 min.

Scheduling must be sufficiently flexible that any child with a special problem can have a conference the day it is needed. Teachers will be able to note certain skills which more than one child needs to improve; the teacher can form them into a group then and teach these skills.

Some attention must be given to specific work on skills, and the teacher may wish to draw upon programmed materials other than basal reading workbooks for this work. How the teacher plans to keep large numbers of children busy while giving attention to one at a time will be discussed later in this chapter.

While some teachers plan one specific day in the week for skills enrichment, others plan for students to work on skills on two or three days during the week although the teacher may discuss them with the group on only one day. (See figure 6.4.)

Figure 6.5 suggests one method of record-keeping. The teacher keeps a five-by-eight-inch card for each child on which to make notes in brief diary form. The teacher will try to record such observations as: "misses many basic sight words in reading," "cannot divide words into syllables," "had a book that was a bit too difficult this morning," "gets implied meanings well."

Individualized reading implies that children are not in a reading circle in front of the teacher, they are at their desks or at tables with books selected

Figure 6.5 A diary record for individualized reading.

	Std. Tst.		
Name: _____	Score: _____	Date: _____	Grade: _____

September 25:	Is reading *Little House in the Big Woods.* Visited the Laura Ingalls Wilder home in Missouri in the summer. Thoroughly enjoys the story. Will plan a report on Friday recommending it to others. Is beginning SRA: RFU with card No. 26 (Gr. Pl. 5.7).
October 2:	Is working with Betty on a special display and report about the Wilder books and the Wilder Home Museum.
October 9:	

by themselves. They receive help from the teacher or a helper only when they ask for it. There will be a time to share with the others what they have read, but, some skills the children need in order to grow in reading independence will be taught to subgroups as occasions arise.

The social interaction in a class with subgroups can teach children that one group is *average,* one group is *inferior,* and one group is *superior.* It is argued that this problem does not exist with individualized reading. This is only partially valid. It would *not* be a serious problem in regularly assigned groups *if* children understood why they were reading far below grade level, *knew* that they were making good growth at that level, and *felt* they would be rehabilitated.

Knowing that the range of ability within any group of thirty children may have a spread of five to seven grade levels, the teacher uses interest and specified routine to allow children to conduct their own free reading practice. Children read what they *want* to read. They learn how to choose books, how to handle the books, how to come and go in the room, how to get help when it is needed; that is, they learn to function independently. The individualized conferences provide opportunity for the teacher to keep a check on sight vocabulary in the primary grades. If the book is at a child's instructional level, the child will not meet too many *hard* words. The teacher will pronounce the words the child doesn't know and provide opportunities for the child to read these words in many situations. If children are selected to be helping teachers, they will tell words to those who need more assistance.

To help children become acquainted with a wide variety of books, the teacher might encourage the class to share them with and advertise them to one another in interesting ways. The children thus, incidentally, have opportunities to show their ingenuity and creative ability in art, writing, dramatic arts, and other fields while stimulating each other to read more books of good quality.

A *Practical Guide to Individualized Reading* is an excellent source book for teachers.[4] Carlton and Moore[5] raise a list of pertinent questions for the classroom teacher to consider:

1. What is individualized reading?
2. What is the teacher's responsibility?
3. What is the best time to begin an individualized program?
4. Are there any special materials needed for an individualized reading program?
5. How does a teacher acquire enough materials for an individualized reading program?
6. How does a teacher know which books to give a pupil?
7. How can a teacher be sure a child is reading at the level where he should be?
8. Can children be expected to select their own reading material wisely?
9. How do pupils develop a basic vocabulary in an individualized reading program?
10. How are word recognition skills incorporated into individualized reading programs?
11. What is the advantage of using individualized reading instead of the basal reader approach?
12. How does the teacher evaluate pupil progress in an individualized reading program?
13. Why do some studies show little difference in results between individualized reading programs and the more traditional approach of using basal reading with the groups?
14. What are some of the advantages of the individualized reading approach?

Experienced teachers will probably plan a reading program in such a way that more emphasis is given to individualized reading and language-experience reading than to using a basal reader. However, at times they need to rely on the stories in basal readers for group reading practice—for instance, when library books are returned and not reissued on time, or when language-experience writing is not serving a purpose. Teachers need many techniques to maximally develop all children requiring individual programs (see figure 6.6).

Language-Experience Approach

In the language-experience approach, the children dictate stories based upon their activities during or after school hours. Experience stories may be individual, small group, or planned and dictated by the class as a whole.

Early in the first grade year a kitten may be brought to school for sharing time. If the group shows enthusiasm, the teacher may catch some of their sentences and make a story on the chalkboard.

A Kitten
Tim has a kitten.
It is all black.
It came to school.
Tim likes his cat.

Or one child may tell the teacher:

My Toys
I have a ball.
I have a wagon.
I have a tractor.
I have a car.
I like to play with them.

The language-experience approach is the most promising method of meeting the reading objectives to help the child relate the written form of language to the spoken form. Experience stories written in the language of the child will demonstrate that reading is useful for remembering things; they will make reading rewarding because they preserve the child's ideas; and they will provide good practice for all the skills required later for more formal reading.

Twenty elements that constitute the language-experience approach to reading are:[6]

Converting experiences to words:
1. Sharing experiences
2. Discussing experiences
3. Listening to stories read
4. Telling stories
5. Dictating
6. Summarizing
7. Making and reading books
8. Writing independently

Studying the words themselves:
9. Developing word recognition skills
10. Developing basic sight vocabulary
11. Expanding English vocabulary concepts
12. Studying words

Recognizing words and relating them to experience:
13. Improving style and form
14. Using a variety of resources
15. Reading a variety of symbols: facial expressions, pictures, calendar, clock, map, road signs
16. Reading whole books
17. Improving comprehension
18. Outlining
19. Integrating and assimilating ideas
20. Reading critically

Research and Writing

The research and writing method is useful for later grades, as the language-experience method is useful for beginning readers.

Good writing skills strengthen reading power. Of course, all of the four skills of communication—listening, speaking, reading, and writing—are interrelated. Optimal communication skill requires that they all function well. But

Figure 6.6 A reading program based primarily on the individualized reading approach.

Individualized Reading

Requires resources of a well stocked school library. Minimum of 100 selected books in the classroom at one time—to be changed each month—range of difficulty to fit the entire class.

Most books will be trade books, but good stories in readers are fine too.

Minimum of one individual conference weekly; both child and teacher keep records.

Must provide opportunity for class reporting, discussing, and evaluating.

Basal Readers

The teacher organizes small groups and uses basal readers to teach skills. This is especially necessary for students in any grade whose instructional level of reading is third grade or below.

Interesting stories in readers should be shared as oral reading practice.

Programmed Texts

Sequenced skill development is well worked out in *Programmed Reading* and *Programmed Remedial Reading* (McGraw-Hill); SRA *Reading for Understanding* and SRA Elementary Labs; EDL *Study Skills; Standard Test Lessons in Reading* and *Practice Exercises in Reading* (Teachers College Press.)

Corrective Reading

Corrective reading is the remedial work done by the regular class teacher to help children develop sequentially their reading skills—filling in what has been missed and relearning what has been forgotten.

Language-Experience Reading

Writing original stories; writing illustrated content lessons; reporting.

the research and writing way to reading, when well motivated, has especially great value. It is the most useful means of expanding horizons—and, indeed, is used throughout a child's school career.

Especially when used in elementary school, the research and writing method requires that the teacher be sophisticated in what word-recognition and comprehension skills the children need and how best to teach them. An experienced teacher who feels confident about the skills and work habits children need can encourage development of these skills and work habits through work produced by the children themselves. Of course, such a program is supplemented with a great deal of reading, including basal readers. But the primary objective is for the children themselves to produce stories, articles, and small illustrated books worth reading. Such a program is also dependent upon a teacher who has a broad knowledge of children's literature so that children will be encouraged to pursue their own individualized reading programs (see figure 6.7).

| Programmed Reading Materials | Teachers should have available many exercises that teach developmental reading and study skills. The SRA Reading Laboratories,[7] the EDL Laboratories,[8] *New Practice Readers,*[9] *McCall-Crabb Test Lessons in Reading*[10] are some of these. Kits such as these make it possible for sophisticated teachers to assemble individualized developmental reading programs as diversified as they are capable of directing. Under the impetus of the Elementary Secondary Education Act, Title I, with large amounts of money available to aid in the purchase of materials, publishers have provided text films, film strips, recordings, word and phrase cards, and many other supplementary reading materials. |

However, teachers are cautioned that materials highly phonemically oriented which require extensive and continued phonics practice as programmed exercises or independent seatwork are profitable only under the close supervision of skilled teachers. Schools are ill-advised to spend large sums of money on systems predicated on teaching primarily the decoding process.

| USSR: Uninterrupted Sustained Silent Reading | Uninterrupted sustained silent reading is an activity assigned at a specific time each day when *everyone* reads silently for a predetermined amount of time. It may seem strange, but is undisputably true, that such a designated period is necessary in order to provide the opportunity for *all* students to read *some*thing of their choosing and to persist at it for a given amount of time. One might think, since school success depends to a high degree on reading ability, that everybody has the opportunity to read. Because there are problems in all schools with unmotivated students, with reluctant readers, and with disabled readers, teachers must be continually seeking out ways to cause students to read because they want to, not because they must. |

Teachers must be models to establish the sincerity of the objectives of USSR. Teachers, becoming engrossed in their own books and magazines, constitute an essential feature of the activity.

Figure 6.7 A reading program emphasizing students writing text material.

The Research and Writing Way to Reading

Through a series of planned lessons in keeping written records of their work—for example, of the fifth grade year—the primary reading job could be the production of stories and well illustrated books related to the fifth grade course of study for the school year.

For beginning readers, this is a language-experience approach to reading: talking about interesting or common experiences and then writing about them; building sequences of such stories into interesting little booklets; also reading carefully written reading charts that repeat vocabulary learned.

Individualized Reading

Self-motivation, self-selection, and self-pacing are the key words in helping children develop individual reading habits. Each child reads what he or she enjoys, wants to learn about, and finds useful.

Lots of trade books and some kind of reading record are important.

Basal Readers

The teacher organizes small groups and uses basal readers to teach skills. This is especially necessary for students in any grade whose instructional level of reading is third grade or below.

Interesting stories in readers should be shared as oral reading practice.

Programmed Texts

Sequenced skill development is well worked out in: *Programmed Reading* and *Programmed Remedial Reading* (McGraw-Hill); SRA *Reading for Understanding* and SRA Elementary Labs; EDL *Study Skills; Standard Test Lessons in Reading* and *Practice Exercises in Reading* (Teachers College Press.)

Corrective Reading

Corrective reading is the remedial work done by the regular class teacher to help children develop sequentially their reading skills—filling in what has been missed and relearning what has been forgotten.

There must be guidelines. Everybody needs to be involved in the reading activity. Everybody must keep the same book through the reading period so as not to disturb others. A timer or alarm clock can be used to mark the end of the reading so no one need watch the clock. No book reports or detailed records of any kind are required.

Sustained silent reading should have many positive values. Students select what they wish to read. They should develop some permanent reading habits if they find value in what they read. And they learn that "free reading" is a pleasurable, fulfilling activity.

Initiating such a daily activity requires trust on the part of the adults that children will respond positively as a total group. The period can be short the first day and lengthened as the abilities of the group merit. However, USSR can be only one of several vital parts of a total reading program.

Reading in the Teacher's Daily Schedule

Most state courses of study recommend the minimum amount of time that teachers should spend teaching developmental reading in the elementary classroom. The amount is usually longer for the primary grades and somewhat less for the intermediate grades. Many teachers in the primary grades spend more than the minimum recommended time teaching reading and may, in fact, spend more than half their teaching day in the teaching of reading. Upper grade teachers are apt to feel pressured to teach a great deal of content material in various subjects. Often, to the detriment of the children, they concentrate more on the subject than upon the student. The individual teacher needs to adapt the quantity of work to be done to the amount of time available. And unless the teacher adapts the teaching of content to the particular children being taught, confusion rather than learning results.

This discussion now focuses on management of the classroom for efficient teaching, since it is not possible to teach small groups in the room effectively if the teacher has not provided for relatively quiet, constructive work for all those not responding directly to the teacher.

Probably the most difficult task for new teachers to master is keeping two-thirds or more of the group actively working and motivated while they teach or lead a worthwhile discussion with a small group in the class. If the teacher plans to spend one hour teaching reading to the class, this hour must be broken down into plans for the activities of each group of children. The lesson plan will be sufficient to keep the teacher busy teaching, checking other groups, and managing the room. The problem is very different from each child's point of view. If the teacher works directly with one group for fifteen minutes, what will that group do the rest of the hour? They will not be busy very long doing the two or three pages provided in the workbook if they know how to do it when they begin. If they do not know how to do it when they begin, they will either need to interrupt the teacher to ask questions, talk to their neighbors, or do the work incorrectly.

How do teachers develop independence in children so they keep working when there are, of necessity, long periods when the teacher cannot directly supervise their work?

First of all, they should not be given *busywork* that only keeps their hands occupied. Coloring, cutting, and pasting are not instructive after the child knows how to do them. Constructive seatwork that has a purpose must be planned. Children must understand what they are doing and see sense in the assignment.

Such routine directions as "Draw a picture about some part of the story that you liked" soon get tiresome for even young children. And as the children see less value in such a task, they will require less and less time to complete it.

It is apparent that the teacher can be very busy teaching during the hour allotted to teaching reading, but *unless careful planning is done with the entire class, many boys and girls may not use much of this time profitably.* Some of the cautions that might be stated then, in summary, are:

1. With respect to improving reading ability, the teacher must be concerned with what *each child needs* and that the child is provided with exercises that help to meet these needs.
2. The teacher's biggest job is to *manage* the total reading program by selecting appropriate methods of teaching. Keeping the individuals in the group busy and interested is the best assurance that discipline does not become a problem.
3. No child is going to profit from trying to handle material at the child's frustration level; children cannot work quietly at their seats without asking questions if they neither understand the instructions nor are able to read the material required for completion of a given task.
4. If children understand their assignment, they are able to use their time wisely and can continue with the job the next day if they need to.

Children carrying on activities worthwhile to them need to have freedom to move about, and they will need to talk quietly to one another occasionally, so there *will be* noise in the classroom. If it is work noise, and the teacher's tolerance level is sufficiently high, this is no problem. Teachers must establish the kind of room climate in which they can function efficiently.

The following activities are suitable for the period of independent study. Some are more suitable for one grade level than another.

1. After appropriate preparation while in the reading group, children may complete the exercises in the reading workbook.
2. If the group wishes to prepare a series of pictures to tell a story, they may each draw a designated scene from the story in the day's lesson.
3. Some children like to be encouraged to write their own stories. They may or may not relate to the day's lesson. All need to be urged to do some writing of original paragraphs. In writing original paragraphs, the primary consideration should be having ideas to write about. However, it provides a teacher an excellent diagnostic instrument to determine which children lack sentence sense, which omit all mechanics of writing, which cannot spell common words, and which have special difficulties with the order of letters in words. At any grade level, a teacher will occasionally have a student who has an extremely poor sense of phoneme-grapheme relationship and needs intensive training in auditory discrimination.
4. The reading table should contain appealing books so that any child who finishes work can read, browse, or study pictures, charts, graphs, and maps. Also, each child can always have a library book checked out and kept in his or her desk.
5. There are many word games that can be kept in one corner where small groups of children can utilize them. Such games as *Go-Fish,* first and second series; *Vowel Dominoes,* from Remedial Education Center, Washington, D.C.; *Take,* from Garrard Publishing Co., Champaign, Ill.; and *Old Itch, Bingobang, Full House,* and *Syllable Count,* from Rand McNally, Chicago, are excellent for this purpose. (See chapter 9.)

6. Each child may choose a partner to study with, for example, by writing regular spelling words or mastering the multiplication facts or division facts.

7. If some unit construction work, murals, models, or dioramas are in progress in the room, it may be desirable for children with individual assignments there to work on them in their free time.

Use of Workbooks

In order to find time to individualize instruction in the classroom, the teacher will need to have seatwork exercises that can be done by children independently while the teacher is busy with subgroups in the room. Workbooks that accompany basic reading series provide some of the necessary practice children need in order to acquire the word analysis and comprehension skills of reading. Wisely used, they have a definite place in the reading program. The quality of exercises they contain, and the quality printing and format provided by publishers are both undoubtedly superior to the majority of teacher-made exercises quickly prepared and reproduced.

Criteria for the Selection of Workbooks or Other Seatwork

1. The workbook exercises the child does are usually related to the reading lesson of the day. In primary reading, this gives the child needed repetition in a new context of vocabulary being taught. With emphasis on context reading situations, this further practice helps to fix vocabulary for the child.

2. The workbooks for a class must be geared to the reading levels to be found in that class. Thirty identical workbooks for thirty third grade children who have a reading range of at least five years is completely unjustifiable. Workbooks have no value unless they vary in relation to the reading ability levels of the boys and girls using them.

3. Workbook exercises should be used for groups that need them, can profit from them, and can complete them successfully. Exercises that are not needed and do not teach needed skills should not be used. The workbook itself does not take care of individual differences in the class, but judicious use of the exercises in selected workbooks may make it possible for the teacher to accommodate differences.

4. Workbooks must not be given an undue amount of time in a child's working day. They tend to be mechanical and stereotyped and are apt to crowd out more active and enriching experiences the child should have. Workbooks leave little opportunity for a child to express initiative and to be creative in communication skills. If the teacher recognizes such limitations of workbooks and is providing these other experiences for the child, the role of the workbook falls into proper perspective.

5. In general, workbooks provide good practice with developmental reading skills. The gradual introduction of skills in a specifically planned sequence makes it possible for the child to learn to read by reading. Study skills, selecting titles for paragraphs, judging whether an anecdote is fact or fancy, and giving definitions for new words are all skills introduced early.

6. It is necessary that children be able to accomplish work assigned in the workbook. They must *feel* that they can do it. If a child has had unfortunate failures, or just marks answers without reading the exercises, the work may be too difficult for the child's reading power. Children cannot work independently for any length of time until they have sufficient reading power to keep them motivated.

A workbook that accompanies a basic reader can have many advantages for the student if it is well taught. Presented in good format, with clearly stated instructions, the exercises are likely to be superior to those prepared by the classroom teacher. Boys and girls can learn work habits and personal responsibility with attention to duty for extended periods of time while the teacher is busy with other individuals or subgroups in the class.

Workbooks can teach such study skills as following directions and using general reference materials. They can help children improve their organizational ability and develop and expand their vocabulary.

In the primary grades, workbooks have an added value of reteaching and giving the child practice on the sight vocabulary being taught in the stories in the child's reader.

Teachers are misusing them, however, if they are "using workbooks indiscriminately with all children; failing to check workbook activities; failing to develop workbook pages with children who are not able to work independently with them without preceding explanations."[11]

Smith suggests *desirable* uses of workbooks:

Use workbooks as they are needed as a whole or in parts, the latter being more desirable. With slower children develop new workbook activities before leaving children to work by themselves. By all means *check* the workbook results carefully after each use. Study these results to ascertain skills needed. Follow up with additional help for children whose workbook activities reveal special needs.[12]

The cost of buying workbooks for every child in a class could be greatly reduced. Individual worksheets classified by skill to be developed and sequenced in order of difficulty of exercise could be used much more flexibly than workbooks by any teacher who knows the study skills and level of difficulty needed. Such worksheets need to be so programmed that the child can check his own work as soon as he finishes it. Individual teachers have built such files of materials by removing pages from many workbooks, mounting them, sequencing them into a skills program, and placing each one in a plastic envelope so that the child writes on the plastic with a grease pencil.

Teachers may consider the following statements in judging the value of workbooks:

1. Workbooks give more practice on the vocabulary in the readers.
2. Workbooks teach word-attack skills in sequence to give the child greater independence in reading.
3. The systematic approach to reading skills is more expertly done than a classroom teacher will likely be able to do.
4. The teacher must rely on seatwork to keep many children working independently while he gives his direct attention to subgroups in the room.
5. Workbooks provide *some* exercises to teach skills and concepts; children may need much more practice with some types of skills than workbooks provide.
6. The teacher needs a greater *variety* of approaches to learning than daily use of workbook exercises alone will provide.
7. If an exercise is not appropriate, or for any reason it serves no purpose for a given child, it need not be used.

Materials for Independent Seatwork

Anderson, Donald G. *New Practice Readers,* 2d ed. New York: Webster Division, McGraw-Hill, 1978. Grades 1–6.

Barnell Loft Specific Skills Series. Baldwin, New York: Barnell Loft, Ltd., 1965–77. Workbook format. *Detecting the Sequence, Using the Context, Working with Sounds, Following Directions, Locating the Answer, Getting the Facts, Drawing Conclusions,* and *Getting the Main Idea.* All books grades 1–6 and advanced.

Boning, Richard A. *Supportive Reading Skills.* Baldwin, New York: Barnell Loft, Dexter and Westbrook, 1965–1978. Grades 1–6 and advanced.

Bracken, Dorothy Kendall. *Bracken Specific Reading Skills Program.* Kankakee, Ill.: Imperial International Learning, 1973. Grades 1–8, three levels for each grade.

Gates, A.I., and Celeste Peardon. *Gates-Peardon Reading Exercises.* New York: Bureau of
    Publishers, Teachers College, Columbia University, 1963. Introductory, Levels A and
    B; Preparatory, Levels A and B; Elementary, SA, What is the Story About?
    Elementary, RD, Can you Remember Details? Elementary, FD, Follow Precise
    Directions; Elementary, PO, Predict Outcomes of Given Events.
Johnson, Eleanor, ed. *Reading Skill Texts* (workbooks). 400 S. Front St., Columbus, Ohio:
    Charles E. Merrill, 1970. Grades 1–6.
Lessons for Self-Instruction in Basic Skills. Monterey, California: California Test Bureau,
    McGraw-Hill, 1965. Programmed. Comprehension, reference skills, mechanics of
    English, from about third to ninth grade levels of difficulty.
Liddle, William. *Reading for Concepts.* New York: Webster Division, McGraw-Hill, 1977.
    Levels A through H teach a variety of comprehension skills. The child reads a short
    story and answers a set of questions. Reading levels grades 2–6.
McCall, William A. and Lelah Mae Crabbs. *Standard Test Lessons in Reading.* New York:
    Teachers College Press, Columbia University, 1979. A series of six levels, from grade 3
    through high school.
SRA, Junior Reading for Understanding. 259 E. Erie St., Chicago, Ill.: Science Research
    Associates, 1963.
Wolfe, Josephine B. *Merrill Phonics Skilltext Series: The Sound and Structure of Words.*
    Columbus: Charles E. Merrill, 1973. Grades 1–6, Books A–F.

Summary

This chapter discusses the reading period in the teacher's daily teaching schedule. Using the recognized principles of child growth and development, the
teacher remembers that the longer children go to school, *the more different*
they become. The teacher must therefore plan for a wider and wider span of
reading abilities as the children progress through school. New teachers are
apt to rely more heavily on basal readers and well planned teachers' manuals.
Experienced teachers are more likely to base challenging, motivated developmental reading instruction on individualized reading programs, language-
experience reading and writing, combinations of these approaches, and programmed study materials to teach skills. Children's skills should improve
during the school year, and teachers need to monitor their programs carefully
to make sure this happens. To achieve this, children must have materials they
can read successfully, and they must be rewarded for successful work.

**Questions for
Discussion**

1. Using what you learned in your course in human growth and development, explain why differences in achievement in a given class get greater
   as children progress through elementary school.
2. Do you believe the basal reader approach is the best approach to teaching
   reading for inexperienced teachers? Why or why not?
3. How can teachers make sure they are planning adequately for the students performing above grade level, those at grade level, and those below
   grade level so that each group is receiving its fair share of the teacher's
   time and attention?

For Further Reading

Allen, Roach Van. *Language Experiences in Communication.* Boston: Houghton Mifflin, 1976.

Ganz, Paul, and Mary B. Theofield. "Suggestions for Starting USSR." *Journal of Reading* 17 (May 1974):614–16.

Hall, Maryanne. *Teaching Reading as a Language Experience.* Columbus: Charles E. Merrill, 1976.

Hunt, Lyman C., Jr. et al. *The Individualized Reading Program: A Guide for Classroom Teaching,* vol. 2, part 3, Proceedings. Newark, Del.: International Reading Assn., 1967.

Lee, Dorris M., and Roach Van Allen. *Learning to Read Through Experience.* New York: Appleton-Century-Crofts, 1963.

McCracken, Robert A., and Marlene J. McCracken. *Reading Is Only the Tiger's Tail.* San Rafael, Calif.: Leswing Press, 1972.

Mork, Theodore A. "Sustained Silent Reading in the Classroom." *The Reading Teacher* 25 (February 1972):438–41.

Quandt, Ivan J. *Teaching Reading: A Human Process,* pp. 134–36. Chicago: Rand McNally, 1977.

Ramsey, Wallace, ed. *Organizing for Individual Differences.* Newark, Del.: International Reading Assn., 1968.

Rogers, Vincent R. *Teaching in the British Primary School.* New York: Macmillan, 1970.

Sartain, Harry W. *Individualizing Reading, An Annotated Bibliography.* Newark, Del.: International Reading Assn., 1970.

Schwartz, Judy I. "A Language Experience Approach to Beginning Reading." *Elementary English,* 52 (March 1975):320–24.

Stauffer, Russell G. "Language-Experience Approach." In Perspectives No. 5, *First Grade Reading Programs,* pp. 86–118, edited by James Kerfoot. Newark, Del.: International Reading Assn., 1965.

———. *The Language-Experience Approach to the Teaching of Reading.* New York: Harper & Row, 1970.

Veatch, Jeannette, et al. *Key Words to Reading: The Language-Experience Approach Begins.* Columbus, Ohio: Charles E. Merrill, 1973.

———. *Individualizing Your Reading Program.* New York: G. P. Putnam's Sons, 1959.

Vilschek, Elaine C., ed. *A Decade of Innovations: Approaches to Beginning Reading.* Newark, Del.: International Reading Assn., 1968.

Notes

1. Martha Dallmann, Roger L. Rouch, Lynette Y. C. Chang, and John J. DeBoer, *The Teaching of Reading,* 4th ed. (New York: Holt, Rinehart & Winston, 1974), p. 521.

2. The tape recorder will be mentioned many times throughout the text. It is an excellent self-teaching device. Upper elementary children can operate it themselves and practice oral reading in any quiet corner or empty closet space.

3. Theodore Clymer, Virginia Jones, Roger Shuy, and Paul Torrance, *Seven Is Magic,* Teacher's ed., *Reading 360* (Boston: Ginn, 1969).

4. Board of Education of the City of New York, *A Practical Guide to Individualized Reading* (Board of Education, Bureau of Educational Research, 110 Livingston St., Room 732, Brooklyn, New York, 1960).

5. Lessie Carlton and Robert H. Moore, "Individualized Reading," *NEA Journal* 63 (November 1964):11–12.
6. Wilhelmina Nielsen, "Twenty Language Experiences which form the Framework of the Experience Approach to the Language Arts," *Claremont Reading Conference: On Becoming A Reader* (Claremont, Calif.: Claremont Graduate School, 1965), pp. 168–74.
7. Chicago: Science Research Associates, Inc., various dates.
8. Huntington, New York: Educational Development Laboratories, Inc., various dates.
9. New York: Webster Division, McGraw-Hill, various dates.
10. New York: Teachers College Press, Columbia University, various dates.
11. Nila Banton Smith, *Reading Instruction for Today's Children* (Englewood Cliffs, N.J.: Prentice-Hall, 1963), p. 100
12. Ibid., p. 102.

7

Interaction in the Classroom

An *effective teacher* needs to be aware of the interpersonal relations among the members of a class. The teacher is therefore continually assessing the emotional and social climate in the room.

Many young teachers working in a departmentalized program with older children have experienced frustration with groups of sixth or seventh graders who are noisy, somewhat tense, and brusk when they storm into the classroom to start a new class period.

Mr. Jones noted such behavior early in the year when his seventh grade groups came to reading-language class. He responded by listening long enough to pick up some thread of the conversation. Then, instead of moving directly to the day's lessons, he chaired a discussion with the boys and girls about their behavior. After perhaps ten minutes, several gripes had been aired and the class settled down to work.

In a casual conversation with Miss Quiet, a colleague who taught these groups the previous period and who had taught in the school system more than twenty years, Mr. Jones related the episode about the very restless behavior.

Miss Quiet assured him they were *not* restless in her room, that they worked very quietly, and that she tolerated no impudence from youngsters who tried to talk back.

Mr. Jones soon learned from colleagues of the pin-drop silence in Miss Quiet's room and the rules about "no pencil-sharpening," "no whispering," and the introduction of *no* topic except the day's lesson.

It was not difficult to understand that after a twenty-minute home room study period and a fifty-five minute recitation and study period with Miss Quiet just prior to reading-language with Mr. Jones, many of the twelve-year-olds had been "still and quiet" about as long as was physically possible.

Mr. Jones accepted the problem of a sudden transition from a highly authoritarian teacher for one long, quiet period to a period which he hoped would be a free, interacting, group-planning, group-conversation atmosphere. With this in mind, he closed his classroom door when the bell rang for classes to begin and planned for a controlled conversation period that could last ten minutes if necessary, in order to reduce tensions and let the held-in exuberance escape. Only then did he get the group back to the assignments of the hour.

It is hoped that most new teachers will not face such extreme teacher-behavior environments. However, just as teachers are admonished to accept children *as they are,* so faculties must accept teachers as *they* are. Teachers naturally range from extremely authoritarian to extremely democratic. Some, confused about the two ends of the continuum, invite chaos because they fail to teach such discriminations as the difference between freedom and license, privilege and irresponsibility, decision-making based on logical reasoning or fact and decision-making based on personal whim.

Yet the primary purpose of education as a socializing institution is to foster intelligent decision-making. Therefore, finding ways to become sensitive to people's feelings, attitudes, and needs is basic to providing for social and intellectual needs in all human interaction.

Teachers probably tend to feel that they have a great deal of information (facts) which they must convey to a group of students in a short period of time. For this reason, they are inclined to use oral language as their means of *telling* boys and girls what they *need* to know. They overlook the need for students to communicate with each other and with the teacher. Learners must have the chance to think through a problem, exchange ideas, and talk to their peers in order to crystallize their thoughts and correct some of their fallacious thinking. Teachers sometimes forget that communication has to be a two-way process if it is to be effective.

This chapter presents information in four sections: (1) discipline and techniques that can influence student behavior; (2) student-teacher communication; (3) learning centers; and (4) interaction analysis as a way of measuring teacher-student interchange.

Discipline and Techniques That Can Influence Student Behavior

The word *discipline* suggests that there has to be a response to negative behavior. All teachers know, of course, that when thirty or more youngsters are working, living, and playing together in one room for a school year, negative behavior is sure to appear occasionally. The danger is, though, that teachers have in mind a specific standard of behavior that is acceptable to them and they wish to "demand" this standard of behavior from everyone. Mature, confident teachers who feel secure in their work do not *fear* the impudence of an *anxious child* or the aggressive, impulsive response of an *angry one.* Rather, they accept these behaviors as normal and maintain a room climate in which these behaviors can be tolerated by the group.

Mental hygienists have taught us the dangers of impulsive, punitive behavior on the part of the adult. Far too many adults judge the ability to discipline a class by just what they see on the surface.

"He used a naughty word so I washed his mouth out with soap. That worked!"

"He was impudent and sassed me so I slapped him. That worked!"

These responses to overt behavior treat *symptoms,* not *causes.* They force the pain, the hurt, the anger (the cause of this behavior) to be more deeply repressed by the offender, thereby practically guaranteeing recurrence in some form eventually.

In helping children to grow in positive directions, in giving positive emphasis to expected behavior, teachers must look for the kinds of *influence techniques*[1] that will help children to help themselves in exercising self-control.

Teachers need a repertoire of techniques so they can anticipate difficulty and perhaps avoid it while at the same time giving children assistance or support when they are apt to get into trouble or are in a crisis. They need to know how to work through a situation without threatening, nagging, or becoming demanding. Some influence techniques are described below.

1. Get the child's attention if he or she is about to commit an antisocial act. If the teacher catches the child's eye and can convey a message by frowning, shaking the head, raising a finger, or clearing the throat, this may be a *warning* that helps the child to exercise self-control. Many children forget, and trouble is avoided by merely helping them remember to conform.

2. Place yourself in close proximity to the child. If the teacher remains cautiously in a position to be tripped by a pair of legs extended across the aisle, the legs are likely to be retracted and placed under the seat. A pat on the shoulder or a friendly reminder spoken in an undertone would not be used to make the child fearful, but rather would help the child find the strength of self-control.

3. Make sure the assignment the child is attempting to do is one the child has the ability to do. Much classroom disorder results from children not being able to cope with the problem in front of them at the moment. Children who can't read need to be taught how, not punished for squirming, making noise, or leaving their seats too much.

4. Encourage children to talk about their feelings. Then accept the feelings and evaluate them. Such frankness from a confident teacher can reduce tension.

5. Humor is a good way to change a tense situation into a face-saving reduced-tension atmosphere. Boys and girls consider humor evidence of poise and self-confidence based on security.

6. A certain amount of routine so that children have some idea of *how* the day is going to be spent is a steadying influence. The younger the class, the more important is knowing "what are we going to do next?" Everyone needs a certain amount of routine in his life.

7. Isolating a child is occasionally a necessity, for many reasons. It is important that teachers not evince anger, hostility, or rejection in doing the isolating. A hyperactive child often needs to be encouraged to work in a quiet, sheltered corner—not as a punishment but because he or she will be able to concentrate better, will be able to attend to the learning task, and will be able to regain self-control.

Occasional temper tantrums, kicking, name-calling, or just "uncontrollable giggles" are all reasons for isolating a child. The important thing is the teacher's behavior in doing the isolation. It should not be punishing but rather should be seen as allowing the child opportunity to regain self-control. If occasionally an industrious child wishes to get a task finished when considerable activity is going on and the teacher can *permit* one child to leave the group, this is not only a good reason for isolation, it also demonstrates that isolation is not punishment but a constructive way to help. Frequent isolation of one child from a class to sit in the corridor for long periods of time is a crass misuse of this technique. Isolation without constructive help for such a child is only avoiding the real problem and encouraging more negative attitudes.

8. The teacher should try to help class members anticipate, as much as possible, changes in their routine. New situations create some anxiety and tensions. The first time a group goes to the auditorium to practice, to the dark room to see a movie, or on a field trip, getting set in advance will pay dividends.

9. Changing activity when everyone is beginning to get tired is a good way to avoid trouble ahead. With younger children, if the job needs to be done that day, it may be well to say something like this: "Let's leave everything just where it is and line up by the door." Or, "Let's move the papers over to the library table so we are free to march up and down the aisles here." Five minutes of brisk walking, singing favorite tunes, formal arm and leg exercises, and time for drinks and toilet may revive almost everyone so that finishing the job doesn't look so forbidding. With older students, it may be necessary only to say, "We have this much more to get done before lunch. If you need to stand up and stretch or get a drink, do it quietly and let's give it a hard try." If most of the group want to finish (are allied with the teacher), this may be all the encouragement they need.

10. Having a fairly well understood way of operating without getting bogged down with too many rules to quibble about will help children define their own limits. Because the teacher has to be at different times a judge, a referee, a detective, a helper, an ego-supporter, or a leader of a group, children need a mature adult whose reactions to behavior situations are reasonably consistent, fair, supportive, and not punitive. Adults who basically do not like children have no business in the classroom.

Specific
Suggestions to
Help New
Teachers with
Discipline

When teachers talk about behavior of boys and girls in their classes, they reveal a great deal about their philosophy of classroom discipline. In this respect, teachers place themselves on a long continuum from strictly enforced discipline to constructively guided discipline. This writer is deeply committed to the philosophy of constructively guided discipline. Children are encouraged to express their attitudes, feelings, and ideas and are then guided in directing them in socially acceptable ways according to the standards of conduct understood by their local environment. Industry, cooperation, and acceptance of a plurality of ideas are desirable ends. The desirable goals may be contrasted with such undesirable ones as *passive* children in very quiet, orderly rooms dominated by an authoritarian teacher.

The discipline recommended here is more difficult to maintain since it is based on a friendly, cooperative spirit prevailing and on a consensus about such matters as behavior, values, and the importance of knowledge. In such an atmosphere, good, effective teaching generates good discipline in most boys and girls. Well planned lessons, careful attention to individual differences in both achievement and behavior, and a constructive, optimistic, worklike atmosphere will eliminate emphasis on behavior *per se* most of the time.

The new teacher may profit from a careful perusal of the following suggestions in preparation for the very complex job of guiding the learning of a roomful of boys and girls for the first time.

1. Learn as quickly as possible to call the boys and girls by their names. Study their names on the class roll before they arrive and connect name to child as quickly as you can.

2. Take charge of the room by talking in a strong, confident voice; present definite plans of work for each hour the first day; conduct business in an impartial, confident way; and provide a variety of tasks and keep everybody busy *all the time* the first day.

3. Accept the standard of conduct for the group that fits the neighborhood in which you teach. While you *must not permit* children to continually tell you "Miss Smith let us do that last year," or "We never did it that way last year," so too, you *must not admonish* your group to behave the way you did when you were a child—or the way children do out in a city suburb.

4. Use every opportunity to make friendly comments throughout the day. These interchanges will cause the boys and girls to feel that you have a personal interest in them. Tell Mary she has a pretty ribbon in her hair, tell John that you appreciate the way he came in very quietly for a change, or write a one-sentence note to Jack's mother and tell her the first time Jack gets all his spelling words right.

5. Begin every class promptly and enthusiastically. Being businesslike, however, does not change the fact that a good sense of humor and a friendly smile are two of your greatest assets. Knowing the lesson well will win respect for you as the teacher. A courteous use of enthusiasm, businesslike behavior, knowledge of the subject matter, and a good sense of humor are sure to win the confidence of the group in the long run.

6. Don't talk too much. Many a sixth grade boy has explained to his mother about his teacher who talks much too much. "We just turn off our hearing aids!" The lecture method has *no* place in the elementary school. This arbitrary point of view is intended to mitigate the far too prevalent situation in which teachers spend long periods of time telling students

what is important and on what content they will be examined. The less response teachers stimulate or accept from the group, the more they are apt to carry on an interminable monologue.

7. Sometimes teachers use words and sentence patterns that the children do not even understand. One third grade teacher teaching children for whom English was a second language in the Southwest asked the boys and girls to be quiet while she talked to a visitor. They were soon talking with each other instead of working. The teacher turned to them and said in a firm voice, "It seems that I cannot relax my vigilance for one minute!" They became quiet for a second, so she turned back to talk to the visitor. Then they continued their conversations in an undertone.

8. When a situation arises that must be handled by the teacher, be sure to keep calm, dignified, and select something that you can carry through to resolve the problem. The child may be asked to take a chair and sit outside the room *once* until the child and the teacher can have a private conference. *But* no child gets an education sitting out in the hall every day.

9. From the first hour of the day, your eyes must be skilled at catching each child's variant behavior no matter where you are standing in the classroom. The first few days, *do not* plan to turn your back on the class for such activities as writing extensively on the blackboard. If material needs to be written on the board, it can be done before the group comes in. Later in the year you may be able to select a mature student to put things on the board for you. Little elementary school teaching is done in a sitting position. The first week you probably shouldn't sit down at all.

10. When you are having a large group discussion, or when you are teaching subgroups, develop the practice of asking the daydreamer or the mischievous one a question, speak the child's name, or make a casual comment about whether or not "X" is going to get the work done today. When a child's attention is beginning to waver, a reminder may be all that is needed.

11. When a fracas has taken place, either between two students or between a student and teacher, don't insist on apologies. An insincere apology teaches hypocrisy.

12. Do not punish the whole class for a mistake committed by one or a few.

13. As a class proceeds, the teacher should note the number of *indifferent* pupils. In a class of twenty-nine fifth graders studying topic sentences for paragraphs, only five girls near the front were paying attention. This teacher needed to reevaluate her goals.

14. Do *not* end the lesson on a sarcastic note: "Nobody had the lesson well prepared today." "Most of you didn't get it—but then I didn't think you would!" Under such conditions, each succeeding lesson will probably get *worse*.

Student-Teacher Communication

One kind of teacher promotes integrative social forces in the classroom through stimulating, clarifying, encouraging, and reflecting feelings and attitudes expressed by students either verbally or behaviorally. Another kind of teacher exercises those skills that control or manage the class much more in a superior-subordinate kind of relationship. The two patterns are characterized below:[2]

The indirect, integrative, pattern:
a. Accepts, clarifies, and supports the ideas and feelings of pupils.
b. Praises and encourages.
c. Asks questions to stimulate pupil participation in decision-making.
d. Asks questions to orient pupils to school work.

The direct, dominative, pattern:
a. Expresses or lectures about own ideas or knowledge.
b. Gives directions or orders.
c. Criticizes or deprecates pupil behavior without intent to change it.
d. Justifies own position or authority.

When the curriculum is based more upon process and less upon content, the teacher operates as a group-centered person. This situation may be contrasted with a classroom climate that is teacher-dominated. The first teacher may be thought of as a leader, who relies mainly on indirect influence; the second teacher relies on direct influence.

Direct influence—through lecturing, giving directions, criticizing, and justifying one's own use of authority—restricts freedom of action by focusing attention on the problem or on the teacher's authority.

Indirect influence—asking questions, accepting and clarifying ideas and feelings, and encouraging student response—consists of the verbal statements of the teacher that expand a student's freedom of action by encouraging verbal participation and initiative. Higher classroom behavior standards can be achieved by asking questions and then using student ideas, perceptions, and reactions to build toward greater student self-direction, responsibility, and understanding.[3]

One might hypothesize that indirect teacher influence increases pupil learning when the student's perception of the objective is clear and acceptable.

Lindgren has illustrated four types of teacher-student language interaction in figure 7.1.[4] Type 4 allows free and open discussion, which provides, each member of the group the opportunity to participate, to answer any other member of the group, and to continue the discussion indefinitely without domination by the teacher.

Figure 7.1 Various types of communicative relationships between teachers and students, in order of their effectiveness.

From Henry C. Lindgren. *Educational Psychology in the Classroom* (New York: John Wiley and Sons, 1956), p. 266.

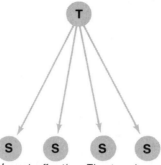

1. *Least effective.* The teacher attempts to maintain one-way communication with individual students.

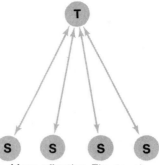

2. *More effective.* The teacher tries to develop two-way communication with individual students.

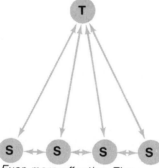

3. *Even more effective.* The teacher maintains two-way communication with individual students and also permits some communication among students on a rather formal basis.

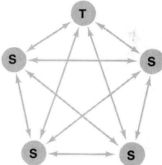

4. *Most effective.* The teacher becomes a member of the group and permits two-way communication among all members of the group.

The kind of language communication within the group should be determined by the objectives to be met during a specific period of time. Certainly there are a few periods of time when the teacher should be imparting needed information to the class, with every member of the group giving the teacher undivided attention. However, the statement sometimes made by junior high school teachers that they lecture to their classes for a forty-minute class period suggests that these teachers do not recognize that boys and girls of that chronological age can neither concentrate on an abstract academic lecture that long nor take adequate notes to have a record of the material covered. For the great majority of elementary and junior high students, lecturing by the teacher is a sheer waste of effort. Many elementary teachers, as well as students, talk too much.

In unit teaching, there is need in the beginning to arouse interest based on what everybody already knows and what everybody would like to learn. This requires free discussion. Then there is need for organized, fairly formal planning so that everyone can go to work efficiently to find information. Next, the unit plan requires sharing in committees, writing about information gained, discussing in small groups, and talking together quietly to crystallize thinking. Then, the entire group is ready to share, question, agree or disagree, and summarize. Finally they need some method to demonstrate that the original objectives for the unit of study have been met. These five steps in the development of a unit of work are presented in table 7.1 with types of interaction of teacher and students.

Simon and Sarkotich[5] have suggested nine skills that need to be strengthened if teachers are to be sensitive to individual students' verbal needs and aware of positive group interaction in the class.

1. Growing accustomed to being nonjudgmental with one another's ideas.
2. Allowing the other person to have attitudes and feelings different from one's own.
3. Growing in the skill of asking and answering questions—without being defensive.
4. Learning to listen for clues in responses.
5. Using neutral questions to expand the responses or to turn attention in new directions.
6. Learning how to report, diagnose, and evaluate classroom problems in group interaction.
7. Using open-ended questions: "How do you feel about this?" "Is there something else important?"
8. Learning that observation, participation, and feedback have real meaning in problem-solving situations.
9. Learning to use "acceptance" and "silence" when useful in getting both participation and interaction.

Table 7.1 Formal steps in development of a unit of work suggesting significant teacher-pupil interaction at each step.

Orientation to the Unit of Work	Teacher-Pupil Planning of Assignments	Information Gathering Time	Information Sharing Time	Culmination
Problem identification.	Problem selection.	Planning and organizing.	Synthesis of ideas.	Evaluation.
Problem exploration.	Goal setting.	Coordinating and communicating.	End product.	Demonstration that objectives have been met.
Informal class interaction.	Teacher-directed discussion.	Committees, small groups, and some individuals doing research and writing activities.	Informal class interaction: sharing information; correcting erroneous ideas; summarizing; selecting important ideas to remember.	Student performance: making and explaining a mural; preparing and performing a play; giving a panel discussion; performing a unit test.

Classroom verbal interaction is a complex process and determines many important aspects of teacher-pupil interaction. Observers can categorize behaviors as arising in the cognitive domain or in the affective domain.

The cognitive system deals with the thinking process. Different kinds of teacher information, teacher questions, pupil responses are differentiated.

The four dimensions of affective behavior are:

1. teacher reaction to pupils' ideas or cognitive output;
2. teacher reactions to pupils' feelings or emotional output;
3. teacher reactions to pupils' attempts to manage classroom procedure and set standards;
4. teacher reactions to pupils' nonverbal behaviors.

Affective behavior can be rated on a continuum from *accepting-praising, encouraging, neutrally accepting, ignoring,* to *rejecting.*

Learning Centers and the Learning Laboratory Concept

The desired teaching-learning environment is one in which both teacher and children are motivated and actively learning. The less experienced teacher is sure to need a less complex environment and enough sense of "control" to have some security. Experienced teachers should be able to allow the group itself to evolve the structure it *needs* in order to permit each of its members to be active, creative learners. A great deal of wisely used freedom is necessary if the teacher is to encourage different behaviors, keep natural curiosity alive and working, and provide the educational resources children need to keep on learning, questioning, problem-solving.

In spite of how different the learning tasks of first and sixth graders are, we traditionally expect them to operate in very similar settings: uniform physical spaces; similar teacher behavior; formal school tasks to be achieved. To accommodate the extreme differences in children—and this includes all types of difference: aptitude, motivation, intelligence, etc.—all teachers need classroom arrangements that allow maximum flexibility so individuals can work undisturbed and at tasks where they have reasonable assurance of success.

Loughlin says:[6]

The arranged environment consists of extensive learning materials and furnishings, their physical organization for access by the learner, and the spaces created by the organization. The arranged environment is organized to respond appropriately to the specific learning needs of the individuals who work in it. As growth and learning occur, changes in the resources, the equipment, and the space patterns meet the increasing maturity and the changing activity needs of the learners. The arranged environment is in a continuing state of adaptation. . . . The teacher works with the arranged environment by arranging places to work, choosing materials, and organizing them to support purposes of teacher and learner.

Such a teacher is prepared from day to day to give necessary directions, ask appropriate questions, help the child who is confused about the work, and encourage students when they are moving in promising directions.

It is important to have a variety of learning centers in an active environment. We must remember that the purpose of any arrangement of classroom space is to facilitate movement within the room and to allow grouping so children can work together and interact in accordance with principles we have known for a long time: that we learn to do by doing; that learning is an active process, not passive.

"Children do not arithmetic, science, or phonic."[7] Rather, they experiment, they argue, they interact, they build, they measure, they chart courses of activities, they write, they read, and they calculate.

If there is no classroom library for children to browse in, the environment is inadequate. If the classroom bookshelves are in a corner behind the teacher's desk and accessible for only brief moments at dismissal time, the environment is still inadequate.

When the teacher arranges learning centers, they should be easy to supervise, easy for small groups of children to use, and materials and equipment should be accessible. Care should be taken not to have long, straight aisles that can become runways, or large empty spaces that can facilitate "horseplay."

When the learning environment is arranged to accommodate a wide selection of on-going activities (see figure 7.2), it is no longer necessary for every student to have a "permanent station," a personal desk. Each student can follow a daily schedule of planned work, moving about the room as the day progresses. However, all students need places for their own things, which can be supplied by a chest providing small drawers or by a series of cardboard boxes that can be easily stacked along one wall of the classroom.

The learning laboratory is the conceptual counterpart to the learning center kind of physical arrangement. If teachers are going to take seriously the principle that great differences in intellectual, social, emotional, and physical maturity exist in every group, then the classroom in the elementary school must become a learning laboratory where children can carry on a wide variety of learning activities simultaneously. In a challenging learning laboratory, children can experiment with a wide variety of avenues to learning. A variety of equipment and materials and a well stocked library must be provided if the classroom is to be a learning laboratory.

In a learning laboratory, there are jobs to do for which children see real purpose; jobs that will satisfy those who need immediate goals and those who can work toward long-range goals; jobs that are easy and jobs that are difficult; jobs that can be performed by individuals and jobs that will be performed by groups. Planning time is crucial, for the teacher must feel sure that each child has definite goals in mind for the work period. Planning time should be a structured period when questions are asked freely and arrangements are made to help those who will need either student or teacher help in finishing tasks.

The learning laboratory has another basic criterion: there are no minimum or maximum levels of performance set as standards for any class group for any given year. Learning is an active, participating process. Problem-

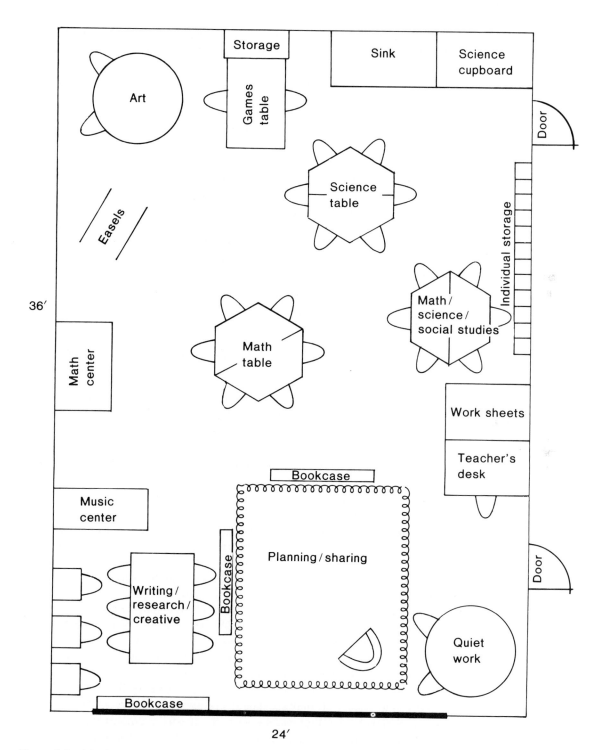

Text labels within the figure:

- Storage
- Sink
- Science cupboard
- Art
- Games table
- Door
- Science table
- Easels
- Individual storage
- 36′
- Math center
- Math table
- Math/ science/ social studies
- Work sheets
- Teacher's desk
- Music center
- Bookcase
- Planning / sharing
- Bookcase
- Writing/ research/ creative
- Door
- Quiet work
- Bookcase
- 24′

Figure 7.2 A learning center arrangement for the classroom.

solving, creative thinking, memory work, and drill are all engaged in—at all levels of difficulty, from readiness (if indicated) to mature levels of reading, evaluating, reporting, and discussing.

Operating this kind of classroom requires maximal group interaction yet leaves the teacher free to work with small groups within the class during the greater part of the school day. In this kind of a classroom, a clear understanding of interaction analysis and how it works is very important.

Interaction Analysis as a Way of Measuring Teacher-Student Interchange

Teacher-pupil interaction can be altered by changing the climate of the classroom. Likewise, through improving the teacher's ability to ask meaningful questions, conduct in-depth discussions, and prepare better lectures, the classroom climate may be improved. If the teacher teaches a curriculum which is geared to memorizing facts; or controls behavior by keeping students afraid of being scolded, sent out of class, failed, or even expelled; or uses direct influence behaviors—clearly, a new approach is needed.

The term "classroom climate" refers to generalized attitudes toward the teacher and the class that the pupils share in common despite individual differences. The development of these attitudes is an outgrowth of classroom social interaction. As a result of participating in classroom activities, pupils soon develop common attitudes about how they like their class, the kind of person the teacher is, and how he will act in certain typical situations. These common attitudes color all aspects of classroom behavior, creating a social atmosphere, or climate, that appears to be fairly stable, once established. Thus, the word "climate" is merely a shorthand reference to those qualities that consistently predominate in most teacher-pupil contacts and in contacts among the pupils in the presence or absence of the teacher.[8]

If teaching behavior is to be changed, teachers must have opportunity to study their own teaching and evaluate what they did and why they did it. The teaching act itself must be brought into focus so it can be evaluated.

Interaction analysis should help teachers develop sensitivity to children's needs, with all the intellectual, physical, emotional, and social differences which they bring to school. It also offers a systematic way to analyze teacher behavior during the teaching act, and may make it possible for teachers to study their personal behavior and teaching strategy to overcome weaknesses and emphasize strengths.

Interaction analysis can be used to study the spontaneous verbal communication of the teacher in a classroom. The purpose of such study is to analyze the role of the teacher in classroom management.

Systems for evaluating teacher behavior should provide two dimensions for growth. (1) Teachers should get feedback on their classroom interaction with students so they can "take stock" and look for new directions to move. (2) Also, the system of analysis should presuppose a theoretical model such that teacher behavior that agrees with the model promotes pupil growth. Because the comparison of present behavior with a standard may indicate that specific new behaviors need to be learned, use of the system may give developmental direction to the teacher.

The Flanders system of interaction analysis provides a method for teachers to study their own teaching behavior in terms of the behavioral objectives they establish for themselves. Actual performance is fed back to them so they have the opportunity to change their own behavior based on data about what they are doing in the classroom.

The Flanders system of interaction analysis involves learning ten categories of classroom verbal behavior (see figure 7.3). The observer judges the strategy of verbal behavior in the class. Pupils, content, teacher's objective, and length of time are evaluated to determine whether learning is taking place to accomplish the behavioral change anticipated in the lesson objective.

The Flanders technique shows how behaviors are linked, and the reader can tell what preceded and what followed in teacher behavior. An observer records interaction in the classroom by writing down a number every three seconds that signifies which of the ten categories of teacher or student verbal behavior is occurring. The result will be a series of numbers such as the following:

10 6 1 3 3 4 8 8 8 7 5 5 3 3 8 8 8   etc.

Then the adjacent numbers are linked into pairs as follows:

10–6 6–1 1–3 3–3 3–4 4–8 8–8 8–8 8–7 7–5 5–5 5–3 3–3 3–8 8–8 8–8 etc.

These linkages are plotted on a matrix of ten rows and ten columns, as in figure 7.4 (the first number along the vertical y-axis, the second number along the horizontal x-axis).

If 400 tallies are plotted for a twenty-minute observation, one can quickly determine the proportion of time devoted to teacher talk and the proportion devoted to student talk. For example, if 260 tallies are in columns 1 through 7, 65 percent of the time was devoted to teacher talk. If 120 tallies are numbers 8 and 9, 30 percent of the time was devoted to student talk.

At least 400 tallies should be recorded, a minimum of twenty minutes of observation, before any attempt is made to interpret teacher and student behavior.

The matrix may be divided into areas that represent types of teacher influence (see figure 7.5). The following list characterizes ten such areas.

Areas Differentiating Types of Teacher Response
Area A. Indirect teacher talk.
Area B. Direct teacher talk.
Area C. Student talk.
Area D. Silence or confusion.
Area E. Acceptance of feelings, offering praise, using student ideas.
Area F. Giving criticism or offering self-justification. May suggest problems in classroom discipline or resistance on the part of the students.
Area G. Teacher responding to termination of student talk with indirect influence.
Area H. Teacher responding to termination of student talk with direct influence.

Figure 7.3 Summary of categories for classroom interaction analysis.

From N. A. Flanders, *Teacher Influences, Pupil Attitudes, and Achievement,* Cooperative Research Monograph, No. 12, O.E.–25040 U.S. Department of Health, Education, and Welfare, 1965.

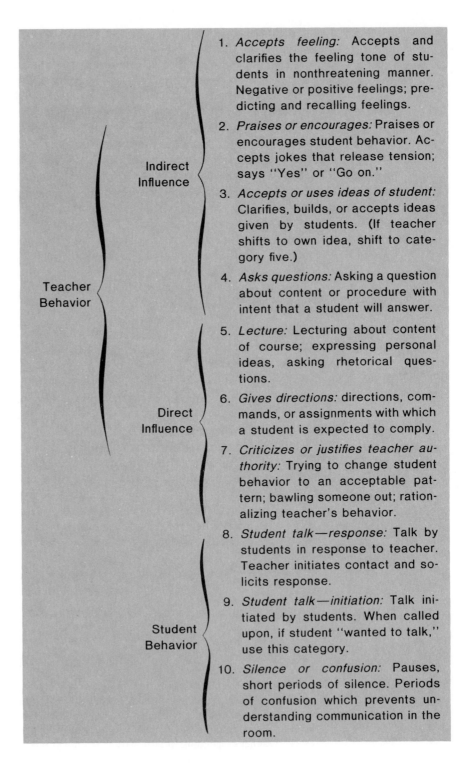

Teacher Behavior

Indirect Influence

1. *Accepts feeling:* Accepts and clarifies the feeling tone of students in nonthreatening manner. Negative or positive feelings; predicting and recalling feelings.

2. *Praises or encourages:* Praises or encourages student behavior. Accepts jokes that release tension; says "Yes" or "Go on."

3. *Accepts or uses ideas of student:* Clarifies, builds, or accepts ideas given by students. (If teacher shifts to own idea, shift to category five.)

4. *Asks questions:* Asking a question about content or procedure with intent that a student will answer.

Direct Influence

5. *Lecture:* Lecturing about content of course; expressing personal ideas, asking rhetorical questions.

6. *Gives directions:* directions, commands, or assignments with which a student is expected to comply.

7. *Criticizes or justifies teacher authority:* Trying to change student behavior to an acceptable pattern; bawling someone out; rationalizing teacher's behavior.

Student Behavior

8. *Student talk—response:* Talk by students in response to teacher. Teacher initiates contact and solicits response.

9. *Student talk—initiation:* Talk initiated by students. When called upon, if student "wanted to talk," use this category.

10. *Silence or confusion:* Pauses, short periods of silence. Periods of confusion which prevents understanding communication in the room.

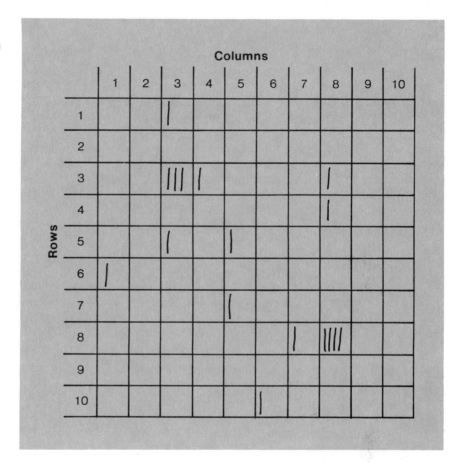

Area I. Pictures the types of teacher's statements that stimulate student participation. High tallies in 8–4 and 4–8 cells indicate question-answer emphasis by teacher.
Area J. Indicates lengthy student responses or student-to-student conversation.

High frequencies in Area C but not in Area J indicate short answers, usually in response to teacher-stimulation. One would normally expect to find high frequencies in Area C closely related to high frequencies in Area J.

There is no single best kind of interaction. What best fits the objectives of a particular lesson is best. Is a lesson best taught with a high percentage of teacher talk or with a low percentage of teacher talk?

The matrix analysis will show whether there has been a predominance of teacher talk, indirect teacher influence, direct teacher influence, student talk in response to teacher questions, or student talk in which students are discussing points with each other. The only person who can decide whether the behavior shown on the matrix is desirable or undesirable is the teacher, who evaluates the behavior in terms of the purpose set in planning the lesson.

Figure 7.5 Areas of matrix analysis.

From N. A. Flanders, *Teacher Influences, Pupil Attitudes, and Achievement,* Cooperative Research Monograph, No. 12, O.E.–25040 U.S. Department of Health, Education, and Welfare, 1965.

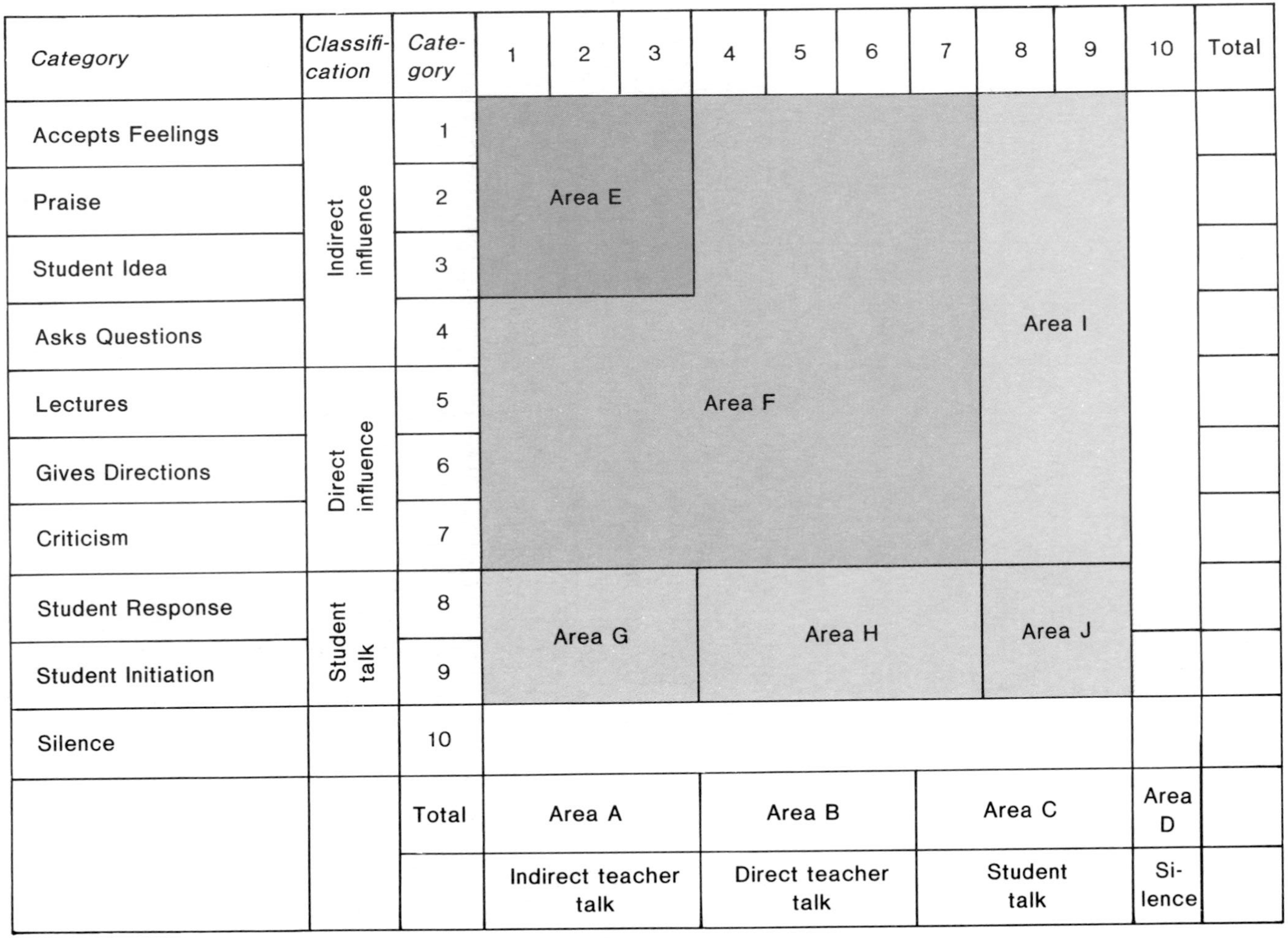

Percentages of time devoted to different kinds of teacher behavior as recorded in actual classrooms are shown below.[9] These are categorized averages reflecting current practices in classrooms. However, current practice may not be the best or more desirable in specific instances.

Category
1. Direct teachers use 0.1 percent of the time, on the average; indirect teachers, 0.5 percent of the time.
2. Both direct and indirect teachers use 2 percent of the time.
3. Direct teachers use 2 percent; indirect, 9 percent of the time.
4. Direct teachers use 8 percent; indirect, 11 percent of the time.
5. Both direct and indirect teachers use 25–50 percent of the time.
6. Direct teachers use 8 percent; indirect, 4 percent of the time.
7. Direct teachers use 5 percent; indirect, less than 1 percent of the time.
8. Direct teachers have most in 4–8 cell; indirect teachers have most in 8–8 cell.
9. Much greater use made by indirect teachers.
10. More heavily loaded for direct teachers.

Gathering and interpreting verbal interaction data in the classroom can provide very useful feedback for teachers who wish to improve teaching performance.

Variability in teacher influence—flexibility—is associated with teachers whose students learned the most.[10]

Teachers can decide what they think their verbal behavior ought to be in a given teaching situation. Then they can tape record a sample of their teaching for at least twenty minutes in that type of situation and analyze their own behavior by replaying the tape and tallying the verbal activity at three-second intervals. With this evidence they can find out whether their behavior was what they desired. Thus, it is clear that, while the use of interaction analysis technique has much value as an assessment of teacher behavior, it can have greater value for teachers in helping them achieve what they wish.

Summary

Classroom management skills are prerequisite to efficient teaching. This chapter presents four major concepts directed toward acquiring such management skills. Teachers are advised to pay more attention to strengthening their repertoire of influence techniques that cultivate positive behavior than to being concerned about disciplining students. Several influence techniques were presented in this chapter along with suggestions for developing open two-way communication. Teachers must provide learning opportunities that keep all their students, with all their differences, interested. Interaction analysis provides one method of studying teaching. Teachers can use the technique to analyze their own classroom behavior.

Suggested Activities

1. Ten influence techniques for managing classroom behavior were discussed. Draw upon your experience and be prepared to discuss a teacher's use of five of them.
2. Four types of teacher-student language interaction were detailed in the text. Discuss the importance of effective two-way communication. What does the teacher do with students who do not conform to classroom behavior?
3. Observe classroom learning centers. Then prepare at least three activities that you could use in learning centers in your classroom.
4. Evaluate the interaction analysis technique as an important way to study teacher behavior.

For Further Reading

Amidon, Edmund J., and Ned A. Flanders. *The Role of the Teacher in the Classroom.* 1040 Plymouth Bldg., Minneapolis, Minn. 55402: Association for Productive Teaching, 1967.

Amidon, Edmund J., and John B. Hough, eds. *Interaction Analysis: Theory, Research, and Application.* Reading, Mass.: Addison Wesley, 1967.

Amidon, Edmund J., and Elizabeth Hunter. *Improving Teaching: Analyzing Verbal Interaction in the Classroom.* New York: Holt, Rinehart & Winston, 1966.

Bierly, Ken. "Taking a New Look at Learning Centers." *Instructor* 87 (January 1978): 80–84.

Charles, C. M. *Individualizing Instruction.* St. Louis: C. V. Mosby, 1976, pp. 133–54.

Flanders, Ned A. "Intent, Action and Feedback, A Preparation for Teaching." *Journal of Teacher Education* 14(1963):251–60. Reprinted in Amidon and Hough, eds. *Interaction Analysis,* pp. 283–94.

Furst, Norma, and Marciene S. Mattleman. "Classroom Climate." *NEA Journal* 57 (April 1968):22–24.

Jones, Elizabeth. *Dimensions of Teaching-Learning Environments.* 714 West California Blvd., Pasadena, Calif.: Pacific Oaks, undated.

Kritchevsky, Sybil, and Elizabeth Prescott. *Planning Environments for Young Children: Physical Space.* Washington, D.C.: National Association for the Education of Young Children, 1969.

Loughlin, Catherine E. "Understanding the Learning Environment." *Elementary School Journal* 78 (November 1977):124–31.

Simon, Anita, and E. Gil Boyer. *Mirrors for Behavior: An Anthology of Classroom Observation Instruments.* Philadelphia, Pa.: Research for Better Schools, 1968.

Simon, Dan, and Diane Sarkotich. "Sensitivity Training in the Classroom." *NEA Journal* 56 (January 1967):12–13.

Taba, Hilda. *Thinking in Elementary School Children.* San Francisco: San Francisco State College, 1964.

Notes

1. Fritz Redl and W. W. Wattenberg, *Mental Hygiene in Teaching* (New York: Harcourt, Brace, 1951), Chapter 12, "Influence Techniques."

2. Ned A. Flanders, "Teacher Influences, Pupil Attitudes, and Achievement," in *Studying Teaching,* ed. James Raths, John R. Pancella, and James S. Van Ness (Englewood Cliffs, N.J.: Prentice-Hall, 1967), p. 46.

3. Ibid., p. 64.

4. Henry Clay Lindgren, *Educational Psychology in the Classroom* (New York: John Wiley & Sons, 1956), p. 266.

5. Dan Simon and Diane Sarkotich, "Sensitivity Training in the Classroom," *NEA Journal* 56 (January 1967):12–13.

6. Catherine Loughlin, "Understanding the Learning Environment," *Elementary School Journal* 78 (November 1977):127, 128.

7. Ibid., p. 128.

8. Flanders, "Teacher Influences," p. 44.

9. Edmund Amidon and Ned Flanders, "Interaction Analysis As a Feedback System," in *Interaction Analysis: Theory, Research, and Application,* eds. Edmund Amidon and John Hough (Reading, Mass.: Addison Wesley, 1967), pp. 137–39.

10. Flanders, "Teacher Influences," p. 64.

8

Parent-Teacher Cooperation

The title of this chapter is meant to emphasize that teaching children is a cooperative venture between parents and teachers. Teachers should recognize that parents are not just people to work *with* or counsel, parents have both information and concerns that can be most helpful in careful planning for a child.

As the school has come to take a more and more important place in the education of children, the parents' roles have become, perhaps, less well defined. Sometimes parents are criticized by teachers, and at times teachers are criticized by parents. Stereotyped and prejudiced attitudes can develop on both sides. Sometimes parents are indifferent to school; sometimes they misunderstand the policies of the school.

Teachers must exercise caution in carrying out their responsibility when having parent conferences about the academic progress of their children. A teacher once said to half a dozen parents in her classroom prior to the regular PTA meeting, in response to a question about the school testing program: "Oh, our testing program. We've been giving some IQ tests." Then after a slightly embarrassed laugh, she continued, "But none of you folks have anything to worry about."

The teacher might more constructively have said something like: "The tests are being given to obtain more information about the children's general abilities and to help us in future planning both *for* and *with* the children."

An educator once mimicked the jargon a teacher is said to have used during a conference with a boy's parents: "He's adjusting well to his peer group and achieving to expectancy in skill subjects. But I'm afraid his growth in content subjects is blocked by reluctance to get on with his developmental tasks." Parent-teacher conferences need to adhere to language clearly understood by both teachers and parents.

It has been suggested that there is an imperative fourth *R* to be added to *Readin', 'Ritin',* and *'Rithmetic.* It is *Relationships,* focusing on a clearer relationship between teacher and child, teacher and parent, and the child's school life.

The conflicts pointed out by Redl and Wattenberg[1] are very real conflicts. Parents who fear trouble for their children in school are apt to be the parents who feared trouble for themselves when they were children in school. And teachers who hope to maintain a safe distance between themselves and parents may remember unpleasant experiences from their past in dealing with adults. Many teachers and principals have, in the past, been predisposed to think that parents who come to the school are in trouble, apt to expose trouble, or predisposed to make trouble.

Merrill has suggested:

> Some of the negative undercurrents in parent-teacher relationships come from feelings most of us have about authority. We normally respond to those in authority in various ways, mixing hostility and submissiveness, the anxiety to please, awe, respect, and perhaps fear. . . . Parents and teachers tend to see each other as authority figures. . . . Many teachers and parents feel ambivalent about being cast in an authority role. They enjoy the prestige but do not wish to cope with negative feelings directed toward those in authority.[2]

Insights into these ways of feeling may be helpful in accepting and dealing with them.

While these comments may seem negative to the beginning teacher, they reflect situations as they exist in some schools. However, increasingly, parents are finding their way into the classrooms and offering their services in constructive ways to further the educational experiences of their children. They want cooperative sharing and planning in order to best structure the total environment of their children.

School-Home Cooperation

Schools need to join forces with parents, first, in order to help parents understand more about the growth and development of their own children and children in general. Some parents need to learn that children are not miniature adults. They need to learn that a continuous growth process starts at birth and goes on during all the waking hours of a child, wherever the child is. Actually, it began long before birth, but perhaps for the teacher's purposes this will be an adequate place to start. Being ready for school requires that from infancy a child be taught the meaning of things in the environment, taught what the environment is, and taught how to use it. Language—not just words, but cognitive growth of concepts—is of first importance in the preschool years.

Schools also need to extend parents' knowledge of availability of services of many community agencies which serve families, adults, or children. This includes making parents aware of their own need for services which they may have felt were only needed by people other than themselves. It may also include acquainting parents with the importance of encouraging children to have library cards in their community library, taking their children to the city museum, or subscribing to, and reading, the P.T.A. magazine.

Further, schools should try to cement mutual understanding and acceptance between teachers and parents. When teachers and parents meet and talk, the face-to-face acquaintance permits building the kind of partnership that works for positive results. Written reports and report cards are, at best, limited in helping parents understand their child's progress in school. Parents should have an opportunity to talk directly with the teacher about their child's academic progress.

Negative reactions and feelings are more apt to be engendered when teachers say, "I sent a note asking the mother to come in but she never did," or when mothers say, "I couldn't write her a note; I couldn't spell the words." It is much better to establish friendly relations on a face-to-face basis early in the year so that parent and teacher feel they know each other *before* there is any need to meet to thresh out a difficult problem that neither adult understands and that each might like to blame the other for.

A further by-product of school-home cooperation is that often teachers can make use of many parents of the children in their rooms. Some fathers could help the third grade boys make bird houses more easily than the teacher could. Some mothers could teach sixth grade girls how to knit. Many mothers would be glad to drive a carload of children to the airport, to the museum, or to the public library. At the same time, when parents have opportunities to meet and talk with other parents, they often find that they have many common interests and aspirations for their children.

Parent-Teacher Conferences

There are a few important points for the teacher to have in mind when a conference with one or both of a child's parents is to be held. It is hoped that the conference will begin and end on a pleasant and constructive note and that it will be held in a comfortable place that makes constructive conversation feasible. Both parent and teacher must feel at ease in the conversation, and the teacher must be a good listener. The teacher must be alert to comments that may have hidden meanings—*other* meanings than the specific references in an anecdote the parents may relate. The teacher must be able to ask appropriate questions, make tactful answers, and extend the parent's conver-

sation, or just listen. The teacher should be constructive if the parent asks direct questions but should be careful to convey to the parent that in the area of serious learning problems, there may be a need for help from specialists. The teacher should follow up constructively on questions, information, or further testing, referrals, or any other result of the conference.

The following general suggestions may be helpful in planning initial contacts with parents or in working out informal ways of keeping them involved in the school program of their child.

1. Plan an opportunity to meet the parents of the children in your room as early in the school year as is convenient. Explain in general terms to the parents in a total group about the work for the year. Emphasize the extent of individual differences and how the range of achievement increases within a class as boys and girls progress through the school.

2. Invite parents to bring individual questions to private conferences. If individual kinds of questions are raised in group discussions, the teacher should make a constructive statement but arrange for a private conference later to discuss the specific problem.

3. To keep channels of communication open, send short informal notes home with the child whenever there is an occasion—to report a good performance some day, to offer encouragement, or to suggest a way for mother to help with a special assignment.

4. Encourage parents to visit the classroom to observe the children at work. Do not permit parents to carry on a conversation with you about children in front of them. But, do plan to meet a parent in a suitable conference environment and allow sufficient time for questions and discussion.

5. Discuss freely with the parents the meaningful records that the school has in the child's cumulative folder. If the child is performing below grade level in reading, for example, make sure that parents understand that the class average, or median, represents that level below which half

of the class achieves. A sample performance on the informal reading inventory would provide a concrete illustration of how well the child reads context and what kinds of errors are made. When parents ask about intelligence tests, teachers must explain their limitations. Group intelligence tests are dependent upon reading ability and sample a child's performance for only a short period of time in a special situation. At best, such a test can only predict whether a child is a rapid learner, above average, average, below average, or a possible slow learner. Neither the teacher nor the parent should accept a group test result as a diagnosis of the limit of intellectual ability of a child. An individual intelligence test provides a much more reliable estimate of general learning ability. Parents are entitled to the best information the school can provide if they are to plan realistically for the future education of their children.

6. Encourage parents to give their children enriching learning experiences that are available to them. Studying the TV guides to seek out worthwhile educational programs will improve the quality of the viewing of many school children. Traveling with parents and learning about places first hand will make reading about them later more meaningful. A library card at the local public library can be an enriching opportunity for any child.

Ways Parents Should Help

A few other specific suggestions that teachers may recommend to parents are:

1. Be sure your child is in an optimal state of physical health and gets adequate sleep and rest. Pay attention to hearing, vision, and neurological problems or symptoms.
2. Be sure the child feels secure and confident in both the home and school environment.
3. Provide the child a reading environment and a positive attitude toward reading at home. This means a place to study and evidence that adults in his home also read. Parents should read aloud to their children; and children should be encouraged to read aloud to their parents. Children will likely favor this if they are successful. Encourage parents to always tell children unknown words when they are reading. If the child misses too many, the material is too difficult and he should seek out easier stories to read.
4. Encourage the child to purchase paperbacks and join book clubs for exchanging them with others to provide wider reading.

There are also ways in which parents should *not* help. The emotional involvement of being the parent of a child who has problems in learning how to read often causes the parent to be anxious or frustrated. In such a situation, the parent may overtly express the idea that the child is stupid or convey it in nonverbal ways. Parents should take heed of the following admonitions:

1. Do not compare the child with siblings who are more successful in school.
2. Do not punish the child for making poor marks in school.
3. Do try to avoid losing patience, raising voices, or otherwise causing the child anxiety.
4. Do not try to teach phonic elements, new words, or other reading skills without fairly clear instructions from the teacher as to suitable methods.
5. Do not try to work with the child when he or she is upset, anxious, or feeling pressured about school.

A Seminar for Parents: How the Developmental Reading Process Works

Parents often have vague notions about how the reading process is being taught but inadequate understanding of many of the things they have "heard." Is phonics being taught? Why can't my boy spell? "Look-say" is inadequate. Is the controlled vocabulary necessary?

Six-week, eight-week, and ten-week seminars have been planned for parents in which the methods of teaching reading in a given school are explained with opportunity for questions.[3]

Similarly, a series of tapes for studying "The Ways of Teaching Children to Read"[4] has been made available. Tapes that could serve as bases for discussion include: (1) "Major Methods of Teaching Children to Read"; (2) "What Parents Need to Know about Child Development and Reading"; (3) "Helping Your Child with Reading."

Parents as Auxiliary Teachers

Wilson and Pfau have suggested that since there are so many more children with reading problems than there are clinicians to help them, perhaps teachers should take another look at ways parents might be able to help.

1. There are types of instruction in remedial reading that are reinforcing practice, and these might be done by parents if they were helped to distinguish these from other types of instruction to be done only by teachers. Such things as mother helping seven-year-old Billy list all the things in the kitchen that start with *P* or *C*, or playing *Go-Fish* or *Vowel Domino* are examples.
2. The teacher must teach the parent how to do correctly the activity he is to enjoy with the child. If the parent is going to listen to the child read, he must be a good listener, give his undivided attention, and be interested in discussing the story after it is read. He should tell the child the word he doesn't know, not make him "sound it out."
3. Parents should have a chance to try the activity; if a game, to play it with the clinician and child; if an exercise in the workbook, to ask the clinician any question they may have.
4. Let the parent decide whether he can establish a good working relationship with his own child. If frustration mounts or the parent is too emotionally involved—still too concerned about possible mental retardation—still burdened with some guilt about the child's failure—then he should understand that it is better to discontinue parent help.[5]

Parents can be a valuable resource, collectively, for all the teachers in a building. One elementary school made a brief survey of the special skills, abilities, travel experiences, hobbies, and other interests which the parents in the district possessed. A surprising number of parents had traveled to Europe and returned with boxes of excellent colored slides which they were happy to show and talk about to a class; others had traveled to many other interesting places and returned with artifacts, costumes, furniture, books, pictures, and musical instruments of endless variety. One man was a glassblower. One could demonstrate and teach elementary judo. Several women could knit, crochet, tat, weave, braid, do textile painting, and one had learned flower-arranging skills in Japan.

In helping children to succeed in school, parents and teachers play similar roles. Both need to offer the child a warm, supportive climate; opportunities for success; a variety of experiences; and above all, a chance to become actively involved in his own learning.[6]

Reports from Teachers of Home-School Cooperation

The more parents there are who come to the school so that they actually see the school program in operation and participate in some activity, the more the total community is apt to think the school does the best it can under the circumstances.

In a community with a wide range of cultural systems, a somewhat transient population, disparity in family incomes, and widespread lack of interest in school, a group of teachers wanted to identify basic behavior problems. They found that inconsistencies within the school staff as well as inconsistencies between home and school with respect to rules and expectations created many of the problems.

The student council in the school, a committee of parents chosen to represent all socioeconomic areas of the district, and a teacher committee laid the foundation for working on the problem:

1. Teachers and children should work together to establish realistic goals and standards.
2. Conflict areas should be analyzed for causes and reasons.
3. Role-playing procedures should be used to analyze discipline and behavior problems.
4. School behavior units should be developed at each grade level.
5. Pupil interests and special abilities should be utilized.
6. Children, teachers, and parents need to understand all discipline regulations.
7. A conference and home visitation program should be developed.
8. Existing teaching methods and the curriculum should be evaluated.

When report cards were distributed through parent-teacher conferences, 96 percent of the parents responded to the invitation for such a conference. Observable changes in attitude and behavior were evident in not only the boys and girls, but also teachers and parents![7]

To provide for personal communication with parents of her fifth grade class, one teacher gave each child a folder in which to file day-to-day exercises, homework exercises, study sheets, tests, and quizzes. At the end of each month the children write their parents letters describing interesting happenings at school, the program in physical education, music, art, and other special subjects, as well as explaining the papers in the folders. The teacher also includes in the folder a note to the parents.[8] This effort is time-consuming but pays big dividends in promoting the desirable team effort of parent-child-teacher in encouraging child growth in academic skills. Typical parent comments reinforce the teacher's evaluation:[9]

About all we can say for the spelling is that it's original. At least 'Duey Desmal Sistom' surpasses them all!

I was disappointed that he hadn't shown much improvement over last month.

For the first time since my son started school, I finally know what is going on.

Just before report cards were due, one primary teacher invited parents to come to school to observe their children for a complete day. She gave those who came a list of things to look for:[10]

How well does he seem to know what to do?
Does he work steadily at a given task?
What distracts him?
What response does he make to his teachers?
What troubles does he have and how does he solve them?
Who does he play with?
Does he seem to have special friends?
Does he play alone or with other children?
Is his work the best he's capable of?
Are you satisfied with his progress?

Such visitations were sufficiently encouraging to cause the teacher to plan for other all-day visits before succeeding report card days.

One school has a parents' waiting room with comfortable arm chairs, tables, exhibits of children's work, announcements, and magazines for parents. A nursery school encourages mothers to bring a child for visits, both staying only a short time at first. In some schools, parents are encouraged to visit often in their child's classroom. They see their own child in contact with and in comparison with other children. The teacher helps them enlarge their perceptions of their child.[11]

In some schools, parents are often called on to give minor assistance, helping to make or repair something, assisting with school excursions, teaching skills the teacher lacks. One school arranged parent-teacher conferences during the school day and asked mothers to come to school to monitor classroom activities while the teacher conferred with other parents.

The child should not be lost sight of in parent-teacher conferences. Three-way conferences of child-parent-teacher are sometimes needed too. Teachers are occasionally able to enjoy such a conference with both parents and their child when they are invited into the home either for a meal or just to visit in the living room when the child feels free to participate in the conversation. Many conferences in the intermediate grades might be more profitable if the student, parents, and teacher all met together.

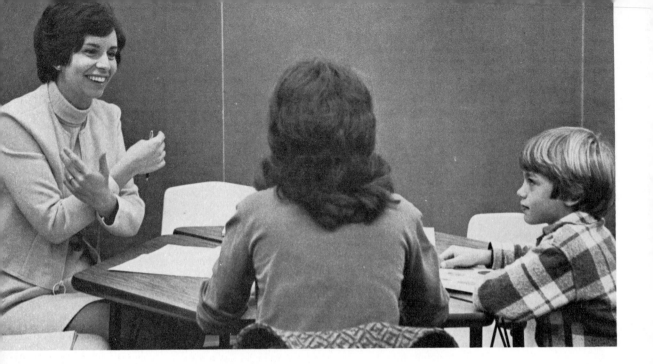

Economic changes in family life have transferred much of the traditional work of the home to outside agencies. Industrial technology has not only decreased the tasks of running the household and providing the food for the family, but also permitted millions of mothers to work outside the home. In this kind of home, children have become an economic burden where once they were an economic asset. Child labor laws, compulsory education, and social and humanitarian motives of society have freed the child from work responsibilities—but may also have created some anxieties for children about loss of independence, concern about personal security in the family, and many other problems.

When parents ask how they can best help their child, some of the following suggestions may be appropriate:[12]

1. Demonstrate an appreciation of books: (a) set up a library shelf; (b) plan regular trips to the library; (c) ask the librarian for lists of recommended books; (d) use books as gifts; and (e) let your children see *their* parents use reading as *their* enjoyable activity.

2. Read to your children often. Make it an enjoyable experience.

3. Accept each child as he or she is, understanding the child's strengths and weaknesses. Avoid comparing siblings. Praise when it is earned.

4. Include your children in shopping excursions. Initiate conversation and keep the dialogue going.

5. Plan little excursions to points of interest where you live. Use them for extending vocabulary.

6. Include your children in decision-making processes where they can participate. If you give them alternatives from which to choose, then abide by their choices.

Summary   Teachers and parents must work cooperatively in a relationship of mutual respect and dependence. Parents do have a great deal of information about their children. They need an opportunity to talk with someone who can help them evaluate this information and plan how to use it to effect behavior change. Suggestions below summarize how parents can best prepare their children for success in school; how teachers may counsel with parents about their child's behavior; and how to conduct successful parent-teacher conferences.

Parents are doing their part when they make sure that their children:

Are in an optimal state of physical health.

Feel secure and confident in the family circle.

Live in a reading environment.

Have a rich background of first-hand experiences.

Get undivided attention when reading aloud to either parent.

Parents must be counseled by teachers to modify their behavior toward their children if they:

Take a punitive attitude toward a child who fails.

Think a child is lazy or unwilling to try.

Force a child to study when it is playtime.

Nag, scold, or punish because a child fails.

Compare a child with siblings.

Feel guilty and defensive about a child's lack of success.

In conducting a parent-teacher conference, the teacher should:

Try to meet parents early in the school year to get acquainted.

Put parents at ease during the conference.

Assure parents of concern for their child.

Open the conference by giving a parent the opportunity to talk first.

Give an honest evaluation of the child's reading status: Does the child know basic sight words? Does the child know phonics and structural analysis? Does the child know how to write and spell (in manuscript or cursive) and at what level?

Discuss anecdotal records with parents.

Assure parents that it takes a long time to learn how to read.

If other services are indicated, either in the school or elsewhere (psychological, medical, speech and hearing, remedial reading, or other), discuss these candidly with the parent.

**Suggested
Activities**

1. In your acquaintance find a mother of an elementary school age child whom you can interview briefly to find out the extent to which she feels the school is meeting the educational needs of her child. Make a brief check list, including the child's reading ability, study habits, interaction in play and games, and general satisfaction with school. Try to obtain some information related to all these areas.

2. If you have a student teaching assignment, or if you have any current assignment where you work directly with children, try to arrange an interview with one of the mothers to discuss her child's status in your group.

3. If you are working in an elementary school, try to arrange with your principal to sit as an observer when parents are in the office to discuss some academic or disciplinary problem of their child.

4. Using the information given by Redl and Wattenberg and Merrill relative to possible conflicts in parent-teacher interaction, plan to role-play situations in which (a) the mother feels her child needs more individual help; (b) the teacher feels insecure and is unable to make any constructive suggestions; (c) neither mother nor teacher can overcome her anger with Tommy, who has refused to obey the teacher's instructions; and (d) both mother and teacher have concern for Mary's poor school work and they have a constructive conversation about specific steps to try to help her.

**For Further
Reading**

Breiling, Annette. "Using Parents as Teaching Partners." *The Reading Teacher* 30 (November 1976): 187–92.

Cassidy, Jack. "Reporting Pupil Progress in Reading—Parents vs. Teachers." *The Reading Teacher* 31 (December 1977): 294–96.

Flood, James E. "Parental Styles in Reading Episodes with Young Children." *The Reading Teacher* 30 (May 1977): 864–67.

Kroth, Roger. *Communicating with Parents of Exceptional Children.* Denver: Love Publishing Co., 1975.

Kroth, Roger, and Richard Simpson. *Parent Conferences as a Teaching Strategy.* Denver: Love Publishing Co., 1977.

Quisenberry, Nancy L., Candace Blakemore, and Claudia A. Warren. "Involving Parents in Reading: An Annotated Bibliography." *The Reading Teacher* 31 (October 1977): 34–39.

Smith, Carl B., ed. *Parents and Reading.* Perspectives in Reading No. 14. Newark, Del.: International Reading Assn., 1971.

Smith, Nila Banton. "Parents Are People." *The Reading Teacher* 18 (May 1965):624–28.

Unruh, Glennys G. "Parents Can Help Their Children Succeed in School." *NEA Journal* 55 (December 1966):14–16.

Wilson, Robert, and Donald W. Pfau. "Parents Can Help." *The Reading Teacher* 21 (May 1968):759–60.

Zintz, Miles V. *Corrective Reading*, 3d ed., chap. 10, "Working Cooperatively with Parents," pp. 279–92. Dubuque, Ia.: Wm. C. Brown, 1977.

Notes

1. Fritz Redl and William W. Wattenberg, *Mental Hygiene in Teaching,* 2d ed. (New York: Harcourt, Brace & World, 1959), Chapter 17, "Working with Parents," pp. 452–76.
2. Barbara W. Merrill, "Under the Surface of Parent-Teacher Relationships," *The Instructor* 75 (November 1965):35.
3. Alma Harrington, "Teaching Parents to Help at Home," in Carl B. Smith, ed., *Parents and Reading* (Newark, Del.: International Reading Assn., 1971), pp. 49–56.
4. The Jab Press, Inc., Box 213, Fair Lawn, New Jersey 07410, 1976.
5. Robert M. Wilson and Donald W. Pfau, "Parents Can Help," *The Reading Teacher* 21 (May 1968):759–60.
6. Glennys G. Unruh, "Parents Can Help Their Children Succeed in School," *NEA Journal* 55 (December 1966):14–16.
7. Jack L. Roach, "We Found Better Ways to Improve Pupil Behavior," *The Instructor* 76 (February 1967):29.
8. Martha J. Hamblet, "Keeping in Touch with Parents," *The Instructor* 77 (January 1968):34.
9. Ibid.
10. Magdalen Eichert, "Parents Come to School," *The Instructor* 75 (October 1965):50.
11. H. H. Stern, *Parent Education, An International Survey* (173 Cottingham Road, Hull, England: Institute for Education, University of Hull, 1960), p. 41.
12. Pat Koppman, San Diego, Calif. City Schools. Lecture, Sixth Annual New Mexico International Reading Association Convention, Jan. 15, 1977.

4

The Skills of Reading

Part 4 contains the chapters that discuss the various developmental skills necessary for children to become independent readers. It begins with teaching word-recognition skills, comprehension skills, and study skills. These three chapters give the teacher guidelines for helping children develop (1) a stock of sight words, (2) phonic and structural analysis skills, (3) comprehension of the ideas contained in material read, and (4) acquaintance with a great deal of easy reading material.

At the same time, helping children learn to exercise critical judgment while reading, develop oral reading skills, and establish permanent habits of reading are other essential aspects of a developmental reading program. There is also a renewed emphasis on teaching reading skills in the content fields.

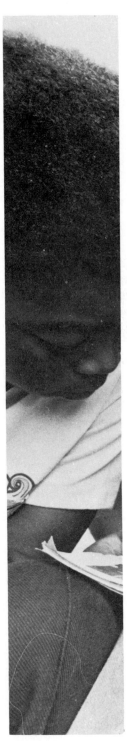

9
Word-Recognition Skills

Growth in the ability to recognize words in print is the most basic skill in learning how to read. None of the other necessary abilities can develop until the child has an accessible stock of words in a reading vocabulary.

In beginning reading the child needs to know the meaning of a word when pronouncing it in order to grasp the principle of demanding meaning from what is read. This presupposes an adequate listening and speaking vocabulary so that all the concepts the child tries to read will be understood.

The typical middle-class, first grade child comes to school with a relatively large vocabulary. Actually the child has not one but several vocabularies. Of these, at age six, the *listening* vocabulary is likely to be the largest. That means that the child understands many words spoken in context that he would not use in his own *speaking* vocabulary. Typically, the *reading* vocabulary will be limited to a very few words, if it exists at all. And most six-year-olds do not have a *writing* vocabulary. It has been estimated that a typical middle-class six-year-old child may have as many as 8,000 to 10,000 words in a listening vocabulary; 5,000 to 7,000 in a speaking vocabulary; and, at the beginning of school, no reading or writing vocabulary of significance. As the child progresses through elementary school, these vocabularies change greatly. The sizes of reading vocabularies vary greatly with children after they have learned word-attack skills for discovering new words for themselves. By grade five or soon thereafter, the reading vocabulary will become larger than the speaking vocabulary for the able reader. Eventually, too, the reading vocabulary will become greater than the listening vocabulary, and the child must develop the dictionary habit in order to find quickly meanings of new words or meanings of old words in new contexts.

Methods of Teaching Word Recognition

Historically, teachers have used several different methods in trying to help children learn word-recognition skills. When Bible reading was the main purpose for learning to read and the Bible was the source used, learners probably resorted mostly to configuration clues and repetition to remember words. They could then learn to recognize syllables and sound out words by syllables. Undoubtedly, many children learned by this method, but there are few statistics to show how many boys and girls *did not learn* to read by it.

Synthetic methods, on the other hand, may be defined as building larger elements (the word) from simpler elements (the letters), or "going from the parts to the whole." The alphabet-spelling and phonics methods are synthetic methods, both based on putting letters together to make words.

The Alphabet Method

In the alphabet method, the letters in the word are named in sequence and then the word pronounced. One difficulty of using this method in English is that the names and the sounds of the letters have little similarity. *Bat* would be spelled as *bee aye tea* and then pronounced *bat*. In languages where the letter names are essentially the same as their sounds, this is much more effective, as, for example, in Spanish.

The Phonics Method

The phonics method introduces many of the sounds of letters and letter combinations so the child can put them together to make words. The 1912 *Beacon Primer* introduced the child to some 150 phonetic elements on large charts, which the child could practice sounding. After mastering the charts, the child was ready to begin reading context. For example, having learned the sounds *ra, ha, ma, ta,* and *sa,* the child could use the consonant *t* and pronounce *ra-t, ha-t, ma-t, ta-t,* and *sa-t,* which, by pronouncing more rapidly, then became the words *rat, hat, mat, tat,* and *sat* (see figure 9.1).

In the *Gordon Primer* one learned initial consonant sounds and joined them to a "family" to make long lists of words (see figure 9.2). For the *at* family, for example, the child combined it with the sound of *m* and pronounced *mat.* Then, with *r,* the child could build *rat,* and with *h, hat.*

Some controversy continues about which of the two approaches to sounding is better. Should one read *ra-t* or *r-at* as the word *rat?* Does it make a great deal of difference so long as children know what they are doing? There is one problem in sounding consonants separately at word beginnings. The child is probably sounding *b* as if it were *be* as in *but* and saying *be-at* for *bat.*

Emphasis on *sounding,* or phonics, as a method of introducing reading to young children has appeared, disappeared, and reappeared through the years. There are undoubtedly several reasons. The most significant reason is that most primary teachers have not been aware of the contribution that some understanding of linguistics could make to reading instruction. Chapter 3 is devoted to that topic. But even if reading teachers have some linguistic background, the question of what children should learn first—how to decode words, or that reading is an intellectual thought process—has still not been satisfactorily resolved. How can both of these jobs be accomplished to the greatest advantage for the child? This writer believes that heavy emphasis on phonics early in the typical child's school life will be much less meaningful or intrinsically interesting than putting reading sentences to work to manipulate ideas. There is also the possibility that some children, not highly motivated with abstract phonics drills, will become word-callers and exhibit labored attempts at reading.

Figure 9.1 The Beacon system used the initial blends *ra, ha, la, ma, ta* as the basis for sounding out words. This may be contrasted with the final blends used similarly in the *Gordon Primer*.

Beacon Primer, page 1, copyright 1912 by Ginn and Company. Reprinted by permission.

BEACON PRIMER

PHONETIC TABLES

This book is planned to be used in connection with the Phonetic Chart. The following tables and exercises should not be taught until the Phonetic Chart is completed.[1]

After finishing the tables found in the chart, the child should come to this work with considerable phonetic power. The following words should be recognized silently and given as wholes at the rate of thirty to forty per minute.

had	map	rag	cat	had
ham	mat	ran	fan	lap
hat	pad	rat	fat	man
lad	pan	tag	bad	sat
lag	sad	tan	bag	rap
lap	sap	tap	nag	bag
man	sat	can	nap	fan

[1] If it is impossible to use the Phonetic Chart, teach the sounds of the following letters: *s, f, h, t, b, r, n, m, c, k, g, d, l, p*, and the short sound of *a*; also *ba, ha, la, ma, na, pa, sa, ra, ta, ca, ga, fa*. When the child has mastered these, build groups upon the blackboard as follows:

ra-n	ha-d	la-d	ma-d	ta-g
ra-p	ha-m	la-g	ma-n	ta-n
ra-t	ha-t	la-p	ma-t	ta-p

1

The Word-and-Sentence Method

The word-and-sentence method may be illustrated from a page taken from the Aldine Primer (figure 9.3). When children read such sentences as "Rain, rain, go away/Boys and girls want to play," they learned the few new words they needed as sight words. Then the sentences on the remainder of the page gave some practice with the same vocabulary. One shortcoming with this attempt to put words in context was that it provided insufficient practice on the new sight vocabulary. Also, the pages provided isolated practice on a few words and did not tell a story so that reading did not have a meaningful purpose.

"I will make a picture of what each word says after you sound it."

Children sound : Teacher draws with simple outlines :

First method				*Second method*	
1 2	3			1	2
m-at	mat			at	mat
r -at	rat			at	rat
h -at	hat			at	hat
c -at	cat			at	cat
s -at	sat			at	sat

Require each child to sound one of these illustrated words before passing to his seat. Those who have gained perception of the blend will do this with little difficulty, as the picture helps in getting the word.

LESSON 26.—BLENDING OF INITIAL CONSONANT

Write family names upon the blackboard : *an, at, ash, op, eet, ilk.* By means of the letter squares, present a succession of initials to be used with them as in the previous exercises, or prefix the same initial to each family name ; as,

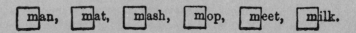

☐man, ☐mat, ☐mash, ☐mop, ☐meet, ☐milk.

Rain, go away.
Boys and girls want to play.
Boys want to jump.
Girls want to run.

The girls want to come with me.
The boys want to go away.

The girls want to play with me.
The boys want to run away.

Go away, boys.
Run away to the tree.

Come with me, girls.
Come and play with me.

The word method was based on the point of view that the word was the smallest thought unit that the child needed to read for meaning. Proponents of the word method believed that a beginning reader need not already know the letters of the alphabet in order to read the whole word. The reader could learn to recognize the word *look* as easily as he or she can learn the letter *k*, for example. With the severely controlled vocabularies in present-day preprimers, a child learns enough words in a relatively short time to read an entire book. The child's memory of visual configurations is sufficient for this beginning.

As early as 1838, Horace Mann recognized the advantage of the whole-word method over the phonics or the spelling approaches to teaching reading. He wrote:

Presenting the children with the alphabet is giving them what they never saw, heard, or thought before. . . . But the printed names of known things (dog, cat, doll) are the signs of sounds which their ears have been accustomed to hear, and their organs of speech to utter. Therefore, a child can learn to name 26 familiar *words* sooner than the unknown, unheard of and unthought of letters of the alphabet.[1]

The Story Method The story method of teaching beginning reading was based on the belief that, from the beginning, children should be exposed to good literature. The authors of these series believed that such material could be written within the vocabulary reach of beginning readers. Free and Treadwell rewrote nine old folk tales,[2] including "The Little Red Hen," "The Gingerbread Boy," and "The Old Woman and Her Pig," so they became the beginning reading lessons.

The teacher would read a complete story from the reader while the children followed along or listened. They learned the story sequence as it was reread so they were able to retell it in detail. Also, as the teacher read, the children joined her in chorus on the many repetitions in such a story. The story was then dissected into episodes, sentences, phrases, and finally words. After a few weeks, the child was expected to be able to read the story and recognize the individual words.

If the study of one story continues for many days, it is questionable whether many children continue to find it interesting.

Such folktales as "The Little Red Hen," "The Billy Goats Gruff," or "The Gingerbread Boy" do provide much repetition of sight words as the sequences in the stories unfold. They are stories that provide conversation parts for dramatization or dialogue reading, and children can illustrate sequence of ideas in pictures.

The story of the gingerbread boy is a classic example of vocabulary practice provided in repetitive episodes as the gingerbread boy runs away. Examine the section of the story as the gingerbread boy came to the fox:

> The gingerbread boy
> came to a fox.
> The gingerbread boy said,
> "Good morning, Fox.
> I am a gingerbread boy,
> I am, I am, I am.
> I ran away
> from the little old woman.
>
> I ran away
> from the little old man.
> I ran away from the hen.
> I ran away from the duck.
> I ran away from the goat.
> I ran away from the dog.
> I can run away from you.
> Here I go."[3]

Basal Readers Basal readers utilize what might be called an *eclectic* approach to reading. Such a method utilizes desirable attributes of all other methods. The child masters a sight vocabulary *first* in order to be able to read stories written with a severely limited number of words. Second, he begins learning about auditory discrimination of sound, which is the beginning of word-attack skills. The effective teacher achieves an appropriate emphasis in each of these jobs. To

Word-Recognition Skills

keep interest in reading at a high level so that children find it exciting to move on to new stories requires that they acquire sufficient phonic and structural analysis skills so they can increase their independence in attacking new words and reading harder material independently. Unless there is attention to getting meaning, reading may degenerate into a word-calling process. However, without word-attack skills, reading can be a word-guessing game.

The child learning a basic sight vocabulary of about fifty words is also beginning phonics training by hearing words that begin the same, hearing rhyming words, and finding pictures of things that begin with the same sound. Whenever words the child is learning have characteristics in common, the teacher points them out. Even in kindergarten, the teacher will help children to see that Mary, Mike, and Michele all have names that begin alike. When three or four words that begin with *d—dog, down, doll, duck—*have been learned, the child is ready to see that they have the same beginning letter and to hear the same sound at the beginning of each.

In summary, the eclectic method attempts to:

1. Emphasize the meaningful nature of reading as the most important factor in reading.

2. Teach an initial vocabulary of sight words learned (memorized) as visual configurations. This is achieved through chart reading, experience stories, labels in the room, blackboard work, workbook lessons, and direct teaching of the words in the first preprimer.

3. Begin systematic teaching of phonic and structural analysis skills simultaneously with the reading of preprimers.

4. Include in the child's reading basal preprimers, experience stories, chart reading, reading labels, and following directions.

5. Encourage children to "write books" of their own that can be bound by the teacher and kept on the reading table.

6. Emphasize the developmental, functional, and recreational nature of a balanced reading program.

Seven Word-Recognition Skills

Word-recognition skills are all those skills and abilities the student must acquire in order to be able to unlock words independently and rapidly while reading. Memorizing a small stock of sight words may work very well for many children to be able to read the first preprimers in a reading series, but extending independent reading requires additional skills. Picture clues are also useful in the beginning and may be effectively used if the reading materials are well illustrated. However, the reader must be prepared to continue reading when there are no illustrations to convey the story theme. There are some other skills, then, that the teacher must develop with boys and girls to give them the independence in word recognition that is imperative for reading success.

Techniques for mastering a sight vocabulary may or may not include extensive study of word patterns or word structure as emphasized by a linguistic approach to reading. Similarly, a linguistic approach emphasizes patterns of speech, systems of phoneme-grapheme relationships, and word order in sentences. These points are mentioned under different subheadings that follow.

The following discussion covers seven word-recognition skills. While the first two are of considerable initial value, they are of little value in helping a student establish good permanent reading habits:

1. Remembering visual cues in a small number of words.
2. Using picture clues for story meaning and word recognition.
3. Building a large stock of common words recognized at sight.
4. Identifying new words by using context clues in the rest of the sentence.
5. Using a sequence of phonic analysis skills.
6. Using structural analysis skills.
7. Learning to use the dictionary for help in both pronunciation and word meaning.

Visual Configuration

Young children are more motivated to read a story in the process of learning to read than they are in learning all the language, word analysis, and word identification that are involved in independent reading. If the teacher can help boys and girls to successfully read a story containing twenty words, and they can then successfully read that story to their mothers, they have reached one of their primary objectives in really reading. The first preprimer in most basal reading series is prepared with a severely controlled vocabulary so that no more than fifteen to thirty words are used in the entire little book. By combining the picture clues that convey the story element and the noun words, visual configuration makes the early reading of such a book easily possible. The child will rely on the look-and-say method for recognizing these few words at this time.

As indicated in the preceding section, it is as easy for the child to learn *look* as a sight word as to remember the letter *k* as the last letter in the word. For a young child, learning the whole word is probably easier since the word is a concept while the letter *k* is not. From a typical first preprimer, as in figure 9.4, one can see that the child can learn these words by their differing configurations without too much confusion. When printed in lowercase characters, the letters provide some cues from ascenders (stems above the line) and descenders (stems below the line). Children can see that *come* and *ride* or *come* and *can* have different configurations. More important for beginners may be the more gross differentiations. *Tomorrow* or *grandmother* may be much easier to remember because of the length of the words compared to *come* or *can*. Also, long words with many ascenders and descenders may be easy to differentiate visually.

Ability to notice the different shapes of words may be of some value to readers if it teaches the habit of observing visual characteristics of new words that need unlocking. It must be pointed out, however, that visual configuration is not helpful to young children with pairs of words like *house* and *horse, these* and *those, tired* and *tried.*

Figure 9.4 Printing in lowercase letters provides children some clues because words have different shapes.

Odille Ousley and David H. Russell, *My Little Red Story Book*, First Preprimer, the Ginn Basic Readers (Boston: Ginn, 1948).

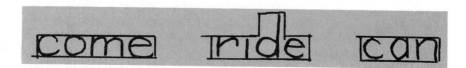

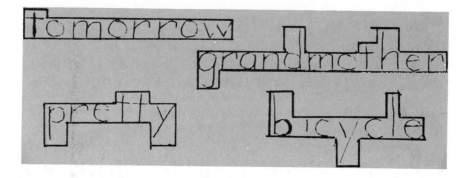

Picture Clues

Picture context can be as helpful to the beginning reader as sentence context is helpful later on. A picture portraying action can help the reader identify verbs in sentence structure. Teachers should utilize pictures more than they now generally do. In the intermediate grades, for example, social studies material will be understood if teachers discuss the pictures contained in the reading as a readiness activity. Questions which the teacher can raise about pictures may help to motivate students to study. The picture in figure 9.5 from the book *Fox and the Fire* by Miska Miles will help a child anticipate meaning if the teacher asks the appropriate questions before the child reads.

Picture dictionaries can be useful in helping children recognize words through the use of picture clues. Young children can learn more from a picture dictionary than to associate a printed word with a picture representing it. They learn that they can find information for themselves by going to the dictionary. Some picture dictionaries available are the following:

Word-Recognition Skills

The fox galloped along beside the fence. He crashed under a clump of blackened brush and leaped to the top rail of the fence.

The dog went racing past.

The fox went on along the fence. The charred wood crumbled between his toes. He jumped down and raced lightly through the vineyard.

Now, far in the distance, he could hear the unhappy yelps of the dog.

Then there was silence.

Back in the barnyard, the dog trotted up, panting loudly, and the chickens scolded softly and settled down again to sleep.

The fox did not return.

A. Y. Bennett, *Picture Dictionary, ABC's Telling Time, Counting Rhymes, Riddles and Finger Plays* (New York: Grosset & Dunlap, 1970).

William A. Jenkins and Andrew Schiller, *My First Picture Dictionary* (Glenview, Ill.: Scott, Foresman, 1975).

William A. Jenkins and Andrew Schiller, *My Second Picture Dictionary* (Glenview, Ill.: Scott, Foresman, 1975).

Marian Monroe, W. Cabell Greet, and Andrew Schiller, *My Pictionary* (Glenview, Ill.: Scott, Foresman, 1975).

Lucille Ogle and Tina Thorn, *The Golden Picture Dictionary: A Beginning Dictionary of More Than 2500 Words* (New York: Western Publ. Co., 1976).

Hale C. Reid and Helen W. Crane, *My Picture Dictionary* (Lexington, Mass.: Ginn, 1977).

Huck Scarry, illus., *My First Picture Dictionary* (New York: Random House, 1978).

Dan Siculan, illus., *Picture Book Dictionary* (Chicago: Rand McNally, 1970).

Developing Sight Vocabulary

The first problem in learning to read is that the learner must *know some words*. As the definition of reading in figure 1.1 shows, word perception is the first element of the four-step process of reading.

Early in the school year in first grade, children generally become word-conscious as a result of various techniques used by the teacher. One of these techniques is labeling many things in the classroom. Each child's name written in manuscript and taped to his or her desk is useful in classroom management, but it is also a way to help children fix the idea that everything has a name that can be written on a label. The labels *door, window, desk, toy box, teacher,* and *reading table* confirm the idea that printed or written words correspond to real objects.

The best way for children to learn a small stock of sight words is by using them to read for meaningful purposes. As soon as they have a small stock of words, there are many interesting little stories and books which they can enjoy. *Using* reading is basic to developing the habit of reading.

By using the most common service words in group and individual experience stories, by labeling objects in the classroom, and by using the vocabularies in the first books to be read, the teacher helps children build a small stock of words they will encounter frequently in their reading.

One of the teacher's most difficult tasks is fitting this phase of beginning to learn a sight vocabulary to the wide range of differences in the reactions of first graders learning the vocabulary. Children who do not have well developed spontaneous oral language abilities should certainly have an extended oral language program before attempting to read. Children who lack the visual motor coordination skills required in writing and in following consecutive lines of print may profit from special readiness teaching to promote these abilities. Children with poor auditory discrimination need to develop these skills. Even among children who possess all these readiness skills, there will be some who

find little interest in learning to read just because the teacher considers it important. Other children will have problems in the affective domain that will influence their adjustment to school. Many children are fearful, others are anxious, some are hostile. These children need understanding and attention to their emotional adjustment before they will successfully retain what the teacher teaches.

Among the children who are not handicapped by the limitations just mentioned, the teacher will find fast learners, adequate learners, and slow learners in the different kinds of tasks in the school curriculum. A few first graders may already possess a sizable sight vocabulary. The teacher must identify these students and encourage their continued growth in reading skills.

<table>
<tr><td>*The High-Frequency Service Words of Reading*</td><td>Stone[4] compiled a list of 100 high-frequency words in children's beginning reading. It is useful for teachers to be able to identify which of the words used in children's stories are the ones the children most need to master. This list is as follows:</td></tr>
</table>

a	dog	I	not	the
after	doll	in	now	then
am	down	into	oh	they
and	father	is	on	this
are	find	it	one	three
at	for	jump	out	to
away	fun	kitten	play	too
baby	funny	laughed	rabbit	two
ball	get	like	ran	up
big	girl	little	red	want
blue	go	look	ride	was
bow-wow	good	make	run	we
boy	good-by	may	said	went
came	had	me	saw	what
can	have	milk	school	where
car	he	morning	see	who
cat	help	mother	she	will
color	here	my	some	with
come	home	new	something	yes
did	house	no	stop	you

The teacher may record the children's dictation as follows:

Tom said, "May I go with you?"
George said, "Where are we going?"
Tom said, "Let's go to the park.
We can play ball in the park."
"OK," said George, "I'd like to go."

It is apparent that several words in the story are high-frequency service words. The following sixteen are on Stone's list:

said	with	are	the	ball
may	you	we	can	in
I	where	to	play	like
go				

Below is another story that might be dictated by first grade boys and girls:

Kee is a Navajo boy.
He lives in a hogan in the canyon.
He lives with his mother and father.
Kee has a pony.
It is a red pony.
He likes to ride his pony.
His pony can run fast.

The following seventeen words are on Stone's list.

is	in	and	red	ride
a	the	father	like	can
boy	with	it	to	run
he	mother			

All of the high-frequency words from the Stone list except nouns are also among the 220 words in the Dolch Basic Sight Vocabulary.[5] It is another list of service words every child must know as sight words in order to read well. The words are those common to three lists containing words used or understood by primary grade children.[6] No nouns are included since nouns change with subject matter and can be illustrated. Dolch also selected ninety-five common nouns as a useful list for teachers.

Below is a child's story about dinosaurs.

This is a dinosaur.
It is an animal *of long, long* ago.
Dinosaurs grew *very* large.
Dinosaurs laid eggs.
Dinosaurs *ate and ate.*
Some dinosaurs *ate only* plants.
Some dinosaurs *ate only* animals.
Maybe *little* animals *ate the* dinosaur eggs.
Maybe *the* land dried *up.*
Maybe *there was not* enough food.
Maybe *the* climate changed *to very cold* winters.
All the dinosaurs died.

There are sixty-three words in this story: thirty-three, or 52 percent, are words from the Dolch Basic Sight Word List. They are italicized.

Preprimers and their accompanying teacher's manuals provide teachers with a sequenced introduction of vocabulary to be learned by the children preparatory to reading a first book with twenty or fewer different words.

Based on 1,000-word samplings from elementary school texts, Dolch found that 70 percent of the words in grade one readers were on the Dolch list; 66 percent in the second grade readers; 65 percent in the third grade readers; 61 percent in the fourth; 59 percent in the fifth and sixth (see table 9.1).

Table 9.1

Percentage of words in school textbooks which are basic sight vocabulary.

From E. W. Dolch, Teaching Primary Reading (Champaign, Ill.: Garrard, 1941), p. 208.

Textbook	No. of Series Used	Grade I	II	III	IV	V	VI
Reading	4	70	66	65	61	59	59
Arithmetic	2			62	63	57	57
Geography	2				60	59	54
History	2				57	53	52

Fry's Instant Words

Fry selected a list of most frequently used words that could be mastered in remedial reading situations to give the child maximum flexibility in reading.[7] By arbitrarily combining and selecting from several word lists, Fry compiled a list of 600 words which he divided into twenty-four groups of twenty-five words each. He attempted to arrange them in graduated difficulty from easiest to hardest to learn. The lists from which Fry selected included the Lorge-Thorndike, Rinsland, and the Dolch service words. His first 300 words will be very useful to all classroom teachers.

The first 100 words of the Fry list include 95 of the Dolch service words; the second 100 include 55 of the Dolch words; and the third 100 include 56. Thus, 206 of the total 220 Dolch service words are among the first 300 Fry instant words. These 300 can serve the same purposes as the comparable list prepared by Dolch.

The following lists are Fry's first hundred instant words, second hundred, and third hundred, each group being arranged in alphabetical order:

First Hundred

a	did	if	on	this
about	do	in	one	three
after	down	is	or	to
again	eat	it	other	two
all	for	just	our	up
an	from	know	out	us
and	get	like	put	very
any	give	little	said	was
are	go	long	see	we
as	good	make	she	were
at	had	man	so	what
be	has	many	some	when
been	have	me	take	which
before	he	much	that	who
boy	her	my	the	will
but	here	new	their	with
by	him	no	them	work
can	his	not	then	would
come	how	of	there	you
day	I	old	they	your

Second Hundred

also	each	left	own	sure
am	ear	let	people	tell
another	end	live	play	than
away	far	look	please	these
back	find	made	present	thing
ball	first	may	pretty	think
because	five	men	ran	too
best	found	more	read	tree
better	four	morning	red	under
big	friend	most	right	until
black	girl	mother	run	upon
book	got	must	saw	use
both	hand	name	say	want
box	high	near	school	way
bring	home	never	seem	where
call	house	next	shall	while
came	into	night	should	white
color	kind	only	soon	wish
could	last	open	stand	why
dear	leave	over	such	year

Third Hundred

along	don't	grow	off	stop
always	door	hat	once	ten
anything	dress	happy	order	thank
around	early	hard	pair	third
ask	eight	head	part	those
ate	every	hear	ride	though
bed	eyes	help	round	today
brown	face	hold	same	took
buy	fall	hope	sat	town
car	fast	hot	second	try
carry	fat	jump	set	turn
clean	fine	keep	seven	walk
close	fire	letter	show	warm
clothes	fly	longer	sing	wash
coat	food	love	sister	water
cold	full	might	sit	woman
cut	funny	money	six	write
didn't	gave	myself	sleep	yellow
does	goes	now	small	yes
dog	green	o'clock	start	yesterday

Techniques for Teaching Sight Words

Most reading series provide children the opportunity to discover new words for themselves if they have already learned the necessary skills to do so. For example, using sight words already known, the child can be shown how to make the following new words.

From the *T* in *Tom* and the *oy* in *boy*, make the new word *toy*.

From the *fl* in *fly* and the *ing* in *sing*, make *fling*.

From the *sh* in *show* and the *ore* in *tore*, make *shore*.

From the *tr* in *tree* and the *end* in *send*, make *trend*.

From the *ch* in *children* and the *ance* in *dance*, make *chance*.

The teacher can use language like the following to give children practice.

Take *b* away from *boy*, put in *t* and you have *toy*.

Take *s* away from *sing*, put in *fl* and you have *fling*.

Take *t* away from *tore*, put in *sh* and you have *shore*.

The Reading for Meaning Series[8] of basal readers provides the teacher with a number of models for reference in planning word recognition exercises:

1. Recognizing capital and small letters: Are *print* and *Print* the same?

2. Recognizing long vowel sounds: Does *idea* begin with the same sound as *island* and *idle?*

3. Discriminating between beginning sounds: Do *ice, iris, make,* and *isle* all begin with the same sound?

4. Hearing consonant clusters at the beginnings of words: Put *br* and the word *bridge* on the board; say a list of words—*brown, brook, could, letter, brave*—and ask the class to identify the *br* words.

5. Discovering new words: From the word *say* take away *s*, put in *pr* and make *pray*.

6. Substituting final sounds: Take *d* away from *bud*, put in *t* and make *but;* put in *n* and make *bun;* put in *s* and make *bus.*

Some Problems That May Be Encountered

Some boys and girls have much difficulty with the abstract service words or often confuse certain pairs of words.

Since many structure words in sentence building are abstract and very difficult to illustrate visually, it is imperative that children learn them early in reading. Such words as *of, the, on, since,* and *because* were presented as "markers" in chapter 3. They are necessary sight words for early meaningful reading.

Children often confuse words like *then* and *when, where* and *there, what* and *that.* The question words *which, what, where, when,* and *why* also cause some children difficulty. These words appear over and over in reading at the second grade level, so teachers should use whatever devices they have found successful to help children distinguish them.

Exercises can be prepared by the teacher to give the child practice reading a troublesome word in context in sentences, having been told that the word will be used; practice reading sentences in which the correct word must be supplied; and, later, practice reading sentences in which the word appears randomly as well as words with which it is often confused.

A child who has much difficulty confusing *then* and *when* might first complete exercises that use only one of these words; then complete exercises that use only the other one; and finally complete exercises in which a choice between the two words must be made. Teachers can prepare sentence exercises like those shown in figure 9.6.

Minimal Pairs   Hearing differences in words that sound almost alike is another difficulty with which teachers must help some boys and girls. Failing to discriminate the proper vowel sound within a word or consonant sound at the end of a word may cause a child to misunderstand or be misunderstood. Discriminating minimal pairs is discussed in chapter 3. Minimal pairs are word pairs that sound exactly alike except for one phoneme that differs. For example, *look* and *book* constitute a minimal pair because they differ only in initial consonant sound. However, the minimal pairs that present difficulty are likely to involve vowel or final consonant or consonant cluster differences.

While these difficulties in perceiving differences in sound are very common with children learning English as a second language, they are by no means limited to them. Common errors are final *g* and *k* confusion, as in *pig* and *pick;* *th* and *f* as in *death* and *deaf;* *s* and *z* as in *rice* and *rise;* *f* and *v* as in *leaf* and *leave.* Vowels such as *ee* and *i* as in *sheep* and *ship;* and *a* and *e* as in *age* and *edge* also cause difficulty.

A short list of minimal pairs follows:

pi*g*—pi*ck*	du*g*—du*ck*	wrea*th*—ree*f*
be*t*—be*d*	*c*old—*g*old	bu*zz*—bu*s*
*p*each—*b*each	*r*ope—*r*obe	play*s*—pla*ce*
cu*p*—cu*b*	p*oo*l—p*u*ll	ri*se*—ri*ce*
ca*p*—ca*b*	li*fe*—li*ve*	boa*t*—bo*th*
lea*f*—lea*ve*	sh*ee*p—sh*i*p	*th*ick—*t*ick
toe*s*—toa*st*	b*i*t—b*ea*t	*p*a*i*n—*p*en
*a*ge—*e*dge	dea*th*—dea*f*	

In teaching phonic analysis skills, teachers will provide practice in the auditory discrimination of such word pairs.

Figure 9.6 Practice for overcoming "when-then" confusion.

1. Write *then* in the blank and read the sentence.
   a. Put the book on the table, _____ bring me your paper.
   b. What will you do _____ ?
   c. _____ the teacher told us a story.

2. Write *when* in the blank and read the sentence.
   a. _____ is Bill coming home?
   b. _____ will it be time to go?
   c. Tell me _____ you are ready to go.

3. Read the sentence. Decide whether *when* or *then* belongs in the blank. Write in the correct word:
   a. I don't know _____ he is coming.
   b. He did his work; _____ he went home.
   c. The flowers will be blooming _____ .
   d. Apples are ripe _____ they are red.

Word-Recognition Skills

Word perception and pronunciation is the first step in the reading process. If the process stops with word calling, then reading as defined in chapter 1 does not take place. For hard-of-hearing and deaf children, modes of learning must maximize other avenues than auditory.

The next step is to use meaning or conceptual skills to relate what is being read to what is already known. This may be thought of as comprehension of the idea. It is depicted in figure 1.1 as the second step in the four-step process of reading.

The reader constructs a concept or a meaning when the last word in a sentence is perceived:

bank

John played the drums in the band

bang

bond

The reader first perceives that the four-letter word *is* ban*d* and not ban*k* or ban*g* or b*ond*. Step one requires the proper *pronunciation* to match the graphic form of *band*.

At the *comprehension* level, the reader must, in this case, know what a *band* is. However, this word has more than one meaning. Before moving to step three in the reading process to *react* to the sentence as a unit, the reader must understand the use of the word *band* in the sentence and the use of all the words in the sentence as they relate to the meaning stored in the concept *band*.

This comprehension of words in any context necessitates a great storehouse of word meanings readily available to the reader. Children must be taught many ways of arriving at adequate meanings. Techniques for doing so will be explored in greater depth in later chapters, but at the elementary level they include teaching multiple meanings of common words, synonyms, homonyms, antonyms, perceiving word relationships in the sentence, and choosing the best dictionary definition. At the same time, a linguistic approach to reading points out the importance of word order in an English sentence, which is a further context clue.

Multiple Meanings of Common Words

The printed form of the word *run* represents many different words in our language. Horn illustrated:[9]

The disease has *run* its course.	To *run* a risk.
The fence *runs* east and west.	To *run* up a bill.
To *run* to seed.	To *run* across a friend.
To *run* a garage.	To knock a home *run*.
To *run* a splinter in a finger.	A *run* on a bank.
To *run* out of money.	The common *run* of persons.
To *run* to ruin.	

Note the elementary uses of *down:*

I will walk *down* the stairs.
Jack likes to sleep under a *down* comforter.
The boy went *down* town.
The struggling swimmer went *down* for the third time.
The boxer was *down* for the count.
Jack fell *down.*
Elevators go up and *down.*

Teachers' guides and preparatory books provide many exercises to help children understand the variant meanings of common words by asking them to match meanings, as in the following exercise:

Directions: Read the sentences in group 1. Then find the sentence in group 2 that uses the word in italics in a similar way. Put the appropriate matching letter on the line in front of the sentence.

Group 1
a. Did you pay the gas *bill?*
b. Uncle *Bill* came to see us today.
c. Did you *bill* them for the medicine?
d. The bird's *bill* was broken.

Group 2
_____ The boy paid the grocery *bill* today.
_____ The chicken pulled the worm out with his *bill.*
_____ Will *Bill* go to school tomorrow?
_____ He *billed* us for the things we bought today.

Comparing and Contrasting Word Meanings

The teacher can provide exercises to develop children's abilities in giving synonyms, antonyms, or deciding whether words presented in pairs are alike or opposite in meaning.

1. Exercises giving synonyms:

    We followed a winding _____ . (path, trail, road)
    We brought water in a _____ . (bucket, pail, container)
    Snow sometimes _____ the trail. (hid, covered, concealed)

2. Exercises identifying antonyms:

    John went *up* the hill. I wanted to go _____ .
    That rose was *rare* around here. It is getting more _____ .
    The light was *red;* it changed to _____ .
    He was *tired* last night but this morning he seemed _____ .

3. Exercises deciding whether words are synonyms or antonyms. For the child the instructions will read: "Write *s* on the line if the two words mean the same; write *o* if the meanings are opposite."

large	small	o
huge	gigantic	s
conceal	hide	s
common	rare	o
try	attempt	s

Word-Recognition Skills

4. Worksheet exercises could ask the child to choose the correct spelling from among groups of homophones to fit a particular context.

scent	to	their	pear	sew
cent	two	there	pair	sow
sent	too	they're	pare	so
sight	right	rowed	vane	rain
site	rite	road	vein	reign
cite	write	rode	vain	rein

5. Perceiving relationships between/among words. Use the words in each group in *one* sentence.

harvest, sale, cotton
teacher, student, principal
seed, irrigation ditches, planting

6. Choosing the best meaning in a given context. The child is asked to read the definitions and match the appropriate one with each example below:

Scale: 1. Instrument for weighing
2. Covering of the fish
3. Size represented on a map

_____a. The *scale* used was 1 mile equals 1 inch.
_____b. They removed the *scales* with sharp knives.
_____c. They weighed the fish on the *scale*.

Phonic Analysis

Many phonic generalizations have been taught in an effort to help boys and girls anticipate pronunciation in new situations. However, some word-count studies have indicated less than complete effectiveness in selected generalizations taught. Those considered most useful are presented. However, if one hopes that phonics will be the child's answer to word recognition, the poem "Our Queer Language" shows some of the difficulties and inconsistencies in grapheme-phoneme relationships in the vocabulary to be mastered.

Our Queer Language

When the English Tongue we speak
Why is "break" not rhymed with "freak"?
Will you tell me why it's true
We say "sew" and likewise "few"?
And the maker of the verse
Cannot cap his "horse" with "worse"
"Beard" sounds not the same as "heard"
"Cord" is different from "word"
Cow is "cow" but low is "low"
"Shoe" is never rhymed with "foe"
Think of "hose" and "dose" and "lose"
And think of "goose" and not of "choose"
"Doll" and "roll," "home" and "some"
And since "pay" is rhymed with "say"
Why not "paid" with "said" I pray?
"Mould" is not pronounced like "could"
Wherefore "done" but "gone" and "lone"
Is there any reason known?
And in short it seems to me
Sounds and letters disagree.

Source unknown.

Smith describes how phonics instruction has been emphasized and deemphasized in cycles through the past two centuries.[10] The misplaced heavy emphasis on phonics in learning to read has already been discussed.

With the new emphasis on reading for meaning in the mid-thirties and concomitant attention to silent reading exercises to emphasize understanding, the teaching of phonics was deemphasized to the point of neglect. Of course, the pendulum has swung back now so that *phonics is being taught today*. The great majority of teachers are teaching phonic and structural analysis skills. Today teachers use a number of methods to reinforce the phonic skills taught—context clues, analyzing word structure, checking for meaning, and using the dictionary.

Phonic skills are now taught to children with a different emphasis. They are taught sequentially throughout the reading program and with spaced reviews. The sequence is designed to develop all the necessary abilities to unlock new words. Phonic skills are introduced gradually in reading series as an integral part of the complete set of techniques in the eclectic approach. This approach was identified and developed by Gates as the intrinsic approach to teaching phonics. Teaching phonics functionally in relation to the reading children are doing and as a way of attacking difficulties as they arise is a defensible practice.

Beginning in the kindergarten, children have a great deal of informal practice in auditory discrimination. (1) They hear how each other's first names begin, as in Carl, Carolyn, Kate, and Karen. (2) They hear Mother Goose rhymes, as in "Jack and *Jill* went up the *hill*." (3) They hear the teacher call attention to words used in their own conversations, as when one child says, *"home, house, and hospital,"* and the teacher points out that all begin with *h,* or that a string of words rhyme, as in *at, bat, cat, dat, gat, lat.*

The phonic elements to be taught include:

1. The sounds of the single consonant letters. (*Q, X, Y,* and *Z* will not be needed early in the program.)

2. The consonant cluster sounds in both initial and final positions in words:

   Initial position: s*m*art, s*k*ill, s*t*ick, *tr*ain, s*w*eep, s*tr*ing.
   Final position: cha*sm*, whi*sk*, ta*sk*, mou*nds*, fore*sts*, mea*sles*.

3. The consonant digraphs: *ch, sh, th, wh* in initial and final positions in words:

   Initial position: *ch*eck, *sh*all, *th*ink, *wh*en.
   Final position: bu*nch*, wa*sh*, ba*th*.

4. The short and the long sounds of the vowels:

   Short vowel words: b*a*g, b*e*g, b*i*g, b*o*g, b*u*g.
   Long vowel words: m*a*te, m*e*te, m*i*te, b*o*ne, m*u*te.

5. The consonant-vowel-consonant (CVC) generalization:

   The vowel in a closed syllable usually has its short sound, as in f*i*n ish, c*a*n dor, l*o*t tery, b*u*t ter, g*e*t ting.

6. The vowel digraphs: *ay, ai, au, ee, ea, ei, eu, ew, ie, oa, oo, ow.*

7. The vowel diphthongs: *oi, oy, ou, ow.*

8. In a syllable ending in a vowel, the vowel is usually long, *he, she.* (This is the consonant-vowel [CV] generalization.)

9. In a short word with a middle vowel and ending with *e,* usually the *e* is silent and the middle vowel is long. (This is the CVCV generalization.)

10. The schwa sound: (ə), as in *a*bout, penc*i*l. It occurs only in unstressed syllables. The following list of words containing the schwa are taken from Cordts:[11]

    | ə bout | fath ə r | Sat ə rn | cupb ə rd |
    | at ə m | doct ə r | tap ə r | surg ə n |
    | circ ə s | doll ə r | fash ə n | tort ə s |

11. The clues to silent letters in words. Silent consonants designate those letters in syllables that are not sounded when the syllable is spoken. Cordts gave the following generalizations:[12]

The letter *b* is silent after *m* and before *t:* debt, doubt, climb, comb.

The letter *g* is silent before *m* and *n:* gnat, gnu, sign, diaphragm.

The letter *h* may be silent before any vowel or when preceded by *r:* rhyme, rhinoceros, honest, herb.

The letters *gh* are silent after *a, i,* or *o:* high, eight, bought, caught.

The letter *k* is silent before *n:* knock, know, knife, knee.

The letter *l* is silent before *k, d,* or *m:* talk, would, calm, salmon.

The letter *p* is silent before *s, t,* or *n:* psalm, pneumonia, ptomaine.

The letter *t* following *s* or *f:* listen, often, thistle, soften.

The letter *w* before *r:* wrist, write, wren, wrong.

12. Several consonant sounds have more than one sound:

The hard sound of *g*, when *g* is followed by *a, o,* or *u*.

The soft sound of *g*, when *g* is followed by *e, i,* or *y*.

The hard sound of *c*, when *c* is followed by *a, o,* or *u*.

The soft sound of *c*, when *c* is followed by *e, i,* or *y*.

The *s* sound as *z* in *fuse; sh* in *sugar;* and *zh* in *treasure*.

The *x* sound as *ks* in box; *gz* in *exact;* and *z* in *xylophone, Xerxes*.

13. Syllabic consonants. There are many words in which there is no vowel in the unaccented syllable. The consonants *l, n,* and *m* sometimes function as syllables by themselves. In the word *little, lit* forms one sounded syllable and the letter *l* forms the other. In the word *garden, gard* forms one sounded syllable and the letter *n* forms the other. In the word *rhythm, rhyth* forms the first sounded syllable and the letter *m* forms the other. Because *l, m,* and *n* are capable of forming a syllable by themselves, they are known as syllabic consonants.

Figure 9.7 Many teachers help boys and girls learn letters by collecting pictures of things whose names begin with the same letter. These pictures were used for the ''B'' page in a first grade book of sounds.

Word-Recognition Skills

There are many examples in English words where phoneme-grapheme relationships are irregular or inconsistent. However, when there are few examples in children's work, it seems best not to teach an element, or its exceptions, until needed. Examples include *ph* as *f; qu* always sounds like *kw;* the *s* is silent in *isle, aisle,* and *island.*

The pronunciation of suffixes beginning with *t,* as in *tion, tious, tial,* must also be taught as a special sound of *sh* for the letter *t.*

By second grade the child has met at least six spellings for long *a* (ā)—p*a*per, *a*te, pl*a*y, pr*ai*se, f*ai*l, gr*ea*t—and eight different sounds spelled by *ea*—gr*ea*t, br*ea*d, w*ea*r, *ea*t, h*ea*rt, s*ea*rch, b*ea*uty, bur*ea*u.

Cordts found forty-seven different sound-letter associations for the letter *a* in words actually occurring in first, second, and third readers.[13]

Fifty years ago Horn raised the question whether English spelling is so unphonetic as to make teaching phonic generalizations in the primary grades impractical.[14]

English spellings often seem irregular—even irrational—and are therefore difficult to teach. The seeming lack of correspondence between the sounds and the spellings of the English language is a product of the history of the language. The spelling of *knight* is an example. It fully corresponded to speech

at the time the *k* was pronounced and the *gh* represented a phoneme of English which has since gone out of the language.

Most phonic generalizations that have been developed take into account only surface details, not underlying historical facts about the language. They have limited scope, therefore.

The value of teaching rules for phonic and structural analysis is open to serious question if some of the first words the child reads and tries to apply the rule to happen to be exceptions. For example, the child may learn that "when two vowels go walking" the first one has its long sound—but then must learn to cope with *bread* and *break* about as soon as with *team* and *cream*.

Oaks[15] in 1952 found that vowel situations requiring explanation appear as early as the primer in basal readers.

Clymer[16] in 1963 found that many generalizations being taught had limited value and that teachers must teach many exceptions to most generalizations being taught. Of forty-five generalizations which he found in primary grade teachers' manuals for basal readers, when checked against all the words in a composite word list, the percent of utility was too low to justify teaching many of them. Using 75 percent as an arbitrary criterion value of usefulness, he found only eighteen generalizations worth teaching.

Burrows and Lourie[17] found that teachers might look for other ways to pronounce double vowels than to try to use the "when two vowels go walking" generalization.

Emans[18] studied the applicability of Clymer's generalizations in grades four and above and found that a few of Clymer's generalizations had less applicability above fourth grade and that there were a few not included by Clymer that had more applicability.

Bailey[19] evaluated the utility of Clymer's forty-five generalizations and found some of them clearly stated and especially useful. She found some less useful, and others difficult to interpret.

Burmeister[20] sifted results from the studies of Oaks, Clymer, Fry,[21] Bailey, Emans, and Winkley, combined them with her own data, and developed a list of especially useful generalizations. The following are selected from that list:

The behavior of consonants:

When *c* and *h* are next to each other, they make only one sound.

Ch is usually pronounced as it is in mu*ch*, *ch*eck; not like *sh*.

When *c* or *g* is followed by *e, i,* or *y,* the soft sound is likely to be heard; otherwise they will have a hard sound.

When *ght* is seen in a word, *gh* is silent.

When a word begins with *kn,* the *k* is silent.

When a word begins with *wr,* the *w* is silent.

When two of the same consonants are side by side, only one is heard.

When a word ends in *ck,* it has the same last sound as in *look.*

The behavior of vowels:

If the only vowel is at the end of a one-syllable word, the letter usually has its long sound.

The *r* gives the preceding vowel a sound that is neither long nor short.

When the letters *oa* are together in a word, *o* gives its long sound and *a* is silent.

Words having double *e* usually have the long *e* sound.

When *y* is the final letter in a word, it usually has a vowel sound.

When *a* is followed by *r* and final *e,* we expect to hear the sound heard in *care.*

Rationale for Vowel Spellings

It is not possible to offer a helpful and simple set of generalizations for the spelling-sound correspondences of the five English vowel graphemes. Generally, the spelling-sound relationships of the vowel letters show little regularity. Nevertheless, there are some patterns that teachers of reading, especially in the early elementary grades, will find helpful.

1. The one-syllable word ending in a consonant—the closed syllable, CVC—will contain a vowel that usually uses its short sound; for example: c*a*n, m*e*n, f*i*n, c*o*t, b*u*t, c*a*ndle, m*e*ntion, f*i*nishing, c*o*ttage, b*u*tterfly.

The many three-letter words fitting the pattern below suggest that this is a very important generalization for boys and girls to learn early in the reading program:

bad	bed	bid		bud
bag	beg	big	bog	bug
bat	bet	bit		but
		dig	dog	dug
Dan	den	din	don	dun
fan	fen	fin		fun
ham	hem	him		hum
hat		hit	hot	hut
lad	led	lid		
mad		mid		mud
mat	met	mit		
	net	nit	not	nut
pan	pen	pin		pun
pat	pet	pit	pot	put
	red	rid	rod	
sat	set	sit		
tan	ten	tin		
tap		tip	top	

2. The vowel followed by a consonant followed by final *e* (V + C + e) usually has its long sound, c*a*ne, m*e*te, f*i*ne, r*o*te, m*u*te.

   The teacher may teach many short sounds of the vowels first. However, children do learn from contrasting too. It may be helpful for some children to contrast *not* and *note, hat* and *hate,* etc. by listening to the separate sounds of the vowels as they look at both words together. A short list of common pairs in this pattern are given below:

tap	tape	plan	plane	mop	mope	rid	ride
can	cane	bad	bade			dim	dime
pan	pane	fat	fate	pin	pine	fin	fine
man	mane			slid	slide	rip	ripe
hat	hate	not	note	win	wine	kit	kite
mad	made	hop	hope	bit	bite	hid	hide

3. The vowel may retain its long sound if the vowel is followed by a consonant followed by another vowel within the word:

   c*a*nine   l*a*dle   p*i*lot   m*e*ter   p*o*tent   m*u*sic

   The vowel sound is short if the vowel is followed by a consonant cluster (*dg, x*) or by geminate consonants (*dd, gg, nn*). Geminate means occurring in pairs—as twin consonants, ca*bb*age, ru*bb*ed, and se*tt*ing.

   ba*dg*e   sa*dd*le   e*x*it   ante*nn*a   ta*x*i   co*gn*ate

4. The long vowel sound in V + C + e changes to a short sound in words that add syllables like *ic* or *ity* or when geminate consonants (twin consonants) appear:

sane	sanity	later	latter
mete	netting	caning	canning
cone	conic	hoping	hopping
rose	roster	motel	mottle
site	sitting	super	supper
induce	induction	biting	bitter
		tubing	tubbing

5. The V + C + e pattern may also produce long vowel sounds in poly-syllabic words:

file	domicile	late	matriculate	size	nationalize
fume	resume	gene	gangrene	robe	microbe

6. Boys and girls need direct teaching of specific application for much of their beginning work with double vowels in one-syllable words. Double *e* producing long *e* and *oa* producing long *o* will be consistent in the words in the elementary school.[22] But *ea* may be long *e* in *lean* and *beat*, short *e* in *bread*, and long *a* in *break*. The double vowel *oo* uses one of its sounds in *book* and the other in *moon*. *Ou* and *aw* sound alike in a few words but have variant sounds in others.

Structural Analysis

Structural analysis is the means by which the parts of a word which form meaning units or pronunciation units within the word are identified. Structural analysis includes recognizing the root word as a meaning unit, identification of compound words, prefixes and suffixes, and generalizations about syllabication. Very important in this task is appreciating the influence of stress on syllables as spoken.

Dictionaries usually attempt to retain the base word or the root as nearly as possible in its original form when showing how words can be divided at the end of a line of print. In other words, dictionaries show primarily how the written, not the spoken, word is divided. Cordts says:[23]

The syllabication of the spoken word may or may not coincide with the way the word is divided when the word is written. The simple word *selfish* offers an example. When writing the word, it is correctly divided as *self'ish*, but the spoken word is *sel'fish*.

Inflectional Variants

1. Possessive forms: John's, the man's.

2. Plural nouns with *s* or *es:* apples, cups, boxes, bananas.

3. Verbs changed by:

   s or *es:* walks, finishes, takes, jumps
   d or *ed:* walked, finished, hoped, filed
   ing: walking, finishing, hoping, filing
   n or *en:* taken, given, loosen, tighten

4. Comparison using *er* and *est:*

   faster, fastest, taller, tallest.

5. Dropping final *e:*

hope	hoping	tape	taping
bare	baring	mope	moping
cane	caning	stare	staring
mate	mating	pine	pining

6. Doubling final consonant:

hop	hopping	tap	tapping
bar	barring	mop	mopping
can	canning	star	starring
mat	matting	pin	pinning

7. Changing *y* to *i:*

happy happiest	crazy craziest	pretty prettiest

8. Changing *f* to *v:*

half halving	shelf shelving	calf calving

Independent Parts of Compound Words

The parts of compound words are, by definition, complete words by themselves:

something	became	broadcloth
grandmother	lifelike	newcomers
airplane	outlaw	wanderlust

Roots, Prefixes, and Suffixes

Each italicized root has both a prefix and a suffix:

en *camp* ment   dis *approv* ing   in *adequate* ly

Fifteen common prefixes constitute the majority of prefixes used in writing for elementary school children.[24] It is important that they be taught meaningfully to boys and girls in the fifth and sixth grades. Boys and girls need to learn that just because these letters appear at the beginning of a word is not a definite indication that they represent a prefix. Learning the meanings and selecting examples is a suitable exercise for sixth graders who perform at grade level. In the lists below, the most common meaning of the prefix or suffix is given and one or two examples:

Prefix	Meaning	Examples
ab	from	abnormal
ad	to	admit, adhere
be	by	bedecked
com	with, together	compact, commiserate
de	reversal	deduct, depose
dis	reversal	disappear, disengage
en	in	enjoy
ex	out	exhale, export
in	inside	inhabit, inhibit
in	not	incorrect, inadequate
pre	before	preview, prediction
pro	for, forward	propel, pronoun
re	again	renovate, reconsider
sub	under	submarine, subjugate
un	not	unhappy, uncommon

Suffix	Meaning	Examples
able	having the potential	suitable
al	having the property of	magical, national
ance	act, process, or fact of being, quality, state of	disappearance
ant	promoting an action	assistant, observant
ary	belonging to, or connected with	legendary, momentary
en	consisting of, or cause to be	wooden, sweeten
ful	full of or characterized by	sorrowful, healthful
hood	a state or condition of	manhood, falsehood
ion	result of an act or process	expression, perfection
less	without	needless, regardless
ly	in the manner of	gladly

Children should be asked to complete exercises like the following:

Choose *less, like, ful, ness,* or *ly* as a suffix to make the word being defined:

In a cruel manner _____(*cruelly*)
Without hope _____(*hopeless*)
Full of being good _____(*goodness*)
Like a bird _____(*birdlike*)
Full of peace _____(*peaceful*)

Greek and Latin Combining Forms

Making charts like the following is helpful to boys and girls:

Combining Forms			Literal Meanings		
bio	+	logy	life	+	science of
geo	+	graphy	earth	+	to write about
thermo	+	meter	heat	+	to measure
tele	+	scope	far away	+	to view

Exercises to Develop Understanding of Structural Analysis

Exercises like the following are useful:

Copy the word that is italicized. Write down what it means.

Everyone needs a *friend.*
I lost my *friend's* address.
He is a *friendly* person.
Jim acts *friendlier* than Ted.
Ed is sometimes *unfriendly.*
I hope I never am *friendless.*
I admire his *friendliness.*
I need your *friendship.*
The Red Cross will *befriend* the flood-stricken people.[25]

The teacher or the students can make charts like the following:

Building inflected and derived forms with root words:

	come				cross	
	come	s		a	cross	
	com	ing			cross	es
be	come				cross	ed
be	com	ing			cross	ing
	come	ly		un	cross	
in	come				cross	section
wel	come				cross	country
	come	back		double	cross	
over	come			hot	cross	buns
					cross	wise
					cross	eye
					cross	roads
				criss	cross	

Syllables are classified as open or closed and as accented or unaccented. Open syllables are those that end with a vowel sound; closed syllables are those that end with a consonant sound.

Open Syllables		**Closed Syllables**	
se′	cret	sun′	set
po′	nies	mon′	key
ti′	ger	but′	ter
sto′	ries	rain′	bow
pota′	to	dif′	ferent
fa′	mous	cir′	cle

Rules for Syllabication

Students must understand that the rules of syllabication which indicate how a written or printed word may be broken are not applicable to spoken words. The following rules are the conventions followed by most publishers.

1. When there are two consonants between two vowels in a polysyllabic word, the syllables will divide between the two consonants unless the first vowel has its long sound. VCCV indicates letter order: vowel-consonant-consonant-vowel in words.

VCCV Words	**VCCV Words with the First Vowel Sound Long**
mon·key	se·cret
ob·li·gate	mi·crobe
cir·cum·fer·ence	
per·fect	
mis·take	

2. When there are twin consonants between the separated vowel sounds, the word is divided between the consonants:

but·ter	lad·der	skim·ming
cab·bage	cop·per	com·mon
sum·mer	cot·tage	bal·loon

3. When a word is composed of two complete words—that is, a compound word—it is first divided between the two words that make up the compound word:

any·one	grand·mother	bird·house
some·where	sun·set	school·yard
any·thing	pop·overs	air·plane
who·ever	cow·boy	tooth·brush

4. Syllables usually do not break between consonant cluster letters or special two-letter combinations:

chil·*dren*	an·*gry*	leath·*er*	broth·*er*

5. When there is one consonant between two vowels, the consonant usually goes with the next syllable if the preceding vowel has its long sound, and with the preceding syllable if the vowel has its short sound or some other sound (VCV indicates letter order—vowel-consonant-vowel in words):

VCV Words, Consonant Begins Second Syllable		VCV Words, Consonant Remains with Preceding Syllable		
fa·tal	to·tal	shiv·er	tax·i	per·il
pa·per	a·muse	nov·el	ex·ert	rock·ets
de·lay	a·corn	trav·el	mim·ic	mon·ey
o·ver	po·lite	sol·id	ban·ish	fath·er
be·gin	ti·ger	rap·id	rob·in	sec·ond
sa·ble	gro·cer		cour·age	com·et
pro·vide	be·tween			

In most of these examples, if the first syllable retains the long vowel sound, the consonant begins the second syllable. Also, if the consonant between the two vowels is either *x* or *v,* this letter often remains with the preceding vowel to form a syllable.

6. When two adjacent vowels in a word form separate syllables, the word is divided between the two vowels. For example, *ru·in, gi·ant, fu·el, Su·ez, cre·ate, li·on, po·etry.*

It is not expected that boys and girls will attempt to learn rules of syllabication until they have derived the generalization based on seeing a large number of words syllabicated in each of the various ways provided by these rules.

Little words in big ones. Children cannot generalize about finding little words in big words:

At is not *at* in attack, dated, eat, fatal, fathom, material, patriot, path, patrol, station, water, watch.[26]
Up is not *up* in pupil, puppet, rupee, supervisor, superman, cupid, cupola, duplicate, duplex.

Stress   Teachers need to give some consideration to stress in pronunciation. Some general statements are possible about the use of stress even though there are few widely applicable rules that can be taught.

In a two-syllable word, one syllable is usually stressed more than the other. In many polysyllabic words, one syllable gets a primary emphasis or stress and another gets a secondary stress. Boys and girls will best learn about stress by generalizing from the examples in which they apply stress to make the intonation and rhythm of their spoken language communicate properly. A vowel grapheme usually has a distinctive sound only when in an accented syllable. It usually has the schwa sound (e) when in an unaccented syllable.

In a two-syllable word in which the first syllable is *not a prefix*, the stress usually falls on the first syllable. For example, *res'cue, stu'pid, fun'ny.*

In a polysyllabic word with a root and prefixes and suffixes, the root of the word is often stressed: *en camp' ment, im prove' ment, sur round' ing.*

In a polysyllabic word ending in *tion, cion, sion, tious, cious*, stress usually falls on the next to the last syllable: pre ven' tion, grav i ta' tion, pre ten' tious, un con' scious.

Cordts recommends three generalizations about placing stress in polysyllabic words but emphasizes that all such generalizations will have exceptions:[27]

1. Two-syllable words that are used as both nouns and verbs will likely be stressed on the first syllable as nouns and on the last syllable as verbs: *per' fume* is a noun; *per fume'* is a verb.

Nouns	Verbs
rec' ord	re·cord'
prog' ress	pro·gress'
pro' test	pro·test'
sur' vey	sur·vey'
per' mit	per·mit'
in'sult	in·sult'
con' flict	con·flict'

2. Words having three or more syllables are apt to have both a primary stress (') and a secondary stress ("), as in *con" sti tu' tion, mul" ti pli ca' tion.*

3. In counting, the first syllable of a number name is stressed, but in saying the numbers, both syllables are accented. One counts *fif' teen, six' teen, sev' en·teen, eigh' teen;* but one says *fif' teen', six' teen', sev' en·teen'.*

There are many words which have an accented syllable in which the vowel sound changes to an unaccented sound—that is, the schwa—when another form of the word is used:

Vowel Sound	Schwa Sound
at' om	ə·tom' ic
cor' al	kər·ral'
up' per	əp·on'
par' ti·cle	pər·tik' yə·lər

Winkley attempted to find out whether stress generalizations should be taught.[28] Using the eighteen stress generalizations listed by Gray,[29] Winkley prepared a test requiring students in the intermediate grades to underline the stressed syllables, select the correct vowel sound for the stressed syllable, and choose the correct meaning of the word. As a result of her testing, she concluded that the following generalizations should be taught in grades four to six:

1. When there is no other clue in a two-syllable word, the stress is usually on the first syllable. Examples: *ba'sic, pro'gram.*

2. In inflected or derived forms of words, the primary stress usually falls on or within the root word. Examples: *box'es, untie'.*

3. If *de-, re-, be-, ex-, in-,* or *a-* is the first syllable of a word, it is usually unstressed. Examples: *delay', explore'.*

4. Two vowel letters together in the last syllable of a word may be a clue to a stressed final syllable. Examples: *com·plain', con·ceal'.*

5. When there are two like consonant letters within a word, the syllable before the double consonants is usually stressed. Examples: *be·gin'ner, let'ter.*

6. The primary stress usually occurs on the syllable before the suffixes *-ion, -ity, -ic, -ian, -ial,* or *-ious,* and on the second syllable before the suffix *-ate.* Examples: *af·fec·ta'tion, dif·fer·en'tiate.*

7. In words of three or more syllables, one of the first two syllables is usually stressed. Examples: *ac'ci·dent, de·ter'mine.*

Use of the Dictionary

To find words needed, determine proper pronunciation of words and establish meanings appropriate to the context in which the word is being used, every child must achieve proficiency in use of the dictionary. Third grade boys and girls who read at or above grade level should be developing some of the dictionary skills outlined in this section. Much time will be devoted to teaching dictionary skills in both fourth and fifth grade because all children will not acquire the skills when they are taught, and the teacher must provide for much reteaching and review.

The skills needed for dictionary usage have been classified as location, pronunciation, and meaning skills (see table 9.2).

In order to find words quickly in the dictionary, children need to know how entries are made and how different forms of a word are handled in the dictionary. If a child is looking for *reporting* and there is no entry for this word, the child must know that *reporting* is derived from *report* and that the word must be looked for under the *report* entry.

A number of dictionaries are designed for elementary school children. Classrooms should have sufficient copies of a good one so that they are easily accessible to each child. This is necessary in order to develop the dictionary habit.

A few of the elementary school dictionaries of recent copyright are:

Scott Foresman Beginning Dictionary. E. L. Thorndike/Clarence L. Barnhart. Glenview, Ill.: Scott, Foresman, 1979.
Scott Foresman Intermediate Dictionary. Clarence L. Barnhart, ed. Glenview, Ill.: Scott, Foresman, 1978.
The HBJ School Dictionary. New York: Harcourt Brace Jovanovich, 1977.
Ginn Intermediate Dictionary. Lexington, Mass.: Ginn, 1977.

Table 9.2 Location, pronunciation, and meaning skills needed by boys and girls in the elementary school in the use of the dictionary.

Adapted from *Scott Foresman Beginning Dictionary*, E. L. Thorndike/Clarence L. Barnhart (Glenview, Ill.: Scott Foresman, 1979).

Location Skills	Pronunciation Skills	Meaning Skills
1. Ability to arrange words in alphabetical order from the initial letter to the fourth letter.	1. Ability to use the pronunciation key at the bottom of each page.	1. Learning meanings of new words by reading simple definitions.
2. Ability to find words quickly in an alphabetical list.	2. Ability to use the full pronunciation key in the front of the dictionary.	2. Using pictures and definitions in the dictionary to arrive at meanings.
3. Ability to open the dictionary quickly to the section in which the desired word is to be found—to the proper fourth of the book.	3. Ability to use and interpret stress marks, both primary and secondary.	3. Using an illustrative sentence to arrive at meanings.
4. Ability to use the two guide words at the top of the page.	4. Ability to select the correct pronunciation for a homograph; for example, rec′ord or re·cord′, ob′ject or ob·ject′.	4. Using two different meanings for the same word.
5. Ability to think of the names of letters immediately preceding and immediately following the letter being located.	5. Ability to identify silent letters in words pronounced.	5. Ability to approximate real life sizes by using dictionary pictures and explanatory clues.
6. Ability to use special pronunciation-meaning sections of the dictionary; for example, medical terms, slang expressions, musical terms, and foreign words and phrases.	6. Ability to recognize differences between spellings and pronunciations (lack of phoneme-grapheme relationship).	6. Ability to select the specific meaning for a given context.
	7. Ability to use phonic spelling for pronunciation.	7. Understanding special meanings: idioms, slang expressions, and other figures of speech.
	8. Ability to discriminate vowel sounds.	8. Use of the concept of *root word*.
	9. Ability to use diacritical marks as an aid in pronunciation.	9. Interpreting multiple meanings of words.
	10. Understanding how syllables are marked in dictionaries.	10. Ability to know when meaning has been satisfied through dictionary usage.
	11. Ability to identify unstressed syllables in words.	
	12. Arriving at pronunciation and recognizing it as correct.	

| Games and Devices | Games and devices, if they are carefully chosen, can provide some of the necessary drill in reading skills. If they offer the child an opportunity to win, they may even provide motivation. Winning the game will be its own reward. At the same time, the child will experience success in learning a reading-related skill. |

Games and Devices

Games and devices, if they are carefully chosen, can provide some of the necessary drill in reading skills. If they offer the child an opportunity to win, they may even provide motivation. Winning the game will be its own reward. At the same time, the child will experience success in learning a reading-related skill.

The mechanics of the game should *not* be such that little time is spent on the learning of the skills needed in reading. The fun part should center around a reading skill rather than a physical skill not related to the reading act.

Available commercial games, a few selected games that teachers can devise, and a brief list of sources of good games and devices are given below.

Commercial Games

1. The *Group-Sounding Game* gives the child practice in self-help sounding at different levels (Champaign, Ill.: Garrard).

2. *Go-Fish* is a card game for practicing and reinforcing auditory discrimination of initial consonant sounds (first series) and consonant blend sounds (second series) (Kingsbury Center, 2138 Bancroft Place, N.W., Washington, D.C. 20008: The Remedial Education Press).

3. *Vowel Dominoes* is a card game played like dominoes that practices and reinforces the short vowel sounds (Kingsbury Center, 2138 Bancroft Place, N.W., Washington, D.C. 20008: The Remedial Education Press).

4. *Take* is a card game designed to practice hearing the sounds at the beginning, in the middle, or at the end of the word (Champaign, Ill.: Garrard).

5. *Quizmo* is a bingo game designed to practice hearing initial consonant, consonant blend, and initial short vowel sounds. The box contains directions, a list of words for the teacher to call, and thirty-eight bingo cards (Springfield, Mass.: Milton Bradley).

6. *The Syllable Game* is a card game in which words from the intermediate grade vocabulary are divided into syllables. Designed to help the student recognize and remember the commonest syllables in words. Like syllables become matched pairs. It may be played as a form of *solitaire* or as a group game (Champaign, Ill.: Garrard).

7. *Word Wheels.* A word wheel is usually two circles of different diameters fastened together at the center. They rotate in such a way that initial consonants and consonant blends on the smaller circle can be matched to family words on the larger circle. Also, prefixes or suffixes can be matched to root words. *Phono Word Wheels* are available from the Steck Company, Box 16, Austin, Texas. *Webster Word Wheels* are available from the Webster Division, McGraw-Hill, New York.

8. *Phonic Rummy* is a game played by matching vowel sounds. There are four sets of cards with sixty cards in each set. One set is for grades 1 and 2; one set is for grades 2 and 3; one set is for grades 2, 3, and 4; and one for grades 3, 4, and 5 (Buffalo, N.Y.: Kenworthy Educational Service).

9. *Phonics We Use Learning Games Kit.* Games for two or more players reinforce primary phonics skills: *Old Itch*—for initial consonant sounds; *Spin-a-Sound*—initial consonant sounds, symbols; *Blends Race*—initial consonant blends, symbols; *Digraph Whirl*—initial consonant digraphs, symbols; *Digraph Hopscotch*—initial and final consonant digraphs, symbols; *Vowel Dominoes*—long and short vowels, symbols; *Spin hard, Spin soft*—hard and soft *c* and *g* sounds; *Full House*—vowels, vowel digraphs, diphthongs; *Syllable Count*—syllabication and stress (Chicago: Rand McNally, 1967).

Games for the Teacher to Make

1. *This to That.* Starting with one word, one of the letters in the word is changed each time, making a series such as: *his, him, ham, ram, ran, run.* The game can also be played by changing one- or two-letter combinations, as: *sheep, sheet, shoot, shook, spook, spoke, broke.*

2. *Fishing.* One word, a phrase, or a short sentence is printed on each of a number of small cardboard cutouts in the shape of fish, to which paper clips are attached. The child picks up a fish by means of a tiny horseshoe magnet on a string (his fishing pole). He may keep his card if he can read it correctly. The one with the most fish wins the game. Similar games can be devised doing such things as pulling leaves off trees, etc.

3. *I'm thinking of a word that begins like . . . :* (a) Use sight words learned and put them in the chart holder. One child says, "I'm thinking of a word that begins like *run.*" The second child says, "Is it *ride?*" The child who guesses the right word gives the next clue. (b) This game also can provide practice in auditory discrimination. The child says, "I'm thinking of a word that begins like *dog.*" This child then whispers his choice to a scorekeeper. Children then may respond with any word that begins with *d.*

Books of Good Suggestions

Selma Herr. *Learning Activities for Reading.* Dubuque, Iowa: Wm. C. Brown, 1976.

Mary E. Platts. *Anchor.* Stevensville, Mich.: Educational Service, 1970.

Mary E. Platts, Sister Rose Marguerite, S.G.C., and Esther Schumaker. *Spice. Suggested Activities to Motivate the Teaching of the Language Arts in the Elementary School.* Benton Harbor, Michigan: Educational Service, 1960.

David Russell. *Listening Aids Through the Grades.* New York: Bureau of Publications, Teachers College, Columbia University, 1959.

David Russell, Etta Karp, and Anne Marie Mueser. *Reading Aids Through the Grades.* New York: Teachers College Press, 1975.

Delwyn Schubert and Theodore Torgerson. *Improving the Reading Program,* 4th ed. Dubuque, Iowa: Wm. C. Brown, 1976.

Evelyn Spache. *Reading Activities for Child Involvement,* 2d ed. Boston: Allyn & Bacon, 1976.

Guy Wagner and Max Hosier. *Reading Games: Strengthening Reading Skills with Instructional Games.* Darien, Connecticut: Educational Publishing Corporation, 1968.

Guy Wagner et al. *Listening Games: Strengthening Language Skills with Instructional Games.* Darien, Connecticut: Educational Publishing Corporation, 1966.

The following book has an inclusive list of kits, games, toys, and workbooks in an appendix:

Lawrence Hafner and Hayden B. Jolly. *Patterns of Teaching Reading in the Elementary School.* New York: Macmillan, 1972. Appendix D, pp. 299–312.

Summary

This chapter has contained a discussion of the skills in word recognition. The techniques discussed were teaching a basic sight vocabulary, recognizing that meaning is essential to develop reading as a thinking process, using phonic and structural analysis clues, and learning to use the dictionary. Studies that review the usefulness of phonic generalizations presented in teachers' manuals accompanying basal readers were summarized. Games and devices for strengthening word recognition abilities were discussed, and a brief list of resources for teachers was presented.

Suggested Activities

1. Administer a phonics test to a child in third grade or above.

2. Take an adult reading test such as the Durkin's Phonics Test for Teachers[30] and interpret the results.

3. Using a teacher's manual for one grade level in the elementary school, outline the phonics skills being taught and reinforced in that textbook.

4. Using the form in figure 9.8, study a teacher's manual for a basal reader and summarize what specific word recognition and word analysis skills are involved in lessons planned for the basal reader.

5. Be prepared to present and teach to your classmates selected games described in this chapter.

6. Develop an experience story with a primary school child and then identify all the words used that also appear in the Fry 300 word list.

For Further Reading

Bagford, Jack. *Phonics: Its Role in Teaching Reading.* Iowa City, Ia.: Sernoll, 1967.

Bailey, Mildred Hart. "The Utility of Phonic Generalizations in Grades One Through Six." *The Reading Teacher* 20(February 1967):413–18.

Burmeister, Lou. "Usefulness of Phonic Generalizations." *The Reading Teacher* 21(January 1968):349–56.

Clymer, Theodore L. "The Utility of Phonic Generalizations in the Primary Grades." *The Reading Teacher* 16(1963):252–58.

Cordts, Anna D. *Phonics for the Reading Teacher.* New York: Holt, Rinehart & Winston, 1965.

Durkin, Dolores. *Phonics and the Teaching of Reading.* New York: Bureau of Publications, Teachers College, Columbia University, 1965.

————. *Strategies for Identifying Words.* Boston: Allyn & Bacon, 1976.

————. *Teaching Them to Read*, pp. 233–21 (chapter 10, "Teaching Phonic Analysis: The Content"; chapter 11, "Teaching Phonic Analysis: The Procedures"; and chapter 12, "Teaching Structural Analysis"). Boston: Allyn & Bacon, 1970.

Figure 9.8 A worksheet for identifying which word-recognition skills which are involved in basal reader lessons as planned in teacher's manuals.

Your name _____	Title of reading text _____	
Date _____	Grade level of reading text _____	
Type of Skill	**Example**	**Example**
(For example: "Using context clues"; "Strengthening memory of word forms"; "Applying phonetic understandings"; etc.)	(Give example and page no. in teacher's manual where found.)	

Emans, Robert. "The Usefulness of Phonic Generalizations Above the Primary Grades." *The Reading Teacher* 20(February 1967):419–25.

————. "When Two Vowels Go Walking and Other Such Things." *The Reading Teacher* 21(December 1967):262–69.

Fuld, Paula. "Vowel Sounds in VCC Words." *The Reading Teacher* 21(February 1968):442–44.

Gray, William S. *On Their Own in Reading,* rev. ed. Glenview, Ill.: Scott, Foresman, 1960.

Hafner, Lawrence, and Hayden B. Jolly. *Patterns of Teaching Reading in the Elementary School,* pp. 89–117 (chapter 5, "Patterns of Teaching Word Identification Skills"). New York: Macmillan, 1972.

Harris, A. J., and E. R. Sipay. *Effective Teaching of Reading.* New York: David McKay Co., Inc., 1970.

———. *How to Increase Reading Ability.* "Developing Word Recognition Skills." New York: David McKay, 1975.

Heilman, Arthur W. *Phonics in Proper Perspective,* 3d ed. Columbus, Ohio: Charles E. Merrill, 1976.

———. *Principles and Practices in Teaching Reading,* 4th ed. Columbus, Ohio: Charles E. Merrill, 1977.

Oaks, Ruth. "A Study of the Vowel Situation in a Primary Vocabulary." *Education* 71(May 1952):604–17.

Otto, Wayne, Richard McMenemy, and Richard Smith. *Corrective and Remedial Teaching,* 2d ed., pp. 155–84 (chapter 7, "Word Attack Skills in Reading"). Boston: Houghton Mifflin, 1973.

Sansbury, Russell J. "Seven Steps for Teaching the Use of the Dictionary as a Word Attack Skill." *Academic Therapy* 8(Summer 1973):411–14.

Schell, Leo M. "Teaching Structural Analysis." *The Reading Teacher* 21(November 1967): 133–37.

Smith, Nila B. *Reading Instruction for Today's Children,* pp. 167–253 (chapter 8, "Word Identification"). Englewood Cliffs, N.J.: Prentice-Hall, 1963.

Spache, George D. *Reading in the Elementary School,* pp. 280–317 (chapter 12, "Word Recognition Techniques and Skills"). Boston: Allyn & Bacon, 1964.

Winkley, Carol K. "Which Accent Generalizations Are Worth Teaching?" *The Reading Teacher* 19(December 1966):219–24.

Notes

1. Lillian Gray, *Teaching Children to Read,* 3d ed. (New York: Ronald Press, 1963), p. 47, citing Horace Mann's *Report to the Board of Education in Massachusetts in 1838.*

2. Harriette Taylor Treadwell and Margaret Free, *Reading-Literature: The Primer* (Evanston, Ill.: Row-Peterson, 1910).

3. Miriam Blanton Huber, Frank Seely Salisbury, and Mabel O'Donnell, *I Know A Story* (New York: Harper & Row, 1962), pp. 20–21.

4. Clarence R. Stone, *Progress in Primary Reading* (New York: McGraw-Hill, 1950).

5. E.W. Dolch, *The Dolch Basic Sight Word Test* (Champaign, Ill.: Garrard, 1942).

6. A.I. Gates, *A Reading Vocabulary for the Primary Grades* (New York: Teachers College, Columbia University, 1926); The Child Study Committee of the International Kindergarten Union, *A Study of the Vocabulary of Children Before Entering First Grade* (1201 Sixteenth St., N.W., Washington, D.C.: International Kindergarten Union, 1928); and H.E. Wheeler and Emma A. Howell, "A First Grade Vocabulary Study," *Elementary School Journal* 31 (September 1930):52–60.

7. Edward Fry, "Developing a Word List for Remedial Reading," *Elementary English,* November, 1957, pp. 456–58.

8. Paul McKee, M. Lucile Harrison, Annie McCowen, and Elizabeth Lehr, Teacher's edition for *Come Along,* rev. ed. (Boston: Houghton Mifflin, 1957), pp. 478–83.

9. Ernest Horn, "Language and Meaning," *NSSE Yearbook. The Psychology of Learning* (Chicago: University of Chicago Press, 1942), pp. 398–99.

10. Nila B. Smith, *American Reading Instruction* (Newark, Del.: International Reading Assn., 1965). Also, Nila B. Smith, *Reading Instruction for Today's Children* (Englewood Cliffs, N.J.: Prentice-Hall, 1963), pp. 187–95.
11. Anna D. Cordts, *Phonics for the Reading Teacher* (New York: Holt, Rinehart & Winston, 1965), p. 162.
12. Ibid., pp. 134–35.
13. Ibid., p. 164.
14. Ernest Horn, "The Child's Early Experience with the Letter A," *Journal of Educational Psychology* 20(March 1929): 161–68.
15. Ruth E. Oaks, "A Study of the Vowel Situations in A Primary Vocabulary," *Education* 71(1952): 604–17.
16. Theodore L. Clymer, "The Utility of Phonics Generalizations in the Primary Grades," *The Reading Teacher* 16(1963):252–58.
17. A.T. Burrows and Z. Lourie, "When 'Two Vowels Go Walking,' " *The Reading Teacher* 17 (November, 1963):79–82.
18. Robert Emans, "The Usefulness of Phonic Generalizations Above the Primary Grades," *The Reading Teacher* 20(February 1967): 419–25; "When Two Vowels Go Walking and Other Such Things," *The Reading Teacher* 21(December, 1967): 262–69.
19. Mildred Hart Bailey, "The Utility of Phonic Generalizations in Grades One Through Six," *The Reading Teacher* 20(February, 1967): 413–18.
20. Lou Burmeister, "Usefulness of Phonic Generalizations," *The Reading Teacher* 21(January 1968): 349–56; "Vowel Pairs," *The Reading Teacher* 21(February 1968): 445–52.
21. E. A. Fry, "A Frequency Approach to Phonics," *Elementary English* 41(1964): 759–65ff.
22. A few exceptions to this valid *oa* generalization are *boa,* as in boa constrictors; *goa,* the gazelle of Tibet; or, *Goa,* a small land area in India.
23. Cordts, *Phonics,* p. 172.
24. Russell C. Stauffer, "A Study of Prefixes in the Thorndike List to Establish a List of Prefixes that Should be Taught in the Elementary School," *Journal of Educational Research* 35(1942):453–58.
25. *100 Good Ways to Strengthen Reading Skills* (Chicago: Scott, Foresman, 1956), p. 16.
26. William S. Gray, *On Their Own in Reading* (Chicago: Scott, Foresman, 1948), p. 80.
27. Cordts, *Phonics,* p. 178.
28. Carol K. Winkley, "Which Accent Generalizations are Worth Teaching?" *The Reading Teacher* 20(December 1966): 219–24.
29. William S. Gray, *On Their Own in Reading* (Chicago: Scott, Foresman, 1960), pp. 66–199.
30. Dolores Durkin, *Phonics Test for Teachers* (New York: Teachers College Press, Columbia University, 1964).

10

Comprehension Skills

Developing meaningful concepts is the primary concern of the classroom teacher. Harrison illustrates clearly why the teacher must be sure that children are developing understanding when they become absorbed in interesting classroom activities:

The children in a second grade had elaborately and painstakingly set up an Eskimo village on the floor of their schoolroom. The teacher had explained the igloo to the children and then proceeded to show them how they might make a satisfactory representation of an igloo from cornstarch and salt. The children molded the mixture on the inside of a bowl, cut out a low door, and turned it out upside down for the igloo. They were delighted with the result and showed it to visitors with pride. One visitor said, "And of what is an Eskimo igloo made?" to which an interested and enthusiastic pupil replied, "Cornstarch and salt." The teacher, very much chagrined, attempted to right the concept formed.[1]

Most teachers agree that pronouncing words correctly without getting meanings from the context is *not* reading. Boys and girls must learn to synthesize meanings as they read through the passages in their textbooks; otherwise, they have wasted their time. At the same time, teachers know that some children may pronounce words well and comprehend little or they may comprehend much but have great difficulty reading the words. For the majority, naturally, there is a positive relationship between the ability to handle the mechanics of the reading process and the ability to interpret the ideas in the passage read. Making sure that skills in comprehending what is read are developed in all elementary classrooms is one of the most basic jobs of the classroom teacher. What good can possibly result from accurate application of the necessary phonic or structural skills in pronouncing words if one cannot understand or interpret the ideas in a paragraph one reads? Techniques for arriving at adequate meanings constitute the comprehension skills in reading.

An Outline of Comprehension Skills

Comprehension, or the understanding of what the author has written, takes place at different levels of complexity, according to the nature of the material and the purposes for which the reading is intended. Horn has written that boys and girls "understand at different levels" whatever content they attempt to read. He classified four types of readers deficient in comprehension abilities: those who comprehend only a small portion of the ideas that a selection contains; those who can answer comprehension questions only by using the words of the textbook, verbatim or in slightly paraphrased form, with little or no understanding of their significance; those who make no overt response or say "I don't know"; and those who make interpretive responses that are partially or wholly erroneous.[2]

Stauffer places students on a long continuum with respect to comprehension abilities—all the way from one extreme of reproducing the exact words of the textbook, or "parroting back what the book says," to producing mental constructs creatively and with originality. The latter are the thinkers. The ability of boys and girls to comprehend is distributed along this long continuum.[3]

Taba's hierarchy of cognitive tasks in the development of thinking in children is applicable to levels of understanding in reading. Taba says that concept formation requires at the primary level three sequential mental operations: differentiation, abstraction, and ordering items in subordinate-superordinate positions. The next level of abstraction in this process requires arriving at inferences and generalizations. Generalizing requires separating relevant and irrelevant information, establishing cause and effect relationships, and perceiving implications beyond what is explicitly stated.[4]

In this text, comprehension skills are classified into three kinds—literal comprehension, or the preinterpretive skills; interpretive skills; and evaluation skills. They are outlined below. Critical reading ability is the application of these skills in reading and applying judgmental, evaluative, and selective skills while reading. These complex skills are discussed in chapter 12.

Literal comprehension requires basic skills in understanding vocabulary, remembering and using what one has read, finding details, following directions, and understanding paragraph organization. Literal comprehension also requires getting meanings from the context through finding the main idea, putting ideas in proper sequence to tell a story, or finding pertinent information in paragraphs to answer questions.

The interpretive skills include learning to anticipate meanings, drawing inferences, drawing generalizations, and selecting and evaluating. An outline of comprehension skills would be as follows:

I. Literal comprehension
    A. Foundation skills
        1. Expanding vocabulary concepts
           a. Using the rest of the sentence to determine meaning
           b. Matching word meanings
           c. Putting words in categories
           d. Choosing synonyms
           e. Recognizing sequence of ideas within a sentence
           f. Determining whether sentence explains *why, when, where*
           g. Understanding referents of pronouns

2. Finding and remembering details
3. Understanding and following directions
   B. Getting meaning from the context
     1. Reading to find answers
     2. Finding the main idea in a paragraph or a story
     3. Putting ideas in proper sequence in a story
II. Interpretive skills
   A. Learning to anticipate meanings
     1. Demonstrated by the cloze procedure
     2. By predicting what will happen next
   B. Drawing inferences
   C. Drawing generalizations
III. Evaluation skills
   A. Fact vs. fancy
   B. Selecting material pertinent to a given topic
   C. Overstatement or unfounded claims
   D. Judging emotional response to what is read

Distinguishing Comprehension Skills from Study Skills

Reading, comprehending, and making use of context constitutes the range of skills described above. In order to *study* successfully in the content areas, other skills are necessary. They are: (1) learning to locate information; (2) learning to read graphs, charts, maps, and tables; and (3) learning organization skills for outlining, summarizing, and notetaking. These skills for study reading are reviewed in greater detail in chapter 11.

Later in this chapter, illustrative exercises for the items listed in the outline of comprehension skills will be provided.

Helping Children with Meaning in Reading

Writers for children need to make use of techniques that will help children learn meanings of new words within the context of what they are reading. Such techniques have been prescribed by Artley and McCullough.[5] They include:

1. A brief explanation of the word can be given in parentheses or in a footnote:

   The *cacique* ordered an inquisition of the intruders who came into the village. (The *cacique* is the chief, or person of the highest authority in the village.)

2. A phrase which explains the meaning of the word can be inserted in the sentence:

   At certain times during the year in the northern skies one can see the *aurora borealis,* a colorful display of flickering, shifting lights.

   Moss, grass, and flowers grow in the *tundra,* the treeless plains found in arctic regions.

3. A synonym or substitute phrase is used to indicate the meaning:

   shrimp, a small shellfish
   the *lobby,* a small waiting room
   the *cacique,* the chief of the tribe

4. A new word is *emphasized* by using italics, quotation marks, or boldface type to call attention to it:

The farmer uses a machine called a *combine* to harvest the wheat.

Pioneer farmers used a "cradle," a scythe with a wooden frame attached, to harvest the grain.

Farmers who shared their crops with the landowner were called **sharecroppers.**

5. A direct explanation of the word can be presented in a full sentence:

In the hot desert, the man makes his garden in an oasis. An oasis is a green spot where there is a water supply.

The nomads of the desert are coming to the trading center. Nomads are people who constantly move about and who have no settled home.

The farmer could guide his oxen by shouting "Gee!" or "Haw!" The oxen had learned that *Gee* meant to turn to the right and *Haw* meant to turn to the left.

The examples above will help children develop the ability to anticipate meanings while reading in the following ways:

1. Sometimes a new word is set off by boldface type, italics, or quotation marks to call attention to it.
2. Sometimes the new word is followed by a parenthetical expression explaining its meaning.
3. Sometimes the new word is followed by a less technical or more generally known synonym or substitute phrase.
4. Sometimes the new word will be defined in the sentence following.
5. Sometimes the new word is one with several meanings, but in its current context it can have only one intended meaning.
6. A pictorial illustration may help clarify a new concept.

Boys and girls will profit from directed practice in arriving at meanings through such techniques as the following:

1. Study the context to look for clues to the meanings.
2. Relate the word to previous content in the subject.
3. Study the word structure. If it has a prefix, root, or suffix that is already known, combine context and word structure to arrive at specific meaning.
4. Read the dictionary meanings; find the one that fits.
5. Once the word is understood, think of synonyms or antonyms.
6. Once the word is understood, use it purposefully in several situations.

Vocabulary Development

Extending children's vocabularies should be a continuing objective of every teacher. There are many ways in which teachers can motivate growth in vocabulary skills. The development of good vocabularies is encouraged by:[6]

1. Wide reading.
2. Association with people who have a wide vocabulary.

3. Travel.

4. Varied experiences such as excursions, activities, industrial arts projects, laboratory experiments.

5. Talking over what one has read.

6. Giving conscious attention to new words when one encounters them.

7. Asking for the meaning of nonunderstood words.

Suggestions to teachers for improving children's vocabularies:

1. Teach children to ask about any new or unusual or nonunderstood words as they encounter them.

2. Put such words on the board, and encourage their frequent use.

3. Enrich the curriculum generally, so that children have much material to talk about and think about. Encourage the reading of other books and magazines. Nothing can take the place of varied experience and of wide reading in building up meanings.

4. Have frequent oral tests covering new words, using them in sentences and discussing their meanings.

5. As any unit of subject matter is finished, children may, alone or with the teacher, make lists of words or phrases which have been learned by the study of the unit.

6. Work on word meanings in specific contexts, not in isolation.

7. Keep the emphasis upon meaning rather than upon mere recognition or mechanical pronunciation of words.

8. Make definite provision for word study in the upper grades; that is, study of roots, prefixes, and suffixes.

9. Make specific attempts to break the habit of skipping over unknown words in reading. Develop the "dictionary habit."

10. Provide practice in giving synonyms and antonyms, both for words and for phrases.

11. Give considerable practice in deriving meanings from the context.

Deighton outlined the following procedure in teaching for vocabulary development in the classroom.[7]

1. Students must understand what word meanings are and how they are determined. Dictionary definitions are only points of departure and do not circumscribe the word.
   What must be explained is the interaction of the reader's experience, the context, and the dictionary entry in deriving the meaning of a particular word in a particular context.

2. Students must be prepared to get the meaning out of unfamiliar words as they meet them. This includes prefixes, suffixes, and combining forms with specific meanings. Establishing meanings of root words from context or the dictionary is also important.

3. Students need instruction in ways meanings can be derived from the context: by definition, by example, by restatement, by qualifiers, and by inference.

4. Understanding figures of speech will require some special attention. They appear frequently and are a source of confusion to young readers.

5. Students need their attention called to ways some words operate in the language: judgment words, relationships in time and space, words of indefinite quantity, and words of an absolute nature.

In summary, then, children are helped to improve their vocabularies by all of the following:

1. Provision of a wide background of first-hand experiences.
2. Use of visual aids.
3. Provision of many opportunities for oral language expression and listening.
4. Careful explanation of concepts by the teacher.
5. Use of oral reading and story telling by the teacher.
6. Use of pupil-made materials.
7. Emphasis upon concept-building in the content fields.
8. Provision for wide reading experiences.
9. Use of the dictionary: picture dictionaries and standard elementary dictionaries.
10. Informal word study: thinking of many multiple meanings, compound words, word opposites, synonyms, classifying words, using descriptive words, knowing plurals of words where spelling changes.

Levels of Questioning

The Questions Teachers Ask

Guszak visited second, fourth, and sixth grade classrooms and recorded the reading lessons for all the groups. The tapes were analyzed to evaluate the types of questions asked in the reading groups. He found that 56.9 percent of the questions were simple recall (How many cats did Katy have? What color were they?); 13.5 percent were recognition questions (Which sentence tells the names of all the seven cats?). This total of 70.4 percent of all questions suggests the heavy emphasis on literal comprehension. Higher levels of thinking required for making inferences or evaluating were too infrequently asked for. Guszak found 13.7 percent inferential and 15.3 percent evaluative questions. He concluded that teachers lack understanding of the reading-thinking-questioning hierarchy and suggests that textbooks need to present a model for reading-thinking skills and a methodology for developing such skills.[8]

Asking appropriate questions can be a way of motivating boys and girls to acquire better vocabularies. Fitzpatrick has suggested the following types:[9]

1. The Definition Question. Example: What does *school* mean in this sentence? As he glided through the water, he met a *school* of small, flat fish.

2. The Semantic Question. Example: What other meanings do you know for the word *school?*

3. The Synonym Question. Example: Look at the *italicized* word in the sentence: Jefferson began a policy of *strict* economy. What other word(s) could be substituted for *strict* without changing the meaning of the sentence?

4. The Antonym Question. Example: What word(s) could you use for *strict* in the above sentence to make it have an opposite meaning?

5. The Homonym Question. Example: Look at the *italicized* word in the sentence: The *seams* of the boat were leaking. What other word(s) sounds the same but is spelled differently and has a different meaning?

6. The Key Word Question. Example: What is the meaning of the italicized word in this sentence: The Russians have placed the first man-made planet in *orbit?*

In short, one way to develop vocabulary is to ask questions about words appearing in written material being studied in every subject area. The advantage of this integrated approach is obvious. Not only is the teacher improving vocabulary, but also general comprehension of the material.

Following Written Directions

Newcastle identified five reasons why children do not follow written directions:[10]

1. Inability to read and understand the words used in written directions.
2. Poorly written directions.
3. Little systematic instruction in reading and following written directions.
4. Conditioned and reinforced habits of inattention to teachers who repeat directions a second or even a third time.
5. Self-defeating practices that condition children to rely on using the teacher-given oral directions.

Some remedies for this problem would be:

1. Simplify directions by rewriting them in a simple, direct manner to make them easier for children to read and follow.
2. To give practice in reading and following directions, ask children to read simple, concisely stated directions and then explain in their own words what to do.
3. Be sure the words frequently used in directions are understood by your students who read them.
4. Have a few practice sessions in how to read, explain, and execute written directions.

After a study of the ability of third grade children to utilize directions found in reading workbooks, Willins[11] offered the following recommendations to teachers who want to help their pupils learn how to follow directions:

1. Directions should be short.
2. If the exercise as presented on the page is apt to be confusing, the directions should be more complete than necessary in standard formats.
3. Especially if the exercise to be done is not in view when directions are presented, the directions should be simply worded.
4. If long directions are required, an example should be provided for the child to insure understanding.

Concepts

Concepts are personal meanings held by an individual. Woodruff defines concepts as "mental images of life accumulated from personal experience with life itself."[12] Figure 10.1 illustrates such a definition. Billings says that "concepts are the cues to the proper understanding of the situations to which they apply. Thus, a concept is both a summary of meaning gleaned from past experience and a cue to the meaning of the present situation."[13]

Concept development is the greatest problem in the teaching of reading to all children. Readiness for reading necessitates the development of vocabulary concepts, use of language to discuss and solve problems, and even, for the six-year-old child, some appreciation of the fact that "the ability to communicate has permitted each generation to rise on the shoulders of the thinkers

Trees provide:

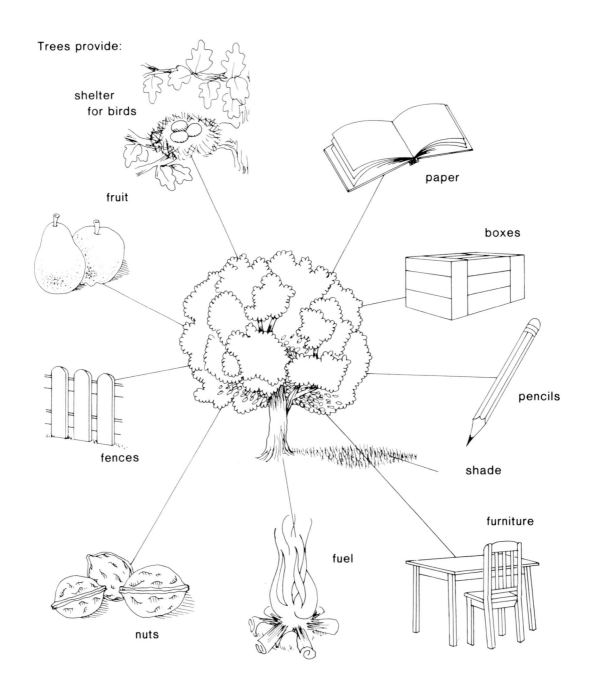

shelter
for birds

fruit

paper

boxes

pencils

fences

shade

furniture

nuts

fuel

Figure 10.1 Concept:
trees are useful to
man.

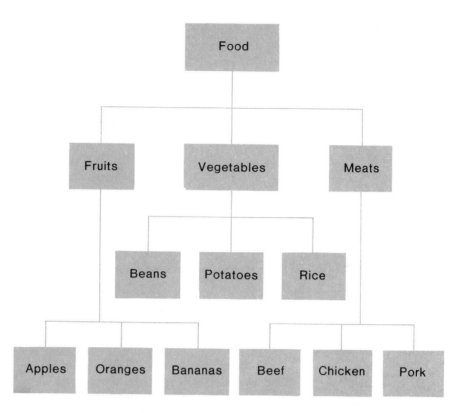

Figure 10.2
Elementary concepts have a three-part structure: differentiation, abstraction, and ordering. Differentiating involves distinguishing apples from oranges, bananas, chicken, rocks, or water, for instance. Abstracting from such elements a concept that some are food and some are not food would be another mental operation. Ordering things that are conceptualized as food into different categories of food, such as fruits, vegetables, and meat, is yet another mental operation. Whether these three operations follow a fixed sequence is not clear, although they are often diagrammed in a hierarchy as here.

Diagram from Margaret Greer, "The Effect of Studying the Structure of Concepts and Cognitive-Emphasis Social Studies Units on Selected Cognitive Processes of Fifth-Grade Children," Unpublished doctoral dissertation, Graduate School, University of New Mexico, Albuquerque, New Mexico, 1969, p. 70.

and achievers who have gone before, to profit from their gains, to avoid their mistakes, and to pursue their dreams and aspirations and make some of them realities."[14]

Elementary concepts have a three-part structure: differentiation, ordering, and abstraction. This is illustrated in figure 10.2. (See also chapter 15, Teaching Reading in the Content Fields.)

Work of curriculum experts in elementary education has emphasized the job of the classroom teacher in developing understandings, concepts, and generalizations. Taba states that the content of learning for the child consists of various levels of thinking:

One level is that of specific facts, descriptive ideas at a low level of abstraction, and specific processes and skills. . . .

Basic ideas and principles represent another level of knowledge. The ideas about causal relationships between human culture and natural environment are of this sort. So are scientific laws and mathematics principles, the ideas stating relationships between nutrition and metabolism of the human body, or ideas about how such factors as climate, soil, and natural resources produce unique constellations of a geographic environment. . . .

A third level of content is composed of what one might call concepts, such as the concept of democracy, of interdependence, of social change, or of the "set" in mathematics.[15]

Comprehension Skills

Taba's levels of thinking are basic theoretical material for the reading teacher who is going to help boys and girls develop reading skills that embody the full definition of reading: comprehending, reacting, and integrating. Levels of questioning as prescribed in Bloom's taxonomy and the refining of conceptual thinking for critical reading ability are positively related.

Bloom's
Taxonomy

Bloom analyzed the intellectual activity involved in reading into the following six types.[16]

1. *Comprehension* represents the most elementary level of all the intellectual skills. It includes skills that explain or translate, or merely reproduce in oral language ideas that are written. Some of the words teachers might use to formulate statements or questions to students at this level are: *tell, describe, make a list of, identify, memorize, recall, repeat, reproduce.*

2. *Interpretation* represents skills that serve to establish relationships between dates, principles, generalizations, or values. Some of the words teachers might use to begin statements or questions to students at this level are: *show the relationship, associate, classify, compare, characterize, differentiate, distinguish, categorize.*

3. *Application* represents skills that facilitate transfer—the application of experiences already acquired to new situations or new relationships. Some of the words teachers might use to begin statements or questions to students at this level are: *apply, experiment, exercise, organize, systematize, practice, utilize.*

4. *Analysis* represents a more complex level of judging or valuing a point of view. Some of the words teachers might use to begin statements or questions to students at this level are: *analyze, discover, determine, observe, examine, investigate.*

5. *Synthesis* represents the ability to create new and personal forms of expression and reasoning. Originality and creativity are a part of synthesis. Some of the words teachers might use to formulate statements or questions to students at this level are: *synthesize, conceive, conclude, create, construct, imagine, ideate, summarize, invent, theorize.*

6. *Evaluation* represents the highest level of skill in the hierarchy. The student utilizes methods, materials, ideas, values, and techniques for learning how to learn. He draws conclusions based on his ability to utilize all of these skills. Some of the words teachers might use to begin statements or questions to students at this level are: *calculate, consult, criticize, decide, discuss, estimate, judge, measure, accept/reject, value.*

Convergent and
Divergent Thinking

Convergent thinking is directed toward finding a correct answer to any question or problem. It has been overused in elementary school to the extent that children often think there has to be a right answer to whatever question the teacher may ask. As suggested by Guszak's report[17] on levels of teachers' questioning, the students are apt to become habituated to unproductive, closed, *convergent* types of thinking, reasoning, and responding.

Divergent thinking, on the other hand, encourages children to respond to different types of questions and problems with open, creative, and imaginative answers. Such a question as, "How many different uses can you think of for a brick used by a brick mason?" may produce a dozen valid uses other than just the construction of sturdy homes. Naturally, people do both convergent and divergent thinking in life outside the school. However, it behooves the school system to encourage the openness and the creativity of divergent and speculative thinking.

Again, levels of questioning and questioning strategies assume primary importance, as pointed out by Taba:

The role of questions becomes crucial and the way of asking is by far the most influential single teaching act. A focus set by the teacher's questions circumscribes the mental operations which students can perform, determines what points they explore, which modes of thought they learn. A question such as "What are the important cities in the Balkans?" provides poor focus in several respects. Because no criterion of importance is available, such questions develop an unproductive mode of thinking, in addition to training in arbitrary judgment. Such questions (1) suggest that one can judge the importance of cities without a criterion. For example, does one look for large cities, capitols, ancient ones or what? Most students faced with such questions have only two alternatives: guessing what the teacher wants, or trying to recollect what the book said, both cognitive not productive. Asking "right" answer questions also (2) builds a "convergent" mind—one that looks for simple right answers, and which assumes that "right" answers depend on authority rather than on rational judgment.[18]

Illustrative Exercises for Teaching the Skills of Comprehension

Foundation Skills: Literal Comprehension

Expanding Vocabulary Concepts

Example 1. Using the rest of the sentence to determine the meaning.[19]

Mrs. James was *puzzled* by Joyce's idea and even more *bewildered* by her actions.

Mrs. Collins *praised* her daughter, *saying that her idea was very good.*

Mr. Warren kept a plow, a hayrake and other *implements* in the barn.

George *looked over* the cleaning job, and when he had completed his *survey*, he said, "I think this basement looks fine."

"See how *sleek* Danny looks after he's curried," said Art as he eyed the pony's *smooth, glossy* coat.

Example 2. Matching word meanings.

What does each worker do? Read carefully through the list of workers:

minister	shoemaker	surveyor	student	author
farmer	swimmer	sculptor	general	actress
fireman	magician	doctor	artist	grocer
teacher	miner	clown	king	conductor

In the list below find the matching word for each word above. On your paper, write the words that go together, for example, "1. minister preaches."

digs	preaches	sells	commands	paints
dives	reigns	juggles	studies	cultivates
measures	collects	acts	rescues	heals
writes	carves	jokes	mends	instructs

Example 3. Putting words in categories.

All of the words below can be classified as four types: flowers, foods, animals, and ways of describing behavior. Rule your paper as shown below, and put each of the words in its proper category.

Flowers	Foods	Animals	Describing behavior

The words are: primrose, kangaroo, prunes, happy, beets, peony, healthy, butter, helpful, tulip, tortoise, buffalo, kind, pansy, donkey, dahlia, zebra, salad, giraffe, cocoa, busy, mule, polite, cheese, chimpanzee, generous, cheerful, brave, thrifty, lilac, interesting, careful, soup, punctual, dandelion, industrious, cauliflower, sandwiches.

Example 4. Choosing synonyms.

Read the list of words below:

finally	entrust	gradually	comment
declared	resented	despair	surveyed
grumbled	difficult	ridicule	compliment

Now read the list of words or expressions below and find one that means the same or nearly the same as each of the words above. On your paper, match the word above with its synonym below:

complained	was angry at	at last	hopelessness
remark	give	said	hard
make fun of	term of praise	looked at	little by little

Example 5. Recognizing the sequence of ideas within a sentence.[20]

Each group of words here is a part of a sentence—a beginning, a middle, or a last part. When you put them in the right order, they make a sentence. In each box you are to put *1* in front of the first part, *2* in front of the middle part, and *3* in front of the last part of the sentence.

_____ Friday was the day
_____ on her vacation
_____ that Miss Spruce started

_____ clear the table
_____ Patty helped
_____ and wash the dishes

_____ and disappeared
_____ the starving beast
_____ leaped from the cage

_____ these new books in the right order

_____ on the bookshelf"

_____ Ruth said, "I'm going to put

_____ so that the bee would fly out

_____ the window of the bus

_____ Mr. Hunger was going to raise

Example 6. Deciding whether the sentence explains when, where, why, how, or who.

Read the sentence on the left and then write in the blank space on the right whether it tells *when, where, why, how,* or *who.*

The man sat *in the shade of the house.*   _____

Mary cried *because she could not go.*   _____

Tell me *when you have finished.*   _____

They lived *happily* ever after.   _____

The boys won the ball game *easily.*   _____

Do you always work so *rapidly?*   _____

McKee introduced the following type of exercise at the second grade level.[21]

In each sentence the part that is italicized tells where or when or how. Read each sentence. After the sentence you will see three words. Draw a line under the one word that shows what the underlined part of the sentence tells:

A golden coach came *down the street.*	When	Where	How
Our cat likes to stay out *at night.*	When	Where	How
I went to the store *in a hurry.*	When	Where	How
Bob ran *as fast as he could go.*	When	Where	How
Last summer I drank some goat's milk.	When	Where	How
Would a goat ride *in a golden coach?*	When	Where	How

Example 7. Understanding antecedents or pronoun referents in the sentence.

Directions: In each sentence below two pronouns are *italicized.* These pronouns refer to a person or thing in the sentence. Read each sentence. Write in the blank the name of the person or thing to which the pronoun refers.[22]

A stranger asked the policeman, "Can *you* tell *me* where Pennsylvania Street is from here?"

you_____

me_____

George saw at a glance that *his* boat had broken away from the dock and that *it* was stuck on a sand bar.

his_____

it_____

Jane carefully put *her* scrapbook on the highest bookshelf so that *it* would not be lost.

her_____

it_____

The girls *who* belonged to the drama club asked the principal for permission to have *their* cake sale.

who_____

their_____

Finding and
Remembering
Details

The kind of questioning that teachers probably emphasize too much is recalling all the details in a short passage.

Example 1.[23]

Henry plowed his way through the snow to the barn. There he got a hammer, some nails, and a wide box, and filled a small sack with cracked grain. He then went to an open shed which was built near the woods and used as a shelter for cows in the summer. When he reached the shed, he saw that a flock of snowbirds had already come to live there for the winter. He nailed the box under the shed and then filled it with the cracked grain. As he hurried back through the snow, he heard the birds chirping their thanks.

The shed was built near the (a) barn (b) house (c) woods (d) box

The grain was to feed the (a) cows (b) pigs (c) birds (d) chickens

Henry put the grain (a) in the barn (b) in the box (c) on the ground (d) on the snow

The birds that came to the shed were (a) snowbirds (b) bluejays (c) sparrows (d) robins

The birds chirped because they were (a) cold (b) warm (c) happy (d) sad

Henry carried the hammer and nails to the (a) house (b) barn (c) woods (d) shed

The box was (a) deep (b) wide (c) narrow (d) long

The birds came to the shed to spend the (a) spring (b) summer (c) fall (d) winter

To get to the barn Henry had to (a) shovel a path through the snow (b) wade through the snow (c) go through the woods (d) go through the shed

Henry nailed the box (a) under the shed (b) to a tree (c) to the roof (d) outside the barn

What kind of person was Henry? (a) considerate (b) skillful (c) hardy (d) devoted

Which sentence isn't true? (a) Henry made use of nails and box. (b) The snowbirds were accustomed to winter. (c) The closed shed was warm. (d) The snow lay thick on the ground.

Example 2.[24]

People used to think that night air was bad for them. They thought it was full of sickness and they kept their windows shut at night. We know that night air is good and that we should keep our windows open. We should keep our windows open even in winter. If our bodies are warmly covered, no cold air we breathe can hurt us.

People thought that night air was full of—
    health   stars   sickness   airplanes

At night we should keep our windows—
    closed   shut   broken   open

Even on cold nights we should keep open our—
    mouths   windows   gates   doors

**Understanding
General
Significance of a
Paragraph**

Example 1.[25]

Ben was a city boy who had never been to the country. He had lived all of his short life in city streets. One summer some friends took him to the country. He was shown the animals, the meadows, and the woods. He looked at them all in silence. Suddenly he looked up with tears in his eyes and asked, "But where are the streets to play in?"

Draw a line under the word that best tells how Ben felt.
excited   homesick   happy   joyful   weary

The little country boy had been brought to the city. He had been shown the high buildings. He had ridden in the subways and had seen bright electric signs at night. But after three days he began to grow weary of the sights of the city. He longed to go back to the country. "Oh, how I wish I could see a little running brook!" he sighed.

Draw a line under the word that best tells how the country boy felt.
angry   afraid   homesick   happy   playful

**Understanding and
Following
Directions**

Example 1.[26]

A long time ago people used weather cocks to tell about the weather. When the wind blew from the north and it was to be cold, the weather cock faced the north. Draw a line around the letter that shows the way the weather cock should face when a cold wind is blowing.

Example 2.

James and Mary go to a funny school. Instead of Saturday or Monday being their holiday, they have Wednesday and Sunday. They have to go to school on Saturday. Draw lines around the days of the week that James and Mary do not go to school.

SUN	MON	TUES	WED	THURS	FRI	SAT

Punctuation

Punctuation marks in written material give meaning to connected written discourse. Reading the punctuation accurately, quickly, and meaningfully enhances comprehension of material read significantly.

Failure to give proper attention to punctuation is certain to weaken meaningful understanding of sentences and longer reading units. Underachievers in reading often fail to read smoothly and fluently and need help in establishing the practice of watching for and using punctuation. Children need to learn precise uses of periods, question marks, commas, colons, semicolons, and exclamation marks. McKee suggested teaching seven uses of the comma.[27]

1. To separate words or groups of words written as a series:

   We usually carry a lunch of sandwiches, fruit, cookies and milk.

2. After the words *Yes* or *No* when either of these words answers a question and the words following merely give additional information:

   Yes, I'm planning to go.

3. To set off an appositive:

   DiMaggio, a great baseball player, was a star for the Yankees.

4. To set off a parenthetical expression in a sentence:

   Rip Van Winkle, a lazy citizen of the town, liked only to hunt or fish.

5. To set off an expression of address:

   I'm sorry, Dad, I won't be able to do that.

6. To separate a dependent clause which precedes its principal clause:

   Despite their efforts to escape, the boys were well cared for by the kidnappers.

7. To set off an adverbial clause when it contains a verb or verbal form:

   When I entered the little store, Mr. Davis smiled warmly.

The words "You want to go to the football game" may be merely a statement in a conversation acknowledging someone's desire to see the game. The same words may be asking if one does, in fact, want to go. Or, they may be voiced in considerable surprise that this individual does wish to see the football game.

You want to go to the football game.
You want to go to the football game?
You want to go to the football game!

Clearly, the use of commas and quotation marks changes the meaning in the following sentence:

Mary said Grace failed the test.
"Mary," said Grace, "failed the test."

Without the comma, the following sentence may be momentarily confusing:

When the hailstorm hit the large picture window was broken.
When the hailstorm hit, the large picture window was broken.

Heilman[28] suggested giving boys and girls material to read in which the punctuation has been put in the wrong places or omitted entirely. This will emphasize for them how easily the meaning is diminished. In the first of the following two paragraphs commas have been deleted and periods and capitalization appear in the wrong places. If the first paragraph is meaningless, perhaps the second will be more easily read.

In the American Southwest there is much talk. About cultural diffusion it has been suggested. That traditional cultures of the Indian and the Spanish-American. Have much to offer the truth of this statement. Is not contested nevertheless. It is difficult to imagine. The typical middle-class Anglo internalizing values. Of life based on the economy education religion or health practices. Of a traditional minority group the diffusion usually talked about is the more obvious. Observable and superficial type. Eating green chili-mutton stew on feast days. In a pueblo with friends wearing fiesta dresses with ostentatious jewelry. Owning a ring with a large turquoise set or an attractive squash blossom. Necklace or decorating a room in one's house. With Navaho rugs and an assortment of Pueblo Indian pottery it is highly questionable. Whether many people would change basic thinking patterns. Or would be willing to give up their two-bathroom houses. And thermostat-controlled central heat!

In the American Southwest, there is much talk about cultural diffusion. It has been suggested that the traditional cultures of the Indian and the Spanish-American have much to offer. The truth of this statement is not contested. Nevertheless, it is difficult to imagine the typical middle-class Anglo internalizing values of life based on the economy, education, religion, or health practices of a traditional minority group. The diffusion usually talked about is the more obvious, observable, and superficial type: eating green chili-mutton stew on feast days in a pueblo with friends, wearing fiesta dresses with ostentatious jewelry, owning a ring with a large turquoise set or an attractive squash blossom necklace, or decorating a room in one's house with Navaho rugs and an assortment of Pueblo Indian pottery. It is highly questionable whether many people would change basic thinking patterns or would be willing to give up their two-bathroom houses and their thermostat-controlled central heat![29]

Getting Meaning from the Context

Reading to find answers.   The following exercise lends itself to factual questioning which reconstructs the story content.

"Dingdong Bell"[30]

Dingdong, dingdong! Sunday morning bells ring out, calling people to church. These bells are heard in both city and country.

Fire engines still carry a bell. Firemen pull a rope to ring the bell when they go racing off to a fire. They also sound their sirens.

On board ship, bells ring every hour and half-hour to tell sailors the time.

In the old days children came into their schoolroom when the teacher rang a bell. Sometimes this was a big handbell. Sometimes the bell was on the roof of the school house.

The most musical bells were the old sleigh bells. You heard them when the horse trotted over the snow, pulling the sleigh. Their merry tinkling, jingling sound in the frosty air is almost forgotten now.

Depending upon the maturity of the student who reads the story, there are many questions possible. For example: "What is the story about?" The story tells about five kinds of bells. The question "What kinds of bells are told about?" could lead to making a simple outline:

Different kinds of bells
1. Church bells
2. Fire engine bells
3. Ship bells
4. School bells
5. Sleigh bells
   Or,
1. The church bell calls _____ .
2. The fire bell tells _____ .
3. The bell on the ship tells _____ .
4. The school bell told the children _____ .
5. Sleigh bells made music when _____ .

Selecting the best title for a paragraph.   After boys and girls read a paragraph or story, they can (1) select the best title from a number of suggested titles, (2) decide whether or not the title given tells what the paragraph or story is about, or (3) think of a good title. This will help to develop understanding of paragraph meaning and organization. The following exercise is an example of providing the student practice in selecting the best title after reading a paragraph:[31]

Fresh vegetables for a salad should be washed and dried carefully. Then they should be placed in a refrigerator for a time. Just before the salad is to be served, the greens should be broken into pieces and put into a salad bowl. Then strips of carrot, rings of onions, or other vegetables may be added. Next, a small amount of French dressing should be poured over the contents of the bowl. The salad should be tossed lightly until each part of it has become coated with dressing.

Put a check (✓) before the title that tells the main idea of the paragraph.
_____1. Preparing a Salad
_____2. How to Toss a Salad

Identifying the topic sentence of a paragraph.   Boys and girls should learn that a good paragraph deals with only one topic, and the paragraph contains a topic sentence which tells what the paragraph is about. All the details of a good paragraph develop the topic sentence. Being able to identify the topic sentence will help a reader understand and organize the ideas being read.

However, children must also learn that not all writers are careful in their writing, and many paragraphs in the textbooks they read will not have a topic sentence. Further, they will have to accept paragraphs that contain details (extra sentences) that do not amplify the topic sentence for the paragraph.

Generally, in the elementary school, children will find that paragraphs contain a topic sentence, which may be the first sentence in the paragraph. Sometimes the topic sentence is a kind of summarizing sentence placed at the end of the paragraph. Boys and girls need practice identifying topic sentences found at either the beginning or the end of the paragraph.

In the paragraph below, the first sentence tells what the whole paragraph is about. Since it states the topic of the paragraph, it is called the topic sentence.

The separate bones are held together by joints in ways that help make movement of the body possible. The joints in the neck make it possible for a person to move his head up or down as well as from side to side. The joint at the shoulder makes it possible for him to move his arm in a round-the-circle manner. It is because of joints that we are able to bend the back, pick up articles with our fingers, and perform other actions.[32]

In the following example, the topic sentence is at the end of the paragraph.

Each person was in his proper place. Flags were flying. The band had begun to play a lively march. Suddenly there was a burst of applause as the marching began. The Fourth of July celebration was starting off with a big parade.[33]

In the following paragraph all the sentences relate to the general topic of roasting corn. The whole paragraph tells two ways to roast corn. The first sentence is the topic sentence because it indicates that the paragraph will tell about two ways to roast corn over an open fire.

I know two different ways to roast corn on an open fire. One way is to dip the ears, husks and all, in water. Then you put the ears on a grill over the fire to steam. These are good, but I like the second way even better. You take off the husks and put butter and salt on the ears. Then you wrap them in aluminum foil and roast them in the coals.[34]

Boys and girls in the intermediate grades should be able to underline the topic sentences in material like the following paragraphs.

When Marco Polo was seventeen years old, he went to China with his father and uncle. While there, he traveled through many little-known parts of the country in the service of the ruler. Many places he visited were very wild, and Marco had some exciting times. Then, three years after he returned to his homeland, he was called on to serve in a war. He was captured and was imprisoned for nearly a year. Marco Polo had many interesting adventures during his life—both in foreign lands and in his homeland.[35]

By following a few simple directions, anyone should be able to raise lettuce. Light, well-fertilized soil should be used. The lettuce seeds should not be dropped too close together. If they are dropped close together, some of the young plants should be thinned out. There should be frequent stirring of the soil to encourage growth of the plants. Large amounts of water are not necessary for growing lettuce.[36]

One of the oldest and most common of the human qualities is that of wanting animals as pets. Children at an early age learn to love pets. A small child will hug his toy dog and love it, but he will gladly exchange it for a live pet. Although we think of children as the persons who most desire and need pets, most older persons also love pets. Those who lose a pet are often very sad, until they get another, or until they become accustomed to being without a pet.[37]

Outlining.   As an initial step in helping children learn to outline, the teacher needs to guide the discussion about the content of the paragraph and to list, perhaps on the chalkboard, the main points, the subordinate points, and the details that the paragraph contains.

Growing and Exporting Bananas

Growing and exporting bananas is the most important industry in Ecuador. Bananas require both a tropical climate and hard work. The plants grow in the lowlands near the Pacific coast, where the temperature is always hot and there is abundant rainfall. The farmers must care for the plants many months before the fruit is mature. Then they select the largest bunches to sell. The bunches are cut from the stalk, and the stalk is then cut off near the ground. Trucks drive to the edge of the fields, and men load the heavy stalks of bananas by hand. If the bananas must be carried any distance to the truck, men carry them on their backs or tie them on the backs of burros. Exporting, or the marketing process, requires hauling the crop to the seaport and loading it on ships. The trucks carry the bananas to the docks in Guayaquil. At the docks, the bananas may be carried by hand and put into large nets that will be lifted by crane and lowered into the holds of ships. These vessels carry great quantities of green bananas to many parts of the world. Some weeks later, the fruit, now ripened and yellow, is ready to be sold in fruit markets and supermarkets in your hometown. Many people never think about the thousands of miles the delicious banana on their breakfast table had to travel to get there.

Growing and Exporting the Banana

Growing Conditions	Farmers	Transporting	Exporting
climate	planting	hauling to trucks	throughout the world
tropical	cultivating	to docks in	food markets
lowlands	harvesting	Guayaquil	eating
rainfall	selling	filling large nets	
		loading into holds of ships	

This list can be rearranged into a topical outline:

Growing and Exporting the Banana in Ecuador

I. Growing bananas
   A. Climate
      1. Tropical
      2. Lowlands
      3. Rainfall
   B. Farmers at work
      1. Planting
      2. Cultivating
      3. Harvesting
      4. Selling
II. Exporting bananas
   A. Transporting
      1. With trucks from farm to docks
      2. Loading on ships
   B. Marketing
      1. Distributing throughout the world
      2. Food markets
      3. Eating the banana

Putting ideas in proper sequence in a story. Boys and girls need practice in remembering significant details and the sequential order of events in material they read. It will be helpful to give special attention to the order of events in a story. The following proverb is a brief example of a crucial sequence of events.

> For want of a nail the shoe was lost,
> For want of a shoe the horse was lost,
> For want of a horse the rider was lost,
> For want of a rider the battle was lost,
> For want of a battle the kingdom was lost,
> And all for the want of a horseshoe nail.

Interpretive Skills

Learning to
Anticipate
Meanings: The
Cloze Procedure

Cloze is a procedure in which the reader attempts to anticipate meaning from context and supply words deleted in a message. Taylor defines the cloze procedure as "a method of intercepting a message from a 'transmitter' (writer or speaker), mutilating its language patterns by deleting parts, and so administering it to 'receivers' (readers and listeners) that their attempts to make the patterns whole again potentially yield a considerable number of cloze units."[38]

The cloze procedure does not require special expertise in test construction. It merely presents the reader with a series of contextually interrelated blanks in a passage. A cloze test is constructed by selecting a passage of a minimum of 250 words and mutilating it by (1) omitting every *nth* word throughout and leaving in their places blanks of some standard length, or (2) omitting every *nth* noun or every *nth* verb. Students read the passage and write in the missing words. It follows that the better the passage is understood, the more likely the reader can anticipate what words are missing. Schneyer found that cloze tests have adequate validity for evaluating reading comprehension for most general uses.[39] The first type of omission correlates more highly with vocabulary and reading comprehension; the second with story comprehension.[40]

The generally acceptable criteria for developing cloze exercises include the following:[41]

1. Every "nth" word is deleted. (N may equal any number between 5 and 12.)
2. The minimum passage length must be 250 words.
3. At least fifty deletions are used to insure adequate sampling of content.
4. For scoring for determining instructional level, the exact word deleted must be used by the reader in order for the scoring criteria to be valid.
5. Other scoring systems (synonyms, form classes) provide less interscorer reliability and require substantially more time.
6. The separate scoring of form classes or content and function words may provide specific information for specialized purposes.

While the cloze has been evaluated as a testing device, little has been said about its use as a teaching device. Sentences with blank spaces in which children write the word that best completes the thought, or sentences in which the children think of synonyms for the underlined word are types of exercises that develop skill in the use of this technique.

An individual's performance on a cloze test is a measure of ability to understand the meaning of the material being read. Meaning is based upon general language facility, vocabulary relevant to the material, native learning ability, and motivation.[42]

In evaluating the cloze test results, the percentage of correctly completed cloze units is used to assign levels of reading comprehension. For example, a percentage of correct answers of forty or below is equated with the frustration level of reading comprehension; a percentage of correct answers between forty and fifty is equated with the instructional level of reading comprehension; a percentage of correct answers above fifty is equated with the independent level of reading comprehension.

Practice exercise 1.

Directions: In this exercise you will use context clues to think accurately and to supply the missing word to give the meaning. Read the selection all the way through before filling in the blanks. You will need only *one* word for each blank.

Life in the Desert[43]

In the northern part of Africa is a great amount of hot, dry (1) _____ called desert. This desert is larger than our (2) _____ . The driest parts of the desert have hills and (3) _____ of sand. No one tries to live there. In some other parts, most of them where the (4) _____ is higher, there is enough rain for some plants to grow.

In these desert (5) _____ , there are hundreds of places where water (6) _____ from springs or wells throughout the year. Such a place (7) _____ called an oasis. At an oasis we find palm trees and (8) _____ . Sometimes several hundred or even several thousand people live near a place with water.

Many of the (9) _____ of the desert lands move about from one place to another. They do so to (10) _____ more water and grass for their animals. These traveling people (11) _____ called nomads.

Most of the land in desert country (12) _____ not owned by anyone.

Cloze Scoring Key.* (Grade level = 4.5)
1. *land,* country, area, region, sand
2. *United States,* country, land, nation, deserts, state
3. *drifts,* dunes, abundance
4. *land,* altitude
5. *lands,* wastelands, areas, regions, parts, places
6. *comes,* spurts, collects, splashes, flows, pours
7. *is*
8. *gardens,* plants, shade, water, spring
9. *people,* nomads, occupants, natives, tribes
10. *find,* supply, get, gather, have, locate, provide, fetch
11. *are*
12. *is*

*The word used by the author is in italics.

Practice exercise 2.

Directions: This is an elementary story about a woodsman who lost his ax. Read the story all the way through quickly and then fill in the blanks. Use only one word for each blank.

The Octopus and the Ax[44]

Once upon a time there was a poor man who lived near the sea. In summer, he fished for a (1) _____ . In winter he cut wood to (2) _____ .

One day, as he was working, (3) _____ ax fell into the water.

"Help!" (4) _____ the man. "I have lost my (5) _____ ." To his surprise, an octopus came (6) _____ . He was waving a gold ax (7) _____ one of his long, black arms.

(8) "_____ this the ax you lost?" asked (9) _____ octopus.

"No," said the man. "My (10) _____ is made of wood."

The octopus (11) _____ down again. This time he brought (12) _____ a silver ax.

"Is this the (13) _____ you lost?" asked the octopus.

"No," (14) _____ the man again. "My ax is (15) _____ wood."

Again the octopus went down. (16) _____ time he came up holding an (17) _____ of wood.

"Is this the ax (18) _____ lost?" asked the octopus.

"Yes! That (19) _____ it!" cried the man. "How can (20) _____ ever thank you?"

"Your honesty is (21) _____ the thanks I need," said the (22) _____ . He gave the man the lost (23) _____ , and the gold and silver ones, too.

Then, with a wave of his (24) _____ black arms, he went back to (25) _____ bottom of the sea.

Key:

1. living	6. up	11. went	16. this	21. all
2. sell	7. in	12. up	17. ax	22. octopus
3. his	8. is	13. ax	18. you	23. ax
4. cried	9. the	14. said	19. is	24. long
5. ax	10. ax	15. only	20. I	25. the

A cloze test.

Directions: In the following story, every seventh word has been left out. Read through the whole story quickly to see what the general idea is. Then anticipate the meaning the author had in mind by using all of the context clues you can find. Write the appropriate word on each blank. Remember you will need only one word for each blank.[45]

Outwitting Brindle

Uncle Hyatt Frame bought a cow named Brindle. He was pleased with his buy (1) _____ he milked her for the first (2) _____ . It took only two minutes for (3) _____ to discover that she was (4) _____ "switcher." Now, it is bad enough (5) _____ have a cow that keeps her (6) _____ going in fly time, but in (7) _____ there is not a bit of (8) _____ excuse for it. A blow in (9) _____ face from a long, stringy tail (10) _____ sure to cause a strong feeling (11) _____ to anger.

At the first switch (12) _____ Brindle's tail, Uncle Hyatt shouted, "Hey!" At (13) _____ second, he hit the cow in (14) _____ . At the third, he got off (15) _____ milking stool, found a piece of (16) _____ , and tied the tail to a (17) _____ .

Warm weather came. Uncle Hyatt moved his (18) _____ outside. At the first switch, he (19) _____ the tail and tied it to (20) _____ boot strap. When he finished the (21) _____ , he got up and picked up (22) _____ pail of milk. Then he gave (23) _____ a slap. Brindle moved away, taking (24) _____ left leg with her. His right (25) _____ followed.

Looking from the kitchen window, Aunt Emily (26) _____ amazed. She saw Uncle Hyatt hopping quickly (27) _____ the yard after the cow. Milk (28) _____ from the pail. Aunt Emily had no (29) _____ what the trouble was. The only (30) _____ she could see was that a (31) _____ milking was rapidly going to waste. (32) _____ called loudly from the open window, (33) " _____ out for the milk!" Then she (34) _____ to the door.

By this time, (35) _____ and Brindle had reached the farther (36) _____ of the yard. They had even (37) _____ on the return trip. Brindle had (38) _____ air of someone who knew where (39) _____ was going. Uncle Hyatt hopped after her, (40) _____ holding the milk pail, which grew (41) _____ and lighter.

"Stop her!" cried Uncle Hyatt.

(42) _____ was between them, so Aunt Emily did (43) _____ know the reason for Uncle Hyatt's strange (44) _____ . She ran through the gate, waving (45) _____ apron and calling, "Whoa, Brindle."

The (46) _____ cow began to run. The milk (47) _____ flew off to one side. Uncle Hyatt (48) _____ and moved quickly along at Brindle's (49) _____ , grabbing at anything in sight.

Finally (50) _____ boot strap broke. Brindle ran to (51) _____ farthest corner of the yard. Aunt Emily (52) _____ Uncle Hyatt to his feet, took him

(53) _____ the kitchen, and worked over him (54) _____ liniment. "Tell me something, Hyatt," she (55) _____ . "If you had to tie the (56) _____ to a leg, why didn't you (57) _____ it to Brindle's?"

Key:

1. until	16. rope	30. thing	44. behavior
2. time	17. rafter	31. whole	45. her
3. him	18. milking	32. She	46. frightened
4. a	19. grabbed	33. Look	47. pail
5. to	20. his	34. hurried	48. fell
6. tail	21. milking	35. Uncle Hyatt	49. heels
7. winter	22. the	36. end	50. his
8. an	23. Brindle	37. started	51. the
9. the	24. Uncle Hyatt's	38. the	52. helped
10. is	25. leg	39. she	53. into
11. leading	26. was	40. still	54. with
12. of	27. about	41. lighter	55. said
13. the	28. splashed	42. Brindle	56. tail
14. anger	29. idea	43. not	57. tie
15. the			

Learning to Anticipate Meanings: Predicting What Will Happen Next

Example 1.[46]

Read the paragraph and two sentences in each column below. Then draw a line under the sentence that answers the question correctly.

The red fox was clever and full of tricks, and never had trouble finding something to eat. In summer he caught small animals and birds. In winter he caught fish through a hole in the ice.

How will the red fox get along without the white fox?

He will go hungry. He will have all that he needs.

The white fox did very little. He sunned himself in front of the den in summer. He slept in his warm bed during the cold, dark winter. Every day he waited for the red fox to come home.

How will the white fox get along without the red fox?

He will go hungry. He will have all that he needs.

1. What the white fox did _____ .
2. What the red fox did _____ .

Example 2.[47]

Read each of the next two paragraphs and the statements which accompany them. Underline the statement that best predicts the outcome for each paragraph.

One winter day a country boy was driving a team of horses. It began to snow, and the wind blew the snow in his face. All around him the falling snow was like a thick curtain. He drove the horses where he thought the road was. Soon he knew he was lost. Then he remembered that horses always know the way home, even in a bad storm.

The horses ate the grass by the road.
He let the horses find the way home.
He made the horses stand still.
He took his sister in out of the storm.

A boy who had never seen snow was taken to a place where snow fell every winter. He could hardly wait to see the snow for he had heard how fluffy and white

Figure 10.3 An exercise requiring the student to process given information and draw the appropriate conclusion.

From Guy L. Bond, Marie C. Cuddy, and Leo C. Fay, *Fun to Do Book* to accompany *Stories to Remember* (Chicago, Ill.: Lyons and Carnahan, 1962), p. 95.

Read Carefully

Science reading must be done carefully. To show that you can read carefully, do what each paragraph tells you to do. You may wish to refer to *Stories to Remember*.

Uranium is used in the production of atomic energy. If both *pitchblende* and *uranite* are rich sources of uranium, draw a line around those words at the right. If uranium is sometimes found in petrified wood, draw a line around the word *petrified*. If it is not found in all three, put a line around *dynamite*.

carnotite	dynamite
uranite	petrified
pitchblende	bauxite
cryolite	probe

A Geiger counter detector is a box with earphones, dials, and other gadgets on it. It is used to detect uranium. If it does this by making a red light show when the probe is near uranium, draw a line around the picture of the Geiger counter at the right. If by making a clicking sound it shows that uranium is near, write the word *demonstrated* under the picture.

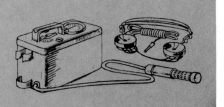

it was. He had been told that it made fences, roads, and even trash heaps beautiful. One morning when he opened his eyes he saw a strange white world through the window. It had snowed.

He turned over and went back to sleep.
He pulled down the window shade at once.
He ran to the window and looked out.
He waited until the winter came.

Drawing Inferences

Based on factual information.   In order to draw inferences based on factual information, it is necessary for the reader to retain, select, and evaluate the information read and then follow the directions to draw conclusions based on the evidence. The exercise presented in figure 10.3 is based on a story in a sixth grade reader.

Ideas implied but not stated.   A student able to evaluate while reading—that is, able to read critically—will be able to draw inferences and arrive at conclusions. Such an ability is achieved by practice. This skill is necessary in evaluating the characters in a story, with just descriptions of their behavior given. In the story presented in figure 10.4, sixth graders are asked to infer appropriate meanings or to draw conclusions based on the reading.

Figure 10.4 Critical reading requires the student to extend the given information to formulate proper conclusions.

From Guy L. Bond, Marie C. Cuddy, and Leo C. Fay, *Fun to Do Book* to accompany *Stories to Remember* (Chicago, Ill.: Lyons and Carnahan, 1962), p. 60.

Read and Think

Read the story and be ready to answer some questions about it.

Part I

Obed Swain was an old sailor, or, as he would have put it, "an old sea dog." He had once been captain of the good ship *Catawba* and had sailed the seven seas. Now that he was old, he had settled down to life in a village. The only difficulty which he had not been able to surmount was that of monotony. The captain had been accustomed to monotony at sea, but had always found diversion in regaling his shipmates with tales of his adventures. People in the village, which Obed Swain called a "landlocked town," did not seem to understand his seafaring language. At first they found it a diversion just to listen to the old captain talk, but soon they lost interest in his tales.

Mark your answer with a check (✓).

What is an "old sea dog"?

___ 1. A dog that goes to sea

___ 2. A worn-out ship

___ 3. An old sailor

What do you think Obed Swain meant by a "landlocked town"?

___ 1. A town with no land to sell

___ 2. An inland town away from the sea

___ 3. A town far away from other towns

Part II

Shortly after the captain settled down in his new home, a railroad was built through the village. Almost everyone was excited about it, but Obed Swain had paid no attention to the event until the day the first train came in. The sight had an electrifying effect on the captain.

"What kind of contrivance is that?" he asked. Then, seeing the smoke pour from the smokestack, he exclaimed, "See that black smoke! That contrivance must burn sperm oil!"

When the train stopped, the captain went over to look at the locomotive. As he approached it, a jet of vapor issued from the side of the engine.

"Thar she blows!" shouted the captain. "Thar she blows on the larboard side!"

When the vapor had disappeared, Captain Swain talked to the engineer.

"Ho, there! Are you the captain of this craft?" inquired Obed. "Where's your ratlines? I want to come aboard."

The engineer did not know what ratlines were, but he helped the old gentleman get up into the locomotive. Obed Swain asked questions about different devices he saw. He understood engines, so he and the engineer had an enjoyable time.

From that day on, the captain looked forward to train time.

Mark your answer with a check (✓).

Which of the following show that the story probably did not take place in recent times?

___ 1. A railroad was just being built into the town.

___ 2. The old man did not know a locomotive when he saw it.

___ 3. Black smoke was coming out of the smokestack.

60

Drawing Generalizations

One lesson in generalizing is being able to read material such as a fable and decide what it illustrates.[48]

1. One sunny day two ducks went out for a walk. "Child," said the mother duck, "you're not walking very prettily. You should try to walk straight without waddling so."

"Dear Mother," said the young duck, "if you'll walk the way you want me to walk, I'll follow you."

2. A lamb on a rooftop saw a wolf pass by on the ground below. The lamb shouted, "Get away from here, you terrible creature! How dare you show your face here!"

   "You talk very boldly," replied the wolf. "Would you be as bold if you were down on the ground?"

3. After fishing for a whole day, a fisherman caught only a single small fish. "Please let me go," begged the fish. "I'm too small to eat now. If you put me back into the pond, I'll grow. Then you can make a meal of me."

   "Oh, no!" said the fisherman. "I have you now. I may not catch you again."

4. One warm day a hungry fox spied a delicious-looking bunch of fruit. It was hanging on a vine that was tied to a high fence. The fox jumped and jumped, trying to reach the fruit. But each time he just missed it. When he was too tired to jump again, he gave up.

   "I'm sure that fruit is spoiled," grumbled the fox as he went away.

   A bird in the hand is worth two in the bush.

   It is easy to dislike what you cannot get.

   Setting a good model is the best way to teach.

   It is easy to be brave from a safe distance.

Evaluation Skills

Exercises like the following are useful.[49]

Separating Fact from Fancy

Telling Which Could Happen

Read the paragraph and accompanying sentence in each section below based on the article about Johnny Appleseed. Then draw a ring around the word *Yes* if the sentence is true according to the article and around the word *No* if the sentence is not true.

One day Johnny Appleseed came to a clearing in which a family had built a cabin. He stopped to plant some apple seeds, and the family asked him to stay for the night. The next morning after breakfast he continued on his way.

This little story could be true.
Yes   No

Johnny stopped beside a stream one day to eat some lunch. As he was sitting under a tree, a squirrel came up and sat on his knee.

"May I have something to eat, too?" asked the squirrel. "I'm hungry."

This little story could be true.
Yes   No

Selecting Material Pertinent to a Given Topic

Determining whether all the sentences relate to a topic sentence in a paragraph is a skill children may develop from exercises like the following.[50]

Directions: Read each of the following paragraphs and find one sentence that does not belong in each one.

As we shot up in the elevator to the top of the Empire State building in New York, I began to realize how high one hundred two stories are. We walked out upon the balcony from which we could look in all directions over the great city below. I caught my breath because of the distance I could see, and because the air seemed thin away up so high. I marveled at the huge tower of steel and concrete under me. We went aboard an ocean liner while we were in New York.

The Indians were friendly toward the earliest settlers in America. They taught the Pilgrims how to plant corn and how to hunt the deer for food. If the Indians had been hostile, they could have destroyed the tiny settlement, but they allowed the pioneers to build their homes and plant crops on the land that had been their hunting ground. King Philip later became the enemy of the whites.

A simple test will tell you whether or not silk has been woven with lead or other metals to make it seem of better quality than it really is. Flowered silks are pretty. Burn a sample of the material. If the silk burns up completely as if it were paper, it is probably pure silk. If a hard substance is left in the ashes, the material is not pure silk.

On our way home from the picnic Oliver stumbled and sprained his ankle. He could not walk, and we had to get to the nearest farmhouse to telephone for a doctor. We had taken bacon and eggs for our lunch. We made a chair for Oliver by crossing our hands and taking hold of each other's wrists. Our progress was slow, but we were able to reach the farmhouse and secure a doctor's services before the painful ankle had swollen badly.

Overstatement or Unfounded Claims

Since the first sentence below is a direct quote from another source, and the sentence following it is not, one may conclude that the writer of the second statement is pointing out that it is really an unfounded claim. The writer is also implying that there is no evidence to substantiate the claim.

"The good teacher of beginning reading, where she is not bound by an imposed methodology, operates on the theory that *beginning* reading is not a thought getting process but is based on translating letters into sounds." No evidence was cited as to source of this data.[51]

Judging Emotional Response to What Is Read

Examples like the following could be used as exercises.[52]

1. If you were sitting on the roof of a house floating down toward the sea in a terrible storm, how would you feel?
   shy   terrified   sleepy
2. If you knew that a policeman was coming to take your pet away, how would you feel?
   smart   alarmed   thirsty
3. If you thought you were very beautiful but no one talked to you or wanted to be around you, how would you feel?
   happy   limp   lonely
4. If a green-and-silver airplane popped out of a blackberry pie that you had bought at the bakery, how would you feel?
   stupid   surprised   chilly
5. If you were the manager of a bus company and people called you all day about a queer-acting bus, how would you feel?
   puzzled   cunning   gay

Summary

Comprehension skills have been defined and illustrated as understanding literal meanings, formulating interpretive meanings, and evaluation. Literal comprehension was defined as understanding vocabulary concepts, integrated ideas in sentences, and paragraph organization. Literal comprehension also involves getting ideas from the context. Some exercises to practice such skills are reading to find answers to questions, finding main ideas, and arranging ideas in proper sequence to tell a story.

Interpretive skills include anticipating meanings, drawing inferences, drawing generalizations, and evaluating with respect to what is read.

Evaluation skills are required to distinguish fact from fancy, select ideas pertinent to a topic, react to overstatements or unfounded claims, and judge emotional response to what is read.

Suggested Activities

Prepare a list of skills to be taught, then find in a teacher's manual for a graded reader two examples of each skill being emphasized in a lesson plan. Identify the book and page number of each lesson plan. You may wish to organize your paper like this:

Skill:	Example 1:	Example 2:
1. Predicting what will happen next.		
2. Reading to appreciate the general significance.		

For Further Reading

Bond, Guy, and Miles Tinker. *Reading Difficulties: Their Diagnosis and Correction.* "Development of the Basic Comprehension Abilities." New York: Appleton-Century-Crofts, 1973.

Bormuth, John. "Cloze as a Measure of Readability." In *Reading as an Intellectual Activity,* edited by J. Allen Figurel. International Reading Assn. Conference Proceedings 8(1963): 131–34.

Dallman, Martha, et al. *The Teaching of Reading,* 4th ed. New York: Holt Rinehart & Winston, 1974, chapter 6, "Comprehension," pp. 164–212.

Gallant, Ruth. "Use of Cloze Tests as a Measure of Readability in the Primary Grades." In *Reading and Inquiry,* edited by J. Allen Figurel. International Reading Assn. Conference Proceedings 10 (1965):286–87.

Glock, Marvin D. "Developing Clear Recognition of Pupil Purposes for Reading." *The Reading Teacher* 11 (February 1958):165–70.

Green, Richard T. *Comprehension in Reading: An Annotated Bibliography.* Newark, Del.: International Reading Assn., 1971.

———. "Ten Information Sources on Comprehension in Reading." *Journal of Reading* 16(October 1972):55–57.

Harris, A. J., and E. R. Sipay. *Effective Teaching of Reading,* chapter 11, "Building Comprehension in Reading." New York: David McKay, 1971.

Henderson, Richard L., and Donald R. Green. *Reading for Meaning in the Elementary School.* Englewood Cliffs, N.J.: Prentice-Hall, 1969.

Huus, Helen. "Basic Reading Skill Instruction in the Total Curriculum." In *Reading and the Elementary School Curriculum,* pp. 25–33, edited by David Shepherd. Newark, Del.: International Reading Assn., 1969.

Jongsma, Eugene. *The Cloze Procedure as a Teaching Technique.* Newark, Del.: International Reading Assn., 1971.

Kennedy, Dolores. "The Cloze Procedure, Use It to Develop Comprehension Skills." *Instructor* 84 (November 1974):82–86.

McKee, Paul. *Reading: A Program of Instruction for the Elementary School,* chapter 8, "Coping with Meaning Difficulties," pp. 255–315. Boston: Houghton Mifflin, 1966.

Rankin, Earl F. "The Cloze Procedure—A Survey of Research." *Yearbook of the National Reading Conference* 14(1965):133–50.

Robinson, Richard D. *An Introduction to the Cloze Procedure, An Annotated Bibliography.* Newark, Del.: International Reading Assn., 1972.

Schell, Leo M. "Promising Possibilities for Improving Comprehension." *Journal of Reading* 15(March 1972):415–24.

Schneyer, J. Wesley. "Use of the Cloze Procedure for Improving Reading Comprehension." *The Reading Teacher* 19 (December 1965):174–80.

Smith, Nila B. *Reading Instruction for Today's Children,* chapter 9, "Getting Meanings from Reading," pp. 255–303. Englewood Cliffs, N.J.: Prentice-Hall, 1963.

Taylor, Wilson L. "Cloze Procedure: A New Tool for Measuring Readability." *Journalism Quarterly* 30(Fall 1953):415–33.

Tinker, Miles A., and Constance McCullough. *Teaching Elementary Reading,* 3d ed., chapter 9, "Comprehension and Interpretation," pp. 185–203. New York: Appleton-Century-Crofts, 1968.

Weaver, W. W., and A. J. Kingston. "A Factor Analysis of the Cloze Procedure and Other Measures of Reading and Language Ability." *Journal of Communications* 13(1963):252–61.

Notes

1. M. Lucile Harrison, *Reading Readiness* (Boston: Houghton Mifflin, 1936), p. 37.
2. Ernest Horn, "Language and Meaning," *The Psychology of Learning,* Forty-First Yearbook of the National Society for the Study of Education, Part II, Nelson B. Henry, ed. (Chicago: University of Chicago Press, 1942), p. 402.
3. Russell G. Stauffer, *Directing Reading Maturity as a Cognitive Process* (New York: Harper & Row, 1969), p. 59.
4. Hilda Taba, *Teaching Strategies and Cognitive Functioning in Elementary School Children.* U.S. Office of Education, Cooperative Research Project No. 2404. (San Francisco: San Francisco State College, 1966), pp. 36–43.
5. A. S. Artley, "Teaching Word Meaning Through Context," *Elementary English Review* 20 (1943):68–74; Constance M. McCullough, "The Recognition of Context Clues in Reading," *Elementary English Review* 22 (1945):1–5.
6. *Manual for Interpretation of Iowa Every-Pupil Tests of Basic Skills* (Iowa City, Ia.: College of Education, State University of Iowa, 1947), pp. 42–43.
7. Lee C. Deighton, *Vocabulary Development in the Classroom* (New York: Bureau of Publications, Teachers College, Columbia University, 1959), pp. 56–59.
8. Frank J. Guszak, "Teachers' Questions and Levels in Reading Comprehension," in *Perspectives in Reading: The Evaluation of Children's Reading Achievement,* ed. James F. Kerfoot (Newark, Del.: International Reading Assn., 1967), pp. 97–109.

9. Lecture by Dr. Mildred Fitzpatrick, 1967, Director, New Mexico Title I Program, State Department of Education, Santa Fe.

10. Helen Newcastle, "Children's Problems with Written Directions," *The Reading Teacher* 28 (December 1974):292.

11. Patricia McCalmont Willins, "The Effects of Variable Directions and Formats in Reading Workbooks upon Oral Responses, Visual Cue Use, and Error Scores," an unpublished doctoral dissertation, The Graduate School, The University of New Mexico, Albuquerque, 1977, p. 105.

12. A. D. Woodruff, *Basic Concepts in Teaching* (San Francisco: Chandler Publishing Co., 1961), p. 57.

13. N. Billings, *Determination of Generalizations Basic to Social Studies* (Baltimore: Wardwick & York, 1929), p. 243.

14. Ruth G. Strickland, *The Language Arts in the Elementary School* (Boston: D.C. Heath, 1951), p. 3.

15. Hilda Taba, *Curriculum Development: Theory and Practice* (New York: Harcourt, Brace & World, 1962), p. 175, 176, 178.

16. Benjamin S. Bloom et al., *Taxonomy of Educational Objectives* (New York: Longman, Green, 1956; 17th printing, New York: David McKay, 1971).

17. Guszak, "Teachers' Questions."

18. Hilda Taba, S. Levine, and F. F. Elzey, *Thinking in Elementary School Children* (San Francisco: San Francisco State College, U.S. Office of Education, Cooperative Research Project No. 1574, 1964), pp. 53–54.

19. William S. Gray and Gwen Horseman, *Basic Reading Skills for Junior High School Use* (Chicago: Scott, Foresman, 1957), p. 13.

20. William S. Gray, Marian Monroe, and Steryl Artley, *Think-And-Do Book* to accompany *Just Imagine!* Teacher's Edition (Chicago: Scott, Foresman, 1953), p. 24, and Guidebook to accompany *Basic Reading Skills for Junior High School Use,* Teacher's Edition (Chicago: Scott, Foresman, 1957), p. 19.

21. Paul McKee et al., *Workbook for On We Go* (Boston: Houghton Mifflin, 1963), p. 25.

22. William S. Gray and Gwen Horseman, *Basic Reading Skills for Junior High School Use* (Chicago: Scott, Foresman, 1957), p. 21.

23. William A. McCall and Lelah Mae Crabbs, *Standard Test Lessons in Reading,* Book B (New York: Bureau of Publications, Teachers College, Columbia University, 1961), p. 9.

24. Arthur I. Gates, *Gates Silent Reading Test, Type D: Reading to Note Details,* Form 1, Grades 3–8 (New York City: Bureau of Publications, Teachers College, Columbia University, 1926).

25. Ibid., *Gates Silent Reading Test, Type A: Reading to Appreciate General Significance,* Form 2, Grades 3–8.

26. Ibid., *Gates Silent Reading Test Type C: Reading to Understand Precise Directions,* Form 1, Grades 3–8.

27. Paul McKee, *The Teaching of Reading in the Elementary School* (Boston: Houghton Mifflin, 1948), p. 87.

28. Arthur Heilman, *Principles and Practices of Teaching Reading* (Columbus, Ohio: Charles E. Merrill, 1972), pp. 374–76.

29. Miles V. Zintz, *Education Across Cultures* (Dubuque, Ia: Kendall/Hunt, 1969), p. 45.

30. Arthur I. Gates and Celeste C. Peardon, *Reading Exercises, Preparatory, Level A* (New York: Bureau of Publications, Teachers College, Columbia University, 1963), story no. 5.

31. Guy L. Bond, Marie C. Cuddy, and Leo C. Fay, *Fun to Do Book* to accompany *Stories to Remember* (Chicago: Lyons & Carnahan, 1962), p. 22.

32. Ibid. p. 34.

33. Ibid.

34. Harold Shane et al., *Using Good English, Book Five* (River Forest, Ill: Laidlaw Brothers, 1961), p. 84.

35. Guy L. Bond, Marie C. Cuddy, and Leo C. Fay, *Fun to Do Book* to accompany *Stories to Remember* (Chicago: Lyons & Carnahan, 1962), p. 35.

36. Ibid.

37. Harold Shane et al., *Using Good English, Book Six* (River Forest, Ill.: Laidlaw Brothers, 1961), p. 81.

38. Wilson L. Taylor, "Cloze Procedure: A New Tool for Measuring Readability," *Journalism Quarterly* 30(Fall 1953):416.

39. Wesley J. Schneyer, "Use of the Cloze Procedure for Improving Reading Comprehension," *The Reading Teacher* 19(December 1965):174.

40. W. W. Weaver and A. J. Kingston, "A Factor Analysis of the Cloze Procedure and Other Measures of Reading and Language Ability," *Journal of Communications* 13 (1963):253.

41. Thomas C. Potter, *A Taxonomy of Cloze Research, Part I, Readability and Reading Comprehension* (11300 La Cienega Blvd, Inglewood, Calif. 90304: Southwest Regional Laboratory for Educational Research and Development, 1968), pp. 39–40.

42. Taylor, "Cloze Procedure," p. 416.

43. Marian Tonjes, "Evaluation of Comprehension and Vocabulary Gains of Tenth Grade Students Enrolled in a Developmental Reading Program," M.A. thesis, The Graduate School, The University of New Mexico, Albuquerque, 1969, pp. 66–67.

44. Clarence R. Stone and Ardis Edwards Gurton, *New Practice Readers,* Book A (New York: Webster Division, McGraw-Hill, 1960), pp. 90–91.

45. Clarence R. Stone and Charles C. Grover, *New Practice Readers,* Book D (New York: McGraw-Hill, 1962), pp. 82–83.

46. William Burton et al., *Flying High,* Developmental Reading Text Workbook, Grade Five (Indianapolis, Ind.: Bobbs-Merrill, 1964), p. 98.

47. Arthur I. Gates, *Gates Silent Reading Test, Type B: Reading to Predict the Outcome of Given Events,* Form 1, Grades 3–8 (New York: Bureau of Publications, Teachers College, Columbia University, 1926).

48. *Think and Do Book* to accompany *Just Imagine* (Chicago: Scott, Foresman, 1953), p. 42.

49. Burton et al., *Flying High,* p. 95.

50. R. W. Bardwell, Ethel Mabie, and J. C. Tressler, *Elementary English in Action,* Grade V (Boston: D.C. Heath, 1935), p. 286.

51. Arthur W. Heilman, *Principles and Practices of Teaching Reading,* 2d ed. (Columbus, Ohio: Charles E. Merrill, 1967), p. 260.

52. W. S. Gray et al., *Think and Do Book* to accompany *Just Imagine* (Chicago: Scott, Foresman, 1953), p. 55.

11

Study Skills

Study skills, sometimes identified as the *functional skills of reading,* deserve greater emphasis in the developmental reading program than is often given to them. The level of mastery of these skills will determine how efficiently a student will be able to learn in all the content areas of the curriculum.

Some elementary teachers have failed to accept responsibility for the planned, sequential development of specific abilities such as making outlines, locating information, or learning to read maps, graphs, and charts efficiently. A detailed outline list of such specific skills is presented at the end of the chapter.

Teachers must be mindful not only of the need to teach study skills, but also of the importance of spaced review and reinforcement later in the school program to insure that the skills are practiced and retained.

Reading in Subject-Matter Areas

The reading in subject-matter areas is generally more difficult than the reading in organized reading classes. Such reading requires special vocabulary; comprehension of concepts; ability to locate and read maps, graphs, and charts and apply their content in further reading in the text; and organization and evalution of the reading.

Fay identified the following difficulties with reading in the content areas.[1]

1. There is an unduly heavy load of facts and concepts.
2. Variations in typographical arrangement from one area to another may confuse the pupil.
3. All too frequently the materials are uninteresting to the pupils.
4. Materials are often less readable than are basic readers.
5. Many writers tend to assume the children have more background than is the case.

Fay concluded that materials to be read for subject matter should be carefully fitted to children and instruction in reading such materials carefully organized.

Are there specific steps that might help anyone get more out of reading? Robinson has suggested an easy-to-remember formula that has proved very useful.[2] He calls it the SQ3R method of study—*Survey, Question, Read, Recite,* and *Review.* It can be summarized as follows.

Survey: Glance over the headings in the chapter to see the main points that will be developed. Also read the final summary paragraph if the chapter has one. This survey should not take more than a minute and will show the three to six core ideas around which the discussion will center. This orientation will help to organize the ideas as you read them later.

Question: Now begin to work. Turn the first heading into a question. This will arouse your curiosity and so increase your comprehension. It will bring to mind information already known, thus helping you to understand that section more quickly. And the question you have raised in your mind will make important points stand out while explanatory detail is recognized as such. Turning a heading into a question as it is read is not difficult, but keeping the question in mind as one reads to find the answer requires a conscious effort.

Read: Read to answer that question, at least to the end of the section. This is not a passive plodding along each line, but an active search for an answer.

Recite: Having read the section, look away from the book and try to recite briefly the answer to your question. Use your own words and include an example. If you can do this, you know what you have read; if you can't, glance over it again. An excellent way to do this reciting from memory is to jot down cue phrases in outline form on a sheet of paper.

Review: When the lesson has been completely read, look over your notes to get a bird's eye view of the points and their relationship and check your memory as to the content by reciting the major subpoints under each heading.

Using the Newspaper to Teach Skills

Newspapers offer a continuous source of material for teaching skills as well as content. Piercey[3] has pointed out several specific ways newspapers can be useful to teachers. They can help students strengthen comprehension skills, critical reading, study skills, vocabulary and creative writing. News stories are tailor-made to help students extract main ideas because they give the important facts in the first one or two paragraphs. In the opening of a news story, called the lead, are answers to who? what? where? why? and when?

Newspapers can help students find supporting details. After a couple of paragraphs covering the main facts, details are usually unfolded in an organized way. Also, by-line columns on and opposite the editorial page offer good debate material for critical readers.

Sample Lessons

Outlining

By studying children's workbooks and teachers' guides, teachers will find graduated sequences of exercises helpful for teaching outlining. It is clear that authors intend boys and girls to have a great deal of guidance before they are expected to make outlines independently. The following two lessons are examples.

Sample Lesson 1[4]

Read the following essay.

How to Become a Good Oral Reader

Good readers select very carefully what they are to read. They try to choose an interesting story or a worthwhile article, one which their listeners will surely enjoy. If they are reading to prove a point, they read only the sentences that are necessary. If they are reading an interesting story or part of a story, they select one which is not too long to be interesting. Here is the first rule: If you want people to like to hear you read, select your story or article carefully.

Good readers know well the story or article which they are to read. In the first place, they know the exact meaning of what they are to read. It would be hard to give the meaning to other people if the readers themselves did not know the meaning. In the second place, they know the words in the selection so that they do not pronounce them incorrectly and spoil the meaning for the listeners. This all takes time and study, but it is necessary if people are to read aloud well. The second rule is: Know well the selection you are to read aloud.

Good readers keep their audience interested in what they are reading. They read loudly enough to be heard easily. They read clearly, so that the listeners do not have to guess what they are saying. They make the important points in the selection stand out plainly, and they read with expression so that the characters talk like real people. Good readers work and practice to do all these things well, in order to keep their audience interested. And so the last rule is: Keep your listeners interested to the very last of what you read.

Directions to the student:

In this article, you have read three rules for reading aloud well to others. Perhaps you noticed that the topic sentence at the beginning is the same as the rule stated at the end of each paragraph. The skeleton outline below tells you to find three details in paragraph one, two details in paragraph two, and four details in paragraph three. Complete the skeleton outline.

How to Become a Good Oral Reader

I.
   A.
   B.
   C.

II.
   A.
   B.

III.
   A.
   B.
   C.
   D.

Sample Lesson 2 Read the following essay.

The Monarch Butterfly

General description

The male monarch is one of the most beautiful of all the butterflies. He is not only neat looking and pretty, but on each hind wing he carries a little pocket of perfume to help get the attention of the female monarch. She is as brilliant as he but lacks the perfume pockets. Birds do not like to eat monarchs either as adults or as larva, probably because the monarch feeds on the milkweed which is a very distasteful plant.

Migration in winter; evidence of traveling long distances

The monarchs are great travelers. They travel north during our growing season but must go back south when we have winter. In the early spring, the mother butterfly flies north as far as she can find milkweeds growing and lays her eggs on the milkweed plant. These eggs hatch and the larva soon become adults and fly farther north because later in the summer the milkweed will be growing still farther north. Sometimes monarchs are found as far north as the Hudson Bay. When cold weather comes, these butterflies gather in great flocks and move back south. It is impossible for us to know how flocks of butterflies are guided in their migration. The monarch is the strongest flyer of all the butterflies. He has been seen flying out over the ocean five hundred miles from land.

Body parts and how they function

The monarch butterfly, like other insects, breathes by means of a system of air tubes through the sides of his body. The body is divided into three parts: the head, the thorax, and the abdomen. He has one pair of antennae, three pairs of legs, and two pairs of wings. He has two large compound eyes but no single eyes. The monarch has sucking mouth parts to draw the honey out of the flower, for example, but he cannot bite.

Metamorphosis; life stages

There are four stages in the monarch's life: egg, larva or caterpillar, chrysalis or pupa, and adult. When the egg hatches into a larva, the larva is very small. This larva molts, just as grasshoppers do, before it becomes as large as it will get. After molting out of its skin four or five times, the larva spins itself a cocoon and in about two weeks hatches out of the cocoon as an adult monarch. The adult monarch is a beautiful brown with the border and veins black and with two rows of white spots on the outer borders. If the adult does not meet with an accident, it will likely live for from four to six years.

Study Skills

Directions to the student:

The four major headings have been selected for you. Using the outline form provided, complete the following topical outline:

A topical outline

The Monarch Butterfly

I. General description
   A. _____
   B. _____
   C. _____

II. Migration
   A. _____
      1. _____
      2. _____
   B. _____
   C. _____
      1. _____
      2. _____
   D. _____

III. Structure and function
   A. _____
      1. _____
      2. _____
      3. _____
   B. _____
   C. _____
      1. _____
      2. _____
      3. _____
      4. _____
      5. _____

IV. Life stages (metamorphosis)
   A. _____
   B. _____
   C. _____
   D. _____
      1. _____
      2. _____

A Time Line

A time line is a graphic presentation of a chronological outline showing important facts in outline form. By the fourth grade the child should have had the concept of time introduced to him in terms of his own experience, such as the passing of a day as the earth rotates once, weeks, months, seasons, and his own birthdays. He will thus be ready for historical time lines in fifth and sixth grade. The time line in figure 11.1 shows many of the "events" presented in a fifth grade social studies program.

Greer suggests that the child at the sixth grade level can see the analogy between the chronology of mankind's history and the chronology of the child's personal history.[5]

Before you were born, your parents were children and lived with their parents; later your parents had a home of their own; then you were born; you learned to walk, to talk, and started to school. In your lifetime there have been special events you remember most vividly.

Mankind's history is divided into two parts: B.C. and A.D. In history, man lived in caves. He learned to make tools and use them in hunting. He began to live in groups called tribes. After Christ was born many events occurred in man's history. America was discovered; people came to live here; cars and planes were invented.

```
5    4    3    2    1    0    1    2    3    4    5
                      your birth
                    Christ's birth
```

Using Climatic Charts in the Study of Geography

The climatic chart is an excellent aid to guide intermediate grade students in generalizing about a geographic location. They need to study first the climatic chart representative of the area where they live so they can use it as a reference point in later work. They learn to notice the length of the frost-free, or growing, season; the amount of cold, cool, warm, and hot weather throughout the year, and during which months; and the amount of rainfall and its distribution throughout the year. The students can then learn to generalize. The example in figure 11.2 of a climatic chart for Chicago, Illinois illustrates how the basic elements of climate appear when graphed.

Conceal the station information at the top of the chart and see if you can answer the following questions by studying only the rainfall, temperature, and growing season.

1. Is the growing season long enough to grow different cereal crops?
2. Is there sufficient annual rainfall to grow different cereal crops?
3. Is there sufficient hot weather at one time to ripen crops?
4. Would you expect to find four distinct seasons in this place?
5. Is this place north or south of the equator?
6. Will tropical fruits grow in this place?
7. What kind of vegetation would you expect to find here? Desert, mountain, tropical, or temperate zone?
8. Might there be snow here to add to the annual precipitation?
9. Since there is sufficient moisture, could two crops be produced annually on the same soil?

Interpreting Maps and Globes

Maps are very common in the everyday experiences of boys and girls in the elementary school, beginning with the road map that helps the family plan the vacation trip. Maps on television newscasts show where major events are happening. Newspapers, magazines, and advertising material present outline maps that pinpoint events and commercial products. Even restaurants are apt to have placemats that are printed with an outline map that locates the place where you are now eating and the one where you should eat next!

Prudence Cutright, A. Y. King, Ida Dennis, and F. Potter, *Living Together in the Americas* (New York: Macmillan, 1960), Teachers Guide, pp. 59, 61; text, p. 63.

| 1000 | 1100 | 1200 | 1300 | 1400 | 1500 | 1600 | 1700 | 1800 | 1900 |

(1000) Leif Ericson discovers America

(1260) Marco Polo's journey to China

(1492) Columbus discovers America

(1519) Magellan circumnavigates globe

(1609) Hudson discovers River and Bay

Make a time line (A.D. 1000–1875) like the one above and add the following events:

1420	Prince Henry establishes a school for sailors	1534 Cartier explored Gulf of St. Lawrence
1486	Dias sailed to Cape of Good Hope	1541 DeSoto discovered Mississippi
1497	Cabot explored North America	1577 Drake began world voyage
1498	Columbus made third voyage	1608 Champlain founded Quebec
1500	Cabral claimed Brazil	1620 Mayflower Compact signed
1513	Balboa discovered the Pacific	1623 New Netherland settled
1513	Ponce de Leon explored Florida	1630 Massachusetts Bay Colony settled

1636 Williams founded Rhode Island
1647 First public school in America
1664 New Netherland seized by English
1682 Pennsylvania settled by Penn
1814 First Power Loom built
1825 Erie Canal opened
1831 Steam locomotive pulled train
1859 First oil well drilled in U.S.

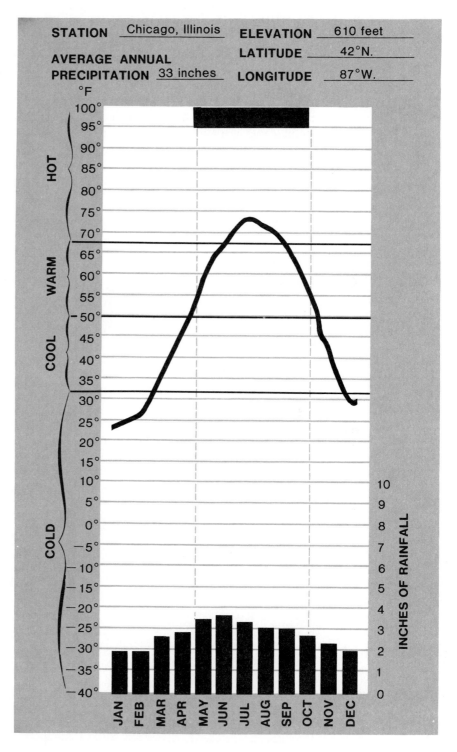

Figure 11.2 Climatic chart for Chicago, Illinois. Average monthly rainfall is represented by the bar graph; average monthly temperatures are represented by the line graph; and the length of the growing season is represented by the rectangle at the top (end of April to early October).

From H. L. Nelson, *Climatic Data for Representative Stations of the World* (Lincoln: University of Nebraska Press, 1968), p. 69.

Yet many boys and girls learn to pay little attention to these maps because they do not understand the legend or the vocabulary and they do not understand the map form of representation. If adults do not take the necessary few minutes to orient children, then the children are missing a very useful lesson that could make maps and diagrams meaningful to them. The nine-, ten-, and eleven-year-olds in the intermediate grades are apt to be very interested in the symbols, signs, and codes in the legends that make maps meaningful if they are guided in their understanding.

Children need to understand projections so that the difference between a Mercator and a polar projection is clear to them. It has been suggested that cutting an orange peel in sections so it can be flattened will show the polar

Figure 11.3
Distribution of some agricultural products in the United States.

From Prudence Cutright, Allen Y. King, Ida Dennis, and Florence Potter, *Living Together in the Americas* (New York: Macmillan, 1958), pp. 199, 251.

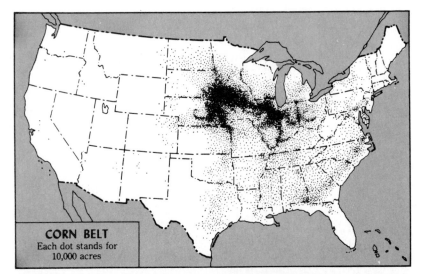

CORN BELT
Each dot stands for 10,000 acres

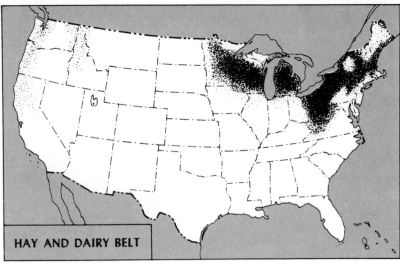

HAY AND DAIRY BELT

projection when the world is produced on a flat map. A hollow rubber ball could also be used and could be preserved indefinitely.

Teachers will find useful the Maps and Globes Kit marketed by Science Research Associates. It provides skills practice for effective use of maps and globes for grades 4–8. The kit contains exercise cards, resource cards, and skills starter cards.

A careful look at the maps in figures 11.3 and 11.4 can suggest to boys and girls questions about which they can do their own research.

1. In which states are both corn and wheat important crops?
2. In which states are both corn and cotton important crops?
3. Which states produce large quantities of corn, wheat, hay, and dairy products?

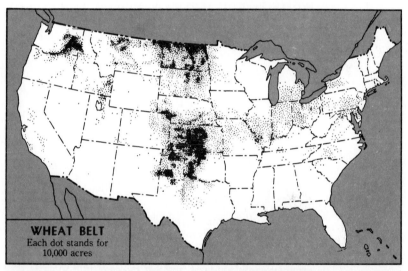

WHEAT BELT
Each dot stands for
10,000 acres

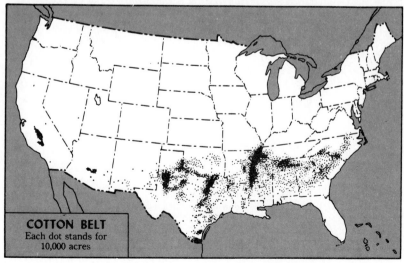

COTTON BELT
Each dot stands for
10,000 acres

Study Skills

Figure 11.4
Distribution of coal deposits in the United States.

From Cutright, King, Dennis, and Potter, *Living Together*, p. 110.

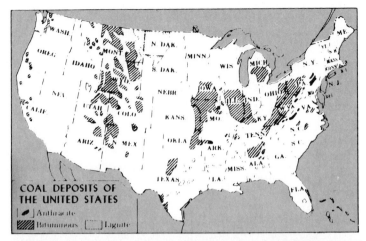

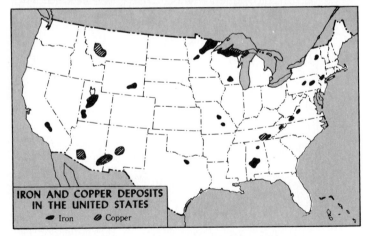

The Skills of Reading

4. Why are *hay* and *dairy* together on one map?
5. Can you state that there is no corn grown anywhere in the dairy belt? Why or why not?
6. Does the location of the iron ore and the bituminous coal deposits suggest why Pittsburgh, Pennsylvania became one of the greatest steel-producing centers in the United States? (Consider the location of the ore, the Great Lakes as inexpensive transportation, and the dense population of the metropolitan areas.)
7. Locate the state in which you live. Which ores are mined there? How significant is mining in the economic life of your state?

How to Teach a Unit of Work

The teacher may think of the unit as having five distinct steps, as shown in the outline below.

I. *Orientation*
   A. Create interest on the part of the class.
   B. Give the class some notion of the scope of the problem involved.
   C. Discuss with the group the purpose and possibilities of the unit so they can see the kind of problem the unit will help them solve.
   D. An orientation period may require varying lengths of time, from a day to a week.

II. *Teacher-pupil planning*
   A. Set down in writing the questions or problems to be answered by completing the unit of work.
   B. Many of the questions will be raised by the members of the class.
   C. The teacher is also a participating member and should raise questions not raised by the class.
   D. A teacher-pupil planning period may evolve a number of experiments to be performed, a list of questions to be answered through reading, or a study guide to provide direction to the *gathering information* phase of the unit.

III. *Gathering information*
   In the lower grades, children will work for short periods with frequent questioning and evaluation. In the higher elementary grades, a class may work for several class periods gathering information from a variety of sources in a variety of ways.

IV. *Sharing information*
   A sharing period would make it possible for the students to share information they have obtained from different sources, so that all members of the class need not read the same thing. The sharing period is especially important, too, for correcting any erroneous ideas children may have gotten in their reading.

V. *Culminating activity*
   There needs to be some way to summarize what the group has learned with the completion of each unit of work. This may be done in any one of several ways.

A. Prepare a program of reports for another group of children, for the class, or for the parents.

B. Make notebooks which compile summary statements about work done in the unit.

C. Take a unit test covering the information that has been taught in the class.

D. Discuss, plan, and draw a mural that tells the story of the unit. The discussion of what the class has learned is very important, since they need to handle the concepts of the unit through oral discussion.

The teacher-pupil planning period can be the most important both in setting up the objectives to be met, and in guiding the students in planning what they think is important—how they can carry out the activities of the unit, and which of them can exercise leadership in working with the teacher.

This method of teaching affords the teacher excellent opportunities for students to work together in small groups or committees and help each other. Organizing committees in the intermediate grades can be frustrating for a teacher if the boys and girls have never worked in this manner before. Yet, once they have learned to study together efficiently, many very important social interaction skills and social values are learned that are just as important as the subject matter being studied. If group work is new to the children, the teacher must guide the process skillfully. For example, groups can be set up for just one short period with no indication of their continuing after this first meeting. Then if the groups have a clear purpose for meeting and the teacher has planned ahead with the chairmen of the groups, the teacher can move from group to group and lend assistance where needed. The boys and girls themselves must evaluate the technique afterward as a total group and reveal their own weaknesses and decide how to move ahead.

The Study Guide

Graded study guides can help give children specific direction for doing silent-study exercises. They are one of the best ways for children to study their content subjects such as science, history, geography, or hygiene. The tasks to be outlined in the study guide will be determined by the planning done by the group with the teacher.

A study guide should be just what the name implies, a *guide* to help children understand, organize, and remember what they are reading. It should concentrate primarily upon thought processes, understanding, relating reading to children's experiences, seeing relationships, and paraphrasing ideas to insure retention.

The detailed suggestions given here about making and using study guides as an aid in studying the material are presented as general suggestions or ideas. They are intended to be useful to a teacher who must plan many types of job-sheets, study sheets, or test-exercises to help boys and girls better understand what they are studying.

Five points to keep in mind are:

1. If a child cannot pronounce the words, he or she needs word recognition exercises over the material before trying to read it silently.

2. If a child does not know the meanings of words, he or she needs vocabulary-building exercises before reading silently to try to understand.

3. In most textbooks, the hard new words are introduced too fast and not repeated often enough for children to learn them. Study guides should require close reading of small amounts of material and also rereading for different purposes.

4. Textbook sentences may sometimes have unusual or difficult syntax. Study-guide exercises should require some restating or paraphrasing of ideas in the text.

5. Often children have not had enough experience with the ideas in the reading material. For example, children may have difficulty with the sentence "Joe's father is working on the ditches that carry the water to irrigate the vegetable fields." If they have not had experience with ditches, irrigation, or vegetables raised in large areas, they need experience, either firsthand or vicarious, to remove this difficulty. Pictures in film, filmstrip, or a flat-picture collection; going to see the thing described; or reading easy material which describes it in terms the child already knows are ways of removing the difficulty.

The study guide should help the child think about and use the material read. Some of the reasons why a child cannot, or does not, think about and use material after reading it are these:

1. The child may have had no clear-cut purpose in reading the material other than to get through the lesson.

2. A child may be so engrossed with the details of every sentence, such as pronouncing hard words, that he or she does not see the larger purposes of the material being read.

3. The child may consider all the sentences of equal value and therefore will need to be taught that some ideas have more importance while others are subordinate. Study sheets are needed which require a child to identify the main ideas and minor ideas and to outline, summarize, and evaluate a selection.

Durrell, in his book *Improving Reading Instruction,*[6] suggests that the teacher needs to plan *levels* and *types* of study tasks in social science and science. The following suggestions will help in such planning.

1. A series of short tasks is easier than a single long task.

2. Multiple-choice answers or short oral answers are easier than unaided summaries.

3. Questions posed prior to reading provide more help than questions asked after reading.

4. Evaluation of the material immediately following the reading is more beneficial than evaluation at a later time.

A study guide for a unit of work needs to be prepared at two or three levels. It can be used in several ways, depending upon the group and their needs. The easiest level may be presented in the form of a list of questions for which children can find specific answers in a text; or they read the text and then select the right choice in multiple-choice questions. This task is easier when the answers are given orally than when they are written. At a more difficult level of functioning, the children are asked to write a summary paragraph about a lesson they have read and discussed.

Below are illustrative questions for a study guide for American history 1860–1865 in fifth grade. The level I questions represent literal comprehension; level II, interpretive comprehension; and level III, evaluation.[7]

Three-Level Study Guide, Fifth Grade

Level I. Check the statements that are accurate and appeared in the reading selection.

1. Hamilton believed that small farmers and merchants should be protected by the government.

2. The majority rules in our democratic form of government.

3. Jefferson formed a new political party to represent his ideas about government.

4. The Southern states controlled the House of Representatives in the fight over slavery.

5. The tariff benefited the North and hurt the South; so the Southern states threatened to ignore the tariff.

6. The cotton gin was an example of Northern industrialism.

7. The cotton gin increased the South's need for slavery.

8. With the expansion of the U.S. territory, states were being forced to enter the Union as either free or slave states.

Level II. Check the statements that are correct *interpretations* of the reading selection.

1. Southerners felt slaveholders should have more rights than free men.

2. A political party holds a common set of beliefs and goals.

3. In a democracy, people in the minority on an issue may not feel their needs are being met.

4. The tariff actually benefited the South.

5. The power of the federal government vs. the state government became a large issue in the Civil War.

6. The cotton gin probably was a factor in causing the Civil War.

7. The Missouri Compromise was a permanent solution to the free vs. slave state issue.

8. Popular sovereignty (the right of a state to decide) agrees with the Constitution, so the Missouri Compromise must be unconstitutional.

Level III. Which of the following statements best expresses or summarizes the meaning of the reading selection?

1. Compromise cannot work unless it deals with the real problems, not just symptoms.
2. Our federal Union should be like a happy marriage.
3. States' rights vs. federal control was one of the real issues of the Civil War.
4. When emotional discussions overrule rational thought and discussion, a break becomes inevitable.

Since study guides require time to prepare, they should be saved for future use as a reference to assist the teacher in updating and improving future lessons. Until study guides are provided with textbooks, teachers—individually or in groups—will have to prepare them. A few have been prepared and are provided commercially, but there is the problem of fitting the guide to the specific activities you wish to complete in your classroom.

Rate of Reading

While rate of reading is unimportant unless the student comprehends the material, it is certain that most people could read much more efficiently than they do and obtain just as much from their reading. It is safe to generalize that fast readers get more from their reading.

In the elementary school, however, it is necessary to establish mastery over the mechanics of reading before giving attention to the rate of reading. Until the child has mastered the words to use in reading, he cannot hurry up the process of assimilating the ideas expressed in those words.

Many adults, unsophisticated in the complexities of the reading process, think about reading speed when they talk about reading problems. If a child is already tense in the reading situation because he does not know how to break words into syllables, or because parts of words reverse themselves in the line of print (quiet—quite; form—from; angel—angle), or if he occasionally reads a word from the line above and then one from the line below the one he is really reading, to challenge him at that point with "Now, read faster!" the teacher is creating emotional problems that may be difficult to overcome.

Average rates of reading at each grade level in the elementary school have been provided by Harris and McCracken. These are given in table 11.1.

By November, Tom was well into his senior year of high school. He was being pressured to get ready to go to the university the next year in spite of serious reading difficulties. His parents were college graduates and expected Tom and his brother to complete college also. In his first interview, Tom discussed his difficulties with reading, writing, and spelling. In his second session in a reading clinic, he read material of approximately sixth grade level of difficulty at a speed of 111 words per minute with 65 percent comprehension.

During the six months that followed, Tom worked on the following elements.

1. Word forms. He faced problems of reversals of word parts by comparing, pronouncing, writing, and spelling many paired words commonly confused.

Table 11.1 Average rates of reading with comprehension in grades 1–6.

*Robert A. McCracken, "The Informal Reading Inventory as a Means of Improving Instruction," *Perspectives in Reading: The Evaluation of Children's Reading Achievement* 8 (1967):85. **Albert J. Harris and Edward R. Sipay, *How to Increase Reading Ability,* 6th ed. (New York: David

Grade	McCracken* Words per Minute		Harris and Sipay**
	Oral	Silent	Silent
1	60	60	—
2	70	70	86
3	90	120	116
4	120	150	155
5	120	170	177
6	150	245	206

The Skills of Reading

2. Word meanings. He learned about roots, prefixes, suffixes, and Greek and Latin combining forms.

3. Writing original paragraphs. He selected philosophical or esoteric topics according to his ephemeral interests and wrote short paragraphs which he and the tutor analyzed and corrected.

4. Rate of reading. He kept graphs of his speed and comprehension in reading Simpson's *Reading Exercises,* Books I and II.[8] From a speed of 111 words on the first story, he improved to a rate of 328 words per minute on one exercise. By graduation time, he was maintaining a speed of about 290 words per minute, which is adequate for college success if other study conditions are satisfactory. The graphs of his speed and comprehension are shown in figures 11.5 and 11.6.

Ideally, Tom's rate of reading will approximate his rate of thinking, since the rate of comprehension is basically being considered. Because of the wide individual differences within peer groups in ability to read silently and identify both literal and implied meanings in a passage, there is no *standard* or *best* rate of reading for all children. However, there are some generalizations that may be made about the individual and his silent reading:

1. Speed of reading should be partially determined by the purpose one has in mind when reading. Children need to adjust their speed in reading to their purpose. They will learn to "shift to a lower gear" when they are attempting to solve a verbal problem in arithmetic or general science. But they can "resume full speed" when they are enjoying an exciting story and wish to know the outcome.

2. Growth in reading efficiency—i.e., at rates appropriate to the material and the purpose—is most easily achieved by good teacher guidance.

3. Clear-cut purposes that are understood beforehand enable the reader to decide whether he can skim rapidly to acquire the general idea or whether he must read slowly for details that must not be missed.

An Outline of Basic Study Skills

Van Dongen surveyed several graded series of readers to find out which study skills are commonly taught.[9] From this research he synthesized the following outline.

I. Ability to locate information
   A. Ability to locate information by using the aid of book parts
      1. cover, title page, title, author, publisher, location of publisher, editor's name, name of series, and edition
      2. copyright page and date of publication
      3. preface, introduction, foreword
      4. table of contents and locating topics by pages
      5. table of contents to locate topical organization of book or determine importance of topic by number of pages devoted to it
      6. locating specific pages rapidly

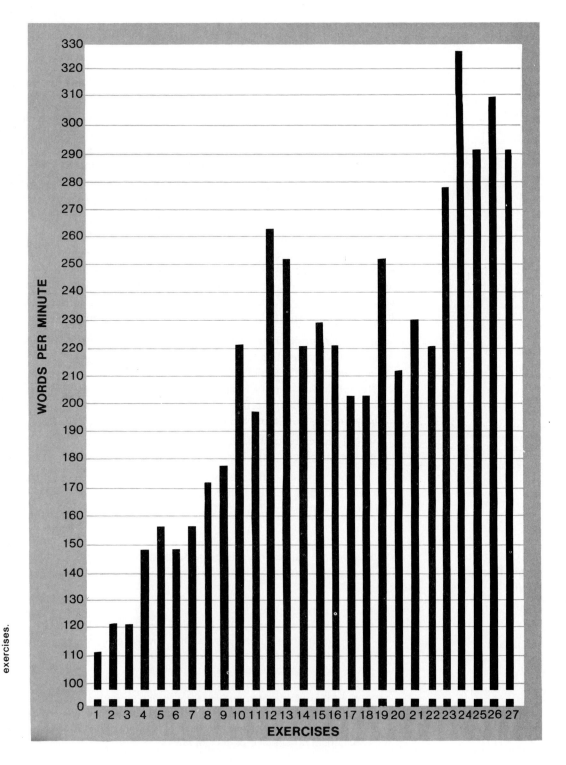

Figure 11.5   A graph of Tom's reading speed on the twenty-seven exercises.

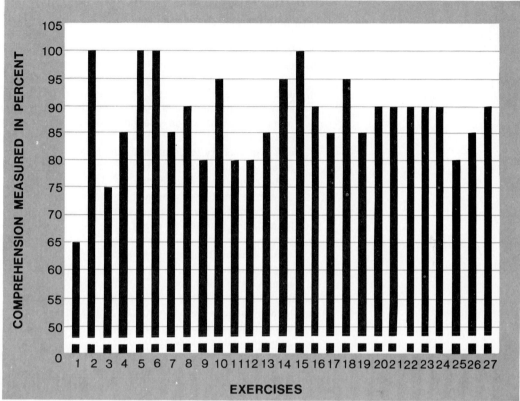

Figure 11.6

A graph of Tom's comprehension on tests over twenty-seven reading exercises.

7. lists of illustrations, maps, figures
8. chapter headings, main headings, section titles, subtitles
9. footnotes and references at end of chapters
10. glossary
11. indexes, select and use key word, cross-references
12. locate and use the appendix
13. locate and use the bibliography
B. Ability to locate information by using knowledge of alphabetizing
1. ability to locate any given letter quickly
2. knowing sections: beginning, middle, end
3. arranging words by initial letter
4. arranging words by second letter
5. arranging words by third or following letters
6. alphabetizing any given list of words
7. locating words or titles with *Mc* or *Mac*
8. use of articles *a, an,* and *the* in locating words or titles
9. alphabetizing people's names when first and last names are given
C. Ability to locate information by using references
1. locate information by using the dictionary
a. finding words quickly

Study Skills

opening the dictionary close to the desired word

using the guide words

using a thumb index

    b.   locate the pronunciation key

    c.   use of special sections of dictionary—geographical terms, biographical dictionary, foreign words and phrases

    d.   ability to use the dictionary as an aid in pronunciation; ability to interpret phonetic spelling and diacritical marks determining pronunciation of words spelled alike; determining preferred pronunciation

    e.   use of dictionary to determine meanings

select meaning from context

pictorial or verbal illustrations

determine what part of speech a word is

    f.   use of dictionary as an aid in checking spelling

    g.   locate base word as an entry

    h.   derivations of the base word

    i.   noting syllabic divisions of a word

    j.   origin of words

    k.   synonyms or antonyms

2.   locating information in the encyclopedia

    a.   locating volume from information on the spine of the book

    b.   using initial letters and guide words

    c.   using the index in the last volume

    d.   using specialized encyclopedias

3.   ability to use and locate other references

    a.   selecting appropriate references for locating information

    b.   locate and use various guides and sources:

        (1) almanac

        (2) atlas

        (3) city directory

        (4) government publications

        (5) junior book of authors

        (6) newspapers and periodicals

        (7) posters

        (8) radio or television schedules

        (9) telephone directory

      (10) time schedules

      (11) yearbooks

4.   ability to use textbooks and trade books for locating information

D. Ability to use the library and its aids for locating information

1.   card catalog

    a.   desired topic, author, or title

    b.   alphabetical arrangement in card catalog

2.   organization of the library for locating material

    a.   shelf plans, labels, and floor plans

    b.   Dewey-decimal system, Library of Congress, or other methods

    c.   locate reference books

    d.   locate and use the magazine file

    e.   locate and use appropriate indexes

          (1) *Readers' Guide to Periodical Literature*
          (2) *Who's Who*
          (3) Biographical dictionaries
          (4) Thesaurus
          (5) Unabridged dictionary
          (6) *Subject Index to Poetry for Children and Young People, 1957-1975*

  E. Locate information by using maps, graphs, charts, pictorial material

II. Ability to organize information

  A. Use knowledge of alphabetizing or organizing information

  B. Construct an outline

    1. ability to put material in sequence

      a. arrange steps of a process in order

      b. construct a time line

    2. classify information on two-way charts, tables

    3. construct an outline

      a. find main headings

      b. give main and subordinate topics

      c. provide subordinates when given main heading or provide main heading when given subordinates

      d. outline single paragraphs

      e. outline short selections

      f. outline more complex selections

      g. put ideas together from various sources in outline form

      h. outline what has been read and use outline in a presentation—either written or oral

  C. Ability to summarize material

    1. summary statement for a paragraph

    2. write summary statements for a short selection

    3. write summary statements for more complex selections

    4. use a summary as data for oral or written reports

    5. bring together information from several sources

    6. write a summary using an outline

    7. construct maps, graphs, charts, or pictorial material as a summary of information

  D. Ability to take notes

    1. take notes in brief—they may be grammatically incorrect and abbreviated

    2. in outline form—formal or informal

    3. in précis writing (spaced intervals of listening or reading)

    4. take notes in fact-inferences charts

    5. note origin of information for footnotes and bibliography

III. Ability to use and interpret maps, graphs, charts, and other pictorial material

  A. Use and interpret maps and globes

    1. ability to locate desired information

      a. interpret key and map symbols

      b. use map scales

      c. interpret directions

    2. ability to demonstrate understanding of map distortions or type of projection

B. Use and interpret graphs, tables, diagrams, and other pictorial material
  1. interpret graphs
     a. bar graphs
     b. circle graphs
     c. line graphs
  2. interpret tables
  3. interpret diagrams
  4. interpret time lines
  5. interpret other pictorial material
C. Read and use charts

Summary

The abilities needed to put reading to work identifying and solving problems are called the study skills. Study skills utilize all the abilities of the student in vocabulary and concept development and are dependent upon mastering comprehension skills of reading. A detailed outline of study skills mentioned in teachers' guides for basal readers is included in this chapter.

Suggested Activities

1. Study the materials in the curriculum center in your campus library or in an elementary school and select an annotated list of sources which will be useful to you in planning the long seatwork periods for children during the language arts periods in the grade which you teach.
2. Select one skill that is of major importance at the grade level you teach. Prepare a sequence of exercises graduated in difficulty which you could use as seatwork during the independent work periods.
3. Teachers refer to exercises that can be used over and over as *permanent* seatwork. Prepare a set of materials for permanent seatwork in your room. You may use separate answer sheets for recording answers; you may provide grease pencils for writing on plastic-covered exercises; or you may devise some other means for the child to complete and check his work.

For Further Reading

Bond, Guy L., and Eva B. Wagner. *Teaching the Child to Read.* 4th ed. Chapter 11, "Basic Study Skills," pp. 225–39. New York: Macmillan, 1966.

Burron, Arnold, and Amos Claybaugh. *Using Reading to Teach Subject Matter.* Columbus, Ohio: Charles E. Merrill, 1974.

Carpenter, Helen McCracken, ed. *Skill Development in Social Studies.* National Council for the Social Studies, 33rd Yearbook. Washington, D.C.: National Education Association, 1963.

Coleman, Mary E. "How to Teach Dictionary and Index Skills." In *New Perspectives in Reading Instruction,* edited by Albert J. Mazurkiewicz, pp. 425–36. New York: Pitman, 1964.

Harris, Albert J., and E. R. Sipay. *How to Increase Reading Ability.* 6th ed., pp. 488–96. New York: David McKay, 1975.

Heilman, Arthur W. *Principles and Practices of Teaching Reading.* Chapter 13, "Teaching Reading-Study Skills," pp. 457–500. Columbus, Ohio: Charles E. Merrill, 1977.

————. "Teaching the Reading Skills." In *New Perspectives in Reading Instruction,* edited by Albert J. Mazurkiewicz, pp. 418–24. New York: Pitman, 1964.

Horn, Ernest. *Methods of Instruction in the Social Studies.* Chapter 5, "Reading in Relation to Learning in the Social Studies," pp. 151–205. New York: Charles Scribner's Sons, 1937.

McKee, Paul. *Reading: A Program of Instruction for the Elementary School.* Chapter 9, "Studying Informative Material," pp. 316–76. Boston: Houghton Mifflin, 1966.

Smith, Carl B. *Teaching Reading in Secondary School Content Subjects: A Book-Thinking Process.* Chapter 9, "Study Skills: The Key to Independent Learning," pp. 251–81. New York: Holt, Rinehart & Winston, 1978.

Smith, Nila B. *Reading Instruction for Today's Children.* Chapter 10, "Study Skills Needed in Reading Content Subjects," pp. 305–52. Englewood Cliffs, N.J.: Prentice-Hall, 1963.

Smith, Richard, and Thomas C. Barrett. *Teaching Reading in the Middle Grades.* Reading, Mass.: Addison-Wesley, 1974.

Tinker, Miles A., and Constance M. McCullough. *Teaching Elementary Reading.* 3d ed. Chapter 10, "Comprehension and Study Skills," pp. 204–23. New York: Appleton-Century-Crofts, 1968.

Notes

1. L.C. Fay, "What Research Has to Say About Reading in the Content Areas," *The Reading Teacher* 8 (1954): 68–72.

2. Francis P. Robinson, *Effective Reading* (New York: Harper & Bros., 1962), p. 31.

3. Dorothy Piercey, "Teachers Use Newspapers as Aid to Reading," *The Arizona Republic,* Sunday, March 6, 1966.

4. Ernest Horn, Bess Goodykoontz, and Mabel I. Snedaker, *Progress in Reading Series: Reaching Our Goals,* Grade Six (Boston: Ginn, 1940), pp. 271–73.

5. Margaret Smith Greer, "The Efficiency of the Use of Analogy in Teaching Selected Concepts at the Sixth Grade Level," M.A. thesis, The Graduate School, University of New Mexico, 1966, p. 40.

6. D.D. Durrell, *Improving Reading Instruction* (New York: Harcourt, Brace, & World, 1956), pp. 285–308.

7. I am indebted to Mrs. Anne M. Anderson, Reading Consultant, State Department of Education, Santa Fe, New Mexico, for the list of questions presented in three levels. They are based on the text *The Social Sciences: Concepts and Values,* Grade 5 (New York: Harcourt Brace Jovanovich, 1970, pp. 248–50).

8. Elizabeth Simpson, *SRA Better Reading Books I and II* (Chicago: Science Research Associates, 1951).

9. Richard D. Van Dongen, "An Analysis of Study Skills Taught by Intermediate-Grade Basal Readers," M.A. thesis, University of New Mexico, August, 1967, pp. 47–54.

12

Developing Critical Reading Abilities

We do not believe everything we read. If we tried to, we would become hopelessly confused. We relate new ideas that we hear, see, or read with our previous knowledge, or prejudice, and then accept or reject the new idea.

Politicians try to say what they think people want to hear. Many compromises are made with the whole truth, and many promises made can be only partially fulfilled.

Reread some of the lines from the "Ballad of Davy Crockett."

Born on a mountaintop in Tennessee
Greenest state in the land of the free
Killed him a b'ar when he was only three.
Raised in the woods so he knew every tree.
Fought single-handed through the Injun war
'Till the Creeks was whipped and peace was in store.

He went off to Congress and served a spell
Fixing up the government and laws as well
Took over Washington so we heard tell
'N patched up the crack in the liberty bell.[1]

Was he born on a mountaintop? Is Tennessee the greenest state? Can anyone kill a bear when he is only three years old? Does one know the names of all the trees in a forest just because he lives there and sees them? Could anyone fight a war single-handed? Does any *one* person do much to stabilize or improve the government of the country? And the crack in the Liberty Bell is not patched!

The ballad is intended to honor the legendary hero, of course, without being taken literally. Teachers might explain that the author was not trying to relate facts, but rather portray a heroic, gallant spirit to whom all good citizens can respond emotionally, with warmth and affection. Education should help us distinguish between what is intended as figurative and what factual and should teach us that different kinds of evaluation are called for.

The Socratic method taught people to demand accurate definition, clear thinking, and exact analysis.[2]

Socrates collected opinions, asked questions, clarified terms and ideas, and indicated commitments. That is all he did. All that was required of those who took part with him was that they should try to think and to understand one another. They did not have to agree among themselves. If they came to conviction, they did so by their own free will. The only constraint upon them was the law of contradiction. They could not answer "Yes" and "No" to the same question at the same time.[3]

Today educational literature stresses that the primary aims of education are to teach problem-solving approaches, the decision-making process, weighing and evaluating, and making logical use of knowledge.

. . . while a good education can be a great good, a bad education can be a very great evil; it can be infinitely worse than no education at all. With a good education a child learns to think clearly and to draw sound conclusions from evidence; with a bad education he will learn to accept plausible falsehoods, to confuse propaganda with truth. With a good education he will come to cherish what is most worthwhile; with a bad education he will learn to value the trivial. With a good education he will learn to make ethical judgments even when they are unpopular; with a bad education he will learn to follow the crowd wherever it may lead him and to be convinced that he is right in so doing.[4]

To achieve such educational aims, we must go well beyond the Socratic method. We must, above all, help boys and girls develop critical reading abilities.

"Critical reading," as the term is used here, encompasses both of the following broad definitions.

. . . merely getting the facts is not critical reading. The reader must first determine whether he is reading facts or merely opinions and/or assumptions. Sensing the relationships among the facts, comparing the facts with experience, knowing when the facts are relevant, evaluating these facts against other facts to arrive at some conclusion, and going beyond the facts to get the inferred, but not explicitly stated, meaning are aspects of critical reading.[5]

To really think while reading, to evaluate, to judge what is important and unimportant, what is relevant or irrelevant, what is in harmony with an idea read in another book or acquired through experience, constitutes critical reading.[6]

Teachers must themselves possess those virtues of attention, curiosity, courage to be themselves, and adherence to high standards that they try to nourish in their students. They must know how to accept and evaluate opposing points of view or dissenting opinions. Teachers must have knowledge. They can guide discussion properly only if their own information and skill in thinking are adequate.

The student who is not taught the habit of critical attention is apt to arrive at adulthood with superficial knowledge and, in turn, base poor judgment on inadequate knowledge.

Critical reading cannot be done without *knowledge*. Through knowledge, the reader is able to make comparisons and judge relevance. If judgments are not based on knowledge, the judgments will not be valid.

Much stress must be placed on the need to organize information. Organizing clearly helps one to reject irrelevant information and helps prevent misuse of information. By the time boys and girls have finished elementary school, they should be well practiced in developing skeleton outlines.

Social studies programs offer teachers excellent opportunities to help students develop critical reading skills. In one elementary school classroom, a watchword committee was set up for the purpose of looking for *loaded* words used in reporting research. Building informational background and eliminating prejudices, comparing different authors' conclusions on controversial issues, recognizing authenticity and authors' specializations, and detecting emotionally charged words that tend to bias the reader are all tasks of the critical reader. Teaching critical reading skills is possible only with adequate library resources.

Extending Language for Critical Reading

Figures of speech, foreign words in English language context, and prefixes, suffixes, and combining forms all require precise understanding on the part of the critical reader.

Figures of Speech

Expressions and words used for other than their ordinary or literal meaning add beauty and force to our language. Yet, many adults use such expressions without knowing their origin. "Mad as a hatter," "my man Friday," "sour grapes," or "a Pandora's box" would all be more meaningful if we were familiar with the source of the expression.

Many such figurative expressions are derived from the Bible, and teachers should remind themselves that many boys and girls grow up without hearing references to the Old or the New Testament. Some biblical expressions commonly used as figures of speech are given below:

as old as Methuselah
as patient as Job
whither thou goest I will go
there entered into the garden a snake
the golden rule
doubting Thomas
the land of milk and honey
it was a David and Jonathan friendship
a voice crying in the wilderness
the wailing wall
they crucified her
vanity, vanity, all is vanity, saith the preacher
it's a whited sepulchre
like the seven plagues
though your sins be as scarlet
the wisdom of Solomon
and the walls came tumbling down

One of the causes of misinterpretation in reading is taking figures of speech literally. The reader may take seriously something that the author intended to be taken humorously.

Strang and Bracken point out difficulties students may have with literary allusions:

Unless the student knows the history of certain literary allusions, he will miss the meaning of the passage. For example, "He's a Jonah" would not be understood by a person who did not know the Bible story of Jonah and the whale. When selections from the Bible, mythology, and other frequently quoted literary sources are included in the English course of study, they have double value—the value inherent in the selections themselves and their future usefulness in helping the reader to interpret allusions in other books.[7]

In *Miracle on 34th Street,* after Fred had promised Kris Kringle his freedom and gone to unlimited detail to prove him competent, he found that Mr. Kringle had deliberately failed the test he had been given. Fred *"had talked himself way out on a long, long limb,* and now he felt it cracking." Later, before Mr. Kringle's trial, Mr. Sawyer *"placed himself in a frying pan and . . . was squirming and wriggling to get out."* Later when Fred is talking with his girl friend, he says, *"Well, it all boils down to this:* You don't have faith in me."[8] Literal meanings of words used in the italicized idiomatic expressions are of no help in understanding the meanings intended.

Seven Types of Figures

Simile. A simile expresses a likeness between two things that in most respects are totally unlike:

After one day on his new job, Jack said the next morning, "I'm *stiff as a board* today."

In making his choices, he was *as sly as a fox.*

Metaphor. A metaphor is an implied comparison which omits the words *like* or *as:*

He has a *heart of stone.*

Tom stood *rooted* to the spot.

Irony. Irony is a method of expression in which the ordinary meaning of the words is the opposite of the thought in the speaker's mind (subtle sarcasm):

Thanks for forgetting to show up to help with all this work!

You are setting a *fine* example for the rest of the class!

Hyperbole. Hyperbole is a figure of speech which uses exaggeration for effect:

Waves *mountain high* broke over the reef.

The horses sped *like the wind* over the prairie.

Personification.   Personification is endowing animals, plants, and inanimate objects with personal traits and human attributes:

> Death won in the traffic race.
>
> Duty calls us.

Synecdoche.   The figure of speech that puts a part for a whole *or* a whole for a part is called synecdoche:

> She had lived in the house fifty springs.
>
> Two heads are better than one.
>
> *Or:*
>
> The world is too much with us.
>
> Modern medicine has virtually conquered the scourge of malaria.

Metonymy.   Using the name of one thing for another, of which it is an attribute or with which it is associated, is a further kind of figure of speech, called metonymy:

> Handsome is as handsome does.
>
> The White House announced a new energy policy.

Foreign Words in English Context

Many expressions in common use are borrowed directly from other languages. The selected list below contains some that are sure to appear occasionally in the reading done by critical readers:

Expression	Language	English dictionary meaning
à la mode	French	in the fashion
a priori	Latin	deductive argument from self-evident propositions
a posteriori	Latin	inductive argument from observed facts
ad infinitum	Latin	to infinity
ad valorem	Latin	according to the value
alma mater	Latin	a school, college, or university one has attended
coup d'état	French	violent overthrow of government
e pluribus unum	Latin	one composed of many
esprit de corps	French	the shared spirit and enthusiasm of a group
ex cathedra	Latin	by virtue of high authority
ex officio	Latin	by virtue of one's office
ex post facto	Latin	after the fact; retroactively
in loco parentis	Latin	in the place of a parent
in memoriam	Latin	in memory of
ipso facto	Latin	by the nature of the case
laissez-faire	French	philosophy of noninterference

modus operandi	Latin	method of procedure
noblesse oblige	French	the obligation of a person of high rank to behave generously
nom de plume	French	pseudonym
non sequitur	Latin	a statement that does not follow from preceding statements; unwarranted conclusion
papier-mâché	French	a light, strong molding material made of paper
par excellence	French	being the best of a kind
per diem	Latin	by the day
poco a poco	Spanish	little by little
pro rata	Latin	in proportion
sine qua non	Latin	an indispensable condition
status quo	Latin	the existing state of affairs
sub rosa	Latin	secret or confidential
tabula rasa	Latin	the hypothetical blank mind before receiving outside impressions
tempus fugit	Latin	time flies
terra firma	Latin	solid earth; a safe footing
vice versa	Latin	the terms being exchanged
vis-à-vis	French	face to face with; in relation to

Prefixes, Suffixes, and Combining Forms

Linguists use the term *morpheme* to refer to parts of words that carry meaning in their own right. Prefixes, suffixes, and what are called here "combining forms" are such parts.

Common Prefixes

Prefix	Meaning of prefix	Example	Literal meaning of example
in	in	inhabit	to live in
com con col	together with	collaborate	to labor together
dis	not	disapprove	not approve
pre	before	prejudice	to judge before
sub	under	submarine	under the water

Common Suffixes

Suffix	Meaning of suffix	Example	Literal meaning of example
ive	relating to	decorative	relating to decoration
ful	full of	helpful	full of help
less	without	needless	without need
ship	state of being	friendship	having friends
tion	act, state of being	conjunction	act of joining with

Combining Forms

Word parts	Meaning	Example	Literal meaning of example
bio	life	biology	study of living things
logy	study of		
geo	earth	geography	write about the earth
graph	write		
therm	heat	thermometer	measure the heat
meter	measure		
poly	many	polygon	having many sides
gon	angle		
tele	far	telephone	sound from far away
phone	sound		

Evaluating Authorities and Evidence

Blough raises the question of what to do when the community disagrees with the principle the elementary teacher wishes to teach. Teachers should remember that young children are not, generally, ready to be asked to choose between "what father says" and a scientific principle in the textbook. Blough suggests that teachers may point out that scientists *search for answers*. Scientists themselves do not claim to know all the answers. Many statements in textbooks are tempered with, "It is generally believed that . . . ," "Evidence seems to show . . . ," "Some scientists think . . . ," or "Probably. . . ." Teachers can keep the conversation open with comments such as, "Everyone has a right to his or her own belief. As time goes on, most of us keep on thinking and learning, and we often change our thinking about some things."[9]

The ultimate goal of the school is to help the student find his or her own defensible position between the conformist on the one hand and the nonconformist on the other. Students will conform to the standards they accept based on careful evaluation of the situation in terms of what they have learned.

Conformity to the group without *basis in reason* implies lack of creative thinking and is the result of too much dependence on the teacher as a voice of authority or the textbook as the source of fact.

Critical reading requires all the steps in problem-solving: (1) knowing where to go to find information; (2) knowing how to select the specific information needed from various sources; and (3) knowing how to evaluate the adequacy, validity, and relevance of information. It also requires separating fact from opinion even when opinion is subtly disguised as fact, determining the author's legitimate authority and his biases, and recognizing propaganda.

Criticism, to be valid and consistent, must be based on specified criteria. Teachers and children should set up their criteria for evaluating oral reporting, story telling, units of work, and many other activities throughout the year.

Developing critical reading abilities means (1) establishing standards of judgment; (2) developing the ability to make comparisons; (3) judging the authority and background of the source; (4) recognizing relevance and irrelevance, fact and opinion; and (5) making inferences and drawing conclusions.

Elementary school children must be provided opportunities for making judgments. They can be asked to rate each other on some performance, such as giving an oral report. Probably children should be asked to evaluate each other's work periodically. If work has been done by committees so that groups rather than individuals are being evaluated, it may be easier to keep the discussion on relative merits on the project itself rather than personalities.

Social studies projects lend themselves to such evaluation. Children may be severely critical of each other at first, and always forget to mention desirable qualities of work, but this is the method by which they eventually learn to evaluate on more objective bases. When the peer group evaluates, benefits accrue to both the judges and the judged.

Teachers are apt to feel that quiet time with each student performing individually in writing is more profitable learning time than an unstructured guided discussion. But time is well spent in class discussion of such problems as one student monopolizing class time, decisions being based on personal feelings about individuals, and arguments being proposed without supporting facts. Many adults exhibit similar behavior; possibly they might have developed better ways of solving problems if time had been given to these types of discussion in their schoolrooms.

Much too much time is spent in traditional schools making children's minds act like sponges that will accept authority of parents, teachers, and textbooks without question.

The mythical "cherry tree story" can be put in proper perspective by a more mature evaluation of the character and leadership qualities of the first president.

Is the story of Lincoln's undying love for Ann Rutledge another myth? Was the story started by Lincoln's law partner, William Herndon, because he had such an active hatred for Mary Todd Lincoln and wanted to discredit her? Do the historians agree?[10]

The period of the Civil War can be used to sample and evaluate differing viewpoints. Students might find any one of the following statements in their reading. They should decide which of the contradictory statements in each of the following pairs has the most supporting evidence.

One opinion	A differing opinion
John Brown was insane.	John Brown was a great abolitionist.
The South had superior leadership.	The South was led by unrealistic cavaliers.
The North did not know what it was fighting for—therefore there were many desertions and much lack of interest.	The North was fighting a moral battle to free the U.S. from slavery.
The *Merrimac* was victorious!	The *Monitor* was victorious in the famous sea battle of the iron clads.
The South did not lose, she simply stopped fighting.	The North won the Civil War.

In summary, all of the following kinds of evaluation are important in critical reading.[11]

1. Identifying and selecting material directly relevant to a given topic.

2. Selecting material appropriate for a particular assignment, audience, or occasion.

3. Distinguishing fact from opinion; sense from nonsense.

4. Comparing the ideas in different sources of information; finding contradictions to a given point of view.

5. Considering, and accepting or rejecting, new ideas or information in light of previous knowledge.

6. Sensing biases in an author's point of view.

7. Identifying and rejecting gross overstatements and dogmatic statements with unfounded claims. (Many advertisements discussed in the following section of this chapter illustrate this point.)

Detecting and Resisting Propaganda Influences

Are most people able to make critical evaluations? The testimony that many are not can be found in the full-page advertisements in color in all of the popular magazines and the frequency of advertising spots on radio and TV. Their high cost is readily paid for by the gullibility of the audiences.

By helping children develop critical reading ability, we also help them achieve critical judgment about appeals through all media, including TV and radio.

How do people learn to *see through* the propaganda techniques in constant use all about us? We may doubt that millions of people will respond to such phrases as "Be the first in your block to own a Volkswagen!" or "And nothing but nylon makes you feel so female!" or "Remember how great cigarettes *used* to taste? Luckies still do!" But the advertisers who pay for them must find them profitable!

Attitudes, beliefs, and biases interfere more with critical reading than they do with literal comprehension. The cognitive process is colored by the affective process.[12]

Henry writes of the psychology of advertising.[13] Through television, advertisers whet children's appetites for certain toys. Children then let their parents know that nothing else will do for Christmas, and desperate parents comb stores, for they *do want to* buy what their children want! "Deprive business of its capacity to appeal to children *over the heads of their parents,* and what would happen to most cereals, some of the drugs, and many toys?"[14]

Most boys and girls, by the time they pass to the sixth grade, have had the personal experience of being a victim of rumor in the course of their school life. "The teacher said . . ." "The coach is going to . . ." "Anybody who can't work these problems in arithmetic. . ." These and many similar expressions implying threat or instilling anxiety or fear are often passed around. The one who has little to fear from the threat may be the one who most enjoys spreading it among the less fortunate, for whom it was probably an agonizing experience for a short time.

Propaganda is defined as "any plan or method for spreading opinions or beliefs." The definition makes it apparent that advertisements and rumors have much in common with propaganda.

Frequently propaganda is sincere, or at least harmless; sometimes, however, it deliberately skirts or conceals the truth. One needs to be alert to the devices and able to evaluate them. Propaganda devices that can mislead have been described by the Institute for Propaganda Analysis, New York City.

1. *Name calling* consists of using labels instead of discussing the facts. This technique usually involves attaching a negative symbol to someone—for example, calling a politician a crook, or labeling a person whose ideas are unpopular a fascist. By branding a person with these negative symbols it is often possible to avoid citing facts. The names, not facts, are used to get the desired reaction.

2. *Glittering generalities* implies use of vague phrases that promise much. They usually try to associate positive symbols, slogans, and unsupported generalizations with an idea or person—as for example, saying in a political campaign that "this act will benefit all Americans and will enhance our position abroad." Only a careful weighing of the facts will determine whether such a glittering generality has any substance.

3. *Transfer* means applying a set of symbols to a purpose for which they are not intended. This method of convincing people consists primarily of transferring the attraction of strong positive symbols or the repulsion of strong negative symbols to some person, group, or idea. For example, a subversive group might display the American flag and pictures of Washington and Lincoln at their meetings. These positive symbols help gain public support. Only careful thinking on the listener's part can determine whether these symbols are compatible with the situation.

4. *Testimonials* involve getting some prominent person to endorse an idea or product in order to induce others to react favorably to it. Motion picture stars and outstanding athletes are often used for this purpose.

5. *Plain folks* device requires pretending to be "one of the folks." People are sometimes persuaded to vote for a candidate for office because he takes a "folksy" approach to problems. In other words, he uses simple language and repeats old proverbs. Sometimes the plain folks approach includes kissing babies, wearing Indian feathers, or posing with a fishing rod in hand. Although very common in American politics, it proves little, if anything, about the qualifications of a candidate for office.

6. *Bandwagon* means claiming that "everyone is doing it." The bandwagon method of persuading people is effective because many people don't make up their own minds and instead follow the lead of the majority. The bandwagon approach consists of giving the impression that everyone is doing it, or voting a certain way, or buying some product, and so one should get on the bandwagon if one wants to keep up with the crowd. It is an appeal to the desire to conform. To resist this approach, one must stand firmly on one's right to make up one's own mind. Appealing to the desire to "keep up with the Joneses" is one of the most common methods used to persuade people to do certain things, and is one of the *most difficult to withstand.* Boys and girls in the intermediate grades have already learned to use the "getting on the bandwagon" technique. How many mothers have allowed themselves to be coaxed and wheedled in that way to say "yes" to something when, if they had telephoned other mothers, they would have found more than enough agreement to have said "no" with no ill effects. Boys and girls will acknowledge to a teacher whom they trust and in whom they have confidence that it is very necessary to know how to "play the game." They can cite examples of specific situations where they and their friends achieved their goal by convincing their separate parents that everyone else highly approved of something. Occasionally a child has felt *pressure* on the one hand to do what the rest of the group wants to do, but felt considerable anxiety on the other hand because he or she didn't really want to be a participant at that time.

7. *Cardstacking* is presenting only facts that favor one side. Examples are using quotations out of context, omitting key words from a quotation, or using favorable statistics while suppressing unfavorable ones. The important thing to keep in mind is that a series of half-truths usually add up to a complete lie. And, since cardstacking usually involves citing some reliable facts, one must be astute to see the flaws and falseness of this approach. In other words, cardstacking is one of the most effective propaganda devices; effort and intelligence are required to see through it.

Reading is become increasingly important in our society, and its ultimate end is to make the reader ably critical. Any thinking, participating citizen in our free society must read critically and make value judgments all the time.

Resisting propaganda, discarding irrelevant information, choosing between two opinions when both are strongly supported, and being able to change one's thinking patterns when new evidence proves an old idea wrong or obsolete are all benefits of well developed critical reading ability.

Teaching Critical Reading

Piekarz reports asking teachers in graduate classes in reading to read a passage and construct five questions that they might ask pupils. The result: about 97 percent of all questions are of a literal nature, 2.7 percent are of an interpretive nature, and .3 percent are of an evaluative nature. She concludes:

Students who spend 97 percent of the time answering literal questions during the twelve years of elementary and high school should expect to experience difficulty with critical reading and thinking when they reach college. Expecting otherwise is unrealistic.[15]

Teaching critical reading can begin very early and should continue throughout the child's school career.

In intellectual development, the child is increasingly able to understand cause-effect relationships, to form generalizations, and to think logically. He makes amazingly clear distinctions between fact and fancy. When problems are within his experience, his thinking appears to be like that of an adult.[16]

Providing an environment that enhances learning is one of the teacher's primary goals. As has already been stated, the attitude of the teacher in the class sets the climate for the thinking of boys and girls.

The teacher introduces the children to the world of thought through the kinds of rules and rituals with which she surrounds the thinking process; the kinds of content she introduces, accepts, and rejects from the children; the kinds of approaches to problem solution she encourages and sustains; the amount of freedom she allows for independent and explanatory thinking; the speed with which she closes down inquiry; the respect she shows for their fumbling, their confusion—all create for them an image of that world and a set of expectations about their own potency as learners and thinkers.[17]

Although critical reading is the most difficult of all reading skills to teach, a checklist of elements can be made. Boys and girls in the elementary school can learn to read carefully for the following:

1. Unwarranted generalizations
2. Making everything a dichotomous—either/or—situation
3. Half-truths
4. Quoting words or sentences out of context
5. Emotionally charged words
6. Sensing biases in writer's accounts

Other critical reading skills that can be taught in the developmental reading program are:

7. Investigating sources
8. Comparing and contrasting different reports
9. Searching for the author's purpose
10. Separating fact from opinion
11. Forming judgments
12. Detecting propaganda

Among the most difficult skills needed for critical reading are:

13. Determining the relevance of the material
14. Evaluating the reliability of authors
15. Examining assumptions
16. Checking data
17. Detecting inconsistencies
18. Drawing conclusions, based upon gathering of adequate information; testing possible conclusions in the light of the data; or reaching tentative conclusions subject to revision if new information is discovered.[18]

Summary

Foundation skills in developing the ability to read critically include (1) extending language concepts in figures of speech, knowing commonly used words borrowed from other languages, and understanding prefixes, suffixes, and combining forms; (2) evaluating authorities; and (3) detecting and resisting propaganda influences.

Critical readers are those who, in addition to identifying facts and ideas accurately as they read, engage in interpretive and evaluative thinking. They project the literal meanings of what they read against their own background of experience, information, and knowledge, *reasoning with and reacting to the stated facts and implied ideas.* Non-critical readers, on the other hand, are those who restrict their thinking to the identification of the clearly stated facts and accept these facts literally and unquestioningly . . . critical reading is the most difficult of all reading skills to teach.[19]

Suggested Activities

1. Take the Watson-Glaser *Test of Critical Thinking*[20] and compare your results to the national norms. According to this test and its interpretation, are you able to read critically?

2. Observe in a classroom during a class discussion. For a 30-minute period, determine the percent of questions that fall in each of the following categories: memory of facts, interpreting facts, evaluation of the written statements, and application of principles.

3. Recall and describe in writing an experience where word meanings caused someone to completely misunderstand or have to ask for an explanation (a figure of speech, idiomatic language, or words borrowed from another language). If each student contributes, the class should then have many meaningful examples.

For Further Reading

Artley, A. Sterl. "Critical Reading in the Content Areas." *Elementary English* 36 (1959): 122–30.

Burrus, Dorothy. "Developing Critical and Creative Thinking Skills Using the Newspaper." *Elementary English* 47 (1970): 978–81. Reprinted in *Readings on Reading Instruction,* 2d ed., pp. 280–83, edited by Albert J. Harris and E. R. Sipay. New York: David McKay, 1972.

Dechant, Emerald V. *Improving the Teaching of Reading,* 2d ed., chapter 13, "Advancing the Pupil's Comprehension Skills," pp. 400–48. Englewood Cliffs: Prentice-Hall, 1970.

Ennis, Robert H. "A Definition of Critical Thinking." *The Reading Teacher* 17 (1964): 599–612. Reprinted in *Reading Instruction: Dimensions and Issues,* pp. 146–59, edited by William K. Durr. Boston: Houghton Mifflin, 1967.

Harris, Larry, and Carl Smith. *Reading Instruction: Diagnostic Teaching in the Classroom,* 2d ed., chapter 12, "Critical Reading," pp. 261–79. New York: Holt, Rinehart & Winston, 1976.

Heilman, Arthur. *Principles and Practices of Teaching Reading,* 4th ed., pp. 474–87. Columbus, Ohio: Charles E. Merrill, 1977.

Henderson, Richard L., and Donald R. Green. *Reading for Meaning in the Elementary School.* Englewood Cliffs, N.J.: Prentice-Hall, 1969.

Karlin, Robert. *Teaching Elementary Reading: Principles and Strategies,* 2d ed., pp. 239–46. New York: Harcourt Brace Jovanovich, 1975.

King, Martha L., Berniece Ellinger, and Willavene Wolfe. *Critical Reading: A Book of Readings.* Philadelphia: J.B. Lippincott, 1967.

Lundsteen, Sara W. "Procedures for Critical Reading and Listening." *Contributions in Reading* 34 (1964): 1–7. Reprinted in *Readings on Reading Instruction,* 2d ed., pp. 270–77, edited by Albert J. Harris and E. R. Sipay. New York: David McKay, 1972.

Olson, Joanne, and Martha Dillner. *Learning to Teach Reading in the Elementary School,* chapter 14. New York: Macmillan, 1976.

Painter, Helen W. "Critical Reading in the Primary Grades." *The Reading Teacher* 19 (1965): 35–39. Reprinted in *Individualizing Reading Instruction: A Reader,* pp. 263–68, edited by Larry Harris and Carl Smith. New York: Holt, Rinehart & Winston, 1972. Also reprinted in *Reading Instruction: Dimensions and Issues,* pp. 160–64, edited by William K. Durr. Boston: Houghton Mifflin, 1967.

Russell, David. *Children's Thinking.* Boston: Ginn, 1956.

Stauffer, Russell G. *Directing Reading Maturity as a Cognitive Process,* chapter 11, "Critical and Creative Reading." New York: Harper & Row, 1969.

Strang, Ruth, et al. *The Improvement of Reading,* 4th ed., pp. 272–79. New York: McGraw-Hill, 1967.

Taba, Hilda. "The Teaching of Thinking." *Elementary English* 42 (1965): 534–42.

Turner, Thomas N. "Critical Reading as a Values Clarification Process." *Language Arts* 54 (1977): 909–12.

Notes

1. Words by Tom Blackburn. Copyright 1954 by Walt Disney Music Company, 800 Sonora Ave., Glendale, Calif. Used by permission.

2. Will Durant, *The Story of Philosophy* (New York: Pocket Books, 1953), p. 6.

3. Robert M. Hutchins, *The Conflict in Education* (New York: Harper & Bros., 1953), p. 96.

4. Paul Woodring, *A Fourth of a Nation* (New York: McGraw-Hill, 1957), p. 4.

5. Ruth K. Flamond, "Critical Reading," in *New Perspectives in Reading Instruction,* ed. Albert J. Mazurkiewicz (New York: Pitman Publishing Corporation, 1964), p. 256.

6. Walter T. Petty, "Critical Reading in the Primary Grades," *Education Digest* 22 (October 1956): 42–43.

7. Ruth Strang and Dorothy Kendall Bracken, *Making Better Readers* (Boston: D. C. Heath, 1957), p. 216.

8. Valentine Davies, *Miracle on 34th Street,* A Special Scholastic Book Services Edition (New York: Pocket Books, 1962), pp. 77, 82, 90.

9. Glenn O. Blough, Julius Schwartz, and Albert J. Huggett, *Elementary School Science and How to Teach It,* rev. ed. (New York: Holt, Rinehart & Winston, 1958), pp. 77–78.

10. William Herndon, *Life of Lincoln* (Fine Editions Press, 1949), p. 106; Ruth P. Randall, *Lincoln's Sons* (Boston: Little, Brown and Co., 1955), p. 242; Benjamin P. Thomas, *Abraham Lincoln* (Knopf, 1952), p. 51.

11. The reader may also wish to read: Donald D. Durrell, *Improving Reading Instruction* (New York: Harcourt, Brace & World, 1956), pp. 305ff; Albert J. Harris, *How to Increase Reading Ability,* 5th ed. (New York: Longman, Green, 1970), p. 431ff.

12. Anne S. McKillop, *The Relationship Between the Reader's Attitude and Certain Types of Reading Responses* (New York: Teachers College Press, Teachers College, Columbia University, 1952).

13. Jules Henry, *Culture Against Man,* chapter 3 (New York: Random House, 1963).

14. Ibid., pp. 75–76.

15. Josephine Piekarz Ives, "The Improvement of Critical Reading Skills," in *Problem Areas in Reading—Some Observations and Recommendations,* ed. Coleman Morrison (Providence, R.I.: Oxford Press, 1966), p. 56.

16. Nelson B. Henry, ed. *Development In and Through Reading,* 60th Yearbook, National Society for the Study of Education, Part I (Chicago: University of Chicago Press, 1961), p. 288.

17. Edna Shapiro, "Study of Children Through Observation of Classroom Behavior," in *Theory and Research in Teaching,* ed. Arno A. Bellack (New York: Bureau of Publications, Teachers College, Columbia University, 1963), p. 101.

18. Dorothy Fraser and Edith West, *Social Studies in Secondary Schools* (New York: Ronald Press, 1961), pp. 222–27.

19. Ives, "Improvement of Critical Reading Skills," p. 5.

20. Goodwin Watson and Edward M. Glaser, *Watson-Glaser Critical Thinking Appraisal,* forms Ym and Zm (757 Third Avenue, New York, New York 10017: Harcourt, Brace & World, 1964).

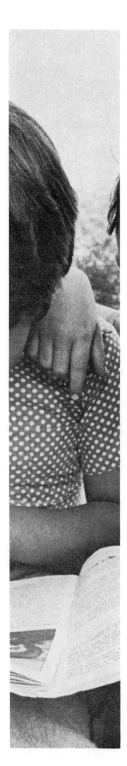

13

Oral Reading

Prior to 1930 the emphasis in teaching children to read was largely on "good oral reading." Correct enunciation and pronunciation and proper inflection, emphasis and feeling tone were primary goals. McCutchen stressed oral reading skill in the preface of his fourth reader, published in 1883, as follows:

A critic of the day has observed that "in the great Republic of North America reading aloud is justly considered to be one of the most important elements of a child's education."

Reading aloud, if properly directed, serves a double purpose: it tends to correct errors in articulation and pronunciation, and to break up certain careless habits of speech; and it also enables the teacher to see whether the pupil *comprehends* what he is reading.

It is the business of the teacher to insure exactness in articulation and pronunciation purely by the force of example; the class thus become mere imitators of a good model. . . . It is only when the meaning is too abstruse for the pupil, or when it is desirable to give examples of modulation or style for those pupils who rarely hear good reading, that the teacher may read for the class and let them imitate his emphasis, his pauses, his inflections, as well as his articulation and pronunciation.[1]

In 1911 Baldwin and Bender were emphasizing oral reading skill as follows:

The design of this series of School Readers is to help children to acquire the art and the habit of reading so well as to give pleasure not only to themselves, but also to those who listen to them. The selections have been chosen and arranged with strict reference to the capabilities and tastes of the pupils who are to read them, thus making every exercise in oral reading both easy and enjoyable as well as instructive.

The notes under the head of "Expression," which follow many of the lessons, are intended to assist in securing correctness of pronunciation and enunciation, a clear understanding of what is being read, and the intelligible and pleasing oral rendering of the printed page. These notes should be carefully studied by both teacher and pupils.[2]

By 1930 emphasis was changing. Silent reading, comprehension, and study skills were being emphasized.

At the present time some teachers devote too much class time to oral reading under poor conditions.[3] Also, many teachers could do more effective *teaching* of oral reading. Ability to read aloud well is, after all, often necessary in adult life. It is still important to be able to read aloud—for such purposes as reading the minutes of a meeting, reading stories to one's children, or participating in group reading in church or social gatherings.

It is regrettable but true that oral reading can be one of the most abused aspects of the reading program. Some teachers ask children to read by turns just so everyone in the group reads one page. When such reading serves no other purpose, the result is fruitless for everyone. Children should have an opportunity to read silently any material they are expected to later read orally, but a group should not be asked to sit and listen quietly while one child reads something they have all already read and discussed. With new material, taking turns around the group is sure to frustrate the fast readers, who are "sneaking" ahead, and to embarrass the slow readers, who cannot read fluently or pronounce all the words. An authoritarian teacher who demands that all the class listen quietly while one person struggles through a paragraph is teaching many negative values and few, if any, positive ones.

The Place of Oral Reading

There seems to have been for the past few years, and continues to be today, considerable controversy about the place of oral reading in the reading program. Part of this controversy is because some people feel that if children are put in an oral reading situation in which they do not do well, the result will be very damaging to their personalities. And, of course, if they are expected to read at their frustration level all the time, it will do such damage. Another argument in the controversy goes as follows: People do no oral reading outside the school setting—that is, all their outside reading will be silent reading; therefore, they should do only silent reading in school. These two arguments have some validity.

Valid criticisms can be leveled against oral reading in situations that are *not oral reading situations.* (1) If children do not have a purpose for reading or do not understand the purpose; if they are given too little help on technical difficulties prior to oral reading; if a selection is not suitable for audience reading because of either type of material or level of difficulty for the reader, then the oral reading will be neither helpful to the reader nor interesting to the listeners. (2) Situations in which all the people in the audience have copies of the material which the child is reading are *not* audience situations. (3) Many teachers now evidence little interest in oral reading. Teachers themselves may be deficient in oral reading ability. Oral reading that the child does under such adverse conditions as those described here will not constitute a worthwhile experience for him.

These criticisms can be overcome by teachers who acknowledge a legitimate place for oral reading in the total reading program for all children. Oral

reading has a place for any student who is reading at a *primary reading level,* no matter what the grade placement may be. First of all, oral reading is more like talking, something the child does all day long in and out of school. When children begin a formal reading program in first grade, they may feel that it is less strange if it continues to be a talking kind of language. In first grade, the teacher can expect to commit about 50 percent of the time to oral reading and 50 percent to silent reading. From the beginning of formal reading through the first grade, the teacher will have reading groups first read silently whatever story they are learning how to read. They will reread most of these stories orally during the first year. While the teacher will set up new purposes for the child for the second reading, one of *the teacher's purposes* is to provide the child reading practice on the basic sight vocabulary.

Oral reading, when it is effective, gives students opportunity to entertain others. The child's self-confidence is strengthened too when he or she reads well to an appreciative audience. For the alert teacher, the child's oral reading gives an opportunity to evaluate the quality of the reading performance.

In second grade, children reading at second grade reader level should have more time for silent reading and less time for oral. Perhaps those children now able to do independent reading should spend two-thirds of their reading time on silent reading and one-third on oral. This provides time for all children to have an opportunity to read aloud. After children establish an independent third grade reader level, the amount of time spent on oral reading is sure to decrease. Probably not more than 20 percent of the time in developmental reading classes above third grade level will be given to oral reading. This should include the teacher's evaluation of reading in all subjects, not just in the reading class itself.

Children should have an opportunity to entertain others by their reading. But when are others entertained? Not when the reading is the wrong kind of material or the reader cannot read it well. When do children get satisfaction and security in oral expression? Only when they express themselves reasonably well. Children can get satisfaction through group participation only when giving something that the group anticipates or understands. Children get effective speech practice only when they have poise, self-confidence, and the feeling that they are doing a good job.

The following poems can serve these objectives for many children, but probably not *all* the children in a group.

Mice

I think mice
Are rather nice.

Their tails are long,
Their faces small,
They haven't any
Chins at all.
Their ears are pink,
Their teeth are white,
They run about
The house at night.

They nibble things
They shouldn't touch
And no one seems
To like them much.

But *I* think mice
Are nice.

Rose Fyleman[4]

Galoshes

Susie's galoshes
Make splishes and sploshes
And slooshes and sloshes,
As Susie steps slowly
Along in the slush.
They stamp and they tramp
On the ice and concrete,
They get stuck in the muck in the mud;
But Susie likes much best to hear

The slippery slush
As it slooshes and sloshes,
And splishes and sploshes,
All round her galoshes.

Rhoda Bacmeister[5]

Eletelephony

Once there was an elephant,
Who tried to use the telephant—
No, No, I mean an elephone
Who tried to use the telephone—
(Dear me, I am not certain quite,
That even now I've got it right.)

Howe'er it was, he got his trunk
Entangled in the telephunk;
The more he tried to get it free,
The louder buzzed the telephee—
(I fear I'd better drop the song
Of elephop and telefong!)

Laura Elizabeth Richards[6]

Arbuthnot[7] suggests that the poem "Where's Mary?" be called a study
in irritability. The woman searching for Mary gets angrier with each succeeding line.

Where's Mary?

Is Mary in the dairy?
Is Mary on the stair?
What? Mary's in the garden?
What is she doing there?
Has she made the butter yet?
Has she made the beds?
Has she topped the gooseberries
And taken off their heads?
Has she the potatoes peeled?
Has she done the grate?
Are the new green peas all shelled?
It is getting late!
What! She hasn't done a thing?
Here's a nice to-do!
Mary has a dozen jobs
And hasn't finished two.
Well, here IS a nice to-do!
Well, upon my word!
She's sitting on the garden bench
Listening to a bird!

Ivy O. Eastwick[8]

Arbuthnot has done as much as any other teacher of children's literature
to emphasize the effective use of oral reading to encourage boys and girls to
read freely from the great storehouse of well written children's books available
to them today.

Certainly reading aloud is the way to introduce children to exceptional books that
they might not choose for themselves or might not enjoy without this added lift
of family enjoyment and the reader's enthusiasm. *The Wind in the Willows, The*

Children of Greene Knowe, The Gammage Cup, Rifles for Watie, Smoky . . . just a sampling of the choice books. . . . To hear *Penn* or *Johnny Tremain* beautifully read is a literary treat; and to read *Winnie-the-Pooh* silently, in solitude, isn't half the fun as to read it aloud or to listen to it read aloud.[9]

In summary, the place of oral reading in the reading program can easily be justified. Teachers recognize that oral reading is more difficult than silent reading. In order to be effective, it not only presupposes the ability to understand and appreciate the selections that one reads, but also involves the attitudes and abilities for portraying these ideas to other people.

Modeling Oral Reading

Teachers are urged to read aloud to the boys and girls in their classes. If they need to improve their oral reading ability, they should practice first. If they read well, they should read something every day to the children. There are many good reasons. There is a direct relationship between reading aloud to children and the children's own reading performance, their language development, and growth of their reading interests.[10] Reading to young children both acquaints them with the syntactic patterns encountered in book language and exposes them to a wide vocabulary, thereby increasing their own repertoire of words.[11]

Listening to good oral reading is not only a pleasant experience, it provides opportunity for the listeners to enlarge their acquaintance with literature and it motivates individuals to read for themselves. Too many parents neglect the opportunity to make reading to their children an intellectually stimulating activity that they can enjoy together.

Lamme developed a "Reading-Aloud-to-Children Scale" to analyze videotapes of teachers reading aloud to children. These are some of the elements she identified as important.[12]

1. Involving the child in the reading (the most influential item).
2. Amount of eye contact between reader and audience.
3. Reading with good expression.
4. Reader's voice showing pleasing variety in pitch and volume.
5. Reader pointing to pictures and words in the books.
6. Familiarity with a story which increases the reader's ability to make it interesting to others.
7. Selection of appropriate books, with size and quality of illustrations two important criteria.
8. Grouping the children so all can see the pictures and hear the story.
9. Highlighting rhyming elements, unusual words, or repetitive refrains.

Larson has suggested a "reader's theater" as an innovative technique for improving oral reading in the classroom. She defines a reader's theater as a medium in which two or more oral interpreters cause an audience to experience literature. Of course, the passages read need to be primarily dialogue.

The basic characteristics of such a theater are: (1) few props; (2) projecting the mood by voice, restrained gestures, and facial expressions; (3) a narrator who speaks to the audience and unites characters and audience; (4) each reader has a copy of the script; and (5) developing a close relationship between the performers and the audience.[13]

The Task of Oral Reading

Children need the opportunity to do a great deal of oral reading until they have established an independent reading level of second grade or above. Of course, this category would include children in the first grade, most of the children in the second grade, many children in the third grade, and also some in the fourth, fifth and sixth grades.

The "real-life" purpose of reading aloud to others is to convey information to them, to entertain them, or to share a good story which they do not have. Under such circumstances, then, the audience being read to will not have copies of the material in their hands. Similarly, oral reading is best used in the classroom, not for its own sake, but, rather, for achieving other purposes. Some of these might be as follows:

1. Giving a report, either individual or committee.
2. Giving specific directions to be followed, sharing announcements of interest to the group, or sharing special items of interest.
3. Trying to prove a point, settle an argument, or give evidence of a different point of view.
4. Sharing the many aspects of recreational reading.

For good oral reading the reader must be prepared beforehand. This means that the reader has help with technical difficulties in the reading, understands the content of the passage very well, and can pronounce all the words. A child may practice reading orally before his or her own reading group.

The selection to be read should lend itself to the oral reading situation. If it will not generate interest, if it will not easily appeal to the listeners, the teacher may suggest other content to be read.

Children enjoy sharing their reading when they have confidence in their ability to read well and they find the story interesting. This sharing an enjoyable experience has much affective value for boys and girls. Oral reading also makes it possible for the teacher to enjoy with the reading group the most interesting parts of stories they have read.

For several reasons, it is important that the teacher hear each child read orally on occasion during the school year. By evaluating the kinds of errors a child makes in reading—word recognition errors, punctuation errors, omissions and insertions, failure to use context clues, or inability to attack unfamiliar words—the teacher can arrange teaching emphasis to help the child. For the child in trouble, the teacher can interject questions, stop the reading to discuss or clarify a point, take turns reading pages or paragraphs, and generally lend encouragement. The teacher can promote the child's optimal growth by helping the child build confidence.

On-going evaluation also has diagnostic value in helping the teacher appraise pupil growth throughout the year. Until children have established at least a fluent second grade level of reading, the teacher needs a careful check on how accurately they read. Some kind of checklist which could be easily kept up to date would be helpful for recording evaluative impressions of each child's oral reading. The teacher can develop with the children criteria for improvement in abilities to read well for others. The two conditions under which the child reads orally should be distinguished: (1) reading *at sight* (without first reading silently), as in the informal reading inventory; and (2) reading something aloud which the child has had an opportunity to read silently first.

Improving Oral Reading

Reading aloud to an audience requires, first, a purpose that is meaningful to the listeners and to the child who is doing the reading. Ideally, the reading shares information which the members of the audience want and do not already have, and they do not have a copy of whatever is being read to them.

Second, the selection read should be appropriate as well as interesting in an audience situation. It should be on the level of difficulty that the child can handle as his independent or instructional level of reading.

Third, adequate preparation is important. That usually involves preliminary silent reading with some attention to vocabulary difficulties, followed by oral reading practice, before the selection is read to the entire class.

If these conditions are present, the quality of the reading can then be analyzed into the following components:

1. Adequate phrasing.
2. Voice modulated to comfortable speech.
3. Opening the mouth so enunciation is clear.
4. Recognizing punctuation marks.
5. Eliminating distracting mannerisms.
6. Flexible use of stress, intonation, and pitch appropriate to the content of the story being read.
7. Developing a comfortable stance or sitting position.
8. Developing the ability to enjoy the story with the audience.

Children need guidance in these details to become satisfactory oral readers. Tape recorders can be very useful tools.

Greer recommends the following procedure:

Ask the student to read a few paragraphs from the Gilmore Oral Reading Test and then analyze the tape with him. Together, compile a list of items which he should check in his oral reading. Paste this check list in the front of his notebook (so it will not be lost) and he can use the list to check subsequent recordings of oral reading.

Save the original tape and let him listen when he likes. After a while he forgets about this tape but continues oral practice. Then near the end of the semester the teacher can bring out the first tape for comparison with his present reading.

In sixth grade, I've had some really excellent results in oral reading improvement with this technique. An advantage is that the child can take care of much of the practice on his own because he knows how to operate the tape recorder.[14]

Use of tape recorders in classrooms makes it possible for children to record their oral reading, to practice a passage under strong motivation, and to prepare tapes of their best reading for the teacher to save. When holding parent-teacher conferences, the teacher can let the parent listen to a sample of the child's oral reading.

The contribution oral reading can make to personality development will evidence itself in clear speech, self-confidence, poise, and an in-group feeling that results from contributing to the pleasure of a group.

Using Oral Reading As a Diagnostic Tool

Oral reading practice is very important in helping the poor reader establish a level of fluency in reading. Children whose reading ability is limited may never have enjoyed silent reading as a means of acquiring new ideas. Such children must be convinced that reading can be fun and a revealing, informative way to learn. It will be helpful for poor readers to have some lessons read to them. Also, interesting books with a low level vocabulary load are useful to help such children strengthen their reading power because they motivate them to read more. The teacher helps make the reading pleasurable and rewarding by enjoying with the child the point of an interesting, easy story that he does read.

If the child has difficulty giving his attention to the job of reading, the teacher can interject questions or stop to discuss points in the story or lend ego-support with encouraging remarks. As the reader's skill in the mechanics of reading improves, less support is needed from the teacher. Poor readers may have developed poor speech habits because they cannot read. If so, they need help in general speech improvement as they gain confidence and begin making reading progress. They may need help with several components of reading: accurate phrasing; modulating the voice to a comfortable level; opening the mouth sufficiently for clear enunciation; putting zest and confidence into the reading; recognizing punctuation marks; eliminating distracting mannerisms developed in the period of frustration about reading; and getting inflection into character parts.

The Word-by-Word Reader

Oral reading allows the teacher to follow the child's reading word by word, syllable by syllable, to find out exactly what kinds of errors are being made. Two common problems in oral reading are word-by-word reading and "guessing-in-context" reading. In word-by-word reading, word-callers plod along slowly, tending to make a noticeable pause after each word. When they do attempt to phrase the reading, the wrong words may be grouped together or punctuation marks may be disregarded or misinterpreted. Keeping the place with a finger is a common practice of word-by-word readers. Children who are word-by-word readers can be helped by being given easier material so they will have to think less about how they read and more about what they read. Thus they will improve memory of the details in what they are reading, and understanding should be somewhat better.

The Context Reader

Context readers, in contrast to word-callers, may sound fluent but be inaccurate in what they are trying to read. They may skip over words, add words, or substitute one word for another. They may be unable to attack any words not already in their sight vocabulary except as they guess at them from context.

Some examples will show the typical kind of reading the context reader does. A sentence may read, *The little rabbit went down the road.* The context reader, studying the picture at the top of the page and then looking at the words in the sentence, may say, *The little bunny hopped down the lane.* The idea is correct, but three basic words in the sentence have been changed. Or a sentence may read, *Behind the band came a man on a big elephant.* But the context reader reads, *After the bandwagon went, a man came by on an elephant.*

Children who are context readers probably need easy material to read for practice. Then their attention should be directed to word-attack skills and to phonic and structural analysis. They should also be encouraged to read with complete accuracy for part of the lesson. The teacher could say, for example, "Now, on the next page I'm going to watch to see if you pronounce every word exactly as it is in the story." Such a case was a sixth grade boy who was reading an easy second grade reader and making several errors. At the end of a page, the teacher said to him, "You are getting the idea across to me, and that is the important thing. But since we are reading an easy book this morning, let's just reread these two pages and be sure we read completely accurately." Without much difficulty, this boy was able to concentrate both on the story, which was elementary, and on the mechanics of how he was reading. He was able to pay more attention to how he was reading and soon stopped reconstructing the sentence the way he thought it ought to be or the way he thought it probably was according to the picture.

A good reader knows how to use context and visual clues, as well as word-attack skills and phonic and structural analysis. A poor reader is apt to have only the visual method of attack, and may often use it incorrectly.

The classroom teacher should keep records such as are suggested in chapter 19 for the Informal Reading Inventory in order to help children analyze specific faults so they can be specifically addressed.

Teachers should also become skilled in using a marking technique such as is suggested for administering the Informal Reading Inventory. Then any oral reading the student does—not just in the reading class but in all subjects of the school curriculum—can be quickly marked and scored to determine how it relates to the student's instruction and frustration reading levels.

Rate of Oral Reading

The average oral reader who enunciates clearly is probably reading at a rate of between 150 and 170 words per minute. This is about as fast as oral reading will be done. By third or fourth grade, the child should begin to perform more rapidly in silent reading than oral. By the end of the sixth grade, the child should have developed a silent reading rate about double his or her oral reading rate. See Table 11.1 for comparative rates of silent and oral reading through the elementary school.

Price and Stroud reviewed investigations of children's oral reading and concluded that there was little, if any, evidence to show that oral reading has much effect on silent reading rate.[15] Teachers have two distinct problems: the teaching of silent reading skills on the one hand, and the teaching of oral reading skills on the other. The way to develop good oral reading is to practice reading orally; the way to improve silent reading is to practice reading silently and to work on the necessary skills.

However, effective oral reading habits take time to develop. That time should not be allowed to conflict with the time necessary for developing competent silent reading abilities.

Innovative Programs Developing Oral Language

Teachers of young children must be alert to different types of materials being made available to them each year. While only two are mentioned here, several publishers are producing programs that emphasize intrinsically interesting ways to learn language and understand the relationships between oral and written forms of language. *The Sounds of Language*[16] by Bill Martin, Jr., for instance, is a set of little books that uses colorful illustrations and graphic design to show word, phrase, and sentence patterns as meaningful equivalents of oral language. The child can either hear the teacher read the story first or listen to a phonograph record of the story that includes signals telling him when to turn the pages. Then he may relisten and help tell the story. Finally, he can read the story for himself. Such materials are excellent supplements for a classroom interest center designed to build positive attitudes toward reading. *The World of Language*[17] by Muriel Crosby stimulates oral language for young children through poems, stories, and plays and such concepts as rhyme, imagery, mood, and human interaction. Interwoven is considerable emphasis on self-concept and positive attitudes toward self and others. Such oral language stimulation provides for one of children's very important needs. Some techniques are included in this volume in chapter 7, "Assessment of Prereading Skills" (see the section on "Language and Concept Development").

Summary

The major purposes of oral reading have been presented as (1) to entertain; (2) to give personal enjoyment and satisfaction; (3) to encourage effective group participation; (4) to provide effective practice for speech improvement; and (5) to provide for the teacher a diagnostic measure of the strengths and weaknesses in children's oral reading abilities.

Other important ideas discussed in the chapter included (1) criteria of what constitutes an oral reading (audience) situation; (2) the need for teachers to be able to read well orally; (3) the use of oral reading practice to improve word-recognition skills of poor readers; (4) the use of the tape recorder to allow children to practice oral reading independently; (5) the importance of the teacher understanding the *child's purpose* in oral reading as well as the teacher's purpose; and (6) the use of oral reading to open the doors to the great exciting world of children's literature for all boys and girls.

Suggested Activities

1. Practice and read a story on the tape recorder that you would read to a class in the elementary school.
2. Ask three children to read something they each think is easy. Record their oral reading on the tape recorder. Listen to each one as many times as necessary and judge the suitability of the material for instructional or independent reader levels.
3. Prepare and read an appropriate story to a class in the elementary school. Evaluate your success in helping them enjoy the story.

For Further Reading

Bond, Guy L., and Eva B. Wagner. *Teaching the Child to Read,* 4th ed., chapter 12, "Oral Reading," pp. 240–49. New York: Macmillan, 1966.

Bush, Clifford, and Mildred Huebner. *Strategies for Reading in the Elementary School,* chapter 7, "Oral Reading," pp. 159–72. New York: Macmillan, 1970.

Dallman, Martha, et al. *The Teaching of Reading,* 4th ed., chapter 10A, "Oral Reading" and chapter 10B, "Developing Skill in Oral Reading." New York: Holt, Rinehart & Winston, 1974.

Faller, Bernard A., Jr. "The Basic Basic: Getting Kids to Read." *Learning* 6 (1978): 100–101.

Frierson, Edward C. "The Role of Oral Reading." In *Individualizing Reading Instruction: A Reader,* pp. 244–47, edited by Larry Harris and Carl Smith. New York: Holt, Rinehart & Winston, 1972.

Harris, Larry, and Carl Smith. *Reading Instruction Through Diagnostic Teaching,* chapter 12, "Oral Reading," pp. 281–310. New York: Holt, Rinehart & Winston, 1972.

Heinrich, June Sark. "Elementary Oral Reading: Methods and Materials." *The Reading Teacher* 30 (1976): 10–15.

Horn, Ernest, and James Curtis. "Improvement of Oral Reading." In *Reading in the Elementary School,* pp. 254–65, edited by Nelson B. Henry. Chicago, Ill.: University of Chicago Press, 1949.

Lamme, Linda Leonard. "Reading Aloud to Young Children." *Language Arts* 53 (1976): 886–87.

Larson, Martha L. "Reader's Theatre: New Vitality for Oral Reading." *The Reading Teacher* 29 (1976): 359–60.

McCormick, Sandra. "Choosing Books to Read to Preschool Children." *Language Arts* 54 (1977): 543–48.

———. "Should You Read Aloud to Your Children?" *Language Arts* 54 (1977): 139–43.

Tinker, Miles, and Constance M. McCullough. *Teaching Elementary Reading,* 3d ed., chapter 11, "Reading Aloud," pp. 224–36. New York: Appleton-Century-Crofts, 1968.

Wildebush, Sarah. "Oral Reading Today." *The Reading Teacher* 18 (1964): 139.

Notes

1. Samuel McCutchen, ed., *The Fourth Reader* (Philadelphia: E. H. Butler and Co., 1883), pp. 7, 8, 10.

2. James Baldwin and Ida C. Bender, *Reading with Expression: Second Reader* (New York: American Book Company, 1911), pp. 5, 6.

3. Sarah W. Wildebush, "Oral Reading Today," *The Reading Teacher* 18 (November 1964): 139. Wildebush states that many precious hours are being "consumed in the round robin of continuous oral reading."

4. Rose Fyleman, *Fifty-One New Nursery Rhymes* (New York: Doubleday & Company, Inc., 1932). Reprinted by permission of Doubleday & Company, Inc.

5. From Rhoda W. Bacmeister, *Stories to Begin On* (New York: E. P. Dutton, 1940. Renewal © 1968 by Rhoda W. Bacmeister). Reprinted by permission of the publishers.

6. From Laura E. Richards, *Tirra Lirra* (Boston: Little, Brown and Co., 1935). Reprinted by permission of the publisher.

7. May Hill Arbuthnot, *The Anthology of Children's Literature: Book I, Time for Poetry* (Chicago: Scott, Foresman, 1952), p. 8.

8. From Ivy O. Eastwick, *Fairies and Suchlike* (New York: E. P. Dutton, 1946). Reprinted by permission of the publishers.

9. May Hill Arbuthnot, *Children and Books,* 3rd ed. (Chicago: Scott, Foresman, 1964), pp. 647–48.

10. Sandra McCormick, "Should You Read Aloud to Your Children?" *Language Arts* 54 (1977): 143.

11. Sandra McCormick, "Choosing Books to Read to Preschool Children," *Language Arts* 54 (1977): 545. See also Bernard A. Faller, Jr., "The Basic Basic: Getting Kids to Read," *Learning* 6 (1978): 100–101.

12. Linda Leonard Lamme, "Reading Aloud to Young Children," *Language Arts* 53 (1976): 886–87.

13. Martha L. Larson, "Reader's Theatre: New Vitality for Oral Reading," *The Reading Teacher* 29 (1976): 359–60.

14. Margaret Greer, Assoc. Prof. of Education, University of Alaska, Anchorage.

15. Helen Price and James B. Stroud, "Note on Oral Reading," *Quarterly Journal of Speech* 31 (1945): 340–43.

16. Bill Martin, Jr., *The Sounds of Language* (New York: Holt, Rinehart & Winston, 1967).

17. Muriel Crosby, *The World of Language* (Chicago: Follett, 1970).

14

Developing Permanent Reading Habits

All teachers want children to develop permanent interests in reading. Attractive bulletin boards showing new book acquisitions, a free reading table, children's book reviews—all are ways teachers try to help children establish a permanent interest in reading. To make reading a permanent habit is, actually, the overall goal of the school's reading program for boys and girls.

Generally, the attitude should be that to read is pleasant. Schools must provide for reading opportunities for all children; children must be guided in making wise choices about which reading materials best serve their purposes; and adequate provision must be made by each teacher to move children toward permanent interests and habits in reading. Reading opportunities for *all* children *require* that:

1. Materials have high interest appeal and be of appropriate difficulty so that children can read with relative ease.
2. Wide ranges of choices be provided: both fact and fiction; travel, history, myth, science, legend, biography, poetry, and plays.
3. They live the incident meaningfully. They must learn to empathize, internalize the feelings, see the sights, smell the smells, hear the sounds.
4. Each child's individual interests be given consideration. Materials can be recommended and made available, but each child will have individual interests, so the teacher should not expect that all children will find particular books, stories, or poems equally appealing just because the teacher feels they have special merit.

Encouraging Extended Reading

The teacher's ability to motivate children to want to read will be dependent both upon personality interaction with the students and on the teacher's awareness of what conditions work most effectively. The reader is encouraged to reread the comments on motivation found in chapter 2. Some basics include:

1. Knowledge about the child's home life, intelligence, general maturity, and independent reading power.

2. As wide acquaintance as possible with the children's literature available to the child.
3. Knowledge of standard references in juvenile libraries that will help the teacher find, or find out about, the wealth of interesting reading material now available for boys and girls.
4. An inviting reading corner that will entice children to browse when they have the liberty to do so.
5. A provision in every school day that makes it possible for each student to have some time in a pleasant, independent reading environment.
6. Opportunities for children to share what they have read, whether it be through discussion, role-playing, or shared reading.
7. Awareness of the many audiovisual aids that can awaken in reluctant readers a desire to read. For example, all the Newbery Award books are now available on long-playing records. Teachers need to be alert for radio and television programs and films and filmstrips that will help promote reading interests.

Activities to promote growth in reading interests:

1. Individual card files: annotations about books read
2. A structured plan for record keeping such as "My Reading Design"
3. Group discussion once a week or once every two weeks
4. Oral reporting
5. Recommending books to others
6. Oral reading by the teacher
7. Oral reading by individual children

Use of "My Reading Design"

"My Reading Design" is a structured plan to help boys and girls broaden and extend their reading interests. In the circle graph (figure 14.1) the child keeps a record of the reading done in all the different subject areas of the school curriculum. In a four-page folder designed by Simpson,[1] one page is for a list of all the titles of books read. Another page is for a list of topics that are represented in each book, to help the child decide how a book relates to the topics around the edge of the circle graph.

The number of the book on the child's list is then recorded in the small circles nearest the center of the design under each major topic the reader enjoyed in the book. Some books relate to only one topic, others may relate to two or three. As children read more and more books and record each one on the graph, they will no doubt be pleased to see how their patterns grow in the "Reading Design."

Teachers sometimes use excellent bulletin board devices for this same motivation. The segmented book worm, bar graphs made by using tiny construction paper folders for each book read by each child, and other similar visual aids are often seen in elementary classrooms.

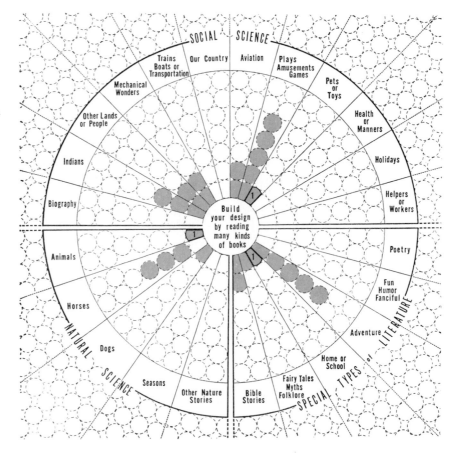

The Interest Inventory

Teachers need to learn as much as possible about the personal interests of the boys and girls in their classrooms. This can be accomplished by taking a few minutes to talk privately with each student and make notes when the time is appropriate. Also, children may write autobiographies which reveal interests or attitudes toward themselves and others. Responding to incomplete sentences (I wish. . . . When I was little. . . . I do my best when. . . . What annoys me. . . . When I grow up. . . .) may reveal directions in which the teacher can interact with a student.

A more systematic inventory of a child's interests and background can be obtained by asking boys and girls to complete short interest inventories. What does the student do after school, on Saturdays, or during the winter evenings? What is the student's relationship with siblings and parents? Does the student have special hobbies or collections or take private lessons of any kind? Learning whether the child has taken interesting trips by train, plane, bus, or car and the kinds of places the child's family visits when they travel is important.

A teacher can prepare an inventory of no more than one page that can provide such information. Current events newspapers like the *Weekly Reader* occasionally have interest inventories for boys and girls to use. All information may be useful to the teacher. It may reveal the adequacy of sleep, rest, diet, play, and work in the student's living habits. The more the teacher knows about the interests, activities, and abilities of the student, the more he or she is able to understand the student's behavior. And all such information will provide the teacher useful background information for planning ways to extend the student's reading environment.

The Elementary School Library

The basic purpose of the school library is to expose children to much good literature and to develop permanent interest in reading—and in reading a wide variety of materials. It is hoped that good school library experiences will also help develop a child's taste for literature worth reading.

If teachers are to find suitable materials to accommodate the wide ranges of ability in any class, they must rely on the centralized library in the school. Adams urged this function for the school library as follows:[2]

If each child is to reach his highest potential in every subject area at the elementary school level he must have access to vastly different materials and instruction than were offered to that grade level in previous years. A multi-level approach is required and multi-level materials must follow this thinking. Although the multi-level materials are maintained in part within the classroom, it has become evident that many supplementary materials must be utilized, and budgetary consideration makes it advantageous to place them in some type of central repository. The obvious choice for this centralization is the elementary school library.

Arbuthnot reminds us:

One tremendous service a library can render both homes and schools is to supply quantities of those books which bridge the gap between reading ability and reading skill. That lag can, by third or fourth grade, assume discouraging proportions for some children. For instance, a child may be reading at first or second grade level but be capable of comprehending and enjoying books which he can't possibly read for himself at fifth, sixth, or even seventh grade level. Then the experts, among other recommendations, advise that the child be given a lot of practice reading and that he be provided with easy-to-read books in order to acquire the confidence that comes from a sense of comfortable fluency.[3]

And Adams explains:

In the child's mind the library is no longer merely a place where he goes once a week to change a book (or get a book for a book report he must write). It is still a place where a child may on any day take out and return books, but it is also a center of information, a place for leisure time activities, for story hours, for discussion of books and a place to listen to music or view filmstrips.

The teachers, the librarians, and the reading consultant see the library as the center of multi-level materials, the research center and training center for the advancing skills of the students.[4]

The library provides a *comfortable* learning situation where children can "learn how to learn." If children are responsive to this learning environment, they will move easily to junior high, high school, and public library situations the way "life" situations ought really to keep encouraging them to read.

The library is planned to meet the individual differences in the reading abilities of large groups of children. The fourth grade boy with third grade reading power can read on his level pursuing his interests; the fourth grade girl reading independently at the sixth grade level can pursue learning much higher on the scale of developmental skills.

A good central library contains no less than 6,000 volumes, made available to all the students and teachers during the entire school day. A balance is maintained between nonfiction books and books for recreational reading and in the various subject fields and fields of children's interests. Intelligent and effective use of available book selection aids will insure the necessary variety of books to extend the experiences of every child. Table 14.1 shows a breakdown of a basic juvenile library book collection suggested by the American Library Association.

If the weeding-out process is properly done, about ten percent of the books will be discarded annually. The most-used books and those with poor quality bindings will have to be replaced or renovated often.

The issue today is not whether to have either good classroom libraries or a good, well stocked central library in the elementary school. It is absolutely necessary to have a good central library to be sure a given classroom in the school has interesting, changing library shelves.

Librarians and teachers together select a shelf of books needed for each new social studies unit and make them readily available to the room teacher. The shelf of books that is no longer needed from the previous unit is returned.

Table 14.1 Analysis of Book Collection.

From American Library Association, *A Basic Book Collection for Elementary Grades* (Chicago, Ill.: American Library Association, 1960), p. 10.

Subject	Percent of Total
Reference Books	1.2
Religion and Mythology	1.2
Social Sciences and Folklore	9.1
Language	0.3
Science	23.0
Fine Arts	5.0
Literature	3.2
History and Biography	22.5
Fiction	21.5
Picture and Easy-to-read Books	13.0
	100.0%

Library Skills to Be Learned

Boys and girls can begin early learning to use the card catalog, to locate a book on the shelf, and to recognize quickly the ascending and descending Dewey Decimal or Library of Congress numbers in the area where the book sought is shelved. Special designations can be learned if pointed out to the children. Certain behaviors will enhance both the child's confidence in using and finding the time to use the library. He needs to be able to locate easily the books and magazines he likes and wants. He should be able to withdraw and return on time all the books he can make effective use of. He needs to know how to take care of books and to practice good "library behavior."

Greer has suggested seven specific information skills to be taught to elementary school boys and girls.[4]

1. How to locate books by author, title, and subject headings.

2. How to find information in alphabetical order to third or fourth letter.

3. Kind of information on a card in the file: full name of author or authors, complete title, publisher, copyright date, whether or not illustrations are included, and a call number, either Dewey Decimal or Library of Congress.

4. Books are filed by call numbers.

5. Every library book has an accession number, which indicates how many volumes have already been cataloged. If the accession number is 50,000, then the library has already cataloged 49,999 before it arrived.

6. The Library has a reference legend explaining which subject headings are assigned to which call numbers on the shelves.

7. Special designations need to be learned: "B" is biography; "F" is fiction; "R" is reference; and "Zi" or "Cla" represents first letters of author's last name.

A number of general reference books must be available to teachers in order for them to select books to meet the needs and interests of boys and girls and to supplement the units of work being taught in their classrooms.

All, or as many as possible, of the following general reference books will be useful to classroom teachers and should be available in the elementary school library.

Arbuthnot, May Hill, et al., eds. *Children's Books Too Good to Miss,* 6th ed. Cleveland: Case Western Reserve University, 1971.

Baker, Augusta. *The Black Experience in Children's Books,* rev. ed. New York: New York Public Library, 1971.

Cianciolo, Patricia J., ed. *Adventuring with Books: 2400 Titles for Pre-kindergarten through Grade Eight.* New York: Scholastic Book Services, 1977.

Council on Interracial Books for Children. *Human (and Anti-Human) Values in Children's Books.* New York: Racism and Sexism Resource Center for Educators, A Division of the Council on Interracial Books for Children, 1976.

Dill, Barbara E., ed. *Children's Catalog,* 13th ed. New York: H. W. Wilson, 1976, with annual supplements.

Eakin, Mary K., ed. *Good Books for Children, Nineteen Fifty–Nineteen Sixty Five,* 3rd ed. Chicago: University of Chicago Press, 1966.

Eakin, Mary K., and Eleanor Merritt, eds. *A Subject Index to Books for Primary Grades,* 3rd ed. Chicago: American Library Association, 1967. Indicates independent reading level and interest level of trade books and readers.

Field, Elinor W., ed. *Horn Book Reflections on Children's Books and Reading.* Boston: Horn Book, 1969.

Gillis, Ruth J. *Children's Books for Times of Stress: An Annotated Bibliography.* Bloomington: Indiana University Press, 1978.

Horn Book. Magazine published by Horn Book, Inc., Park Sq. Bldg., 31st St. & James Ave., Boston, Mass. 02116. Includes discriminating reviews of children's books and an annual list of outstanding books.

Kearney, Ruth Carlson. *Emerging Humanity, Multi Ethnic Literature for Children and Adolescents.* Dubuque, Ia.: Wm. C. Brown, 1972.

Larrick, Nancy. *Parent's Guide to Children's Reading,* 4th ed. New York: Doubleday, 1975.

Latimer, Bettye I., ed. *Starting Out Right: Choosing Books about Black People for Young Children.* Madison, Wisc.: Dept. of Public Instruction, 1972. Presents criteria for judging; 200 books annotated.

Reid, Virginia, ed. *Reading Ladders to Human Relations,* 5th ed. Washington, D.C.: American Council on Education, 1972.

Rudman, Masha K. *Children's Literature: An Issues Approach.* Lexington, Mass.: D. C. Heath, 1976.

Spache, George. *Good Reading for Poor Readers,* rev. ed. Champaign, Ill.: Garrard, 1974.

Sunderlin, Sylvia, ed. *Bibliography of Books for Children,* rev. ed. Washington, D.C.: Assoc. for Childhood Education International, 1971.

Organizing Enriching Resources for Unit Teaching

Methodology in the form of sample lessons and organizing the teaching of a unit of work was discussed in chapter 11. Methodology is brought in here for the purpose of pointing out how the well stocked library enriches the teacher's resources for social studies units especially that he or she may be teaching.

The fifth grade unit on the westward movement is used to exemplify some of the kinds of library materials that can be drawn upon to make the unit challenging and interesting to boys and girls.[5] Folklore and folk songs, student reading materials, teacher reading materials, sources of free materials, audiovisual aids, and (because this unit includes the Southwest) a limited Spanish vocabulary are all resources that might be used to develop understandings in the unit. Clearly, librarian-teacher cooperation is necessary to organize such resources.

Behavioral objectives can be formulated in teacher-pupil planning sessions:

1. Each child learns about faith in our American heritage by _____ .

2. Class members learn greater awareness of and respect for ethnic groups and their beliefs and values by _____ .

3. The United States extended its boundaries to the West Coast through buying land, exploring new territory, importing the total economic life of the nation, and removing Indians to reservation lands. Children understand these happenings by _____ .

4. Society is always changing. Children sense this by observing _____ .

5. Even in pioneer days, there was a social and recreational life for the people. Children will learn about this by _____ .

6. Education moved with the families. Children can observe the extension of public education to the west by _____ .

7. The connecting of the East to the West was accomplished by _____ .

8. Extending law and order to the far west was a complex operation. Children can understand many of the problems by _____ .

A. Folklore and folk songs.
   1. How folklore, ballads, and literature began.
   2. What folklore, ballads, and literature used as their subject matter.
   3. What is folklore and folk music?
      a. Folklore.
         (1) It includes all the customs, beliefs, and stories that people themselves have handed down through the years.
         (2) When people didn't have printing or when printing wasn't used as widely as it is today, people recounted orally stories from generation to generation.
      b. Folk music.
         (1) Music which has grown up among the people as an important part of their life.
         (2) It is often very old and was never written or printed until recent years.
         (3) Usually it contains unusual rhythms and unusual scales, with frequent changes between major and minor modes.
         (4) The author unknown.

(5) The language and customs of the people are reflected in this kind of music. The American folk song is generally narrative and tells the story of a person or an event.

    4. Examples of folklore and folk music.

B. Selected student readings grades 3–4.
1. *I Am a Pueblo Indian Girl.* Abieta. Cadmus.
2. *Wild Bill Hickok.* A.M. Anderson. Harper & Row.
3. *Portugee Phillips and the Fighting Sioux.* A. M. Anderson. Harper & Row.
4. *In My Mother's House.* Ann Nolan Clark. Viking.
5. *A Child's Story of New Mexico.* Clark. University Publishing Co., 1960.

C. Selected student readings grades 5–6.
1. *Kit Carson, Mountain Man.* Margaret Bell. Morrow.
2. *Buffalo Horse.* Cardell D. Christenson. E. M. Hale and Company.
3. *Sam Houston, The Tallest Texan.* Wm. Johnson. E. M. Hale and Company, 1953.
4. *The Lewis and Clark Expedition.* Richard Neuberger. Random House.

D. Teacher's background reading.
1. "Frontier Lawman." William G. Bell. *The American West,* 1 (Summer 1964): 5–13.
2. *Indian Legends from the Northern Rockies.* Ella E. Clark. University of Oklahoma Press.
3. *Of Men and Rivers.* Virginia Eifert. Dodd, Mead.
4. *New Mexico's Troubled Years.* Calvin Horn. Albuquerque: Horn and Wallace.
5. *Tales of the Frontier: From Lewis and Clark to the Last Roundup.* E. Dick. University of Nebraska Press.

E. Audiovisual aids: educational motion pictures.
1. "Northwest Territory"; "The Louisiana Purchase"; "Texas and Far West"; "Settling the West"; "The Oregon Country" (U.S. Expansion Series). Chicago: Coronet Films.
2. "Indian Influences in the United States"; "Spanish Influences in the United States" (Cultural Influence Series). Chicago: Coronet Films.
3. "Johnny Appleseed: A Legend of Frontier Life." Chicago: Coronet Films.
4. "Indians of the Southwest." New York: William Claiborne.
5. "How the West Was Won—and Honor Lost." New York: McGraw-Hill Films.
6. "The Oregon Trail." Chicago: Encyclopaedia Britannica.

F. A glossary of western words: Spanish.
acequia irrigation ditch
adobe unburnt brick dried in sun used for building

angoras   chaps made of goat hide with hair retained

broncho-busting   horse-breaking

bronco; broncho   unbroken Mexican or California horse

buckaroo; buccarro   cowboy (Northwest)

caballada   band of horses

caballero   Spanish knight or horseman; happy cowboy; expert horseman

caballo   horse

cabestro   rope; horsehair rope halter

calabozo   Spanish name for jail

caracole   to make a half turn to the right or left on horseback

cataloes   cross-breed of cattle and buffaloes

cholla   type of large cactus with sharp spines

compadre   boon companion; pal

conchas   silver disks worn for decoration on chaps, hats, etc.

corral   pen for livestock

dinero   money

frijole, frijol   type of bean much cultivated in Mexico for food

hacienda   in Spanish America, a large plantation on which the owner is resident; an establishment for raising stock

jacal   small hut or cabin

javalina   a wild boar

junta   the junction; sometimes refers to business meeting

latigo   leather strap attached to girth and used to fasten saddle on horse's back

lobo   wolf

loco   crazy; foolish

maguey   a century plant from which the fibers are used in making rope

mañana   tomorrow; late

mantas   type of blanket or wrap

mesa   elevated tableland

mestizo   half-breed

peso   Mexican dollar; hence, any dollar

pinto   piebald; small calico horse of the Western plains

pueblo   group of buildings constructed by Indians of the Southwest

ranchero   rancher; especially Mexican rancher

reata   leather rope; lariat

remuda   band of saddle horses; extra mounts

romal   whip fashioned from leather thongs and attached to bridle or saddle

serape   blanket worn as cloak by Mexicans

sudaderos   leather lining or underside of saddle

vaquero   cowpuncher; cowboy

vara   Spanish measure of length equal to about a yard

Values of the People Studied

Social studies textbooks designed to provide the overview of a full year of work for any given grade level must, of necessity, be digests of much factual material. If teachers rely heavily on basic text material, boys and girls will be attempting to absorb many facts for which they may not always see relevance. Typical kinds of abbreviated facts for almost any geographical area include: the important crops, the major cities, the chief industries, the latitude and longitude, the mountain ranges, and the navigable rivers.

To illuminate the cultural, social, and economic values of the people about whom the social studies text is written, teachers need to seek out those fiction and nonfiction accounts that will teach something of the affective life of the people. What was daily living like for the pioneers? What was fun? What games did they play? What were the causes of happiness or unhappiness? What about the fears and anxieties of boys and girls? For historical fiction or biography, the questions need to be in the past tense. Of course, for stories about boys and girls today, the questions should be asked in the present tense.

A special bibliography of such books for children in which Indians are main characters is appended to this volume. The selections were made by Dr. Juanita Cata, Chief, Division of Education, Albuquerque Area Office, Bureau of Indian Affairs.

Cavanah has written a book about Abraham Lincoln's boyhood that many boys and girls enjoy.

Abe Lincoln was hired to work as a clerk in Denton Offut's general store. Customers could buy all kinds of things there—tools and nails, needles and thread, mittens and calico, and tallow for making candles. One day a woman bought several yards of calico. After she left, Abe discovered that he had charged her six cents too much. That evening he walked six miles to give her the money. He was always doing things like that, and people began to call him "Honest Abe."[6]

Laura Ingalls Wilder has made pioneer days in the Middle West live for many boys and girls in the intermediate grades with her *Little House in the Big Woods, On The Banks of Plum Creek, The Long Winter, Farmer Boy, Little House on the Prairie, By the Shores of Silver Lake, Little Town on the Prairie, and These Happy Golden Years.*[7]

The book *Fifth Chinese Daughter* has many episodes that reveal the strong conflict between the parents and the children growing up as first-generation immigrants in San Francisco.

Jade Snow was seventeen and had just arranged her first date without her mother's or father's permission. Her very traditional father chastised her in this way:

"Where and when did you learn to be so daring as to leave this house without permission of your parents? You did not learn it under my roof."

When Jade Snow tried to explain her behavior to her parents, her father became very angry and continued:

"Do I have to justify my judgment to you? I do not want a daughter of mine to be known as one who walks the streets at night. Have you no thought of our reputations if not for your own? If you start going out with boys, no good man will want to ask you to be his wife. You just do not know as well as we do what is good for you."[8]

Louise Stinetorf has written delightfully of the experiences of Abed, a Sudanese boy who lived in the Nubian Desert in North Africa. He took his donkey loaded with his parents' ceramic pots to the marketplace in Fadwa and found a little empty space and began calling out his wares.

Presently a woman stopped in front of the pots and began looking them over. As she moved, Abed heard a little tinkling sound, and although her dress was so long he could not see her feet, he knew she was wearing iron anklets. He knew also, that this meant that God had given her many children, but that God had also taken them away from her.

There was no choice among Abed's wares. Every pot was exactly the same size and shape and color. In Africa, a potter makes exactly one size and kind of pot. If the customer wants something different, he goes to another potter. Abed knew his pots were good ones. His father and mother were careful workmen. They chopped the straw they used until it was almost as fine as flour, and they used enough of it to make their wares good and strong. Their clay, too, was not half sand, but a good red product carried half way across the Sahara Desert on the backs of strong camels.

In spite of all this, the woman lifted up one pot, then another, and examined them all carefully. One pot was too heavy and too shallow, and another made from the same mold was too thin and too deep. At last she chose a pot and offered a price.

Abed took the pot away from the woman, dusted it off carefully, and put it back on the pile. To offer such a tiny price for so excellent a pot was an insult to his ancestors, he told her. The woman seized the pot and pointed out all the rough spots. Abed patted it lovingly as though it were a kitten. The woman thumped the pot with the flat of her hand. See, she cried, it sounded as though there were weak spots in it. It would probably crack wide open the first time she put it over the fire. But she was a charitable woman, and she would offer a little more money for it.

Abed plinked the pot with his thumb nail and cocked his head on one side. It had the ring of strength and purity, he answered. It was sweet toned like a metal camel bell. It had been in the glazing kiln over a fire of hot sheep's dung for two days. It would give hard service for years. Possibly this woman's children would cook in the same pot long after she was dust! But he, too, was charitable and he would take a little less money for the pot although, he assured his customer, it was a very jewel of a pot.

Abed and his customer haggled for some time. She found every possible fault with the pot—and finally every possible fault with Abed and his family, shrieking at him that he was a thief and the child of a family of thieves. But little by little she raised her price.

And the more fault the woman found with the pot, the more Abed praised it. Finally he, too, began to berate her, telling her she was surely blind to find fault with such an excellent pot and saying that if he sold his wares at her price his father and mother would without any doubt starve to death. But little by little he lowered his price.

Then, just when the woman was calling terrible curses down upon Abed's donkey's eyebrow, and it seemed as though they would come to blows, they agreed upon a price. The woman paid Abed, and just as softly as they had sounded loud and angry before, they asked God's blessing on each other and parted good friends. No one seemed disturbed at the shouting nor surprised at the sudden calm and friendship—that is just the way marketing is done in Fadwa![9]

Two recent books about Navaho children provide some insights into the thinking of young Navaho in relatively recent times.

Grandmother decided that Sad-Girl must go away to the off-reservation boarding school to learn the white man's reading and writing. She arranged with the trader at the trading post to have her registered for school, then arranged for her to ride to the trading post at the appointed time with the neighbors, the Yuccas. Enroute to the trading post, the Yucca children explained that the Navaho name was not sufficient in the white man's school and, after due deliberation, named her Rose Smith.

At the boarding school she was awakened one night by the crying of her roommate in the lower bunk. She had been a bit frightened by the strange, muffled sound of the crying. Her first thought was that it might be the ghost of an earth person, because she knew that ghosts appear only after dark and only on moonless nights. Rose must help her friend Isobel.

If Isobel had contracted sickness or disease it was because she had violated a taboo or had been attacked by a ghost or a witch. If the latter was the case and the spectral attack was very recent, it could be averted or lessened by certain precautions.

She fumbled her way through the darkness to the dresser. Her fingers slipped down, counting, until they arrived at her own drawer. Inside, carefully laid away with her change of underwear and her sweater, was a tiny sack of gall medicine. Grandmother had made it for her just before she left home, so it was fresh and potent. It was composed of dried and pulverized galls of many animals and was a sure cure for anyone who had unknowingly absorbed a witch's poison.[10]

In a book titled *Owl in the Cedar Tree*, Mrs. Momaday presents a conflict between the culture of the Indian and the culture of the white man. Haske, a little boy who rides the bus each day to school from his mother's hogan, makes a painting at school that wins him a prize and allows him to buy the horse that he had wanted for a long time. But woven into the story is the cultural conflict between Old Grandfather and Haske's father. Old Grandfather tells Haske he should become a medicine man when he grows up and that he should start now by going into the hills for four days to fast and pray. His father, however, is determined that Haske must go to school every day and learn the white man's language and culture. One day Haske asks his father to tell the bus driver that he will not be there that day, or the next three days. The father is indignant and tells him that he most certainly will go to school as usual. He also says that the Old One has not given Haske good advice. When Haske returns from school, only his mother and sister are there. He knows that his father has gone to sing for a sick friend and will not return. But he also knows that since Old Grandfather is not there, his father has spoken to him and he has gone away feeling unwanted.

Then Mrs. Momaday explains how the mother resolves the situation:

At supper Riding Woman saw that Haske was not eating his food. By the light of the center fire she saw that her son was troubled, and she understood how he felt.

Finally she said, "Your father told me all about it, my son. This morning he spoke to the Old One and tried to explain that school is good. But Old Grandfather could not understand. He was hurt and offended. He left without saying goodbye."

Haske did not try to hide his tears. He kept his eyes on his mother's face. For the first time in his life he saw the strength and courage in her face. Until now he had seen only the beauty and tenderness. Suddenly he was ashamed of his tears. He stopped crying and smiled at his mother.

Riding Woman said, "Now you feel better and must eat your supper." She put hot food on his plate and warmed his coffee. While Haske ate hungrily, his mother explained all the things he needed to know.

She said, "My son, you have made an anthill look like a mountain. You have worried about which trail to follow. There is only one trail. You have come to believe that some things are all good and some things are all bad. This is not true. The Indian and the white man are not so different as you might think. Both have the same needs, and each must try to understand the other. This is why school is important. At school you learn the white man's language. You cannot understand another person until you can talk with him. By speaking with others you learn what they are thinking and how they feel. This brings understanding between people."

Riding Woman saw that Desbah had gone to sleep by the fire. She picked up the little girl and wrapped a blanket about her. Then she tucked Desbah into her sheepskin bed and sat down again beside Haske.

"So you see, my son, there is only one trail," she continued. "Follow it and keep the best of the old ways while learning the best of the new ways."

Haske felt very happy. His mother had made him understand, and he no longer felt that he was being pulled in two directions. She had set his feet upon the trail as surely as the Navaho gods could have done. And he would make it a trail of beauty.[11]

Reading Good Books to Children

Especially good books may well be read in their entirety to children. Good books that supply background information for units of work but that are too difficult for children to read alone should be read, in whole or in part, to the class.

Books of story type that present such a vivid picture of life in other times and places that the reader is able to recreate them in imagination lend reality to social studies and help children to realize their drama and romance. The voyages of Columbus . . . told by Armstrong Sperry in *The Voyages of Columbus* . . . become a thrilling adventure.[12]

McKee provides a long list of books for teachers to read aloud to first grade boys and girls.[13]

One fifth grade teacher reported reading the following books to her class during the school year. All had a high interest level for the group.

Esther Forbes, *Johnny Tremain* (New York: Houghton Mifflin Co., 1943).
Sterling North, *Rascal* (New York: E. P. Dutton Co., Inc., 1963).
James Daugherty, *Daniel Boone* (New York: Viking, 1939).
Carol Brink, *Caddie Woodlawn* (New York: Macmillan, 1935).
Joseph Krumgold, *And Now Miguel* (New York: Crowell, 1953).
Elizabeth G. Speare, *The Bronze Bow* (New York: Houghton Mifflin, 1961).

The same fifth grade teacher reported that the first two or three chapters of the following books were read and considerable interest generated. Then the book was given to an individual student who wanted to finish it.[14]

Laura Ingalls Wilder, *On the Banks of Plum Creek* (New York: Harper, 1953).
Laura Ingalls Wilder, *The Little House in the Big Woods* (New York: Harper, 1951).
May McNeer, *Armed with Courage* (Nashville: Abingdon, 1957).
Anna Sewell, *Black Beauty* (New York: Macmillan, 1877).
Scott O'Dell, *Island of the Blue Dolphins* (New York: Houghton Mifflin, 1960).
Joseph Krumgold, *Onion John* (New York: Crowell, 1959).
Lois Lenski, *Strawberry Girl* (New York: Crowell, 1945).
Alice I. Hazeltine, *Hero Tales from Many Lands* (Nashville: Abingdon, 1961).

Julie is explaining about her life at school with her teacher-aunt Cordelia, with whom she also lived. Julie makes clear that Aunt Cordelia was *only* the teacher at school and pretended to know her no better than the other children.

. . .She read aloud to us on Friday afternoons, and she read beautifully; I came very close to loving Aunt Cordelia during those long afternoons when I rested my arms upon the desk in front of me and became acquainted with Jim Hawkins and Huck Finn, with little David and Goliath, with Robinson Crusoe on his island, and with the foolish gods and their kinfolk somewhere above the clouds on Mount Olympus.[15]

The Wind in the Willows is one of the children's classics that should be read aloud too, and enjoyed with children. Mole, Water Rat, Badger, and Toad are *gentlemen* of the woods and river. Children do enjoy the subtle humor in the behavior of the characters. Peter Green wrote:

The book for me is notable for its intimate sympathy with Nature and for its delicate expression of emotions. When all is said, the boastful, unstable Toad, the hospitable Water Rat, the shy, wise, childlike Badger, and the Mole with his pleasant habit of brave boyish impulse, are neither animals nor men, but are types of that deeper humanity which sways us all. . . . And if I may venture to describe as an allegory a work which critics, who ought to have known better, have dismissed as a fairy-story, it is certain that *The Wind in the Willows* is a wise book.[16]

Fisher evaluated the book for children in this way:

The Wind in the Willows is a wise book; it is a complicated book; yet it has given more pleasure to children than almost any other. Firm and strong it certainly is in its implications. Grahame's story will not push philosophy or satire at a child. It will arouse in him, at different times, pity and anger, enjoyment and laughter; it will satisfy the desire for these things as it satisfied Grahame when he wrote it; and it will leave the animal world where it was, untouched by human sentiment or speculation. The animals return to the river and the wood unchanged; but the reader, young or old, can never again feel blank or indifferent towards them.[17]

Newbery Medal Books

Since 1922, a Newbery Medal Book has been selected annually by a committee of competent librarians as "the most distinguished juvenile book written by a citizen or a resident of the United States and published during the preceding year." The award is made at the annual meeting of the American Library Association.[18]

John Newbery (1713–1767) has come to be known as the father of children's literature. As a London bookseller, he worked diligently to promote the idea that children needed their own shelves of books written especially for them. He printed in all about two hundred little books selling for about six pence each.[19]

The books that have won the Newbery award are, for the most part, excellent books of classic and enduring qualities. Teachers will do well to know these books and use each opportunity to recommend the appropriate book to individuals in their classes. The list of Newbery Award Books is presented below:

1922 *The Story of Mankind*, by Hendrick Van Loon (Liveright).
1923 *The Voyages of Dr. Dolittle*, by Hugh Lofting (J. B. Lippincott).
1924 *The Dark Frigate*, by Charles B. Hawes (Little, Brown).
1925 *Tales from Silver Lands*, by Charles J. Finger (Doubleday).
1926 *Shen of the Sea*, by Arthur B. Chrisman (E. P. Dutton).
1927 *Smoky, the Cowhorse*, by Will James (Charles Scribner's Sons).
1928 *Gayneck: The Story of a Pigeon*, by Dhan Gopal Mukerji (E. P. Dutton).
1929 *The Trumpeter of Krakow*, by Eric P. Kelly (Macmillan).
1930 *Hitty: Her First Hundred Years*, by Rachel Field (Macmillan).
1931 *The Cat Who Went to Heaven*, by Elizabeth Coatsworth (Macmillan).
1932 *Waterless Mountain*, by Laura Adams Armer (David McKay).
1933 *Young Fu of the Upper Yangtze*, by Elizabeth F. Lewis (Holt, Rinehart & Winston).
1934 *The Story of the Author of Little Women: Invincible Louisa*, by Cornelia Meigs (Little, Brown).
1935 *Dobry*, by Monica Shannon (Viking Press).
1936 *Caddie Woodlawn*, by Carol Ryrie Brink (Macmillan).
1937 *Roller Skates*, by Ruth Sawyer (Viking Press).
1938 *The White Stag*, by Kate Seredy (Viking Press).
1939 *Thimble Summer*, by Elizabeth Enright (Holt, Rinehart & Winston).

1940 *Daniel Boone,* by James Daugherty (Viking Press).

1941 *Call It Courage,* by Armstrong Sperry (Macmillan).

1942 *The Matchlock Gun,* by Walter D. Edmonds (Dodd, Mead).

1943 *Adam of the Road,* by Elizabeth Janet Gray (Viking Press).

1944 *Johnny Tremain,* by Esther Forbes (Houghton Mifflin).

1945 *Rabbit Hill,* by Robert Lawson (Viking Press).

1946 *Strawberry Girl,* by Lois Lenski (J. B. Lippincott).

1947 *Miss Hickory,* by Carolyn Sherwin Bailey (Viking Press).

1948 *Twenty-one Balloons,* by William Pene DuBois (Viking Press).

1949 *King of the Wind,* by Marguerite Henry (Rand McNally).

1950 *Door in the Wall,* by Marguerite de Angeli (Doubleday).

1951 *Amos Fortune, Free Man,* by Elizabeth Yates (Aladdin).

1952 *Ginger Pye,* by Eleanor Estes (Harcourt, Brace & World).

1953 *Secret of the Andes,* by Ann Nolan Clark (Viking Press).

1954 *And Now Miguel,* by Joseph Krumgold (Thomas Y. Crowell).

1955 *The Wheel on the School,* by Meindert de Jong (Harper & Row).

1956 *Carry On, Mr. Bowditch,* by Jean Lee Latham (Houghton Mifflin).

1957 *Miracles on Maple Hill,* by Virginia Sorenson, illustrated by Beth and Joe Kruch. (Harcourt Brace & World).

1958 *Rifles for Watie,* by Harold Keith (Thomas Y. Crowell).

1959 *The Witch of Blackbird Pond,* by Elizabeth George Speare (Houghton Mifflin).

1960 *Onion John,* by Joseph Krumgold (Thomas Y. Crowell).

1961 *Island of the Blue Dolphins,* by Scott O'Dell (Houghton Mifflin).

1962 *The Bronze Bow,* by Elizabeth George Speare (Houghton Mifflin).

1963 *A Wrinkle in Time,* by Madeleine L'Engle (Farrar, Strauss).

1964 *It's Like This Cat,* by Emily Neville (Harper & Row).

1965 *Shadow of a Bull,* by Maia Wojciechowska (Atheneum).

1966 *I, Juan de Pareja,* by Elizabeth B. deTrevino (Farrar, Strauss, & Giroux).

1967 *Up a Road Slowly,* by Irene Hunt (Follett).

1968 *From the Mixed-up Files of Mrs. Basil E. Frankweiler,* by E. L. Koenigsburg (Atheneum).

1969 *The High King,* by Lloyd Alexander (Holt, Rinehart & Winston; also, Dell paperback).

1970 *Sounder,* by William H. Armstrong (Harper & Row).

1971 *Summer of the Swans,* by Betsy Byars (Viking Press).

1972 *Mrs. Frisby and the Rats of NIMH,* by Robert C. O'Brien (Atheneum).

1973 *Julie of the Wolves,* by Jean C. George (Harper & Row).

1974 *The Slave Dancer,* by Paula Fox (Bradbury Press).

1975 *M. C. Higgins, The Great,* by Virginia Hamilton (Macmillan).

1976 *The Grey King,* by Susan Cooper (Atheneum).

1977 *Roll of Thunder: Hear My Cry,* by Mildred Taylor (Dial).

1978 *Bridge to Terabithia,* by Katherine Paterson (Crowell).

Bibliotherapy and Personal Values

When a person who has a problem follows a planned course of reading about characters in stories who have analogous problems in order to gain insights for better self-understanding, the process is termed bibliotherapy. The term literally means therapy through books.

Russell and Shrodes have described bibliotherapy in this way:

[Bibliotherapy is] . . . a process of dynamic interaction between the personality of the reader and literature . . . interaction which may be utilized for personal assessment, adjustment and growth. This definition suggests that bibliotherapy is not a strange esoteric activity but one that lies within the province of every teacher of literature in working with every child in a group. It does not assume that the teacher must be a skilled therapist, nor the child a seriously maladjusted individual needing clinical treatment. Rather, it conveys the idea that all teachers must be aware of the effects of reading upon children and must realize that, through literature, most children can be helped to solve the developmental problems or adjustment which they face.[20]

Personal values can be cultivated through reading since children strongly identify with story characters they like and strongly reject those they dislike. Empathy, understanding life experiences of others very different from ourselves, and acceptance of other people's values, attitudes, and beliefs are all character traits desired in the whole generation of elementary school children. Reading can help them develop these traits, especially with respect to handicapped people of all kinds—physically handicapped, economically handicapped by poverty, socially handicapped by loneliness. Such reading may help the nonhandicapped *more* than it does the handicapped.

Nancy Larrick expresses clearly and concisely how teachers help children grapple with the "personal touch" in their affective lives:

Personal problems are not solved by applying a lotion advertised over television. And a lifetime set of values is not established in a day. Countless factors exert influence. Probably the most effective are the personal ones.

The way a word is spoken may decide the way it is heeded. And the way a book is introduced may make or break its influence on a child. This is particularly true of the books which might have special meaning for a child with problems. Certainly it will not help to say, "Here's a book about a boy who is shy, too." That simply hits where it hurts, and wounds are not healed that way.

But if you read *Crow Boy* in class and show your children those extraordinary pictures, the shy one will hear. The others, not so shy, may realize that their own Chibi yearns for friendship. No word need be said about a lesson in the story unless the children bring it up. If they do, let their discussion flow naturally. As they talk, they may be forming conclusions important to them.[21]

Malkiewicz used Jerold Beim's *Mister Boss* and *Shoeshine Boy* (both Morrow, 1954), Pearl Buck's *The Big Wave* (Day, 1948), and Byrd Baylor Schweitzer's *Amigo* (Macmillan, 1963) with fifth graders. The books helped them identify and discuss social and emotional issues raised in the stories and learn that sometimes problems which seem to be unique are, instead, universal.[22]

A few books that many teachers use to develop affective values in all children are listed below with annotations.

The Hundred Dresses, by Eleanor Estes (Harcourt, Brace & World, 1944). Wanda, a little Polish girl who always wears the same faded blue dress, is ridiculed by the other children.

Blue Willow, by Doris Gates (Viking Press, 1948). With her father and stepmother, Janey moves from one crop to another, always hoping there will be work and shelter. The blue willow plate which she carries as her one treasure is all she has to remind her of better days.

Johnny Tremain, by Esther Forbes (Houghton Mifflin, 1943). The moving story of an
apprentice silversmith of Paul Revere's day, whose maimed hand causes deep bitterness.
Excellent details about the Colonists' fight for independence. Newbery Medal winner in
1944.

Crow Boy, by Taro Yashima (Viking Press, 1955). Picture story of a shy Japanese boy who
withdraws to a world of daydreams until his teacher makes him feel at home.
Distinctive drawings.

Door in the Wall, by Marguerite DeAngeli (Doubleday, 1949). A crippled boy in Old England
wins the right to knighthood.

Two Is a Team, by Lorraine and Jerrold Beim (Harcourt, Brace, & World, 1945). A little
Negro boy and a white boy learn that each can help the other and that they can have
more fun together.

Old Rosie, The Horse Nobody Understood, by Lilian Moore and Leone Adelson (Random
House, 1952). Farmer Dilly thought he was doing Rosie a favor when he stopped
working her and turned her out to sleep, eat, and rest. Rosie became very lonesome and
really missed doing all the things she'd been used to. She made a great nuisance of
herself until the day she happened in at just the right time to frighten away burglars.

Kintu, by Elizabeth Enright Gilham (Holt, Rinehart & Winston, 1935). Kintu, who lives in
the African Congo, overcomes his fear by making himself venture into the jungle,
finding that he knew what to do to keep himself safe.

Yonie Wondernose, by Marguerite DeAngeli (Doubleday, 1944). The story of a Pennsylvania
Dutch boy whose curiosity was never satisfied.

| Personal Ownership of Books | The child who grows up in a reading environment, seeing adults read, is apt to develop an early interest in reading. The importance that parents attach to books will be learned very early by children. |

Personal Ownership of Books

The child who grows up in a reading environment, seeing adults read, is apt to develop an early interest in reading. The importance that parents attach to books will be learned very early by children.

Children imitate the adults around them whom they love and respect. If mother or father often has something interesting, funny, or unusual to read aloud to the rest of the family, it is likely that sooner or later the child will appear with something to share too. Becoming confident in one's ability to read makes it possible for children to use reading as a pleasant way of filling periods of free time.

Some of the books children read will be more appealing, seem more worthwhile, than others. The home has an important responsibility in encouraging not only reading as a permanent habit, but reading books of lasting value. Ideally, the home library will contain a set of encyclopedias and a few other reference books which the child may use in pursuing his school assignments and personal interests. Parents who help children begin to accumulate good books as personal possessions are wise. Many youngsters have proudly collected the "Little House" books[23] and read and reread them throughout their childhood years. Inexpensive paperback books make it possible for children to build their own libraries at no greater cost than can be a part of their regular weekly allowance. Scholastic Book Service has made many excellent book choices available to boys and girls—Tab Books for the junior high school level and Arrow Books for the elementary school level. Group orders in classrooms encourage children to obtain books which they would probably not get otherwise. Preparation of the group order is a good school exercise, and the boys and girls enjoy the anticipation of receiving the order. Reading the books in order to evaluate them for the group and recommend them to others is a motivating experience.

The child who has a shelf of books of his own is more apt to have and use a public library card. Caring for one's own books makes one more apt to exercise proper care of borrowed books.

Summary

This chapter has emphasized all the facets of the child's experience that would build permanent interest in reading by the time the child leaves elementary school. Aside from parents, the key person will be the classroom teacher for most children. The teacher must be sufficiently acquainted with children's literature to be able to recommend "the right book for the right child." This ability requires more than a casual, "Why don't you read this one; it looks interesting." The teacher should be able to tell the child why the book is interesting by describing a few episodes or giving a brief synopsis of the whole story.

In order to build broad, permanent reading interests, the school must have a well stocked central library staffed by a competent librarian; standard references for teachers to use in seeking out the particular materials that fit their courses of study; adequate reading materials so that teachers can draw shelves of books related to social studies units being taught.

Teachers and parents who read well to children will encourage them to be curious about the great wide wonderful world of books.

Suggested Activities

1. Using the general references listed in the chapter as sources of books for children, find books related to a social studies unit which you expect to teach in the elementary school. Make a bibliography of fifty books or stories related to this unit topic. Make sure you have selected reading material that covers a wide range of levels of difficulty. For example, if you teach fourth grade, you need materials that range from easy second grade to sixth or seventh grade level. Write brief annotations of the books that will help you to distinguish their value at a later time. If the book was rated by a committee of readers and especially recommended, note that also, for your later use. A useful bibliography identifies books by author, exact title, publisher, and copyright date.

2. Make a list of topics about library books to be used for bulletin board displays; for example, "Animals," "Space Travel," or "Pioneer Days." Plan a variety of media in the displays—make use of book jackets, children's summaries of different books, felt cutouts, yarn, and/or any other materials often found in collages.

3. Have children plan a bulletin board or set up a table display illustrating a scene or depicting the characters from a particular book.

For Further Reading

Arbuthnot, May Hill. *The Arbuthnot Anthology of Children's Literature,* 4th ed. revised by Zena Sutherland. Glenview, Ill.: Scott, Foresman, 1976.
————. *Children and Books.* 4th ed. Glenview, Ill.: Scott, Foresman, 1971.
Arnsdorf, Val. "Selecting and Using Collateral Materials in Social Studies." *The Reading Teacher* 20 (April 1967):621–25.
Catterson, Jane, ed. *Children and Literature.* Newark, Del.: International Reading Assn., 1970.
Cianciolo, Patricia Jean. "A Recommended Reading Diet for Children and Youth of Different Cultures." *Elementary English* 48(Nov. 1971):779–87.
Dallmann, Martha, et al. *The Teaching of Reading.* 5th ed. chapter 11A, "Children's Interest in Reading"; Chapter 11B, "Promoting Children's Interests in and Through Reading," pp. 352–96. New York: Holt, Rinehart & Winston, 1978.
Dietrich, Dorothy, and Virginia Matthews, eds. *Development of Lifetime Reading Habits.* Newark, Del.: International Reading Assn., 1968.
Edwards, B. S. "Therapeutic Value of Reading." *Elementary English* 49 (February 1972):213–18.
Harris, Albert J., and E. R. Sipay. *How to Increase Reading Ability.* Chapter 18, "Fostering Reading Interests and Tastes," pp. 511–43. New York: David McKay, 1975.
Hoaglund, J. "Aiding Children in Personality Development." *Elementary English* 49 (March 1972):390–94.

Huus, Helen. "The Effects of Reading on Children and Youth." In *Reading for All,* edited by Robert Karlin, pp. 132–41. Newark: International Reading Assn., 1973.

————., ed. *Evaluating Books for Children and Young People.* Perspectives No. 10. Newark, Del.: International Reading Assn., 1968.

Larrick, Nancy. *Parents' Guide to Children's Reading,* 4th ed. New York: Doubleday, 1975.

Malkiewicz, J. E. "Stories Can Be Springboards." *Instructor* 79(April 1970):133–34.

Newton, E. S. "Bibliotherapy in the Development of the Minority Group Self-Concept." *Journal of Negro Education* 38(Summer 1969):257–65.

Painter, Helen W., ed. *Reaching Children and Young People Through Literature.* Newark, Del.: International Reading Assn., 1971.

Russell, David, and Caroline Shrodes. "Contributions of Research in Bibliotherapy to the Language Arts Program." *School Review* 58(September 1950):335–42.

Sebesta, Sam Leaton, ed. *Ivory, Apes, and Peacocks: The Literature Point of View.* Newark, Del.: International Reading Assn., 1968.

Smith, Dora V. *Communication, The Miracle of Shared Living.* New York: Macmillan, 1955.

————. *Fifty Years of Children's Books.* Champaign, Ill.: National Council of Teachers of English, 1963.

Smith, Nila B. *Reading Instruction for Today's Children.* Part 3, "Developing Interest and Taste in Reading Literature," pp. 385–442. Englewood Cliffs, N.J.: Prentice-Hall, Inc., 1963.

Stauffer, Russell G. *Directing Reading Maturity as a Cognitive Process.* Chapter 8, "Libraries and Reading Instruction," pp. 355–403. New York: Harper & Row, 1969.

Tinker, Miles A., and Constance McCullough. *Teaching Elementary Reading.* Chapter 15, "Interests and Tastes," pp. 309–26. Englewood Cliffs: Prentice-Hall, 1975.

Whitehead, Robert. *Children's Literature: Strategies of Teaching.* Englewood Cliffs, N.J.: Prentice-Hall, Inc., 1968.

Notes

1. G. O. Simpson, "My Reading Design" (Defiance, Ohio: The Hubbard Co., P.O. Drawer 100, 43512, 1962).
2. Hazel Adams, "The Changing Role of the Elementary School Library," *The Reading Teacher* 18 (April 1965):563
3. May Hill Arbuthnot, *Children and Books,* 3d ed. (Chicago: Scott, Foresman, 1964), p. 654.
4. Margaret Greer, "The Efficiency of the Use of Analogy in Teaching Selected Concepts at the Sixth Grade Level," pp. 44–50, Masters thesis, University of New Mexico, Albuquerque, 1966.
5. These suggestions for teaching a unit on *the Westward Movement* have been used by Dr. Jean Legant in her methodology course "Social Studies in the Elementary School."
6. Frances Cavanah, *Abe Lincoln Gets His Chance* (Chicago: Rand McNally, 1959), p. 78.
7. Harper & Row, 1953.
8. Jade Snow Wong, *Fifth Chinese Daughter* (New York: Scholastic Book Services, 1963), pp. 163–65.

9. Louise A. Stinetorf, *Children of North Africa* (Philadelphia: J. B. Lippincott Company, 1943), pp. 53–55.

10. Evelyn Lampman, *Navaho Sister* (New York: Doubleday and Co., Inc. 1956), p. 93.

11. Natachee Scott Momaday, *Owl in the Cedar Tree* (Flagstaff, Ariz.: Northland Press, 1975), pp. 82–84.

12. Mabel I. Snedaker, "The Social Studies Curriculum in the Elementary School," *Report of the 36th Annual Conference on Administration and Supervision* (State University of Iowa: Epsilon Chapter of Phi Delta Kappa, College of Education, 1952), p. 6.

13. Paul McKee and William K. Durr, *Reading: A Program of Instruction for Elementary School* (Boston: Houghton Mifflin, 1966), pp. 91–98.

14. Mildred Hillyer, "A Report of a Supervised Recreational Reading Program," unpublished masters thesis, Graduate School, The University of New Mexico, 1968, p. 39.

15. Irene Hunt, *Up a Road Slowly* (Chicago: Follett, 1966), p. 20.

16. Peter Green, *Kenneth Grahame* (Cleveland, O.: World Publ. Co., 1959, p. 259).

17. Margery Fisher, *Intent upon Reading, A Critical Appraisal of Modern Fiction for Children* (New York: Franklin Watts, 1962), p. 64.

18. Lillian Hollowell, ed., *A Book of Children's Literature* (New York: Rinehart, 1959), p. 649.

19. Ibid., p. 8.

20. David Russell and Caroline Shrodes, "Contributions of Research in Bibliotherapy to the Language Arts Program, I," *The School Review* 58(September 1950):335.

21. Nancy Larrick, *A Teacher's Guide to Children's Books* (Columbus, Ohio: Charles E. Merrill, 1969), p. 104.

22. J. E. Malkiewicz, "Stories Can Be Springboards," *Instructor* 79 (April 1970):133–34.

23. Laura Ingalls Wilder, *Little House in the Big Woods; On the Banks of Plum Creek; Little House on the Prairie; The Long Winter* (New York: Harper & Row, 1951, 1953, 1953, 1953).

15

Teaching Reading in the Content Fields

Susan is now in the sixth grade and is having some difficulty with the study assignments in science class. Susan has always perceived herself as a "good" student who follows the teacher's precise directions and works diligently to complete her written assignments. She has never had any difficulty with reading *in reading class*. But this year the science units have been demanding of considerable vocabulary, and they presupposed some previous knowledge of concepts and generalizations. Susan can remember that she memorized quite a few things last year before unit tests in science, but the teacher hadn't sounded so "scientific" as this year.

Susan's new unit is about rockets and space travel. Tomorrow she needs to know how to explain things like: "For every action, there is an opposite and equal reaction," and words like "gravity," "centrifugal force," "inertia," and "escape velocity."[1] The words have definitions in the glossary of her textbook, and she knows she could memorize them, but the teacher wants everyone to give examples and ask questions.

Susan is not the only child having such problems in the sixth grade world. But because she is conscientious and habitually tries to please the adults in her world, she may *feel* very much alone. Actually she is studying very abstract subject matter. The teacher may need to provide much more time for some of the students to assimilate elementary concepts than is necessary for the "real scientists" in the class. Also, the teacher should have quite different expectations for different students at the end of the unit.

Susan needs to be reassured that she *can* read many of the things she needs to read. She needs her confidence restored so she can approach science work positively. And she needs to get a "picture" of what is expected of her in the science class.

The teacher may build background—through reading to the class, asking those who have had more experience with Newton's Laws to do experiments for the others, or presenting an educational motion picture that shows how a rocket works. New vocabulary presented first orally in meaningful context, then in written context will help some of the class to assimilate it.

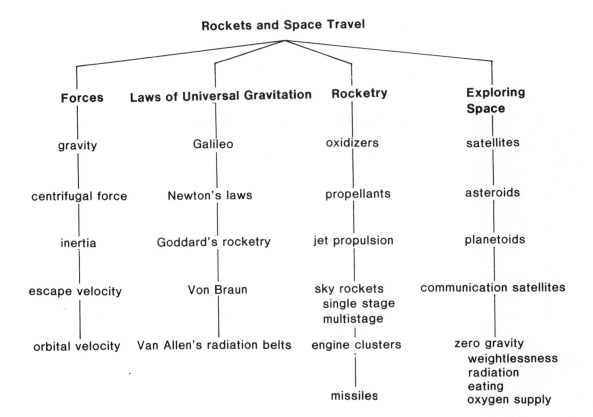

Rockets and Space Travel

Forces	Laws of Universal Gravitation	Rocketry	Exploring Space
gravity	Galileo	oxidizers	satellites
centrifugal force	Newton's laws	propellants	asteroids
inertia	Goddard's rocketry	jet propulsion	planetoids
escape velocity	Von Braun	sky rockets single stage multistage	communication satellites
orbital velocity	Van Allen's radiation belts	engine clusters	zero gravity weightlessness radiation eating oxygen supply
		missiles	

Figure 15.1 A structured overview of concept relationships in rocketry and space travel.

Based on John G. Navarra and Joseph Zafforoni, *The Young Scientist: His Predictions and Tests* (New York: Harper & Row, 1971), chap. 11.

It may help if the teacher were to present an overview in diagrammatic form for the whole unit and then keep the overview handy for reference as the unit progresses. Such an overview might be structured like the one in figure 15.1.

Then perhaps Susan could begin by reviewing what she was previously taught about gravity. Or she could read elementary biographies of scientists who were interested in conquering space. Or she could participate in some experiments to demonstrate how jet propulsion works.

Reading is a very elaborate procedure, involving a weighing of each of many elements in a sentence, their organization in the proper relations one to another, the selection of certain of their connotations and the rejection of others, and the cooperation of many forces to determine final response. In fact we shall find that the act of answering simple questions about a simple paragraph . . . includes all the features characteristic of typical reasoning.[2]

Teachers must not consider the reading of a textbook or related assignment as a passive, undiscriminating task. Reading a textbook assignment requires the exercise of critical skills, judgment, and organization and association of ideas. It is no small task for the student to really learn what the book is saying. The teacher's primary problem is to be inventive or stimulating enough to cause students to become sufficiently *interested* and *motivated* that they will want to make the necessary effort.

Reading skills include: (1) word recognition, context clues, word structure, and dictionary techniques; (2) understanding meanings, which involves literal comprehension, interpretation, critical judgment, and knowing specific word meanings; and (3) flexibility of rate so that it can be accommodated to the reason for reading the material and the nature of the subject matter.

Study skills include: selecting and evaluating; organizing; recalling; locating information; and following directions in order to make use of information gained.

Teachers must be aware of which students can already apply all of these reading and study skills; which students are in need of additional instruction; and which students do not have any of these skills. Illustrative lessons for developing these skills are presented in earlier chapters of this text.

Comprehension Skills for Reading

Reading in the content fields requires the use of all of the comprehension skills that have already been presented and illustrated in the chapters on comprehension and study skills. Literal, interpretive, and applied comprehension levels have already been presented. All these levels have a part to play in critical reading of content. The study skills, including many subskills, of locating information, organizing information, and interpreting graphs, maps, and charts are discussed in chapter 11. Application of these study skills is basic to meaningful study in the content fields.

Also, the expansion of vocabulary, the ability to identify purposes, and concept building that have been discussed previously, will be used daily by teachers and students as they study the content subjects.

This chapter will include the following sections:

1. Attention to specialized and technical vocabulary.
2. The structured overview as a technique for understanding unit organization and interrelationships of concepts.
3. How to study an assignment.
4. Study strategies in content subjects.
5. Awareness of bias, prejudice, discrimination.
6. Summary.
7. Suggestions for further reading.

The Specialized Vocabulary

Each student has several different vocabularies: his oral vocabulary which he uses in conversation; his listening vocabulary which enables him to understand what others say; his reading vocabulary which he, generally speaking, *begins* when he learns how to read at school; and his writing vocabulary which enables him to communicate on paper with others and to record his own thoughts. Generally for young children the listening vocabulary is the largest and, if the youngster has lived with adults who use a diversified vocabulary, he may enter school with a very large listening vocabulary. The reading vocabulary for the successful reader will, by fifth or sixth grade, begin to equal and surpass the listening and speaking (oral) vocabularies.

The student's reading vocabulary must assimilate many types of words. Structure words, or transition words, predetermine the facility of the reader to assimilate the ideas expressed in writing. Such structure words include: *however; in the first place; finally; moreover; nevertheless; therefore; as well as; because; when; but; as . . . as; if . . . then; not only . . . but also.*

Each subject has its own specialized vocabulary. Attention must be directed to the science vocabulary, the mathematics vocabulary, or the history vocabulary.

In addition, there are some problems to be dealt with in the multiple meanings conveyed by many commonly used words in children's vocabularies. These are the *common* words that have very different meanings when used in different subject matters. For example, children soon learn from both home and school that they must pick up the *litter* they normally leave about. They evolve a meaning for *litter* that says: "Litter is the disorder created when little things are left lying around or in a state of disorder." However, children will soon add another meaning when they learn that Sally's dog has a new *litter.* A third meaning of *litter* may be "straw or hay used as bedding for animals." Then, eventually, the student will add the additional meaning "a stretcher used for carrying a sick person."

Such concepts need to be developed through guided instruction just as understandings for *centigrade* or *Celsius, theocracy,* or *kinetic energy* need to be developed.

A comb is an instrument for arranging the hair or for holding the hair in place. But it can also mean "to search through" as in, "We *combed* the whole library to find the lost book." Or it can be the red, fleshy piece on a rooster's head, or the cellular structure in which bees store honey.

Young children understand: "I got it right"; "I'm all right, mother"; "He did the right thing." Then meanings expand to: "He has his rights"; "I have the right to vote"; "She always does the right thing"; "Tommy looked all right; I didn't know he'd been sick"; "It's on your right side"; "Is this the right side of the cloth?"; "He writes with his right hand"; "Turn right"; "They set it upright"; "Your book is right where you left it"; "Look me right in the eye!"

The word *foot* has several common meanings:

He has frozen his left *foot.* (a part of the body)
The army moved on *foot.* (a means of travel)
The *foot* of the hill. The *foot* of the page. (the base or bottom of something)
Who will *foot* the bill? (to have to pay)
Twelve inches make a *foot.* (a measure of length)
The lines of poetry were each four *feet.* (a unit of poetry)

In addition, *foot* combines with other words to determine meanings of new words: *foot*ball, *foot*board, *foot*hill, *foot*hold, *foot*ing, *foot*man, *foot*note, *foot*pad, *foot*path, *foot*print, *foot*rest, *foot* soldier, *foot*step, *foot*stool, *foot*work.

Technical Vocabulary

Technical vocabulary needs to be presented in context and practiced to allow students to gain familiarity with it. Perhaps it might be well to have a quiz or play a game using some of the new terminology even before it appears in silent reading.

Pictures from science texts may offer suggestions for projects youngsters might work on in groups of three or four to prepare, demonstrate, and explain such things as the following:

A child's balloon and a piece of aluminum foil can show how jet propulsion works. How?

Centrifugal force can be demonstrated with a ball and a string. How?

In science, Greek and Latin combining forms include:

bio (life) and *logy* (study of)	biology
geo (earth) and *graph* (write)	geography
pan (all-everything) and *chrom* (colors)	panchromatic
micro (small) and *meter* (measure)	micrometer
tele (far) and *phon* (sound)	telephonic

In mathematics:

octo (eight) and *gon* (angle)	octagon
dia (through) and *gon* (angle)	diagonal
peri (around) and *meter* (measure)	perimeter
quadri (four) and *lateral* (side)	quadrilateral
bi (two) and *sect* (separate)	bisect

In social studies:

demo (people) and *crat* (government)	democratic
mono (one) and *theist* (belief in God)	monotheism
epi (over) and *dem* (people)	epidemic
sub (under) and *terra* (earth)	subterranean
trans (across) and *globe* (world)	transglobal

In general use:

bio (life) and *graph* (write)	biography
gen (beginnings) and *logy* (study of)	genealogy
crypt (secret) and *ic* (being)	cryptic
em (put into) and *path* (state [disease]) and *ic* (being)	empathic
psych (mind) and *social* (relating to)	psychosocial

Teachers will find Burmeister's article "Vocabulary Development in Content Areas Through the Use of Morphemes" useful.[3] Figure 15.2 illustrates her use of a morpheme tree or mobile for teaching specialized vocabulary.

Figure 15.2 A morpheme tree bulletin board display or mobile would be a useful addition to a classroom. The trunk of the tree would be labeled with two or more morphemes in a subject being taught. Students can be asked to contribute words based on the morphemes as labels for the tree's branches or as leaves or ornaments for the tree.

Adapted from Lou E. Burmeister, *Journal of Reading* 19 (March 1976): 481–87.

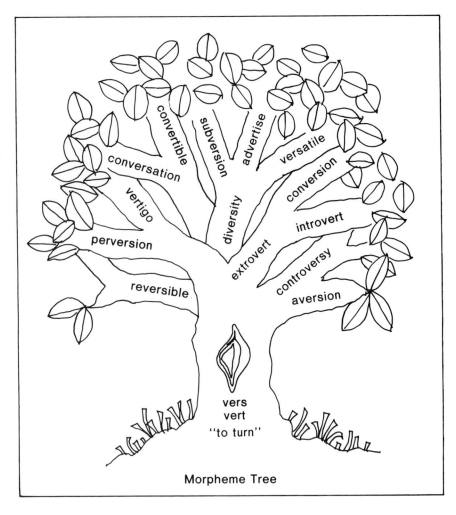

Morpheme Tree

In an article in *The Journal of Reading* Vacca suggested an interesting way to use the magic square to reinforce specialized vocabulary.[4] Students should enjoy doing such exercises in small groups.

The following sources offer word lists related to specific subjects:

Willmon, Betty. "Reading in the Content Area: A 'New Math' Terminology List for the Pr. Grades." *Elementary English* 48 (May 1971):463–471. Reprinted in Earle, Richard A., *Teaching Reading and Mathematics,* Appendix B. Newark, Del.: International Reading Assn., 1976. Contains 473 words appearing most frequently in primary mathematics texts, compiled from eight basal arithmetic series, grades 1–3.

Thelen, Judith. *Improving Reading in Science.* Newark, Del.: International Reading Assn., 1975.

Aukerman, Robert C. *Reading in the Secondary Schools.* New York: McGraw-Hill, 1972.

Burmeister, Lou E. In *Reading Strategies for Secondary School Teachers,* pp. 298–308. Reading, Mass.: Addison-Wesley, 1974.

| The Structured Overview | A structured overview, developed with the students when possible, is an excellent readiness experience for students before they read a lesson. It is a diagram that attempts to give students a *visual* approach to the structure of a unit. It presents key vocabulary to be taught and suggests ways technical terms may be related to each other. Preparing a brief overview also helps the teacher define the purposes in conducting the lesson.[5] |

Such an overview should help students understand the objectives of a particular lesson. It can also provide the stimulus for discussion of relationships between terms. And it can help students see the interrelationships among separate parts of reading assignments. While any overview may appear to be oversimplified, its usefulness in the classroom depends upon its being used as a stimulus for the teacher and students to *question* sufficiently to clarify concepts and add supporting details to the outline. The teacher needs to be a good questioner, to be able to elicit information from the group, and to be able to supply explanations.[6]

Two structured overviews are presented here. Figure 15.3 is designed to help eleven-year-olds understand an abstract term such as *democracy* as it is exemplified by the government of the United States of America.

Figure 15.4 presents a structured overview that could be the basis for a discussion prior to reading about the problem of hunger throughout the world.

How to Study a Lesson

Students need guidance in their preparation for study, they need suggestions from teachers in ways to read more efficiently, and they need to be taught new techniques that work in different subject areas.

Readiness usually incorporates establishing purposes, building some background for understanding, and teaching unfamiliar vocabulary.

Most students will profit from being given an oral summary of key points contained in text material before they begin reading. Especially if the text contains two or three major issues to be evaluated, students will grasp them more quickly if the teacher presents them briefly beforehand and permits a few minutes of discussion. Background information presented to make reading the lesson easier for students to understand is called an *advance organizer*. Or students will profit from *directed prereading activities* such as seeing a film or filmstrip or listening to a tape or seeing a *structured overview* of the major or minor topic. Also, a few guide questions can make the purposes for reading much more specific.

The extent of previous learning that a student brings to the reading determines how well the reading will be understood. Big differences in quality of reading done by students in a given class relate to a large extent to differences in the readers' background information.

It may be necessary to develop concepts and ideas in some detail to insure that the lesson is understood. Enlarging the context of the topic is the responsibility of the teacher *before* the reading is done. Such preliminary activities as locating places on maps or a globe, comparing new places with

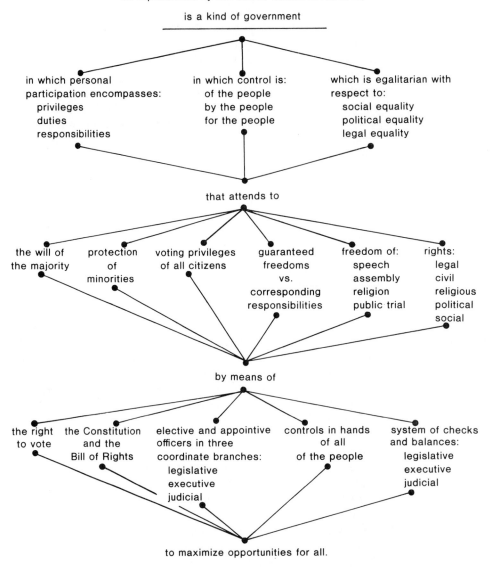

A democracy,

as represented by the United States of America,

is a kind of government

in which personal
participation encompasses:
  privileges
  duties
  responsibilities

in which control is:
  of the people
  by the people
  for the people

which is egalitarian with
respect to:
  social equality
  political equality
  legal equality

that attends to

the will of
the majority

protection
of
minorities

voting privileges
of all citizens

guaranteed
freedoms
vs.
corresponding
responsibilities

freedom of:
  speech
  assembly
  religion
  public trial

rights:
  legal
  civil
  religious
  political
  social

by means of

the right
to vote

the Constitution
and the
Bill of Rights

elective and appointive
officers in three
coordinate branches:
  legislative
  executive
  judicial

controls in hands
of all
of the people

system of checks
and balances:
  legislative
  executive
  judicial

to maximize opportunities for all.

Figure 15.3 A structured overview for the concept of democracy.

Figure 15.4 A structured overview relating to the problem of hunger throughout the world.

Adapted from the Starting Points Learning Activity Poster, "Hungry People in a Rich World." Special permission of *Learning, the Magazine for Creative Teaching,* December 1976. © 1976 by Education Today Company, Inc.

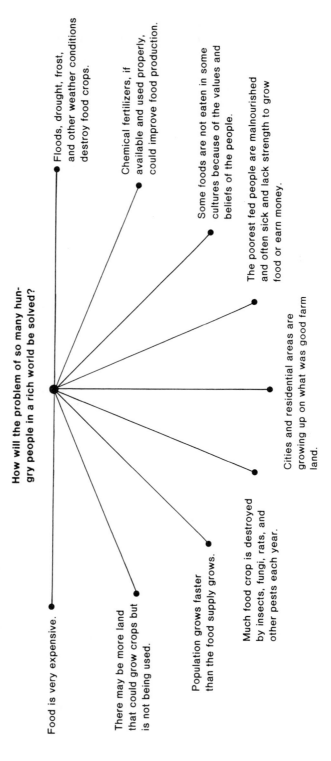

How will the problem of so many hungry people in a rich world be solved?

Floods, drought, frost, and other weather conditions destroy food crops.

Chemical fertilizers, if available and used properly, could improve food production.

Some foods are not eaten in some cultures because of the values and beliefs of the people.

The poorest fed people are malnourished and often sick and lack strength to grow food or earn money.

Cities and residential areas are growing up on what was good farm land.

Food is very expensive.

There may be more land that could grow crops but is not being used.

Population grows faster than the food supply grows.

Much food crop is destroyed by insects, fungi, rats, and other pests each year.

familiar *reference points,* seeing an educational motion picture, and studying pictures, travel posters, and illustrations in magazines may all help students.

In order to compare new places with familiar reference points, students need to understand physiographic concepts such as altitude, longitude, latitude, equator, rainy season, growing season, frost-free season, weather, and climate. Once they understand each of these terms with reference to where they are, they can then compare or contrast their own region with another region.

When one basic text has been provided for the entire class, the teacher should identify which students cannot read it with understanding and should provide other reading materials for them. This may be done by (1) finding alternative books at lower readability levels, (2) selecting additional texts with lower reading levels, (3) making different assignments for different children, and (4) rewriting textbook materials at easier reading levels. Each teacher should be continuously selecting and adding to the classroom library books which relate to any subject matter being taught. These materials should be available to all students and should span a wide range of levels of difficulty and interests. Hansell[7] makes some excellent suggestions for teachers who wish to help students improve their reading skill when reading in content areas.

Once students have been introduced to a unit of work, have been motivated to find information, and have specific objectives for reading, they should be allowed to proceed on their own. They need opportunity to work alone or in small groups, opportunity to talk informally about what they are finding, and opportunity to question or to verify facts. Then the teacher needs to provide for sharing information, interpretations, analyses, syntheses, and evaluation of concepts and generalizations presented. Reviewing and summarizing are final steps. Table 15.1 shows six steps by which a teacher can guide students through a unit of work: (1) overview; (2) development of vocabulary; (3) sample content to motivate study; (4) read, study, and share; (5) do further research; and (6) summarize and review. When children have little background for a lesson, these steps cannot be covered hurriedly.

The common reading skills which students should be using need to be consciously reinforced over and over by the teacher. These include separating main ideas and details; drawing inferences; recognizing the author's purpose; using a table of contents, index, appendices, and standard references to locate information.

Specific lessons need to be provided for *subgroups* in the class to allow practice in (1) reading to grasp the general significance of the argument; (2) selecting generalized statements and then searching for objective proof; (3) identifying problems and then finding solutions or summarizing evidence for decision-making; and (4) identifying an effect as given in the reading and then looking for causes that lead to this effect.

Teachers should also teach the *specific study skills* needed in a unit of study. Will sequencing in a chronological timetable be useful? Will compar-

Table 15.1 A plan for helping students study the content material in subject fields.

Step 1	Step 2	Step 3
An overview.	Teach the vocabulary of the unit.	Read *short passages* of specific information to find answers to questions.
What is the present unit going to be about?	Discussion should come first, followed by several kinds of matching exercises.	*Discussion* needs to be emphasized here.
Study pictures, illustrations, maps, or see an educational motion picture.	Some work on roots, prefixes, suffixes, as needed.	All students need *not* read the same text.
Listen to a recording or anecdotes read to the class by the teacher.	The class, under teacher guidance, formulates a list of questions based on the overview and vocabulary study.	Some may *listen* to tapes of the text read aloud.
		Some may read *more elementary material* that does not answer all of the questions.

Step 4	Step 5	Step 6
By now the class may be able to set up a list of questions that require *interpretation* and *application* on what is read and to use maps, charts, globes, diagrams, or tables to help *explain* the narrative.	*Individual research* or reading or study, fiction or nonfiction, in the library. Some means for keeping a record of *extensive related* reading.	*Summarizing* activity.
Discussion in which students *share* with each other is very important.		May be *generalizing* kinds of questions.
A shelf of books at *many levels of difficulty*—fiction and nonfiction—related to the subject may be available. Biography is important here.		May be *diagrammatic* or schematic *presentations*.
		May be *reports* on special books or articles read and interpreted.

ison and contrast be a primary focus? Will categorizing, enumerating, or solving problems be important?

Teachers can give suggestions and can demonstrate to boys and girls how to study a reading assignment. Following are some steps that most students should follow as they study a lesson. Teacher guidance will be necessary in order for students to establish the habits.

1. Look through all the pages of the assignment. Chapter headings, chapter subheadings, guide questions, and captions for pictures, maps, and tables should be read because they begin to circumscribe the topic under study. They will provide some information that should later fit into an organized unit plan.

2. Read the introductory paragraphs at the beginning of the chapter and at the beginning of each subsection of the assignment. Find the last paragraph in each subsection and read this summary. A good summary will present important points that have been made.

3. If there are questions at the end of the assignment, or if the teacher has given a list of questions to be answered, the student should read them carefully now, *before reading the assignment,* because they will pinpoint what the author or the teacher thinks is important.

4. If words have been identified which are not in the students' vocabulary, a dictionary or glossary definition should be consulted before reading the assignment.

5. If main ideas are explained by presentation of details, notes in outline form should be made after each subsection is read. Writing down information helps one to remember it.

6. When an assignment has been read, the student needs to take a few minutes to *reflect* on the reading, to decide whether preliminary questions posed were answered, and to think through the major points covered.

7. Notes taken during reading need to be compared with the teacher's explanation later, and if they are to be remembered, they need to be reviewed.

The "SQ4R formula" is probably the most often referred to specific study technique which the teacher can demonstrate with the class: *Survey, Question, Read, Reflect, Recite, Review.* SQ4R is an adaptation of Francis Robinson's SQ3R formula, to which the word *Reflect* has been added.[8] It has direct application to much of the studying students do.

Survey: The survey may well be a part of the readiness—that is, before reading/study begins. Chapter title and subtitles should be looked at, opening and closing paragraphs should be skimmed, bold face type noticed, and captions for illustrations read. A careful look at all the pictorial material in the chapter will prepare the reader for chapter content. In such a class period survey, the teacher can judge whether the students have prior experiences that relate to or help clarify concepts needed.

Question: What is the author telling me that I should believe? Reread the question to determine what specifically is asked.

Read: Reread looking for specific phrases and sentences that relate to or clarify the question.

Reflect: Think about the question being asked. What type of question is it? Will charts or diagrams clarify understanding? How can I make sure I remember this? What does it relate to that I already know about?

Recite: Answer the question in the text or provided by the teacher. Is the meaning clear?

Review: Without review, what we learn is gradually forgotten. What one needs to "keep" must be reviewed now and then.

Methods of Writing in Subject Matter Areas

Even though children have succeeded in reading the basal readers, they may run into serious difficulties in fourth or fifth grade when they are expected to read the content of science, social studies, and mathematics. That is sufficient reason for teaching specialized skills for those content subjects.

One of the student's problems is that the textbook is more difficult to read than the basal reader. It has greater frequency of unknown technical words and a more academic approach to topic presentation. Another problem is that more complex skills are required of students to enable them to keep their purposes in mind while they cope with the written material.

The subject matter teacher who can select what is cognitively important in the subject is the logical person to provide some appropriate reading and study strategies to insure efficient learning. Burmeister has outlined specific techniques for helping students understand some material through sequencing.[9] She has suggested, helpfully, that sequencing may be chronological, spatial, or expository and can be expressed accordingly as follows:

Sequencing
    Chronological order
        Flow chart
        Outline
        Time line
        Tree chart
    Spatial Order
        Sketch
        Map
        Floor plan
    Expository order
        Outline
        Chart
        Graphs
            Map
            Pie
            Bar
            Line
            Pictograph

Fay[10] has recommended the specific study skill SQRQCQ to increase the student's problem-solving ability. It is an adapted form of SQ4R and involves the following steps:

Survey: The material is read quickly to determine its nature.
Question: What is the problem presented in the reading?
Read: Reread for details and interrelationships.
Question: What process will I use?
Compute: Carry out the computation.
Question: Is the answer correct?

Another technique involves recognition of major patterns commonly used in content writing. *Enumeration* is a pattern that presents descriptions or attributes to help the reader understand and remember subtopics. For example, the following quotation about clouds defines three main cloud types by describing their characteristics.

Clouds

Clouds come in many different shapes, sizes, and colors and are found at different heights. By knowing what to look for, you can tell what kind of weather each kind of cloud may bring.

There are three main cloud shapes:

1. *Cirrus* means feathery. How does their name describe their shape? These clouds are found very high up . . . up to 40,000 feet high. They are made of ice crystals. Why do you think ice crystals form instead of water drops? Cirrus clouds are formed in fair weather, but often mark a change in the weather.

2. *Stratus* means layer. Why is this a good name for this type of cloud? Stratus clouds form an overcast-looking sky which often turns to rain or drizzle.

3. *Cumulus* means heap. These white, billowy clouds are seen in fair weather.[11]

Sequence is a pattern that presents the steps of a process. The following quotation, "How coal was formed," is an illustration. The reader should be able to identify the several steps.

How coal was formed

If you like to collect ancient things, you should have a lump of hard coal in your collection. Most hard coal is over two hundred million years old!

Scientists believe that coal was made long ago, in the Paleozoic era. This was a time very long ago when the climate was hot and steamy, like a tropical rain climate. There were many large swamps in many parts of the earth. Treelike plants and huge ferns grew and died and sank into the water. Others grew on top of these dead plants, died, and sank into the water, too. The dead plants were covered with water.

For many centuries the layers of dead plants piled up, thicker and thicker. In places the land sank. The swamps became lakes or seas. Through many centuries destructional forces washed sediments over the dead plants.

Pressure and the heat of the sediments changed the plant material.

What happens when plant material is heated without air? You can find out.[12]

Generalizations as a pattern may be based on supporting or clarifying information. The example quoted below, "Chemical energy in living things," first states the importance of green plants to all living things. Then the process of photosynthesis is explained. Finally the generalization is made: "Photosynthesis is the most important energy transfer in the world."

Chemical energy in living things

A fuel is a high-energy substance. You take in a fuel called food. In your body the fuel combines with oxygen. The fuel is oxidized. During the oxidation there is an output of heat energy. This is what keeps your body warm. There is also an output of mechanical energy. This is what makes your muscles move.

Of course, this is just a very bare outline of how chemical energy is used by your body. You know that your body needs food for other purposes besides releasing energy. You will find out in a later chapter about the chemical changes that prepare food and change it into body materials.

Living things get their energy by feeding on high-energy substances. The cat feeds on a mouse that ate the cheese that was made from the milk that came from the cow that ate the grass. Mouse, cheese, milk, grass—these are all high-energy foods.

No matter what food chain you follow, you come to green plants.

Green plants make food for all other living things. They make it out of substances that animals cannot use as food.

Plants take molecules of water from the soil and molecules of carbon dioxide from the air. These are low-energy substances. With the energy of sunlight, the plants separate these molecules into their atoms and then combine them into new molecules with high energy—molecules of sugar and oxygen.

This process is called **photosynthesis.** *Photo* means "light"; *synthesis* means "put together."

Photosynthesis is the most important energy transfer in the world. Can you tell why?[13]

In *cause-and-effect* the reader is typically presented with an effect, such as in the following passage.

Lincoln was a minority president—not the first and not the last. But far worse, in the eyes of Southerners, he was also a sectional President. Not a single southern or border state had voted for him. Southern leaders had long been prepared to leave the Union rather than be ruled by the North. Now they did it. Less than eight weeks after Lincoln's election, the people of South Carolina voted to secede from the Union. Georgia, Florida, Alabama, Mississippi, Louisiana, and Texas quickly followed.

In February 1861, delegates from these states met and formed their own government. They called it the Confederate States of America. Its Constitution was much like that of the United States. But it stressed the right of each state to decide most of its own laws. It also protected slavery wherever it existed. Jefferson Davis of Mississippi was elected president of the new Confederacy.[14]

These two paragraphs give several causes for an effect. The teacher could ask the student to list the causes under the effect in their order of importance, as in the following example.

Effect: Seven Southern states seceded from the Union.
Causes: 1. _____ [sectionalism; not be ruled by a Northerner]
           2. _____ [supremacy of states' rights]
           3. _____ [maintain slavery]

Some other writing patterns are *classification, comparison and contrast,* and *problem-solving.*

Awareness of Author Bias or Prejudice in Textbooks

Cultural pluralism has been accepted theoretically as the objective of American education. The melting pot theory has proved unworkable and, instead, the tremendously rich ethnic diversity in America is now being recognized. But present-day education lags behind, partly because it relies to a great extent upon the written word. Therefore, cultural pluralism must get so deeply imbedded in all the reading materials of boys and girls that its values, attitudes, beliefs, cognition, and affect are learned right from the beginning and throughout their school years.

Much of the reading material now available to students still represents only the dominant culture. It needs to be completely rewritten to delete subtle biases and judgmental descriptive words which attribute such values as right and wrong, good and bad, or civilized and uncivilized to one or another set of cultural traditions.

Evaluating textbooks for such biases is a very time-consuming task. Many of the objectionable words, phrases, and illustrations are not readily detected by all teachers. We need to make this transition and achieve a more acceptable library of reading materials as quickly as possible and with maximum fairness and good judgment.[15]

Recent analyses of social studies books used in schools indicate that the great majority are still presenting a view of the world, both historically and

currently, which is largely white, Anglo-Saxon, and Protestant. Since textbooks are, and will continue to be in the foreseeable future, the most universally used teaching tool, it is imperative that they be carefully evaluated not only for *what they contain,* but also for *what they imply subtly* and *what they omit.* A monograph by Marcus sets forth seven evaluative criteria:[16]

1. *Inclusion.* (Students need to read the truth about the Nazi persecution before and during World War II.)

2. *Validity.* (Statements need to present accurate, pertinent information.)

3. *Balance.* (Both sides of an issue should be presented fairly.)

4. *Comprehensiveness.* (Encourage diversity; eliminate stereotyping.)

5. *Concreteness.* (The material should be factual and objective.)

6. *Unity.* (Information about a topic should be unified, coherent, and concentrated in one place.)

7. *Realism.* (Social evils must be presented frankly and openly with students encouraged to think individualistically about better ways to solve them.)

A fifth grade social studies book asks the question: "Can you see one reason why North American Indians never had cities?"[17] It is not true, according to modern archaeology, that North American Indians never had cities. In the twelfth century a community of 30,000 people lived at Cahokia, Illinois (near present-day St. Louis).[18] The same book states a few pages later: "The man who discovered America was an Italian sailor, Christopher Columbus." Josephy[19] has suggested that perhaps nearly a million Indians were living in what is now the United States when Columbus came to America. Another fifteen million may have lived in Mexico and Central and South America. Didn't *they* discover America?

The subtle implications of such statements are unacceptable. It behooves teachers to become critical, discerning readers. And they must help students develop their own critical, evaluative skills so they can recognize such writing.

The Council on Interracial Books for Children has suggested some ways to analyze books for racism and sexism that may be helpful:[20]

1. Check the illustrations for stereotypes, tokenism, life styles.

2. Check the story line—relationships, measure of success, viewpoint.

3. Check the author's perspective.

4. Check the author's competency to write about this minority.

5. Check for the effect on self-image, self-esteem.

6. Check the copyright date. The minority experience is recent—late '60s and early '70s.

7. Watch for loaded words.

Similarly, Rudman raises the following pertinent questions: "How aware are we of the connotations and innuendos in the books that our children read? . . . What of the popular fantasies and novels and even works of so-called nonfiction that are rife with racist ideas? . . . How can we recognize our acts of omission?"[21]

Stereotypes

Cata analyzed children's fictional literature in which one main character was an Indian. She identified 89 verbal stereotypes used to describe North American Indian characters in 401 fictional stories for children. Eight negative stereotypes that appeared thirty or more times were: superstitious, stolid, revengeful, savage, warlike, cruel, physically dirty, and hostile.[22]

According to Klineberg, "the existence of ethnic stereotypes may play an important part in preventing the improvement of race relations on the basis of increased contact between two conflicting groups. It may result in a literal inability to see those things which do not fit into the stereotype."[23]

The following paragraph by Rogers and Muessig was characteristic of findings a decade ago:

Too many texts are filled with slanted "facts," stereotypes, provincial and ethnocentric attitudes, and superficial, utopian discussions which skim over conditions as they actually exist today. Texts which have sections devoted to life in our United States, for example, too often portray "Americans" as white, Anglo-Protestant, white-collar, and middle class. Perusing a number of books, one gets the impression that all Americans live on wide, shady streets in clean suburban areas, occupy white Cape Cod houses, drive new automobiles, have two children (a boy and a girl, of course), and own a dog. Characters in texts have first names like Bill, Tom, and John, rather than Sid, Tony and Juan and last names like Adams, Hill, and Cook, rather than Schmidt, Podosky, and Chen.[24]

McDiarmid and Pratt, in a monograph entitled *Teaching Prejudice,* ask the serious question whether *teaching children to be prejudiced* may not be exactly what we are doing.[25] They identified six categories of people: Christians, Jews, Moslems, blacks, Indians, and immigrants. They then asked students to select from a list of descriptive words the ones that most frequently applied to each group. The result was that Christians are devoted, Jews are a great people, Moslems are infidels, blacks are primitive, Indians are savage, and immigrants are hard working. In a study of pictorial stereotypes of Africans, Asians, and Indians, the Native Americans emerged as the least favored and were portrayed as primitive, unskilled, aggressive, and hostile.[26]

In 1973 the Manitoba Indian brotherhood evaluated a number of social studies textbooks used in sixth grade classes across Canada. They titled their monograph *The Shocking Truth About Indians in Textbooks*.[27] They quoted from a text that told sixth graders about the use of tobacco:

Raleigh was also responsible for making tobacco fashionable in England. Tobacco is a New World plant that was not known in Europe until after the discovery of America. Sir Walter Raleigh introduced the custom of smoking to his friends, and it was not long before elegant Englishmen were puffing away as contentedly as the naked savages of North America. [p. 21]

And from another text:

Perhaps the sailors made friends with the Indians as you would make friends with a puppy—by offering them something to eat. [p. 93]

Champlain grew fond of the Indian people as one grows fond of children, and he made plans to help them. [p. 96]

Such statements demean the dignity of Indians as people. They demonstrate one of the most objectionable attitudes: that Indians are childlike, and therefore others *must decide* what is best for them and do things *for* them.

Yet another text contained these statements:

The Pueblo Indians had even learned how to dig ditches to bring water to their fields from the nearby streams and rivers, to keep crops growing when there was no rain. It is interesting to think that this art, which is called irrigation, was already known in North America when the white man came. [p. 13]

Use of the word "even" conveys no historical information, but it certainly emphasizes a patronizing attitude toward the Indians. The whole paragraph seems to express great surprise that another group of people could possibly know about such technology before the white man arrived. Contrast the above paragraph with the following in the book by Josephy:

The Pueblo people depended primarily on intensive agriculture with corn as the principal crop. In the west, where matrilineal clans were important social units, the women owned the crops, as well as the houses and furnishings. . . .

Along the Rio Grande, in the east, Pueblos planted their crops in the river bottoms near their towns and irrigated their fields. The people also raised squash, beans, cotton, tobacco, and gourds, using wooden sticks and hoes with which to cultivate their plots. Farm work was difficult in a country with an average of only 13 inches of rain a year and the men did all the labor in the fields.[28]

It is no wonder that Mary Gloyne Byler, a member of the eastern band of Cherokees of North Carolina, after analyzing hundreds of children's books about Indians written by non-Indians, wrote the following:

There are too many books featuring painted, whooping, befeathered Indians closing in on too many forts, maliciously attacking "peaceful" settlers or simply leering menacingly from the background; too many books in which white benevolence is the only thing that saves the day for the incompetent, childlike Indian: too many stories setting forth what is "best" for the American Indian.

It is time for American publishers, schools, and libraries to take another look at the books they are offering children and seriously set out to offset some of the damage they have done. Only American Indians can tell non-Indians what it is to be Indian. There is no longer any need for non-Indian writers to "interpret" American Indians for the American Public.[29]

It is apparent that there is need for criteria by which to judge writing for American school children. The criteria might include such questions as these:

1. Is there any way the gist of what is written could deprive *anyone* of his or her human rights?
2. Does the author develop the role of American minority groups in a scholarly, factual, and effective manner?
3. Is the context a balanced treatment?
4. Is there any chance that the context can create or increase race or class hostility, national rivalries, prejudice, or religious bias?
5. Does the text adequately emphasize the pluralistic nature of our multiracial, multiethnic, and multireligious society?
6. Are all groups of people represented in varied and diverse settings?
7. When individuals are recognized, are there only white middle-class *men* or are all minority groups and women properly represented?

Summary

Reading with competence in the content fields of the curriculum necessitates the reader acquiring study skills so that assignments can be completed without undue frustration. To achieve these ends, the reader needs:

1. to understand the specialized vocabulary used in a given subject field;
2. to grasp an overview of the material presented;
3. to know how to study a lesson;
4. to recognize how specific strategies can be used in studying different kinds of material; and
5. to know how to recognize author bias or prejudice when it appears.

It is the job of the teacher to help students develop these techniques.

Suggested Activities

1. Apply Burmeister's morpheme tree model and develop a vocabulary lesson for your grade level.
2. Anticipate a unit of study you will teach. Decide the scope of content to be included. Make a structured overview that you could develop with your students.
3. Select a lesson to be taught in a subject of your choice. How will you teach the application of SQ4R?
4. Find a current professional journal article that discusses bias, prejudice, or discrimination in children's books. What are the conclusions of the author?
5. Find examples in the textbooks of writing patterns using: enumeration, sequence, generalization, and cause-and-effect.

For Further Reading

Allington, Richard L. "Improving Content Area Instruction in the Middle School." *The Journal of Reading* 18 (March 1975): 455–61.

Billig, Edith. "Children's Literature as a Springboard to Content Areas." *The Reading Teacher* 30 (May 1977): 855–59.

Bullerman, Mary, and E. J. Franco. "Teach Content Material But Teach Reading, Too." *Journal of Reading* 19 (October 1975): 21–23.

Burmeister, Lou E. *Reading Strategies for Secondary School Teachers,* 2d ed. Reading, Mass.: Addison-Wesley, 1978.

———. "Vocabulary Development in Content Areas Through the Use of Morphemes." *The Journal of Reading* 19 (March 1976): 481–87.

Burron, Arnold, and Amos L. Claybaugh. *Using Reading to Teach Subject Matter: Fundamentals for Content Teachers.* Columbus: Merrill, 1974.

Costo, Rupert, ed. *Textbooks and the American Indian.* San Francisco: Indian Historian Press, 1970.

Dallmann, Martha, et al. *The Teaching of Reading,* 5th ed. New York: Holt, Rinehart & Winston, 1978, chapter 10A, "Reading in the Content Areas," pp. 322–33.

Duffy, Gerald, ed. *Reading in the Middle School.* Newark: International Reading Assn., 1974.

Earle, Richard A. *Teaching Reading and Mathematics.* Newark: International Reading Assn., 1976, especially chapter 6, "Analyzing Relationships," which discusses the structured overview.

Fay, Leo, and Lee Ann Jared. *Reading in the Content Fields: An Annotated Bibliography.* Newark: International Reading Assn., 1975.

Forgan, Harry, and Charles Mangrum II. *Teaching Content Area Reading Skills: A Modular Preservice and Inservice Program.* Columbus: Merrill, 1976.

Gerhard, Christian. *Making Sense: Reading Comprehension Improved Through Categorizing.* Newark: IRA, 1975. Chapter 5: "Writing Topic Sentences," and Chapter 6: "Completing Paragraphs from Specific Items of Categories."

Hansell, T. Stevenson. "Increasing Understanding in Content Reading." *The Journal of Reading* 19 (January 1976): 307–11.

Herber, Harold L. *Teaching Reading in Content Areas,* 2d ed. Englewood Cliffs, N.J.: Prentice-Hall, 1978.

Karlin, Robert. *Teaching Elementary Reading: Principles and Strategies,* 2d ed. New York: Harcourt Brace Jovanovich, 1975. Chapter 7: "Reading in the Content Fields," pp. 249–315.

Kirkness, Verna J. "Prejudice about Indians in Textbooks." *The Journal of Reading* 20 (April 1977): 595–600.

Lees, Fred. "Mathematics and Reading." *The Journal of Reading* 19 (May 1976): 621–26.

Manitoba Indian Brotherhood. *The Shocking Truth about Indians in Textbooks.* Winnipeg: Manitoba Indian Brotherhood, 1974.

Marcus, Lloyd. *The Treatment of Minorities in Secondary School Textbooks.* New York: Anti-defamation League of B'nai B'rith, 1963.

McDiarmid, Garnet, and David Pratt. *Teaching Prejudice.* Toronto, Canada: Ontario Institute for Studies in Education, 1972.

Palmer, William S. "Teaching Reading in Content Areas." *The Journal of Reading* 19 (October 1975): 43–50.

Piercey, Dorothy. *Reading Activities in Content Areas.* Boston: Allyn & Bacon, 1976.

Robinson, H. Alan. *Teaching Reading and Study Strategies in the Content Areas,* 2d ed. Boston: Allyn & Bacon, 1978.

Staton, Thomas F. *How to Study,* 5th ed. P.O. Box 6133, Montgomery, Ala., 36106: How to Study, 1968.

Troy, Ann. "Literature for Content Area Learning." *The Reading Teacher* 30 (February 1977): 470–74.

Tutolo, Daniel J. "The Study Guide—Type, Purpose, Value." *The Journal of Reading* 20 (March 1977): 503–507.

Vacca, Richard T. "Readiness to Read Content Area Assignments." *The Journal of Reading* 20 (February 1977): 387–92.

————. "Reading Reinforcement through Magic Squares." *The Journal of Reading* 18 (May 1975): 587–90.

West, Gail B. *Teaching Reading Skills in Content Areas: A Practical Guide to the Construction of Student Exercises,* 2d ed. P.O. Box 19225, Orlando, Florida 32814: Sandpiper Press, 1978.

Notes

1. John G. Navarra and Joseph Zafforoni, *The Young Scientist: His Predictions and Tests* (New York: Harper & Row, 1971), Chapter 11: "Travel Beyond the Earth," pp. 338–72.

2. Edward L. Thorndike, "Reading as Reasoning: A Study of Mistakes in Paragraph Reading," *Journal of Educational Psychology* 8 (June 1917): 323.

3. Lou E. Burmeister, *Journal of Reading* 19 (March 1976): 481–87.

4. Richard T. Vacca, "Reading Reinforcement through Magic Squares," *The Journal of Reading* 18 (May 1975): 587–90.

5. Richard T. Vacca, "Readiness to Read Content Area Assignments," *The Journal of Reading* 20 (February 1977): 387–92.

6. Richard A. Earle, *Teaching Reading and Mathematics* (Newark, Del.: International Reading Assn., 1976), p. 34.

7. T. Stevenson Hansell, "Increasing Understanding in Content Reading," *Journal of Reading* 19 (January 1976): 307–11.

8. Francis P. Robinson, *Effective Study* (New York: Harper & Row), 1962, p. 31. Ellen Lamar Thomas and H. Alan Robinson, *Improving Reading in Every Class* (Boston: Allyn & Bacon, 1972), p. 70.

9. Lou E. Burmeister, *Reading Strategies for Secondary School Teachers* (Reading, Mass.: Addison-Wesley, 1974), pp. 163–179.

10. Leo Fay, "Reading Study Skills: Math and Science," in *Reading and Inquiry,* ed. J. A. Figurel (Newark: International Reading Assn., 1965), pp. 92–94.

11. Herman and Nina Schneider, *Science in Our World,* 4th ed. (Lexington, Mass.: D. C. Heath, 1973), p. 20.

12. Ibid., p. 332.

13. Ibid., p. 135.

14. *Social Sciences Concepts and Values,* Grade 5 (New York: Harcourt, Brace, Jovanovich), p. 241.

15. Paula Grinnell (chairperson, Textbook Committee, Dallas Chapter, The American Jewish Committee, Southwest Office, 1809 Tower Bldg., Dallas, Texas 75201), "A Study of Racial Bias in Social Studies Textbooks," undated.

16. Lloyd Marcus, *The Treatment of Minorities in Secondary School Textbooks* (New York: Anti-Defamation League of B'Nai B'rith, 1515 Madison Ave, 1963), p. 9.

17. Gussie M. Robinson, *Man and Society* (Morristown, N.J.: Silver Burdette, 1972), pp. 37, 48.

18. George E. Stuart, "Who Were the Moundbuilders?" *National Geographic* 142 (December 1972): 789.

19. Alvin M. Josephy, Jr., *The Indian Heritage of America* (New York: Bantam Books, 1968), pp. 50–51.

20. Council on Interracial Books for Children (1841 Broadway, New York, N.Y. 10023), "Ten Quick Ways to Analyze Books for Racism and Sexism," *The Bulletin* 5 (March 1974): 1, 6.

21. Masha K. Rudman, *Children's Literature: An Issues Approach* (Lexington, Mass.: D. C. Heath, 1976), pp. 173–74.

22. Juanita O. Cata, "The Portrait of American Indians in Children's Fictional Literature," unpublished doctoral dissertation, Graduate School, University of New Mexico, 1977, p. 67.

23. Otto Klineberg, *Social Psychology* (New York: Henry Holt, 1954), p. 489.

24. Vincent R. Rogers and Raymond H. Muessig, "Needed: A Revolution in the Textbook Industry," *The Social Studies* 54 (October 1963): 169.

25. Garnet McDiarmid and David Pratt, *Teaching Prejudice* (Toronto: Ontario Institute for Studies in Education, 1972).

26. Cited in Verna J. Kirkness, "Prejudice About Indians in Textbooks," *The Journal of Reading* 20 (April 1977): 597.

27. The Manitoba Indian Brotherhood, comp., *The Shocking Truth About Indians in Textbooks* (Winnipeg, Canada: The Manitoba Indian Brotherhood, 1974).

28. Alvin M. Josephy, Jr., *The Indian Heritage of America* (New York: Alfred A. Knopf, 1971), pp. 163–64.

29. Mary Gloyne Byler, *American Indian Authors for Young Readers, A Selected Bibliography* (432 Park Ave., New York, N.Y. 10016: Association on American Indian Affairs, 1973), pp. 5, 11.

Part 5

Provision for All the Children

Many adults have arrived at their station as classroom teachers without having acquired much understanding of the **one** language that is their only vehicle of communication. The structure of every language conforms to **definite** principles which the teacher should understand. These principles are broken down into the categories of phonology, morphology, syntax, and semantics. In second language learning, contrastive analysis of language differences can be a very useful tool when described within these categories. Contrastive analysis of phonemic differences especially is helpful.

At present, most schools are wrestling with teaching **all** children **in only the English language medium.** Good techniques in teaching English to speakers of other languages will facilitate this process. However, in the relatively near future, it is hoped that bilingual schools will have a place in the public school system. Only in this way can the school help children develop and extend their fluency in two or more languages.

Diagnostic teaching has been tragically neglected in work with children for whom English is a second language. The accepted communication skill hierarchy of listening-speaking-reading-writing has often been violated.

Chapter 3, "Linguistic Foundations for Reading Instruction," has prepared the reader for the next two chapters. Chapter 16 is concerned with teaching reading to the bilingual child and chapter 17 with teaching reading to the child who speaks nonstandard English.

Chapter 18 is devoted to children who need rehabilitative services in order to succeed in the school program. Children with learning problems are described, and the need for diagnosis is shown by examination of the many causes of reading disability.

Many of the children not functioning as well in the reading process as their capacity for learning would suggest would profit greatly from the teacher's use of corrective techniques in the classroom. Special programs must be provided for the intellectually gifted, the mentally retarded, and the few who have special learning disabilities rooted in neurological impairment or emotional disturbance. Children with learning disabilities are, more often than not, receiving no special help today. They desperately need special methodologies. When a school system makes no provision for their diagnosis and teaching in special clinics, classroom teachers must arrange special reading programs for them. Many professionals can and should help teachers better understand and work with the handicapped child.

Through continuous diagnosis and identification of children's abilities, disabilities, and possibilities, the teacher will be able to formulate measurable behavioral objectives so that tangible results will reveal whether learning is taking place or whether there is need for further study.

Bond and Tinker* estimate that seventy-five percent of the children who become remedial reading cases could be helped successfully by the classroom teacher before they reach that stage. The necessary conditions are as follows:

1. All **pressure** from the teacher for every child to complete the same work in the same amount of time with the same amount of practice be **eliminated;**

2. Each child be accepted as an **individual** and permitted to work at his or her **instructional** level of reading, moving only as fast as the child is able to learn;

3. The teacher's effort be bent toward providing many learning activities at many levels of difficulty so that each child would be challenged at his or her growing edge of learning;

4. The philosophy of the school be that other personnel are also concerned about each child's learning so that no teacher need operate alone.

*Guy L. Bond and Miles A. Tinker, *Reading Difficulties: Their Diagnosis and Correction* (New York: Appleton-Century-Crofts, 1967), p. 245.

16

Teaching Reading to the Bilingual Child

Cultural Differences and English Language Learning

At recess time one cold day in December, a teacher told her class of boys and girls that no one should leave the room until they had put on their *wraps*. Everyone got in line except five little Spanish-speaking children. She questioned why they were not in line, and they said, "But Mrs. Williams, we don't have any wraps." As soon as she said that she really meant to get their *caps* and *coats,* they *wrapped* up and got in line.

Many children who must learn English as a second language after they enroll in school develop negative attitudes and fail to achieve academically. These problems are rooted in the differences of culture, language, and experience.

In a publication entitled *Educating the Children of the Poor,*[1] it is pointed out that adequate theory requires integration of the wisdom of sociologists and psychologists so that environmental factors and personality variables will each receive proper attention. If applied anthropology is left out, a very important portion of the total appraisal of the child has been omitted.

One's cultural heritage shapes all the values, ideals, aspirations, anxieties, taboos, and mores that are represented by a person's behavior. Behavior is the internalized response one makes to the demands placed upon one by the culture.

While this cultural heritage is expressed in many ways, language is probably the most apparent and significant medium of expression. The interdependence of language and culture is discussed throughout this chapter.

Some excerpts from the literature will make clear the anthropological contribution to understanding behavior.

Salisbury describes the Alaskan Indian child's problem understanding and relating to the middle-class Anglo-oriented course of study:

By the time the native child reaches the age of seven, his cultural and language patterns have been set and his parents are required by law to send him to school. Until this time he is likely to speak only his own local dialect of Indian, Aleut, or Eskimo, or if his parents have had some formal schooling he may speak a kind of halting English.

He now enters a completely foreign setting—the western classroom situation. His teacher is likely to be a Caucasian who knows little or nothing about his cultural background. He is taught to read the Dick and Jane series. Many things confuse him: Dick and Jane are two gussuk[2] children who play together. Yet he knows that boys and girls do not play together and do not share toys. They have a dog named Spot who comes indoors and does not work. They have a father who leaves for some mysterious place called "office" each day and never brings any food home with him. He drives a machine called an automobile on a hard covered road called a street which has a policeman on each corner. These policemen always smile, wear funny clothing and spend their time helping children to cross the street. Why do these children need this help? Dick and Jane's mother spends a lot of time in the kitchen cooking a strange food called "cookies" on a stove which has no flame in it.

But the most bewildering part is yet to come. One day they drive out to the country which is a place where Dick and Jane's grandparents are kept. They do not live with the family and they are so glad to see Dick and Jane that one is certain that they have been ostracized from the rest of the family for some terrible reason. The old people live on something called a "farm," which is a place where many strange animals are kept—a peculiar beast called a "cow," some odd looking birds called "chickens" and a "horse" which looks like a deformed moose.

And so on. For the next twelve years the process goes on. The native child continues to learn this new language which is of no earthly use to him at home and which seems completely unrelated to the world of sky, birds, snow, ice, and tundra which he sees around him.[3]

Evvard and Mitchell analyzed concepts in the stories in the Scott-Foresman basic readers.[4] They contrasted the beliefs and values the books contained with traditional Navajo beliefs and values and found many that conflicted with the young Navajo child's concepts of himself, his family, and his community.

Middle-class, urban values	*Navaho values*
Pets have humanlike personalities.	Pets are distinct from human personality.
Life is pictured as child-centered.	Life is adult-centered.
Adults participate in children's activities.	Children participate in adult activities.
Germ-theory is implicitly expressed.	Good health results from harmony with nature.
Children and parents are masters of their environment.	Children accept their environment and live with it.
Children are energetic, out-going, obviously happy.	Children are passive and unexpressive.
Many toys and much clothing is an accepted value.	Children can only hope for much clothing and toys.
Life is easy, safe, and bland.	Life is hard and dangerous.

Too many teachers are inadequately prepared to understand or accept cultural values that are different from their own. They come from homes where the drive for success and achievement is internalized early, where "work for work's sake" is rewarded, and where time and energy are spent building for the future. Many children come to the classroom with a set of values and a background of experience radically different from the American middle-class standard. To teach these children successfully, teachers must be cognizant of these differences and must, above all else, seek to understand and not disparage ideas, values, and practices different from their own.

The following paragraph has for *too* long accurately expressed the viewpoint of too many Anglo-American teachers toward Mexican-American students and their parents:

They are good people. Their only handicap is the bag full of superstitions and silly notions they inherited from Mexico. When they get rid of these superstitions, they will be good Americans. The schools help more than anything else. In time, the Latins will think and act like Americans. A lot depends on whether or not we can get them to switch from Spanish to English. When they speak Spanish they think Mexican. When the day comes that they speak English at home like the rest of us, they will be part of the American way of life. I just don't understand why they are so insistent about using Spanish. They should realize that it's not the American tongue.[5]

The attitude of the teacher toward language and other cultural differences is crucially important. Unless the teacher is patient and understanding, the student who must learn English as a second language "develops insecurity instead of security, worry instead of certainty, fear instead of competence, and the teacher makes enemies instead of friends for the English language."[6]

Teachers must be continually alert to the differences in languages, values, customs—the whole cultural heritage. They must seek to understand the students they teach as people whose feelings, attitudes, and emotional responses make them behave the way they do. Most important, they must realize that one way of life is not better, not superior, and not "more right" than another.

Dora V. Smith tells a story of a little Japanese girl who was spending a year in the United States attending an elementary school:

At Christmas time her American classmates sent a package to her school in Tokyo. They decided to write a letter to accompany it. When Reiko was asked whether she wished to add a line, this is what she wrote: "The boys and girls in America sound funny when they talk. We have to read in English, too. But they laugh and cry and play in Japanese.[7]

All teachers should learn what Reiko expressed—that laughing, crying, and playing are a universal language. Time to laugh together and play together allows a kind of communication that helps to counteract the tensions that result from language differences.

Cultural Expectations of the School

Children whose cultural heritage is different from that of the value system perpetuated by the school they attend are in need of special educational services. They need help to master the cultural and language demands of the school *before* they can profit from the typical course of study with which they are apt to be confronted.

Each child coming to the school is expected to become oriented to certain values emphasized in the dominant culture. Some of these values are:[8]

1. Everyone must climb the ladder of success and must place a high value on competitive achievement.

2. Everyone must relate to time by being precise to the hour and minute and must also learn to place a high value on looking to the future.

3. The teachers' reiteration that there is a scientific explanation for all natural phenomena must be accepted.

4. Everyone must become accustomed to change and must anticipate change. (The dominant culture teaches that "change" in and of itself is good and desirable!)

5. Shy, quiet, reserved, and anonymous behavior must be traded for the aggressive, competitive behavior that is socially approved.

6. Everyone must believe that, with some independence, one can shape one's own destiny rather than follow the tradition of remaining an anonymous member of society.

Earl Kelley, in the yearbook of the Association for Supervision and Curriculum Development (ASCD), *Perceiving, Behaving, Becoming,* describes the behavior of the fully functioning self in present-day society:

We live in a moving, changing, becoming-but-never-arriving world. . . . He needs to see process, the building and becoming nature of himself. Today has no meaning in the absence of yesterdays and tomorrows. The growing self must feel that it is involved, that it is really a part of what is going on, that in some degree it is helping shape its own destiny.

The acceptance of change as a universal phenomenon brings about modifications of personality . . . one who accepts change and expects it, behaves differently. . . .

He sees the evil of the static personality because it seeks to stop the process of creation. . . . Life to him means discovery and adventure, flourishing because it is in tune with the universe.[9]

But the Indian child has probably already learned that nature provides what people need, and the objective is to remain in harmony with nature. The dances, the rituals, the seasonal prayers, and the chants are learned perfectly and passed from one generation to another in the hope of maintaining and restoring harmony.

Indians believe that time is always with us. Life is concerned with the here and now. Accepting nature in its seasons, they will get through the years one at a time.

The Indian child is early made to feel *involved* and personally responsible for doing his part so that all of life—in the village and throughout the natural order—all the cosmic forces—are kept running smoothly and harmoniously. *But,* not with the goal of changing the destiny determined for one by those who are older and wiser. The Indian child best fulfills his destiny by remaining an anonymous member of the social group, accepting group sanctions and placing primary emphasis on conformity.

The Indian child will be able to understand the values of his teacher much better if the teacher has some understanding and acceptance of the child's values. Robert Roessel, formerly director of the community school at Rough Rock, Arizona, attempted to give his staff an awareness of the peculiar texture of Navajo life. He described the following small-scale tragedy that resulted from a teacher's inexperience at a reservation school and thereby hoped to avert just such episodes in the future.

Her credentials were excellent, but she had never taught Navajo children before. She noticed one morning that the face and arms of one of the third grade boys were covered by something that looked like soot. In his hair was a substance that resembled grease. With a normal respect for cleanliness, the teacher asked the boy to wash himself. When he refused, she took him to the washroom and washed him.

The boy never returned to school. It turned out that his family had conducted an important healing ceremony on his sick sister, the "soot" and "grease" being part of the ceremonial painting. With her soap and water, the teacher destroyed the healing powers of the ceremony. The girl died and the parents could not be shaken in their belief that it was the teacher's fault. No member of the family has set foot in a school since.[10]

Developing Language Arts Skills in Bilingual Children

To be a good teacher of bilingual children requires more than a set of classroom techniques. Above all, the teacher should have tact, common sense, and sympathetic understanding of problems the children may have. It has already been stressed that the teacher should also know something of the language of the child's parents and should know something about the cultural practices and contribution of that culture. It is a good idea for the teacher to visit the child's home, not once, but many times. Such visits make it possible for the teacher to explain the basic purposes of the school and clarify erroneous concepts the child may have brought home. It is important for the teacher to feel and to show genuine appreciation for the values of the culture of the parents. Good teaching techniques will produce the best possible results when grounded on such a firm emotional base.

How shall primary teachers develop the language arts in bilingual boys and girls during the primary grades? The first task is to teach the child learning English as a second language the necessary oral language skills so that he can function more nearly the way the native speaker functions.

Finocchiaro has described the second-language teaching-learning process as follows.[11]

1. Learning a language means forming new habits through intensive practice in hearing and speaking.
2. It is deemed advisable that the teacher use and repeat a limited number of sentence patterns and give the children intensive practice in those patterns only. The teacher should learn to pronounce these patterns as perfectly as possible. He should learn when to use them and with which other combinations they are normally used. He should learn how to develop and how to judge accurate pronunciation in his pupils. Too, he should learn how to give varied, interesting practice in the limited patterns being taught. Improvisation by teacher and pupils at this level is not recommended.
3. *Habitual use of the most frequently used patterns* and items of language should take precedence over the mere accumulation of words. The acquisition of vocabulary should be a secondary goal at the beginning stage. Vocabulary will increase rapidly when reading is begun. To reiterate the same principle—because it is of utmost importance—*learning a foreign language is not primarily acquiring vocabulary,* as necessary as that is. It is much more important for the student to engage in practice which will most quickly form habits of articulation, stress, intonation, word-order, and word formation. The sooner these patterns become habit and not choice, the sooner mastery of the language will be achieved.
4. Vocabulary should be taught and practiced only in the context of real situations so that meaning will be clarified and reinforced.
5. Classroom activities should center about authentic speech situations—dialogues, interchanges (I'm six. How old are you?), descriptions, rejoinders ("Are you ready?" "Of course.")—where two or more children are involved.

6. Speech should not be slowed down nor the rhythm distorted because of the mistaken idea that it will increase understanding.
7. New patterns of language should be introduced and practiced with vocabulary that students already know. For example, if one were teaching the interrogative form, "Do you have _____?" the point of departure would be a sentence the children already know, e.g., "I have a dog at home."

Children cannot *read* a language they cannot use orally. They must be able to express themselves well in oral English before they can read it with any satisfaction. Even many concepts describing everyday activities will be meaningless if met the first time in textbooks. The teacher's effort will be totally nonproductive if reading and writing are taught before listening and speaking. The *pressure* to move children into formal reading groups before they have learned listening and speaking habits in the language is one of the gravest errors teachers continue to make with young non-English-speaking children.

The aural-oral method of learning a language is a method of instruction that emphasizes *hearing and speaking* the new language, especially in the beginning rather than learning grammatical structure, translation, reading, or writing. When this method is correctly followed, learners say only what they have heard (and understood); read what they have said; and write what they have heard, said, and read.

Cognitive Learning

Hildreth, in *The Reading Teacher,* makes some generalizations about teaching beginning reading in English and Arabic. This one generalization is pertinent in teaching all bilingual children:

Oral language readiness appears to be the most important aspect of readiness and beginning reading, both because reading is a form of language and because a pupil's linguistic maturity reflects his thought level and his experiential background. Responses in beginning lessons should be primarily oral. If the reading deals with situations that are meaningful to the children, there is nothing in daily oral practice to prevent the pupils from developing into good silent readers. Children the world around retain best the words in print that they can pronounce and commonly use in conversation.[12]

Stauffer discusses the problem of concept development:

Concept development merits a first order rating in the teaching of reading as a thinking process. This is so because concepts are cognitive structures acquired through a complex and genuine act of thought, and they cannot be absorbed ready-made through memory or drill. A concept is symbolically embodied in a sign, usually a word, and, as such, a word represents an act of generalization.[13]

For example, very young children can eat and enjoy apples. They can also learn to describe them as *round, red,* and *shiny.* They can learn other pertinent adjectives: *delicious, juicy,* or *Jonathan.* Or an apple may be described as *spotted, shriveled,* or *soft.* It might even be called *rotten, spoiled,* or *bad.* The word *apple* first signifies a concrete object, the apple itself, and then it could signify a wax imitation of the real thing. Both are three-dimensional. Then the word can apply to a two-dimensional picture, which is only semi-concrete. This is as far as abstraction goes for most children in the early years. When they are introduced to reading they can learn that the combination of letters *a-p-p-l-e* stands for the object. It is very important for teachers to recognize that *the spelling of the word using the letters of the Roman alphabet is an extremely abstract process.* The high degree of abstractness of this process for young children is very often missed completely by literate adults.

At age four, five, or six, children can learn many other things about apples. They can learn to classify them as fruit, to know that they are good for boys and girls, that they grow on trees, that they may come from Uncle Jim's apple orchard, and that they sometimes produce a million dollar crop in the Rio Grande Valley in New Mexico. So, this developmental process utilizing concepts is a thinking process—in which children put words to work solving problems. Stauffer says:

If children are to acquire concepts and words to represent them, they must make use in varying degrees of efficiency of such intellectual functions as deliberate attention, logical memory, abstraction, the ability to note likenesses and differences, and so on. To successfully instruct a school child, methods must be employed that will require pupils to be articulate about and put to deliberate use such intellectual functions.[14]

Special Aspects of Vocabulary

Through several years of personal observation, the writer has been both amazed and frightened to see dozens of ethnically mixed elementary, junior high, and senior high classes using traditional textbooks devised for unilingual, English-speaking, middle-class students—and the teacher carrying out traditional lesson plans *as if all the students were profiting* from them. The evidence is clear, derived from observation of teachers carrying on interminable monologues and from casual, friendly conversations with the boys and girls from minority ethnic groups whose first language is not English: much of the English is very difficult to understand and the student has far too limited language-power to comprehend either the teacher or the written text.

Without first mastering the sound system of the language, the student gets hopelessly lost and, if he stays in school, his achievement level drops farther and farther below that of the English-speaking students.

To demonstrate empirically that the language was severely limited, a number of language tests were devised and administered to large groups of these boys and girls. A few selected test items are presented here:[15]

1. In this story Betsy *turned the tables* on several people.
   a. made the people move over
   b. changed her mind
   c. surprised everyone
   d. turned the tables around

2. The black clouds let fall *sheets of rain.*
   a. squares of rain
   b. solid rain
   c. heavy downpour of rain
   d. white rain
3. Uncle Ben started *in a beeline* for the river.
   a. following an imaginary line
   b. straight and fast
   c. busy like a bee
   d. with a bee after him
4. But Mother, who understood thoroughly how Lucy was feeling, tried *to turn the matter off lightly.*
   a. to turn away
   b. to turn off the lights
   c. to dismiss the matter without seriousness
   d. to turn the matter off quietly
5. The old lady was kindhearted, but a bit *sharp-tongued.*
   a. her tongue was too long
   b. she talked too much
   c. her tongue was too sharp
   d. she spoke harshly

On tests prepared to measure responses to antonyms, simple analogies, and multiple meanings of words, fourth grade Anglo children who constituted normative groups performed statistically significantly better than sixth grade students from the minority groups.

The following are sample items from the multiple meanings test developed by Cox:[16]

Directions: Select the correct definition above the sentence to replace the word in the sentence which appears in italics. (The first one is done for you)

1. (a) place where liquor is sold, (b) fasten, (d) ale, (d) barrier, (e) the court
   __b__ 1. Don't *bar* the door.
   __a__ 2. The men had a drink in the *bar*.
   __d__ 3. The class constructed a sand *bar*.
   __e__ 4. The lawyer pleaded the man's case at the *bar*.
2. (a) snouts, (b) chests, (c) axle, (d) shorts, (e) bases
   _____ 1. The athletes wore white *trunks*.
   _____ 2. They bore holes in the *trunks* of the trees.
   _____ 3. The elephants picked up the sugar with their *trunks*.
   _____ 4. *Trunks* of gold were found in the cave.
3. (a) square designs, (b) figures, (c) ticket showing price, (d) mark, (e) control
   _____ 1. She placed a red *check* on the best paper.
   _____ 2. The matron had to keep *check* on the girls.
   _____ 3. She prefers *checks* to stripes.
   _____ 4. The man waited until the waitress gave him his dinner *check*.
4. (a) lower, (b) remove, (c) weapon, (d) knotted ribbon, (e) front of a ship
   _____ 1. They have learned to use a *bow* and arrow.
   _____ 2. Janet always wears a *bow* in her hair.
   _____ 3. The minister asked them to *bow* their heads as he prayed.
   _____ 4. Water seeped into the *bow*.
5. (a) church, (b) festival or exhibition, (c) just, (d) average, (e) light haired
   _____ 1. The judge asked the jurors to be *fair*.
   _____ 2. His mother is very *fair* and dainty.
   _____ 3. The children had fun at the *fair* in Window Rock.
   _____ 4. Timothy made *fair* grades in school.

Lessons for Developing Aspects of Vocabulary

Teachers can devise many lessons using improvised audio and visual aids to motivate language learning.

Elementary stories and poems can be used to establish meanings. For example, the poem "What Is Black?" could reinforce many meanings for the word *black* if the teacher gathers some pictures from the vertical picture file and some three-dimensional toys from ten-cent stores, drug stores, and department stores.

What Is Black?[17]

Black is good earth where little seeds grow;
Black is the bird that we call a crow.
Black is a berry which grows on a vine;
Black is the night, unless moon and stars shine.
Black are the shoes that you wear on your feet;
Black is the pepper on food that you eat.
Black is sweet licorice—yum, yum, yum!

Black is the spot of ink on your thumb.
Black is the skunk with stripe down his back;
Black is the engine that runs on a track.
Black is a fierce old Halloween cat;
Black is a witch's steeple hat.
Black is the marker with which you write;
Black is the opposite of white!

Louise Binder Scott

The picture illustrating "helpful little words," figure 16.1, can make common prepositions meaningful and be useful for review. The teacher must be careful to present such abstract words *one at a time* and to fix their meanings in a way that will not confuse the child.

Find pictures of natural pairs of objects in magazines and catalogs and mount them on 3-by-5 or 4-by-6-inch cards. Some possible pairs would be:

cup—saucer	fork—knife	ball—bat
pen—pencil	boy—girl	shirt—tie
doll—doll carriage	chair—desk	comb—hair
broom—dust pan	light bulb—lamp	hammer—nail
pan—lid	ring—finger	football player—football
mare—foal	baker—cake	fire fighter—fire truck
cat—dog	nose—face	letter carrier—letter
leaf—tree	paint—brush	dog—bone

Pictures that associate opposite concepts can be collected and mounted. Reading readiness books and picture dictionaries are among sources that should be looked at. Some possible pairs would be:

empty—full	above—below	large—small
in—out	cold—hot	on—off
inside—outside	left—right	tall—short

Pictures that represent seasons of the year can be compiled and classified into spring, summer, fall, winter. Similarly, pictures can be found to represent action verbs: swinging, sitting, reading, pasting, cutting, playing, falling down, getting off of, reaching, falling, kneeling, running, standing, painting, leaning over, setting, jumping, flying, sliding down.

Pictures of clothing we wear can be put in categories of things for mother, father, brother, sister. Catalogs of the big mail order companies are excellent sources for pictures of tools.

Dogs, toys, furniture, time pieces, different kinds of chairs, different kinds of lamps, ways we travel, domestic animals, dishes, money, sharp objects, musical instruments. All such things are categories of pictures that might be compiled in packets for different kinds of games or drills that might be planned with or without direct teacher supervision.

Children are not *functioning* in a language until they can generate sentences of their own. One technique that may be helpful is the use of pictures without background detail. Question words such as *who, what, why,* and *where* can then be used to elicit the necessary parts for constructing complete sentences.

Figure 16.1 The common prepositions must be taught one at a time in meaningful situations and with sufficient review provided so that the child uses them confidently.

From Hale C. Reid and Helen W. Crane, *My Picture Dictionary* (Boston, Mass.: Ginn, 1965), p. 37.

Helpful Little Words

The suggestions given here all emphasize the oral language and language-experience approach. That means teaching language patterns and providing the children much opportunity to talk about their experiences, with the teacher doing the little writing that needs to be done.

Six-year-olds can learn orally why irrigation is necessary in much of the Rio Grande Valley for growing garden vegetables. One kindergarten class became interested in a new house that was being built near the school so were taken to visit the house several times. They discussed how water would be piped into it, how the electricity would work, and all the kinds of skilled workmen who helped to build a house. Because one child was especially interested in the water pipes, a trip was arranged to the city water works department to see a large wall map that showed how the water lines were laid throughout the city.

Through meaningful experiences like these, a teacher can develop a language-experience approach to reading with children learning English as a second language in the same way as she does with children whose native language is English. The children soon learn that:

1. Reading is nothing more than talk written down.
2. Once written down, it can be read back exactly as it was said.
3. The printed word and a picture can mean the same thing.
4. Punctuation can change meaning in written language.

Some Methodology in TESOL

The main methodology of TESOL (Teaching English as a Second Language) includes oral drills in sentence patterns that involve substitutions, expansions, and transformations, among other things. Following are some examples.

Substitutions

The teacher models a sentence, such as "The school is just around the corner." The whole class repeats it, then, small groups, and then individuals. Then the teacher says only the word *store,* and in sequence, the class, small groups, and then individuals respond, "The store is just around the corner." The teacher says "restaurant," and the class etc. respond, "The restaurant is just around the corner," etc.

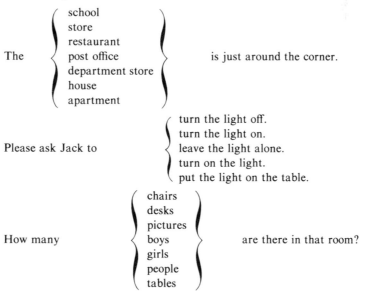

The ⎰ school / store / restaurant / post office / department store / house / apartment ⎱ is just around the corner.

Please ask Jack to ⎰ turn the light off. / turn the light on. / leave the light alone. / turn on the light. / put the light on the table. ⎱

How many ⎰ chairs / desks / pictures / boys / girls / people / tables ⎱ are there in that room?

Basic sentence patterns are, of course, made to serve their purposes more clearly for speakers by being expanded. Boys and girls who are native speakers of the language get much practice in this in English lessons. Speakers of nonstandard English will need a great deal of help with these exercises.

	Dogs bark.
	Dogs bark loudly.
The people's	dogs bark loudly.
The people's	dogs bark loudly every night.
We could hear the people's	dogs bark loudly every night.
We could hear the people's	dogs bark loudly every night when we were at grandmother's house.

The roses	are beautiful.
The red roses	are beautiful.
The red roses near my window	are beautiful.
I gave the red roses near my window	to the elderly couple next door.

I can play.	
I can play	this afternoon.
I can play	this afternoon for a while.
I can play	until five o'clock this afternoon.
I can play in the park	until five o'clock this afternoon.

Transformations

All English sentences are derived, by transformation and combination, from a few basic sentence types. So the sentence "Four chairs are in the room" can be transformed into a question by changing the positions of the subject and verb: "Are four chairs in the room?"

Lenneberg defined *transformation* in this way.[18]

We have illustrated a universal principle of grammatical knowledge or understanding: there must be lawful ways in which certain types of structure may be related to other types of structure. The grammatical laws that control these relations have come to be called *transformations.*

Transformations are statements of grammatical as well as semantic and phonological connections.

Observe the many transformations of the sentence "The girl knits her sweater."

The girl knitted her sweater.
The girl did knit her sweater.
The girl was knitting her sweater.
The girl didn't knit her sweater.
The girl wasn't knitting her sweater.
Wasn't the girl knitting her sweater?
Did the girl knit her sweater?
Didn't the girl knit her sweater?
The sweater was knitted by the girl.
Was the sweater knitted by the girl?

More basic sentences and transformations are presented below.[19]

Basic sentence structure	Passive transformation
They built a house.	A house was built by them.
John shot a deer.	A deer was shot by John.
Our country fought a civil war.	A civil war was fought by our country.
The third grade worked that problem.	That problem was worked by the third grade.
The old man planted the garden.	The garden was planted by the old man.

	Verb-to-noun transformation
John works.	John is a worker.
Julio gardens.	Julio is a gardener.
Mary teaches.	Mary is a teacher.
Ramon farms.	Ramon is a farmer.
Enrique drives a truck.	Enrique is a truck driver.
Mr. Jones practices law.	Mr. Jones is a lawyer.
Marianna cooks.	Marianna is a cook.
Mrs. Chacon makes dresses.	Mrs. Chacon is a dressmaker.
Mr. Acosta plays chess.	Mr. Acosta is a chess player.
Larry studies at the university.	Larry is a student at the university.

Basic sentence structure

I go to work.

I need help.

I walk to class.

I bring my books.

I eat lunch at school.

I work.

He works.

She works.

You work.

We work.

They work.

I go.

He goes.

John works here.

Robert lives in *Arizona*.

The books should have cost *ten dollars*.

Bill is in his *office*.

He studies *geography*.

He *works* in an office.

He studies in the *afternoon*.

He writes letters *at night*.

A man is at the door.

Four chairs are at the table.

Three boys are in the principal's office.

The day is warm.

The job is tough.

He reads fast.

Past transformation

I went to work.

I needed help.

I walked to class.

I brought my books.

I ate lunch at school.

I worked.

He worked.

She worked.

You worked.

We worked.

They worked.

I went.

He went.

Question-word transformation

Who works here?

Where does Robert live?

How much should the books have cost?

Where is Bill?

What does he study?

What does he do?

When does he study?

When does he write letters?

"There," "it," or "does" transformation / Question transformation

There is a man at the door./
Is there a man at the door?

There are four chairs at the table./
Are there four chairs at the table?

There are three boys in the principal's office./
Are there three boys in the principal's office?

It is a warm day./
Is it a warm day?

It is a tough job./
Is it a tough job?

He does read fast./
Does he read fast?

He is at school.

He is going now.

Is he at school?

Is he going now?

**Tag question, negative tag/
Tag question, positive tag**

You can go.

You can go, can't you?/
You can't go, can you?

He has the book.

He has the book, hasn't he?/
He doesn't have the book, does he?

He is working today.

He is working today, isn't he?/
He isn't working today, is he?

He was in your office.

He was in your office, wasn't he?/
He wasn't in your office, was he?

He will come back soon.

He will come back soon, won't he?/
He won't come back soon, will he?

Coordination

It is the end of summer.
School will begin soon.

It is the end of summer and school
will begin soon.

Girls work.
Boys play.

Girls work and boys play.

Coordination with deletions

The teacher was fair.
The teacher was helpful.
The teacher was completely honest.

The teacher was fair, helpful, and
completely honest.

Subordination

The book was lost.
The book was *The Wind in the
Willows.*

The book which was lost was *The
Wind in the Willows.*

The man in the library reads almost
every evening.
He knows a great deal about Mexico.

The man who reads in the library
almost every evening knows a
great deal about Mexico.

Some pupils know the story already.
They should not tell the ending.

Pupils who know the story already
should not tell the ending.

**Subordination using *because, until,
when*, etc.**

I came home early.
The library was closed.

I came home early because the library
was closed.

The farmer didn't plant potatoes.
The ground was too wet.

The farmer didn't plant potatoes
because the ground was too wet.

Mother complained.
I didn't help get dinner.

Mother complained because I didn't
help get dinner.

I didn't finish.
The bell rang.

I didn't finish because the bell rang.

Basic sentence structure	Subordination using *because, until, when,* etc.
I can't go with you.	I can't go with you until my homework
My homework isn't finished.	is finished.
I have to wait.	I have to wait until I get paid on
I get paid on Friday.	Friday.
I can't buy the groceries.	I can't buy the groceries until she
She didn't give me the list.	gives me the list.
I'll stay here.	I'll stay here if the library stays open.
The library stays open.	
José will work every day.	José will work every day if his brother
His brother can work too.	can work too.

A year—or longer—much longer if necessary—may be required to teach the most common sentence patterns with dialogue practice, substitution drills and questions and answers. Such lessons are now commercially available to all teachers. Of course, each teacher will adapt any text to fit the needs and specific experiences of the students being taught.

Contrastive Analysis of English and Spanish

Most teachers of native Spanish-speakers in classrooms where English is the medium of instruction have heard sentences like the following: "We went through the rooms bigs"; "Mary is wear a dress red"; "He no go to school"; "Yesterday your brother I saw"; "I am ready for to read"; "I see you later"; "Is Tuesday"; and "This apple is more big than that one." Usually such sentences represent Spanish structure combined with English vocabulary. It is useful to analyze such sentences in those terms for the students in order to demonstrate *why* Spanish-speakers tend to produce certain kinds of mistakes in English.

The following examples of contrast in structure are adapted from *Teaching English as a New Language to Adults:*[20]

Native English-Speaker	Spanish-Speaker Learning English
Not is negative used with verb forms: "Mary is not here."	Spanish negation of verb is *no;* hence, "Mary is no here."
Verb is inflected with *s* in English third person simple present: "The boy eats."	Spanish verbs are fully inflected; hence, in learning our comparatively uninflected English, the student tends to drop even the inflections which persist, to say: "The boy eat."
Negatives are formed with *do, does, did:* "He *did* not go to school."	Spanish has no auxiliaries; hence, "He no go/went to school."
English adjectives usually precede the noun: "The red dress."	Spanish adjectives usually follow the noun; hence, "The dress red."
Going to to express future time: "I am going to sing."	Comparable Spanish construction uses the simple present; hence, "I go to sing."

The auxiliary *will* in English future: "I will see you later."	Tendency is to omit auxiliary and to say: "I see you later.
Use of *it* to start a sentence: "It is Tuesday."	Spanish does not have the "It . . ." construction; hence, "Is Tuesday."
Use of *to be* to express age: "I'm twenty years old."	Spanish uses *to have;* hence, "I have twenty years."
Use of *to be* to express hunger, thirst, etc. "I am thirsty."	Spanish uses *to have;* hence, "I have hunger"; "I have thirst."
English negative imperative: "Don't run!"	Spanish does not have the auxiliary *do;* hence, "No run!"
Questions with *do, does,* and *did:* "Does this man work?"	No auxiliaries exist in Spanish. Tendency is to say: "This man works?" or "Works this man?"
Indefinite article used in front of noun identifying occupation: "She is a nurse."	Spanish does not use the indefinite article; hence, "She is nurse."

The following English-Spanish language differences cause particular problems.

English often uses the single phonological feature of voiced vs. voiceless sounds (e.g., *z* vs. *s*) to distinguish spoken words. For example: race-raise; lacy-lazy; niece-knees; seal-zeal; price-prize. This difference in sound is never the sole feature to separate meanings in Spanish.

English uses the phonological difference between *n* and *ng* to distinguish meanings while Spanish does not. For example: ran-rang; sin-sing; kin-king; thin-thing; fan-fang; ban-bang.

The Spanish speaker learning English must learn many new consonant sounds. *Sh* in *shine* and *wh* in *when.*

While Spanish uses only five vowel sounds, English uses many more *to distinguish meanings.* Practice is necessary for the Spanish-speaking person to develop auditory discrimination of such pairs as the following: heat-hit; met-mate; tap-tape; look-luck; pin-pine; hat-hot; sheep-ship; mit-meet; eat-it; late-let; bed-bad; fool-full; coat-caught; caught-cut.

Distinguishing between some consonant sounds can cause trouble too: pig-big; pig-pick; thank-sank; then-den; place-plays. Also, clusters like *ts* in *hats; lpt* in *helped; lkt* in *talked.*

Modifiers do *not* follow the noun in English:

The blue sky, not *the sky blue.*
The juicy apples, not the apples juicy.
The bus station is not the same as *the station bus.*
The pocket watch is not the same as *the watch pocket.*

Word order in sentences has more flexibility in Spanish than in English. For example, any of the following Spanish sentences is correct but only one of the literally translated English.

Ayer vine aquí.	Yesterday I came here.
Aquí vine ayer.	Here I came yesterday.
Vine ayer aquí.	I came yesterday here.
Ayer aquí vine.	Yesterday here I came.

The irregularity of some words causes difficulty after children learn to generalize from regular forms: I *teared* the paper. I *throwed* the ball. I *dood* it.

Intonation and stress are very important in conveying meanings:

Which book did *you* buy?
Which book *did* you buy?
Which book did you *buy?*
Are *you* going back to school this fall?
Are you going back to school *this* fall?
Are you going *back to school* this fall?

Programs that teach English as a second language in the United States have been based generally upon contrastive analysis of Spanish and English. Weaver has pointed out that this bias does not fit the needs of the Indian child. The points of contrast between English and Indian languages that cause most difficulty are not at all like the English-Spanish contrasts. The difficulties that Navajo children, for example, are most likely to encounter are:

1. Distinction of number.
2. Expression of possession.
3. Application of adjective to noun.
4. Distinction of gender.
5. Usage of subject and object.
6. Usage of definite and indefinite articles.
7. Usage of definite and indefinite pronouns.
8. Usage of correct verb inflections.
9. Usage of negative questions.[21]

Indian languages need the same contrastive study with respect to English as European languages have had so educators can improve English language instruction for Indian people.

TESOL Text Materials

A selected list of texts available to teachers of English as a second language includes the following:

Boggs, Ralph, and Robert Dixson. *English Step by Step with Pictures,* rev. ed. New York: Regents Publ. Co., 1971.

Dixson, Robert, J. *Complete Course in English,* rev. ed. New York: Regents Publ. Co., 1972. Four books in series. (Cassette tapes are available.)

English Language Services, Inc. *New English 900.* New York: Macmillan, 1973.

English Language Services, Inc. *English This Way.* New York: Macmillan, 1964. Twelve textbooks in series. (Tapes are available.)

Hall, Eugene J. *Practical Conversation in English for Beginning Students.* New York: Regents Publ. Co., 1972.

The Institute of Modern Languages, Inc. *Contemporary Spoken English.* A five-book series prepared by John Kane and Mary Kirkland. New York: Thomas Y. Crowell, 1967–1968.

Lado, Robert. *English Series: A Complete Course in English as a Second Language.* New York: Regents Publ. Co., 1977–1979. Six books in series.

Mackin, Ronald. *Exercises in English Patterns and Usage.* London: Oxford University Press, 1969. Five books in series.

Mellgren, Lars, and Michael Walker. *New Horizons in English.* Reading, Mass.: Addison-Wesley, 1973. Three books in series.

National Council of Teachers of English. *English for Today.* William R. Slager, general editor. New York: McGraw-Hill, 1973–1976.

Taylor, Grant. *Practicing American English.* New York: McGraw-Hill Book Co., 1962.

Wheeler, Gonzales. *Let's Speak English.* New York: McGraw-Hill, 1967. Six books in series.

"Linguistic" Reading Programs

By 1968 three or four sets of so-called "linguistic readers" were published. They were based on the general principle that the spelling patterns of new words introduced to beginning readers must be rigidly controlled. The decoding process was thus emphasized to the exclusion of teaching reading as a meaningful process. These books have nothing to offer the classroom teacher of reading. They contradict any first grade teacher's efforts to encourage good oral language and expanded usage in conversations and to enlarge vocabulary and attention span by reading good stories to children. These books offer as a lesson only uninteresting, artificial bits of text containing, for example, no vowel except short *a*. Few teachers could motivate much interest in "day-after-day" reading of such passages as this:

> A cat sat.
> A fat cat sat.
> A cat had a hat.
> A man had a cat.
> A cat had a fat rat.

A remedial reading clinician once used such books in individual tutoring situations with youngsters to encourage them to read either silently or orally. At the next session many children asked if they could please have a different book to read.

Loban[22] and Strickland[23] have helped teachers to understand how the English language is used by children for whom it is the first language. The fact that only a few basic patterns are used in ordinary conversations provides a basis for English language practice that will help other children learn it as a second language. Similarly the sentence word order of children's oral usage probably should be carried over into written material used for teaching reading. Reading comprehension should be greater in materials that utilize high frequency sentence patterns from oral language structure than in materials using unusual or unfamiliar types of sentence patterns.

Goodman has questioned the types of controlled sentences used in primers and preprimers.[24] He points out that the reading process requires, beyond word recognition, that the reader understand both the semantic meaning of the word and the syntactic use. In other words, beyond the recognized word as it comes into focus in the line of print, lie all the contextual clues which the child is anticipating—clues from all the determiners and structure words. Even beginning readers project ideas ahead of the print as they read. This point relates to an important problem in writing preprimers and primers for young children. Children can much more easily anticipate meanings in "fully formed English language" sentence structures—

Betty said, "I am going with my mother to the store."
Pete said, "May I go along with you?"

—than they can in the types of controlled sentences which Goodman has called "Name the Word Game"—

"Come here, Betty."
"Here I come," said Betty.

Certain types of limitation might be useful in the materials used by beginning readers, however. The number of personal pronouns and also the number of verb forms could be limited in first readers. This degree of restriction might facilitate the children's understanding without violating the current emphasis on meaningful language.

Craker[25] studied the personal pronoun occurrences in recommended instructional talk in three reading-readiness programs. The purpose was to investigate how many personal pronouns forms were used in listening material that it was assumed the children understood. She counted each form of personal pronoun used and how frequently it occurred in the first twenty pages of reading-readiness instruction in the teacher's manuals. No one series used all twenty-three forms of personal pronouns. The *Scott, Foresman Readers*[26] used seventeen, the *Bank Street Readers*[27] used sixteen, and the *Miami Linguistic Readers*[28] used six.

The *Scott, Foresman Readers*, designed for middle-class children, provide much teacher talk and utilize pronouns in a greater range of grammatical form, case, and number than do the other two series. The *Bank Street Readers*, designed for inner-city children with culturally disadvantaged backgrounds, reduce the listening load by making more limited use of pronouns in basic sentences. However, they use almost as many different pronouns as do the *Scott, Foresman Readers*.

The discussion of linguistic foundations presented in chapter 3 points out that new understanding of how language is acquired and how children are motivated to develop and extend their communication skills significantly influenced the way reading was taught in the 1970s. Emphasis was on the importance of enriching children's oral language experiences and encouraging children to record their own ideas and experiences in written form. It is to be hoped that out of studies in descriptive linguistics, psycholinguistics, and sociolinguistics, we can distill principles for an educational linguistics that will help all children achieve more success in learning the language arts.

Bilingualism in the Southwest

The word *bilingual* is used very loosely because it is applied wherever children in school must use a second language as the language of instruction whether they know anything about the language. The word is applied as readily to children who know only a nonstandard dialect of English as to those who come to the English-speaking school without ever having used English as a means of communication. Although the real meaning of *bilingual* is "being able to speak in two languages," the term is applied to anyone who is in a two-language environment, even if the person can say only "hello," "thank you," and "good-by" in the second language.

In the Southwest, children are spoken of as bilinguals if they speak an Indian tongue or Spanish until they enroll in a school where English is the medium of instruction. Naturally, these children are not *bi*lingual by any stretch of the imagination. In the past they were *not* given systematic instruction in the second language so they had little opportunity to become bilingual.

Were the school to take advantage of the child's native language to help him become proficient in the language of the school, the child would then be truly bilingual. With the needs around the world as great as they are today for peoples to be able to communicate across language barriers, it seems extremely foolish that in the United States the child who brings a language other than English to school has been asked to forget it. If current trends toward bilingual/bicultural programs continue, such children can finish the sixth grade with competent literacy skills in two languages.

The basic problem in the Southwest is *biculturalism,* not bilingualism. Language expresses the values of a culture; culture, by determining behavioral practices and goals, limits the connotations and denotations of the language. The limitations of bilingualism are illustrated in the use of the word *father* in Anglo-American culture and in Zuni Indian culture. For Zuni children, the word *father* represents their mother's husband—a man who enjoys his children as companions. He takes no part in disciplining his children, nor does he have any concern for their economic security. In this matrilineal society, the mother owns the property and her brothers assist in the rearing and disciplining of children. Further, it is said that she may divorce her husband by leaving his shoes and ceremonial garb outside the door while he is away and that this act will be his cue to gather up his belongings and return to his mother's house. The extended family organization does not decree that the marriage relationship is more important than the consanguinal mother-son or sister-brother relationship.

Father for the Anglo middle-class child represents the legal head of a household who is held responsible for the rearing and disciplining of his children. The father's marriage to the child's mother is based, at least theoretically, on a love relationship, and even if dissolved in a court of law, the father may still be held accountable for the full support of the mother and children. It is thus apparent that the term *father* has quite different meanings for the Anglo and for the Zuni child.[29]

The interdependence of language and culture for the young child has been well stated by Davies:

To change a child's medium of instruction is surely to change his culture; is not culture bound up with language? And if the language should disappear, can the culture remain? Everyone must have his own orientation to life, and language provides the most natural means of reacting to life. In the deepest things of the heart, a man or woman turns naturally to the mother tongue; and in a child's formative stages, his confidence in that tongue must never be impaired.[30]

It is hoped that children hold two psychological values about their language and family who speak that language. First, they should feel that their language is a good one, that it expresses their ideas and wishes adequately, and that they may be justly proud to use it. Second, all the people in their extended family use the language which they have learned as their first language, and they derive their ego strength and sense of personal worth as members of their particular ethnic groups. However, if the school teaches that English is the only acceptable language there, and that use of another language even during free play on the playground will be punished, children can only conclude that their school feels that their language is inferior to the one that must be used *all the time* during the school day.

If the teacher reacts negatively to a child's first language, the child will further conclude that only people who speak English are adequate in the teacher's eyes. Both of these things were done to children in the Southwest for many years. They were denied the use of their own language and subtly taught that their language and their people were inferior. One example of this very bad kind of teaching can be cited. A counselor in a border town dormitory for Indian students is reported to have met a bus load of boys and girls at his school in the fall of the year and to have asked them to group themselves around him so that he might say a word to them. He then made the following announcement: "The first thing I want you to do here is to forget that you are an Indian, and the second thing I want to tell you is that we speak only English around here."

Bilingual schools taught in Spanish and English would be natural, workable solutions in many schools in the Southwest. Since Spanish is a major language of the world, books, newspapers, and periodicals are readily available in that language. There are some 200,000,000 speakers of the language in the many nations in the Americas, with libraries, government, business, and schools functioning in Spanish.

The question of young Navajo children receiving instruction in school in the Navajo language is an entirely different matter though no less important. Although there are no libraries and there is no indicated future literary use, the two psychological values are just as valid for Navajo as for Spanish children. At ages five and six, the school should provide for the Navajo language to be used two-thirds or more of the day and planned, sequenced English taught as a spoken means of communication. Learning concepts and reading readiness in Navajo would save children some time later on. At age eight or nine, they would begin learning to read in English, and English would be used as the medium of reading and writing instruction. Thus, the behavior of the adults at school during the first three years would show the children that the school valued their language and cultural heritage, and they might well participate in a Navajo conversation class throughout their school life.

What Is a Bilingual School?

Few truly bilingual programs operate in the public schools of the United States. A bilingual school is one which offers instruction during the school day in more than one language. This means that content subjects are taught in both languages. A child might study mathematics in English and history in Spanish in a Spanish-English bilingual school. In contrast, having children study Spanish for one period of the day as a foreign language, with little attention given to that language except in the class period, does not constitute bilingual education. Furthermore, bilingual education must begin before high school. Few students who begin to study a foreign language in high school are able to master the sound system of that language so they can understand native speakers of that language.

Davies has described a second language learning situation in Wales:[31]

A pleasing feature of parallel-medium or "two-stream" schools in Wales is their complete lack of separatism. The Primary School, Aberystwyth, reorganized in 1948, has 340 pupils, of whom 225 are English- and 115 Welsh-speaking. The staff is bilingual, and the spirit of the school on the whole is Welsh, with Welsh the language of the staff and staff meetings. English is used as the medium of instruction for the English-speaking section throughout, with Welsh introduced as a subject in the second year and taught in every subsequent year. For the Welsh-speaking section, English is introduced during the second half of the first year, the time devoted to it being increased during the second and subsequent years; by the third year, the medium of instruction has become 50% Welsh, 50% English, and by the fourth, equal facility in the use of both languages is aimed at.

Peal and Lambert demonstrated that bilingual children are superior on both verbal and nonverbal intelligence tests when compared with monolinguals. They compared monolingual and bilingual groups of ten-year-old children who were students in six French schools in Montreal, Canada. The groups were matched on age, sex, and socioeconomic status. They concluded that the bilingual subjects had greater mental flexibility than did the monolingual children and, in addition, demonstrated superiority in concept formation.[32]

Richardson reported that bilingual classes in Dade County, Florida achieved as well, on the average, as the monolingual English-speaking classes and had as a bonus their acquired fluency in the Spanish language.[33]

Modiano did a comparative study of two approaches to the teaching of reading in the national languages.[34] She studied reading achievement of native Indians in the Chiapas highlands in southern Mexico, where some of the Indian children are taught to read first in their native Indian languages while others are immediately taught in Spanish. In each of three tribal areas studied, the researcher found significantly better reading ability among children who were first taught to read in their native language.

Modiano's findings are applicable to all schools, and to test this hypothesis she urges experimental programs in schools in the United States having large linguistic minorities. She found no school system in the nation employing the native-language-first approach when she was ready to conduct her study in 1965.

Rock Point Bilingual Program

Rock Point Boarding School is located on the Navajo Reservation near Chinle, Arizona. Several years ago this school passed from the Chinle Agency of the Bureau of Indian Affairs (BIA) to the local community and became a community-controlled "contract" school. The school began developing a bilingual program in 1967 when Title I funds became available for that purpose. However, from 1967 until 1971 the local school board exercised little control and those years were spent developing oral Navajo and oral English, reading readiness in Navajo, and doing a great deal of thinking about initial literacy. Little material was available in Navajo then, so just planning the curriculum one year at a time was a monumental task. However, the first results of the bilingual program at Rock Point are now in print. Rosier and Farella reported:[35]

A basic assumption of the bilingual program at Rock Point is that learning to read in Navajo will probably result in better reading skills, which will later result in better reading results in English achievement tests. Critical thinking, developed through language and cognitive development, can be better nurtured by teaching first in the child's vernacular. Nevertheless, good reading skills in English are important. The 1975 testing program showed significant increases in English reading test scores for fourth and fifth grade students who learned to read in Navajo and had instruction in the subject matter areas in Navajo while they learned English. The biliterate Navajos at Rock Point scored significantly higher in reading on the Stanford Achievement Tests than did Navajo students in monolingual English-speaking BIA schools on the Navajo Reservation. At fifth grade level, the growth of Rock Point students was almost double that of the BIA sample population. Apparently the effects of initial literacy in Navajo are cumulative. Rock Point's bilingual-biliterate program demonstrates the instruction in Navajo is both practical and beneficial for Navajo-speaking students.

Materials for Bilingual Schools

Schools interested in finding text materials for elementary school classes will be able to find an adequate supply. Since the passage of funding for the Bilingual Education Act, more than a hundred federally funded programs in bilingual education have been in progress for four or five years. The large majority have been Spanish-English bilingual, although more than twenty different native American languages were used in 1973–74 in developing Indian language-English bilingual programs. Anyone seeking sources of available materials could address inquiries to:

Center for Applied Linguistics
1611 N. Kent Street
Arlington, Virginia 22209

U.S. Commission on Civil Rights
Washington, D.C. 20425

Materials Acquisition Project
2950 National Avenue
San Diego, California 92120

Dissemination Center for Bilingual Bicultural Education
6504 Tracor Lane
Austin, Texas 78721

Summary

. . . There is general agreement all over the educational world that the child should begin his education in his mother tongue or . . . the language he most easily understands.

. . . we are not producing bilingual school children and we never shall, as long as the second language is *not* used as an instrument of expression and *not* merely as a subject to be learned for an examination. In other words, the second language must be used as a medium in the school.[36]

Thompson and Hamalainen stated:

In the ever shrinking world the attainment of goals of communication and understanding among its people is imperative if we are to live in peace and security. It is an obvious fact known to almost everyone that we are only one day's distance from every place in the world. Not only are we this close to each other in time, but in increasing numbers we are establishing contact with each other.[37]

The United States government, aware of the importance of foreign languages to the national interest, enacted pertinent legislation to provide support for research and training. The National Defense Education Act (NDEA) of August 1958 in its Title VI promoted the study of foreign languages and the quality of instruction. NDEA has provided more schools and colleges with the opportunity to teach foreign languages more effectively than any other measure in recent years.

The focus on foreign language study has shown that learning a second language is very difficult. The learner must follow many of the same steps children take in learning their native language. However, adult learners experience much interference from previously learned speaking and reading and writing habits. Yet, they must learn to hear and to discriminate the significant sounds of that new language as used by its speakers. The learner must produce sound units that are new and, therefore, difficult because these sounds are not found in the structure of his native language. Since the learner is fluent and at ease in the use of his native tongue, there are additional barriers to overcome: feelings of awkwardness, of inhibition, and limitations in language expression.

The communication explosion presents promises and problems. While it makes the world one village, technology alone cannot bring about human understanding. Knowledge of one or more foreign languages has become a practical necessity.[38]

Teaching reading in English to the bilingual child will not differ as a process if the child has an opportunity to master the sound system of the English language before he is expected to learn to read and write it. Teachers need to understand and appreciate the cultural background of the child, the cognitive learning processes for all children, some of the phonemic and syntactical differences between their language and the child's, the present-day methods of teaching the reading and writing skills and the contribution of linguistics to this process, and the problems of vocabulary expansion for the second language student. In addition, where children already understand the sound system of another language, opportunity should be found for them to retain and develop it. If large numbers of children have a common *other* language, a successful bilingual school has deep significance to the community and to the larger society.

Suggested Activities	1. If you teach in a classroom where children are learning English as a new language, prepare text exercises to measure understanding of idioms, multiple meanings, and antonyms appropriate to your grade level.
	2. Ask three children to discuss something in the regular school work on the tape recorder. Allow a prescribed amount of time—for example, two minutes—then evaluate the quantity and quality of language (total number of words, mean length of sentence, modifiers, and verb forms).

For Further Reading

Abrahams, Roger D., and Rudolph C. Troike, eds. *Language and Cultural Diversity in American Education.* Englewood Cliffs, N.J.: Prentice-Hall, 1972.

Allen, Harold B., and Russell N. Campbell. *Teaching English as a Second Language: A Book of Readings,* section II, "Methods, Techniques, and Materials," pp. 81–170. New York: McGraw-Hill, 1972.

Carroll, John B. *Language and Thought.* Englewood Cliffs, N.J.: Prentice-Hall, 1964.

Cazden, Courtney B. *Child Language and Education,* chapter 7, "Dialect Differences and Bilingualism," pp. 143–81. New York: Holt, Rinehart, & Winston, Inc. 1972.

Davies, R. E. *Bilingualism in Wales.* Capetown, South Africa: Juta, 1954.

Goodman, Kenneth S. "The Linguistics of Reading." *Elementary School Journal* 64 (April 1964):355–61.

———. "Reading: A Psycholinguistic Guessing Game." In *Theoretical Models and Process in Reading,* 2d ed. edited by Harry Singer and Robert Ruddell, pp. 497–508. Newark, Del.: International Reading Assn., 1976.

Hall, Edward T. *The Silent Language.* Greenwich, Conn.: Fawcett Publications, 1966.

Horn, Thomas D., ed. *Reading for the Disadvantaged, Problems of Linguistically Different Learners.* New York: Harcourt, Brace & World, 1970.

Lamb, Pose. *Linguistics in Proper Perspective.* Columbus: Charles E. Merrill, 1967.

LeFevre, Carl A. *Linguistics and the Teaching of Reading.* New York: McGraw-Hill, 1964.

Liebert, Burt. *Linguistics and the New English Teacher.* New York: Macmillan, 1971.

Loban, Walter. *The Language of Elementary School Children.* Champaign, Ill.: National Council for the Teachers of English, NCTE Research Report, No. 1, 1963.

Malherbe, E. G. *The Bilingual School.* Capetown, South Africa: Juta, 1946.

Pearson, P. D., and D. D. Johnson. *Teaching Reading Comprehension.* New York: Holt, Rinehart & Winston, 1978.

Ruddell, Robert B. *Reading-Language Instruction: Innovative Practices,* chapter 9, "Nonstandard Dialects and Second Language Learning: The Instructional Program," pp. 263–89. Englewood Cliffs, N.J.: Prentice-Hall, 1974.

Ruddell, Robert B., Evelyn J. Ahern, Eleanore K. Hartson, and Joellyn Taylor. *Resources in Reading-Language Instruction,* part 3, "Reading-Language Achievement: Socio-Ethnic Variation," pp. 118–68. Englewood Cliffs, N.J.: Prentice-Hall, 1974.

Savage, John F., ed. *Linguistics for Teachers: Selected Materials.* Chicago: Science Research Associates, 1973.

Smith, E. Brooks, Kenneth Goodman, and Robert Meredith. *Language and Thinking in the Elementary School,* 2nd ed. New York: Holt, Rinehart, & Winston, 1975.

Weaver, Wendell W. "The Word As the Unit of Language." *The Journal of Reading* 10 (January 1967):262–68.

Yandell, Maurine, and Miles V. Zintz. "Some Difficulties Which Indian Children Encounter with Idioms in Reading." *The Reading Teacher* 14 (March 1961):256–59.

Zintz, Miles V., *Corrective Reading,* 3d ed. chapter 11, "Teaching the Linguistically and Culturally Different Child," pp. 293–337. Dubuque, Iowa: Wm. C. Brown Company Publishers, 1977.

―――. "Developing a Communication Skills Program for Bilinguals." In *Understanding and Helping the Retarded Reader,* edited by Ruth Strang. pp. 64–75. Tucson, Ariz.: University of Arizona Press, 1965.

―――. *What Classroom Teachers Should Know About Bilingual Education,* ED 028 427. ERIC TESOL. 1969.

Zintz, Miles V., Mari Luci Ulibarri, and Dolores Gonzales. *The Implications of Bilingual Education for Developing Multicultural Sensitivity Through Teacher Education,* SP 005 242 ERIC Clearinghouse on Teacher Education. (September 1971).

Notes

1. Alexander Frazier, ed., *Educating the Children of the Poor* (Washington, D.C. 20036: Assn. for Supervision & Curriculum Development, National Education Assn., 1968).

2. Eskimo term for white person. Derived from Russian word *cossack.*

3. Lee H. Salisbury, "Teaching English to Alaska Natives," *Journal of American Indian Education* 6 (January 1967):4–5.

4. Evelyn Evvard and George C. Mitchell, "Sally, Dick and Jane at Lukachukai," *Journal of American Indian Education* 5 (May 1966):5.

5. William Madsen, *The Mexican-American of South Texas* (New York: Holt, Rinehart and Winston, 1964), p. 106.

6. Robert Hall, *Linguistics and Your Language* (Garden City, New York: Doubleday, 1960), p. 193.

7. Dora V. Smith, *Communication: The Miracle of Shared Living* (New York: The Macmillan Co., 1955), p. 51.

8. Miles Zintz, *Education Across Cultures* (Dubuque, Ia.: Kendall/Hunt Publishing Co., 1969), p. 28.

9. Earl C. Kelley, "The Fully Functioning Self," in *Perceiving, Behaving, Becoming, A New Focus on Education* (Washington, D.C.: Assn. for Supervision and Curriculum Development, National Education Assn., 1962), pp. 10–12.

10. Paul Conklin, "A Good Day at Rough Rock," *American Education* (Reprint) (February 1967). Unnumbered pages.

11. Mary Finocchiaro, *Teaching Children Foreign Languages* (New York: McGraw-Hill, Inc., 1964), pp. 26–28.

12. Gertrude Hildreth, "Lessons in Arabic," *The Reading Teacher* 19 (December 1965):210.

13. Russell Stauffer, "Concept Development and Reading," *The Reading Teacher* 19 (November 1965):101.

14. Ibid., p. 102.

15. Maurine Yandell, "Some Difficulties Which Indian Children Encounter with Idioms in Reading," Masters thesis, University of New Mexico, Albuquerque, 1959.

16. Clara Jett Cox, "An Experimental Study in the Teaching of Certain Facets of the English Language to Navajo Pupils in the Sixth Grade," paper, College of Education, University of New Mexico, July, 1963.

17. Louise Binder Scott and J.J. Thompson, *Talking Time,* 2d ed. (New York: McGraw-Hill, 1966), p. 327.

18. Eric H. Lenneberg, *Biological Foundations of Language* (New York: John Wiley & Sons, 1967), pp. 291–92.

19. Paul Roberts, *English Sentences* (New York: Harcourt, Brace & World, Inc., 1962).

20. Board of Education of the City of New York, *Teaching English as a New Language to Adults,* Curriculum Bulletin No. 5, 1963–1964 series (Publications Sales Office, 110 Livingston Street, Brooklyn, New York: Board of Education of the City of New York), pp. 7–9.

21. Yvonne Weaver, "A Closer Look at TESL on the Reservation," *Journal of American Indian Education* 6 (January 1967):28.

22. Walter Loban, *The Language of Elementary School Children* (Champaign, Illinois: National Council of Teachers of English, NCTE Research Report, No. 1, 1963).

23. Ruth Strickland, *The Language of Elementary School Children: Its Relationship to the Language of Reading Textbooks and the Quality of Reading of Selected Children* (Bloomington, Ind.: Indiana University Bulletin of the School of Education, Vol. 38, No. 4, 1962).

24. Kenneth S. Goodman, "Reading: A Psycholinguistic Guessing Game," in *Theoretical Models and Processes in Reading,* Harry Singer and Robert Ruddell, eds. (Newark, Del.: International Reading Assn., 1970) pp. 359–72.

25. Hazel Craker, "Personal Pronoun Occurrences in Recommended Instructional Talk in Three Reading Readiness Programs," paper, College of Education, University of New Mexico, 1968.

26. Scott, Foresman and Company.

27. Macmillan Company.

28. D. C. Heath and Company.

29. Miles V. Zintz, "Cultural Aspects of Bilingualism," in *Vistas in Reading,* ed. J. Allen Figurel, 11th Annual International Reading Assn. Proceedings, p. 357, 1967.

30. R. E. Davies, *Bilingualism in Wales* (Capetown, South Africa: Juta, 1954), p. 14.

31. R. E. Davies, *Bilingualism in Wales* (Capetown: Juta, 1954), pp. 17, 90.

32. Elizabeth Peal and Wallace Lambert, "The Relationship of Bilingualism to Intelligence," *Psychological Monographs: General and Applied,* No. 76:1–23 (Washington: American Psychological Assn., 1962).

33. Mabel Richardson, "An Evaluation of Certain Aspects of the Academic Achievement of Elementary Pupils in a Bilingual Program," (Coral Gables, Fla.: Graduate School, University of Miami, 1968).

34. Nancy Modiano, "A Comparative Study to Two Approaches to the Teaching of Reading in the National Language," New York University School of Education, 1966.

35. Paul Rosier and Merilyn Farella, "Bilingual Education at Rock Point—Some Early Results," *TESOL Quarterly* 10 (December 1976): 379–88; Paul Rosier and Lillian Vorih, "Rock Point Community School: An Example of a Navajo-English Bilingual Elementary Program," TESOL Quarterly 13 (September 1978) 263–69.

36. T. J. Haarhoff, "Introduction," in *The Bilingual School* by E. G. Malherbe (Capetown: Juta, 1946), pp. 5, 8.

37. Elizabeth Thompson and Arthur Hamalainen, "Foreign Language Teaching in the Elementary Schools," *An Examination of Current Practices* (Washington: Assn. for Supervision and Curriculum Development, National Education Association, 1958), p. 9.

38. Dolores Gonzales, "Auditory Discrimination of Spanish Phonemes," Ed. D. dissertation, University of Pennsylvania, 1967, pp. 4–5.

17

Teaching Reading to Children Who Speak Nonstandard English

A few years ago a kindergarten teacher in an inner-city kindergarten wanted to develop some feeling about the importance of George Washington and Abraham Lincoln during the month of February. On Lincoln's birthday, the concept that Mr. Lincoln had been president of the United States was discussed and his picture was displayed. The comment was made that Mr. Kennedy was now president of our country.

Mark asked: "Why Lincoln not president now?"

Teacher: "Mr. Lincoln is dead now."

Mark persisted: "Why he daid?"

The teacher realized that these children knew something of the reality of life and that shooting was not uncommon in the neighborhood, so she said, "A man shot him."

The kindergartners looked big-eyed at the teacher and asked, "Who?" "Why?"

Mark said, unbelieving, "He shot him daid?"

Mr. Booth was discussed briefly as a man who thought some of the things President Lincoln had done were not right and that he had become mentally ill and committed the act of violence.

Mark continued all day to go and look at the picture of President Lincoln and repeat to himself, "He shot him daid." He took the teacher's hand and led her to the picture several times and said, "That good man. He shot him daid."

The teacher responded calmly, "Yes, Mark, he shot him dead."

Mark responded, "That good Mr. Lincoln. [Pause.] Bastard!"[1]

Any kindergarten teacher distressed with the vivid way Mark characterized John Wilkes Booth must first understand why "bastard" is the word that Mark brings easily to the conscious level. If he has heard it often at home or near home, should she tell Mark it is "bad" language or "wrong" for him to say it? How soon should Mark learn there is one language spoken at school and another at home? If the teacher wishes to encourage Mark to use language, to expand language, and to evaluate through language, she must start where he is with the language he has.

This chapter presents briefly (1) the problems of people who live in poverty; (2) the problems of elementary school children who live in these homes; (3) the problems of language and concept development to improve literacy skills; and (4) teaching reading to children who speak nonstandard English.

The Culture of Poverty

Among the fifty million people in the United States who fit into the classification of poor, Lewis estimates that perhaps one-fifth, or ten million, live in a "culture of poverty." The largest numbers of this group are made up of Negroes, Puerto Ricans, Mexicans, American Indians, and Southern poor whites.[2]

The hard-core poor in the United States are said to live in a culture of poverty. The *culture of poverty,* in this sense, indicates that they are caught in a vicious circle—with no solution to meeting even minimum economic needs. The individual who grows up in the culture of poverty develops attitudes of fatalism, helplessness, and inferiority. Such a person's primary concerns are immediate, and a strong present-time orientation is characteristic of his or her behavior. With a weak ego structure, the person has little disposition to defer personal gratification or to think about the future.[3]

Miller has characterized the hard-core lower class in our country as being primarily female-based households as the basic child-rearing unit and as having "serial monogamy" mating as the primary marriage pattern.[4]

The lower-class Negro family pattern commonly consists of a female dominated household, with either the mother or the grandmother acting as the mainstay of the family unit. The husband, if present, is often an ineffective family leader. The boy growing up in a Negro family frequently perceives his father as a person with a low-status job, who is regarded with indifference or varying degrees of hostility by members of the out-group. In short, the lower-class Negro adult male is seldom regarded as a worthwhile masculine model for the boy to emulate.[5]

Harrington has described the insoluble economic problems that keep the poverty cycle operating:

Here is one of the most familiar forms of the vicious circle of poverty. The poor get sick more than anyone else in the society. That is because they live in slums, jammed together under unhygienic conditions; they have inadequate diets, and cannot get decent medical care. When they become sick, they are sick longer than any other group in the society. Because they are sick more often and longer than anyone else, they lose wages and work, and find it difficult to hold a steady job. And because of this, they cannot pay for good housing, for a nutritious diet, for doctors. At any given point in the circle, particularly when there is a major illness, their prospect is to move to an even lower level and to begin the cycle, round and round, toward even more suffering.[6]

After describing how the family structure of the poor is different from that of the rest of society, Harrington went on to contrast the attitudes of the middle class and the urban poor toward the city policeman:

For the middle-class, the police protect property, give directions, and help old ladies. For the urban poor, the police are those who arrest you. In almost any slum there is a vast conspiracy against the forces of law and order. If someone approaches asking for a person, no one there will have heard of him, even if he lives next door. The outsider is a "cop," bill collector, investigator (and in the Negro ghetto, most dramatically, he is "the Man").[7]

People in the culture of poverty talk about the middle-class values as if they accept them, but, in day-to-day living, they fail to live by most of them. Poverty forces them to buy small quantities of goods at high prices, to pawn personal goods often, and to pay usurious rates of interest on bits of borrowed money.

All children learn very early in life, in the home, about help from adults, security with adults, trust of others, and the extent to which life is pleasant or painful. Communication develops early too. Words, intonation, gesture, inhibitions, listening with care, or withdrawing are all learned as children observe and experience how they are valued in the family and how they are to value others—both peers and adults.

One mother, speaking of a previous Parents Association meeting, said, "In that there meeting the principal and all the teachers called us dopes—poor slobs that don't know what our kids are getting from school." To which the principal immediately countered: "Why, Mrs. _____ , you know very well that no one said anything of the kind in that meeting," and the mother in question replied, "Maybe you didn't say it, but that's what the atmosphere said." However correct or incorrect this parent was in her perception, it is clear that communication between her and the professional staff would be difficult.[8]

Conflicts in values between the lower-class child and the middle-class teacher are *inevitable*. The concepts of authority, education, religion, goals, society, delinquency, time orientation, violence, sex, and money are viewed very differently by the middle-class teacher and the families of the inner-city poor.

Since many parents are reluctant to come to school until they know and trust the people there, it is necessary for the school to go to the parents. Visiting in the homes gives each teacher an opportunity to see a child in the family setting. Parents are usually convinced that the teacher is interested in learning ways to work successfully with their child. Such visits need to be made when there are no pressing negative problems needing solutions. Schools should do everything possible to help parents help their children learn in school. Even though parents look to the school with hope, many are fearful and confused in relation to the school. Principals who wish to bring about change are often baffled by what seems to them to be teacher indifference.

Many of the undesirable characteristics of the poor of Appalachia are common to the inner-city poor. Scarnato reported from Appalachia:

A few years ago, a public spirited group of doctors in Kanawha County, in which the state capitol is located, gave a physical and psychiatric examination to some

329 welfare clients listed as totally disabled, and they found no cases of conscious malingering and found that strong and conscious feelings of inferiority and guilt were resulting in depressive apathy and serious physical illness. The result of their findings was summed up in the graphic phrase, "Idleness is a disease."[9]

Urban ghettos are a world incomprehensible to many beginning middle-class teachers who may be selected to teach them. Hilliard found that for millions of the hard-core poor in Chicago, their ghetto segregated them, unemployment was very high, and many, many adults lacked adequate literacy skills for even unskilled employment. Lost in a feeling of hopelessness, discriminated against in many subtle ways, and without resources to climb out of the deep rut that entombs them, these people have no way to become sufficiently integrated into the mores and culture of the middle class. Yet, Hilliard found also that when these people were offered literacy education, their response as a group was enthusiastic, their attendance was excellent, their personal appearance indicated a strong desire to conform, and the adult education classes had few discipline problems.[10]

The Child in the Learning Situation in the Inner-City School

Ausubel considered the motivational aspects of learning as an integral part of the real life learning situation:

Doing without being interested in what one is doing results in relatively little permanent learning, since it is reasonable to suppose that only those materials can be meaningfully incorporated on a long-term basis into an individual's structure of knowledge that are relevant to areas of concern in his psychological field. Learners who have little need to know and understand quite naturally expend little learning effort; manifest an insufficiently meaningful learning set; fail to develop precise meanings, to reconcile new ideas with existing concepts, and to formulate new propositions in their own words; and do not devote enough time and energy to practice and review. Material is therefore never sufficiently consolidated to form an adequate foundation for sequential learning.[11]

Motivation to learn is derived generally from a child's natural curiosity and predisposition to explore, to manipulate, and to cope with the environment. Theoretically, meaningful school learning, when successful, furnishes its own reward. Teachers should never completely give up the idea that if children achieve adequate success in the learning situation, the success will in turn generate motivation. This is most apt to happen when teachers are able to generate contagious excitement and enthusiasm about the subjects they teach, and when they are people with whom the learners can identify.

Because lower-class students often have an anti-intellectual and pragmatic attitude toward the academic purposes of the school, it may be much harder for the teacher to motivate them. For this reason, such intrinsic motivation is even *more* necessary for inner-city children than for middle-class children. For the motivation to be intrinsic to the learning probably requires that rewards be more immediate and experiences be more concrete.

McCreary observed:

Early in the school careers of many socially disadvantaged youths, teachers notice an eagerness, a very great responsiveness to new experiences and especially to the kindness, personal attention, and assistance that some teachers give. Some children come to school very early in the morning, because they like the teacher and the warmth, physical and personal, that they find in the classroom. Some want to stay on after school to help the teacher or to talk with her. But for far too many, the early responsiveness to affection and to learning is destroyed by experiences of failure. Teachers need to find ways to strengthen and maintain the initial enthusiasm for school characteristic of many disadvantaged children by providing continuing opportunities for success and recognition.[12]

Levy studied elementary education at Harvard and did student teaching in a middle-class school in Lexington, Mass. Then she wrote of her experience as a fourth grade teacher in Harlem:

What impressed me most was the fact that my children (9–10 years old) are already cynical and disillusioned about school, themselves, and life-in-general. They are hostile, rebellious, and bitter. Some belong to gangs, some sniff glue, and some even have police records. They are hyperactive and are constantly in motion. . . .[13]

Most teachers . . . grow up in and are trained to work in a middle-class environment. Working in a Negro slum school is in many ways like going to a foreign country. The values, interests, goals, experiences, and even language of the children are quite different and often in conflict with the middle-class oriented school and its teachers.[14]

Levy emphasized two points in teacher education:

. . . need to train teachers to be able to deal with an attempt to overcome their own "culture shock" and "culture bias" . . . need to be prepared to deal with parents who may be illiterate or partly illiterate, concerned but helpless, or hostile and abusive.[15]

Deutsch, studying underprivileged children in New York City, found that early in life these children develop a "negative self-image." His observers recorded derogatory remarks made by teachers toward individual children:

The most frequent such remark was to call a child "stupid," and as a result, the teacher, and through the teacher, the school played a role in reinforcing the negative self-image of the child, and contributed a negative reason for learning.[16]

Bettelheim suggested that occasionally teachers misread children's behavior and do not really understand the deep-seated feelings children have. He counseled teachers to take seriously the remarks of the hurt child:

If a child says to you, "I hate your ugly white face," you are certainly going to be bothered unless you don't take the child seriously. . . . If we don't take a person's nasty remarks seriously, that means that we really don't take him seriously. It implies, "You're irresponsible, no good, of no account." Because if a person is of any account, then it seems to me that we must take seriously what he says.[17]

Henry, in an article called "White People's Time, Colored People's Time," said:

Poor children often come to school unfed, after wretched nights torn by screaming, fighting, bed-wetting; often they cannot sleep because of cold and rats. They come to class hungry, sleepy, and emotionally upset. To start routine schoolwork effectively at once is impossible.[18]

To attempt, constructively, to meet this problem, he suggested:

Their teachers should breakfast with them at school. The school should, of course, furnish the food, perhaps out of government surplus. School breakfast would accomplish two things: it would feed hungry children, otherwise unable to concentrate adequately on their work; and it would bring teacher and pupil together in an informal and friendly atmosphere, associated with satisfaction, before the strain of classroom constriction and peer-group pressures dictate that teacher become an enemy. It is essential, therefore, that the teacher be present.[19]

A program like this suggested by Dr. Henry in Kansas City brought about immediate and sharp improvement in attendance, behavior, and in schoolwork. The more the teachers know about the emotional management of these children, the better.

The President's 1969 message to Congress on the Economic Opportunity Act emphasized the importance of providing intellectual stimulation during the early years to enable children of the inner-city poor to interact with middle-class children when in the public school:

We have learned . . . that environment has its greatest impact on the development of intelligence when that development is proceeding most rapidly—that is, in those earliest years. . . . So crucial is the matter of early growth that we must make a national commitment to providing all American children an opportunity for healthful and stimulating development during the first five years of life.[20]

| **Sociocultural Problems in the School That Cause Failure** | The school has been aware for decades that large numbers of minority group children—blacks, Latins, Indians—fail or become severely retarded educationally as they are promoted through the public schools. Expenditures for additional instruction materials and for small-group remedial teaching have not solved the problem. |

McDermott has argued that the cleavage between the teacher, with one set of values and behaviors, and the minority child, with a quite different set of values and behaviors, may actually be contributing to the school failure. McDermott attributed this failure to something he called "the politics of everyday life." By that term he meant that the patterns of attention or inattention, of motivation to learn or resistance to learning, and of feeling "with the teacher" or "against the teacher" are actually a child's rational adaptation to the subtle messages transferred from teacher to child all day in the classroom. Support vs. antagonism, trust vs. deference, respect vs. anxiety, and success vs. failure—all are learned responses in a mutually misunderstanding social atmosphere. In such an atmosphere the student can learn how not to see—or, more specifically, how not to look in order not to see. In this politics of everyday life, minority children may learn how *not* to read; *not* to attend to printed information. Once the teacher treats the child as inadequate, the child will find the teacher oppressive. Once the child finds the teacher to be oppressive, the child will start to behave inadequately. Once behaviors become dichotomized, as two opposing forces in the school, the student can take sides by attending or by not attending. Those who attend learn to read; those who do not attend do not learn to read.[21]

Language and Concept Development to Improve Literacy Skills

Inner-city children may have gone to school at age six without ever having had their mothers sing them traditional lullabies and with no knowledge of nursery rhymes. Similarly, they may not have been told any of the fairy stories or folklore of their country. They may have taken few trips. Deutsch found many children had not been farther than two miles from home even in downtown New York City. They may well be children of a minority group, sent to inferior schools, taught by indifferent teachers. As early as age six, they had been isolated from many rich experiences that other children their age had enjoyed. Their isolation may have been caused by poverty, meagerness of intellectual resources at home, or the incapacity, illiteracy, or indifference of the adults with whom they have lived.

Brooks recommended:

1. Standard English should and can be taught successfully as though it were a second language to children who speak nonstandard English as a result of cultural differences or cultural deprivation.

2. If standard English is taught as a second language, it is not necessary to insist that the child reject entirely the other or "first" language.[22]

Language serves different purposes for lower-class, inner-city children. For them, language controls others more than it conveys information. They learn to respond because the speaker is a figure of authority. Verbal interchange is apt to be an order, request, or threat expressed in a single word, an idiomatic expression, or a short sentence.

This language is considered substandard by middle-class employers. It might better be considered *non*standard since it is an effective way for children to communicate at home and with their friends. Effective communication is the primary goal of language. However, if disadvantaged children are to have a fair chance in our mobile society, they must learn standard English for use in school and on the job. They may retain their dialect for use with family and close friends.[23]

There must be increased coordinated effort among schools, local government, and other social and civic agencies. School faculties must carry out academic studies of the impact of social-class differences on students and teachers. These studies need to be done community by community. And there must be direct teaching aimed at changing attitudes and self-concepts for the students, for the teachers, and for the parents.[24]

Teaching strategies should follow three basic guidelines. (1) Initial teaching should be geared to the learner's state of readiness. (2) It should provide the necessary foundation for successful sequential learning. (3) It should provide structured learning materials that will facilitate efficient sequenced learning.[25] Such a teaching plan demands that all subject matter that learners cannot economically assimilate at their present level of academic functioning be eliminated. One of the Philadelphia programs provides for an on-school-time, in-service training program for teachers. While the teachers are attending in-service sessions, their classes participate in a carefully planned program of storytelling, literature films, filmstrips, and recordings. Library books have been provided to support the special literature program. This program has been very effective in raising reading achievement levels.[26]

The Junior High School 43 Project in New York City was designed as a comprehensive approach to effective education of culturally different children. It provided the following services: systematic guidance and counseling; clinical services when indicated; a cultural enrichment program which included trips to the theater, museums, opera, college campuses; a parent-education program; and a systematic supplementary remedial program in reading, mathematics, and languages.[27]

When teachers have a low expectation level for their children's learning, the children seldom exceed that expectation. The process may well represent a self-fulfilling prophecy.

Acceptance of the child is of vital importance. It is based on a firm belief that the child is capable of self-determination. It seems to be a respect for the child's ability to be a thinking, independent, constructive human being.[28]

When a teacher respects the dignity of a child, whether or not he be six or sixteen, and treats the child with understanding, kindliness, and constructive help, she is developing in him an ability to look within himself for the answers to his problems, and to become responsible for himself as an independent individual in his own right.

Possibly the greatest contribution that educators can make to the younger generation is the type of guidance that places the emphasis on self-initiative and transmits to the young people by living example the fact that each individual is responsible for himself. In the final analysis, it is the ability to think constructively and independently that marks the educated man. Growth is a gradual process. It cannot be hurried. It comes from within the individual and cannot be imposed by force from without.

It is the relationship that exists between the teacher and her pupils that is the important thing. The teacher's responses must meet the real needs of the children and not just the material needs—reading, writing, arithmetic.[29]

Our inner-city schools contain thousands of culturally different boys and girls who are innately bright. The schools must identify those individuals and challenge and stimulate them so that they will be sure to overcome the shackles of poverty and keep alive their intellectual curiosity. Perhaps these highly intelligent students have been the most neglected in our system of mass education. Stimulation for them in enriched programs in language, social studies, and general science early in the elementary school may keep them motivated to succeed in the intellectual life.[30]

Teaching Reading to Children Who Speak Nonstandard English

The language model that a person has always used in communications with other people should not be considered a substandard version of school language. It is *neither wrong nor substandard.* It is a different dialect of the language. Every dialect is a complete, systematic, functioning language which is correct for the speaker who uses it at certain times, in certain places, and under certain circumstances.

The language that the child learns before coming to school is a valuable personal possession. Likewise, the people about whom the child cares most are not to be labeled *incorrect* or *inferior* because they do not use the language of the school.

A few suggestions for the teacher:

1. The best way to reflect both the language and the experience of a child is to *record them as he or she brings them* to the classroom.

2. The closer the language of the material in the book matches the language the child would customarily use, the easier the reading task will be, especially for beginning readers.

3. When a child's nonstandard language is intact, systematic, and organized, and the child's experiences are known, these are the strengths he most needs in learning to read.

4. But after the child has read his own stories, in his own dialect, there is probably no need for the creation of specific dialect materials for wide-scale use in teaching beginning reading to speakers of nonstandard dialects. Of course, we need to use trade books such as *Stevie*[31] and *Train Ride,*[32] which reflect the everyday nonstandard language of their characters. Such books are fun to read or listen to but are not meant to serve as basal readers. Pilon provides a short list of such books. She further discusses working with *is* and *are* and the inflectional endings *s* and *ed* and provides specific methodology for the teacher and lists of materials to use with children.[33]

Seymour provides numerous exercises to help the nonstandard language user with consonant clusters, tense and person markers, and plurals and possessives.[34]

Baratz does not accept the idea that there is no need for dialect-specific materials in basal readers. She wrote in the early '70s that school use of dialect readers was "an idea whose time has not yet come," but she believed that it would come in the future.[35]

5. Reading is not *really* "talk written down." Notice, for example:

The "Sounds" We Speak	The Words We Write
Itzabook.	It is a book.
nooshooz	new shoes
plejeleejens	pledge allegiance
Juwannago?	Do you want to go?

The root of the problem is not in the nonstandard English itself. Rather the problem is embodied in the attitudes expressed about it by teachers and other adults.

Teachers should:

1. Teach Standard English as a second language to those students who have habituated an oral nonstandard language pattern.

2. Use nonstandard dialect in written form for beginning reading. If the teacher begins the reading program with a language-experience approach, this should be no problem.

3. Be sure that the speakers understand clearly that there are two variations of the same language. Their pronunciation "fits" the written-down language too if the teacher emphasizes understanding. Labov wrote:

> There is no reason to believe that any nonstandard vernacular is in itself an obstacle to learning. The chief problem is ignorance of language on the part of all concerned. . . . Teachers are being told to ignore the language of Negro children as unworthy of attention and useless for learning. They are being taught to hear every utterance of the child as evidence of his mental inferiority. As linguists, we are unanimous in condemning this view as bad observation, bad theory, and bad practice.[36]

There is abundant evidence that traditional teaching of "language" to speakers of nonstandard dialects of English has been ineffective. Most culturally different students leave school after twelve years still using the nonstandard variety of English they were using when they came to school. Many teachers *still* project the attitude that the language used by the nonstandard speaker is inferior; that all nonstandard dialects are *substandard*.

Sherk analyzed the language produced by five-year-olds in Kansas City and reported:

> Language is a very personal thing. Pupils whose language is always criticized soon come to feel that it is themselves that are being criticized, and this reflects on their parents, their neighbors, and their whole world. Because teachers refuse to accept their words, pupils feel they are not accepted as persons. In turn, pupils reject their teachers, and thereby in effect they reject school language, textbook language, and the language of the larger society.[37]

A Rationale for the Teacher

Standard English is a language system. So is nonstandard English. Nonstandard English has features which deviate from Standard English in systematic and predictable ways. Nonstandard English provides a functional, efficient, and satisfying means of communication among its users, just as does standard English among its users.

In order to work effectively with children who speak a nonstandard dialect of English, teachers must learn to understand the dialect. Teachers must first accept the language of the students; second, carefully analyze the language they hear children use; and third, decide whether some of the features of the child's language need to be the focus of formal language instruction. Such formal language instruction would likely entail practice exercises patterned after methodology in teaching English to speakers of other languages. Standard English is needed by the student as an alternate dialect. In critical situations, the student must be able to communicate in standard English without embarrassment; he must recognize those situations in which standard English is the only appropriate way to respond.

Black English can generally be described in the following way:

Initial consonants are usually standard except *th*, which is *d*.

A few initial consonant clusters are altered: *stream* for *scream*.

R's are generally omitted: *guard* becomes *god*.

L's are frequently omitted: *tall* becomes *toe; help* becomes *hep; fault* becomes *fought*.

M and *n* are expressed as nasalized preceding vowels: *ram* and *ran* sound alike.

Final consonant clusters are simplified: *past* becomes *pass; bites* becomes *bite; nest* becomes *nes*.

The consonant cluster *sk* becomes *ks: ask* becomes *aks*.

Final consonants may be weak or missing: *ba* may represent *bat, bad*, or *bag*.

Final voiced *th* may be sounded *v: breathe* becomes *breav;* final voiceless *th* may be sounded *f: breath* may become *breaf*.

Before *m* and *n,* the vowels *e* and *i* may be pronounced the same: *Pen = pin; ten = tin*.

Dorothy Seymour has listed a few of the grammatical forms which teachers will find to be typical of Black English.[38]

Grammar	Standard English	Black English
1. Verb usage	He runs.	He run.
Present tense	He is running.	He run.
Present progressive	He took it.	He taken it.
Past tense, irreg.	He has taken it.	He have took it.
Past perf., irreg.	I will do it, or I am going	I'm a do it.
Future	to do it.	
Present habitual	He is (always, usually) doing it.	He be doing it.
Past habitual	He (always) used to do it.	He been doing it.
2. Negation	I don't have any.	I don't got none.
	He hasn't walked.	He ain't walked.
3. Question	How did he fix that?	How he fix that?
Indirect question	I asked if he fixed that.	I asked (aksed) did he fix that.
4. Treatment of subject	My brother is here.	My brother, he here.
5. Noun plural	those books; men	them book; mens
6. Pronouns	We have to go.	Us got to go.
7. Possessive	Jim's hat	Jim hat
	The hallway of Jim's family's building	Jim and them hallway

Summary

Teachers of students who habitually use nonstandard English must study and accept the children's language and, in due course, help them to use both nonstandard and Standard English efficiently and appropriately. Some of the generalizations upon which this statement is based are:

1. There is such a thing as Black English. Black English and standard English differ phonologically and syntactically. They also differ in vocabulary.
2. Generally, in the past, nonstandard English was rejected. However, insistence by teachers on the use of only standard English has not led to satisfactory achievement in curriculum practice.
3. A child brings to school at least six years of life experience, which embody the cultural, social, economic, and other values the child has acquired.
4. Rather than deny any value of the language, teachers must encourage students to use it in positive ways to assure self-confidence and to develop a competent feeling.
5. Teachers must be sensitive when communicating with pupils so they do not convey a nonaccepting attitude toward the language the child speaks. The teacher must also be keenly sensitive to nonverbal clues.
6. Students speaking a nonstandard English dialect have a well structured, sophisticated language and vocabulary which is suited to their everyday needs. They must never be looked upon as having *no* language or an inferior language.
7. In itself, speaking nonstandard English is not detrimental to learning how to read. A child with a nonstandard dialect is likely to have the *same capacity to learn* to read as a user of a middle-class standard dialect.
8. Of course, the standard dialect must be taught, and it should be learned. Even though there is nothing inherently *wrong* or *bad* about using a nonstandard dialect, there will be times when it will be detrimental to the person who cannot use standard English (prevent one from getting the job wanted, for example).

For Further Reading

Abraham, Rogers D., and Rudolph Troike. *Language and Cultural Diversity in American Education.* Englewood Cliffs, N.J.: Prentice-Hall, 1972.

Allen, Virginia French. "Teaching Standard English as a Second Dialect." *Teachers College Record* 68(February 1967):355–70.

Baratz, Joan C., and Roger Shuy, eds. *Teaching Black Children to Read.* Washington, D.C.: Center for Applied Linguistics, 1969.

Burling, Robbins. *English in Black and White.* New York: Holt, Rinehart & Winston, 1973.

Cazden, Courtney, Vera John, and Dell Hymes. *Functions of Language in the Classroom.* New York: Teachers College Press, 1972.

Claerbaut, David. *Black Jargon in White America.* Grand Rapids, Mich.: Wm. •B. Eerdman's Publ. Co., 1972. The author discusses his own frustration in learning to teach black junior high school students in the inner-city and what he did about it.

Cohen, Alan, and Thelma Cooper. "Seven Fallacies: Reading Retardation and the Urban Disadvantaged Beginning Reader." *The Reading Teacher* 26(October 1972):38–45.

Cronnell, B., D. Kilgman, and G. Vern. "Black English; Pronunciation and Spelling Performance." *Elementary English* 49(December 1972):1247–53.

DeStefano, Johanna S., ed. *Language, Society, and Education: A Profile of Black English.* Worthington, Ohio: Charles A. Jones, 1973.

Dillard, J. L. *Black English.* New York: Random House, 1972.

————— . "The English Teacher and the Language of the Newly Integrated Student." *Teachers College Record* 68(February 1967):115–20.

Fasold, Ralph W., and Walter Wolfram. "Some Linguistic Features of Negro Dialect." In *Language, Society, and Education: A Profile of Black English,* edited by Johanna S. DeStefano. Worthington, Ohio: Charles A. Jones, 1973.

Finocchiaro, Mary. *Teaching English as a Second Language,* rev. ed. New York: Harper & Row, Publishers, 1970.

Fries, C. C. *Teaching and Learning English as a Foreign Language.* Ann Arbor, Mich.: University of Michigan Press, 1945.

Gottlieb, David, and Charles E. Ramsey. *Understanding Children of Poverty.* Chicago, Ill.: Science Research Associates, 1967.

Hockman, Carol H. "Black Dialect Reading Tests in the Urban Elementary School." *The Reading Teacher* 26(March 1973):572–80.

Horn, Thomas, ed. *Reading for the Disadvantaged.* New York: Harcourt Brace Jovanovich, 1970.

Houston, Susan H. "Black English." *Psychology Today* (March 1973):45–48.

Jacobson, Rodolfo. "Cultural Linguistic Pluralism and the Problem of Motivation." *TESOL Quarterly* 5(December 1971):265–84.

Johns, Jerry L. "What Do Inner City Children Prefer to Read?" *The Reading Teacher* 26 (February 1973):462–67.

Labov, William. "The Logic of Non-Standard English." In *Language, Society, and Education: A Profile of Black English,* edited by Johanna S. DeStefano. Worthington, Ohio: Charles A. Jones, 1973.

————— . *The Social Stratification of English in New York City.* Washington, D.C.: Center for Applied Linguistics, 1966.

Laffey, James L., and Roger Shuy. *Language Differences: Do They Interfere?* Newark, Del.: International Reading Assn., 1973.

McDermott, Ray P. "Achieving School Failure: An Anthropological Approach to Literacy and Social Stratification." In *Theoretical Models and Processes of Reading,* 2d ed., edited by Harry Singer and Robert Ruddell, pp. 389–428. Newark, Del.: International Reading Assn., 1976.

————— . "The Ethnography of Speaking and Reading." In *Linguistic Theory: What Can It Say about Reading?* edited by Roger Shuy, pp. 153–85. Newark, Del.: International Reading Assn., 1977.

Merriam, Eve. *The Inner City Mother Goose.* New York: Simon & Schuster, 1969.

Reed, Carol. "Adapting TESL Approaches to the Teaching of Written Standard English as a Second Dialect to Speakers of American Black English Vernacular." *TESOL Quarterly* 7(September 1973):289–307.

Rivers, Wilga. *The Psychologist and the Foreign Language Teacher.* Chicago: University of Chicago Press, 1964.

Rystrom, Richard. "Caveat Qui Credit (Let the Believer Beware)." *Journal of Reading* 16(December 1972):236–40.

Savage, John. *Linguistics for Teachers, Selected Readings.* Chicago: Science Research Associates, 1973.

Saville-Troike, Muriel. *Foundations for Teaching English as a Second Language.* Englewood Cliffs, N.J.: Prentice-Hall, 1976.

Seymour, Dorothy Z. "Black English, Black Speech." *Commonweal,* November 19, 1971, pp. 175–77.

————. "Black English in the Classroom." *Today's Education* 62(February 1973):63–64.

Sherk, John K., Jr. "Psychological Principles in a Strategy for Teaching the Reading of a Standard Dialect." In *Reading: Process and Pedagogy,* 19th Yearbook, edited by George B. Schick and Merrill M. May. Milwaukee: National Reading Conference, 1970.

Shuy, Roger, ed. *Linguistic Theory: What Can It Say about Reading?* Newark, Del.: International Reading Assn., 1977.

Smith, Holly. "ERIC RCS Report: Standard or Non-standard: Is There an Answer?" *Elementary English,* 1972.

Stewart, William A. "On the Use of Negro Dialect in the Teaching of Reading." In *Language, Society, and Education: A Profile of Black English,* edited by Johanna S. DeStefano. Worthington, Ohio: Charles A. Jones, 1973.

Wolfram, Walter. "The Nature of Non-standard Dialect Divergence." *Elementary English,* Vol. 47, May, 1970.

————. "Sociolinguistic Premises and the Nature of Non-standard Dialects." *Language, Communication and Rhetoric in Black America.* New York: Harper & Row, 1972.

Zintz, Miles V. *Corrective Reading,* 3d ed., especially chapter 11, Dubuque, Ia.: Wm. C. Brown, 1977. "Teaching The Linguistically and Culturally Different Child," pp. 293–337.

————. *What the Classroom Teacher Should Know About Bilingual Education.* ERIC, TESOL, ED 028427, 57 pp. 1969.

Notes

1. This episode was contributed by Dr. Catherine Loughlin, Professor of Education, University of New Mexico.
2. Oscar Lewis, "The Culture of Poverty," *Scientific American* 215 (October 1966):25.
3. Ibid., pp. 19–25.
4. Walter B. Miller, "Lower-Class Culture as a Generating Milieu of Gang Delinquency," *Journal of Social Issues* (1958).
5. Israel Woronoff, "Negro Male Identification Problems and the Education Process," *Journal of Educational Sociology* (September 1962); reprinted in Staten W. Webster, ed., *Understanding the Educational Problems of the Disadvantaged Learner* (San Francisco: Chandler Publishing Co., 1966), pp. 293–95.

6. Michael Harrington, "The Invisible Land," reprinted in *The Disadvantaged Learner,* ed. Staten W. Webster (San Francisco: Chandler Publishing Co., 1966), p. 17.

7. Ibid., p. 18.

8. John Niemeyer, "Some Guidelines to Desirable Elementary School Reorganization," in *The Disadvantaged Learner,* ed. Staten W. Webster (San Francisco: Chandler Publishing Co., 1966), p. 394.

9. Samuel A. Scarnato, "The Disadvantaged of Appalachia," a presentation made at a meeting of a special language study committee of the National Council of Teachers of English, Champaign, Illinois, July 1968.

10. Raymond M. Hilliard, "Massive Attack on Illiteracy," *American Library Association Bulletin* 57 (1963):1034–38.

11. David P. Ausubel, "A Teaching Strategy for Culturally Deprived Pupils: Cognitive and Motivational Considerations," *The School Review* 71 (Winter 1963):457.

12. Eugene McCreary, "Some Positive Characteristics of Disadvantaged Learners and Their Implications for Education," in *The Disadvantaged Learner,* ed. Staten W. Webster (San Francisco: Chandler Publishing Co., 1966), pp. 51–52.

13. Betty Levy, "An Urban Teacher Speaks Out," in *The Disadvantaged Learner,* ed. Staten W. Webster (San Francisco: Chandler Publishing Co., 1966), p. 430.

14. Ibid., p. 434.

15. Ibid., p. 435.

16. Martin Deutsch, *Minority Group and Class Status as Related to Social and Personality Factors in Scholastic Achievement,* Monograph No. 2 (Ithaca: The Society for Applied Anthropology, Cornell University, 1960), p. 26.

17. Bruno Bettelheim, "Teaching the Disadvantaged," *NEA Journal* (September 1965).

18. Jules Henry, "White People's Time, Colored People's Time," in *The Disadvantaged Learner,* ed. Staten W. Webster (San Francisco: Chandler Publishing Co., 1966), p. 190.

19. Ibid.

20. From the President's message to Congress on the Economic Opportunity Act, *A News Summary of the War on Poverty,* Office of Economic Opportunity, 24 February 1969.

21. Ray P. McDermott, "Achieving School Failure: An Anthropological Approach to Literacy and Social Stratification," in *Theoretical Models and Processes of Reading,* 2d ed., ed. Harry Singer and Robert Ruddell (Newark, Del.: International Reading Assn., 1976), pp. 389–428; Ray P. McDermott, "The Ethnography of Speaking and Reading," in *Linguistic Theory: What Can It Say about Reading?* ed. Roger Shuy (Newark, Del.: International Reading Assn., 1977), pp. 153–85.

22. Charlotte K. Brooks, "Some Approaches to Teaching English as a Second Language," in *Non-Standard Speech and the Teaching of English,* ed. William A. Stewart (Washington, D.C.: Center for Applied Linguistics, 1964).

23. Ellen Newman, "An Experiment in Oral Language," in *The Disadvantaged Learner,* ed. Staten W. Webster (San Francisco: Chandler Publishing Co., 1966), p. 570.

24. Delmo Della-Dora, "The Culturally Disadvantaged: Educational Implications of Certain Social-Cultural Phenomena," in *Education and Social Crisis: Perspectives on Teaching Disadvantaged Youth,* ed. Everett T. Keach et al. (New York: John Wiley & Sons, Inc., 1967), pp. 279–80.

25. David P. Ausubel, "A Teaching Strategy for Culturally Deprived Pupils: Cognitive and Motivational Considerations," *The School Review* 71 (Winter 1963):454–55.

26. Ibid., pp. 329–30.

27. Kenneth B. Clark, "Educational Stimulation of Racially Disadvantaged Children," in *Education and Social Crisis: Perspectives on Teaching Disadvantaged Youth,* ed. Everett T. Keach et al. (New York: John Wiley & Sons, 1967), p. 308.

28. Virginia Mae Axline, *Play Therapy* (Boston: Houghton Mifflin, 1969), p. 21.

29. Ibid., pp. 75–76.

30. Staten W. Webster, ed., *Educating the Disadvantaged Learner* (San Francisco: Chandler Publishing Co., 1966), pp. 580–81.

31. John Steptoe, *Stevie* (New York: Harper & Row, 1969).

32. John Steptoe, *Train Ride* (New York: Harper & Row, 1971).

33. Barbara Pilon, "Culturally Divergent Children and Creative Language Activities," in *Language Differences: Do They Interfere?* ed. James L. Laffey and Roger Shuy (Newark, Del.: International Reading Assn., 1973), pp. 129–45.

34. Dorothy Seymour, "Neutralizing the Effect of the Non-Standard Dialect," in *Language Differences: Do They Interfere?* ed. James L. Laffey and Roger Shuy (Newark, Del.: International Reading Assn., 1973), pp. 149–60.

35. Joan Baratz, "The Relationship of Black English to Reading: A Review of Research," in *Language Differences: Do They Interfere?* ed. James Laffey and Roger Shuy (Newark, Del.: International Reading Assn., 1973), p. 110.

36. William Labov, "Logic of Nonstandard English," in *Language, Society, and Education: A Profile of Black English,* Johanna S. DeStefano (Worthington, Ohio: Charles A. Jones, 1973), p. 43.

37. John K. Sherk, Jr., "Psychological Principles in a Strategy for Teaching the Reading of a Standard Dialect," in *Reading: Process and Pedagogy,* 19th Yearbook, ed. George B. Shick and Merrill M. May (Milwaukee: National Reading Conference, 1970), p. 291.

38. Dorothy Seymour, "Black English in the Classroom," *Today's Education* 62 (February 1973): 63–64.

18

Exceptional Children and Reading Instruction

Any teacher who has spent a few years in elementary school classrooms is well aware from firsthand experience that there are in all heterogeneously grouped classes, a few rapid learners, a few more who are above-average learners, a larger group of middle achievers, a smaller number of below-average achievers, and a few with learning difficulties. Occasionally, the teacher has one whom he considers a *very* rapid learner or a *very* slow learner. While the limitations of intelligence tests in current use are well known, one can accept without qualification the inevitable range of abilities that must be dealt with in any self-contained classroom (see chapter 2).

Bond and Brueckner have presented the possible combinations of rate and accuracy among the students in a given class as shown in table 18.1. Individuals in groups I, IV, and VII are able to perform their work in a highly accurate manner while individuals in groups I, II, and III are all reading at rapid rates but with very different degrees of accuracy. Group V pupils represent those at the middle of the distribution in both rate and accuracy, and those in group IX are both very slow and very inaccurate. This diagram is intended to help beginning teachers appreciate group variability, but it is only *theoretical;* no class really has these nine distinct categories.

If the teacher is going to take into account the basic principle that the longer children attend school, the greater will become the spread of differences in almost any selected ability, then some adaptations of the total program must be made in order to make it fit both the rapid learner and the slow learner. The differences are not *in kinds* of learning, but, rather, *in degree* of children's accomplishments.

Therefore, it is pointed out that the general suggestions offered throughout this book for a developmental reading program apply to the atypical students as well as to the majority of the class.

Some of the characteristics of gifted children, handicapped children, and gifted children with special problems, and some working principles for teachers who have these children in their classes are presented in this chapter. A great deal of literature is readily available in each of these areas, and the teacher will profit greatly from specialized courses in professional schools devoted to gifted children, enrichment programs for all children, and methods of teaching retarded, neurologically impaired, or emotionally disturbed children.

Table 18.1 Spread of abilities in rate and accuracy normally found among the students in a given class.

From *The Diagnosis and Treatment of Learning Difficulties,* copyright 1955, Meredith Corporation, p. 18. Reproduced by permission of Appleton-Century-Crofts.

		Accuracy		
		High	**Average**	**Low**
Rate	**High**	I High in both rate and accuracy	II High in rate; average in accuracy	III High in rate; low in accuracy
	Average	IV Average in rate; high in accuracy	V Average in both rate and accuracy	VI Average in rate; low in accuracy
	Low	VII Low in rate; high in accuracy	VIII Low in rate; average in accuracy	IX Low in both rate and accuracy

Education of the Intellectually Gifted

The goals of education for the able learners, the gifted, are the same as for all children: self-realization, human relationships, economic efficiency, and civic responsibility. For the gifted, greater emphasis may be given to creativity, use of abstract intelligence, critical reading and thinking, growth toward communal versus individual values, and opportunities to experience leadership and develop leadership qualities.

Teachers desperately need to help the general citizenry understand that equality of opportunity in education does not mean identical opportunities for all children of the same chronological age in a community. Gifted children may begin the school year in September with most of the knowledge and skills that other children in the same classroom will acquire during the course of the school year. If the year is to be constructively used, the gifted children too must be challenged to grow. They do not need to do the exercises that many other children do just to demonstrate that *they can do them.* Teachers have inventories, checklists, pretests, and unit tests of skills and abilities which can be administered to find out which children already have the skills. Those children can spend their time on enriching activities that make use of the skills. It is imperative that teachers have many different activities for the children in a class. There is no other way that each individual can have a challenging job to "dig into."

Most schools accept the recommendation that some combination of moderate acceleration and enrichment will produce the best results in the education of gifted children. Each child must have enrichment types of activities that enrich for him or her. Acceleration makes it possible for a child to finish elementary school in five years instead of six; junior high school in two years instead of three; and/or senior high school in two years instead of three. It is better for some children than for others. Similarly, acceleration of two years may be more appropriate for some children than acceleration of one year would be for others.

Acceleration should evolve from staffing conferences at which principal, teacher, psychologist, and parent sit down together to review the case. Information should be available from the school social worker, school nurse, and school physician if it is contributory to the case.

If the so-called normal child spends twelve years going through the public school with its present academic bent, the slow learner should be privileged to spend thirteen years or more, and the gifted ought to be permitted to spend eleven or fewer years. Terman wrote in 1954 about the issue of educational acceleration for the gifted:

It seems that the schools are more opposed to acceleration now than they were thirty years ago. The lockstep seems to have become more and more the fashion, notwithstanding the fact that practically everyone who has investigated the subject is against it. [1]

In his follow-up studies of 1,500 gifted students, Terman found that 29 percent graduated from high school by age 16½ [2]. This group constituted his "accelerated" group. Compared to the remainder (ages 16½ to 18½ at graduation), they made better grades in college, were more apt to complete undergraduate work, and were more apt to go on to graduate school.

The major concern in the school for the gifted child should be to free the child to learn. If schools are able to provide adequate learning experiences, the gifted child will be challenged without respect to acceleration, enrichment, or segregation per se. Children must be *free* to learn outside the classroom, *free* to acquire information apart from formal teacher-pupil efforts, and *free* to work in small groups with good teacher-pupil planning but little teacher supervision. Providing learning experiences for children does not mean necessarily that the child even comes to school to learn—the school may make the experiences available somewhere else.

One of the greatest obstacles to better education of children may be faulty communication between parents and teachers. Parents may be poor communicators, and therefore teachers should go more than halfway. Teachers generally do not communicate nearly well enough with parents, even though they are supposedly prepared, ready, and anxious to do so.

It is especially important that teachers, in their desire to help gifted children, not use certain words that may arouse strong sentiments and negative notions. If teachers are to be challenged about whether they will "enrich," "accelerate," *or* "segregate," they will get nowhere. Maybe schools need to discard these words that have been misused and misapplied so teachers can think clearly about *all the ways* they can bring adequate learning experiences to children. Probably they best meet the needs of gifted children in the elementary school by individual and unique combinations of accelerating, segregating and *always* enriching.

Most of the country's gifted children are the direct responsibility of teachers in regular classrooms. In fact, almost every year each teacher has one or two gifted children enrolled in his or her class.

Teachers' attitudes vary. Some ignore high-ability children and try to teach them as if they were average. Others do nothing *special* to help them and rationalize that in a large class one can't. Some teachers give extra time to slow learners and rationalize that gifted children will take care of themselves.

Havighurst and De Haan reported a case study of a gifted boy in a junior high school social studies class.[3] As his special report, he chose to work alone on a study of national highway construction because the topic was in the news at that time.

An office of a large highway engineering company was located in the city. This company was working on projects in several states and had many books on materials, surveys, machinery, and cost estimates. As James began to develop his project of designing a system of highways, the teacher made appointments for him to go to the offices of the engineers and to laboratories. Soon he was making his own appointments. Sometimes he was gone from her class for as long as two weeks at a time, visiting these offices, making appointments with the engineers, consulting with them, and taking pictures of their models of highways.

He learned how to make maps and drawings on sheets of clear plastic that would overlay each other. He compiled data from the maps, describing how various cities and regions would be affected by the highway plan.

When the time came to make his report, he had a table piled with material and notebooks filled with figures and charts. He used an opaque projector to present his material. The report was a masterpiece. Later he made a report to the regional meeting of the engineers of the company where he had obtained so much help.

The authors point out that the significant aspect of the boy's experience is that the office staff of engineers was an invaluable resource in that community to help this boy in his project in the social studies. In another community, it may not be engineers but rather other specialists who can, in their way, be as helpful to other gifted children.

Havighurst has also stated:

Thinking, then, of the unusual child as the talented child, I suggest that we speak of four areas of talent. We have found this useful in our work: first, the area of intellectual talent—a child with high intelligence or high I.Q.; second, the area of artistic talent—talent in music, drawing or dramatics, and so on; third, the area of social leadership—this is something we sometimes do not think of as a talent, but certainly in our society a gift for social leadership is an important and precious thing; and, fourth, something which I cannot define so clearly but I like to call "creative intelligence" or the ability to find new ways of doing things and solving problems. . . .

The principal factor within the individual which affects the supply of talent is motivation. Motivation is necessary to the development of intellectual or artistic talent—the motivation being a desire to seek training and willingness to sacrifice other desires while undergoing training. Lack of motivation appears to be more powerful than lack of money in reducing the supply of talent.[4]

Pintner reminds school personnel:

Educators at all levels of instruction must divest themselves of the belief that gifted students can get along by themselves and that it is undemocratic to give them special education suited to their particular needs. And we must also dispel the fear sometimes expressed that the gifted may become selfish through too much consideration, for "it is precisely this group of individuals of great ability who, in the long run and as a group, will be the least selfish, the least likely to monopolize the good things in this world, and by their inventions and discoveries, by their creative work in the arts, by their contributions to government and social reform, by their activities in all fields, will in the future help humanity in its groping struggle upward toward a better civilization."[5]

The teacher is the most important factor in the classroom success of the gifted child:

Teachers of gifted children should display unusual sensitivity in recognizing the potentialities of such pupils; they should maintain a balance between individual and group work in the classroom; they should help pupils solve problems and resolve conflicts; they should aid pupils in mastering the knowledge needed for understanding themselves and the world; and they should display a sincere interest which will inspire confidence.[6]

"Young children can be bored by the school work offered to them. One first grader spoke sharply to his teacher, 'Take that pusillanimous primer away!' One can imagine how that teacher warmed up to him!"[7]

The objectives of reading instruction for the gifted are:[8]

1. Gaining proficiency in the techniques of reading and refining these skills in each successive year.

2. Learning how to use books for study projects: outlining, summarizing, and reporting on information gained from reading.

3. Exploring the wide world of reading, discovering the best books for every possible purpose and the books of special interest to the individual reader.

4. Learning how to use the facilities of the school library.

5. Becoming acquainted with the best literature and learning to appreciate the value of reading great books.

Nelson and Cleland list the following implications for the teacher of the intellectually gifted child:[9]

1. The teacher must possess an understanding of self.

2. The teacher must possess an understanding of giftedness.

3. The teacher should be a facilitator of learning rather than a director of learning.

4. The teacher must provide challenge rather than pressure.

5. The teacher must be as concerned with the process of learning as with the product of learning.

6. The teacher must provide feedback rather than judgment.

7. The teacher must provide alternate learning strategies.

8. The teacher must provide a classroom climate which promotes self-esteem and offers safety for creative and cognitive risk-taking.

The Bright Child Who Must Learn English as a Second Language

Many, many of our school children today are blessed with a bountiful amount of innate intelligence and learning ability and so demonstrate on tests which do not involve heavy use of English. Yet in school such children are almost completely unable to function because the school uses some language other than their own.

In many parts of the United States schools have done untold psychological damage to boys and girls, first by devaluing their first language, second by causing children to suspect that the school devalues them and, in turn, their families. If the school denies children the right to speak their own language, they can only conclude that it must be inferior—or at least that the teachers think it is inferior. If their language is no good and it is the only language their parents and whole extended family can use, they can only conclude that they must all be inferior. Such ego destruction can do serious harm to children as they progress through the school.

Native American students in college often have difficulties with the English language. One group of such students entering college expressed need for help in all the following areas: reading skills, vocabulary development, written and oral expression, spelling, taking notes, taking examinations, listening to lectures, and effective studying.

One student wrote about his reading problem in this way:

Looking back to my high school days, I find that the ACADEMIC course that caused the UTMOST agony was English. It was my belief that English was an *insurmountable obstacle;* but after a lengthy discussion with my English tutor, Mr. Charles, who is also a philosopher, I was enlighten *[sic]* that my belief was false. He said that English can be mastered if a student is willing to persistently and diligently works *[sic]* at it. . . . The principle cause of slow reading is lip reading of which I am guilty. To become an efficient reader, I must overcome this impediment. This I did by placing a pencil between my teeth.[10]

In a tutoring-counseling program on the university campus, a number of Native American students were given the Wechsler Adult Intelligence Scale. Almost invariably, there were large discrepancies between the performance scale and the verbal scale. A performance IQ score of 120 and a verbal IQ score of 80 for the same person was not an uncommon result. The low verbal score was attributable in large part to the language, culture, and experience barrier faced by the student.

Such nonsuccess stories testify to the failure of the schools and the teachers, *not* of the students.

A success story, on the other hand, would be more like the following. It is presented here to emphasize the importance of planned, sequenced lessons in order to prevent frustration and failure in learning a second language.

Edna was a thirteen-year-old Japanese girl transplanted suddenly and unexpectedly to a city in the American southwest to live with her uncle's family and attend school. Edna was very bright and spoke Japanese expertly but had heard very little English as spoken by native speakers. She had studied only a few isolated words. This young lady found herself in a junior high school attending eighth grade classes in mathematics, American history, general science, and English grammar and literature—all taught only in English.

Edna's aunt was perplexed that the school had no provision for meeting this problem. Her own difficulty using and understanding English was partly illustrated by an early telephone call with Edna's new language clinician when she was explaining how she was trying to make the young lady feel at home. She said she was "trying to break out the ice."

Edna was enrolled in the remedial reading clinic to study English as a second language. She reported to her school daily at 8:30 A.M. and left at 10:00 to catch a city bus to the reading clinic. Her tutors at the clinic were relatively unskilled in techniques for teaching English as a second language. Their formal education had prepared them to teach developmental reading skills remedially. However, they used the principles of teaching English as a second language (TESOL) as described in chapter 16, and helped Edna develop oral language ability to reproduce the language she heard. Her teachers quickly taught her the common utterances used in casual conversation. Every day for several weeks she practiced all the previously studied questions and answers and substitution drills and added new ones. The most common sentence structures were taught, modeled, repeated, drilled, and reviewed and, because Edna was a very bright girl and living in an environment where remembering the work had such high reward value, she quickly mastered the material.

Special attention was devoted to the common prepositions, verb tenses, homonyms, antonyms, synonyms, and personal pronouns. Dictation of simple sentences was begun early about subject matter to be presented in Edna's history and literature classes. Edna attended her tutoring sessions from early December until the following August.

Humorous moments occasionally broke the sometimes tense feelings Edna had because she wished she could learn English much faster than was humanly possible. One day early in the spring, when Edna was responding to elementary antonyms in English, her tutor gave the stimulus word *noisy*. She looked puzzled, and the tutor said, "The class is very noisy today." Edna's eyes lighted up, and she said in a loud voice, "Shut up!"

For methodology in second language teaching, the reader is referred to chapter 3, "Linguistic Foundations for Reading Instruction," and chapter 16, "Teaching Reading to the Bilingual Child."

Exceptional Children in Regular Classrooms

Classifying some children as having learning or behavior deviations has led to problems in the development of adequate school programs for them.[11]

1. Children so classified are often victimized by stigma associated with the label.
2. Assigning a label suggests that all the children given that label conform to a stereotyped behavioral expectation.
3. Some children who are labeled and placed in special programs may not really need a special education program.
4. Some children have been misplaced or misclassified.
5. Sometimes decisions for assigning children to special programs have been made without adequate data, without legal basis, and without parental involvement.

Public Law 94—142 has clarified several general concepts that all teachers must accept and work very hard to implement:[12]

1. All children can learn.
2. Education is that continuous, developmental process by which individuals learn to cope and to function within their environment.
3. Children with handicaps *may* participate in all programs and activities provided by the schools.
4. Every handicapped child *will be* provided a free appropriate education at no additional expense to the parents or guardian.
5. Diagnosis and evaluation will provide for those children who have different languages and cultures so they will not be discriminated against.

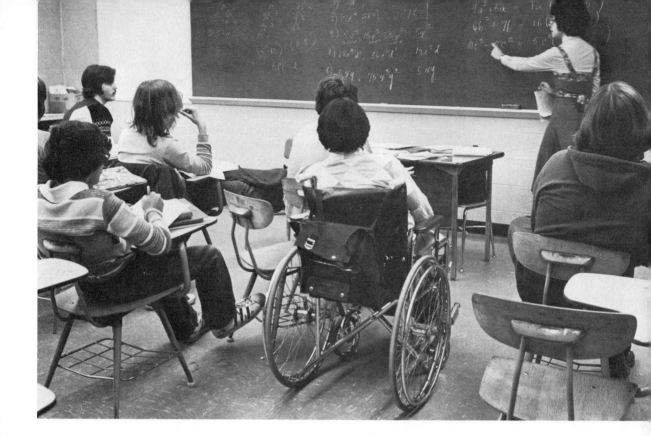

6. To the maximum extent possible, handicapped children will be educated with children who are not handicapped. All children will be provided an optimal learning environment.

7. Handicapped children are *children* first; second, they are children with special learning needs.

Mentally Retarded Children

John is nine and a half years old. He entered kindergarten at five and a half and after several weeks of observation of his intellectual and language immaturity, his kindergarten teacher had referred him to the school psychologist for an evaluation. There were no physical findings in his medical evaluation to indicate lack of development. His muscle tone, vision, hearing, motor coordination, and reflexes all seemed to be within the normal limits for a five-year-old. However, the individual intelligence test was administered and yielded a mental age of three years and nine months although he was five years and nine months at the time of testing. He was permitted to repeat kindergarten at age six and a half and to spend two years in the first grade. At nine and a half, he has been placed in second grade, and because of his physical growth and development, he will be permitted only one year in each grade from now on—unless he should be able to attend classes for the educable mentally retarded at some future date.

When John was retested by the pyschologist at a chronological age of nine years and seven months, the results showed his mental age to be only six years and three months. He comes from an "average" family with two girls ages seven and six who are doing well in school. Even though John is not quite as large as many boys nine and a half, he is one of the largest in his class of seven- and eight-year-olds. His physical skills in active play approximate those of second and third grade children. John is reasonably well accepted in the group but he needs a great deal of help to adjust socially: not to laugh too much, not to pester the other children, and not to put his hands on the others.

Since John will spend the year in the regular class, there are a few cautions the teacher must remember. He or she will try never to think or say aloud: "He doesn't really belong here; he ought to be in a room for the retarded." The teacher will realize that John is only one other different individual in a whole class of different individuals who each need planned, specific objectives. The teacher's attitude about differences is contagious and, for this reason, of primary importance.

The objectives for John's school year include his learning both social behaviors and academic behaviors. The general objectives are to help John in the following ways:

1. adjust to other members of the group;
2. extend reading readiness and develop beginning reading abilities;
3. learn habits of good health and safety;
4. develop personal habits of cleanliness, grooming, and neatness;
5. learn about his immediate environment;
6. build language and quantitative concepts;
7. learn habits of punctuality, orderliness, and following directions.

The teacher's objectives in language arts with respect to John are the following:

1. to use more oral than written language;
2. to give much instruction in following directions;
3. to extend his ability to listen with understanding;
4. to help him develop skills in beginning reading;
5. that he practice reading with another child at a level commensurate with his mental age and understanding in order to get repetition on basic sight words;
6. to teach him to read signs, labels, and brief explanations.

With John's motor coordination, he will be able to write anything he can read. Motivating him to do very well with manuscript writing will be one possible place where John can excel in the class. In the unit work of the class, there will be activities associated with the content in which John should be able to participate with small groups. Generalizations in science, social studies, health and safety that are explained in class may be understood to some degree by all members of the class.

The appreciations—music, art, physical education, and literature—are all areas where John can participate to some degree with the others. The teacher will be able to accept different levels of performance in the same activity.

The most important thing is that in a group of thirty John will not be *the only one* who is different, and the difference is a matter of degree, not kind. He may be more different in some respects than in others, but no two are alike.

The classroom teacher must be alert to the appearance of *slow learners* in the class. If such children can be identified early, their programs can be planned in terms of their functioning levels of ability so that the time in school will be used constructively even though they do not attain the statistical norms for the class. It is likewise extremely important for the teacher to know who slow learners *are not*. They *are not* children who learned another language as their first language and enroll in school as so-called bilinguals with a severe English language handicap. They *are not* children who have speech, hearing, or vision problems or neurological impairment or minimal brain dysfunction, which may or may not have been diagnosed. They *are not* children whose primary problems in school stem from emotional, social, or other personality difficulties. However, any child who is a slow learner may *also* have any of these problems concomitantly. Diagnosis should reveal a child's primary problem, and it should have the attention of the special educator before the secondary problems can be adequately addressed.

Slow learners are students whose general learning ability, as measured by individual intelligence tests, is below average. Slow learners have a degree of mental retardation which, to date, is believed to be a permanent handicap for which they must make the best possible adjustment. Regular classroom teachers, from time to time, will find mentally retarded boys and girls in their classrooms because this is the best provision in the school system. In individual cases, it may be better for such a child to remain with the *regular* class instead of being enrolled in a class for *slow learners* or a class for the *educable mentally retarded.*

Doll gave the following comprehensive definition of mental deficiency:

Mental deficiency is a state of social incompetence obtaining at maturity, or likely to obtain at maturity, resulting from developmental mental arrest of constitutional (hereditary or acquired) origin; the condition is essentially incurable through treatment and unremediable through training except as treatment and training instill habits which superficially compensate for the limitations of the person so affected while under favorable circumstances and for more or less limited periods of time.[13]

The curriculum goals for the mentally handicapped child are theoretically the same as for any child: achievement of self-realization, learning proper human relationships, achieving economic efficiency, and assuming civic responsibility. Achieving behavioral goals of self-discipline, self-development, self-actualization is primary. A life-experience curriculum will help the learner to achieve physical and mental health, useful knowledge and skills, appreciations and worthy use of leisure, and some sense of the interdependence of individuals in their social group. A life-experience curriculum teaches such values, knowledge, skills, and abilities through units built around (1) home and family life; (2) the community, its helpers and its resources; and (3) expanding concepts about the community to the city, the state, and the nation. Activities other than reading from textbooks are utilized as much as possible to enrich these concepts for slow learners.

Functional learning for the slow learner includes tasks in everyday living: filling out an application blank; being able to use telephone directories, road maps, travel schedules, street guides, restaurant menus; understanding written directions of various sorts, radio and TV program schedules, classified ads, and various types of catalogues.

The life-experience approach to teaching retarded children is primarily concerned with helping them understand and cope with practical problems of living that will persist all through life. Such problems include understanding and using money, understanding and making efficient use of time, developing social competencies for all kinds of interaction with people, and learning prevocational skills from as early an age as feasible.

The following generalizations are believed to be true of most slow learners.

1. They are satisfied to continue doing work that is repetitive.

2. They need more drill and practice and are more apt to enjoy it.

3. They need careful guidance in all assignments; goals need to be fairly immediate and carefully explained.

4. They need more help with planning in the form of specific directions to follow, ego-support, and close supervision to see that the directions are carried out.

5. They need success experiences and opportunities to do things they can do well (e.g., handwriting).

6. They have trouble when assignments are abstract, when abstract reasoning is required, or when evaluation "beyond the book" is under discussion.

For slow learners in regular classes, teachers need to remember the following:

1. Formal reading and using reading as a thinking process must be developed in proportion to the extent of mental retardation. A child of six with an IQ of 85 is more like a five-year-old than a six-year-old. An eight-year-old with an IQ of 75 is more like a six-year-old than an eight-year-old. While children at all these ages can profit from any language and concept development experiences which they can understand, expecting them to move to the complex, abstract process of reading should come much later chronologically. When children have sufficient language and understanding of concepts and verbalize freely, they will be ready to move toward the more formal activities of reading and writing. However, when children are provided with compensatory training, increases in mental age—and therefore, by definition, IQ—are sometimes greater than one might expect.

2. The way reading is taught to slow-learning children is very similar to the way it is taught to normal children. However, there are differences. When the child is ready for reading, overlearning the core of basic sight words is important. Slow learners must have all the time they need to master them. This necessitates more books, more stories, and more language-experience reading at the appropriate level before progressing to more difficult levels. And a structured, systematic phonics and spelling program may be indicated. The Hegge-Kirk-Kirk *Remedial Reading Drills*[14] were first prepared for mentally retarded boys. If a child growing at the normal rate requires one year at the second-grade level of difficulty, a retarded child whose growth rate is approximately two-thirds that of a normal child needs perhaps one-third year more time to grow through the same quantity of learning. He is not fundamentally different, he just grows more slowly.

3. The teacher can take advantage of the student's acceptance of repetition and monotony. Stories can be reread for different purposes. He needs few purposes at one time under any circumstances. So he may reread to learn something he missed the first time. Beyond reading to find out what happened in the story, he may practice reading aloud so he can record his *best* reading on the tape recorder. Every rereading provides additional practice on the basic sight words he needs to overlearn.

4. Teachers will probably encourage more oral reading with slow learners.

5. Teachers must give much help in making directions clear in preparation for independent seatwork before leaving slow learners to work on their own.

6. Concrete experiences are more valuable than abstract ones. The reader is referred to Dale's "Cone of Experience" in chapter 2. Pictures, objects, drawings, cartoons, and photographs all help to make words more meaningful.

Slow learners, as a total group, may exhibit behavior characteristics that have resulted from repeated experiences of failure in the classroom, poor motivation, dislike for school, compensations for academic failure, and dropping out of school. Poor health and poor home conditions may be more prevalent among slow learners because of socioeconomic factors in their lives. It is logical that slow learners need a greater number of years of compulsory school attendance than normals if they learn at a slower pace. For too long schools operated on a contradictory principle: that because slow learners were retarded, their formal education was terminated as soon as they passed the age for compulsory attendance.

Schools must anticipate and hasten the day when *all* children will be provided for according to their individual talents. Then there need be *no* forgotten children. Today, however, Rose's experience pointedly suggests she has been forgotten:

Rose was an *unfortunate* retarded child who was assigned to a special room half-days and to a regular class the other half. One day a university student appeared to administer a test to Rose. When he asked for Rose in the special class, he was told she was in another classroom nearby. When he asked there for Rose, he was told there was no one there by that name. He returned to the school office and asked again. Upon returning to the same classroom and stating that the office records indicated that she should be there in the afternoon, the teacher thought a moment, then said, "Oh, that must be her over there. She just sits in the corner."

Children with Learning Disabilities

Children have many problems which affect their ability to read. These problems can be physical, emotional, or cultural. Most often there is a combination of factors. Perceptual and neurological disorders are often misunderstood by the average teacher. What is probably the most frequent cause of learning difficulties, although it is perhaps the least widely recognized of all, is a disturbance of perceptual abilities—visual perception, auditory perception, kinesthetic perception, or a combination of these.

Perceptual Handicaps

Learning disability refers to those children of any age who demonstrate a substantial deficiency in a particular aspect of academic achievement because of perceptual or perceptual-motor handicaps, regardless of etiology or other contributing factors. The term *perceptual* as is used here relates to those mental (neurological) processes through which the child acquired his basic alphabets of sounds and forms. The term *perceptual handicap* refers to inadequate ability in such areas as the following: recognizing fine differences between auditory and visual discriminating features underlying the sounds used in speech and the orthographic forms used in reading; retaining and recalling those discriminated sounds and forms sequentially, both in short- and long-term memory; ordering the sounds and forms sequentially, both in sensory and motor acts . . .; distinguishing figure-ground relationships . . .; recognizing spatial and temporal orientations; obtaining closure . . .; integrating intersensory information . . .; relating what is perceived to specific motor functions.[15]

Frostig has divided visual perception into five component parts:

1. Deficiency in visual-motor coordination results in difficulty in cutting, pasting, drawing, and in learning how to write. The child also displays clumsiness, and even dressing himself can be difficult.

2. Deficiency in perceptual constancy results in inadequate recognition of the adaptation to the environment. The child may learn to recognize a number, letter, or word in one particular form or context but fail to recognize it when seen in a different manner. Learning to read or work with symbols in any way poses many problems.

3. Deficiency in perception of position in space results in difficulty in understanding what is meant by the words up and down, in and out, before and behind, etc. Difficulty becomes apparent in academic tasks—letters, words, phrases, numbers, and pictures appear distorted and confusing. The child may be able to pronounce the sounds *p a t* in "pat," but then, when blending them together, they may come out "tap." The child may perceive *b* as *d, p* as *q, saw* as *was,* and *24* as *42.* This makes it difficult if not impossible to learn to read, write, spell, or to do arithmetic without special teaching.

4. Deficiency in perception of spatial relationships leads to many difficulties in academic learning. They may make impossible the proper perception of the sequence of letters in a word, remembering the sequences of processes involved in long division or understanding graphs.

5. Disability in perception of figure-ground is characterized by inattentive and disorganized behavior, inability to shift attention from one stimulus to another, inability to stay within lines or to form letters correctly, inability to find the place on a page, or words in the dictionary, inability to solve familiar problems on the crowded page in his workbook. Children with such difficulties literally cannot find anything, even when it is right in front of their noses.[16]

Schools need to be prepared to adjust their curricula to enable students to demonstrate their abilities in the most positive way. Learning-disabled students who cannot read fast enough or write correct spellings need to be allowed to use alternative ways to demonstrate their achievements. They could be allowed to respond orally instead of in writing, by, for example, telling answers to questions via a tape recorder instead of writing them. They could tape a teacher's class periods instead of trying to take notes. They could listen to a tutor read aloud just as a blind student would. They could work with another student as a pair, in a "buddy system." All of these techniques may help disabled learners keep up with their age mates.[17]

Cox has presented case histories of two young adults whose school failure as children would today be diagnosed as learning disability. She discusses their rehabilitation in adulthood, when their problems were finally diagnosed. Their success offers much hope for similar students who have not yet been recognized. Cox discusses the need for such techniques as those listed above and the psychological needs of those who have experienced repeated failure.[18]

Kirk and Elkins observed Child Service Demonstration Centers for Learning Disabilities in twenty-one different states. In reviewing the provisions for 3,000 children, they found that: (1) most were enrolled in the lower elementary grades; (2) the ratio of boys to girls was three to one; (3) about two-thirds were rated as reading problems; (4) they were educationally retarded; (5) they were more retarded in reading and spelling than in arithmetic; and (6) assigning children to the resource room was the most commonly used method of delivering services.

On the basis of their observations that 80 percent of the time emphasis was on remedial reading but that deficiencies in spelling and arithmetic were also often given as reasons for assigning children to the resource room, Kirk and Elkins questioned whether underachievement in these three subjects can be considered specific learning disabilities.[19] They concluded that often what was being dealt with was not specific learning disabilities, but rather a *general learning problem* such as found in slow learners or children from environments unlike that expected by the middle-class school.

Lack of school learning opportunities, poor instruction, poor motivation for learning, or poor school attendance are all valid concepts, but they should not be confused with the concept of specific learning disabilities.

Neurological Handicaps

Jill, in the fifth grade, was one of the children who had not made adequate progress in developmental reading despite a great deal of special attention from her teachers and some additional tutoring with a competent clinician during the summer following third grade. Although she was a bright child, her instructional level of reading was only middle-third grade. While she had never repeated a grade, her classroom teachers had observed her carefully and forwarded their observations. From year to year, written anecdotes for her cumulative folder more strongly underscored teacher dissatisfaction with her progress. The teachers noted that after tutoring following third grade, Jill had overcome many of her problems of reversals and confusions. Jill's teachers, in a shared decision, concluded that the basic problem was an emotional instability exhibited at school in a very short attention span, inability to concentrate, and general lack of efficient organization. They reasoned that her father's manner of discipline might be excessively rigid and authoritarian while the mother was too indecisive and used a laissez-faire attitude. Since the father traveled and was away from home at times, this could cause the child to be mixed up about which pattern of values and behaviors to follow. Fortunately, the teachers conveyed, as tactfully as possible, their thoughts to the parents, who insisted on further clinical study.

The Wechsler Intelligence Scale for Children confirmed an above-average IQ reported on a previous group test, the *California Test of Mental Maturity*. However, an especially low score on the block-design test in the performance scale was judged to be clinically significant, and a *Bender-Gestalt Visual Motor Test* was administered. This instrument revealed a tendency for the child to rotate her drawings by ninety degrees when she reproduced drawings from a set of dots on cards—sufficient evidence to recommend a complete neurological examination.

The neurologist discovered an unusual neurological problem. While Jill had never demonstrated any overt symptoms of epilepsy or other convulsive disorder, her electroencephalogram indicated the brain wave pattern of a person with some form of *petit mal* or *grand mal*. The neurologist explained to the parents and the reading therapist that this positive finding might account for the short attention span, flighty behavior, and resultant poor progress in school. After a few weeks of establishing the appropriate anticonvulsant drug therapy, Jill's behavior did change noticeably. Her progress in the reading clinic was rapid, and she was more *conforming and competent* in the regular classroom.

This case study shows how crucial are competent diagnosis and treatment. The implications of not having such a thorough examination and diagnosis are many. Dangerous, unfounded "blaming" assumptions can cause parents to say, "If teachers would only . . .," or teachers to say, "The parents are inconsistent in their discipline, so . . ." Jill's problem also emphasizes that even the most competent classroom teacher, teaching all of the developmental skills of reading in the most commendable way, will probably experience failure in a situation where organic disorders are the primary cause of learning disability.

The following description is a synthesized sketch of a typical hyperactive child:

Charles was nine years old when first seen, and the chief complaint was that he was doing badly in school. He vomited a lot as a baby, banged his head and rocked in his bed for hours, and cried much more than his sister. He walked at eleven months, talked first at two-and-a-half years, did not talk in sentences until four. Always very active, he has broken a bed and a trampoline and wears out the double knees in his jeans before the second washing. At age five, he was constantly turning off the furnace and water heater. He does not learn from punishment, is afraid of nothing, wanders from home and gets lost, dashes into the street without looking. He never completes projects at home and never finishes work at school. Hard to get to bed at night, he takes two hours or more to go to sleep and gets up at six A.M. Neighbors "live in quiet terror" because he has run water into their basements through the hose, ridden his bicycle over their gardens, and blocked their sewers. He fights all the time with the neighborhood children and has no friends. In school he is "creative" in avoiding work, he hides his books, eats crayons, tears papers, and pokes the other children. Every teacher reports that she has to stand over him to get him to do any work. Though bright, he has had to repeat second grade twice and is now in a special school.[20]

Suggestions for Teaching the Neurologically Impaired Child

There are some general principles to enhance instruction for neurologically impaired children.

1. The classes should be small.
2. The room should contain a minimum of distracting stimuli.
3. Activities must be paced at the child's capacity for sustained participation with frequent periods of guided and supervised large-muscle play, such as bicycle riding or running.
4. The children should be permitted to leave the classroom and run about the playground to release mounting tensions.
5. Group discipline must be firm, and clearly defined limits must be set.
6. Children must not be permitted to experience failure regularly or habitually. Success will build self-esteem and enhance the child's ability to try harder the next time.

But it is clear that teachers must be prepared to deal with many kinds of behaviors in the classroom beyond what is characteristic of the normal child. Some specific suggestions about how to handle particular kinds of behavior are offered below.

Hyperactivity and Distractibility

The child may be seated at the front of the room in order to separate him or her as far as possible from classmates without isolation from the group. The room decoration should be minimal, perhaps limited to one wall or area. A quiet corner completely devoid of distracting stimuli where the child can sit when he is particularly excited or irritable may help. Special worksheets that contain small amounts of material and omit extraneous illustrations or designs may help the child learn to pay attention. The teacher should keep his or her appearance plain and should avoid wearing nonessential jewelry.

Some youngsters develop hysterical reactions to stressful situations. The alert teacher tries to anticipate such situations and prevent them as much as possible.

Hyperactive children require a teacher with patience and sympathetic understanding of their problems. This teacher will provide materials which will help slow down and channel their random motor movements. The children will be able to construct many of their own learning devices through such activities as cutting, pasting, and sorting. When purposefully engaged, these children tend to become calmer. Calmer behavior leads to gradually improved attention, increased success experiences, and greater interest in the acquisition of academic skills.

Use of drugs to make it possible for a child to control impulsive behavior or attention to a topic for longer periods of time is now a controversial subject. Divoky discusses the negative aspects in an article entitled "Toward a Nation of Sedated Children,"[21] to which there is an excellent, reasoned reply in the letters to the editor in the October 1973 issue of *Learning*.[22]

Perseveration

To help the child overcome perseveration, the teacher can vary the ongoing task with one that is completely different or provide new materials to encourage the child to change responses. At the same time, the child can be encouraged to *branch out* by generalizing from the first task. These boys and girls must be specifically taught to do these things.

In making shifts of attention from one type of work to another, the teacher must be aware of the child's difficulties in such shifting and help by waiting for the child's attention. The teacher can ask specifically if the child is following or can move closer and put a hand lightly on the child's shoulder or can help put away material or get new materials ready.

Meticulousness

Keep the learning assignment short with a time limit. This requires careful diagnosis of functioning levels, including attention span, to be sure that the task is an appropriate one. The teacher may be able to encourage attending and interacting by using the operant-conditioning technique. Tangible rewards for completion of simple tasks under conditions previously agreed upon are sometimes helpful in establishing the pattern of behavior the teacher desires. Oral work should be emphasized in preference to written, but at all times overstimulation and failure should be avoided in oral as well as written expression.

Withdrawal Tendencies

Be sympathetic. Include the child as a part of the group. Any attempt at group socialization must be carefully controlled by the teacher. It is advantageous to recognize those children with a high social quotient or ability to adapt to differences in behavior. The teacher then manipulates the situation so that communication takes place. For example, "John and Billy, will you please put these notices in their envelopes?" The teacher should strive at all times for achieving insight in learning tasks by concretizing them through visual, tactile, and auditory devices.

| Compulsive Behavior | It is probably desirable to abandon the phonics method of reading with a child who compulsively analyzes words letter-by-letter but has difficulty blending the sounds into words. |

Compulsive Behavior

It is probably desirable to abandon the phonics method of reading with a child who compulsively analyzes words letter-by-letter but has difficulty blending the sounds into words.

Difficulty with Abstraction

Concepts must be broken down into isolated, compartmentalized learning. Concrete representations of numbers, letters, and color cues, for example, are helpful in securing insight. Keying new tasks to what the child is capable of performing will help insure that his responses will be more consistently correct. In self-tutoring activities, the correct answer should be immediately available. Overlearning is important. Responses need to become automatic after insight is achieved. Separate bits of knowledge should chain upon each other in sequential steps until whole concepts are learned.

Language Disabilities

Probably this common language disorder of children prevents them from perceiving and/or accurately recording the symbols of the printed page. They cannot interpret written language in the way unaffected children can. Certain remedial approaches are very effective with these children. Many exercises in proper discrimination of left-right direction will be helpful for those who display letter and word reversals. Shapes and sizes must be perceived. The child will benefit by being taught to look for letter details within a word.

Tactual experiences with letter contours can be gained through using wooden letters upon which sandpaper surfaces are pasted. The child's memory for letter shapes is thus reinforced through the sense of touch. Tracing the word also reinforces memory through the use of muscle or kinesthetic sense. Through writing, tactual, and kinesthetic experiences, he becomes aware of letter details.

Another effective teaching method is to present a word with one or two letters left out. As the child fills in blanks and finds that he is right, he is forced to become aware of the missing details.

Children with Emotional Disturbances

Hewett has found that emotionally disturbed children are usually not ready for "formal" instruction in which skill mastery is the primary objective. He lists *five* readiness levels prerequisite to skill mastery. They are ability to: (1) pay attention; (2) respond to others in learning situations; (3) respond to instructions or follow directions; (4) explore the environment meaningfully; and (5) get along with others and value social approval. Beyond these readiness levels, the school expects (6) mastery of skills and (7) achievement. (See Table 18.2.) Hewett summarized these seven tasks in relation to the child's difficulties with respect to each; the educational goal; types of learner rewards; and the amount of teacher involvement in structuring child behavior.[23]

When the standards others have set for children do not match their own natural way of growing up in their own good time, conflicts will result. "No, no!" "You're a big girl now." "Give that to your little sister!" "I'm not going to let go of you until you apologize to your grandmother!" Many remarks like that will cause anger and resentment and hostility to build up in the child. These moments of "bad feelings" against another child or an adult must not be pushed deep down inside; they need to come out.

If children try to let their feelings come out in drawings or paintings, teachers must not say, "Oh, don't paint such an unhappy picture. Start again and make a nice one."[24] Children could also pound nails, hit punching bags, and tackle dummies to work out some of these feelings. A child may spank a doll, put it in an oven, willing to burn it up, try to flush it down the toilet, stomp on it, or otherwise try to mutilate it. Teachers should keep as neutral as possible and not say, "Oh! the nice dolly. You must be nice to it."[25] The neutral response to the child's expressions of "I hate it" is "You don't like the doll [or whoever the doll represents at the moment] very well today, do you?"[26]

Table 18.2 Description of Educational Tasks.

Adapted from Frank N. Hewett, "Educational Engineering with Emotionally Disturbed Children," *Exceptional Children* 33 (March 1967):461. Used with permission.

| | Readiness Skills | | | | | | |
	Attention	Response	Order	Exploratory	Social	Mastery	Achievement
Child's Problem	Inattention due to withdrawal or resistance	Lack of involvement and unwillingness to respond in learning situations	Inability to follow directions	Incomplete or inaccurate knowledge of environment	Failure to value social approval or disapproval	Deficits in basic adaptive and school skills not in keeping with IQ	Lack of self motivation for learning
Educational Goal	Get child to pay attention to teacher and task	Get child to respond to tasks he likes and which offer promise of success	Get child to complete tasks with specific starting points and steps leading to a conclusion	Increase child's efficiency as an explorer and get him involved in multisensory exploration of his environment	Get child to work for teacher and peer group approval and to avoid their disapproval	Remediation of basic skill deficiencies	Development of interest in acquiring knowledge
Learner Reward	Provided by tangible rewards (e.g., food, money, tokens)	Provided by gaining social attention	Provided through task completion	Provided by sensory stimulation	Provided by social approval	Provided through task accuracy	Provided through intellectual task success
Teacher Involvement	Minimal	Still limited	Emphasized	Emphasized	Based on standards of social appropriateness	Based on curriculum assignments	Minimal

Asquith, Donaher, and Barton have described one emotionally disturbed little girl as follows:

> She is hyperactive, interrupts, cries easily, has temper tantrums and is utterly unpredictable from one moment to another. Recently she climbed on top of her desk and screamed and threw books, crayons, and paper all over the room.[27]

If a class has a student who obviously is emotionally disturbed, it is the teacher's responsibility to assist the remaining students in a subtle manner to accept the defiant child as part of the group. The term "individual differences" in educational jargon does not apply only to academic work. Just as children differ in academic ability, they also differ in the background experiences that cause each one to respond to situations in a unique manner. Therefore, each child must be accepted, with weaknesses as well as strong points, as a person having worth and dignity as a human being. The teacher has the responsibility of encouraging individuality insofar as any one child's behavior does not impinge on the rights of others.

According to national figures, in a class of thirty-five students, the teacher can expect, on the average, from two to five students to show symptoms of some sort of exceptionality. How these exceptional children are handled depends on the teacher's educational background and personal maturity.

The teacher must not only be able to recognize deviant behavior, but also should try to discover the cause. Emotional disturbance is generally expressed by the following four types of behavior: aggression, anxiety, withdrawal, and bizarre behavior. For each type, certain distress signals are given below and appropriate teacher responses suggested.

Aggression

Aggression manifests itself in temper tantrums, bullying, teasing, destroying property of others, being physically abusive to other children, interrupting and disrupting classroom routine, stealing, or lying.

To help the children with certain of these behaviors, the teacher may respond in any of the following ways:

1. Have a corner set aside that is neutral and nondistracting.
2. Separate the child from the group during periods of active aggressive behavior.
3. Be accepting but firm; be matter-of-fact, businesslike, and *fair*.
4. Anticipate aggressive behavior and help the child regain control or select alternate behavior.
5. Set up minimum standards of expected behavior *with* the child, then when corrective measures are taken, the child knows it is his own standard that he has violated.
6. Provide acceptable outlets for tensions that build up aggression: modeling clay, punching bags, nondestructible toys.

The anxious child cries easily, is timid, is afraid to tackle new tasks, is over-anxious about grades, cannot accept less than his understanding of your standards.

To help the child who is anxious, the teacher should respond as follows:

1. Maintain warm rapport with the child.
2. Help the child build self-confidence based on successes.
3. Reassure but do not coddle the child.
4. Help the child minimize stress over grades.
5. Be able to discipline in a kind way, but be firm.
6. Do not allow the child to become overly dependent on a teacher for security.
7. Maintain a sense of proportion by businesslike friendliness.
8. Ask for responses in class when you know the child will be successful.

Withdrawal

The withdrawing child daydreams, prefers to be alone, does not seek the company of anyone, has few friends, maybe only one with whom he or she can feel intimacy. To help the child who withdraws, the teacher can respond as follows.

1. Bring the child into class activities when he is able to handle it emotionally.
2. Make sure that class activities are varied between quiet and active work.
3. Help the child develop interest in school work by varying teaching techniques to include games, giving the child responsibility in group projects, and calling on the child to respond when you know he or she can be successful.

Bizarre Behavior

Bizarre behavior may be unpredictable behavior, nonsense language responses, or "ritual" performed before any action is taken.

If any such symptom persists in spite of firm but kind teacher response, the teacher must feel obligated to seek professional help through the school psychologist or the school social worker.

What's Bothering David?

David was in the fourth grade when his teacher suggested to his mother that he needed special help with his reading. Since his school provided no special help, he was enrolled in a private reading clinic for one session a week. It was the middle of the school year and David had just had his tenth birthday.

The reading clinician found that he could read for instruction at the beginning third-grade level, he knew most of the 220 Dolch Basic Sight Words, and his spelling was adequate for beginning third grade. He could not discriminate many sounds on the McKee phonics inventory; he made many errors in the vowel section. He had difficulty determining that such pairs of words as *puddle-puzzle, clean-cling* were different. He passed the vocabulary item of the Binet Intelligence Test at age 12, and since he was just ten, the clinician felt confident he had at least average intelligence.

After several sessions with David, developing rapport while he wrote some original paragraphs, completed exercises in the easy levels of SRA Reading for Understanding, Junior Edition,[28] and enjoyed some easy oral reading, the clinician began to feel that reading really wasn't David's problem. David had read books in the Deep Sea Adventures series[29] and was presently enjoying *Frogmen in Action* (third-grade level). He was anxious to get each new book in the series.

David had some strange mannerisms—not really bizarre, but different— was afraid of not doing well, and was unable to sit still. These behaviors bothered his clinician the most. She invited him to talk often by leading into conversations that might reveal what he was thinking or feeling.

One day when David was reading, he began to squirm in his seat and his arms were covered with goosepimples. Then he said that every time he started to read, something gave him the chills.

The clinician gave David opportunity to discuss the problem by answering with neutral comments, asking questions that might provide further explanation, or restating some of David's observations. The following running commentary is a report of David's report about "shivering" and having the "chills" when he reads. His ability to discuss his feelings at such length suggests that this is a serious problem to him and that he does need to clear up his feelings before he will be able to apply his best efforts in the reading situation.

I try to hold my hand in a fist to keep from having the shivers. Then I cross my feet and try to hold them still. Then I get nervous and make more mistakes. And then I can't read at all. I don't know why this happens when I read. When I was in second grade, the lady in the administration building [diagnostic testing service] said that the stories weren't interesting. But that's not it.

I really do want to read. I just get the shivers. Lisa and Jamie [little sister and little brother] holler and that gets me, too. But now, my mother and I read early in the morning and it's better. But I still get the shivers.

Well, a long time ago when I was in kindergarten, I don't really think the teacher liked me. She used to say, "Why can't you act like Mark [a big brother]?" But I never did know how I'd acted. Then, one day, you know, she always made us put our heads down, and rest. But one day, she said when we came in, "You've all been so good today, you don't have to put your heads down and rest." Then, all of a sudden, she said, "David Carr, put your head down on that desk and rest." I knew it was me, but I couldn't figure it out. You know, I still don't know what I did or why she made me put my head down.

There's something else that bothers me, too. Sometimes I shut my eyes and when I open them, I don't know where I am. Once, at ten o'clock in the morning, I closed my eyes at school, and I thought I was at home. Then I had to blink and blink and I was at school. I don't know how I got there, I just remembered crossing the fence. You know, that'd happened two times when I was in the car and once when I was playing baseball.

The clinician asked if he could show how this happened.

No, I can't just make it happen, but that's the way it happens when it does happen.

You know how your eyes are when you first wake up, with a light shining in them. Well, that's what happens and I don't know where I am, except everytime so far, I've been able to blink and think "Where am I?" and then I know. [He made motions—waving with the fingers of one hand—to show that his eyes were flickering.]

At a session one week later:

You know, something real nice happened this week. One evening my dad and I sat out on the patio and talked and talked man to man. We stayed out there till nine-thirty. It sure was neat. He explained to me that my uncle—Uncle Davie—had them, too. [Shivers.] And he still makes funny faces! And even my dad, when he was a kid, and my grandpa had them too. And now me. And I think I know why. Maybe not exactly, and I'm just guessing about this, but my brother is the only one that hasn't had them and he's the only one that hasn't had appendicitis. They all had their appendix out and now I've had it out, too. And now I've got them.

At a session one week later:

As David was reading, the clinician notices his shoulders were twitching. She said, "Oh, David, have you got the shivers again?" But David, with that strained, faraway look in his eyes, said, "Oh no, I don't have them anymore. My mom and dad both told me just to tell myself I didn't have them, and so I do, and I don't." But his eyes had a kind of strained, desperate look, as if he feared that the shivers would come right back if he didn't keep telling himself.

The clinician began to wonder whether a new kind of substitute nervous mannerism might replace the shivers. (If the adult insists the child *not* bite his nails, he *can* pick his nose, and if that is stopped, he *can* twist his hair.)

Why would David be afraid? And of what?

Could there be a neurological basis for the "closing of his eyes and not knowing for a minute where he is"?

If there is a problem with either an organic or psychological base, can the parents help him overcome it by denying the symptoms? Why would the classroom teacher have referred him for reading? Reading is the most often reported cause of children's failure in school. In a large class, the most obvious behaviors may be unfinished work, inattention, and, as a consequence, some difficulties in reading situations. When the child is doing unsatisfactory school work for any reason, teachers are probably inclined to look first for inability to do activities associated with reading. The clinician reports that, generally, David is an outgoing boy when talking about most things. Physically, he's "a beautiful specimen." And other than laboring over his problem, he is animated about all the things he talks about. When he reports something that pleases him, his eyes dance. "He does have some slight speech problem. I can't really pinpoint what it is. Sometimes he does a great deal of repeating himself, or sometimes he doesn't enunciate clearly, or sometimes he mixes up the syllables in polysyllabic words."

For David, referral to the school psychologist and his family doctor is indicated.

The Rebus Technique

The rebus technique, among other kinds of structural helps, such as programmed instruction, may be useful for teaching emotionally disturbed children to read. It has also been suggested as a useful reading system for severely retarded children.

The rebus technique uses a combination of pictures or symbols and traditional orthography to represent words. Rebuses are used occasionally in children's magazines and books to make the text more readable for children who have a limited reading vocabulary. For the same reason, preprimers have used rebuses for words children have not yet learned as sight vocabulary. The rebus technique is useful for promoting high interest in stories because it permits the use of words which are in a child's speaking vocabulary but not yet in the reading vocabulary.

The Peabody Rebus Reading Program, illustrated in chapter 8, was intended for use primarily in kindergarten and first grade and with some children having marginal learning abilities. Although three books are available, teachers would not have to use them all. According to Woodcock, the first rebus book presents most of the readiness work of preprimer level instruction; the second rebus book presents most of the skills necessary to begin primer level instruction; and if book three is used, most children can then move easily into the primer level of other reading programs.

Actually, the Peabody Rebus Program materials are less like the rebus technique described above than they are like pictographic writing. Pictographs were developed as a form of writing in several parts of the world independently long before the invention of alphabetic writing. Pictographs illustrate objects or concepts, whereas a true rebus is a picture that represents speech sounds by illustrating an object whose name sounds like the intended word or one or more of its syllables. A rebus is, therefore, more like the symbols of alphabetic writing, which, of course, stand for the sounds which make up the word.

The Peabody Rebus Reading Program uses pictographs primarily as a link between spoken language and alphabetic printing and is organized in programmed text format.[30] The pictographic vocabulary for books one and two and four reading frames are presented in figures 8.6 and 8.7.

Suggestions for the Classroom Teacher

1. The child with deviant abilities should be kept in the regular classroom as much as possible, even if for only a few minutes at a time. The use of programmed materials, paced at the child's performance level, is recommended for some children. Some teachers have successfully used the rebus technique in easy reading.

2. There should be a movable screen in the classroom that can be used to partition off a corner or other working space in order to shut out unwanted stimuli. This is carefully interpreted to the child as a way to make it easy for him or her to work; it is *not a punishment*. The teacher can explain that "Some people need a quiet place where they won't be disturbed if they are to get anything done."

3. The teacher must become skilled in sizing up children's moods early in the day. A child who is upset and having a bad day should be kept in the teacher's line of vision all day long. On bad days the teacher should make a special effort to support the child by any of the following behaviors carried out casually:

    a. close physical proximity;
    b. gentle massage of the shoulder and neck muscles as the teacher passes the child's desk (if the child permits);
    c. talk to the child, even if he or she doesn't respond;
    d. set reasonable limits and hold firmly to them;
    e. check the child's medical record or ask the mother's permission to talk with the child's family doctor.

Channels of communication are very important so that everyone who may have useful information has a way to share it with others who badly need it. Teacher, principal, family doctor, school nurse, social worker, parents, neurologist, school psychologist, and, if indicated, psychiatrist—all need to share information, even though they may not have learned to "talk the same language." It is necessary for them all to exchange ideas and learn how to work together.

Summary

Although Roger is eleven years old *chronologically,* the teacher must not expect him to be eleven *behaviorally*—or *academically.* He may not even seem to be eleven *physically,* although he is most apt to approximate the norm in this respect. Roger may be *eight* behaviorally, or eight academically. What teachers must be able to do is to see through the eleven-year-old exterior and see the eight-year-old inside and work from there. This has been called X-ray vision—to look through the structure to see the *real* child inside.

For the bright child, the problem is comparable. An eleven-year-old exterior can harbor a fifteen-year-old problem-solver. The intellectually gifted child is apt to have a social age above but approximating his chronological age. As emphasized, a bright child who must function in a second language needs technical help to succeed in school.

Special problems of children who are neurologically handicapped or emotionally disturbed have been reviewed in this chapter. It is apparent that most beginning teachers will need expert help and supervision when working with children with these problems. With patience and calmness, many teachers are able to help such children function in regular classes by tailoring their program to fit individual, specific needs.

Although not presented in this chapter, it is extremely important for the teacher to develop the ability to recognize his own emotional needs as well as the child's emotional needs and to be able to separate the two.

Suggested Activities

1. In the school where you teach, ask for permission to give an informal reading inventory to one child with a high IQ score in a given grade, to one child with an average score, and to one with a low score. Evaluate the Informal Reading Inventory results and contrast the performances.
2. Choose a child in the grade you teach who has a high IQ score or gives other indications of keen intelligence. Observe the child with respect to his or her total growth. Evaluate the child's development in leadership, group interaction, aggression, and success in academic areas.
3. Visit a reading clinic and (1) observe children with special problems being tutored; (2) interview the reading clinician and learn (a) causes of the difficulty, (b) diagnosis (medically, psychologically, educationally), (c) remediation planned.

For Further Reading

General Reading about Exceptional Children

Abeson, Alan, and Jeffrey Zettel. "The End of the Quiet Revolution: The Education for All Handicapped Children Act of 1975." *Exceptional Children* 44 (October 1977): 114–28.

Bender, Lauretta. *A Visual Motor Gestalt Test and Its Clinical Use.* New York: American Orthopsychiatric Assn., 1938.

Charles, C. M. *Individualizing Instruction.* St. Louis: C. V. Mosby, 1976.

Gonzales, Eloy, and Leroy Ortiz. "Bilingualism and Special Education: Social Policy and Education Related to Linguistically and Culturally Different Groups." *Journal of Learning Disabilities* 10 (June/July 1977): 331–38.

Harris, A. J. *A Casebook on Reading Disability.* New York: David McKay, 1970.

Kroth, Roger. *Communicating with Parents of Exceptional Children.* Denver: Love Publishing Co., 1975.

Kroth, Roger, and Richard Simpson. *Parent Conferences as a Teaching Strategy.* Denver: Love Publishing Co., 1977.

Reynolds, Maynard, and Jack W. Birch. *Teaching Exceptional Children in All America's Schools: A First Course for Teachers and Principals.* Reston, Va.: Council for Exceptional Children, 1977.

Gifted Children and Reading

Divoky, Diane. "Room 13: Roni Howard's Oasis for Kids." *Learning* 6 (Aug./Sept. 1977): 76–85.

Gallagher, James John. *Teaching the Gifted Child,* 2d ed. Boston: Allyn and Bacon, 1975.

Hauck, Barbara, and Maurice Freehill. *The Gifted: Case Studies.* Dubuque, Iowa: Wm. C. Brown, 1972.

Labuda, Michael, ed. *Creative Reading for Gifted Learners: A Design for Excellence.* Newark: International Reading Assn., 1974.

Renzulli, Joseph S., and Linda H. Smith. "Two Approaches to Identification of Gifted Students." *Exceptional Children* 43 (May 1977): 512–18.

Rowe, Ernest Ras. "Creative Writing and the Gifted Child." *Exceptional Children* 34 (December 1967): 279–82.

Stanley, Julian C., Wm. C. George, and Cecelia H. Solano. *The Gifted and the Creative: A Fifty-Year Perspective.* Baltimore: Johns Hopkins University Press, 1977.

Syphers, Dorothy F. *Gifted and Talented Children: Practical Programming for Teachers and Principals.* Reston, Va.: Council for Exceptional Children, 1972.

Torrance, Ellis Paul. *Gifted Children in the Classroom.* New York: Macmillan, 1965.

Trezise, Robert L. "Teaching Reading to the Gifted." *Language Arts* 54 (Nov./Dec. 1977): 920–24.

Witty, Paul A. *Reading for the Gifted and Creative Student.* Newark: International Reading Assn., 1971.

Slow Learners and Reading

Benyon, Sheila D. *Intensive Programming for Slow Learners.* Columbus, Ohio: Charles E. Merrill, 1968.

Gardner, Wm. I. "Social and Emotional Adjustment of Mildly Retarded Children and Adolescents." *Exceptional Children* 33 (October 1966): 97–106.

Kephart, Newell C. *The Slow Learner in the Classroom.* Columbus, Ohio: Charles E. Merrill, 1970.

Kirk, Samuel, Sister Joanne Marie Kliebhan, and Janet W. Lerner. *Teaching Reading to Slow and Disabled Learners.* Boston: Houghton Mifflin, 1978.

Learning Disabilities and Reading

Book, Robert M. "Predicting Reading Failure: A Screening Battery for Kindergarten Children." *Journal of Learning Disabilities* 7 (January 1974): 43–47.

Cruickshank, Wm. M. "Myths and Realities in Learning Disabilities." *Journal of Learning Disabilities* 10 (January 1977): 51–58.

Divoky, Diane. "Screening: The Grand Delusion." *Learning* 5 (March 1977): 34.

Gearhart, Bill. *Learning Disabilities: Educational Strategies,* 2d ed. St. Louis: C. V. Mosby, 1977.

Hartman, Nancy C., and Robert Hartman. "Perceptual Handicap or Reading Disability." *The Reading Teacher* 26 (April 1973): 684–95.

Johnson, D. J., and H. R. Myklebust. *Learning Disabilities: Educational Principles and Practices.* New York: Grune & Stratton, 1967.

Kirk, Samuel A., and John Elkins. "Characteristics of Children Enrolled in the Child Service Demonstration Centers." *Journal of Learning Disabilities* 8 (December 1975): 630–36.

The Emotionally Disturbed Child and Reading

Axline, Virginia. *Dibs: In Search of Self—Personality Development in Play Therapy.* Boston: Houghton Mifflin, 1964.

———. *Play Therapy.* Boston: Houghton Mifflin, 1969.

Baruch, Dorothy. *New Ways in Discipline.* New York: McGraw-Hill, 1949.

Ephron, Beulah. *Emotional Difficulties in Reading.* New York: Julian Press, 1953.

Gallagher, Patricia A. "Structuring Academic Tasks for Emotionally Disturbed Boys." *Exceptional Children* 38 (May 1972): 711–20.

Hewett, Frank M. *The Emotionally Disturbed Child in the Classroom.* Boston: Allyn & Bacon, 1968.

Long, Nicholas, ed. *Conflict in the Classroom.* Belmont, Calif.: Wadsworth, 1971.

Tift, Katharine. "The Disturbed Child in the Classroom." *NEA Journal* 57 (March 1968): 12–14.

Zintz, Miles V. *Corrective Reading,* 3d ed., pp. 145–55. Dubuque, Iowa: William C. Brown, 1977.

Notes

1. Lewis M. Terman, "The Discovery and Encouragement of Exceptional Talent," *The American Psychologist* 9 (June 1954).
2. Terman used the Stanford-Binet IQ score of 140 as a criterion of giftedness.
3. Robert F. De Haan and Robert J. Havighurst, *Educating Gifted Children* (Chicago: The University of Chicago Press, 1957), p. 151. They recommended that qualities of leadership and special abilities also be evaluated. They believed that the top 15 to 20 percent of the population should be considered talented and that a lower IQ score, perhaps 120, would be sufficient to identify this group.
4. R. J. Havighurst, Virgil M. Rogers, and Paul Witty, "Are the Community and the School Failing the Unusual Child?" University of Chicago Round Table, April 27, 1952, cited in Helen M. Robinson, *Promoting Maximal Reading Growth Among Able Learners* (Chicago: University of Chicago Press, 1954), pp. 29–30.
5. Rudolph Pintner, "Superior Ability," *Teachers College Record* 42 (February 1941): 419, as cited in Paul Witty, ed., *The Gifted Child* (Boston: D.C. Heath, 1951), p. 275.
6. Louise Krueger et al., "Administrative Problems in Educating Gifted Children," in *The Gifted Child,* ed. Paul Witty (Boston: D.C. Heath, 1951), p. 266.
7. Paul Witty, ed., *The Gifted Child* (Boston: D. C. Heath, 1951), p. 151.
8. Gertrude H. Hildreth, *Introduction to the Gifted* (New York: McGraw-Hill, 1966), p. 217.
9. Joan B. Nelson and Donald L. Cleland, "The Role of the Teacher of Gifted and Creative Children," in *Reading for the Gifted and the Creative Student,* ed. Paul A. Witty (Newark, Del.: International Reading Assn., 1971), pp. 48–54.
10. Miles V. Zintz and Joyce Morris, "Tutoring Counseling Program for Indian Students" (Albuquerque: The College of Education, University of New Mexico, 1962), mimeographed, p. 13.
11. Alan Abeson and Jeffrey Zettel, "The End of the Quiet Revolution: The Education for All Handicapped Children Act of 1975," *Exceptional Children* 44 (October 1977): 114–28.
12. Ibid., pp. 122–28.
13. Edgar A. Doll, "Essentials of an Inclusive Concept of Mental Deficiency," *American Journal of Mental Deficiency* 46 (October 1941): 217.
14. T. Hegge, S. Kirk, and W. Kirk, *Remedial Reading Drills* (Ann Arbor, Mich.: George Wahr, 1955).
15. N. Hobbs, ed., *Issues in the Classification of Children,* vol. I (San Francisco: Jossey-Bass, 1975), p. 306.
16. Marianne Frostig, *Administration and Scoring Manual, Developmental Test of Visual Perception* (Palo Alto, California: Consulting Psychologists Press, 1966), p. 5.
17. Frances B. DeWitt, "Tear off the Label: the Older Student and SLD," *Academic Therapy* 13 (Sept. 1977): 69–78.
18. Sheralyn Cox, "The Learning-Disabled Adult," *Academic Therapy* 13 (Sept. 1977): 79–86.
19. Samuel A. Kirk and John Elkins, "Characteristics of Children Enrolled in the Child Service Demonstration Centers," *Journal of Learning Disabilities* 8 (December 1975): 630, 636.

20. Roger Signor, "Hyperactive Children," *News Bulletin Quarterly* 37 (Winter 1967): 19 describes the work of Dr. Mark A. Stewart, Professor of Child Psychiatry, Washington University School of Medicine, St. Louis.
21. Diane Divoky, "Toward a Nation of Sedated Children," *Learning* 1 (March 1973): 7–13.
22. Avrum L. Katcher, M.D., letter to the editor, *Learning* 2 (October 1973): 8.
23. Frank M. Hewett, "Educational Engineering with Emotionally Disturbed Children," *Exceptional Children* 33 (March 1967): 461.
24. James Hymes, *Understanding Your Child* (Englewood Cliffs, N.J.: Prentice-Hall, 1952), p. 147.
25. Ibid., p. 149.
26. Virginia Axline's case study *Dibs* describes dramatically how one little boy's personality was restored to good mental health through play therapy! Virginia Axline, *Dibs* (Boston: Houghton Mifflin, 1967).
27. Melrose Asquith, Mrs. Robert Donaher, and Clifford Barton, "I Have an Emotionally Disturbed Child in My Classroom," *Grade Teacher* 85 (April 1968): 77–80.
28. Science Research Associates, Inc., 259 East Erie St., Chicago, Ill. 60611, 1963.
29. Field Educational Publications.
30. Richard W. Woodcock, *Teacher's Guide, The Peabody Rebus Reading Program* (Circle Pines, Minnesota 55014: American Guidance Service, Inc., 1969), p. 71.

6
Evaluation in the
Reading Program

19

The Informal Reading Inventory

One of the most serious problems in elementary school classrooms today is the very large percentage of children who are kept reading at their *frustration* level. If a book is too difficult, if too many new concepts appear and are not repeated several times, and if the decoding process of unlocking new words has not been learned, boys and girls spend much time in school trying to gain information which is beyond their grasp. When teachers look at standardized test results and on that basis divide all the children in their rooms into three reading groups, they may be asking some children to stay frustrated all day long. Learning does not progress when children work at the frustration level.

Standardized reading achievement tests do have a very important place in assessment of the total school reading program. Also, they provide each teacher with a distribution of his students from best to poorest performer. However, they do not provide an adequate measure by which the teacher can determine which books are appropriate for which children to read at their respective *instructional* levels. "The standardized test, if it is a timed test, is a power test, and may more nearly measure a child's frustration level of reading for a short period of time."[1]

Teachers have found that standardized test scores may yield grade placement equivalents one or even two years higher than children can actually read with understanding.[2]

Wheeler and Smith found that the grade placement scores on standardized reading tests in the primary grades often have little relationship to the child's actual instructional reading level.[3]

The teacher cannot meet each child at his level of functioning and provide instruction from which the child can profit unless he can somehow determine with a fair degree of accuracy what that functioning level is. An informal reading inventory will provide the classroom teacher with this fundamental information.

Betts has pointed out the advantages of the informal reading inventory as the teacher's primary tool in teaching developmental reading skills:[4]

1. The teacher uses the materials at hand; there is little cost.
2. With direct and rapid administration, the teacher gets some needed answers quickly.
3. In terms of textbook reading the child will do, it is more valid than other tests.
4. Informal reading inventories can be either group or individual for appropriate purposes.
5. The student can be made aware of how well he reads.
6. The student can be made aware of progress as he achieves it.
7. As achievement is appraised, specific needs are revealed.
8. Interesting materials can be selected to use in the inventory.
9. Readability of materials can be checked in series of texts.
10. The test situation can be a valuable instructional situation also.

What Is the Informal Reading Inventory?

An informal reading inventory (IRI) is an individual test in which the child reads both orally and silently from increasingly difficult material until he or she becomes frustrated because of not knowing the words, not being able to pronounce them, or not understanding the ideas presented. IRIs are informal tests for reader level, sometimes referred to as "trying on a book for size." The informal reading test is diagnostic in that it reveals many specific areas of difficulty in reading for the observant teacher. Clearly, the value of the IRI depends entirely upon the competence of the teacher to make judgments as the child reads. An informal reading inventory should provide a selection of oral and silent reading at each level from preprimer through the sixth grade. Comprehension questions must be provided to measure the child's understanding of what is read.

The child should read from the book while the teacher has a reproduced copy on which to mark errors and make notes and evaluations. At the level at which the child makes too many errors for his or her instructional level, either in comprehension or pronunciation, the teacher begins reading one passage orally at each reading level and then asks prepared questions to measure the child's capacity for understanding ideas when he listens to someone else read the material. This is referred to as his capacity level, listening level, or hearing comprehension level.

The Four Reading Levels to Be Defined

The IRI will provide the teacher with information about levels of reading appropriate for the child's instructional work in class, the level at which he might most enjoy free reading, and a level of understanding ideas in written context even when it is too difficult for him to read the material himself. These levels are called: (1) independent; (2) instructional; (3) frustration; and (4) capacity levels.

The cloze procedure is also a valid means of determining reading levels. Teachers can easily prepare cloze exercises to measure the student's general understanding of the passage. Cloze is discussed in some detail in chapter 10, Comprehension Skills.

The *independent level* of reading is the *highest* level at which the child can read fluently and with personal satisfaction but without help. In independent reading, the child encounters practically no mechanical difficulties with the words and no problems with understanding the concepts in the context. The level is generally defined as that level where the child makes no more than one error in 100 words in the mechanics of reading and where he has no difficulties in comprehension. Much of the material the child selects for free reading from the library as well as some of the collateral reading he does for unit work in social studies and science should be at this level.

The *instructional level* of reading is the teaching level. This is defined as the *highest* level at which the child makes no more than five uncorrected errors in reading 100 consecutive words with at least 75 percent comprehension. Such materials are difficult enough to be challenging but sufficiently easy that the student can do independent seatwork with only the usual readiness help from the teacher when assignments are made. The most important task of the elementary teacher in all of his work is to establish each child's instructional level of functioning in reading and provide him with work at that level. Material at the child's instructional level should be read silently before it is read orally. Then there should be no difficulties with phrasing, punctuation, finger pointing, or tension. Studies reported here indicate that many children are not given the opportunity to ever read at this level in school. The instructional level is reached when the child uses a conversational tone, without noticeable tension, with satisfactory rhythm, and with suitable phrasing. He also makes proper use of word recognition clues and techniques.[5]

The *frustration level* is the *lowest* level at which obvious difficulties cause confusion, frustration, and tension in the reading situation. Betts lists inability to anticipate meanings, head movements, finger pointing, tension, slow word-by-word reading vocalization, and too many substitutions, omissions, repetitions, and insertions as evidences of frustration.[6]

The teacher understands that a clear line of separation does not exist between the instructional and frustration levels. The teacher's purpose is to keep the child on the growing edge of learning without pushing him along too fast. The teacher will do well to choose the lower of two possible reader levels when there is a question about which is appropriate for a given individual. It is preferable to let him have more practice at an easier level and thus strengthen his abilities and skills than to move him into material too difficult and impede his progress.

The *capacity level* for reading is the *highest* level at which the child can understand the ideas and concepts in informational material that is read to him. In determining this level, the teacher begins reading to the student at the level of difficulty at which he stops oral or silent reading because of reaching his frustration level. The same questions prepared to ask if he read the material are also appropriate to ask him after the teacher reads the material. Comprehension of 75 percent, the same proportion used for establishing instructional level, is the figure used for establishing capacity level. It is important to determine a child's capacity level so it can be compared to the child's instructional level. If the instructional level is only second level of second grade (2^2) and the capacity level for reading is fourth grade, the child's reading retardation is 1.5 years. This is one indication that the child has the innate ability to read much better than he or she is reading.

Limitations of the Informal Reading Inventory

The severest limitation of the informal reading inventory is the competence of the teacher administering it. However, with a minimum amount of practice, any classroom teacher can use the technique confidently and will be convinced that it is a necessity. It is the most accurate test of a child's ability to use textbooks for instructional purposes.

Some classroom teachers who have never administered an IRI expect it to be a technical and complicated instrument. For this reason they avoid it. But being a teacher must involve such responsibility. The reading inventory should be the very core of the teacher's whole reading-work program for the year. A teacher dare not believe that it is too technical and still think that he or she is functioning as a teacher.

Any teacher can learn to prepare that part of a complete reading inventory that meets the immediate need, and with study and practice, learn a great deal about the abilities and disabilities of the boys and girls in his classroom with respect to developmental reading.

Since the child is reading only brief passages and the test situation represents only one small sample of the child's total behavior, it is easily possible that there are facets of reading not adequately assessed and that on another day or at another time, the same individual might perform somewhat differently.

Spache feels that the individual texts in any basal reading series are not accurately graded and that a readability formula needs to be applied to determine the level of difficulty. He also suggests that a passage needs to be sufficiently long to represent four minutes of reading time in order to adequately check comprehension of ideas.[7] Further, Spache reports that classroom teachers have been found to be very inaccurate in recording errors in the informal reading inventory.[8]

While these limitations described by Spache are valid criticisms, they in no way change the fact that it is the classroom teacher who, in the final analysis, *must make all the decisions* about the child's reading ability in day-to-day work. The teacher must, *unavoidably,* select reading materials in language arts, social studies, arithmetic, science, and literature. It is to be hoped that shelves of books of many levels of difficulty will be provided for students to choose from, but the scope of the selections is the teacher's responsibility.

Improvement in the accuracy of the interpretation of the IRI develops with practice—if this practice is guided, or based on further reading and study. An excellent way for a beginning teacher to acquire initial skill in administering an informal reading inventory is to record the child's oral reading on a tape recorder so that it can be played back a number of times. Most clinicians are apt to hear some errors the second time that they missed completely the first time. Without a specific plan of what to listen for, the listener is probably not able to make any kind of objective summary of the results of the oral reading.

Construction of the Informal Reading Inventory

The first step in preparing the inventory is the selection of a series of books, probably a series of readers. Preferably a series of readers not already familiar to the children being tested would be used. While there are many words *not common* to two series of readers, the controlled vocabularies, the picture clues, and the context clues all help the child anticipate meanings, and most of the words are already in the typical English-speaking child's vocabulary.

Selections from preprimers, primers, and first and second readers need to contain 60 to 125 words and to be sufficiently informational so that questions can be constructed to measure understanding of the ideas in what is read. For grades three to six, passages need to be somewhat longer, perhaps 100 to 200 words in length.

One selection must be identified to be read orally and one to be read silently. The selection from each book should be taken from near the end of the first third of the book. It should not be from the first stories, which contain mostly review words from previous books in the series, but should fall close

enough to the front of the book to include the newly introduced words before the progressively more difficult reading which follows.

When the child reads, even if it is at the beginning of a story, the teacher should first give a synopsis of the story, or otherwise clue the child in to the place where the reading begins. It is wise to select for silent reading the selection immediately following the oral reading selection so the child can continue reading without teacher explanation and, thus, save time.

The comprehension questions should be carefully thought out so that they measure understanding as completely as possible. Different levels of questioning are appropriate: factual or memory items; inferential items requiring reading between the lines; vocabulary items to test concepts; and items to test ability to use context clues.

Authors need to provide meaningful definitions for new or difficult vocabulary items: "Erosion, which is the washing or blowing away of the soil, is therefore a serious problem."[9] The careful reader can now answer the question: "What is erosion?" "The stumpage, or timber in standing trees, is sold to lumbermen, who come in and cut the timber which is marked by the rangers for cutting."[10] The careful reader can answer the question: "What is stumpage?"

When choosing selections for the informal reading inventory, teachers should consider the nature of the context material. Can good comprehension questions be framed concerning the story? Vocabulary, sentence structure, human interest, and the number and complexity of the ideas dealt with influence the comprehension level of the material. Complexity of the ideas may be estimated by the number of prepositional phrases. The teacher should prepare questions that can be answered from the reading material, not from what the child already knows. Also, the questions should require recall, not merely a *yes* or *no*. For example, "What color was the hound?" *not,* "Was the hound in the story red?"

Patty, in the fourth grade, was referred for a reading evaluation because she was unable to do her work in her content subjects. When she was reading the Gilmore Oral Reading Test,[11] paragraph 2, she had little difficulty with the words. She read, "The cat is looking at the girl. He wants to play ball, too." But when she was asked, "What does the cat want?" she replied, "Cat food." In paragraph 3, she read, "After father has gone to work, the children will leave for school." To the question, "When will the children leave for school?" she responded, "When they're ready." This child apparently needs much help to improve concentration on what she is reading. If she had been asked *yes-no* questions, her inattention to the content of the story might have been much less evident.

Depending upon the content of the material read, there should be five to seven questions to measure comprehension. If the questions are of different types as suggested, this will provide some measure of the individual's understanding. *New Practice Readers*[12] provide six exercises over each short story read and these exercises have several types of questions.

The child should read from the book itself. This gives him the book format, the appropriate size print, and picture clues. The selections need to be reproduced in order that the examiner has a copy for marking reading errors, making notes in the page margins, checking comprehension, and observing the child's behavior in the reading situation. As teachers develop sophistication in asking a child to "try the book on for size," they need to be able to apply their techniques for marking errors and checking comprehension of the available material in the classroom. The word "informal" in informal reading inventory emphasizes that it allows the teacher to check quickly to see if a book is appropriate for a particular child's functioning reading level.

While any teacher can construct an informal reading inventory, there are a number published for teachers to use. With practice in administering and interpreting them, teachers will develop their own preferences about such inventories. Some of them are:

Botel, Morton. *The Botel Reading Placement Test.* Chicago, Ill.: Follett, 1970.

Johns, Jerry L. *Basic Reading Inventory, Preprimer-Grade 8.* Dubuque, Ia.: Kendall-Hunt, 1978.

La Pray, Margaret. *On-the-Spot Reading Diagnosis File.* New York: Center for Applied Research in Education, 1978.

McCracken, Robert A. *The Standard Reading Inventory.* Bellingham, Wash.: Pioneer Printing Co., 1966.

Silvarolli, Nicholas. *Classroom Reading Inventory,* 3d ed. Dubuque, Ia.: William C. Brown, 1976.

Spache, George D. *The Diagnostic Reading Scales.* New York: McGraw-Hill Book Company, 1972.

Sucher, Floyd, and Ruel A. Allred. *Reading Placement Inventory.* Oklahoma City: The Economy Co., 1973.

Administering the Informal Reading Inventory

Before the teacher can decide what selection to give the child to read, he needs some idea of the child's functioning level. There are several ways to acquire information for making this decision.

1. In September the teacher can check the cumulative record from the previous year to see what book the child was reading when the school year ended and choose accordingly. If the book selected is too difficult, the teacher will simply move to easier material.

2. The teacher may be able to assemble subgroups of children in reading circles very early in the year and ask them to "read around the circle" sampling a story which the teacher has developed readiness for. For children who have difficulty, only one sentence is sufficient. For those who read well, a much longer passage is fine.[13]

3. If the teacher estimates that a book at second level of first grade is appropriate, a sampling of words can be made from the list in the back of the book to make a word recognition test of twenty words. The sample will be obtained by dividing the total number of words in the list by twenty and then selecting words from the list at intervals of that quotient. For example, if there are 200 words in the list, $200 \div 20 = 10$; the teacher will thus select every tenth word in the list. A child who knows at least 80 percent of these words at sight will probably be able to read from the book. The following list of twenty-five words represents every eighth word in a list of 207 new words in the back of the book *Fields and Fences, Readiness Second Reader*.[14]

uncle	sister	people	already	brought
easy	nuts	threw	loud	hopped
getting	hide	shark	send	broke
past	Teddy	paw	held	bumpity-bump
it's	both	branch	whole	drum

If the child can pronounce twenty or more of these words at sight, this would be an appropriate book to sample for the child's instructional level of reading.

4. The teacher can use easy-to-administer word recognition tests to quickly estimate a beginning level for reading in context. The San Diego Quick Assessment or the Slosson Oral Reading Test discussed in chapter 20 will be useful for this purpose.

5. The Dolch Basic Sight Word List can be administered as a recall test. This is done by asking the child to pronounce all the words, line by line, on the *Dolch Sight Word Test*.[15] Generally, the teacher has one copy of the test and writes comments and marks errors as the child works (see figure 19.1). The child needs a three-by-five-inch index card to move down the page and hold under each word as it is being pronounced. The teacher strikes a line through each word recognized *at sight*. The

Figure 19.1 A system of marking sight recognition of the first forty words on the Dolch list.

From E. W. Dolch, *The Dolch Basic Sight Word Test* (Champaign, Ill.: Garrard Press, 1972).

Name _____ Date _____

1.	~~by~~	~~at~~	~~a~~	~~it~~
2.	~~in~~	~~I~~	~~be~~	~~big~~
3.	~~did~~	~~good~~	~~do~~	*good* go
4.	~~all~~ *has*	~~are~~ *had*	*many* any	~~an~~
5.	had	have	~~him~~	~~drink~~
6.	~~his~~ *as*	~~is~~	~~into~~	~~if~~
7.	ask *c*	~~may~~	~~as~~	~~am~~
8.	~~many~~	~~cut~~	~~keep~~	~~know~~
9.	~~does~~ *do*	*good* goes	*doing* going	~~and~~ *for* far
10.	~~has~~	~~he~~	~~his~~	

McBroom-Sparrow-Eckstein scale of known sight words indicates approximately which book in the reading series the child may be able to read.[16] (See table 19.1.) Further use of the Dolch Basic Sight Word Test as a diagnostic instrument is discussed in chapter 20, Corrective Reading.

If the child makes more than five uncorrected errors in reading the first selection attempted, the teacher may select an easier book and have the child continue reading until a satisfactory instruction level is found. Occasionally a child makes more errors on the first passage than on a subsequent more difficult one. The teacher has to be alert to such a possibility and to any psychological factors that may cause it to happen in order to be sure that the child's instructional level is correctly identified.

While the pupil is reading, the teacher should record all word substitutions, hesitations, mispronunciations, repetitions, omissions, and insertions. The method of marking and scoring is discussed in the next section of this chapter. The busy teacher will find it helpful to record the pupil's reading with a tape recorder and replay it when the children are gone so that more concentrated attention can be given to the reading. Sometimes it can be arranged for the rest of the class to work on independent activities so the teacher is free for fifteen or twenty minutes in one corner of the room where the child can complete the inventory. A relatively uninterrupted environment is necessary. Some teachers arrange to test one child each day during a recess

Table 19.1

Approximate reader
levels based on the
Dolch Basic Sight
Word Recall Test.

From Maude McBroom,
Julia Sparrow, and
Catherine Eckstein, *Scale
for Determining a Child's
Reader Level*
(Iowa City: Bureau of
Publications, Extension
Division, University of
Iowa, 1944), p. 11.

Dolch Words Known	Equivalent Reader Levels
0–75	Pre-Primer
76–120	Primer
121–170	First Reader
171–210	Second Reader or above
Above–210	Third Reader or above

period or during the special music or physical education period. A properly conducted informal reading inventory is the best instrument the classroom teacher has for determining what the child can and cannot do in formal reading.

The child continues to read selections until the teacher is certain the child's frustration level has been reached. Then the teacher reads one selection at each subsequent level so long as the child can answer the comprehension questions.

The easiest way to establish rapport with a child is to explain exactly what you are doing and why determining the child's instructional level of reading is so important. If the child is interested, point out how the size of print changes in more difficult books, therefore increasing the amount of reading on a page, and how the use of pictures decreases. The child must not be made to feel that the test is a "threat" to his or her status, and if the child is the type who continually asks for reassurance (Am I doin' good?), the teacher needs to be completely reassuring.

Marking and Scoring the IRI

The system of marking errors in oral reading described by Gilmore will meet the needs of most teachers for scoring the IRI. The errors to be noted include substitutions, omissions, insertions, hesitations, words pronounced by the examiner, and repetitions. The important point is that the teacher have a definite, well learned system of marking that will be meaningful. By such a method, a child may read a passage of 300 words, for example, with twenty errors in the mechanics of reading. Measurable growth is shown if three months later the student can read the same passage with only five errors. However, the system of recording errors must be consistent if the pre-/posttest record is to have value. Durrell[17] and Gates[18] have also provided detailed systems for marking errors. Each teacher must know one system well.

With only a minimum amount of practice, groups of experienced teachers find they mark children's oral reading with a very high percent of agreement. So, even though administering the IRI has subjective elements, and many judgments must be made informally and quickly by the teacher, the results will yield objective data from the competent teacher after some practice.

The following types of oral reading errors represent most of the difficulties children have.[19]

Hesitation. Mark after two seconds of hesitation with a ($\checkmark$). Proper nouns are given to the child as needed and are not scored as errors unless the proper noun is a word that most children would know, like Brown, Green, or Smith.

Word pronounced for the child. If a pupil hesitates for approximately five seconds on a difficult word, the teacher should pronounce it and make a second check mark ($\checkmark\checkmark$).

Mispronunciation. This results in a nonsense word which may be produced by: (1) wrongly placed stress, (2) wrong pronunciation of vowels or consonants, or (3) omission, addition, or insertion of one or more letters without creating a real or new word. Example: *crēt'ik* for *critic.* Write the child's pronunciation above phonetically. Notice word attack methods and enunciation. If errors come too rapidly for recording, draw a line through mispronounced words. Do not count foreign accent or regional speech mannerisms. If a proper noun that most children would know is miscalled several times in one passage, the teacher must decide whether to count this as only one error. For example, the child may have read regularly about Tom and Betty and consistently pronounce Fred as Tom in the IRI reading. This should be counted as only one error.

Omissions. Circle the omitted word, syllable, letter sound, or endings that are omitted. Count as only one error the omission of consecutive words.

Punctuation. Put an X on punctuation marks that the child ignores or passes over.

Substitutions. When one sensible or real word is substituted for the printed word, write the substituted word directly above the word presented in print. Notice whether it makes sense or is irrelevant to the context. If the child makes one substitution error and then in the same sentence makes a second error to get proper grammatical structure with verbs or pronouns, count this as only one error. In basic sight word substitutions, the error should be counted each time it occurs. If the reader says "then" for "when" three times, this is three errors.

Insertions. When the child reads words that do not appear in the printed material, place a caret ($\wedge$) and write the added word or words. Count as only one error the insertion of two or more consecutive words.

Repetitions. Repetition of a word, part of a word, or groups of words may indicate that the child is having trouble understanding what he or she reads. Draw a wavy line under the repeated words.

The teacher must record the child's responses to the comprehension questions as they are given. When the child's comprehension falls below 70 to 75 percent, there is no need to have the child continue reading even if few mechanical difficulties are showing up.

Nervous mannerisms such as fidgeting, hair twisting, nose picking, heavy sighing, or undue restlessness indicate discomfort and frustration and should be noted on the child's test. Some other signs that should be noted are losing the place in the story, holding the book close to the face, finger pointing, or head movements.

In silent reading, the child may vocalize everything he reads, read very slowly, or need encouragement to keep on reading.

Figure 19.2 contains a story passage on which oral reading errors are marked according to the system described for the Gilmore Oral Reading Test (figure 19.3). This exercise does not adequately identify the child's instructional level of reading, however. Before making a firm decision, a classroom teacher should ask the child to read some less difficult selections.

The teacher will be able to summarize the results of the IRI reading in a chart such as the following:

Oral

Level of book	Total words	Total errors	Percent of error	Percent accuracy	Level of difficulty
_____	_____	_____	_____	_____	_____
_____	_____	_____	_____	_____	_____
_____	_____	_____	_____	_____	_____
_____	_____	_____	_____	_____	_____
_____	_____	_____	_____	_____	_____

Silent

Level of book	Total words	Time in seconds	Rate per minute	Percent comprehension	Level of difficulty
_____	_____	_____	_____	_____	_____
_____	_____	_____	_____	_____	_____
_____	_____	_____	_____	_____	_____
_____	_____	_____	_____	_____	_____
_____	_____	_____	_____	_____	_____

The Reading Miscue Inventory

The *reading miscue inventory*[20] is another measure of the accuracy with which a child reads a passage orally. It provides an opportunity to study the "match" or the "mismatch" between the exact wording in the text and the language used by the reader in reproducing that text orally. A miscue is the term used to describe those oral responses that differ from the phrasing in the text. The use of the miscue inventory allows the teacher to make the very important distinction between reading miscues which preserve meaning and should be overlooked and miscues which represent the traditional "inability to read well" examined in the informal reading inventory discussed above. In fact, use of such tools as the miscue inventory offers some understanding of how the process of reading works. It shows, for example, that beginning readers who have strong motivation for interpreting sentence structure and sentence meaning in what they read may be deterred and badly taught by teachers who

Figure 19.2 Recording errors in oral reading.

Adapted, with permission, from John V. Gilmore and Eunice C. Gilmore, *Gilmore Oral Reading Test. Manual of Directions* (New York: Harcourt, Brace & World, 1968), pp. 6–7.

Type of Error	Rule for Marking	Examples
Substitutions.	Write in substituted word.	The boy is back of the girl.
Mispronunciations (nonsense words).	Write in the word phonetically or draw a line through word.	symbolic
Words pronounced by examiner (after hesitation of 5 sec. or more).	Make two checks above the word pronounced.	It is a fascinating story.
Disregard of punctuation.	Mark punctuation disregarded with an *X*.	Jack, my brother, is in the navy.
Insertions (including additions).	Write in inserted word or words.	The dog and cat are fighting.
Hesitations (pause of two or more seconds).	Make a check above the word on which hesitation occurs.	It is a fascinating story.
Repetitions (a word, part of a word, or group of words repeated).	Draw a wavy line beneath the word or words repeated.	He thought he saw a whale.
Omissions (one or more words omitted).	Encircle the word or words omitted.	Mother does all of her work with great care.
Corrections.	Write a *C* next to a mistake when the child corrects the error.	I am too unhappy about leaving you.

Figure 19.3 An example of oral reading errors made by a student reading without previous preparation. Four substitutions were self-corrected, and proper names—Zabriski and Oscar—were not counted. Number of errors are expressed as a percentage of number of words.

Gertrude Hildreth et al. *Enchanting Stories* (Philadelphia: Winston, 1952), pp. 181–82.

Oscar's Airplane Ride

When Mr. Zabriski decided to go to Los Angeles, Oscar *went* wanted to go with him. But Mr. Zabriski only shook his head. "I'm sorry," he said, "but I can't be bothered with a seal on this trip, not even a famous seal. You must stay here in New York. I have secret work to do."

Poor, neglected Oscar! He just couldn't stay in New York all alone! "We always go everywhere together," he said to himself. "I know Mr. Zabriski doesn't mean to be selfish. *He* The first thing tomorrow I'll *think* talk *talking* him into taking me along. I need a vacation."

When Then Oscar got into his bathtub and slept until morning.

The next morning, when the seal climbed from his bathtub, he found that *he* his trainer was gone. In a few minutes, he *was* saw a letter leaning against *the* a large fish - Oscar's favorite food. The letter said:

Dear Oscar:

I can't bear to say good-by. I am *going* too unhappy about leaving you. Take good care of yourself until I come back.

Your Trainer,

Zabriski

What did Mr. Zabriski tell Oscar? *+*	Substitutions *9/5*
What did Oscar think about this? *0*	Hesitations *2*
Where did Oscar sleep? *+*	Words pronounced by examiner *9/7*
What is Oscar's favorite food? *+*	Repetitions *2*
What did the letter tell Oscar? *+*	Omissions *1*
comprehension adequate.	Insertions *0*

TOTAL UNCORRECTED ERRORS *17*

Level of difficulty: 2⁄3   Percentage of error: *11%*

Number of words: 160   Percentage of accuracy *89%*

emphasize the phonic or "sounding out" approaches to word identification. It seems clear that if emphasis were placed on extracting meaning rather than on pronunciation of words, fewer reading problems would develop.

The *Reading Miscue Inventory* provides a view of a student's reading performance that is very different from the ones provided by the traditional standardized reading tests or by informal reading inventories. During the oral reading, the student receives no external help; he must rely on his own strategies. His miscues are evaluated to see if he makes appropriate use of syntactic and semantic information. The results of the inventory register the reader's strengths and give information about ineffective and inefficient uses of strategies. It also provides the teacher with information about causes and quality of miscues.[21]

Classroom teachers who study and practice administering the Reading Miscue Inventory to a few students will be better prepared to evaluate classroom reading episodes with individual students for whom there is not time to complete an inventory.

Summary

The regular classroom teacher has the inescapable responsibility for accurate assessment of each child's oral and silent reading abilities. The informal reading inventory is a useful tool for this purpose.

The IRI is a technique for measuring what the independent, instructional, and frustration reading levels are for a child by having the child read graded material and what the capacity level is by reading to the child. The difference between the instructional level of reading and the capacity level for understanding represents the extent of the child's reading retardation.

The limitations of the informal reading inventory and how to construct, administer, mark, score, and interpret the results in terms of difficulty levels of books for children have been presented.

Suggested Activities

Administer the informal reading inventory to five boys and girls with different levels of reading ability, interpret the results, and make recommendations for the children's reading programs.

For Further Reading

Aaron, Ira E. "An Informal Reading Inventory." *Elementary English* 37 (November 1960):457–60.

Bleismer, Emery P. "Informal Teacher Testing in Reading." *The Reading Teacher* 26 (December 1972):268–72.

Botel, Morton. *Botel Reading Inventory.* Chicago, Ill.: Follett, 1961.

Chall, Jeanne. "Ask Him to Try the Book for Fit." *The Reading Teacher* 7 (December 1953):83–88.

Ekwall, E. E. *Diagnosis and Remediation of the Disabled Reader.* Chapter 11, "Using Informal Reading Inventories, the Cloze Procedure, and the Analysis of Reading Scores," pp. 260–91. Boston: Allyn & Bacon, 1976.

Guszak, Frank J. *Diagnostic Reading Instruction in the Elementary School,* 2d ed. New York: Harper & Row, 1978.

Harris, Albert J., and E. R. Sipay. *How to Increase Reading Ability,* 6th ed. Chapters 8 and 9, "Evaluating Performance in Reading I and II." New York: David McKay, 1975.

Johnson, Marjorie, and Roy Kress. *Informal Reading Inventories.* Newark, Del.: International Reading Assn., 1965.

McCracken, Robert A. "Informal Reading Inventories: Diagnosis Within the Teacher." *The Reading Teacher* 26 (December 1972):273–77.

————. "The Informal Reading Inventory as a Means of Improving Instruction." In *Perspectives in Reading: The Evaluation of Children's Reading Achievement,* pp. 79–95, edited by Thomas Barrett. Newark, Del.: International Reading Assn., 1967.

————. "The Development and Validation of the Standard Reading Inventory for the Individual Appraisal of Reading Performance in Grades One Through Six." In *Improvement of Reading Through Classroom Practice,* edited by J. Allen Figurel. IRA Conference Proceedings 9 (1964):310–13.

Valmont, William J. "Creating Questions for Informal Reading Inventories." *The Reading Teacher* 25 (March 1972):509–12.

Wheeler, Lester R., and Edwin H. Smith. "A Modification of the Informal Reading Inventory." *Elementary English* 34 (1967):224–26.

Zintz, Miles V. *Corrective Reading,* 3d ed., Chapter 3, "Evaluating Oral and Silent Reading," pp. 60–114. Dubuque, Ia.: Wm. C. Brown, 1977.

Notes

1. Emmett A. Betts, *Foundations of Reading Instruction* (New York: American Book Co., 1946), p. 449.

2. William D. Sheldon, "Specific Principles Essential to Classroom Diagnosis," *The Reading Teacher* 14 (September 1960):8.

3. Lester R. Wheeler and Edwin H. Smith, "A Modification of the Informal Reading Inventory," *Elementary English* 34 (April 1967):224.

4. Betts, *Foundations of Reading Instruction,* pp. 478–79.

5. Miles A. Tinker, *Bases for Effective Reading* (Minneapolis: University of Minnesota Press, 1965), p. 274.

6. Betts, *Foundations of Reading Instruction,* p. 448.

7. George D. Spache, *Reading in the Elementary School* (Boston: Allyn & Bacon, Inc., 1964), p. 245.

8. Ibid., pp. 248–49.

9. Ernest Horn et al., *Reaching Our Goals,* Progress in Reading Series (Boston: Ginn, 1940), p. 138.

10. Ibid., p. 145.

11. John V. Gilmore, *Gilmore Oral Reading Test* (New York: Harcourt, Brace & World, 1952).

12. Donald G. Anderson, *New Practice Readers* (New York: Webster Division, McGraw-Hill, 1978), Levels A, B, C, D, E, F, G.

13. E. W. Dolch, "How to Diagnose Children's Reading Difficulties by Informal Classroom Techniques," *The Reading Teacher* 6 (January 1953):10–14.

14. William D. Sheldon, Mary C. Austin, and Richard E. Drdek, *Fields and Fences, Readiness Second Reader* (Boston: Allyn & Bacon, 1957), pp. 188–91.

15. E. W. Dolch, *Dolch Basic Sight Word Test* (Champaign, Ill.: Garrard Press, 1942).

16. Maude McBroom, Julia Sparrow, and Catherine Eckstein, *Scale for Determining a Child's Reader Level* (Iowa City: Bureau of Publications, Extension Division, State University of Iowa, 1944).

17. D. D. Durrell, *Manual of Directions, Analysis of Reading Difficulty* (Yonkers-on-Hudson: World Book Co., 1955).

18. A. I. Gates, *Manual of Directions: Gates Reading Diagnostic Test* (New York: Teachers College Press, 1953).

19. Dianne Brown, "The Preparation, Use and Analysis of the Results of the Informal Reading Inventory" (Masters thesis, Graduate School, University of New Mexico, Albuquerque, New Mexico, 1968).

20. Yetta Goodman and Carolyn Burke, *Reading Miscue Inventory: Procedure for Diagnosis and Evaluation* (New York: Macmillan, 1972).

21. Yetta Goodman and Dorothy J. Watson, "A Reading Program to Live with: Focus on Comprehension," *Language Arts* 54 (Nov./Dec. 1977): 868–79.

20

Corrective Reading

Holt has suggested that the expectations of the school and the efforts of boys and girls are not directed toward the same goals:

When I started, I thought that some people were just born smarter than others and that not much could be done about it. This seems to be the official line of most of the psychologists. It isn't hard to believe, if all your contacts are with students in the classroom or the psychological testing room. But, if you live at a small school, seeing students in class, in the dorms, in their private lives, at their recreations, sports, and manual work, you can't escape the conclusion that some people are much smarter part of the time than they are at other times. Why? Why should a boy or girl, who under some circumstances is willingly observant, imaginative, analytical, in a word, intelligent, come into the classroom and, as if by magic, turn into a complete dolt?[1]

When Carolyn came for instruction in remedial reading, she made it quite evident that she thought neither the teachers' efforts nor the school program were designed to help her.

Carolyn's mother called and asked if her daughter, age fourteen and finishing the eighth grade, might have an evaluation of her reading skills. It was the final week of school late in May, and an appointment was made for early June.

Carolyn came for testing in an obviously belligerent mood. Her mother brought her and waited for her during the testing, and this was an obvious irritation for Carolyn.

Carolyn explained to the clinician that she was stupid. When the clinician raised some doubt about it, Carolyn said, "Just ask all the teachers over at Junior High, they'll all tell you I'm stupid." The clinician presented a brief list of polysyllabic words to be pronounced and divided in syllables, and Carolyn commented, "O.K., so you can see how stupid I really am."

When she defined the vocabulary words in the Stanford-Binet test and earned an "average adult" score on that subtest, the clinician used this bit of evidence to say that she was apparently doing as well as the average on that particular test. At this, Carolyn said acidly, "So that's an intelligence test! I've had those at junior high, too, and the counselor there told me I was stupid."

Later the young lady revealed that, not only was she stupid, but she was also huge. She thought she was as big as a horse. She was a large-boned fourteen-year-old, taller and heavier than the average girl in her class.

On the reading survey test, she scored at beginning fifth grade on vocabulary, speed, and comprehension. This was no surprise to Carolyn and she let it be known that she understood that the clinician was collecting further evidence of her inadequacy.

Carolyn's summer program included one lesson a week, during which she studied spelling, phonic and structural analysis, and syllabication and wrote paragraphs about topics of her choice. In addition, she came twice a week to complete, independently, exercises from the SRA Junior Reading for Understanding Laboratory. She began with card No. 17, at beginning fifth grade level. At this level she was successful, and completed two cards at each level until she reached beginning sixth grade level in about two weeks. When she read the table of grade placement values in the teacher's guidebook, she began to appear much more confident. By the end of eight weeks, she was ready for cards at beginning ninth grade level and appeared confident that she would be able to do her reading work in the fall.

Her summer program had been well planned apart from the reading lessons, too, and she had enjoyed short courses at the YWCA in cheerleading, drama, and charm. In addition, she was an excellent swimmer and participated as a member of a girls' swimming team.

Corrective reading is the instruction provided by the regular classroom teacher during the school day to help individual children overcome whatever stumbling blocks prevent them from achieving appropriate developmental skills in reading. Children who fail to master a basic sight vocabulary, who fail to develop auditory discrimination of the phonemes of the English language, who fail to learn to read fluently enough to read entertainingly to others are in need of remediation, reteaching, special help, or tutoring to master the missing mechanical skills. Of course, adequate comprehension of material read must also be considered. Children who fail to comprehend may or may not have adequate word recognition skills.

To distinguish corrective from remedial instruction is only to indicate that the extra effort to help the child is made by the classroom teacher within the framework of the regular teaching day rather than by a remedial reading clinician who teaches the child at a special time outside the classroom. While no clearcut distinction can be made between what is remedial and what is corrective, the latter term helps us to think specifically about ways the classroom teacher can function *all day long* as a teacher of children with skill deficiencies.

We can hope that corrective reading cases will not be severely complicated by emotional or neurological problems or language deficits, but they very well may be. Hopefully, if the philosophy of teaching throughout the elementary school has been a diagnostic one, many of these problems will have been identified early and deep-seated emotional problems averted.

With early identification, teachers need to emphasize ways in which children learn best, try to strengthen learning styles that are weak, and provide a systematic program of sequenced instruction of skills over as long a period of time as is indicated.

Why Do Children Fail?
It may be well to look first at some erroneous reasons given for why children fail. Although they are often cited, the following are *not* reasons why so many children fail in reading.

1. It is *not* because teachers do *not* teach phonics in the elementary schools today. In the lessons on word-attack skills, specific techniques are presented in all teacher's guides.

2. It is *not* because teachers do not know how to teach reading. If a teacher in a busy, crowded classroom teaches 85 percent of her class to read successfully in terms of their potential ability to achieve, it is unfair to look at the small percentage of children who fail to progress and place all the blame on the teacher. Might it not be much more logical to say that the overcrowded conditions of the classrooms may be a primary cause?

3. It is *not* because schools are progressive and permit anarchy in their classrooms. Sufficient standard test data are available today to prove convincingly that groups of children today read better than comparable groups did at any time in the past. Further, there is evidence to show that children who are taught in classrooms where *activity* work, teacher-pupil planning, and student responsibility are encouraged read better, on the average, than children taught in more formally organized classrooms.

4. It is *not* because too little time is devoted to the 3 Rs. Visits to classrooms would soon show one that teachers still devote much time to the 3Rs—in fact, spend *too much time* working on routine, unmotivating, monotonous lessons in an attempt to help children learn the 3 Rs.

5. It is *not* because parents won't cooperate with the schools. Although there are a few situations where teachers and parents are incompatible, parent-teacher conferences help immeasurably to clarify the problems of children in school.

While none of these five causes should be used as a generalized vague reason for our problems, it is true that any one of them may be a primary contributing factor in individual cases.

The main causes for children failing to learn to read are related to the traditional organization of schools. A school that puts children into classes where *standards* have been defined arbitrarily in terms of grade placement automatically labels as failures all children who do not measure up. All children are expected to come to school when they are six and be enrolled in the first grade. All parents are strongly pressured by the mores of their community to see that their child fits a normal pattern.

The organized school works far too hard trying to make everybody alike—and conform to a preconceived stereotype—rather than encouraging real individuality. Even when schools give lip service to the idea of accepting individuality, they often work against it in practice. Teachers are habituated to a deeply entrenched practice of teaching *books* rather than teaching *children* to read books.

The continuing practice that every first grader read first grade readers, every second grader read second grade readers, and every third grader read third grade readers will never work. Teachers should have children read for regular classes only those books that are appropriate for their instructional level. (Instructional level is that level at which a child fails to pronounce correctly no more than five words in reading a passage of 100 words and can answer questions to show that at least 75 percent of the ideas are understood. (See chapter 19.)

Teachers who do not hold stringently to this standard and allow children to work in books that are too difficult keep the children struggling at their frustration levels. Children can do little more than memorize statements and parrot facts when they are kept reading at this level.

Teachers, generally, have not followed an application of our knowledge of the psychology of individual differences to its logical conclusion. One hears from teachers and administrators, "What are you going to do when they get to the fourth grade?" "What will they do when they get to seventh grade?" or "How about when they come to high school at ninth grade?"

One accepts the situation as he finds it. Two basic principles about learning apply here: (1) the spread of mental ability in any grade is going to increase as children go through school; and (2) no child can read a more difficult book until he or she can read an easier one. If these two principles are accepted, there is no alternative to starting where the child is. Rejecting or not knowing these principles, a few teachers have said, "But I'm a sixth grade teacher and I don't know anything about phonics," or "I'm an upper grade teacher and I don't know how to teach primary reading," or "I teach seventh grade and they're supposed to learn that in the lower grades."

Teachers need to remember that in their classes children exhibit different levels of understanding. Level of understanding is determined by degree of intelligence and previous experiences either firsthand or vicarious. Children may understand a concept very well; or they may understand some things about the concept; or they may have only a vague idea of what the concept is about. It helps little to try to clarify concepts in children's thinking if their chief concern is remembering facts to give back to a teacher. Teachers can best help to clarify concepts by seeing that the same concept is dealt with in many ways, and by using the concept in problems related to the child's life experience.

Finally, many schools do not have an overall school policy that gives teachers confidence in what they do in one calendar year. Overall policy gives continuity to the school program from grade to grade. Present-day school programs must recognize the necessity of teaching reading all the way through the secondary school and having a cumulative record available for each child so that each teacher has access to all the helpful information compiled by the child's previous teachers.

<table>
<tr><td>Does the Work Schedule "Fit" the Child?</td><td>Causes of reading failure will be met only by:</td></tr>
</table>

1. *Doing* something about individual differences. This means doing something about them *all day long.* A child who reads a fourth grade reader much of the year while in the sixth grade should spell fourth grade spelling words and read books no more difficult than fourth grade reader level for factual information in all the content subjects. It means accepting careful measures of readiness for reading before putting all children into a formal reading program in first grade. It means that educators must stop expecting all children in a class to learn the same thing, in the same amount of time, with the same amount of practice.

2. Knowing how to use information about children and where to get it, such as cumulative records, which should include:
   a. Intelligence test records
   b. Health records
   c. Reading record of books previously read
   d. Summaries of personal conferences with child, parent, or other professional
   e. Standardized tests of achievement

3. Having an accepted school policy that everybody is willing to put into effect. The school program should be well enough understood by each teacher to provide a sense of security. Overall school policies should accept these basic principles:
   a. The school exists solely to help children. This means that no child is a misfit. They *all* belong.
   b. Since no two children are alike, the teacher must start to help each child "where the child is." This means that each teacher must feel secure in knowing that each succeeding teacher will also accept the wide range of differences in a class when they are promoted.
   c. Every teacher is a reading teacher. Children must be taught how to read all the different kinds of material with which they are confronted: extensive reading, intensive reading, reading to evaluate critically, reading to remember details, and recreational reading are some of the types.

d. An accepting, analytical approach to existing problems. An open-mindedness and "pooling of ideas" when teacher, principal, and special services representatives discuss a child with a problem. No one should feel insecure in asking for help with children who present difficult problems. (See below, the need for "staffing" case studies.)

4. Having a special services department to analyze problems. This means personnel who are able to analyze problems in the areas of: remedial reading, behavior, mental retardation or acceleration, physical handicaps, speech correction and speech improvement. When a child's problem has been studied and a case study has been prepared, a round table discussion should include as many people as are concerned with the case and will implement the findings. Any or all of the following people should participate in such a discussion: teachers, parents, principal, school guidance counselor, school social worker, school nurse, school psychologist, school doctor, visiting teacher, and special therapists.

5. Having adequate *materials of instruction.* Probably the one greatest obstacle to improvement of classroom instruction today is the lack of adequate materials of all sorts for teacher use (books, magazines, pamphlets, charts, maps, pictures, films, filmstrips, models, workbooks).

6: The best practice in reporting a child's progress to his parents must come by way of some kind of two-way communication. There must be some time and some way that the teacher can discuss in a "face-to-face" situation with the parents the progress in academic work and social development the child is making. The parents can say in the same "face-to-face" situation to the teacher what they are thinking, and then, in this same conversational atmosphere, they can work out any semantic differences. While they may not agree, at least they have a greater degree of understanding of each other's opinions. Sometimes, such a conversation gives them much mutual support.

In summary, then, six suggestions are offered for meeting the problems of reading failure:

1. Recognizing and meeting individual differences.
2. Knowing how to obtain and use information about children.
3. Establishing a school policy that is effective from the first year through senior high school.
4. Utilizing special services and special personnel in studying about children.
5. Providing adequate materials of instruction.
6. Working cooperatively with parents.

Remedial Techniques

The reader will recall from chapter 19, The Informal Reading Inventory, that for each child three reading levels are relevant: the independent level, at which free reading is done; the instructional level, at which classroom reading is done; and the frustration level, at which the child makes too many errors in mechanics of reading and/or comprehends too few of the ideas in the text to profit from the work. For corrective reading materials, the teacher should take every precaution that the reading the child may do outside the classroom is no more difficult than his independent reader level. The child may do easy oral reading practice for parents if they show interest and attention, but unless it is done at the child's independent reading level, the parents may not understand the difficulties and may render a great disservice.

It is generally not recommended that parents try to help their own children who have problems with reading. This recommendation is sound for two reasons. First, without specialized training, a parent is apt not to understand that remedial teaching techniques must fit a specific child. Second, being a parent of a child who is *failing* in a task at which all children *should* succeed creates an emotionally stressful situation. When a child has difficulty with both conditions present, the result is apt to be an emotional scene of belligerence, aggression, crying, or some combination of these.

If a philosophy of diagnostic teaching has been followed, then corrective reading instruction is part of standard operating procedure. Difficulties are worked on as soon as they appear. Difficulties are uncovered, and reteaching is the next order of business. All children need spaced reviews and a great deal of reinforcement of important learnings.

Specific Difficulties

Word Recognition

Many children finish the third grade without establishing mastery of the 220 Dolch Basic Sight Words. Because this list is composed of the service words that constitute half of all the text words in elementary school textbooks, they must be mastered. No nouns were included in the basic sight word list since Dolch did not consider naming words to be service words. But he also identified the 95 most common nouns in children's reading experience. Any corrective reading program must provide for the teaching of these most used words. Suggestions for such teaching are included in chapter 9, Word Recognition Skills.

Figure 20.1 A sample of a child's errors on Part I of the Dolch Basic Sight Word Test. The teacher crosses out all words pronounced at sight and writes in the substitution errors the child makes.

10. has ~~he~~ his far *(his)* *(has)* *(for)*

11. ~~but~~ ~~jump~~ ~~just~~ ~~buy~~ *barked* *came* *fan*

12. black kind ~~blue~~ find

13. ~~fast~~ first ate ~~eat~~ *aren't*

14. ~~help~~ hot both ~~hold~~ *hope* *boat*

Table 20.1 Analysis of errors made on Part I, *Dolch Basic Sight Word Test.*

Wrong Beginnings	Wrong Middles	Wrong Endings	Reversals	Wrong Several Parts	Failed to Pronounce
it for at	hid for had	his for him	me for am	barked for black	drink
brown for down	here for have	bringing for bring	brown for down	came for kind	ask
now for how	my for may	boat for both	now for how	fan for find	as
gray for give	his for has	became for because		aren't for ate	found
gray for gave	has for his	less for let	(3)	hope for hot	eight
	for for far	go for got		get for grow	better
(5)	a boat for about	can for came		a little for always	light
	fall for full			game for again	done
	bean for been			afraid for after	draw
	like for live	(7)		couldn't for clean	get
	din't for don't			four for five	
	came for come			bus for best	(10)
				lake for laugh	
	(12)			hard for hurt	
				could for carry	
				could for call	
				heard for here	
				had for here	
				(18)	

Criteria for knowing a Dolch Basic Sight Word are as follows:

1. The child looks at the word and pronounces it correctly.
2. The child does not sound the word letter-by-letter.
3. The child does not need more than a few seconds to say the word.

A child having difficulty and missing half of the sight words should be allowed to stop the test. With older children making many errors, the teacher may decide to do only Part I or Part II of the Basic Sight Word Test Sheet.

Some sample errors made by a child on Part I are shown in figure 20.1. It is possible to make an analysis of these errors by grouping them into the following categories: wrong beginnings, wrong middles, wrong endings, reversals, wrong several parts, and words not pronounced—as in table 20.1. The analysis shows that the child makes all types of errors. However, if *brown* for *down* is caused by reversing *b's* and *d's,* and *now* for *how* is caused by confusing *n's* and *h's,* there were fewer errors in beginnings. This is significant since, at the level at which the child will be able to read context, attention to "How does the word begin?" seems most appropriate. Since the child has pronounced about 55 of the 110 words in Part I of the test at sight, we could project another 55 out of 110 on Part II. For this estimated score of 110, the McBroom, Sparrow, Eckstein scale (see table 19.2) indicates a primer level of reading.

Wrong beginnings is probably the lowest level of error since first grade teachers work very hard at helping children perceive words from left to right. The teacher will probably want to give the child some help with studying the word all the way through to be sure to get the ending right. The analysis of errors makes it clear that vowel sounds are giving the child a great deal of difficulty in the middle of words. As the child's reading level increases to second grade, complete instruction in the vowel skills will be needed.

The Slosson Oral Reading Test (SORT) (Richard L. Slosson: Slosson Educational Publications, 140 Pine Street, East Aurora, New York) is a quick, easy word list to administer to get some knowledge of a student's word recognition ability. The test can be given and scored in about three minutes. Its worth in evaluating a student's total reading ability is severely limited, but it may be a useful preliminary to other diagnostic testing.

The Slosson Oral Reading Test is given individually and requires only that the student *pronounce* words from graded lists at different levels of ability. There are ten lists of twenty words each: primer, grades one through eight, and high school. The total number of words pronounced correctly plus the number below the individual's starting place is converted by a table to a reading grade level in years and months. For example, a raw score of 86 is a grade equivalent score of 4.3 (third month of fourth grade).

The San Diego Quick Assessment is another very short, easy-to-administer word recognition test. It is included here. It has been found useful for finding a starting place to begin work with a child. Below are the instructions, the steps in administering, and the test itself.

San Diego Quick Assessment[2]

Margaret La Pray and Ramon Ross

Instructions:

1. Have the student read lists until he misses three words in one list.
2. The list in which a student misses no more than one of the ten words is the level at which he can read independently. Two errors indicate his instructional level. Three or more words identify the level at which reading material will be too difficult.
3. Be sure to analyze the errors.
4. Observe behaviors that accompany the reading.

Administration:

1. Type out each list of ten words on index cards, one list to a card. If available, type the first three or four lists with primary type.
2. Begin with a card that is at least two years below the student's grade level assignment.
3. Do not put the reading level on the cards where the student can read it. Do your coding on the back of the card.
4. Ask the student to read the words aloud to you. If he misreads any on the list, drop to easier lists until he makes no errors. This indicates the base level.
5. Write down all incorrect responses or write them on the copy of the test.
6. Encourage the student to read words he does not know so that you can identify the techniques he uses for word identification.
7. Keep reading lists until he misses three words on any one list or all lists are exhausted.

The Test:

PP	Primer	1	2	3
see	you	road	our	city
play	come	live	please	middle
me	not	thank	myself	moment
at	with	when	town	frightened
run	jump	bigger	early	exclaimed
go	help	how	send	several
and	is	always	wide	lonely
look	work	night	believe	drew
can	are	spring	quietly	since
here	this	today	carefully	straight

4	5	6	7	8
decided	scanty	bridge	amber	capacious
served	certainly	commercial	dominion	limitation
amazed	develop	abolish	sundry	pretext
silent	considered	trucker	capillary	intrigue
wrecked	discussed	apparatus	impetuous	delusion
improved	behaved	elementary	blight	immaculate
certainly	splendid	comment	wrest	ascent
entered	acquainted	necessity	enumerate	acrid
realized	escaped	gallery	daunted	binocular
interrupted	grim	relativity	condescend	embankment

9	10	11
conscientious	zany	galore
isolation	jerkin	rotunda
molecule	nausea	capitalism
ritual	gratuitous	prevaricate
momentous	linear	risible
vulnerable	inept	exonerate
kinship	legality	superannuate
conservatism	aspen	luxuriate
jaunty	amnesty	piebald
inventive	barometer	crunch

Measuring Abilities in Phonics and Structural Analysis

The teacher can informally test how well children in a reading group can identify the initial, medial, and final sounds in words by merely asking:

What is the first sound you hear in *book, toy, forest, party, kitchen, candy* (either k or c)?

What are the first two letters in these words *fright, snake, skate, scales* (either sk or sc), *praise, dwelling?*

What is the middle sound you hear in *cabbage, forest, balloon, reading, practice?*

What is the vowel that this word begins with *Indian, olives, elephant, umbrella, apple?*

The teacher needs, however, a more standard measure of which phonic elements a child knows and does not know. There are some inventories available to the teacher for this purpose.

The Inventory of Phonetic Skills[3] is one of these. The inventories are developed for end of grade one, end of grade two, and end of grade three and are called Test One, Test Two, and Test Three. They sample the phonic and structural elements that have been taught in the Houghton Mifflin Reading Program through each respective grade level. Test Two includes seven subtests: initial consonant sounds, final consonant sounds, structural elements, vowel elements, initial consonant sounds (more difficult), structural elements (more difficult), and vowel elements (more difficult). Test Two is reproduced in part in figure 20.2. A teacher's guide contains the rationale for the test, directions for administering and scoring, and suggestions for reteaching items a child misses.

As another source, most series of readers provide at each achievement level adequate tests of the phonic and structural elements taught.

Several subtests of the Silent Reading Diagnostic Tests[4] are also useful for analyzing phonic and structural errors in children's reading test performance. They provide for identifying initial, medial, and final errors in word recognition errors; locating visual elements in words; syllabication; locating root words; hearing beginning sounds; hearing rhyming words; and identifying letter sounds.

Figure 20.2

Inventory of Phonetic Skills, Test Two, Houghton Mifflin, 1972.

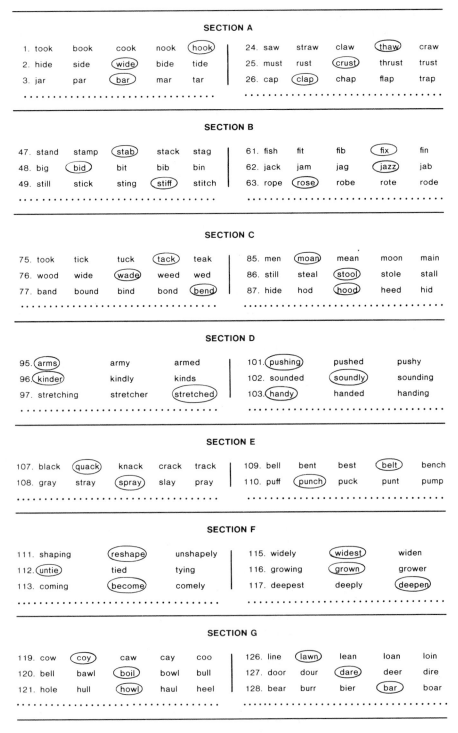

SECTION A

1. took	book	cook	nook	(hook)
2. hide	side	(wide)	bide	tide
3. jar	par	(bar)	mar	tar

24. saw	straw	claw	(thaw)	craw
25. must	rust	(crust)	thrust	trust
26. cap	(clap)	chap	flap	trap

SECTION B

47. stand	stamp	(stab)	stack	stag
48. big	(bid)	bit	bib	bin
49. still	stick	sting	(stiff)	stitch

61. fish	fit	fib	(fix)	fin
62. jack	jam	jag	(jazz)	jab
63. rope	(rose)	robe	rote	rode

SECTION C

75. took	tick	tuck	(tack)	teak
76. wood	wide	(wade)	weed	wed
77. band	bound	bind	bond	(bend)

85. men	(moan)	mean	moon	main
86. still	steal	(stool)	stole	stall
87. hide	hod	(hood)	heed	hid

SECTION D

95. (arms)	army	armed
96. (kinder)	kindly	kinds
97. stretching	stretcher	(stretched)

101. (pushing)	pushed	pushy
102. sounded	(soundly)	sounding
103. (handy)	handed	handing

SECTION E

| 107. black | (quack) | knack | crack | track |
| 108. gray | stray | (spray) | slay | pray |

| 109. bell | bent | best | (belt) | bench |
| 110. puff | (punch) | puck | punt | pump |

SECTION F

111. shaping	(reshape)	unshapely
112. (untie)	tied	tying
113. coming	(become)	comely

115. widely	(widest)	widen
116. growing	(grown)	grower
117. deepest	deeply	(deepen)

SECTION G

119. cow	(coy)	caw	cay	coo
120. bell	bawl	(boil)	bowl	bull
121. hole	hull	(howl)	haul	heel

126. line	(lawn)	lean	loan	loin
127. door	dour	(dare)	deer	dire
128. bear	burr	bier	(bar)	boar

Evaluation in the Reading Program

The arbitrary necessity for reading from left-to-right on the line of print is a learned behavior needed in our culture—although not in all cultures. A number of children have difficulties with this orientation when they come to school, and the difficulty varies in intensity from one child to another. Teachers must have some techniques for helping children overcome their confusion.

Children may reverse whole words: *was* for *saw; ten* for *net.* They may reverse some of the letters inside words: *form* for *from; left* for *felt; tired* for *tried.* Or, they may reverse only one letter: *pig* for *dig; put* for *but; way* for *may.*

It is common for the so-called dyslexic child to have imperfect directional sense—to confuse left and right and up and down. As a result, the child is likely to reverse letters and words, or syllables within words: *b* becomes *d, p* becomes *q; saw* may be written as *was, left* as *felt, on* as *no,* and *sorrow* as *sowro.* Numbers may be similarly reversed, with *42* substituted for *24.* Up and down confusion leads a child to write *M* for *W* and *d* for *p.* All children up to about age six may have a few difficulties of this kind, but the so-called dyslexic child's reversals are far more numerous and persist much longer.[5]

The teacher will utilize any device that will help a child remember always to begin on the left until the habit has been established. Some techniques for teaching directional sense are: uncovering words from left to right; coloring the first letter of a word green and the last letter red; repeatedly moving the hand left-to-right under lines of print when reading with the boys and girls; comparing two words already confused, like *was* and *saw,* to call attention to how they are alike and how they are different. A teacher who knows that a child has such a problem will avoid teaching two words at the same time that are often confused. For example, if the word *left* is being used in reading, the word *felt* should be avoided in writing until emphasis on remembering the word *left* has caused it to be fixed in the child's memory. The teacher will find lists of suggestions in Harris and Sipay[6] and Zintz[7].

Ellingson reports in her book *The Shadow Children:*[8]

A favorite anecdote among the group I have worked with concerns a boy who, after painstaking care, finally learned the composite parts of the word "until," but still could not "pull" the word instantly from memory when he tried to read it. Finally, he said to his teacher, "If I could just *see* an 'until,' I know I could remember it." What was necessary to complete the boy's mastery of the word was an associative method. The boy was instructed to draw, from within himself, his idea of the word—to make a picture to go with a sentence using the word. The boy then carefully drew a picture of a herd of cows, pastureland, a fence with a gate, and a farmhouse in the distance, with the cows going through the gate toward the farmhouse. He then wrote his sentence, "I will wait until the cows come home." For this boy, with this word, "until the cows come home" provided the needed association and visual memory that firmly "set" it in his mind. From then on, whenever he came across the word, no matter how different or complicated the context, he could look at it and say, "Oh, yes, that's until—until the cows come home." This achievement is not inconsequential. The child had used all of his avenues of learning—then added association and was able to read, write, spell, and comprehend the word "until."

Easy Oral Reading Practice

While it is difficult for the teacher to find time, it is necessary for each child to have as much oral reading practice as is possible. Children who do not have mastery over the sight words must read them over and over and over in interesting stories until they do know them. Other children can be pupil-teachers if the teacher plans carefully how children can read in pairs. Older brothers and sisters who read well can be very helpful in listening to a child read. Placing the tape recorder in a quiet corner and stationing one child with it who knows how to operate it makes it possible for children to go there for three or five-minute intervals to record their oral reading. The teacher can then evaluate the results after school or with the child at an appropriate time.

Reading in Phrases

To help children overcome word-by-word reading, practice on reading phrases may help them anticipate endings of prepositional phrases. Such phrases as the following might be used for motivated flash card drill:

On Phrases	*In* Phrases	*To* Phrases
on the house	in a minute	to the river
on the hilltop	in a hurry	to the house
on the mountainside	in the basket	to the window
on the far side	in her pocketbook	to the candy store

Expanding Word Understanding and Comprehension	For techniques to help children use multiple meanings of common words, opposites, homonyms, synonyms, context clues, picture clues, word analysis, selecting appropriate dictionary definition, interpreting figures of speech, simple analogies, putting nouns in categories, see chapter 10.
	For ways to help children improve their ability to comprehend sentence meanings, comprehend paragraphs, evaluate emotional responses, generalize, organize, and summarize, see chapter 11.
Books of High Interest, Low Vocabulary Level	The following list of books should be especially useful to reading teachers in their corrective and remedial work. The high interest appeal of the subjects motivates children and the low vocabulary level used keeps them from becoming discouraged.

American Adventure Series, Lexington, Mass.: D. C. Heath. About twenty titles ranging in difficulty from second through sixth grade.

Animal Adventure Series. Westchester, Ill.: Benefic Press. Preprimary to grade 3. Record or cassette available for each book.

Beginner Books Series. New York: Random House. Dozens of titles of first and second grade levels of difficulty.

Checkered Flag Series. Menlo Park, Calif.: Addison-Wesley. Four books especially designed to appeal to older boys with severe reading handicap.

Childhood of Famous Americans Series. Indianapolis, Ind.: Bobbs-Merrill. More than 100 titles with vocabulary controlled to about fourth grade level.

The Clyde Bulla Books. New York: Thomas Y. Crowell.

Contact, prepared by the editors of Scholastic Scope. Englewood Cliffs, N.J.: Scholastic Book Services.

Cowboy Sam Series. Westchester, Ill.: Benefic Press. Ten titles ranging in difficulty from preprimer to third grade level.

Dan Frontier Series. Westchester, Ill.: Benefic Press. Ten titles ranging in difficulty from preprimer to third grade level.

Deep Sea Adventure Series. Menlo Park, Calif.: Addison-Wesley. Eight books ranging in difficulty from high first to low fifth grade level.

The Dolch Four-Step Reading Program. Champaign, Ill.: Garrard.

Easy Reading Book Bags. Chicago: Children's Press.

Easy Reader Wonder Books. New York: Wonder-Treasure Books. Inexpensive editions with vocabularies controlled to between 100 and 200 words.

Follett Beginning to Read Series. Chicago: Follett. Some preprimer level, first grade level, second grade level, and third grade level.

Interesting Reading Series. Chicago: Follett. Ten titles written for older boys and girls with vocabulary controlled to about third grade reading level.

Jim Forest Reading Series. Menlo Park, Calif.: Addison-Wesley. Six books ranging in difficulty from first grade to third grade.

Landmark Books. New York: Random House. More than 100 titles ranging in difficulty from fourth grade through ninth grade level.

Monster Books. Los Angeles: Bowmar/Noble. Strong appeal for reluctant readers; also available in Spanish.

Morgan Bay Mysteries. Menlo Park, Calif.: Addison-Wesley. Eight mystery stories written at about independent third grade reading level.

Our Animal Story Books Series. Lexington, Mass.: D. C. Heath. Preprimer level vocabulary.

Pioneer Series. Westchester, Ill.: Benefic Press. Many titles with vocabulary controlled to about third grade reading level.

Read-by-Yourself Books. Boston: Houghton Mifflin.

Reading Incentive Program. Los Angeles: Bowmar/Noble.

Sailor Jack Series. Westchester, Ill.: Benefic Press. Ten titles ranging in difficulty from preprimer to third grade level.

Signal Books. Garden City, New York: Doubleday. Ten titles in the series with reader level controlled to about fourth grade level.

Simplified Classics. Glenview, Ill.: Scott, Foresman. Many children's classics rewritten at about fourth grade level of difficulty.

Target Today Series. Westchester, Ill.: Benefic Press. Four books with teachers' manuals, pupils' editions, activity books, and participation and involvement kits.

Venture Books. Leland Jacobs and John McInnes, consultants. Champaign, Ill.: Garrard.

Wild Life Adventure Series. Menlo Park, Calif.: Addison-Wesley. Stories of wild animals written with about fourth or fifth grade reading level of difficulty.

Yearling Individualized Reading Program. Los Angeles: Bowmar/Noble.

Henry Bamman et al. *Kaleidoscope Readers*. Menlo Park, Calif.: Addison-Wesley. Paperback story and workbook type exercises for the elementary grades.

John D. Bushman, Marvin Laser, and Cherry Tom. *Scope: Reading I*, and *Scope: Reading II*. New York: Harper & Row. Short articles and stories of interest to older students.

C. R. Crosher. *Pacemaker Story Books*. Belmont, Calif.: Fearon-Pitman. Short paperback books with high interest appeal for older students.

Jean Darby. *The Time Machine Series*. Menlo Park, Calif.: Addison-Wesley. Science interest for intermediate grades but vocabulary control for first through third grades.

Harvey Granite et al. *Houghton Mifflin Action Series*. Boston: Houghton Mifflin.

Margaret Hillert. *Follett Just Beginning to Read Books*. Chicago: Follett.

Bill Martin, ed. *The Owl Books*. New York: Holt, Rinehart & Winston.

Bill Martin and Peggy Brogan. *The Sounds of Language Readers*. New York: Holt, Rinehart & Winston.

Edith McCall. *Button Family Adventure Series*. Westchester, Ill.: Benefic Press. Twelve titles ranging in difficulty from preprimer to third grade level.

John and Nancy Rambeau. *Better Reading Series*. Oklahoma City: Educational Guidelines Co., A Division of the Economy Co.

William Sheldon et al. *Breakthrough*. Boston: Allyn & Bacon. Easy reading paperback books for junior and senior high pupils.

Gertrude Warner. *The Box Car Children Books*. Glenview, Ill.: Scott Foresman.

Diagnostic Information and Record Keeping

It is important for a teacher initiating a corrective reading program for a child also to try to find out why the child is not learning to read as well as expected. To obtain this information, the teacher will build a kind of case study about the child. Ideally, there will be a school psychologist, a school social worker, and a reading specialist in the school system who can provide much needed information to the teacher. Case history information will relate to intelligence, physical problems, neurological difficulties, and social and emotional factors.

The diagnosis and planning needed are diagrammed in figure 20.3. Five types of information should go into the case history. (1) There should be a parent interview concerning family background, significance of reading success in the family, and probable causes for reading failure. (2) A medical examination should include evaluation of the child's visual and hearing acuity and general health. The family doctor will make referrals to specialists when neurological problems, problems of basal metabolism, or convulsive disorders are present. (3) A psychological evaluation will include both tests of general intelligence and structured or unstructured personality tests. (4) A school history will reveal grades, attendance, persistent problems, teachers' evaluations, and work habits. (5) Guidance information will describe the child's motivation, aptitude, and level of aspiration.

This body of information gathered in the case history must be studied and analyzed by the school psychologist or the school social worker. In turn, it must be interpreted to the pupil, the parents, and the pupil's teacher and principal.

Basic to analyzing problems of specific learning disabilities are four areas of diagnosis:

1. Possible genetic findings. If one or both parents of a child had serious learning problems in school, or if the child has uncles or aunts or brothers or sisters who never learned to read, the possibility that such a trait is inherited gains credibility.

2. The diagnostician will eliminate as many causal factors as possible, such as: emotional disturbance; perceptual defects; low intelligence; poor reading instruction; poor motivation. When such understood factors are known *not* to be related to a child's problem, professionals must search for more adequate answers.

3. The diagnostician examines clues or indications, sometimes referred to medically as *soft signs:* low subtest scores on block design or object assembly on the Wechsler Intelligence Scale for Children; mild but not definitive electroencephalogram abnormalities; lack of cerebral dominance; inefficient eye movements in reading.

4. Do specific teaching methods produce positive results? If techniques help these children, then the clinician categorizes the child's problem with greater confidence.

A teacher can keep a progress report on children having corrective reading instruction by completing a summary of an informal reading analysis every two months or nine weeks throughout the school year. A suggested form is presented in figure 20.4.

Figures 20.5, 20.6, and 20.7 show some suggested forms for keeping records of progress for individuals or small groups. A teacher could adapt them to 5-by-8-inch index cards or loose-leaf notebook sheets.

Summary

One may generalize the following principles of corrective reading for the classroom teacher:

1. Corrective reading instruction must be based on a diagnosis of the reading problem and the instruction must be directed to supplying the missing skills in the developmental sequence.

2. Corrective reading instruction must begin at the level where the child will be successful in whatever he does. The maxim "Nothing succeeds like success" is still true.

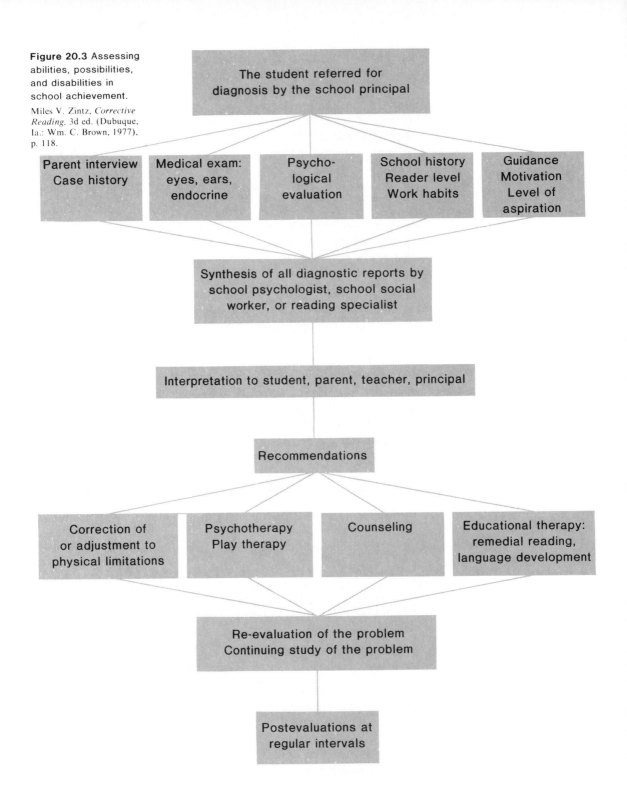

Figure 20.3 Assessing abilities, possibilities, and disabilities in school achievement.

Miles V. Zintz, *Corrective Reading,* 3d ed. (Dubuque, Ia.: Wm. C. Brown, 1977), p. 118.

The student referred for diagnosis by the school principal

Parent interview
Case history

Medical exam: eyes, ears, endocrine

Psychological evaluation

School history
Reader level
Work habits

Guidance
Motivation
Level of aspiration

Synthesis of all diagnostic reports by school psychologist, school social worker, or reading specialist

Interpretation to student, parent, teacher, principal

Recommendations

Correction of or adjustment to physical limitations

Psychotherapy
Play therapy

Counseling

Educational therapy: remedial reading, language development

Re-evaluation of the problem
Continuing study of the problem

Postevaluations at regular intervals

Figure 20.4 Summary
of informal reading
analysis.

Teacher (Clinician) _____ Date _____

Student _____ C. A. _____ Grade _____ Date _____

I. Reader level found in a series of readers

A. Oral reading

Level of book	Total words	Total errors	Percent of error	Percent of accuracy	Suitability of level of difficulty

B. Silent reading

Level of book	No. of words	Time in sec.	Rate of reading	Percent of comprehension	Suitability of level of difficulty

C. Capacity level for material read to student

_____

_____

_____

II. Analysis of errors on sight word test (Dolch, San Diego, Slosson, etc.)

Initial errors (most commonly made)	Medial errors (grade level indicated)	Final errors (comments)

III. Other word perception abilities

Does student always recognize compound words? _____

Errors in any area of phonics survey: _____

At what grade level can student spell (60 percent correct before study)? _____

Does student have reversals and confusions? _____ What kinds?

_____

_____

IV. Summary

Instructional level of reading: _____

Plans for reading progress: _____

_____

Figure 20.5 Initial summary of information about the child who has a reading disability.

Name (last name first)	Date	Grade in school
Parent or guardian	School	Attended kindergarten?
Home address	Home telephone number	Grades repeated
Estimated capacity level	Intelligence level (individual or group test?)	Date of birth
Reading instructional level	Knowledge of phonics	Grade level of spelling
Vision	Hearing	Motor coordination
School absences last year	Socio-economic status	Number of siblings
Report from parents		Report from family doctor
Specific plans for beginning work		Report from previous teacher

Figure 20.6 Record of reading progress throughout school year.

Name (last name first) _____ Date _____ Grade in school _____

Standardized reading test _____ Date given _____ Results (grade placement) _____

Standardized reading test _____ Date given _____ Results (grade placement) _____

(1) IRI (material used) _____ (1) Date of IRI _____ Instructional level _____

(2) IRI (material used) _____ (2) Date of IRI _____ Instructional level _____

(3) IRI (material used) _____ (3) Date of IRI _____ Instructional level _____

Interest inventory findings _____

Personality data _____

Notes: _____

Figure 20.7 Books and materials used for the reading program.

Name	Date	Grade in school
Name of book or program:	Beginning date:	Finishing date:

3. The teacher and the child both need to feel, and to express this feeling, that it is *all right* for the child to begin *where he or she is* and progress from there.
4. Corrective reading instruction teaches the missing skills but takes care to see that all skills needed for successful reading are developed.
5. The key element in corrective reading, as in any teaching of reading, is meaningful practice. The learner must put all the reading skills to work in meaningful situations.
6. Corrective reading materials must be selected both to teach skills and to cultivate the student's interests and aptitudes.
7. In corrective reading, one should build on strengths. If one avenue to learning produces better results, use it.
8. In developmental reading, corrective or otherwise, there is a sequence in levels of difficulty, and the child moves from the simple to the complex.
9. The student must grow toward independence. Long range goals should include preparing the student for longer and longer periods of independent seatwork without direct supervision.
10. Records must be kept to indicate progress, regression, or change, in both the cognitive and the affective areas.

For each child with reading difficulties, the teacher must be prepared to measure his or her (1) instructional level of reading using the IRI; (2) knowledge of basic sight words using an instrument like the 220 Dolch Basic Sight Word Test or Fry's Instant Words as a recall test; and (3) ability to use the phonic and structural skills commensurate with the child's instructional reader level, moving progressively from initial consonant sounds to consonant blend sounds, most elementary suffixes (s, ed, ing), short and long vowel sounds, variant vowel sounds, roots, prefixes, and suffixes.

These three measures will be sufficient to prevent assigning children work at their frustration level. Preventing this frustration will greatly reduce concomitant emotional problems in children.

For Further Reading

Bond, Guy L., Miles A. Tinker, and Barbara B. Wasson. *Reading Difficulties: Their Diagnosis and Correction,* 4th ed. Englewood Cliffs, N.J.: Prentice-Hall, 1979.

Ekwall, Eldon E. *Diagnosis and Remediation of Disabled Readers.* Boston: Allyn & Bacon, 1976.

———. *Locating and Correcting Reading Difficulties.* Columbus, Ohio: Charles E. Merrill, 1976.

Fry, Edward. *Reading Instruction for Classroom and Clinic.* New York: McGraw-Hill, 1972.

Gallant, Ruth. *Handbook in Corrective Reading,* 2d ed. Columbus, Ohio: Charles E. Merrill, 1977.

Guszak, Frank J. *Diagnostic Reading Instruction in the Elementary School,* 2d ed. New York: Harper & Row, 1978.

Harris, Albert J. *How to Increase Reading Ability,* 6th ed. Chapter 8, "Evaluating Performance in Reading, I"; Chapter 9, "Evaluating Performance in Reading, II." New York: David McKay, 1975.

Johnson, Marjorie S., and Roy A. Kress. *Corrective Reading in the Elementary School.* Perspectives in Reading No. 7. Newark, Del.: International Reading Assn., 1967.

Johnson, Robert D. "Reading: A Case Study." In *Reading and Revolution,* pp. 38–44, edited by Dorothy Dietrich and Virginia Matthews. Newark, Del.: International Reading Assn., 1970.

Kennedy, Eddie C. *Classroom Approaches to Remedial Reading.* Itasca, Ill.: F. E. Peacock, 1977.

La Pray, Margaret. *Teaching Children to Become Independent Readers.* New York: Center for Applied Research in Education, 1972.

Otto, Wayne, and Richard A. McMenemy. *Corrective and Remedial Teaching,* 2d ed. Boston: Houghton Mifflin, 1973.

Schubert, Delwyn, and Theodore L. Torgerson. *Improving Reading Through Individualized Correction,* 4th ed. Dubuque, Ia.: Wm. C. Brown, 1976.

Silvaroli, Nicholas. *Classroom Reading Inventory,* 3d ed. Dubuque, Ia.: Wm. C. Brown, 1976.

Strang, Ruth. *Diagnostic Teaching of Reading.* Chapter 4, "Oral Reading as a Diagnostic Technique," pp. 67–73; Chapter 10, "Reading Tests Administered Individually," pp. 187–209. New York: McGraw-Hill, 1964.

Trela, Thaddeus, and George M. Becker. *Case Studies in Reading: An Annotated Bibliography.* Newark, Del.: International Reading Assn., 1971.

Wilson, Robert M. *Diagnostic and Remedial Reading, For Classroom and Clinic,* 3d ed. Columbus, Ohio: Charles E. Merrill, 1966.

Zintz, Miles V. *Corrective Reading,* 3d ed. Dubuque, Ia.: Wm. C. Brown, 1977.

Notes

1. John Holt, *How Children Fail* (New York: Harper & Row, 1964), p. 5.
2. Margaret LaPray and Ramon Ross, "The Graded Word List: Quick Gauge of Reading Ability," *Journal of Reading* 12 (January 1969): 305–7.
3. *The Inventory of Phonetic Skills,* Tests One, Two, and Three (Boston: Houghton Mifflin, 1972).
4. Guy L. Bond, Theodore Clymer, and Cyril J. Hoyt, *Silent Reading Diagnostic Tests* (Chicago: Lyons & Carnahan, 1970).
5. Careth Ellingson and James Cass, "Teaching the Dyslexic Child," *Saturday Review,* April 16, 1966.
6. Albert Harris and E. R. Sipay, *How To Increase Reading Ability,* 6th ed. (New York: David McKay, 1975), p. 414.
7. Miles V. Zintz, *Corrective Reading,* 3d ed. (Dubuque, Iowa: William C. Brown, 1977), pp. 104–5.
8. Careth Ellingson, *The Shadow Children, A Book About Children's Learning Disorders* (Chicago: Topaz Books, 1967), pp. 89–90.

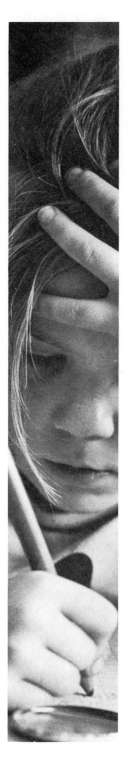

21
Evaluation in the Reading Program

Ongoing evaluation of how efficiently the teacher is teaching and how effectively the child is learning is essential to any successful reading program. Through evaluation the teacher does not only determine the extent to which objectives have been met. Evaluation also identifies the need for corrective and remedial teaching and the extent of review and reinforcement that should be included in the reading program.

Evaluation will be both *formal*, as in the use of standardized measures of achievement, and *informal*, as in the use of subjective judgment, opinions of both students and teacher, and records kept of desired behaviors registered in knowledge, attitudes, and skills. Informal evaluation measures especially involve much more than testing cognitive learning and achievement of specific study skills. Records of the types of library books read during the year kept by means of a technique such as *My Reading Design* (see figure 14.1) are good sources for evaluation of growth of interests. A good way for the teacher to evaluate growth in interpretive abilities and verbal fluency is to have scheduled periods with groups of ten or twelve students to discuss books or stories read.

There are three steps in evaluation:[1]

1. Formulation of objectives to be used. These objectives must be defined clearly in terms of specific behaviors to be achieved.
2. Identification of sources of evidence. Evaluation in the reading program requires information from several sources.
    a. Standardized reading tests would be used as well as tests provided by publishers of graded series of readers to be administered as each book is finished or semiformal tests such as those provided by *My Weekly Reader* or the Student Record Book of the SRA laboratories.
    b. Written work of the children may be summaries of stories they have read, original essays, or answers to questions.
    c. Oral work may include, besides the child reading aloud to the teacher and to groups of children, tape recorded samples of the child reading aloud early in the year compared with samples later

in the year. A tape recorder may also be used to record the child talking about the books and stories read.

    d. The informal checklists used to evaluate individual children from time to time with respect to accuracy in oral reading, attitudes toward reading, and efficiency in silent reading should be included. Other informal techniques are:

    e. Sociometric tests by which the teacher evaluates the extent of personal interaction in the group;

    f. Anecdotal records filed chronologically throughout the year to help the teacher judge progress or lack of it in the child's total growth;

    g. Children's self-evaluations, which help show how successful or profitable they feel their school year has been to them; and

    h. Teachers' evaluations of cognitive and affective growth.

    i. Profiles that evaluate many skills and abilities will also be useful.

3. Interpretation of results. Final outcomes must be interpreted in terms of behavioral objectives established initially. If the reading program has been based on a prescribed set of behavioral objectives from the beginning, in which the teacher has already defined the resulting behavior to be expected if the objectives are met, then final evaluation will be very specific and will have been built into the total program in reading.

Criterion-Referenced Testing

Interest in criterion-referenced testing is related to the ever-increasing emphasis on accountability, on performance-contracting, and on the principle that a child must master one level of learning before being advanced to the next more difficult level.

Programmed instruction, when competently done so that the student is almost sure to be able to move from each frame to the next and continue to make a very high percentage of correct responses, is criterion-referenced for mastery of knowledge about some unit of content or sequence of information.

The principle of teaching reading for mastery at successively more difficult levels is excellent. But whether new criterion-referenced tests can actually measure mastery at specific levels is something else. In reading, it is very difficult to set specific goals to be achieved in a specific sequence within a hierarchy. As a child's reading base widens and the child gets beyond the need to laboriously figure out what the words are, progress will not be measurably comparable to peers around him.[2] Self-motivation and self-teaching will do more for the child's growth in reading than formal instruction. Therefore, there is not much basis for criteria for what is second grade level, third grade level, etc.

An argument sometimes advanced for criterion-referenced testing is that each student competes only with himself or herself and will not be unfavorably compared with others. This argument is not entirely valid, however, since no test can be completely independent of a context. For example, what is appropriate for fourth grade? Or, *at what level* should the boys and girls be able to define the words in a vocabulary list?

Further problems with criterion-referenced testing arise because psychological and environmental factors that influence a child's success in academic learning are ignored. Such factors are: Does the child feel that the content is relevant to his needs? What is the quality of teaching? What is the child's learning aptitude? Ransom[3] cautions the reader that performance objectives must take into account what we know about learning theory; the complete range of learning to read, liking to read, and reading to learn; the child's reaction to print with thought and feeling; and peer group, cross-age, and child-adult interaction in manipulating ideas.

Criterion-referenced tests can provide information which teachers need for both guiding pupil learning and evaluating themselves with respect to their instruction. If teachers have clearly defined the behavioral objectives desired according to the criteria established in chapter 2, then theoretically success in achieving the objectives can be measured.

Standardized Reading Tests

A test becomes standardized by administering it to a large number of subjects of given age and grade status so that the examiner can determine the *expected* performance of boys and girls under given circumstances. Results of such a test are most easily interpreted in percentile ranks.

Any one child's percentile rank is determined by the percent of the total number of children who took the test who perform less well than that child. For example, if 1,000 children in fifth grade complete a given reading test and they are rank-ordered by score, the 500th ranking person is in the fiftieth percentile. Naturally the scores of fifth graders will tend to cluster around an average score. This means that the difference between the fortieth and sixtieth percentiles may be a very small number of raw score points. However, the differences in raw score points between given percentiles are likely to get greater at high and low extremes of the distribution. The seventieth (70th) percentile represents the raw score below which 70 percent of the students scored, the second percentile is the level below which only 2 percent of all the students in a given grade scored, and the 99th percentile is the level below which 99 percent of the children scored.

It is especially important for the classroom teacher to find out which students can perform in the upper third of the distribution, which perform in the middle third, and which perform in the lower third on standardized tests. With this information, the teacher can begin to accumulate many kinds of informal diagnostic information to try to provide instruction in reading skills that will be challenging but not too difficult. In a fifth grade class, for example, the teacher should expect to find one or two children performing at seventh or eighth grade level in reading ability and one or two performing at no better than first or second grade level. (See chapter 2.) Administering an individual oral reading test to a child would provide the teacher with some much-needed information for planning the child's work for the year. This is why it is so important for the teacher to do informal reading inventories as early in the school year as possible. (See chapter 19.) For those few boys and girls with many reading deficiencies, the teacher may wish to administer standardized oral reading tests as pre- and posttests in order to measure progress during the school year.

The Gilmore Oral Reading Test is one of the easiest of such tests to administer. It can be completed with a child in fifteen to twenty minutes and yields a grade placement score for accuracy in mechanics, a grade placement score in comprehension, and a rating for rate of reading (see figure 21.1). The Durrell Analysis of Reading Difficulty and Gray's Oral Reading Test are more diagnostic in nature but can be administered by any classroom teacher who studies the manual of directions carefully and follows the directions as written (see figures 21.2 and 21.3). The Botel Reading Inventory uses word-recognition and word-opposites tests to help teachers place students at appropriate levels of difficulty.

Standardized silent reading tests for use in elementary schools are also readily available. The Gates-MacGinitie Reading Tests are carefully graduated in difficulty levels and can be used with separate answer sheets to allow much easier scoring by teachers. A test summary sheet is shown in figure 21.4. The Nelson Reading Test can also be used with separate answer sheets or self-scoring answer sheets. The Silent Reading Diagnostic Tests, Grades 2–6, provide the teacher with very useful diagnostic information and results that can be presented concisely on a profile provided in the test booklet (see figure 21.5). The selected oral and written standardized tests just described are listed below.

Figure 21.1 The back page of the revised Gilmore Oral Reading test provides for a summary of the student's performance.

Reproduced from John V. Gilmore, and Eunice C. Gilmore, *Gilmore Oral Reading Test,* Copyright 1968 by Harcourt, Brace & World. Reproduced by special permission.

NAME_____

TEST SUMMARY   Form C

PARA-GRAPH	ACCURACY		COMPREHENSION	RATE	
	ERRORS	10 MINUS NO. ERRORS	NO. RIGHT (OR CREDITED)	WORDS IN (	TIME IN SEC.
1				24	
2				45	
3				50	
4				73	
5				103	
6				117	
7				127	
8				161	
9				181	
10				253	
	ACC. SCORE (TOT. "10 MINUS NO. ERRORS" COLUMN)		COMP. SCORE (TOT. NO. RIGHT OR CREDITED)	(1) NO. WORDS READ*	
				(2) TIME IN SEC.*	
STANINE				(1) ÷ (2)	X 60
GRADE EQUIV.				RATE SCORE (WPM)	
RATING					

*Do **not** count "ceiling" paragraph or paragraphs below "basal."

COMMENTS:

493

Figure 21.2 The cover page of the Durrell Analysis of Reading Difficulty Test provides a useful profile of data concerning a child's achievement and possible potential.

Reproduced from *Durrell Analysis of Reading Difficulty*, Copyright 1937, 1955 by Harcourt, Brace & World. Reproduced by special permission.

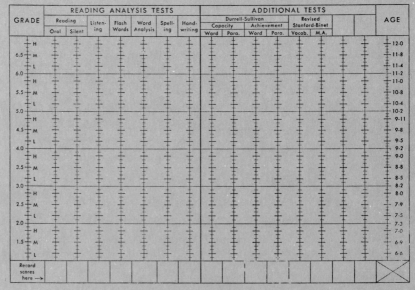

494

Figure 21.3 This Gray Oral Reading Test summary shows that while Charles is in sixth grade, he reads at beginning fourth grade level. He also makes many types of errors.

Reproduced from Examiner's Record Booklet, *Gray Oral Reading Test,* Form A. Copyright 1963 by Bobbs-Merrill Co., Indianapolis, Indiana. Reproduced by permission.

EXAMINER'S RECORD BOOKLET

for the

GRAY ORAL READING TEST

FORM A

Name *Charles* Grade *6* Age *12*
School *Lincoln Elementary* Teacher *Smith* Sex *M*
City State
Examiner *Dale Smith* Date *5-3-68*

SUMMARY

Passage Number	No. of Errors	Time (in Seconds)	Passage Scores	Comprehension
1.	0	8	9	1
2.	0	16	9	4
3.	0	17	9	4
4.	2	28	5	3
5.	5	36	1	2
6.	8	38	0	2½
7.	7	60	0	2½
8.	6	59	0	2½
9.	9	57	0	2½
10.				
11.				
12.				
13.				
Total Passage Scores			33	
Grade Equivalent			4.1	

TYPES OF ERRORS

1.	Aid	
2.	Gross Mispronunciation	7
3.	Partial Mispronunciation	4
4.	Omission	9
5.	Insertion	5
6.	Substitution	4
7.	Repetition	8
8.	Inversion	

OBSERVATIONS
(Check statement and circle each part)

— Word-by-word reading
— Poor phrasing
— Lack of expression
— Monotonous tone
— Pitch too high or low; voice too loud, too soft, or strained
— Poor enunciation
— Disregard of punctuation
— Overuse of phonics
— Little or no method of word analysis
— Unawareness of errors
— Head movement
— Finger pointing
— Loss of place

COMMENTS: *Reads slowly at times. Reads with his teeth clenched (?). When asked if he liked to read he said, "I really don't like reading because it's hard to pronounce the words and I don't understand it so it doesn't give me any fun."*

THE **BOBBS-MERRILL** COMPANY, INC.
A SUBSIDIARY OF HOWARD W. SAMS & CO., INC.
Publishers · INDIANAPOLIS · NEW YORK

Copyright © 1963, The Bobbs-Merrill Co., Inc. Indianapolis 6, Indiana

Figure 21.4 While Ivan is in the sixth grade, he has performed above the eighth grade level on the four measures of the Gates-MacGinitie Reading Test.

Reproduced from Gates-MacGinitie Reading Tests, Primary C, Form 1. Copyright 1964 by Teachers College Press, Columbia University, New York. Reproduced by permission.

Name _____ *Ivan* _____
(LAST)   (FIRST)

Birth date _____ Boy **X** Girl _____
(MONTH, DAY, YEAR)

Grade *6th grade* Testing date *5-9-1968*

Teacher _____

School *Buena Vista* _____

City _____

DIRECTIONS: Read sample paragraph S 1. Under it are four words. Find the word that best answers the question.

S1. Mary pulled and tried to turn the knob. She could not turn it. It was a cold day to be locked outside. What was Mary trying to open?

box   bag   (door)   safe

The word **door** is the best answer to the question. Draw a line under the word **door**.

Now read paragraph S2. Find the word below the paragraph that best completes the paragraph, and draw a line under it.

S2. The huge animals walked slowly, swinging their trunks from side to side. They had big floppy ears and long white tusks. These animals were

tigers   deer   lions   (elephants)

The word **elephants** best completes paragraph S2. You should have drawn a line under the word **elephants**.

On the next two pages are more paragraphs like these samples. When you are asked to turn the page, read each paragraph and find the word below it that best answers the question or completes the paragraph. Draw a line under the best word. Mark only *one* word for each paragraph. Do the paragraphs in the order in which they are numbered: 1, 2, 3, etc. If you can't answer a question, go on to the next one. Work as fast as you can without making errors.

GATES —
MacGINITIE
READING TESTS

SURVEY D, FORM 3

Speed & Accuracy
Vocabulary
Comprehension

□□□   □□□□□□

TEACHERS COLLEGE PRESS
TEACHERS COLLEGE
COLUMBIA UNIVERSITY
NEW YORK

To the Teacher:
BE SURE to follow the directions in the Manual (included in each test package) when giving these tests. The directions will tell you how to explain the tests and how to work the sample items with the students. Allow the exact time specified in the Manual.

		COMPREHENSION	VOCABULARY	SPEED & ACCURACY	
		Number right	Number right	Number right	Number attempted
Raw score		47	39	23	24
Standard score		57	57	53	52
Percentile score		76	76	62	58
Grade score		9.5	8.4	8.9	8.1

© 1964 by Teachers College, Columbia University
Printed in U.S.A.

10   9   8   7   6   5   4   3

Figure 21.5 The profile of the Silent Reading Diagnostic Test provides subtest measures of many phonic and structural abilities in word recognition.

Reproduced with permission of the publisher from the *Silent Reading Diagnostic Tests*. Chicago: Rand McNally, 1970. Reproduced by permission.

Silent Reading Diagnostic Tests
GRAPHIC PROFILE

Name _____ School _____

Grade _____ Teacher _____ Date _____

Grade Equivalent

	Pupil Score	1.5	2.0	2.5	3.0	3.5	4.0	4.5	5.0	5.5	6.0	6.5	7.0	7.5	8.0
BASIC DATA															
Grade in School															
Chronological Grade															
Reading Expectancy															
READING ABILITIES															
Vocabulary															
Literal Comprehension															
Creative Comprehension															
Average Reading															
WORD-RECOGNITION SKILL (Tests 1 and 2)															
Total Right (1 + 2)		11	21	29	38	49	60	65	70	75	77	80	82	84	
Words in Isolation (1)		12	17	23	29	37	42	45	47	49	51	52	53	54	
Words in Context (2)		1	5	7	10	15	18	21	23	25	26	28	30		
ERROR PATTERN (1 + 2)															
Total Omitted (1 + 2)		37	29	17	7	4	1								
Total Errors (1 + 2)		31	29	28	27	22	17	15	13	10	7	4	2	1	
Error Type (1 + 2) — Initial		9	8	7	6	5	4	3	3	2	2	1	1	0	
Middle		10	9	7	6	5	4	3	2	1	1	0			
Ending		8	7	7	6	6	5	5	4	3	2	2	1	0	
Orientation		8	7	7	6	6	5	4	3	2	2	1	0		
RECOGNITION TECHNIQUES (Tests 3, 4, and 5)															
Total Right (3 + 4 + 5)		19	23	27	32	38	44	50	55	58	60	69	78	83	85
Visual-Structural Analysis (3)		3	6	7	8	9	10	12	13	14	16	20	26	28	30
Syllabication (4)		8	11	13	15	17	19	20	21	22	23	25	26	28	30
Word Synthesis (5)		4	6	7	9	12	14	17	19	20	22	25	28	30	
PHONIC KNOWLEDGE (Tests 6, 7, and 8)															
Total Right (6 + 7 + 8)		39	45	51	58	63	66	68	71	73	75	78	83	85	88
Beginning Sounds (6)		9	14	17	20	22	23	23	24	25	26	27	28	29	30
Ending Sounds (7)		8	10	12	15	17	19	20	21	22	23	25	27	28	30
Vowel and Consonant Sounds (8)		16	20	22	23	24	24	25	25	26	26	27	28	29	30
		1.5	2.0	2.5	3.0	3.5	4.0	4.5	5.0	5.5	6.0	6.5	7.0	7.5	8.0

Grade Equivalent

Individually Administered Reading Tests for Classroom Teachers	Botel Reading Inventory. Tests word recognition, word opposites, spelling placement, and phonic ability. Chicago: Follett, 1970.
	Gilmore Oral Reading Test. Ten reading paragraphs of increasing difficulty. Yields separate accuracy of reading mechanics and level of comprehension scores. New York: Harcourt, Brace & World, 1968.
	Gray's Oral Reading Test. Thirteen paragraphs of increasing difficulty. Indianapolis: Bobbs-Merrill, 1963.
Standardized Silent Reading Tests for Elementary School Reading Programs	California Reading Achievement Tests. Separate tests for lower primary, primary, elementary, junior high, and advanced grades. Tests vocabulary and comprehension. New York: McGraw-Hill, 1970.
	Gates-MacGinitie Reading Tests. Tests vocabulary and comprehension in primary grades; vocabulary, comprehension, and speed in upper grades. Primary A: Grade 1; Primary B: Grade 2; Primary C: Grade 3; Survey D: Grade 4, 5, 6; and Survey E: Grade 7, 8, 9. May be machine or hand scored. New York: Teachers College Press, Columbia University, 1965.
	Iowa Tests of Basic Skills. The reading test may be obtained separately from the battery in a reusable booklet. Tests paragraph comprehension and vocabulary. Boston: Houghton Mifflin, 1973.
	Nelson Reading Skills Test. For Grades 3–9. Timed. Eight minutes vocabulary; twenty-five minutes paragraph comprehension. Boston: Houghton Mifflin, 1977.
	Silent Reading Diagnostic Tests. Tests word recognition, left-to-right orientation, syllabication, root words, auditory discrimination, and word synthesis. Provides profile for each child. Chicago: Rand McNally, 1970.

Children's Written Work

There are several means by which the classroom teacher can obtain written expression from children which conveys how well they read, how well they can think about and use what they read, and also how they feel about the material read and how they feel about the job of reading.

Teachers often obtain from children early in the year an original paragraph describing a summer vacation incident. Since children usually need to be helped to delineate specifics and describe them in concrete terms, it would be well for teachers to help them delimit their topic and not use such global titles as "What I Did Last Summer" or "My Summer Vacation."

Writing a summarizing paragraph about a lesson is a difficult assignment in the elementary school. Boys and girls need help and guidance in arriving at the main point with two or three supporting details. They may write paragraphs that follow the suggestion in chapter 10 about understanding the anatomy of a paragraph.

When the primary objective is for the young child to express an idea on paper, the teacher should accept the idea and not judge accuracy in mechanics harshly. After the ideas are on paper, they can be edited as seems necessary to an individual teacher.

Figure 21.6 shows part of a diary kept by a fourth grade boy for several weeks when his teacher found that he needed help to *think about and write* even one complete sentence. The reader will notice that he usually writes down the *topic* of his sentence and then begins the sentence he is planning to write.

Figure 21.7 shows two book reports written by a fourth grade girl after she had read the books and discussed them with her remedial reading teacher. Both children are expressing ideas. If teachers insist primarily on capital letters, periods, and margins and indentations, they may get carefully presented paragraphs without ideas.

The Oral Reading of Children

There are three major reasons why teaching oral reading in the elementary school classroom is important. The first is its usefulness as a testing or evaluation instrument. In the primary grades on a day-to-day basis the child must read aloud so the teacher knows how successful the child is in learning all the basic sight words that must be mastered in order to read anything. In the higher grades, there must also be testing of oral reading ability. Samples of each child's oral reading will help the teacher evaluate how well the child reads so that a reading improvement program can be mapped out with the child. Such individual oral-reading samples can be very useful in parent conferences, too, because they allow the parents to see exactly how well and at what grade level their child reads orally.

The second reason oral reading in a classroom is important is that it allows pleasurable sharing of interesting passages and motivates the reading of good books, thereby firmly establishing the belief that books are treasures of interesting information to be shared and enjoyed. If a teacher is a good oral reader (see chapter 14), the boys and girls can be easily motivated to share interesting anecdotes, jokes, witticisms, and informational materials that add documentary evidence to formal classroom argumentation and debate on issues.

3/15/68 I like planes. They are fun. To ride in I went to D.C. in one. It was fun we left at 2:30 in D. and got in Alb. at 3:00.

3/16/68 Cars I like cars I like racing cars. I like when they go fast. And I like old old cars too.

3/18/68 fish I like fish they are swim in my room. We have two fish a little one and a big one.

3/22/68 Jon is a French boy. I play with him all day long. He can talk French only. He likes to ride bikes all day.

3/23/68 Arithmetic I like arithmetic it is easy to do. Today we did some arithmetic like these one's 7]925] 60- I got a B in arithmetic. 420 / 5]60

3/25/68 Spelling I like spelling it is easy too. We get easy words to spell. I got a B in it too.

3/26/68 Reading I like reading I got a C in it. I like the teacher who teaches me. She is good very good.

3/27/68 Blackbeard's Ghost I saw it Saturday night. It was funny show. It was at Hiland Theater.

3/28/68 I got up at 6:00 and now it is 6:33 right this very min. It is fun to get up at 6:00. I can do my work in 33 min.

Figure 21.7 Book reports prepared by a fourth grade girl in her special reading class.

Walter Farley. *Little Black, A Pony* (New York: Beginner Books, Random House, 1961); and Edith McCall, *Butternut Bill and the Big Pumpkin* (Chicago: Beckley Cardy, Benefic Press).

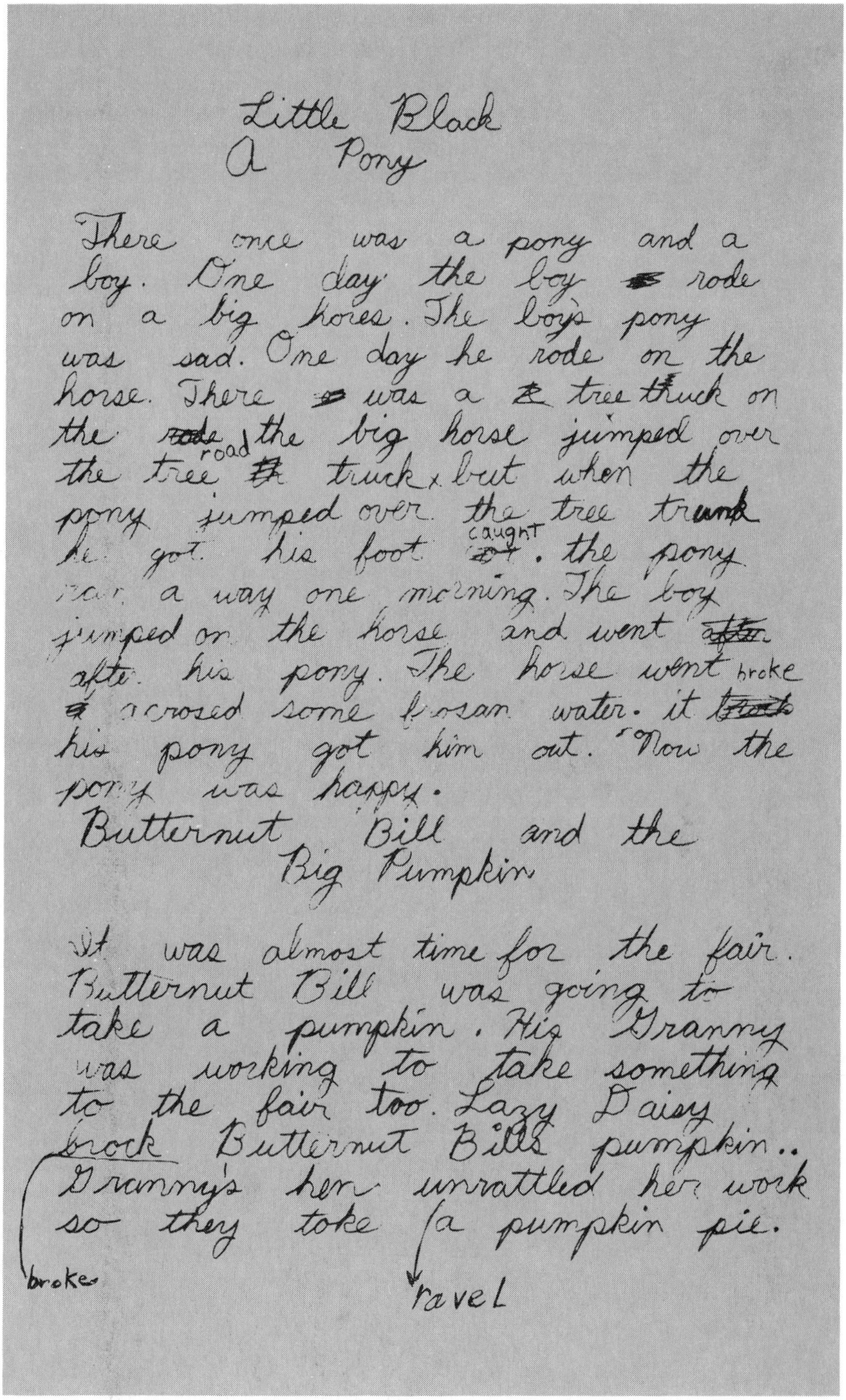

Little Black
A Pony

There once was a pony and a boy. One day the boy ~~was~~ rode on a big horse. The boy's pony was sad. One day he rode on the horse. There ~~was~~ was a ~~tree~~ tree thuck on the ~~rode~~ road the big horse jumped over the tree ~~th~~ truck but when the pony jumped over the tree trunk he got his foot ~~at~~ caught. the pony ran a way one morning. The boy jumped on the horse and went ~~after~~ after his pony. The horse went broke ~~a~~ acrosed some frozan water. it ~~froze~~ his pony got him out. Now the pony was happy.

Butternut Bill and the Big Pumpkin

It was almost time for the fair. Butternut Bill was going to take a pumpkin. His Granny was working to take something to the fair too. Lazy Daisy ~~brock~~ Butternut Bill's pumpkin.. Granny's hen unrattled her work so they toke a pumpkin pie.

broke

ravel

The third reason why oral reading should be taught is that it may help someone present evidence to prove a point, to settle an argument, or to show that a line of reasoning is supported by authorities.

The latter two uses of oral reading are audience situations wherein only the reader has the information being shared.

Checklists and Questionnaires

Teachers should be continuously learning more and more about the boys and girls they teach. How well or how poorly they perform in reading must be seen in relation to the home environment in which they live, the emotional stability of the adults in their lives, the socioeconomic level of the home, the *pressures* on a child for academic success, and other pressures of day-to-day living. At the same time, every day the teacher must make decisions about each child as an integral part of the total classroom.

In the affective domain, the concerns with respect to a child are:

How does the teacher feel about George?

How does George feel about the teacher?

How does George feel about himself in relation to all other people?

How do George's parents feel about George?

How do the other children in the room feel about George?

In the cognitive domain, the concerns are:

How well does George perform on a standardized reading test?

How well can he read aloud?

How well can he read silently?

How well does he retain what he reads?

The teacher can prepare a checklist of behavioral items that will help answer the above questions to some degree. The following items might constitute a checklist of reading behaviors for the classroom teacher. Any checklist can be edited or extended as the teacher uses it.

Does the child:

Read with understanding?

Apply phonics skills?

Read independently?

Finish assignments?

Read well orally?

Use independent study time efficiently?

Follow directions?

Understand reading assignments?

Pronounce new words efficiently?

Work well in small groups?

Bring in new information from outside of school?

Become embarrassed in front of class?

Read in too soft a voice to be heard?

Miss little words (basic sight words)?

Read in a monotone?

Other Informal Techniques in Evaluation

For too long teachers have thought of evaluation only as measurement of cognitive growth. When a unit of work was finished, the test should determine whether the child had absorbed all the facts the teacher had emphasized. There are many other ways, of course, by which a teacher can estimate permanent cognitive learning.

More important, however, is the present-day effort to measure growth in affective behavior. Teachers need to be doing the following also:

Developing appropriate leadership-followership qualities.

Identifying children who are always on the periphery in social situations.

Finding out how a child feels about success or lack of it.

Planning for teacher judgment about both the cognitive and affective changes in child behavior is necessary in the present-day school.

Sociometrics

A sociogram is a chart showing the social interaction among the members of a group at a given time. Sociograms help the teacher to visualize social status of the members of the group. By constructing a sociogram, a teacher can determine cliques, most popular children, isolates, and leaders. Restructuring the room environment through such activities as assigning a leader to work with an isolate on a worthwhile project, the teacher may be able to effect a real change in children's behavior over a period of time. Teachers do not discuss the results of the sociogram with the boys and girls; they never indicate who is the reject, the isolate, or the most popular. Neither do they naïvely urge popular children to be nice to neglected ones. There are many sources of specific information about how to construct the sociogram. Two such sources are:

John U. Michaelis. *Social Studies for Children in a Democracy,* pp. 164–66. Englewood Cliffs, N.J.: Prentice-Hall, 1956.
Miles V. Zintz. *Corrective Reading,* pp. 140–43. Dubuque, Iowa: William C. Brown, 1977.

Anecdotal Records

Anecdotal records are brief descriptions of specific instances of a child's behavior; they are not superficial comments made about a child by a teacher. An anecdotal record may be made more meaningful by exact comments of the child. Well thought-out anecdotal records become very helpful when the teacher holds parent-teacher conferences. Anecdotal records begin to have value as soon as the teacher has recorded enough specific behaviors so that threads or patterns of behavior begin to become evident.

| Children's Evaluations of Themselves | Self-evaluation should guide children in developing self-direction. Helping children learn to analyze their own strengths and weaknesses, successes and failures, means helping them improve their skills in the problem-solving approach to all problems. Thus they develop the ability to set purposes and evaluate end results which represent mature behavior. |

Children's Evaluations of Themselves

Self-evaluation should guide children in developing self-direction. Helping children learn to analyze their own strengths and weaknesses, successes and failures, means helping them improve their skills in the problem-solving approach to all problems. Thus they develop the ability to set purposes and evaluate end results which represent mature behavior.

Children need guidance to learn how to evaluate themselves. Checklists, charts, and development of work standards can provide this guidance.

Children can, with the help of the teacher, prepare their own guidelines for improving study and work habits. The following questions illustrate what such guidelines would be:

Do I do my own work?
Do I finish whatever I begin?
Do I listen to directions?
Do I return materials I have used?
Do I work quietly without asking too many questions?

Teachers' Evaluations

The teacher could check on his own behavior in teaching reading by asking himself such questions as the following:

Do I introduce new words and new concepts in order to teach their meanings?

Do I provide for review and reinforcement after initial teaching?

Do I have informal reading inventory results to show that each child is reading at a level where he or she understands at least 75 percent of the ideas in the materials and makes no more than five uncorrected errors in 100 consecutive words?

When teaching a directed reading lesson, do I have too many interruptions from children working independently? If so, is the material that the children are studying too difficult?

Do any children still need a marker when reading? If so, is there a justifiable reason for it?

Do any children still move their lips when reading silently?

Do my boys and girls see purpose in their work and is the climate a constructive one?

Evaluation Records

A profile is any type of graphic aid that portrays many measures of knowledge, skills, and abilities so that the observer can see in one picture at a quick glance any individual student's strengths and weaknesses or high, average, and low scores. By observing which scores are above and which below the median, the teacher can quickly see how strengths compare to weaknesses.

The profiles of two fifteen-year-old eighth graders are presented in figures 21.8 and 21.9. One has a mental age of only nine years, six months while the other has a mental age equal to his chronological age. The one with normal intelligence is a nonreader *but* with sufficient capacity to read at grade level. The other has a fourth grade reader level, which is approximately equal to

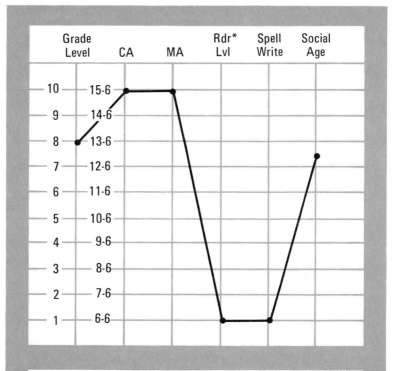

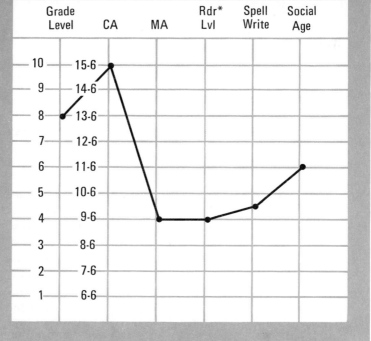

Figure 21.10 Summary of information about reading for each child in my class.

Name of child	IRI Oral Reading	IRI Silent Reading	IRI Capacity Level	Standardized Reading Test[1]	Phonic Skills[2]	Vocabulary Sight Words	Vocabulary Standard Tests[3]	Spelling Ability[4]	Other Information
1.									
2.									
3.									
4.									
5.									
6.									
7.									
8.									
9.									
10.									
11.									
12.									

1. Name of test _____

2. Name of test _____

3. Name of test _____

4. How determined _____

his level of mental ability. The second student is not retarded in reading since he is reading as well as his mental ability indicates. It is clear that the reading teacher needs two entirely different programs for these two students. One student needs an intense remedial reading program, while the other needs an adapted reading program that will provide efficient teaching of skills at the level he can read with understanding.

Busy classroom teachers need ways of keeping records that are as concise and simple as possible. Each one will develop a technique for keeping notes, anecdotes, and needed information to make it as useful as possible. Figure 21.10 has been prepared to show how a teacher might summarize on one sheet of paper some of the important data about individual children. If results of individual intelligence tests are available, that information might be included. If an intelligence test has been administered to all the children at one time by the classroom teacher, the probability of the results being invalid for the lower half of the class are so great that the teacher might indicate on the summary only broad categories, such as "high," "above average," "average," "below average."

Suggested Activities

1. Administer a standardized reading test to a small group of children in the room where you teach or for the grade level you hope to teach. Analyze the results and write your interpretation.
2. Make a sociogram for the class based on choices for working together on reading and writing activities. Evaluate the positions on the sociogram of the best and poorest readers in the class.
3. Teachers can devise subjective ways to compare their evaluations with childrens' self-evaluations and compare both with objective measures of achievement. How do children's expectations of themselves correspond to the idea of the self-fulfilling prophecy?

For Further Reading

Barrett, Thomas C., ed. *The Evaluation of Children's Reading Achievement.* Perspectives in Reading No. 8. Newark, Del.: International Reading Assn., 1967.

Guszak, Frank J. *Diagnostic Reading Instruction in the Elementary School,* 2d ed. New York: Harper & Row, 1978.

Johnson, Marjorie Seddon, and Roy A. Kress, eds. *Corrective Reading in the Classroom.* Perspectives in Reading No. 7. Newark, Del.: International Reading Assn., 1967.

Otto, Wayne; Robert Chester; John McNeil; and Shirley Myers. *Focused Reading Instruction.* Reading, Mass.: Addison-Wesley, 1974.

Rauch, Sidney J. "A Checklist for the Evaluation of Reading Programs." *The Reading Teacher* 21 (March 1968): 519–22.

Tinker, Miles A., and Constance M. McCullough. *Teaching Elementary Reading,* 4th ed. Englewood Cliffs, N.J.: Prentice-Hall, 1975.

Notes

1. Joseph Crescimbeni, "The Need for Diagnostic Evaluation," *Education* 88 (November-December 1967): 161.
2. Frank Smith, *Understanding Reading* (New York: Holt, Rinehart & Winston, 1971), p. 162.
3. Grace A. Ransom, "Criterion Referenced Tests—Let the Buyer Beware," *The Reading Teacher* 26 (December 1972): 282–85. See also George A. Prescott, "Criterion Referenced Test Interpretation in Reading," *The Reading Teacher* 24 (Jan. 1971): 347–54, reprinted in Althea Beery, Thomas C. Barrett, and William R. Powell, *Elementary Reading Instruction: Selected Materials,* 2d ed. (Boston: Allyn & Bacon, 1974), pp. 605–13.

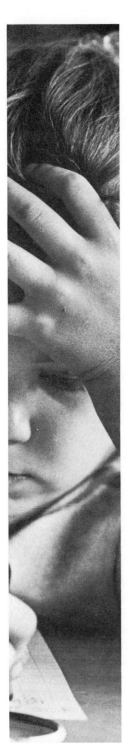

22

Teaching Reading in Proper Perspective

Throughout the text, emphasis has been given to the extent of differences in children's learning. All the principles of learning that cause boys and girls to become more different rather than more alike as they progress through school are in direct contradiction to the organization by chronological-age level and the inflexible patterns deeply embedded in schools today. Having copies of the same textbook for every child in the class is just the opposite of a flexible pattern to encourage teachers to provide for many levels of ability within the class. What is the classroom teacher to do?

A suggestion was made in chapter 4 that inexperienced teachers might rely more heavily than experienced teachers on basal readers and their corresponding manuals to keep several reading groups progressing in the sequential development of reading skills. Experienced teachers will feel more confident about working with individualized reading programs and language-experience types of reading and writing. However, they too will rely on organized, sequenced basal-reader lessons for some children.

In perspective, how can the classroom teacher keep up with each child in the room if nearly all are doing different things? Is the atmosphere one of noise and chaos? How will the principal react to this?

Probably the teacher will not wish to keep up with ten or more separate reading groups day after day if they are all in basal reading series and are dependent upon the teacher for guidance. Yet, with some well planned lessons that include individualized reading for those who really want to read and individualized work-type lessons for those who need planned, guided seatwork, most of the children can work independently for much of an hour that the teacher may have scheduled for reading in the daily program.

Two of the classroom teacher's most valuable tools for diagnostic teaching in primary reading are the informal reading inventory, as discussed in chapter 19, and the Dolch Basic Sight Word Test, as discussed in chapter 20.

Diagnostic Teaching of Reading

Diagnostic teaching of reading requires acceptance and application of the following principles.

1. Children are indivisible entities.

2. No learning takes place without a motive. If something isn't important *to the child,* it won't be learned very efficiently.

3. There is *no necessary relationship* between level of intelligence and being a disabled reader.

4. Differences within a group get greater as children progress through elementary school.

5. Each child has his or her own optimal time for learning.

6. No two children can learn the same thing in the same amount of time with the same amount of practice.

7. No child is inherently lazy. If a child acts that way, there has to be a reason.

8. Almost everything that is learned must be reviewed from time to time or it will be forgotten.

9. When an objective is stated behaviorally for a child, the teacher can determine whether the objective is achieved.

Not all teachers accept these principles, but all recognize that there are problems in applying them in their day-to-day work. Some examples of teacher behavior are discussed below.

A second grade teacher showed the following duplicated letter to her student teacher early in the school year and explained that the second graders were *too far behind* in reading.

Dear Parent:
The attached list of 175 words were taught last year in first grade. In second grade, your child will be expected to know them. Please see that your child knows all of these words so that he or she can do the work in the second grade.

Your child's teacher
Mary Smith

Did all children learn 175, and only 175, service words in first grade? Does forgetting during the summer constitute any problem? Is second grade only for people who have already learned to recognize the 175 words? Or can a child be in second grade and know very few sight words?

If Miss Smith has the *usual* heterogeneous group of thirty children about seven years old, she should expect to find the full range of differences in intellectual, psychological, physical, and social growth usually found in children at this chronological age. Such children became *more different* in first grade, *not more alike.* How they grew in emotional stability and independence varied in relation to how each set of parents applied "individual" quantities and combinations of overindulgence, acceptance, rejection, neglect, punishment, or tender loving care. For the teacher to assume that parents can or will teach their child a basic sight vocabulary implies that their know-how in methodology is equal to that of the teacher. This is occasionally true! However, the letter tells parents nothing about how to proceed; nothing about being sure that learning the words is a meaningful, rewarding kind of experience for the child; nothing about the psychological danger of trying to coerce a child into learning.

A teacher teaching diagnostically in second grade would find out early in the year how many of the 175 sight words each child knew and then arrange for different subgroups to start their reading experiences with materials that took account of how many words they already knew. Some children might learn best with more auditory work to help them hear phonic elements in words. Others might benefit more from practice in writing sentences containing words they have learned. Some might do better with more oral reading practice. And still others might need special attention directed to letters or words often confused (*b* and *d, n* and *m, was* and *saw, and* and *said*). The teacher should also expect the children to show varying degrees of emotional, social, and intellectual maturity. And, as a professional, the teacher will probably know how to accomplish this job better than most parents.

The fact that a student teacher received the "letter to parents" from her supervisor indicates to the young student teacher that such a letter is supposed to represent *good* teaching practice. An example of better teaching practice would be the following case.

A good teacher, knowing that children need a great deal of easy reading practice to become good readers, would do well to ask young children to carry home their textbooks *after* they have learned *all* the new words. The teacher would hope that the mothers or fathers would be good listeners and encourage their children in oral reading practice. But because parents are *not* oriented in teaching methodology, the teacher would send a letter like the following to the parents.

Dear Parent:

Bill has read all of *Peanuts, the Pony*[1] at school and knows all the new words. Of course, he needs much practice to become a good reader. Will you please listen attentively while he reads aloud for you so you can enjoy the story together? After he has read for you, please sign your name below and let *Bill* return the letter to me.

> Thank you for your kind cooperation,
> Miss Smith

Bill has read *Peanuts, the Pony* aloud, and we enjoyed it together.

> Parent _____

Helping the Child Work at His Instructional Level All Day Long

Mrs. Walker has been a sixth grade teacher for many years. She has many pictures which she has beautifully arranged on bulletin boards many times. Her room is clean, efficient, and very quiet. She organizes the work of her student teacher so that the student teacher will learn to perform exactly the way Mrs. Walker performs. This observer believes that such effort will perpetuate indefinitely some bad practices.

In a culturally deprived, low socioeconomic area of the city, Mrs. Walker has grouped her twenty-seven sixth graders into three reading groups. About one-third read from a first-semester fifth grade reader; another third read from a first-semester fourth reader; and the final third read from a first-semester second reader. This last group includes children with many types of reading problems, each of whom needs carefully tailored individual solutions. What they get each day, however, are superficially motivated, directed reading lessons that follow the manual written for second graders.

Paradoxically, each week for spelling class all three groups study the same list of words in *My Word Study Book,* Book Six. Perhaps more than half the class cannot understand the meanings of these words and cannot pronounce them. The most serious result from the mental health point of view is the destruction of ego and devaluation of self when the teacher asks, "How many perfect papers?" after the Friday test and then looks approvingly at the two or three children who always raise their hands. When all those who fail are admonished to study harder or to write each word ten times, it is apparent that this teacher does not follow the practice of teaching diagnostically. No child has a *need* for any spelling words he or she cannot *pronounce and use* in writing. The level of difficulty in spelling that a child is asked to master can hardly be greater than the child's ability to read.

In this same sixth grade, all students used the regular sixth grade arithmetic textbook, and every day *all* tried to learn the same mathematics skills in the same amount of time with the same amount of practice.

Grouping children according to their instructional reading levels makes it possible to provide study activities all day long which the child can do successfully. This is one of the advantages of the self-contained classroom.

Perhaps one way to emphasize the extent of differences in the self-contained classroom is to talk about "The Many Faces of Reading." Figure 22.1 depicts some of the many different attitudes toward reading found in the primary classroom. All classroom teachers teaching heterogeneous groups of boys and girls are sure to have had at one time or another a child who comes from a foreign language background; a fearful child; a child who is already convinced that he or she can't learn; a child who is emotionally disturbed and cannot think logically about immediate problems; a child who thinks that right-to-left direction is as appropriate for reading as is left-to-right; a child who uses all kinds of excuses when the words are difficult but doesn't want to admit it. Then there are children who always know all the words; who have read many interesting stories before they get to the class; who delight in good

Figure 22.1 The many faces of reading.

reading ("Gee, that's a neat story!"); and who overwork the expression "I'm so bored!" A few children have been told emphatically that they have never been taught phonics and that is the reason they are not good readers. With this mixture, the teacher must find constructive ways to group students within the class, ways to identify and develop leadership for groups, and varied activities to make reading fun to do.

Teachers' Questions about the Teaching of Reading

Teaching reading diagnostically requires both ability and judgment on the part of the teacher. Below are many questions for which teachers need answers. They are typical of many other possible questions teachers ask.

1. How will I organize my room for reading in the fall when school starts?

2. How can I get some kind of grouping established early in the year?

3. How will I explain to parents or other teachers what I am doing?

4. What will my basic organization be: basal reader, individualized reading, or language-experience?

5. What will each child be reading at his or her instructional level all the rest of the school day?

6. How can I make sure children are not expected to write and spell words they cannot read?

7. How will I make a daily lesson plan that incorporates everything (including independent seatwork to last long periods of time)?

8. What reading plans do I make for those who *do* almost all read at grade level or above? those in a normal distribution in the achievement range? and those whose achievement is below grade level?

9. Have I made reading just *one* of the parts of a language arts curriculum?

10. How do I teach diagnostically those who speak nonstandard English?

11. How do I first teach English to the student for whom English is a foreign language, the culturally different child?

12. Do I accept and respect the course of study as a guide of what to teach in a given class but recognize the need to adapt it for each child's achievement?

13. The child *never* just all of a sudden "catches on" to reading. If children want to do well, to follow the principles of growing toward maturity, do I know how to find out what is wrong in case of trouble?

14. No teacher can know all the answers. There has to be support from many disciplines. How can I find answers outside the classroom?

15. Will I make sure the child has a good year *in my room* and let next year take care of itself?

16. Will I know what to tell parents who ask, "Does the school teach phonics?"

17. Should the school provide programmed material for independent seatwork? What materials?

18. What is dyslexia? Can I help the child who has it?

19. When should a child repeat a grade in the elementary school?

Some teachers still feel that regardless of what a child has learned or has failed to learn, a book of the grade level to which the child is assigned is what must be used.[2] Such an attitude could hardly be less productive or more inefficient.

English says:

. . . the textbook in its present form is outdated, expensive, and inefficient. The assumptions underlying its present usage are false; they do not explain or foster learning in depth or promote student inquiry. . . . The removal of legal straitjackets [textbooks] will provide the freedom necessary to arrive at modern education in a time when "modern" is woefully out of date.[3]

Soghomonian, in a response to English, says:

There are good and bad textbooks, easy-to-read ones, and hard-to-understand ones. But the major fault, the core of the problem, is not the text *per se,* but that too many teachers have made the text an icon. Therein lies the monster. The text is not protoplasm; the teacher is. The classroom text is inert, as is any tool. It hardly seems fair to criticize the tool and not the operator.[4]

Influence of Expectations

Do a teacher's expectations about a pupil's performance affect that performance? The answer is *yes.* Rosenthal and Jacobson[5] found that when teachers in an elementary school were told that certain children would do especially well, those children—even though they were picked at random—showed significantly greater gains than did others during the school year. This effect of expectation was greater at the primary than at the intermediate levels.

Subjective teacher descriptions of the same designated children at the end of the year rated them as having better chances of success, being significantly more interesting and curious, and being somewhat more adjusted and affectionate.

Two questions follow: (1) How much does a teacher's attitude toward a child influence how successfully the child learns to read? (2) How much do teachers' favorable or unfavorable expectations of individual children influence the results of educational research done by the teachers?

Coopersmith[6] studied behavior patterns in a group of boys, ages ten-to-twelve, in order to evaluate qualities that build self-confidence and feelings of personal worth. Expectation of success, motivation to achieve, initiative, and dealing with anxieties are behaviors necessary for developing self-esteem. Coopersmith found that a boy's behavior was significantly related to the opinion he had of himself.

High self-esteem is associated with academic or social success, confidence, optimism, originality, and having parents who are generally strict and consistent in enforcing rules. Low self-esteem is related to being convinced of inferiority, fear of social encounters, self-consciousness, sensitivity to criticism, lack of confidence, remaining in the shadows, and listening rather than participating.

The relationship between self-esteem and level of aspiration needs to be studied and evaluated carefully. If Coopersmith's study is valid, the crucial role of primary teachers is underscored and reemphasized. The young child who experiences personal failure during the first two or three years of school may be fitting into a behavior pattern of low self-esteem with all the negative behavior that this suggests.

Prevention Is Better Than Remediation

Early identification of difficulties in the school learning situation could prevent much of the painful correction that now takes place in special remedial teaching situations. As was emphasized in the chapter on readiness, the basic idea in evaluation before formal reading should be to study the child's status in school with respect to physical, intellectual, emotional, and social readiness for the complex task of learning to read. Formal reading instruction should be carefully delayed for the child who is immature and can profit from pre-reading development in any of these four major areas.

By the end of the first day of school, in a heterogeneous group of thirty children, there are those individuals who have not completely achieved the objective the teacher had in mind in each of several areas of the school curriculum. In truth, then, one can say that there is remedial work to be done from the first day. The teacher must be alert to failure symptoms in any child—whether he is failing in the area of cognition (learning all the facts the teacher has in mind), the area of affect (developing confidence in himself as a person and acquiring the necessary self-esteem), or in the psychomotor area (being able to demonstrate all the necessary motor skills related to the successful completion of academic tasks).

When failure symptoms first appear is when the alert teacher searches for ways to redirect the child's efforts so that success will be experienced. Strengthening an area of weakness prepares the child for continuous growth.

Diagnostic teaching is the technique whereby each child is taught the specific skills not yet mastered but which must be known before there can be sequential progress to more difficult learning.

Diagnostic teaching begins with attention to one child—each unique one—and that child's individual range of competencies, concerns, enthusiasms, self-concept, learning style, aspirations, and personal way of learning. Learning for each child is a highly personal and affective experience.

Dorris M. Lee reminds us:

Diagnostic teaching employs procedures that are based on the findings of experience and research about children and learning, those that can be effective in attaining the goals of the school, and those that recognize unique personal values.[7]

Olsen and Kelley both emphasize special needs of lower-class children in school. Olsen says:[8]

We have yet to face the fact that lower-class children are socialized in ways that are quite different from those of the middle-class. We have yet to take full account of the differing value patterns, attitudes, and beliefs with which the lower-class child comes to school. The child brings the reality of his own life into the classroom, and to be effective, the school must admit that reality. I suggest that the central challenge that the slum child presents to the school is not only the disadvantages that he brings with him. His challenge to us is much more profound than this. His ambitions, his hopes, his desires, his attitudes toward authority, education, success, and school, his fears, his habits, his hates—in short, his basic orientation toward life—are, in many ways, so different from ours that we do not understand him nor does he understand us.

And Kelley reminds us:[9]

The child born and raised in a lower-class setting derives his perceptions and values, attitudes and habits of living in a cultural setting that teaches, rewards, and reinforces his way of life. His way of perceiving, behaving, and becoming is distinctly different from the school culture.

Finally, the profession needs teachers with the determination which Hunt described in Aunt Cordelia when she explains why she must continue to teach the rural school near her farm:

Aunt Cordelia didn't really have to teach for a livelihood; the income from the farm was sufficient for her needs, and the modest salary she received for each month of the school year was not the incentive which brought her back to her desk year after year. Her reason for teaching was actually the belief that no one else would do the work quite as well, would understand the backgrounds of these children whose parents she had taught when she was young. There was never a doubt in Aunt Cordelia's mind but that *her* teaching was the best to be had, and she would have felt that she was denying something beyond price to the handful of country children who sat in her classroom if she allowed a younger or a less dedicated woman to take over.[10]

For Further Reading

Ashton-Warner, Sylvia. *Teacher*. New York: Simon & Schuster, 1963.

Austin, Mary C., and Coleman Morrison. *The Torch Lighters, Tomorrow's Teachers of Reading*. Cambridge, Mass.: Harvard University Press, 1961.

Bush, Clifford, and Mildred H. Huebner. *Strategies for Reading in the Elementary School,* 2d. ed., chapter 14, "Challenging Every Reader," pp. 363–89. New York: Macmillan, 1979.

Chall, Jeanne S. *Learning to Read: The Great Debate.* "Conclusions and Recommendations," pp. 305–14. New York: McGraw-Hill, 1967.

Daniels, Steven. *How Two Gerbils, Twenty Goldfish, Two Hundred Games, Two Thousand Books and I Taught Them How to Read*. Philadelphia: Westminster Press, 1971.

Downing, John, ed. *Comparative Reading: Cross National Studies of Behavior and Processes in Reading and Writing*. New York: Macmillan, 1973.

English, Fenwick. "The Textbook—Procrustean Bed of Learning." *Phi Delta Kappan* 48 (April 1967):393–95.

Herndon, James. *How to Survive in Your Native Land*. New York: Bantam Books, 1971.

———. *The Way It Spozed to Be*. New York: Simon & Schuster, 1965.

Holt, John. *What Do I Do Monday?* New York: Dell, 1970.

International Reading Assn., P.O. Box 695, Newark, Delaware 19711.
   a. Proceedings of the Annual Convention.
   b. *The Reading Teacher,* eight issues per year.
   c. *The Journal of Reading,* eight issues per year.
   d. *The Reading Research Quarterly*.
   e. *Perspectives in Reading*.

Kohl, Herbert. *36 Children*. New York: New American Library, 1967.

Lee, Dorris M. *Diagnostic Teaching*. Washington, D.C.: National Education Assn., 1966.

Manolakes, George. "Instructional Practices in Reading: An Assessment for the Future." In *New Perspectives in Reading Instruction,* edited by A. J. Mazurkiewicz, pp. 96–111. New York: Pitman Publishing Corp., 1964.

Postman, Neil, and Charles Weingartner. *The Schoolbook*. New York: Delacorte Press, 1973.

Rogers, Vincent, ed. *Teaching in the British Primary School*. London: Macmillan, 1970.

Soghomonian, Sam. "The Textbook—Tarnished Tool for Teachers?" *Phi Delta Kappan* 48 (April 1967):395–96.

Strang, Ruth, Constance McCullough, and Arthur Traxler. *The Improvement of Reading,* 4th ed., pp. 503–14. New York: McGraw-Hill, 1967.

Notes

1. Pre-primer, *Our Animal Story Series* (Boston: D. C. Heath, various states).
2. Madeline C. Hunter, "You—as a Diagnostician," *The Instructor* 76 (February 1967): 31, 126.
3. Fenwick English, "The Textbook—Procrustean Bed of Learning," *Phi Delta Kappan* 48 (April 1967): 395.
4. Sam Soghomonian, "The Textbook—Tarnished Tool for Teachers?" *Phi Delta Kappan* 48 (April 1967): 395.

5. "Science and the Citizen," *Scientific American* 217 (November 1967):54. Reported from Robert Rosenthal and Lenore Jacobson, "Self-Fulfilling Prophecies," *Psychological Reports* 19 (1) (1966):115–18.

6. Stanley Coopersmith, "Studies in Self-Esteem," *Scientific American* 218 (February 1968): 96–102.

7. Dorris M. Lee, *Diagnostic Teaching* (Washington, D.C.: National Education Assn., 1966).

8. James Olsen, "Challenge of the Poor to the Schools," *Phi Delta Kappan* 47 (October 1965):79.

9. Earl C. Kelley, *Perceiving, Behaving, Becoming, A New Focus on Education* (Washington, D.C.: National Education Assn., 1962.)

10. Irene Hunt, *Up A Road Slowly* (Chicago: Follett, 1966), p. 21.

Bibliography

Abrahams, Roger D., and Rudolph C. Troike. *Language and Cultural Diversity in American Education*. Englewood Cliffs, N.J.: Prentice-Hall, 1972.

Alexander, J. Estill, ed. *Teaching Reading*. Boston: Little Brown, 1979.

Aukerman, Robert C. *Approaches to Beginning Reading*. New York: John Wiley & Sons, 1971.

Baratz, Joan C., and Roger W. Shuy. *Teaching Black Children to Read*. Washington, D.C.: Institute for Applied Linguistics, 1969.

Berry, Althea, Thomas C. Barrett, and William R. Powell. *Elementary Reading Instruction: Selected Materials*. 2d ed. Boston: Allyn & Bacon, 1974.

Bond, Guy L., Miles A. Tinker, and Barbara Wasson. *Reading Difficulties: Their Diagnosis and Correction*. 4th ed. Englewood Cliffs, N.J.: Prentice-Hall, 1978.

Bowren, Fay F., and Miles V. Zintz. *Teaching Reading in Adult Basic Education*. Dubuque, Iowa: Wm. C. Brown, 1977.

Bruner, Joseph F., and John J. Campbell. *Participating in Secondary Reading: A Practical Approach*. Englewood Cliffs, N.J.: Prentice-Hall, 1978.

Burling, Robbins. *English in Black and White*. New York: Holt, Rinehart & Winston, 1973.

Burmeister, Lou. *Reading Strategies for Secondary School Teachers*. 2d ed. Reading, Mass.: Addison-Wesley, 1978.

————. *Words: From Print to Meaning: Classroom Activities for Building Sight Vocabulary, for Using Context Clues, Morphology and Phonics*. Reading, Mass.: Addison-Wesley, 1975.

Burns, Paul C., and Betty D. Roe. *Teaching Reading in Today's Elementary Schools*. Chicago: Rand McNally, 1976.

Burron, Arnold, and Amos Claybaugh. *Basic Concepts in Reading Instruction: A Programmed Approach*. 2d ed. Columbus: Charles E. Merrill, 1977.

Bush, Clifford L., and Mildred H. Huebner. *Strategies for Reading in the Elementary School*. 2d ed. New York: Macmillan, 1979.

Cazden, Courtney B., Vera John, and Dell Hymes, eds. *Functions of Language in the Classroom*. New York: Teachers College Press, Columbia University, 1972.

Chall, Jeanne. *Learning to Read: The Great Debate*. New York: McGraw-Hill, 1967.

Cunningham, Patricia, Sharon V. Arthur, and James W. Cunningham. *Classroom Reading Instruction, K–5, Alternative Approaches*. Lexington, Mass: D.C. Heath, 1977.

Dallman, Martha, et al. *The Teaching of Reading*. 5th ed. New York: Holt, Rinehart & Winston, 1978.

Dechant, Emerald V. *Improving the Teaching of Reading*. 2d ed. Englewood Cliffs, N.J.: Prentice-Hall, 1970.

DeStefano, Johanna, ed. *Language, Society and Education: A Profile of Black English*. Worthington, Ohio: Charles A. Jones, 1973.

Dillner, Martha H., and Joanne P. Olson. *Personalized Reading Instruction in Middle, Junior and Senior High Schools.* New York: Macmillan, 1977.

Downing, John. *Comparative Reading: Cross-National Studies of Behavior and Processes in Reading and Writing.* New York: Macmillan, 1973.

———. *The Initial Teaching Alphabet Explained and Illustrated.* New York: Macmillan, 1964.

Drew, Clifford J., Michael L. Hardman, and Harry P. Bluhm, eds. *Mental Retardation: Social and Educational Perspectives.* St. Louis: C. V. Mosby, 1977.

Duffy, Gerald, and George B. Sherman. *Systematic Reading Instruction.* 2d ed. New York: Harper & Row, 1977.

Durkin, Dolores. *Teaching Them to Read.* Boston: Allyn & Bacon, 1974.

———. *Strategies for Identifying Words: A Workbook for Teachers and Those Preparing to Teach.* Boston: Allyn & Bacon, 1976.

Durr, William K. *Reading Instruction: Dimensions and Issues, A Book of Readings.* Boston: Houghton Mifflin, 1967.

Ekwall, Eldon. *Diagnosis and Remediation of the Disabled Reader.* Boston: Allyn & Bacon, 1976.

———. *Locating and Correcting Reading Difficulties.* 2d ed. Columbus: Charles E. Merrill, 1977.

Fernald, Grace. *Remedial Techniques in Basic School Subjects.* New York: McGraw-Hill, 1971.

Frierson, Edward C., and Walter B. Barbe. *Educating Children with Learning Disabilities: A Book of Readings.* New York: Appleton-Century-Crofts, 1967.

Fry, Edward. *Elementary Reading Instruction.* New York: McGraw-Hill, 1977.

Furth, Hans G. *Piaget for Teachers.* Englewood Cliffs, N.J.: Prentice-Hall, 1970.

Gallant, Ruth. *Handbook in Corrective Reading.* 2d ed. Columbus: Charles E. Merrill, 1977.

Gearheart, B. R. *Learning Disabilities: Educational Strategies.* St. Louis: C. V. Mosby, 1977.

Gray, W. S. *On Their Own in Reading.* 2d. ed. Chicago: Scott, Foresman, 1960.

Guszak, Frank J. *Diagnostic Reading Instruction in the Elementary School.* 2d ed. New York: Harper & Row, 1978.

Hafner, Lawrence E. *Developmental Reading in Middle and Secondary Schools: Foundations, Strategies, and Skills for Teaching.* New York: Macmillan, 1977.

Hafner, Lawrence, and Hayden B. Jolly. *Patterns of Teaching Reading in the Elementary School.* New York: Macmillan, 1972.

Hall, Maryanne. *Teaching Reading as a Language Experience.* 2d. ed. Columbus: Charles E. Merrill, 1976.

Harris, Albert J., and Edward R. Sipay. *How to Teach Reading: A Competency-Based Program:* New York: Longman, 1978.

———. *How to Increase Reading Ability.* 6th ed. New York: David McKay, 1975.

Harris, Albert J., and Edward R. Sipay, eds. *Readings on Reading Instruction.* 2d. ed. New York: David McKay, 1972.

Harris, Larry A., and Carl B. Smith. *Individualizing Reading Instruction: A Reader.* New York: Holt, Rinehart & Winston, 1972.

———. *Reading Instruction: Diagnostic Teaching in the Classroom.* 2d ed. New York: Holt, Rinehart & Winston, 1976.

Heilman, Arthur. *Phonics in Proper Perspective.* 3d ed. Columbus: Charles E. Merrill, 1976.

———. *Principles and Practices of Teaching Reading.* 4th ed. Columbus: Charles E. Merrill, 1977.

Henderson, R. L., and D. R. Green. *Reading for Meaning in the Elementary School.* Englewood Cliffs, N.J.: Prentice-Hall, 1969.

Herber, Harold L. *Teaching Reading in Content Areas.* 2d ed. Englewood Cliffs, N.J.: Prentice-Hall, 1978.

Herr, Selma. *Learning Activities for Reading.* Dubuque, Iowa: Wm. C. Brown, 1977.

Hillerich, Robert L. *Reading Fundamentals for Preschool and Primary Children.* Columbus: Charles E. Merrill, 1977.

Hodges, Richard E., and Hugh Rudorf. *Language and Learning to Read.* Boston: Houghton Mifflin, 1972.

Huey, Edmund Burke. *Psychology and Pedagogy of Reading.* New York: Macmillan, 1908; Cambridge, Mass.: M.I.T. Press, 1968.

International Reading Assn., Box 695, Newark, Del. 19711.
  Perspectives in Reading
  Proceedings of the Annual Convention
  Reading Aids
  Annotated Bibliographies
  IRA + ERIC/CRIER
  The Reading Teacher
  Journal of Reading
  The Reading Research Quarterly

Jansky, Jeannette, and Katrina De Hirsch. *Preventing Reading Failure: Prediction, Diagnosis, Intervention.* New York: Harper & Row, 1972.

Karlin, Robert. *Teaching Elementary Reading: Principles and Strategies.* New York: Harcourt Brace and Jovanovich, 1975.

Kean, John M., and Carl Personke. *The Language Arts: Teaching and Learning in the Elementary School.* New York: St. Martin's Press, 1976.

Kennedy, Eddie C. *Classroom Approaches to Remedial Reading.* 2d ed. Itasca, Ill.: F. E. Peacock, 1977.

————. *Methods in Teaching Developmental Reading.* Itasca, Ill.: F. E. Peacock, 1974.

King, Martha L., Berneice Ellinger, and Willavene Wolfe. *Critical Reading: A Book of Readings.* Philadelphia: J.B. Lippincott, 1967.

Labuda, Michael, ed. *Creative Reading for Gifted Learners: A Design for Excellence.* Newark, Del.: International Reading Assn., 1974.

LaPray, Margaret. *Teaching Children to Become Independent Readers.* New York: Center for Applied Research in Education, 1972.

Lee, Dorris M., and Roach Van Allen. *Learning to Read Through Experience.* 2d. ed. New York: Appleton-Century-Crofts, 1963.

Long, Nicholas J., William C. Morse, and Ruth G. Newman. *Conflict in the Classroom: The Education of Emotionally Disturbed Children.* Belmont, Calif.: Wadsworth, 1972.

Lundsteen, Sara W. *Children Learn to Communicate: Language Arts Through Creative Problem-Solving.* Englewood Cliffs, N.J.: Prentice-Hall, 1976.

McCracken, Robert A., and Marlene J. McCracken. *Reading Is Only the Tiger's Tail.* San Rafael, Calif.: Leswing Press, 1972.

Malmstrom, Jean. *Understanding Language: A Primer for the Language Arts Teacher.* New York: St. Martin's Press, 1977.

Mazurkiewicz, Albert J. *Teaching About Phonics.* New York: St. Martin's Press, 1976.

Moffett, James. *A Student-Centered Language Arts Curriculum, K–6.* Boston: Houghton Mifflin, 1976.

Olson, Joanne P., and Martha H. Dillner. *Learning to Teach Reading in the Elementary School, Utilizing a Competency-Based Instructional System.* New York: Macmillan, 1976.

Otto, Wayne, Robert Chester, John McNeil, and Shirley Myers. *Focused Reading Instruction.* Reading, Mass.: Addison-Wesley, 1974.

Pearson, P. D., and D. D. Johnson. *Teaching Reading Comprehension.* New York: Holt, Rinehart & Winston, 1978.

Piercey, Dorothy. *Reading Activities in the Content Areas: An Ideabook for Middle and Secondary Schools.* Boston: Allyn & Bacon, 1976.

Quandt, Ivan J. *Teaching Reading: A Human Process.* Chicago: Rand McNally, 1977.

Ransom, Grayce. *Preparing to Teach Reading.* Boston: Little Brown, 1978.

Robinson, H. Alan. *Teaching Reading and Study Strategies: The Content Areas.* 2d ed. Boston: Allyn & Bacon, 1978.

Roswell, Florence, and Gladys Natchez. *Reading Disability: Diagnosis and Treatment.* New York: Basic Books, 1976.

Ruddell, Robert B. *Reading Language Instruction: Innovative Practices.* Englewood Cliffs, N.J.: Prentice-Hall, 1974.

Ruddell, Robert B., et al., eds. *Resources in Reading: Language Instruction.* Englewood Cliffs, N.J.: Prentice-Hall, 1974.

Russell, David, Etta Karp, and Anne Marie Mueser. *Reading Aids Through the Grades.* New York: Teachers College Press, Columbia University, 1975.

Savage, John F., ed. *Linguistics for Teachers, Selected Readings.* Chicago: Science Research Associates, 1973.

Savage, John F., and Jean F. Mooney. *Teaching Reading to Children with Special Needs.* Boston: Allyn & Bacon, 1978.

Schubert, Delwyn G., and Theodore L. Torgerson. *Improving the Reading Program.* 4th ed. Dubuque, Iowa: Wm. C. Brown, 1976.

Smith, Frank, ed. *Psycholinguistics and Reading.* New York: Holt, Rinehart & Winston, 1973.

Smith, Frank. *Understanding Reading, A Psycholinguistic Analysis of Reading and Learning to Read.* 2d ed. New York: Holt, Rinehart & Winston, 1978.

Smith, Nila Banton. *American Reading Instruction.* Newark, Del.: International Reading Assn., 1965.

Smith, Richard J., and Thomas C. Barrett. *Teaching Reading in the Middle Grades.* Reading, Mass.: Addison-Wesley, 1974.

Smith, Richard J., and Dale D. Johnson. *Teaching Children to Read.* Reading, Mass.: Addison-Wesley, 1976.

Spache, Evelyn. *Reading Activities for Child Involvement.* Boston: Allyn & Bacon, 1976.

Spache, George. *Diagnosing and Correcting Reading Disabilities.* Boston: Allyn & Bacon, 1976.

Spache, George, and Evelyn Spache. *Reading in the Elementary School.* 4th ed. Boston: Allyn & Bacon, 1977.

Stauffer, Russell G. *Directing the Reading-Thinking Process.* New York: Harper & Row, 1975.

———. *The Language-Experience Approach to the Teaching of Reading.* New York: Harper & Row, 1970.

Thonis, Eleanor Wall. *Literacy for America's Spanish-speaking Children.* Newark, Del.: International Reading Assn., 1976.

———. *Teaching Reading to Non-English Speakers.* New York: Macmillan, 1976.

Tinker, Miles A. *Preparing Your Child for School.* New York: McGraw-Hill, 1976.

Tinker, Miles A., and Constance McCullough. *Teaching Elementary Reading.* 4th ed. Englewood Cliffs, N.J.: Prentice-Hall, 1978.

Valett, Robert E. *Developing Cognitive Abilities: Teaching Children to Think.* St. Louis: C.V. Mosby, 1978.

Veatch, Jeannette, et al. *Key Words to Reading: The Language Experience Approach Begins.* Columbus: Charles E. Merrill, 1973.

Wilson, Robert M., and Maryanne Hall. *Programmed Word Attack for Teachers.* 2d. ed. Columbus: Charles E. Merrill, 1974.

———. *Reading and the Elementary School Child: Theory and Practice for Teachers.* New York: Van Nostrand Reinhold, 1972.

Zintz, Miles V. *Corrective Reading.* 3d ed. Dubuque, Iowa: Wm. C. Brown, 1977.

Appendix

Books in Which American Indians Are Principal Characters

Characters in children's fictional literature provide an important avenue through which student self-identification can occur. When literature is used for the purpose of building self-image, it is essential that the characterizations in the stories selected portray a reasonably accurate and positive image with which the reader can identify.

American Indians are used quite extensively as storybook characters in children's literature. Unfortunately, many of the characterizations are inaccurate or portray a negative, stereotyped image. It is important that teachers and librarians carefully preview reading materials before making them available to children.

The following bibliography includes some of the better books using American Indians as characters. The Indian tribe represented and the reading level of the book are indicated in each case. Those books which are starred are especially recommended for classroom use.

Juanita O. Cata
Chief, Division of Education
Bureau of Indian Affairs, Albuquerque Area Office

Agle, Nan Hayden. *Makon and the Dauphin.* New York: Charles Scribner's Sons, 1961. (Woodland; intermediate)

Agnew, Edith J. *Nezbah's Lamb.* New York: Friendship Press, 1954. (Navajo; primary)

Armer, Laura Adams. *Waterless Mountain.* New York: David McKay, 1931. (Navajo; upper)

Baker, Betty. *And One Was a Wooden Indian.* New York: Macmillan, 1970. (Apache/Papago; intermediate)

———. *Killer-Of-Death.* New York: Harper & Row, 1963. (Apache; upper)

———. *Little Runner of the Longhouse.* New York: Harper & Row, 1962. (Iroquois; primary)

———. *The Shaman's Last Raid.* New York: Harper & Row, 1963. (Apache; intermediate)

*———. *Walk the World's Rim.* New York: Harper & Row, 1965. (Southwest; upper)

Balch, Glenn. *Horse of Two Colors.* New York: Thomas Y. Crowell, 1969. (Nez Perce; intermediate)

———. *Indian Paint.* New York: Scholastic Book Services, 1962. (Plains; intermediate)

*Bannon, Laura. *When the Moon Is New*. Chicago: Albert Whitman, 1953. (Seminole; intermediate)

Baylor, Byrd. *Before You Came This Way*. New York: E. P. Dutton, 1969. (Anasazi; primary)

Beatie, Bernadine. *Little Turtle*. Chicago: Scott, Foresman, 1971. (Hopi; intermediate)

Beatty, Hetty Burlingame. *Little Owl Indian*. Boston: Houghton Mifflin, 1951. (Iroquois; primary)

Behn, Harry. *The Painted Cave*. New York: Harcourt Brace Jovanovich, 1957. (Southwest; intermediate)

Bleeker, Sonia. *The Crow Indians: Hunters of the Northern Plains*. New York: William Morrow, 1953. (Crow; intermediate)

———. *The Navajo*. New York: William Morrow, 1958. (Navajo; intermediate)

*Buff, Mary, and Conrad Buff. *Hah-Nee*. Boston: Houghton Mifflin, 1965. (Anasazi; intermediate)

———. *An Indian Boy Before the White Man Came*. Los Angeles: Ward Ritchie Press, 1966. (California; intermediate)

Bulla, Clyde Robert. *Eagle Feather*. New York: Thomas Y. Crowell, 1963. (Navajo; intermediate)

*———. *Indian Hill*. New York: Thomas Y. Crowell, 1963. (Navajo; intermediate)

Carlson, Vada, and Gary Witherspoon. *Black Mountain Boy*. Chinle, Ariz.: Rough Rock Demonstration School, Navajo Curriculum Center, 1974. (Navajo; intermediate)

*Chandler, Edna Walker. *Charley Brave*. Chicago: Albert Whitman, 1962. (Sioux; intermediate)

Christense, Cardell Dano. *Buffalo Kill*. New York: Archway, n.d. (Blackfoot; intermediate)

*Clark, Ann Nolan. *Brave Against the Enemy*. Haskell Institute: U.S. Indian Service, 1944. (Sioux; intermediate)

———. *The Desert People*. New York: Viking Press, 1962. (Papago; primary)

———. *In My Mother's House*. New York: Viking Press, 1972. (Pueblo; intermediate)

———. *Little Boy of Three Names*. Haskell: Bureau of Indian Affairs, Haskell Press, 1959. (Pueblo; intermediate)

———. *Little Navajo Bluebird*. New York: Viking Press, 1943. (Navajo; intermediate)

———. *Little Navajo Herder*. Haskell: U.S. Indian Service Press, 1951. (Navajo; intermediate)

———. *Summer Is for Growing*. New York: Farrar, Straus & Giroux, 1968. (Southwest; intermediate)

*———. *Sun Journey*. Washington, D.C.: Government Printing Office, 1945. (Zuni; intermediate)

Dodge, Carol. *Kine-U*. Washington, D.C.: U.S. Office of Education, 1971. (Menominee; primary)

Feague, Mildred H. *The Little Indian and the Angel*. Chicago: Children's Press, 1970. (Navajo; primary)

Friskey, Margaret. *Indian Two Feet and His Horse*. Chicago: Children's Press, 1959. (Plains; primary)

George, Jean Craighead. *Julie of the Wolves*. New York: Harper & Row, 1972. (Eskimo; intermediate)

Harris, Christie. *Raven's Cry*. New York: Atheneum, 1966. (Haida; upper)

*Harvey, James O. *Beyond the Gorge of Shadows*. New York: Lothrup, Lee & Shepard, 1965. (Anasazi; intermediate)

Hoffine, Lyla. *The Eagle Feather Prize*. New York: David McKay, 1962. (Sioux; upper)

*———. *Jennie's Mandan Bowl*. New York: Longman, Green, 1960. (Mandan; intermediate)

Holling, Holling Clancy. *The Book of Indians*. New York: Platt & Munk, 1962. (mixed; intermediate)

*Hood, Flora. *Pink Puppy*. New York: G. P. Putnam's Sons, 1966. (Cherokee; primary)

*———. *Something for the Medicine Man*. Chicago: Melmont Publishers, 1962. (Cherokee; intermediate)

James, Harry C. *Ovada: An Indian Boy of the Grand Canyon.* Los Angeles: Ward Ritchie Press, 1969. (Havasupi; intermediate)

Katz, Jane B., ed. *Let Me Be a Free Man: A Documentary of Indian Resistance.* Minneapolis: Lerner, 1975. (leadership; upper)

Kendall, Lace (A. Stoutenburg). *The Mud Ponies.* New York: Coward-McCann, 1963. (Pawnee; intermediate)

LaFarge, Oliver. *Cochise of Arizona.* New York: E. P. Dutton, 1953. (Apache; intermediate)

Lampman, Evelyn Sibley. *Cayuse Courage.* New York: Harcourt Brace Jovanovich, 1970. (Cayuse; upper)

*Lauritzen, Jonreed. *The Ordeal of the Young Hunter.* Boston: Little, Brown, 1954. (Navajo; upper)

Marriott, Alice. *Indian Annie: Kiowa Captive.* New York: David McKay, 1965. (Kiowa/Choctaw; intermediate)

Meigs, Cornelia. *The Willow Whistle.* New York: Macmillan, 1931. (Sioux; upper)

Miles, Miska. *Annie and the Old One.* Boston: Little Brown, 1971. (Navajo; primary)

*Momaday, Natachee Scott. *Owl in the Cedar Tree.* Flagstaff, Ariz.: Northland Press, 1975. (Navajo: primary)

Moon, Grace. *One Little Indian.* Rev. ed. Chicago: Albert Whitman, 1967. (Navajo; intermediate)

*Mulcahy, Lucille. *Fire on Big Lonesome.* Chicago: Elk Grove Press, 1967. (Zuni; intermediate)

Nelson, Mary Carroll. *Michael Naranjo: The Story of an American Indian.* Minneapolis: Dillon Press, 1975. (Pueblo; upper)

O'Dell, Scott. *Island of the Blue Dolphins.* Boston: Houghton Mifflin, 1960. (California; upper)

*———. *Sing Down the Moon.* Boston: Houghton Mifflin, 1970. (Navajo; upper)

Penny, Grace J. *Moki.* New York: Avon, 1973. (Cheyenne; intermediate)

Randall, Janet. *The Buffalo Box.* New York: David McKay, 1969. (Nez Perce; intermediate)

Schweitzer, Byrd Bayler. *One Small Blue Bead.* New York: Macmillan, 1965. (Southwest; primary)

Selden, Alice, and Carol Dodge. *One Menominee Boy.* Washington, D.C.: U.S. Office of Education, 1971. (Menominee; intermediate)

Smucker, Barbara C. *Wigwam in the City.* New York: E. P. Dutton, 1966. (Chippewa, intermediate)

*Steiner, Stan. *The Last Horse.* New York: Macmillan, 1961. (Navajo; intermediate)

Thompson, Eileen. *The Blue Stone Mystery.* New York: Abelard-Schuman, 1963. (Pueblo; intermediate)

Waltrip, Lela, and Rufus Waltrip. *Quiet Boy.* New York: David McKay, 1961. (Navajo; intermediate)

Warren, Mary P. *Walk in My Moccasins.* Philadelphia: Westminster Press, 1966. (Sioux; intermediate)

*Especially recommended for classroom use.

Photo
Credits

Name Index

Aaron, Ira E., 462
Abeson, Alan, 442, 444
Abrahams, Roger D., 62, 394, 410, 520
Adams, Hazel, 321, 339
Agle, Nan H., 524
Agnew, Edith J., 524
Alexander, J. Estill, 520
Allen, Claryce, 16, 119
Allen, Harold B., 394
Allen, Roach Van, 6, 16, 119, 149
Allen, Virginia F., 410
Allington, Richard L., 361
Amidon, Edmund J., 170
Anastasiow, Nicholas, 90
Anderson, Anne M., 287
Anderson, Donald, 147, 463
Arbuthnot, May Hill, 91, 308, 317, 321, 324, 338, 339
Armer, Laura Adams, 524
Armstrong, William H., 44
Arnsdorf, Val, 338
Artley, Sterl, 261, 302
Ashton-Warner, Sylvia, 518
Asquith, Melrose, 445
Aukerman, Robert, 119, 346, 520
Austin, Mary C., 518
Ausubel, David P., 413, 414
Axline, Virginia Mae, 414, 443, 445

Bacmeister, Rhoda, 316
Bagford, Jack, 226
Bailey, Mildred H., 214, 226, 229
Baker, Augusta, 324
Baker, Betty, 524
Balch, Glenn, 524
Baldwin, James, 316
Bankson, Nicholas W., 73, 91
Bannon, Laura, 525
Baratz, Joan C., 410, 414, 520
Bardwell, R. W., 263
Barnette, Eleanor, 120
Barnhart, Clarence L., 222
Barrett, Thomas C., 287, 507, 520
Baruch, Dorothy, 443
Bateman, Barbara, 43
Baylor, Byrd, 525
Beattie, Bernadine, 525
Beatty, Betty B., 525
Becker, George M., 488
Behn, Harry, 525
Bender, Ida C., 316
Bender, Lauretta, 442
Bennett, A. Y., 198
Benyon, Sheila D., 443

Berry, Althea, 520
Bettelheim, Bruno, 413
Betts, Emmet, 117, 118, 121, 463
Bierly, Ken, 171
Billig, Edith, 361
Billings, N., 237, 262
Bing, Lois, 90
Birch, Jack W., 442
Bissett, Donald J., 91
Blakemore, Candace, 183
Blakey, Janis, 120
Bleeker, Sonia, 525
Bleismer, Emery P., 462
Bloom, Benjamin, 36, 43, 240, 262
Blough, Glenn, 294, 303
Bond, Guy L., 256, 257, 260, 263, 286, 316, 487, 520
Boning, Richard, 147
Book, Robert M., 90, 443
Bormuth, John, 260
Botel, Morton, 462
Bowren, Fay F., 520
Boyer, E. Gil, 171
Bracken, Dorothy K., 147, 303
Bradford, Arthur, 17, 62
Brieling, Annette, 183
Brooks, Charlotte, 413
Brown, Dianne, 464
Bruner, Joseph F., 520
Buff, Mary, 525
Bulla, Clyde R., 525
Bullerman, Mary, 361
Burke, Carolyn, 7–8, 16, 54, 63, 464
Burling, Robbins, 410, 520
Burmeister, Lou, 214, 226, 229, 346, 361, 363, 520
Burns, Paul C., 520
Burron, Arnold, 16, 286, 361, 520
Burrows, A. T., 213, 229
Burrus, Dorothy, 302
Burton, William, 263
Bush, Clifford, 316, 518, 520
Byler, Mary Gloyne, 360, 363

Campbell, John J., 520
Campbell, Russell, 394
Carlson, Vada, 525
Carlton, Lessie, 137, 150
Carpenter, Helen M., 286
Carroll, John B., 62, 394
Cass, James, 488
Cassidy, Jack, 183
Cata, Juanita O., 328, 363, 524
Catterson, Jane, 338

Cavanaugh, Frances, 38, 44, 328
Cazden, Courtney, 53, 55, 62, 64, 394, 410
Chall, Jeanne, 10, 17, 95, 119, 120, 462, 518, 520
Chandler, Edna W., 525
Chang, Lynette Y. C., 149
Chapanis, A., 91
Charles, C. M., 43, 171, 442
Christense, Cardell D., 525
Cianciolo, Patricia, 324, 338
Claerbaut, David, 411
Clark, Ann N., 525
Clark, Kenneth, 414
Claybaugh, Amos, 15, 286, 361, 520
Clymer, Theodore, 149, 213, 226, 229, 488
Cohen, Alan, 411
Coleman, Mary E., 286
Conklin, Paul, 396
Cooper, Thelma, 411
Coopersmith, Stanley, 519
Cordts, Anna, 212, 216, 226, 229
Costo, Rupert, 361
Cox, Clara Jett, 396
Cox, Sheralyn, 444
Crabbs, Lelah M., 148, 262
Craker, Hazel, 388, 397
Crane, Helen W., 198
Craven, Margaret, 45
Cresimbeni, Joseph, 508
Cronnell, B. D., 411
Crosby, Muriel, 315, 317
Cruickshank, William M., 443
Cuddy, Marie C., 256, 257, 263
Cunningham, Patricia, 520
Curtis, James, 316
Cutright, Prudence, 270, 272
Cutts, Warren G., 92, 97, 120

Dale, Edgar, 28, 29
Dallman, Martha, 16, 120, 125, 149, 260, 316, 338, 361, 520
Daniels, Steven, 518
Darling, David, 43
Davies, R. E., 394, 397
Davies, Valentine, 303
deAngeli, Marguerite, 44
De Boer, John J., 149
Dechant, Emerald V., 302, 520
DeHaan, Robert F., 444
DeHirsch, Katrina, 72, 90, 522
Deighton, Lee, 234, 261
Della-Dora, Delmo, 413
Dennis, Ida, 270, 272
De Stefano, Johanna, 62, 411, 520

Deutsch, Martin, 116, 121, 413
De Witt, Frances B., 444
Dietrich, Dorothy, 338
Dill, Barbara, 324
Dillard, J. L., 411
Dillner, Martha, 302, 521, 522
Divoky, Diane, 442, 443, 445
Dodge, Carol, 525, 526
Dolch, E. W., 202, 228, 463
Doll, Edgar A., 91, 444
Downing, John, 518, 521
Drew, Clifford, J., 521
Duffy, Gerald, 361, 521
Dunn, Lloyd, 90
Durant, Will, 303
Durkin, Dolores, 119, 226, 229, 521
Durr, William K., 340, 521
Durrell, D. D., 277, 287, 464

Eakin, Mary K., 324
Earle, Richard A., 361, 362
Eastwick, Ivy O., 317
Ebbinghaus, H., 30
Eckstein, Catherine, 464
Edwards, B. S., 338
Eichert, Magdalen, 184
Ekwall, E. E., 462, 487, 520
Ellinger, Berniece, 302, 522
Ellingson, Careth, 120, 488
Elliott, Charles, 63
Elliott, Geraldine, 120
Ellis, Henry A., 27, 44
Elzey, F. F., 262
Emans, Robert, 214, 227, 229
English, Fenwock, 518
Ennis, Robert H., 302
Ephron, Beulah, 443
Estes, Eleanor, 44
Evvard, Evelyn, 396

Farella, Merilyn, 397
Farr, Roger, 90
Fasold, Ralph W., 411
Fassett, James H., 120
Fay, Leo C., 256, 263, 287, 361, 363
Feague, Mildred H., 525
Fernald, Grace, 521
Field, Elinor, 324
Finocchiaro, Mary, 396, 411
Fisher, Margery, 340
Fitzpatrick, Mildred, 235, 262
Flamond, Ruth, 303
Flanders, Ned A., 168, 170, 171
Flood, James E., 183

Forbes, Esther, 44
Forgan, Harry, 361
Fraser, Dorothy, 303
Frazier, Alexander, 395
Free, Margaret, 228
Freehill, Maurice, 442
Frierson, Edward C., 316, 521
Fries, C. C., 62, 411
Friskey, Margaret, 525
Frostig, Marianne, 444
Fry, Edward, 228, 229, 487, 521
Fryer, Ann, 16
Fuld, Paula, 227
Furst, Norma, 171
Furth, Hans G., 521
Fyleman, Rose, 316

Gagne, Robert, 18, 43
Gallagher, James, 442
Gallagher, Patricia, 443
Gallant, Ruth, 260, 487, 521
Gans, Roma, 92
Ganz, Paul, 149
Gardner, William I., 443
Garrett, Henry, 31
Gates, Arthur I., 11, 12, 17, 148, 228, 262, 263, 464
Gearhart, Bill, 443, 521
Geismer, Barbara, 91
George, Jean C., 44, 525
Gerhard, Christian, 361
Gillis, Ruth, 324
Gilmore, John V., 463
Gipson, Fred, 44
Glaser, Edward M., 303
Glock, Marvin, 260
Gonzales, Dolores, 395, 397
Gonzales, Eloy, 442
Goodman, Kenneth S., 62, 63, 64, 394, 396
Goodman, Yetta, 464
Goodwin, William, 26, 40
Goodykoontz, Bess, 287
Gottlieb, David, 411
Graebner, Dianne B., 119
Gray, Lillian, 228
Gray, William S., 6, 16, 227, 229, 262, 263, 521
Green, Donald R., 260, 302, 521
Green, Peter, 332, 340
Green, Richard T., 260
Greer, Margaret, 43, 239, 269, 287, 312, 317, 323, 339
Greet, Cabell, 198
Grinnell, Paula, 363

Grover, Charles C., 263
Gunther, John, 45
Gurton, Ardis E., 263
Guszak, Frank J., 16, 235, 240, 261, 462, 487, 502, 521

Haarhoff, T.J., 397
Hafner, Lawrence, 226, 227, 521
Hall, Edward T., 62, 395
Hall, Maryanne, 119, 149, 521
Hall, Robert, 63, 395
Hamalainen, Arthur, 397
Hamblet, Martha J., 184
Hansen, T. Stevenson, 361, 362
Harmin, Merrill, 44
Harrington, Alma, 184
Harrington, Michael, 412
Harris, A. J., 44, 90, 228, 260, 280, 286, 338, 442, 463, 488, 521
Harris, Christie, 525
Harris, Larry, 302, 316, 521
Harris, Stephen G., 16, 94, 120
Harrison, Lucille, 92, 228, 230, 261
Hartman, Nancy C., 443
Hartman, Robert, 443
Harvey, James O., 525
Hauck, Barbara, 442
Havighurst, Robert J., 444
Hegge, T., 444
Heilman, Arthur, 16, 90, 119, 228, 242, 262, 286, 302, 521
Heinrich, June S., 316
Henderson, Richard L., 260, 302, 521
Henry, Jules, 298, 303, 413
Herber, Harold L., 361, 521
Herndon, James, 518
Herndon, William, 303
Herr, Selma, 225, 521
Herrick, Virgil, 120
Hewett, Frank M., 443, 445
Hildreth, Gertrude, 396, 444
Hilgard, Ernest, 18, 43
Hillerich, Robert L., 73, 90, 91, 522
Hilliard, Raymond M., 413
Hillyer, Mildred, 340
Hoaglund, J., 338
Hobbs, Nicholas, 444
Hockman, Carol H., 411
Hodges, Richard, 16, 61, 64, 522
Hoffine, Lyla, 525
Holling, H. C., 525
Holloway, Ruth L., 17
Hollowell, Lillian, 340
Holt, John, 55, 63, 488, 518

Hood, Flora, 525
Horn, Ernest, 10, 17, 45, 212, 228, 287, 316, 463
Horn, Thomas D., 62, 395, 411
Horrocks, John, 32
Horsman, Gwen, 262
Hosier, Max, 225
Hough, John B., 170
Houston, Susan H., 411
Howell, Emma, 228
Hoyt, Cyril J., 488
Huber, Miriam B., 228
Huebner, Mildred, 316, 518, 520
Huey, Edmund B., 522
Huggett, Albert J., 303
Hunt, Irene, 340, 519
Hunt, Lyman, 149
Hunter, Elizabeth, 170
Hunter, Madeline C., 518
Hutchins, Robert M., 303
Huus, Helen, 261, 339
Hymes, Dell, 62, 63, 410, 520
Hymes, James, 445

Irving, Edward B., 63
Ives, Josephine P., 303

Jacobson, Rodolfo, 411
James, Harry C., 526
Jansky, Jeannette, 72, 90, 522
Jared, Lee Ann, 361
Jastak, J. F., 97, 120
Jastak, S. R., 97, 120
Jenkins, William A., 198
Johns, Jerry L., 411
John-Steiner, Vera, 53, 62, 410, 520
Johnson, D. D., 395, 522
Johnson, D. J., 443
Johnson, Eleanor, 148
Johnson, Marjorie, 463, 488, 507
Johnson, Robert D., 488
Jolly, Hayden B., 226, 227
Jones, Elizabeth, 171
Jones, Virginia, 149
Jongsma, Eugene, 261
Josephy, Alvin M., 363
Jucknat, M., 27, 28
Judd, C. H., 27, 44

Karlin, Robert, 302, 362, 522
Karp, Etta, 225
Katcher, Avrum L., 445
Katz, Jane B., 526
Kaulfers, Walter V., 47, 63

Kean, John M., 522
Kearney, Ruth Carlson, 324
Kelley, Earl C., 396, 519
Kendall, Lace, 526
Kennedy, Dolores, 261
Kennedy, Eddie C., 488, 522
Kephart, Newell C., 443
Kerfoot, James F., 114, 115, 119
King, A. Y., 270, 272
King, Martha, 302, 522
Kingston, A. J., 261, 263
Kirk, Samuel A., 91, 443
Kirkness, Verna J., 363
Klausmeier, Herbert, 26, 40, 44
Klineberg, Otto, 119, 363
Knowlton, Clark S., 16
Kohl, Herbert, 518
Koppitz, Elizabeth, 118, 119, 121
Koppman, Pat, 184
Krathwohl, David R., 36, 44
Kress, Roy, 463, 488, 507
Kritchevsky, Sybil, 171
Kroth, Roger, 183, 442
Krueger, Louise, 444

Labov, William, 411, 414
Labuda, Michael, 442, 522
LaFarge, Oliver, 526
Laffey, James L., 62, 411
Lamb, Pose, 395
Lambert, Wallace, 397
Lamme, Linda L., 316, 317
Lamoreaux, Lillian A., 120
Lampman, Evelyn, 340, 526
Langford, William, 72, 90, 91
LaPray, Margaret, 488, 522
Larrick, Nancy, 324, 335, 339, 340
Larson, Martha L., 316, 317
Latimer, Bettye I., 324
Lauritzen, Jonreed, 526
Lee, Dorris, 67, 119, 149, 518, 519, 522
Lees, Fred, 362
LeFevre, Carl A., 395
LeGant, Jean, 339
Lehr, Elizabeth, 229
Lenneberg, Eric H., 396
Levine, S., 262
Levy, Betty, 413
Lewis, Oscar, 412
Liddle, William, 148
Liebert, Burt, 395
Lindgren, Henry C., 171
Loban, Walter, 62, 395, 396
Long, Nicholas, 443, 522

Loughlin, Catherine, 161, 171
Lourie, Z., 213, 229
Lundsteen, Sara, 302, 522
Lyon, D. O., 44

Mabie, Ethel, 263
McBroom, Maude, 464
McCall, William A., 148, 262
McCarthy, James J., 91
McCormick, Sandra, 316, 317
McCowen, Annie, 228
McCracken, Marlene J., 119, 120, 149, 522
McCracken, Robert A., 119, 120, 149, 280,
    463, 522
McCreary, Eugene, 413
McCullough, Constance M., 287, 316, 339,
    507, 518
McCutchen, Samuel, 316
McDermott, Ray P., 411, 413
McDiarmid, Garnet, 362, 363
McKee, Paul, 119, 228, 246, 261, 287, 332,
    340
McKillop, Anne S., 303
McMenemy, Richard A., 228, 488
Madsen, William, 396
Malherbe, E. G., 395
Malkiewicz, J. E., 335, 339, 340
Malmstrom, Jean, 62, 522
Mangrum, Charles, 361
Manolakes, George, 518
Marcus, Lloyd, 362, 363
Marguerite, Sister Rose, 225
Marriott, Alice, 526
Martin, Bill, 315, 317
Martin, Mavis, 90
Maslow, A. H., 25, 26, 27, 44
Matthews, Virginia, 338
Mattleman, Marciene, 171
Mazie, David M., 17
Mazurkiewicz, Albert J., 120, 522
Meigs, Cornelia, 526
Meredith, Robert, 63
Merriam, Eve, 411
Merrill, Barbara W., 173, 184
Miles, Miska, 197–198, 526
Miller, Walter, 412
Mitchell, George C., 396
Modiano, Nancy, 397
Moffett, James, 522
Momaday, Natachee S., 330, 340, 526
Monroe, Marian, 198, 262
Moon, Grace, 526
Moore, Robert H., 137, 150
Mork, Theodore, 149

Morris, Joyce, 444
Morrison, Coleman, 518
Mueser, Anne Marie, 225
Mulcahy, Lucille, 526
Myklebust, H. R., 443

Naiden, Norma, 118, 120, 121
Navarra, John G., 362
Nelson, H. L., 271
Nelson, Joan B., 444
Nelson, Mary Carroll, 526
Nerbovig, Marcella, 120
Newcastle, Helen, 237, 262
Newman, Ellen, 413
Newton, E. S., 339
Nielsen, Wilhelmina, 150
Niemeyer, John, 413

Oaks, Ruth, 213, 214, 228, 229
O'Dell, Scott, 526
O'Donnell, Mabel, 228
Ogle, Lucille, 198
Ojemann, Ralph, 41, 45
Olsen, Arleen, 91
Olsen, James, 519
Olson, Joanne, 302, 521, 522
Ortiz, Leroy, 442
Otto, Wayne, 228, 488, 507, 522

Painter, Helen W., 302, 339
Palmer, William S., 362
Peal, Elizabeth, 397
Peardon, Celeste, 263
Pearson, P. D., 395, 522
Penny, Grace J., 526
Personke, Carl, 522
Petty, Walter, 303
Pfau, Donald W., 184
Piercey, Dorothy, 266, 287, 362, 522
Pilon, Barbara, 414
Pintner, Rudolph, 444
Pitcher-Baker, Georgia, 90
Platts, Mary E., 225
Postman, Neil, 518
Potter, F., 270, 272
Potter, Thomas C., 64, 263
Powell, William, 43, 520
Pratt, David, 362, 363
Prescott, Elizabeth, 171
Pressey, Sidney, 32
Price, Helen, 314, 317

Quandt, Ivan J., 149, 522
Quisenberry, Nancy L., 183

Ramsey, Wallace, 149
Randall, Janet, 526
Randall, Ruth P., 303
Rankin, Earl F., 261
Ransom, Grace A., 508, 522
Raths, Louis E., 44
Rauch, Sidney J., 507
Rawls, Wilson, 44
Redl, Fritz, 171, 184
Reed, Carol, 412
Reid, Hale C., 198
Reid, Virginia, 324
Renzulli, Joseph S., 442
Reynolds, Maynard, 442
Richards, Laura E., 317
Richardson, Mabel, 397
Rivers, Wilga, 412
Roach, Jack L., 184
Roberts, Paul, 396
Robinson, F. N., 63
Robinson, Francis P., 32, 265, 287, 362
Robinson, Gussie M., 363
Robinson, H. Alan, 362, 523
Robinson, Richard D., 261
Roe, Betty D., 520
Rogers, Vincent, 120, 148, 518
Rosier, Paul, 397
Roswell, Florence, 523
Rouch, Roger L., 149
Rowan, Carl, 10, 17
Rowe, Ernest Ras, 442
Ruddell, Robert B., 395, 523
Rude, Robert T., 87, 90, 92
Rudman, Masha K., 324, 363
Rudorf, E. Hugh, 16, 61, 64, 522
Russell, David, 225, 302, 334, 339, 340, 523
Rutherford, William E., 58, 62, 64
Rystrom, Richard, 412

Salisbury, Frank S., 228
Salisbury, Lee H., 120, 395
Sanders, Norris, 43, 44
Sansbury, Russell J., 228
Sarkotich, Diane, 160, 171
Sartain, Harry, 149
Savage, John, 5, 16, 63, 395, 412, 523
Saville-Troike, Muriel, 412
Sawicki, Florence, 120
Sawrey, James M., 28
Scarnato, Samuel A., 413
Scarry, Huck, 198
Schell, Leo, 228, 261
Schiffman, G.B., 83, 91
Schiller, Andrew, 198

Schneider, Herman, 363
Schneider, Nina, 363
Schneyer, J. Wesley, 261, 263
Schubert, Delwyn, 225, 488, 523
Schumaker, Esther, 225
Schwartz, Judy I., 149
Schwartz, Julius, 303
Schweitzer, Byrd Bayler, 526
Scott, Louise Binder, 377, 396
Sebesta, Sam L., 339
Selden, Alice, 526
Seymour, Dorothy, 58, 63, 412, 414
Shane, Harold, 263
Shapiro, Edna, 303
Sheldon, William D., 463
Sherk, John K., 412, 414
Sherzer, Joel, 63
Shrodes, Caroline, 334, 339, 340
Shuy, Roger, 62, 63, 149, 410, 411, 412, 520
Siculan, Dan, 198
Signor, Roger, 445
Silvaroli, Nicholas, 488
Simon, Anita, 171
Simon, Dan, 160, 171
Simon, Sidney, 44
Simpson, Elizabeth, 281, 287
Simpson, G. O., 319, 339
Simpson, Richard, 183, 442
Sipay, E. R., 44, 90, 228, 260, 280, 286, 338, 463, 488, 521
Smith, Carl, 183, 287, 302, 316, 521
Smith, Dora V., 45, 339, 396
Smith, E. Brooks, 63, 395
Smith, Edwin H., 463
Smith, Frank, 16, 43, 63, 64, 508, 523
Smith, Holly, 412
Smith, Nila B., 120, 147, 150, 183, 229, 261, 287, 339, 523
Smith, Richard, 228, 287, 523
Smucker, Barbara, 526
Snedaker, Mabel I., 287, 340
Soghomonian, Sam, 518
Spache, Evelyn, 225, 523
Spache, George D., 228, 324, 463, 523
Sparrow, Julia, 464
Spitzer, Herbert, 31, 44
Stanchfield, Jo, 116, 117, 121
Stanley, Julian C., 442
Staton, Thomas F., 362
Stauffer, Russell, 16, 120, 149, 229, 231, 261, 302, 339, 396, 523
Steiner, Stan, 526
Steptoe, John, 414
Stern, H. H., 184

Stewart, William A., 412
Stinetorf, Louise, 329, 340
Stone, Clarence, 200, 228, 263
Strang, Ruth, 302, 303, 488, 518
Strickland, Ruth, 262, 396
Stroud, J. B., 314, 317
Stuart, George E., 363
Sunderlin, Sylvia, 324
Sustakoski, Henry J., 57, 64
Suter, Antoinette, 91
Syphers, Dorothy F., 443

Taba, Hilda, 171, 231, 239, 261, 262, 302
Taylor, Wilson L., 261, 263
Telford, Charles, 28
Terman, Lewis, 444
Thaddeus, Trela, 488
Thelen, Judith, 346
Theofield, Mary B., 149
Thomas, Benjamin P., 303
Thomas, Ellen L., 362
Thompson, Eileen, 526
Thompson, Elizabeth, 397
Thonis, Eleanor W., 523
Thorn, Tina, 198
Thorndike, E. L., 27, 44, 222, 362
Tift, Katherine, 443
Tinker, Miles A., 16, 90, 120, 260, 287, 316,
        339, 463, 487, 507, 520, 523
Tonjes, Marian, 90, 263
Torgerson, Theodore, 225, 488
Torrance, Paul, 149, 443
Traxler, Arthur, 518
Treadwell, Hariette T., 228
Tressler, J. C., 263
Trezise, Robert L., 443
Troike, Rudolph, 62, 394, 410, 520
Troy, Ann, 362
Turner, Thomas N., 302
Tutolo, Daniel J., 362

Ulibarri, Mari Luci, 395
Unruh, Glennys G., 183, 184

Vacca, Richard T., 362
Valett, Robert E., 91, 523
Valmont, William J., 463
Van Dongen, Richard, 281, 287
Veatch, Jeannette, 120, 149, 523
Venezky, R. L., 63
Vilschek, Elaine C., 149
Vorih, Lillian, 397

Wagner, Eva B., 286, 316
Wagner, Guy, 225
Wagner, Jane, 44
Waltrip, Lela, 526
Wardhaugh, Ronald, 46, 63
Warren, Claudia A., 183
Warren, Mary P., 526
Wasson, Barbara B., 487, 520
Watson, Dorothy J., 464
Watson, Goodwin, 303
Wattenberg, W. W., 171, 184
Weaver, W. W., 261, 263, 395
Weaver, Yvonne, 396
Webster, W. Staten, 414
Weingartner, Charles, 518
West, Edith, 303
West, Gail B., 362
Wheeler, H. E., 228
Wheeler, Lester, 463
Whitehead, Robert, 339
Wildebush, Sarah, 316
Wilder, Laura Ingalls, 328, 340
Willins, Patricia M., 237, 262
Willmon, Betty, 346
Wilson, Robert, 184, 488, 523
Winkley, Carol, 214, 228, 229
Witherspoon, Gary, 525
Witty, Paul A., 443, 444
Wolfe, Josephine B., 148
Wolfe, Willavene, 302, 522
Wolfram, Walter, 411, 412
Wong, Jade Snow, 44, 339
Woodcock, Richard W., 445
Woodring, Paul, 303
Woodruff, Asahel D., 34, 35, 44, 237, 262
Woronoff, Israel, 412

Yandell, Maurine, 395, 396
Yep, Lawrence, 44
Young, Robert, 47, 63

Zafforoni, Joseph, 362
Zettel, Jeffrey, 442, 444
Zintz, Miles V., 16, 262, 395, 396, 397, 412,
        443, 444, 463, 488, 523

Subject Index

abstractness, 434
acceleration, of gifted, 416
accent, 221
accession numbers, 323
acquisition of language, 52
adjusted reading program, 126
adjusting the work of the child, 469
administering the IRI, 455
adult basic education, 10
advance organizer, 347
affective response to reading, 38
affix defined, 51
age, chronological, behavioral, academic, physical, 441
aggression, 436
Aldine Primer, 192
alphabet method, 189
Amos Fortune, Free Man, 38
And Now Miguel, 39, 332
anecdotal records, 503
    Charles, 431–32
    David, 437–40
    Edna, 421
    Jack, 2
    Jill, 430–31
    John, 423–25
    Rose, 428
Anglo course of study, 367
antecedents, 243
anticipating meaning, 251
anticonvulsant therapy, 431
anti-intellectual attitudes, 401
antonyms, 207
anxiety, 436
apologizing, in controlling behavior, 156
arbitrary standards, 468
Armed with Courage, 332
Arrow Books, 337
assessing language levels, 70, 79
assessment, 68, 79
attitudes toward reading, 512
audio-visual aids, 326
auditory discrimination, 83
authoritarian teacher, 151

bandwagon, 299
Bankson Language Screening Test, 73
basal reader approach, 97, 102–5, 114
basal reader program, diagrammed, 133
basal readers, 193
Basic Reading Inventory, Pre-Primer-Grade 8, 454
Beacon Primer, 190
behavioral objectives, 41, 325, 366

Bender-Gestalt Visual Motor Test, 431
bias in textbooks, 356–58
bibliotherapy, 334
biculturalism, 389
bilingualism, 389
bilingual materials of instruction, 392
bilingual school, 391
bizarre behavior, 437
Black English, 93, 409
Blue Willow, 38, 335
book collections, 322
books, high interest, 479
"borrowed" words, 292
Botel Reading Placement Test, 454
bright child in TESOL, 420
Bronze Bow, The, 332

Caddie Woodlawn, 332
capacity for learning, 19
capacity level, 449, 451
card files, library, 319
cardstacking, 299
case history, 480
categorizing, 75, 242
cause and effect, 356
changing activity, in controlling behavior, 154
changing attitudes, 404
chaos in the classroom, 152
Charles, hyperactive boy, 431–32
Charlotte's Web, 38
check lists, in evaluation, 502
children's written work, 498
clarifying responses, 37
classification, 356
classifying things, 75
classroom climate, 164
Classroom Reading Inventory, 454
climatic chart, 269, 271
closed syllables, 219
cloze procedure, 251–54, 450
cloze technique, 60
Clymer-Barrett Prereading Battery, 87
cognition, 34
cognition in second language learning, 373
color blindness, 82–83
combining forms, 218, 294, 345–46
comma, uses of, 246
commercial games, 224
commonest nouns, 471
communication, effective, 159
communication skills, 11
community agencies, 173
comparison and contrast, 356

compound words, 217
comprehension, 6
  evaluative, 231, 278
  interpretive, 231, 278
  literal, 231, 241
  questions, 78
  skills of, 230, 343
compulsive behavior, 434
concept development, 74, 79, 237
concepts, 34, 237
"cone of experience," 29, 428
conferences, parent-teacher, 174, 179
conferencing, 470
conflict, poverty vs. school, 400
consonant substitution, initial, 203
construction of IRI, 452, 453
content reading difficulties, 264
context clues, 206, 241, 247, 479
context reader, 313
contrastive analysis, 365, 384
controlling classroom behavior, 152
conventional grade competence, 127
convergent thinking, 240
convulsive disorder, 431
corrective reading, 126
  defined, 466
Council on Interracial Books for children,
  358
criteria for evaluating books, 357
criterion-referenced testing, 490
critical reading, 289
  ability, 231, 295
  skills, 300–1
  teaching, 300
cross-age grouping, 126
Crow Boy, 336
cues for learning, 22
cultural heritage, 367
cultural pluralism, 356
culture of poverty, 399
cumulative folder, 175
curriculum, life experience, 426
CVC, 214

Daniel Boone, 332
David, emotionally disturbed boy, 437
Death Be Not Proud, 39
deep structure, 51, 58
democracy, structured overview, 348
details, remembering, 244
developmental reading, 14
  problems in, 118
Developmental Survey of Basic Learning
  Abilities, 71

deviant behavior, 436
diagnosis, an outline, 482
diagnosis
  of retardation, 424
  of slow learners, 425
diagnostic information, 480
Diagnostic Reading Scales, The, 454
diagnostic teaching, 67, 365, 471, 510, 517
dialect differences, 48, 51
dictionary skills, 222–23
differences, individual, 12, 468
  in six-year olds, 95
digraph defined, 51
diphthong defined, 51
directed activity, unsupervised, 142–45
directed reading activities, 347
directed reading lesson, 129–32
direct influences, in classroom, 157
directional sense, 447
discipline and the new teacher, 154
discipline in the classroom, 152
discrimination, auditory, 83–84
  visual, 82–83
distractibility, 432
divergent thinking, 240
Dolch Basic Sight Vocabulary, 201
Dolch Basic Sight Word Test, 455, 509
Dolch list, analysis of errors, 472, 473
domains
  affective, 36
  cognitive, 34
  psychomotor, 39
dominant language, 4–5, 93
Door in the Wall, 336
Dragonwings, 39
drawing conclusions, 256
drawing inferences, 256
Durrell Analysis of Reading Difficulty, 492,
  494
dyslexic, 477

Eames Eye Test, 82
eclectic method, 195
Edna, in ESL program, 421
effective communication, 159
"Eletelephony," 308
emotional disturbance, 126, 434
emotionally disturbed, educational tasks, 435
emotionally stressful situations, 471
emotional management, inner city, 403
emotional maturity, 82
emotional response, 259
English as a second language (ESL), 68, 369,
  372, 421

enrichment for gifted, 416
enumeration, 354
environmental experiences, 81
environment for learning, 161–64
epilepsy, 431
errors in oral reading, 460
    on IRI, 461
ethnography defined, 51
evaluation
    of evidence, 294–95
    of first grade programs, 113, 116–18
    formal, informal, 489
    on-going, 489
    of readiness for reading, 70, 79
    skills, 231, 258
    steps in, 489
exceptional children in regular class, 422
expansion sentences, 380
expectations of teachers, 515
expository order, 353

fact vs. fancy, 258
failure, reasons for, 467
features of Black English, 409
feedback, 8, 22
    in controlling behavior, 164
Fifth Chinese Daughter, 39
figure-ground relationships, 429
figures of speech, 290, 479
finger-pointing, 97
Flanders System, 164–70
following directions, 237, 245
foot, multiple meanings of, 344
foreign words, 292
frustration level, 448–49, 451
Fry's Instant Words, 202
functional learning, 426
functional reading, 14
functional skills, 264

"Galoshes," 307
games and devices, 224
Gates-MacGinitie Reading Tests, 492, 496
geminate consonants, 215
generalizations, in phonics, 213
generalizing, 33, 231, 257, 355
general learning problems, 430
gifted children, 416
    acceleration of, 416
    enrichment for, 416
    learning environment for, 416
    segregation of, 417
    talents of, 419
    teachers' attitudes toward, 418

Gilmore Oral Reading Test, 492–93
glittering personalities, 298
globes, 269
goals of education, 416
Gordon Readers, 191
grammar defined, 51
grapheme defined, 51
Gray's Oral Reading Test, 492, 495
Greek combining forms, 218, 294
growing season, 269
guided silent reading, 131

handicaps, perceptual, 429
Harrison-Stroud Reading Readiness Test, 87
hearing comprehension level, 449
helping learning-disabled students, 430
Hero Tales from Many Lands, 332
hierarchy of needs, 26
hierarchy of steps in language-experience
    reading, 138
high-frequency words, 200
homographs defined, 51
homonyms, 77, 479
homophones, 51, 208
hopelessness in the ghetto, 401
Horace Mann, on reading, 192
how to study assignments, 351
humor, in controlling behavior, 153
Hundred Dresses, The, 39, 335
hunger, structured overview, 349
hyperactive children, 431–32
hyperbole, 291

idioms, 374–76
I Heard The Owl Call My Name, 39
Illinois Test of Psycholinguistic Abilities, 70
implied ideas, 256
improving vocabularies, 234
impulsive behavior, 431–33
independent level, 449, 450
Indians' attitude toward time, 371
indirect influence, in classrooms, 158
individual conferencing, 134–35
individual differences, 12, 468
    in sixth grade, 341
individualized reading, 132
    diagrammed, 139
    as method, 97, 115
inflections, 77, 216
influence techniques, 152–54
informal analysis, summary, 483
informal reading at home, 85

informal reading inventory (IRI), 448, 509
  administering, 455
  constructing, 452–53
  defined, 449
  interpreting, 459
  limitations of, 451
  marking, 457–58
  published, 454
  scoring, 458–59
initial consonant substitution, 203, 204
initial summary sheet, 484
initial teaching alphabet, 105
instructional level, 449–50
  through the day, 512
integration, 6
intellectual differences, 13
intelligence classifications, 21
intelligence tests, 74, 79
interaction analysis, 164
  categories of, 166
interdependence of language and culture, 390
interest inventory, 320
interpretive skills, 231, 251
intonation defined, 51
intrinsic motivation, 401
Inventory of Phonetic Skills, 475–76
involvement in learning, 22
IRI. *See* informal reading inventory
irony, 291
Island of the Blue Dolphins, 332
isolating, in controlling behavior, 153

Jack, in the first grade, 2
Jill, a problem in neurology, 430–31
John, a retarded boy, 423–25
Johnny Tremain, 39, 332
J. T., 39
judging authorities, 294
Julie of the Wolves, 39
juncture, 51, 56
Jungle Book, The, 38

Keystone Visual Telebinocular Survey, 82
kindergarten experience, 84
kinesthetic experiences, 434
Kintu, 336

language
  acquisition, 52
  age, 71
  characteristics of, 46
  and concept development, 404
  differences, 367
  dominance of primary, 4–5, 93

  facility, 81
  interference, 393
  problems, Spanish-English, 385–86
  structure of, 50
language-experience approach to reading, 6, 7–8, 55, 97, 98–102, 137, 379
Latin, combining forms, 218, 294, 345
learning centers, 126, 161–64
  arrangement of, 163
learning disabilities, 365, 428
learning language, 372
learning *not* to read, 404
learning principles, 18
learning, programmed, 32
learning to read, 96
left-handed child, 84
left-to-right orientation, 477
level of aspiration, 515
levels of questioning, 235
levels of reading defined
  capacity, 451
  frustration, 451
  independent, 450
  instructional, 450
levels of understanding, 468
lexicon defined, 51
library resources
  minimum collection, 322
  and service, 321
  and skills to be taught, 322
  and weeding process, 322
  well-stocked, 322
life experience curriculum, 426
linguistic reading programs, 387
linguistics
  defined, 46, 51
  in reading, 57–60
  vs. phonics, 58
lip movement, 97
listening level, 449
listening vocabulary, 188
literacy in U.S., 9
literal comprehension, 231
litter, multiple meanings of, 344
Little House in the Big Woods, 332
Little House on the Prairie, 38
little words in big ones, 220
"loaded" words, 290
lockstep promotion system, 417

magic square, 346
main idea, 248
mainstreaming, 422
many faces of reading, the, 512–13

maps, 269
marking errors on IRI, 457
mastery learning, 22
meaning
    in context, 247
    and lessons to teach, 376
    in reading, 232
measuring affective growth, 503
median, 20
medical examination, 480
mental retardation, 423
Mercator projection, 272
metaphor, 291
methods of teaching reading, 97
meticulousness, 433
metonymy, 292
Metropolitan Readiness Test, 87, 88
"Mice," 307
middle-class values, 368
minimal pairs, 56, 205
miscue analysis, 60
miscue inventory, 459–60
modeling oral reading, 309
modified writing systems, 105–7
morpheme defined, 51
morpheme tree, 346
morphology defined, 49, 50, 51
morphophoneme defined, 51
morphophonemics defined, 51
Mother Goose, 81
motivation, 23–26, 401
multiple meanings, 77, 206, 344, 376, 479
*Murphy-Durrell Diagnostic Reading
        Readiness Test,* 87
My Reading Design, 319, 320

name-calling, 298
Navajo bilingual education program, 392
Navajo values, 368
needs, hierarchy of, 26
Nelson Reading Test, 492
neurological handicaps, 430
Newbery medal books, 333–34
newspaper for reading, 266
new teacher and discipline, 154–56
nonstandard English, 398
    attitudes toward, 407
    reading in, 406
normal curve, 19–20

objectives, behavioral, 41
objectives of reading program, 15
Old Rosie, the Horse Nobody Understood,
        336

On the Banks of Plum Creek, 38, 332
Onion John, 332
On-the-spot Reading Diagnosis File, 454
open syllables, 219
opposites, 74, 377
oral language before kindergarten, 2
oral reading, 304
    to diagnose a problem, 312
    as evaluation, 499
    improvement of, 311
    modeling, 309
    practice, 471, 478
    rate of, 314
    as sharing, 307–9, 499
    situations, 305
    the task, 310
    time in school, 305
    time spent on, 306
    and use of clues, 314
    and use of tape recorder, 312
ordering, conceptual, 239
outlining, 250, 266
overstatement, 259
overview, diagrammed, 342, 347–49
ownership of books, 337

parent, initial contacts with, 175
parent interview, 480
parents
    as teachers, 177
    losing patience, 177
    observing at school, 179
    seminar for, 177
    with special skills, 178
parent-teacher conferences, 174, 179
patterning language, 379
Peabody Rebus Reading Program, 107–8,
        440
peer teaching, 126
percentile rank, 491
perception, 6
perceptual constancy, 429
perceptual handicaps, 429
permanent reading habits, 318
perseveration, 433
personification, 292
phoneme defined, 52
phoneme-grapheme relationship, 212
phonetics defined, 52
phonic
    ability, 475
    analysis, 52, 209
    elements, 210–11
    generalizations, 213

phonics
   approach, 97, 108–12, 115
   defined, 52
   vs. linguistics, 58
   method, 189
   and sequenced lessons, 95
phonology, defined, 49, 50, 52
phonovisual charts, 111–12
phrases, common, 478
physical handicaps, 126
picture clues, 197
pitch, 52
"plain folks" propaganda technique, 299
polar projection, 272
"politics of school life," 403
polysemantic words, 344
position in space, 429
poverty, culture of, 399
practice
   distributed, 23
   massed, 23
practice in learning, 23
pragmatics, 52
predicting outcomes, 255
predicting reading failure, 72
"*Prediction with Diagnostic Qualities*"
      (PDQ), 73
prefixes, 217, 294
prejudice in textbooks, 356
prepositions
   common, 76
   teaching, 378
prevention vs. remediation, 515
principles for planning reading program, 125
principles of corrective reading, 481
principles of learning, 18
problem-solving, 356
process vs. content, 30
process methodology, 30
process of reading, 93
profiles, 504–5
programmed learning, 32
programmed reading material, 140, 440
promotion policy, 469
pronoun referents, 243
propaganda, 297
proximity, in controlling behavior, 153
psycholinguistics, 52, 389
psychological evaluation, 480
psychological values of bilingualism, 390
Public Law, 94–142, 422
punctuation, 245

quantitative thinking, 78
questioning, levels of, 235
questionnaires, 502
questions for IRI, 453
questions teachers ask, 513–15
question words, 377

racism, 358
range of abilities, 21, 126–27, 416
Rascal, 332
rate of oral reading, 314
rate of reading, 280
reaction, 6
read around the circle, 455
readers, dialect-specific, 406
reading
   as an active process, 342
   to children, 331
   defined, 5, 7, 10, 11, 342
   developmental, 14
   environment at home, 176
   failure, 13
   to find proper levels, 124
   four-step process of, 7
   functional, 14
   handicaps to, 12
   kinds of, 469
   and major jobs to do, 13, 187
   and nonstandard English, 406
   objectives, 15
   oral, 304
   permanent habits of, 318
   rate of, 280
   recreational, 14
   skills of, 13–14
   vocabulary, 188
   what it is *not,* 12
Reading Placement Inventory, 454
reading programs
   characteristics of, 94
   principles to guide, 125
reading readiness, 4, 69, 79
   abilities, 71, 73
   factors summarized, 89
   quantitative concepts of, 78
   tests, 86
Real Mother Goose, The, 91
rebus reading, 60, 102, 107–8, 440
records
   and diagnostic information, 480
   and evaluation, 504
   of reading, 319, 320
   of reading progress, 485
recreational reading, 14

redundancy, 60
reference points, familiar, 350
reinforcement, 22
remedial instruction, 466
Remedial Reading Drills, 427
remedial techniques, 471
remembering details, 244
reversals, 477
rewards and punishments, 27
rhyming, 78
right, multiple meanings of, 344
Rock Point Bilingual Program, 392
roots, in multisyllabic words, 217
Rose, retarded girl, 428

San Diego Quick Assessment, 455, 473, 475
sarcasm, in controlling behavior, 156
Scholastic Book Service, 337
school-home cooperation, 173
schwa, 221
scoring the IRI, 458–59
screen for partitioning room, 440
seatwork, constructive, 142
segregation of gifted, 417
self-esteem, 515
self-evaluation, 504
self-fulfilling prophecy, 405, 515
semantics, 50, 52, 60
seminar for parents, 177
sentence method, 190
sequence, 355
sequencing, 242, 353
service words, 199
sex differences, 113–18
sexism, 358
shifting gears in reading, 281
siblings, comparing, 177
sight words, 198
    in context, 201
    difficulties with, 204
    teaching, 203
significance of the paragraph, 245
Silent Reading Diagnostic Tests, 475, 492, 497
simile defined, 291
size of groups, 126
skeleton outline, 267, 268
skills of reading, 13–14
    comprehension and, 343
Slosson Oral Reading Test, 455, 473
slow learners, 425
    generalizations about, 427
Snellen chart, 82
social maturity, 74, 82

sociocultural problems, 403
sociogram, 503
sociolinguistics, 52, 389
Socratic method, 289
Sounder, 39
Sounds of Language, The, 315
Spanish vocabulary, 326–27
spatial order, 353
spatial relationships, 429
speaking vocabulary, 188
special ancillary services, 470
specialized vocabulary, 343–45
special writing systems, 97, 105–7
spelling, in English, 212
spread of ability in class, 416
SQ3R, 265
SQ4R, 352
SQRQCQ, 354
SSR, 140
staffing for case studies, 470
standardized reading tests, 448, 491
Standard Reading Inventory, The, 454
standard references, 319
standards, arbitrary, 468
Stanford-Binet Intelligence Test, 74
steps in directed reading lesson, 129
stereotypes, 358
story method, 193
Strawberry Girl, 332
stress, 52, 220
structural analysis, 216
structured overview, 342, 347–49
structure words, 57
study guide questions, 276–78
study of reading assignments, 351–52
study skills, 232
    outline of, 281–86
substitution drills, 379
suffixes, 217, 294
summary of reading abilities, 506
suprasegmentals defined, 52
surface structure defined, 52
syllabication, 475
synecdoche, 292
synonyms, 207, 242, 479
syntactic correctness, 8
syntax, defined, 49, 50, 52
synthetic method, 189

Tab books, 337
tactile experiences, 434
talented child, 419
tape recorder, use of, 456

taping the oral reading test, 456
taxonomy
    affective, 36
    of cognition, 240
    cognitive, 34–36
    psychomotor, 39
teacher-pupil interaction, 154
teachers' questions, 235, 513–15
teaching English as a second language. *See*
    TESOL
teaching the neurologically impaired, 432
Teaching Prejudice, 358
teaching sight words, 203
TESOL, 379, 386–87
testimonials, 298
testing readiness, 86
tests, of reading, lists for classroom teachers,
    498
then-when confusion, 205
thinking, convergent, and divergent, 240
three reading groups, 126, 512
    planning work for, 130
time line, a sample, 268, 270
title, for a paragraph, 248
topical outline, 251
topic sentence, 248
transfer, 298
transfer of training, 27–28
transformations, 380–83
Two Is a Team, 336
two-way communication, 158

understanding, 28
    levels of, 468
unfounded claims, 259
uninterrupted sustained silent reading. *See*
    USSR
units of work
    development of, 160
    enriching resources for, 324
    Spanish vocabulary, 326
    steps in, 160, 275, 350
    and visual aids, 326
universal language of feelings, 369
Up From Slavery, 38
USSR, 140
utterance, 52

values, 37, 328
    Navajo, 368
    personal, 335
V + C+ e spelling regularities, 215
verbal skills in kindergarten, 3
verb-to-noun transformations, 381

vernacular defined, 52
Vineland Social Maturity Scale, 74
visual configuration, 196
visual discrimination, 82–83
visual-motor coordination, 429
vocabulary
    of children, 188, 343
    concepts, 241
    development, 233
    listening, 343–44
    meanings, 374
    specialized, 343–45
    technical, 345–46
vowel spellings, 214

ways parents should help, 176
Wechsler Intelligence Scale for Children, 21,
    74
Westward Movement, 324–27
"What Is Black?" 376
when, where, why, how, who, 243
"Where's Mary?" 308
why children fail, 467
Wind in the Willows, The, 332
withdrawal, 433, 437
writing patterns in texts, 353
writing vocabulary, 188
writing way to reading, diagrammed, 141
word inflections, 77
word recognition, 471
    methods of teaching, 188
    skills to teach, 195
word and sentence method, 190
word-by-word readers, 313
words associated in pairs, 76, 377
Words in Color, 105
workbooks, use of, 145–48
World of Language, The, 315

Yonie Wondernose, 39, 336